A History of Kiribati

From the Earliest Times to the 40th Anniversary of the Republic

A History of Kiribati

From the Earliest Times to the 40th Anniversary of the Republic

Michael Ravell Walsh

Copyright:

Text: Michael Ravell Walsh

Front cover photograph © by Michael Ravell Walsh

Back cover photograph © by Temaia Ereata

All rights reserved.

ISBN: 9-79869535-895-7

Imprint: Independently published

Dewey Decimal Classification 996

Library of Congress Subclass DU – Oceania (South Seas)

For Rotee

And our children:

Sophia / Mamaua
Philip / Tekee
Cordelia / Kabobo

And our grandchildren.

Contents

Foreword by His Excellency Taneti Maamau, President of Kiribati	i
Introduction	iii
Acknowledgements	ix
Glossary of Austronesian terms	xi
Maps of Kiribati	xxiii

PART 1: TUNGARU

Chapter 1.	The islands	1
Chapter 2.	Settlement	14
Chapter 3.	Society	42
Chapter 4.	Religion and magic	60
Chapter 5.	Arts, crafts, competitions and games	75
Chapter 6.	Warfare	90
Chapter 7.	Material culture, technology and the traditional economy	97
Chapter 8.	Early contact with Europeans	127

PART 2: GILBERT AND ELLICE ISLANDS

Chapter 9.	Protectorate to Colony 1892 - 1916	161
Chapter 10.	The Pacific Phosphate Company 1899 - 1920	184
Chapter 11.	The edifice of control 1916 - 1941	199
Chapter 12.	The economy 1916 - 1941	225
Chapter 13.	Japanese, Americans, and the aftermath of WWII	245
Chapter 14.	Separate existences 1949 - 1967	271
Chapter 15.	Centralisation onto Tarawa	301
Chapter 16.	The quest for a modern economy	319
Chapter 17.	The road to political independence	337

PART 3: THE REPUBLIC OF KIRIBATI

Chapter 18.	The newly independent country	367
Chapter 19.	Village and urban societies in 1979	382
Chapter 20.	The Tabai and Teannaki Years 1979 - 1994	399

Chapter 21.	The Tito Years 1994 - 2003	419
Chapter 22.	The Tong Years 2003 - 2015	438
Chapter 23.	The I Kiribati diaspora	459
Chapter 24.	The next 40 years	479
Epilogue		504
Index		507

Foreword by His Excellency Taneti Maamau

As one of the famous Pacific sayings goes, *'without the past there is no future'*, or to put it in the opposite way, *'there is no future without the past'*. Essentially, it is important to understand to where we all are sailing, by knowing where we have been; and it is in this light of philosophy that this new book of Kiribati history should find a pleasant swim in our pristine waters.

A coherent and recent History about Kiribati, in terms of its historical and modern contexts, up to its fortieth anniversary of independence on 12th July 2019, is hardly available at all - albeit a number of fragmented writings and publications already abound.

Access to information is costly, and there is an emerging need for research and development by I Kiribati of the younger generation at home, and in our disjointed diaspora. This book provides easy information and analysis to visitors, including our development partners and friends.

Both of these provide a reason for this important work.

So it is a great honour for me to provide a Foreword to this new book on the history of Kiribati: as it was in the past, before colonial times, then during the protectorate and colonial times until independence in 1979, and the post independent times - to its current status after four decades.

A new account of its history will make Kiribati more appealing, resilient and sustainable, in light of the immense challenges it faces: its scale, isolation, and of course the environmental and climate change issues, to name only a few. The launching of this new book happens at a time of historical transformation in Kiribati. It is timely to publish it during the term of my Government, in which the fortieth anniversary of independence was celebrated, as it is complementary to the Kiribati Vision for the next 20 years - where we hope that optimal use of our natural, human and cultural talents will be the means for a journey to a wealthier, healthier and peaceful Kiribati.

As a predominately Christian country, the number forty also is important. It is a pertinent reminder of the forty years' journey by the Israelites to the Promised Land: another biblical and compelling message that there is no smooth sailing in this life. Reaching forty years is as well important in our Kiribati context, because the age of forty traditionally means reaching full maturity after formative years of ability, hard work and perseverance.

While history is important in its general sense, it can also be controversial, if taken specifically by the respective islanders. I have admired the way the author of this history has delicately addressed this issue, both in his reflections about his personal connections and in the treatment of his sources. As he rightly indicates - in the words of Sabatier - it is not always easy (and more still by a non I Kiribati) to understand clearly an I Kiribati mind and heart in their wholeness.

Important also is the fact that this new publication, based as it is on a proliferation of sources, many of them new works produced by I Kiribati authors, is a demonstration of how innovative talents are pushing into new frontiers of learning, research and development in the Kiribati literature.

My personal encounters with the author, Michael Walsh, have been limited compared to those of my predecessors, since I was still at school when he lived and worked in Kiribati (whilst the first four Beretitenti have been his contemporaries); but I have known him through his professional writings and official publications and communications, as the first ever economist and a founding member of the National Economic Planning Office in 1971. I first became aware of his work when I joined the same office in 1983. I found his writings to be succinct and meticulous then, and, equally, now in presenting this comprehensive summary of the past and contemporary history of Kiribati.

Michael's appointment as Kiribati Honorary Consul in the UK in 1996, a diplomatic assignment he has held from then until now, clearly demonstrates the diligence, capability and dedication he has for Kiribati. His marriage to an I Kiribati lady, Rotee Tekee, has amplified further his passion and love for our nation.

I strongly recommend this book for social as well as academic reading.

Te Mauri Te Raoi ao Te Tabomoa - meaning Health, Peace and Prosperity - to us all.

Taneti Maamau

Beretitenti of Kiribati

December 2019

Introduction

In Kiribati, *'only a slave has no history'*.

The earliest historical accounts of the I Kiribati were closely bound up with the Karangoa *boti* (see pages 51-52 for explanation of the term); and especially an account published as *The Story of Karangoa* in 1991. This had been dictated by an *unimane* on Nikunau in the 1930s, to Tione Baraka, a member of the Karangoa *boti*, and written down by him. As in many cultures, it mixes divine and human stories to explain origins. In ancient times, a person with no *boti* was a 'nobody': literally, a non-person. *Beia mwa Tekaai* spoke in Tarawa tradition of the sons of *Naubwebwe*, who had no *boti*, as *'things'*; but recently, a survey of the roughly 50 members of the I Kiribati diaspora in the UK who were born in Kiribati revealed that only a few were nowadays certain as to which *'boti'* was their own; and some did not even understand the question.

This book is written in the belief that, in part because of the lack of a recent single narrative, there is a continued but unsatisfied hunger amongst I Kiribati people, and those of I Kiribati descent, for historical knowledge - and not only of ancient times, but also of the 300 or so years since explorers and whaling ships arrived off Kiribati and contact began with Europeans, and later Chinese. People of I Kiribati descent who now live elsewhere, and also prospective visitors, have often asked me for advice for a single work to read in order to gain a general historical perspective of both the traditional and the modern country, and how the balance between the two has evolved over these past 300 years. For nearly forty years, I have pointed them to the excellent and pioneering *Kiribati: Aspects of History*, the *'first history of the Gilbert Islands written by Gilbertese'*, which was published in 1979 (and is still in print); or, for those who wished for a more detailed account, Dr Barrie Macdonald's *Cinderellas of the Empire*, which was first published in 1982 (and was also reprinted a decade ago).

However, not only have nearly four decades passed since these were written – almost half the period in which the Gilbert and Ellice Islands Colony existed – but there have been a number of new researches. In this period, no new overall account of Kiribati history has been published. These are the reasons why I have produced this book.

Much of what has been written and published about the first histories – the oral historical traditions - has been the work of outsiders: we owe a great debt to Hamann, Grimble, Maude, Sabatier, Luomala, and Latouche, to name a few. However, most of their researches are now out of print. More recently, *Te Umwanibong*, the Kiribati National Museum and Cultural Centre, has been active in putting together better documentation of I Kiribati oral tradition, and its work (on which I have been able to draw) has been supported by a large number of local community cultural groups.

Only in the past few decades have such oral histories been supplemented by science: genetic analysis (of both humans and plants), geology, and archaeology. These put the dates of Tungaru settlement at around the beginning of the Common Era, two millennia ago.

After first contact by Europeans in the 19th century CE many I Kiribati – not always voluntarily - travelled abroad; but after Britain declared a Protectorate, they were, between 1900 and the mid-1960s, kept largely isolated from the rest of the world. For better or worse, there was a 'museum' policy by successive Resident Commissioners – only briefly interrupted by the shock of the Japanese and American occupations in the 1940s. This was eventually replaced by a very rapid (at least by the standards of most other ex-colonies) evolution of indigenous political control in the 1970s.

During this time, people balanced their own traditional authority and culture against those introduced by two other, often competing, sources of external influence: the Missions and the colonial authorities. In this time also, they effectively contributed an 'aid' package - which was the equivalent in today's values of some AUD$ 750 million - to the then developing economies of Australia and New Zealand. This came about through transfer of phosphate from Banaba to these two countries at cost rather than at world prices; and it was indirectly also to the benefit of Britain, through cheap food. As memories of the British Phosphate Commission (BPC) fade, many have asked for a coherent narrative as to how the BPC effectively 'highjacked' the country in colonial times.

Forty years after its independence from Britain, Kiribati has belied the then common view that the country would be unable to maintain itself as a sovereign nation due to its size, dispersion, and lack of resources other than the phosphate, which was finally mined out in the very year of independence. Kiribati has skilfully managed to exploit its control of a significant part of the world's pelagic tuna fisheries, so that royalties from them now effectively play the role that phosphate exports once did. The government has also prudently invested abroad the proceeds of phosphate in the decade up to independence (when the BPC had been forced to pay world prices for it). In the 40th year of independence, this fund exceeded a billion Australian dollars for the first time.

However, success, and the 'graduation' of Kiribati from the United Nations' list of *'least developed countries'*, is now threatened by other sets of circumstances: of these the two most important are the effects of global warming, and the emergence of poverty - which was unknown in traditional society.

The scope of this book

The book has three Parts:

- Part 1 is about Tungaru, the original name for the sixteen atolls of the Gilbert Islands archipelago and Banaba, from prehistoric times up to the declaration of the Protectorate by Britain in 1892
- Part 2 is about the Gilbert and Ellice Islands Protectorate and then Colony, up to the re-establishment of independence in 1979. I have not however attempted to cover the very different Ellice (Tuvaluan) culture in any detail
- Part 3 is a history of the Republic of Kiribati from its inception to its fortieth anniversary, including the growing diaspora of I Kiribati people, which now equates to about 15% of the home population.

This history is not an original work of scholarship, nor is it the result of extensive new research: it is mostly a synthesis and interpretation of other works. It is my hope that it will be useful, firstly, as a summary of 19th and 20th century publications, many of which are now out of print; secondly, as more accessible to the general reader than the often very specialist journals in which specific aspects of history have been published; and thirdly, as being up to date with such current research. I have, as well, generally preferred to let these sources speak for themselves, rather than to paraphrase them. There are therefore many quotations in the book, sometimes quite lengthy ones. Where I have condensed a longer article, my source is acknowledged in the text.

My principal aim as editor and synthesiser has been to be easily readable. The book is thus not laid out in an academic style, with detailed footnotes accompanying the text to identify the source of each statement. (This is partly because I personally find such documents very tedious to read). Rather, I have at the end of each chapter listed the sources which have been consulted in its production and suggested further reading, and also how to access documents on the internet. I have used footnotes, instead, to add my personal reminiscences and observations to the text. I have as well borne in mind things that I would have liked to have known about when I first went to Kiribati, such as how a coral lens works, or the structure of the language, or the history of the international date line: and I sometimes digress to topics such as these. There is more, too, about the economy than in the earlier works.

I am sure it will be apparent at times also that I have strong views about the I Kiribati, the Europeans with whom they have interacted, and the uniqueness of their culture; but the book is not, I hope, a polemic. I am only too aware, as well, of what Sabatier said about outsiders' views of Kiribati: that *'after ten years in the islands you think you know the local people; after twenty-five years you doubt it, and after forty years you are firmly convinced that you do not know them'*.

My other concern has been to publish at a price which is affordable in Kiribati. I have thus chosen a simple, low cost layout for the book and have not included photographs; and I also drew the maps myself rather than have them professionally done.

New sources

Much has moved on since the authors of *Aspects of History* and *Cinderellas of the Empire* published. The then current theories on the settlement of the Pacific islands have been wholly transformed by many studies, since the 1970s, into the genetics of humans, animals, and plants; through advances in linguistics; through geological and climate studies; and because of the evidence of archaeological digs.

I have been able to draw on Professor J M Massing's uncovering of the seemingly forgotten writings of Nicolas Hamann, a Lay Brother in the Société des Missionnaires du Sacré-Coeur, who resided in the Gilbert Islands between 1901 and 1912. These writings - when published in full - will add enormously to our knowledge of pre- and immediately post-contact Tungaru.

An immense amount of material is now available via the internet, such as the *Journal of the Polynesian Society* and also the *Atoll Bulletin*, in which two publications much early research relating to the Gilbert Islands was published. This has been added to an extensive collection of early contemporary writings about the GEIC that I have managed to collect over the last 45 years, including *'Broken Atoms'* by Edward Eliot, Resident Commissioner from 1913 to 1920, and *'Land Travel and Sea Faring'* by his successor H R McClure, Resident Commissioner from 1921 to 1926, neither of which seem to have been drawn upon before.

The definitive *Winding Up the British Empire In The Pacific Islands,* by Professor W. David McIntyre, adds much to knowledge of the British Government's dealings with its colonies there from WWII and during their progression to independence, including the Gilbert Islands. The UK Government's files for the period up to independence, and a few years after, have also now been declassified and made available to researchers in the UK National Archive. I have spent some time with these, and also the few records that have survived from earlier periods (perhaps 5% of what was once there; for the rest, titles are listed but stamped 'destroyed by permission'). I have equally drawn on reports and studies written by a variety of institutions - governmental, consultant and academic - since Independence. Increasingly, as time has gone on, these have been produced by I Kiribati authors.

A number of memoirs have been published in the past decade that throw light on the period from 1950 onwards, especially *An Island In The Autumn,* by John Smith, Governor of the Gilbert Islands between 1973 and 1978; and (if he will forgive me for calling him so) the midwife of the unique Kiribati Constitution. I have also benefitted from the insights of two other recently published memoirs, *Ghost Stories and Other Island Tales* by the late Ian Butler (about the colony in the 1950s), and *The Last District Officer* by John Pitchford (covering the 1970s to the 1990s).

There are nevertheless some new and unpublished sources. Quentin Peel, son of Sir John Peel who was Resident Commissioner from 1948 to 1950, has kindly donated to me his father's personal papers from that era, and these have informed Chapters 11, 14 and 15 of this work. The late Eric Bailey, before his death, entrusted to me his personal papers relating to the Ellice Separation Referendum and its aftermath, on which I have drawn in Chapter 17.

For the period from the 1950s to the present, I have been able to tap new personal memories. First and foremost of these are those from Nei Rotee Tekee, my wife, who grew up and lived on several 'outer islands' between her birth in 1952 and her marriage to me in 1975. In her childhood, these islands had but sporadic contact with the rest of the then colony, let alone the outside world; and her memories provide a counterpoint to the observations of European writers about these times.

The other set of personal memories are my own. I first went to Tarawa in May 1971, as a founder member of the National Economic Planning Office, and as the first professional economist ever to live and work in Kiribati. I had a ringside seat during the critical period in which the foundations for independence were being laid, and local people began taking control. Rotee and I were living in London at the time of the independence negotiations between 1976 and 1979 and were in close contact with the I Kiribati ministers whenever they visited to negotiate with the British Government (and the Banabans). Through the 1970s and 1980s we also looked after many I Kiribati people who studied in the UK. In 1996, I was asked by the then Beretitenti Teburoro Tito to become the Kiribati Honorary Consul in the UK; and this has encouraged me to keep abreast of developments in the past twenty or so years.

Acknowledgements

Many people have encouraged me to write this book, and have helped with it. I should however like to mention first those who stimulated my interest in I Kiribati history and culture when I lived on Tarawa, most of whom, alas, are no longer alive: Reuben Uatioa; Toamati Iuta (who did his best to teach me to speak the I Kiribati language); Babera Kirata and his wife Nei Oileen; Dr Bwebwentekai Tutu Tekanene and his wife Nei Katherine; my former housekeeper Nei Teurikan and her husband Tomi; Dick and Peggy Turpin; and Rosemary Seligman (née Grimble). The late Ron Crocombe was also both an inspiration and a great supporter of my work in Kiribati in the 1970s.

I have also been fortunate to know personally the first four Beretitenti of Kiribati; and I would like to thank H E Taneti Maamau, their successor, for contributing the Foreword to this book.

I thank especially, as well, those who have reviewed drafts of it. Some have commented on all of it: former Beretitenti Teburoro Tito; former Governor of the Gilbert Islands John Smith; Dr Frank Thomas, of the Oceania Centre for Arts, Culture & Pacific Studies at the University of the South Pacific; and my sister, Anna Baggallay, who read the drafts from the viewpoint of someone who had relatively little prior knowledge of the subject matter, and thus provided a very valuable external viewpoint. She also proof-read the English language text for me. I also thank the following for their direct input on specific topics: Natan Itonga, Richard and Beta Turpin, and David Little.

I must also thank all those who have granted me permission to quote from works which are subject to their copyright, including those already mentioned above: to them I must add especially Dr Barrie Macdonald, Professor J M Massing, John Pitchford, Roniti Teiwaki, Guy Slatter, Katerina Teaiwa, Alaric Maude, Susan Woodward, Keith Dixon, Peter McQuarrie and Guigone Camus. I have done my best to identify and search for all quoted authors with copyright, but have not always managed to contact them; so there must be others whose copyright I may have infringed, for which I apologise (it was not for lack of trying).

Thanks are also due both to Anton Gill for giving me advice on publishing, and to Siân Williams for her sterling (and unexpectedly onerous) work in re-formatting my own draft for publication.

My wife Nei Rotee not only made many useful observations, as interspersed in the book, but was, as always, a great support to me while I have been writing this history. She also proof-read the Kiribati phrases and words scattered through the book.

No-one is however responsible for remaining errors, other than myself.

I should be happy to receive comments on and suggested corrections to this work. Please address them to me at:

The Great House, Llanddewi Rhydderch, Monmouthshire NP7 9UY, WALES

mravellwalsh@btopenworld.com

Glossary of Austronesian terms

Note: the definite article 'te' has been omitted from this Glossary so as to simplify the alphabetical ordering. Terms of non-I Kiribati origin (e.g. Tuvaluan words) are identified as such; otherwise all terms are I Kiribati.

The items are spelled in the main text (or in quotations) as they were at the time the relevant source document was produced, and may not therefore always reflect the most modern orthography (e.g. babai / bwabwai).

aamakai	Stage in the growth of a coconut
Aba n Anti	Land belonging to te anti (q.v.)
aba n nenebo	A piece of land given in compensation for the committing of a crime
aba n riring	On Banaba, a piece of land payable to a bonesetter
aba n tibu	A piece of land given as part of an adoption
Aba Ni Maneka (Mwaneka)	The rock of footprints (at Eita on South Tarawa)
aekia	Person with many tattoos
aia mwaan ikawai (or *ai katei ikawai*)	The customs of the ancients
ai-ni-Kiroro	A technique of steam cooking in an earth oven
ai-n-Nabanaba	A technique of steam cooking in an earth oven; also the shell at the base of the oven which gives its name to the technique
ai-n-umum	The covered hearth of an earth oven
aliki	(Tuvaluan) Hereditary Chiefs
angin te maie	A state of ecstasy (usually engendered by dancing)
ano	A ball made from coconut fronds
anonikai	Corrupt or dishonest behaviour
anti	A God (spirit)
anti ma aomata	Hero (of mixed anti and human ancestry)
aomata	An ordinary person with land; a 'freeman'
ati ni kana	An ordeal as part of the training of a *rorobuaka* (q.v.). Technically, a small fireplace prepared and set for the food to be eaten by a person who is to be initiated into manhood or some extraordinary feat
atu ni kua	Type of tattoo
atua	A totemic object
ba	Midrib of the coconut frond
baa:	Classifier - leaves, and by extension flat objects such as sheets of paper
baabaa	Plaited basket of coconut-leaf used in cooking

baangota	Family altar
babakanikawai	To defraud or cheat, also to sponge off someone
babai (now *bwabwai*)	Giant swamp taro (*Cyrtosperma chamissonis*)
baeao	Mother-of-pearl (*Pinctada marginifera*)
bai	Classifier - fingers, teeth, timbers, and other objects of elongated shape (such as sticks or by extension, bottles)
baneawa	Milkfish (*Chanos chanos*)
banuea	Of royal descent
bara	Lit. a hat. In cooking, a spiral winding of coconut-pinnules round a fish, knotted at the head and tail
bareaka	Coconut thatch for canoe shed
Batabata (now *bwatabwata*) or *Be'e'roro*	A land of black-skinned spirits. The legendary land of black spirits is also called Tebongiroro in some sources
batano	A soil type: a layer of almost clayey consistency
batere	A dance performance
batino	Sea urchin (*Echinozoa spp.*)
batiraku	A traditional weapon
batua or *te ikawei*	Name for the spokesman for a kaainga (q.v.)
baurua	(Prob. Tongan loan word). Large double-hulled, ocean going canoe.
be	Pandanus mat worn as formal clothing by men
Beia mwa Tekaai	An anti, who has a shrine near Buariki on North Tarawa
ben	A ripe coconut
bero	Fig (*Ficus tinctoria*)
beru	Name for several *Labroides* species of geckos
bo maki	Ceremony for recently dead person
bobo	Stage in the growth of a coconut
boboti	Lit. 'put things together' - the I Kiribati name for a Co-operative Society
boi	Purslane of several *Portulaca* and *Sesuvium* species
boka	Stage in the growth of a coconut
bokakua	Stage in the growth of a coconut
bokikokiko	Kiribati reed-warbler (*Acrocephalus aequinoctialis*) the only bird species endemic to the Gilbert islands archipelago
bon, iarauri, ianuri	Types of soil for mulching babai plants (q.v.)
bonotia	Person completely covered in tattoos

bora teuana	Single layer earth oven
bora uoua	Double layer earth oven
boti	A place in the mwaneaba reserved for the members of a particular clan.
Bowi	Name for Courts in the colonial period
buakonikai	Land divided into individually-owned plots, lit. 'the bush'
buatoro	A type of pudding
bubuti	System of mutual obligations; a request for something by a relation that, by custom, could not be refused
buki	A type of dance
bukimaere	Stage in the growth of a coconut
bunia	Coconut with edible mesosperm
bunna	Necklace
buro	Tender white shoot inside a coconut
bwerera	A stick game
dalo	(Fijian) Taro (q.v.)
dugdug	(Chamorro language) Species of breadfruit tree (*Artocarpus mariannensis*)
e ewe te karoro	Lit. 'The fourth generation goes free'. Person who was marriageable
e nananga nako	Stage in the growth of a coconut
E taku te kamitina	'The Commissioner has decreed'. Phrase to describe colonial rule - sometimes ironically
e tangi ni kimoa.	Stage in the growth of a coconut
e tawaa	Stage in the growth of a coconut
e tenatena	Stage in the growth of a coconut
e uraura	Stage in the growth of a coconut
eireti	Form of sexual relationship outside marriage but licensed by custom
en anon nange	Type of tattoo
ena	Stone from the reef used as a sharpener
etete	Armband worn for certain dances
fatele	(Tuvaluan, prob.loan word from I Kiribati *batere*) A dance performance
hura	(Tahitian). A form of dance (cf 'hula')
iam	Yam (*Dioscorea spp.*)
iarauri	A soil type: a humus layer under Te uri (*Guettarda speciosa*)

ibonga	Person who conducted religious rituals
ikaraoi	Variety of babai (q.v.)
ikari	Bone fish (*Albula spp.*)
imaiaki	Variety of babai (q.v.)
Imatang	Name for a European
inaomata	A social class, below Uea but above an ordinary person
inato	*Clerodendron inerme*
ing	The fibrous material which grows at the base of the coconut-leaf
iria	Container for dessicated pandanus fruit
iriba	A fan made from pandanus
kaainga	Family group of several generations who lived together; by extension, the place where they lived
kabanin	Rough mat made from coconut frond
kabe	(Possibly Tongan loan word) Giant taro (*Alocasia macrorrhiza*)
kabirongorongo	Term used for those on the verge of famine, without provisions. Traditionally 'a store of food kept for extreme droughts'
kabubu	Dessicated pandanus fruit
kabue-ari	An ordeal as part of the training of a *rorobuaka* (q.v.)
kabuti	A type of dance
kabwaia	Well-being
kai n oro	(In context) Mid-rib of coconut used as a hammer in tattooing
kai	Classifier - trees, shrubs, land sections and fish-hooks
Kaimaimai (now *kamwaimwai*)	Syrup made from repeatedly boiling coconut toddy. (Also known as 'molasses')
kaimatoa	A type of dance
kain	Belonging to; e.g. someone whose descent is from Abemama will describe themselves as '*kain Abemama*'
kain nano ni kannano	People with no access to land or resources; destitute
kaina	Generic name for pandanus (*Pandanus tectorius*)
kainikamaen	A composer of music
Kaintikuaba	A sacred mythological tree (variously sited according to different family traditions)

Kaitu n Tarawa	A name for the Uea of Tarawa
kakoko	A type of dance
kakoko	Finely woven hat made from white young coconut fronds
kamangao	To cause a disorder
Kamaraia	A cursed piece of land, that must be treated with respect to avoid getting cursed
kanawa	*Cordia subcordata*
kaneati	Bonito lure
kanebu	Name for several species of dragon fly
kanna ni mane	Series of ordeals as part of the training of a *rorobuaka* (q.v.)
kara	A soil type: coral fragments
karababa	Dish made from pandanus fruit
karaebari	Chest ornament
karewe	Coconut toddy
karika-na	Making of a cat's cradle
karinimane	Lit. 'Money that you keep'. A sum set aside for a major future expenditure such as school fees
karikin aomata	A human ancestor (as opposed to a divine one)
karikirake	(Lit. 'Make to happen to get bigger quickly'). An I Kiribati word which at different times was conscripted as a translation of the English words 'promotion' and, later, 'development'
karoro	Type of dancing skirt
karoro	Black grass skirt for certain dances
karuoia	A form of magic
katabwanin	A tradition unique to Marakei; first time visitors need to pay their respects to the four *anti* of Marakei, travelling anticlockwise, before undertaking any other activities. Offerings must be made at the shrines of Nei Reei, Nei Rotebenua, Nei Tangangau and Nei Nantekimam
katake	Type of chant or song
katau	Ornamental belt
katei ni Nikunau kaubai	Rich in resources (on Nikunau)
katua	A stone-throwing game

katura	A technique of steam cooking in an earth oven; also the cockle shell at the base of the oven which gives its name to the technique
katutu	Variety of babai (q.v.)
kaubure	(From English 'Councillor'). Native representatives and Magistrates 1892-1966, thereafter Island Council member.
kaue	Headress or garland, either floral, or made from pandanus strips
kaunikai	A formal dancing competition
kauniman	A weaving pattern
kaura	An ordeal as part of the training of a *rorobuaka* (q.v.)
kaura	Leaf of *Sida fallax*
kaura ni Banaba	Leaf of *Wollastonia biflora*
kava	(Polynesian) A beverage made from *Piper methysticum*, a plant native to the western Pacific islands. The name comes from the word 'awa,' meaning 'bitter'
kawa	Subsidiary kaainga (q.v.) formed when original kaainga became too large
kawa	The status of slave on Butaritari and Makin
kawai	Magical rituals
keketi	Name for several species of dragon fly
kemai	A type of dance movement
kiaou	Leaf of *Triumfetta procumbens*
kie n ataei	Type of pandanus mat (for a baby)
kie ni matu	Type of pandanus mat (for sleeping on)
kimoa	Polynesian rat (*Rattus exulans*)
kirakira	Relation to whom an incest prohibition applies
kiremkirem	Middle finger
kiri	Austronesian dogs brought to Tungaru by the first settlers
Koa Koa	The 'sharp one'. Gilbertese name for the trader Richard Randell
korea n riri	Type of tattoo for women only
kua n en an or *moani kua*	Type of tattoo
kuan nanoa	Type of tattoo
kumara	(Austronesian) Sweet potato (in some languages *kumala*)

kamea	Dog of European variety (lit. '*come here*')
maabubu	Name of a sea mark known to navigators, some 400 km. north of Butaritari
mae	Dance ornament
mae are te nikabono	An ornament with magical significance on Maiana
mae are te tawatawa	An ornament worn by Matang, Uea of Tarawa
mae te nuota	Dance ornament
maeke	Stage in the growth of a coconut
maiu ni Imatang	Things pertaining to Europeans and their way of life
maiu ni Kiribati	Things pertaining to the I Kiribati way of life
mamiraki	(Lit. '*blessed*'). A finished song ready for public performance
man:	Classifier - animate things (people, animals, birds, insects and most fish)
maneapa	(Tuvaluan) loan word from Gilbertese *mwaneaba* (q.v.)
maniba	A well
manoku ni wae	Type of tattoo
maraia	Accursed
Matang	A land of white-skinned spirits
matari	Stage in the growth of a coconut
matauninga	A offence against the mwaneaba (q.v.) 'Matauninga' generally results from an act or behaviour that is not respecful of another person or persons, including the spirits dwelling in a place
maunei	Sedge used in making grass skirts
moa	(Prob. Tongan loan word). Chicken.
moa ni wae	Type of tattoo
moi	Stage in the growth of a coconut
moimoto	Drinking-nut
momoka	Stage in the growth of a coconut
mon-n-taai	The name of a magical fish eaten by the dead
mronron	Lit. '*Round or circular*'. Name for a type of co-operative indigenous enterprise
mtea	Purslane or turtle grass (*Portulaca australis*)
mwaneaba (*previously maneaba*)	Assembly house; figuratively, the 'will of the assembly'

mweaka	To make an offering to the spirit of a place, often in the form of tobacco sticks
mweang	A soil type: decaying plant fragments
mwenga	Sleeping house
nako	To walk
nakonako	To run
Nareau	Ancient Spider, also called Nareau the Elder, a pre-existent being who commanded sand and sea water to bear children. Among these children was Nareau the Younger who killed Nareau the Elder and fashioned the sun and the moon from his eyes. There were several other Nareaus in mythology, including 'The Creator', 'The Wise', 'The Trickster' and 'The Cunning'
nari	A soil type: a hard layer, impenetrable to roots
nati	Child of
Nei Auti	A Goddess; also the name for the Plieades constellation, and for the season of the year associated with poor sailing conditions
nen te boti	Lit. 'the container of the *boti* (q.v.)'. A function of the *mwaneaba* (q.v.)
ni	Generic name for coconut (*Cocos nucifera*)
nikiranroro	Lit. 'left behind their generation'. Name for sexually active unmarried woman
nimataanin	A shell (*Nerita plicata*)
nimoimoi	Stage in the growth of a coconut
nira	Winding of babai-leaf used in cooking
non	*Morinda citrifolia*
non-nabanaba	A cultivar of *te non* (q.v.)
ntabo	Pendant worn at the neck
nouete	A gift given at an event to which one has been invited for that purpose
nuota	Dance ornament
oka	Lit. a rafter; an astronomical term for the celestial equator
onobua	Stage in the growth of a coconut
oudud	(Palauan). Glass and ceramic bead money used on that island group
Palangi	(Tuvaluan) Name for a European
proa	(Austronesian) Double hulled sailing vessel

pulaka	(Tuvaluan) Taro (*Calladium esculentum*)
rai	(Yappese). Stone money used on Yap
rang	A landless but 'free' person
ranimauna	Stage in the growth of a coconut
rao	Leaf of *Hibiscus tiliaceus*
rebwe	A type of dance
ren	*Tournefortia araentea*
renga	(Probably) Betel nut
ribaiai (now *ribwaeai*)	Young coconut tree coming into its first flowering
ribu or *riburibu*	A soil type: sulphur-smelling mud.
Rimwimāta	A God; also the name for the star Antares, and for the season of the year associated with good sailing conditions
riri	A short grass skirt worn by women
ririki	A calendar year
ririko	Sash worn whilst dancing
roata n ni	A weaving pattern
roba	Type of pandanus mat
rongorongo	(Prob. Tongan loan word). News or information
rorobuaka	A warrior who had undergone a severe training programme
ruanuna	A technique of dry cooking in an earth oven
ruoia	Type of dance
ruoia te bino	A seated dance
rurubene	An ad hoc group chosen to perform a new song
Tabakea	A primordial deity of the Gilbert Islands; in some traditions, he was the creator God, and he and his consort Tituabine engendered all the other deities. His physical representation was a turtle.
tabotabo	Index finger
taboua	A traditional weapon
tabu	Prohibition (adopted in English as 'taboo')
tabunea	Magical spells
taitai	Marks made by a *wii n taitai* (q.v.)
Takoronga i Nano	Place in Tabiteuea where, according to local tradition, the world was created
Tama	Father
tangana	A type of pudding

tangauri	Dish made from pandanus fruit
tangitang	Post WWII co-operative society, covering six islands
tani kaiwa	Sorcerers
tannaki	A period of steady wind
tano	A soil type: sand
taona n riri	Ornamental belt
taororo	Taro (*Colocasia esculenta*)
tatanga ni mainiku	Lit. 'the roof-plate of east': the Eastern horizon
taua ni kai	A concubine, usually a sister or cousin of a wife
taubuki	Lit. 'the roof-plate of west': the Western horizon
taumañgaria	A traditional weapon
tausi	(Tuvaluan) Redundant; already taken care of
tauti	Spine of a porcupine fish (*Diodontidae spp.*)
teauabubuti	A traditional weapon
tebakabota	A traditional weapon
tebana	A traditional weapon
tebarantauti	Component of Gilbertese armour
tebaratekora:	Component of Gilbertese armour
teboka-na	Water poured onto an earth oven to create steam
tebutu	A traditional weapon
teie	A traditional weapon
tekatibana	Component of Gilbertese armour
tekoromatan	A traditional weapon
temaran	A traditional weapon
tembo	A traditional weapon
tenea	A traditional weapon
tenikawewe	A 'holy' area
teotana	Component of Gilbertese armour
teronikiri	A traditional weapon
tetana	Component of Gilbertese armour
tetara	A traditional weapon
tetaumanaria	A traditional weapon
tetoanea	A traditional weapon
tetuta	Component of Gilbertese armour
teunun	A traditional weapon
tewinnarei	A traditional weapon
tia kainikamaen	An inheritor of musical tradition
tia tabe atu	A female relative

tiakaba	Canoe builder
tiaki kain au utu	Someone not part of the speaker's utu (q.v.)
Tibu	Grandparents
Tibu mamano	Great-great- grandparents
Tibu tabonibubua	A distant relation with whom an ancestor was shared
Tibu Taratara	A very distant relation with whom an ancestor was shared
Tibu toru	Great-grandparents
tibutibu	Adoption
tikaobion	A scorpion
tikutaungaunga	Species of dragonfly
Tina	Mother
tinaba	Form of sexual relationship outside marriage but licensed by custom
tirere	Type of dance
Toa ake Onoman	Legendary giants on Nuatabu on North Tarawa, who subsequently populated Onotoa
tibwatibwaan raoi	An equitable distribution (of income, resources, etc.)
toañgea	A traditional weapon
toamau	A household which is balanced in age and gender so there is a good division of labour for the tasks needed to be carried out
tongabiri	Ring finger
toro (kawa)	A slave. On Butaritari and Makin the equivalent word was 'kawa'
touru	Species of banana formerly grown in Tungaru, now replaced by other varieties
tuae	Dish made from pandanus fruit
tukunei	A small lizard
ua	Classifier - general classifier, used for common objects, as well as for periods of time
uaa-n-ni	The generic name of the coconut nut
uba	Type of tattoo
uba are te nikabono	An ornament with magical significance on Aranuka
Uea	King (or chief)
Ueanikai	The Tree of Kings (part of creation myths)
Uekera	A sacred mythological tree (variously sited according to different family traditions)
ui n aine	A traditional weapon for women

ukinaba	Thumb
ukirere	Little finger
uma ni borau	Lit. 'roof of voyaging', an astronomical term that describes the night sky and stars
umum	An earth oven (covered hearth)
umuna	To cook in a covered hearth
unaine	Old woman
unimane	Old man
uri	Species of tree (*Guettarda speciosa*),
Uruakin Kain Tiku-aba	Lit the '*breaking of the tree of the resting place of lands*'. Name for civil war in Samoa about 1400 CE
uteute	Generic name for grass species
utu	Extended family, including those not resident in a *kaainga* (q.v.)
utu ae kan	Close relations (defined as those sharing a great-great grandparent)
utuao	Generic name for a kite (usually constructed from a pandanus leaf)
uuan	Ground pumice stone
wa ni banga	A type of dance
waa:	Classifier - canoes
wao	*Boerhavia repens*
warebwi, bwebwe, boiri, oreano	Types of *ano* (q.v.)
wawi	Death magic
wewene	Type of pandanus mat
wii n taitai	Tattooing instrument
yaqona	(Fijian) kava (q.v.)

Maps

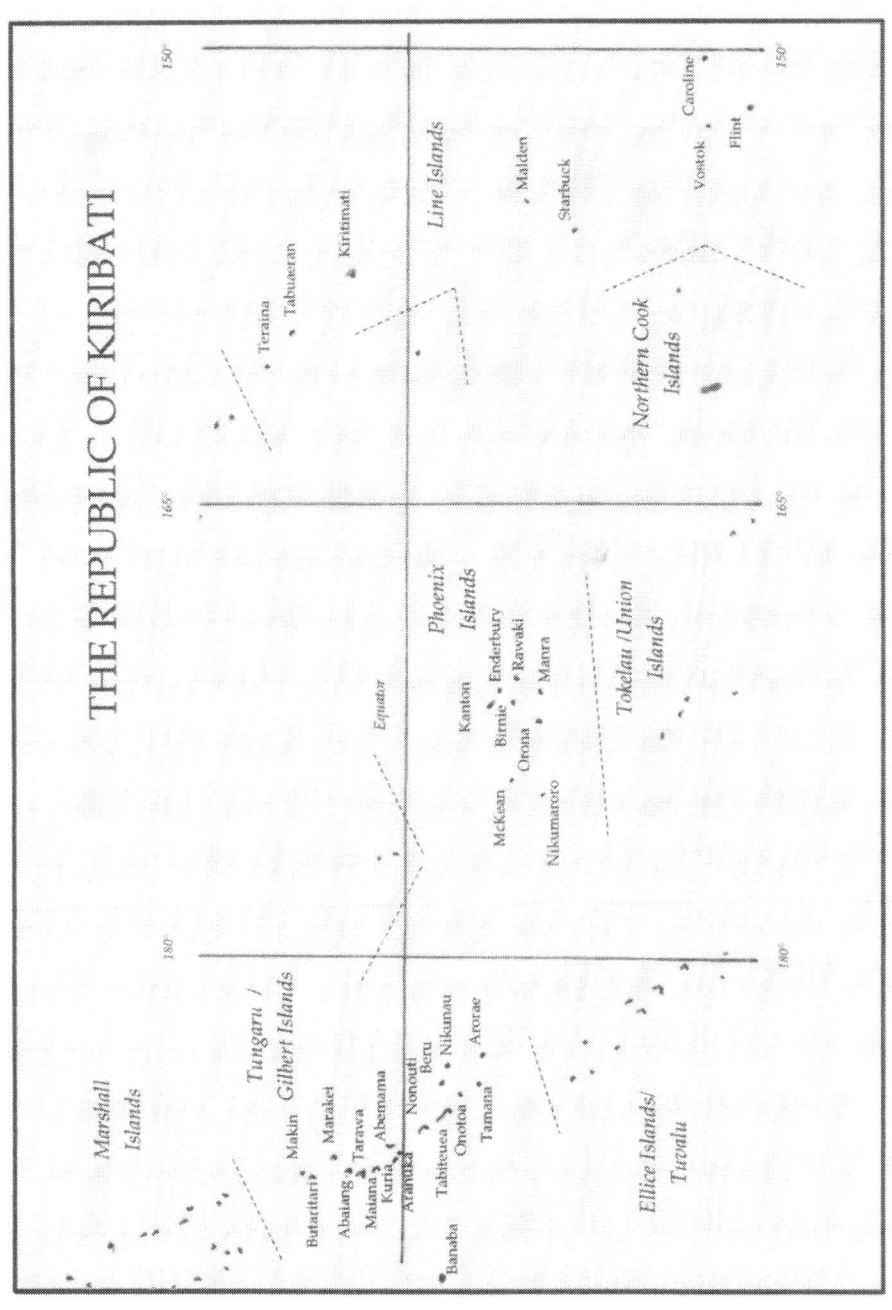

Tarawa Atoll

PART 1
TUNGARU

Chapter 1.

THE ISLANDS

Location

The Republic of Kiribati, as it exists today, comprises 32 atolls and reef islands, and one raised coral island. The islands lie in the middle of a triangle between the Philippines, Hawaii and Australia.

Kiribati is the only country in the world to straddle not only the Equator, but also the Eastern and Western Hemispheres; it has a footprint in all four quadrants. Its islands are scattered over an expanse of the Pacific Ocean equivalent in size to the area from London to Moscow, to Ankara, to Madrid - bigger than the area of the continental United States. Banaba, the most westerly island, is at a latitude of 169.32° degrees east; Teraina, the most northerly, at 4.71° N; Caroline Island is the most easterly, at 150°12'W; and Flint Island the most southerly at 11.43° S.

That the most westerly island has a longitude described as 'east', and the most easterly as 'west', is due to the fact that until 1994, Kiribati was intersected by the International Date Line; so that the Line Islands were a day behind the other two island groupings, the Gilbert Islands and the Phoenix Islands. On December 23, 1994, the Republic of Kiribati announced a change of time zone for the Line Islands, to take effect on January 1st 1995. This adjustment effectively moved the International Date Line over 1,000 km to the east within Kiribati, placing all of Kiribati on the Asian, western, side of the date line, despite the fact that the Line Islands longitude corresponds to UTC−10 rather than its official time zone of UTC+14.

This move made Caroline Island both the easternmost land in the earliest time zone (by some definitions, the easternmost point on Earth); and one of the first points of land which saw the sun rise on January 1st 2000 (at 5:43 a.m., as measured by local time).

However, although there is some disputed evidence of pre-contact Micronesian (as well as Polynesian) settlement in some of the Phoenix Islands, and of Polynesian temporary settlement in the Line islands, Part 1 of this book is only concerned with the sixteen atolls of the Gilberts archipelago, and the raised coral island of Banaba to the west. These islands originally called themselves Tungaru (although there was little sense of their being a single nation).

Under British rule, they were for administrative purposes variously joined with other groups of islands, notably the Ellice Islands (Tuvalu). These arrangements are discussed in Part 2 of the book.

Geology

Kiribati is located within the stable centre of the Pacific tectonic plate, although there is little information on the seismological history of its atoll chains. The Gilbert Islands (and the Phoenix and Line are similar) have been described as:

> *'essentially Holocene carbonate caps resting on a pre-Holocene reef, developed on a NW-trending chain of mid-oceanic volcanoes - a continuous chain of seamounts with that of the Ratak Chain of the Marshall Islands to the north'.*

Each atoll is a ring-shaped coral reef, with a coral rim that encircles a lagoon (partially or completely). The coral of the atoll sits on top of the rim of an extinct seamount (volcano) which has eroded or subsided beneath the water. The lagoon forms over the volcanic crater (*caldera*), while the higher rim remains above water, or at shallow depths that permit the coral to grow and form reefs. Storms then create islets along the reef; for the atoll to persist, continued erosion or subsidence must be at a rate slow enough to permit reef growth upwards. The lagoon may in some instances be filled in or never develop; in the context of Kiribati, these are known as 'reef islands'.

In the islands, the windward reef front is typically a gently seaward-sloping terrace, marked at its seaward margin by a steep drop-off to the reef slope; and at its landward margin by abrupt, coral-algal buttresses.

The reef platform, or atoll rim, extends from the reef crest to the first major break in the slope of the atoll lagoon, or in the case of reef islands, the leeward reef crest. It is the 'substrate' on which the atoll islets and reef islands rest, and its composition varies from eroded rock to a surface which has been built up by sediments washed from the ocean and deposited in the lagoon.

Chapter 1: The Islands

The islands are thus a complex mix of limestone and carbonate sediments, whereby platforms of coral conglomerate have been overlain by sands and gravels, which make up most of the islet surfaces.

These are composed almost entirely of skeletal carbonate material: and both their existence and form are acutely sensitive to climate variations. However, they lie in a tropical zone where environmental conditions such as water clarity, temperature and organic productivity are favourable for vigorous coral growth.

Islets are geologically young, having developed only in the last millennia (mid-late Holocene). The transition from corals to unconsolidated sediments required for islet buildup varied across time and space, even within the confines of individual atolls, and the emergence of land suitable for permanent human occupation appears to have taken place several centuries later. It would then have taken time for the coral lenses (see below) to develop.

The estimated dates of their formation, as measured by radio carbon techniques, are for a quite recent period: between about 2000 BCE and 500 CE. At this time there is evidence of increases in 'storminess', lower sea levels, and increases in carbonate production rates. When the usual easterly trade winds are replaced by strong 'westerlies', the waves that result can produce significant shoreline change over a very short period.

Some beaches are almost completely composed of *Foraminifera* (protozoa) shells, though they may also contain mollusc shells and coraline algae.

Studies have computed a chronology for the decline of sea levels and 'crossover' dates in different parts of the Pacific island region, finding a close correspondence between the availability of suitable landmass and the first appearance of human activities. (The 'crossover' date is when declining late-Holocene sea levels first carried the high tide level below the mid-Holocene low tide level).

Before the crossover date, relict mid-Holocene paleo-reef flats were still overtopped by the sea at high tide. For parts of Kiribati this situation has been estimated as being in place as late as 200 B.C.E, and with a 'crossover date' of 1100 C.E.

Chapter 1: The Islands

Topography

The Gilberts archipelago is composed of five reef islands and eleven pure atolls. These are arranged in an approximately north-to-south line, with some 780 km. distance between the northernmost island, Makin, and the southernmost, Arorae. They consist of strips of land, nowhere more than 400 or so metres wide [1].

The reef islands (Makin, Kuria, Nikunau, Tamana, and Arorae) do not have lagoons; they tend to be slightly higher than the atoll islets, up to 5 m. above sea level. Makin has a central shallow depression connected to the sea by a small tidal channel; and Nikunau contains central ponds which may be lagoon vestiges.

The other islands have a lagoon surrounded by a limestone rim. Marakei is the only 'enclosed' atoll: except for two shallow reef flat channels this triangular-shaped atoll has a continuous landmass around its rim. Of the remaining ten atolls, the land tends to be on the northern and eastern edges of the rim, with many islets which are divided by tidal reef passages from ocean to lagoon. Tabiteuea has more than 60 such islets along a reef of 30 Km.

Aranuka, Maiana, Beru and Onotoa have relatively shallow lagoons (less than 10 metres); Butaritari, Abaiang, Tarawa, Abemama, Nonouti and Tabiteuea have deeper lagoons (more than 10 metres, with Butaritari the deepest, at 33 metres).

Banaba is by contrast a raised coral atoll, that is, an atoll that has been lifted high enough above sea level by tectonic forces to protect it from scouring by storms. The highest point on the island is also the highest point in Kiribati, at 81 metres.

Soils

The soils generally encountered in Kiribati:

> *'may be described as having an AC type profile. The A-horizon consists of sand containing a very variable quantity of humus. It is usually about*

---

[1] When my wife first came to Europe, it took us some months to identify what was 'missing'. We eventually worked out that it was the sound of the surf, which had up until then had formed a constant backdrop to her life. You cannot in Kiribati get away from the sound.

Chapter 1: The Islands

> *25 cm deep, has a pH of 7.6-8.0, and is dark greyish to black in colour. This rapidly gives way to coarse white and pink gravely sand of the C-horizon, which consists almost exclusively of calcium and magnesium carbonates and has a pH of 7.8-8.3.*
>
> *'The soil type is one of coral sediment with varying topsoil that is poor in nutrients. The soil has a high amount of free calcium, locking up most of the necessary nutrients.*
>
> *'The soils are very highly permeable and have a low moisture-retaining capacity. The topsoil may have clay-sized particles constituting up to 5 percent of the volume of soil, but such particles are formed by the breakdown of the algae shells by carbonic acid in humus.*
>
> *'Atoll soils are generally low in N and K, and P tends to be fixed. Deficiencies of micro-minerals (nutrients) such as Cu, Zn, Fe and Mn are very common, however, the levels of sodium, boron and molybdenum are adequate, while sulphur may be borderline in some areas'.*

In other words, soils are thin, alkaline, and deficient in minerals. This severely restricts the range of plants that can survive, as will be seen in the description of the flora of Kiribati below [2].

The people of Kiribati distinguish a number of soil types, for example:

- *Te batano*: a layer of almost clayey consistency
- *Te nari*: a hard layer, impenetrable to roots
- *Te kara*: coral fragments
- *Te tano*: sand
- *Te iarauri*: a humus layer under *Te uri* (Guettarda speciosa)
- *Te mweang*: decaying plant fragments
- *Te ribu* and *Te riburibu*: sulphur-smelling mud.

---

[2] In the early 1970s, a number of soil samples were sent abroad to Germany by the Agricultural Department for analysis. They came back with a curt note: 'these soils are not suitable for growing plants'.

Chapter 1: The Islands

Climate

The climate of the Gilbert Islands is tropical. Temperatures lie within a narrow range, between 26-32°C, with surrounding water temperatures even narrower, at 28-29°C.

The Tungaru people distinguished two seasons: *Te Auti*, which lasts from early December to early June, and *Te Rimwimāta*, which lasts from early June to early December. The year was considered to begin with the appearance of *Nei Auti* (the constellation known in Europe as the Pleiades) to eastward, just after sunset, which takes place by modern calendars at the very end of November, or the first week in December. This season ends when *Rimwimāta* (the star Antares) is observed to appear at the same altitude at 6 p.m., about the second week of June. The second season (*tannaki*) of the year (*ririki*) then began, and lasted until the Pleiades reappeared at sunset.

Te Auti was the season when the trade winds, which blow from the northeast almost continuously, may more commonly turn around and be replaced by westerlies. Heavy rain and squalls then result, and inter-island voyages were not undertaken in this season. By contrast, *Rimwimāta* was the season of 'good sailing' with moderate and consistent winds.

Thus dry seasons are typically encountered at the time of *Rimwimāta*, and wet through *Te Auti*.

However these cannot be relied upon. Rainfall is very much affected by the movement of the South Pacific Convergence Zone (which extends across the South Pacific Ocean from the Solomon Islands to the east of the Cook Islands) and the Intertropical Convergence Zone across the Pacific, just north of the equator. Bands of heavy rainfall are caused by air rising over warm water where these winds converge and create thunderstorms.

This climate varies considerably also from year to year, due to the El Niño-Southern Oscillation (ENSO), the natural climate pattern that occurs across the tropical Pacific Ocean (and affects weather patterns right around the world). There are two extreme phases of the El Niño-South Oscillation: El Niño and La Niña. There is also a neutral phase. El Niño events tend to bring wetter, warmer conditions than normal.

Average rainfall varies from just over 1000 mm/yr. at Tabiteuea to nearly 3100 mm/yr. at Butaritari. However the island of Tarawa has received more than

Chapter 1: The Islands

4000mm in the wettest El Niño years, while in the driest La Niña years as little as 150mm of rain has fallen there.

All of the islands are periodically subject to drought except the two northernmost, but especially the most southern islands, and Banaba. In historical times, severe droughts were noticed by visitors between 1870 and 1876; in 1892; and the random pattern is recorded in successive Colonial 'Blue Books': 1924-5, 1928-9, 1938-39, 1950-52 and 1955-6, and so on [3].

Although the islands owe their existence to debris thrown up by storms, historical records of tropical cyclones are rare. Cyclones normally arise very close to the equator, but build up destructive force only when more than 3 degrees North or South of it. In 1927 a cyclone did considerable damage to Butaritari and Makin, and in 2015 Cyclone Pam to Tamana and Arorae; these are the only ones in the record. In Kiribati, in most years, squalls accompanied by heavy rains and strong winds are more common than storms.

The spring range of the semi-diurnal tides normally varies from a low of about 1.5 m at Beru, to just over 2.2 m at Abaiang. However, and as discussed in Chapter 24, the incidence of very strong 'King Tides' has become significant over the past two or three decades, as the climate has warmed and sea levels have risen.

Fresh water and the coral lens

Fresh water has been, and continues to be, the limiting resource for habitability of the islands. The water supply in pre-contact days came entirely from shallow wells, and, in times of drought, scarcity of water was acute (page 113).

Coral limestone is porous and allows seawater to flow through it. The water table oscillates on a daily basis with the tides, and in the long term with the mean sea level. The wells tap into coral lenses made up of a convex layer of fresh groundwater which is – literally - floating on top of the denser salt water.

The lens arises when rainwater seeps down through the soil surface and gathers over a layer of seawater at or anything up to five feet below sea level.

---

[3] When I first arrived on Tarawa in 1971, there had been virtually no rain for two years and water was being severely rationed.

Chapter 1: The Islands

The sustainable yield of a freshwater lens is dependent on the rate of recharge, and the extent (location, width, depth) and behaviour (response to external influences) of the lens. The recharge of these lenses and therefore their viability as water sources are directly related to rainfall recharge. The other parameters provide information about the storage characteristics of the groundwater and the input (from rainfall) to the groundwater. No permanent freshwater lens can occur, regardless of rainfall, where the island width is less than about 120 m.

The process is illustrated below.

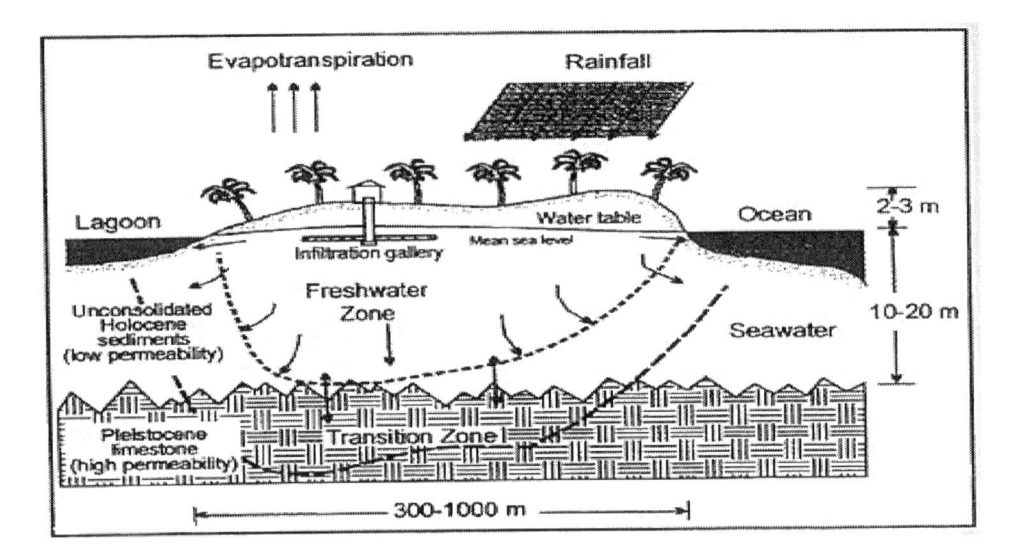

Source: United Nations Environment Programme

Other factors may also have an effect on the occurrence of freshwater lenses (such as the permeability of the coral sediments, or the density of vegetation). Visitors to the island of Marakei are shown one unusual fresh water source which is literally inches from the high tide mark; whereas in other places water remains brackish well inland. Siting of a well may thus involve a certain amount of trial and error, although the presence of loose and permeable coral (and therefore brackish water) is likely to be detected through an exploratory dig.

If too much water is extracted at a location where the lens is not thick enough, saltwater will rise up from below the freshwater lens, making it unusable.

Chapter 1: The Islands

Marine resources

The marine resource groups of the central pacific include: seaweeds, corals, bivalves, gastropods, cephalopods, stomatopods, shrimps, lobsters, crabs, holothurians, sharks, batoid fishes, chimaeras, bony fishes, sea turtles, sea snakes, and marine mammals (and crocodiles, but not in Kiribati!). Amongst all these families, only eleven species are considered as endemic to Kiribati.

Oceania has been described by the UN Food and Agriculture Organisation (FAO) as having *'the richest diversity of marine species in the world'*.

An area of upwelling of nutrient-rich deeper water along the equator, where the Gilbert islands are located, and caused by the diverging flow of the North Equatorial Current and the Equatorial Countercurrent, results in much higher density of marine life near the islands than there is in the surrounding ocean.

Flora

Unsurprisingly, the I Tungaru people had immense knowledge of the ecology, medicinal and cultural uses of their flora. Such knowledge is still common amongst older people in rural areas [4].

The most comprehensive list available contains some 183 I Kiribati names for plants, together with 110 other (mostly recently introduced) species now growing there, for which there are no local names (these numbers disregard names for varieties, such as the many names for types of Pandanus). Some I Kiribati names may also refer to more than one botanically distinct species; for example *te uteute* is the generic name for almost all grasses (which were not of any economic significance in traditional society).

It is estimated that 66 species preceded human settlement, and that a further eight (all food crops) were introduced very early by settlers (see pages 97 - 98 in Chapter 7). None seem to be endemic (i.e. uniquely found in the Gilbert Islands). The indigenous species include: 22 tree species, four of which belong to mangrove associations, whereas the balance are widespread coastal strand species, including Pandanus, which is both indigenous and an aboriginal introduction; 8 shrubs or sub-shrubs; 7 vines or creepers; 7 forbs (non-grass

---

[4] My mother-in-law, who could not read nor write, was a walking encyclopaedia about the growing of and uses of plants; sadly much of this knowledge died with her.

herbs); 12 grasses or sedges; three pteridophytes or fern-like species; two aquatic plants; and three fungi.

Fauna

There were no terrestrial mammals in the Gilbert islands before people, who brought rats and dogs.

A survey in 1969 recorded 79 species of birds in the Marshall and Gilbert Islands, of which 37 are seabirds and 42 are land and fresh-water birds (some of these however are confined to the Northern Marshall islands, see Further Reading).

Studies note the:

- Absence of 'singing' birds
- Few true land birds, by far the majority of species being oceanic birds and migratory shore birds
- Large number of migratory species which make the atolls their winter quarters, or use them as a 'halfway house' on their flights northward and southward
- Noisiness of some species during the night
- Absence of any very small birds.

The study commented that *'perhaps the food-gathering of sea-birds, demanding as it does much time and prolonged journeys on the wing, is the factor which determines their sizes and wing-spans'*.

There are a few species of lizard (such as *te beru* and *te tukunei*); and one type of scorpion (*te tikaobion*).

I have been unable to discover any systematic survey of the insect [5] and arachnid populations of the Gilberts, although the indefatigable René Catala made a preliminary list in his seminal work on the ecology of the Gilbert Islands in 1956 (see Further Reading).

---

[5] Hugh Robinson, who came to advise on setting up the Gilbert Islands Provident Fund in 1974, but whose real passion was the taxonomy of moths, was very surprised and disappointed by his failure to identify a single endemic species of moth on Tarawa.

Chapter 1: The Islands

The creator deity Nareau (Chapter 2) was, of course, a spider; and the I Kiribati distinguish three species of dragonfly: *te keketi, te tikutumauma*, and *te kanebu*; all play a part in mythology.

Mosquitos are very much present in Kiribati, but fortunately they spread neither malaria nor lymphatic filariasis, although the latter is present in neighbouring Tuvalu. Other hazards are stone fish and poisonous sea snakes (although these normally avoid humans).

It seems that the islands are simply too recently formed for evolution to have produced any unique terrestrial species [6].

Summary: the islands before human settlement

There were several important characteristics of the islands that the Tungaru people came to settle:

- The islets above sea level are of recent origin, and (see next Chapter) were probably settled less than 1000 years after they had first emerged from the sea; and their coral lenses would have taken several hundred years after that to establish. If radio carbon dates from the geological survey, and from archaeological digs, are compared, the current shape of the islands, and new islets, must still have been emerging for 1500 years after the first known human settlement of the atolls
- There were few natural terrestrial species, plant or animal, that could be used by humans, other than (probably) pandanus and (possibly) coconut: the settlers had to import the limited range of food crops that could survive in the poor and mineral-deficient soil
- By contrast, marine resources were rich and varied, although the first settlers would have had to work out by painful trial and error which were poisonous
- There were few insect-borne or other diseases

---

[6] There are three recorded exceptions, but they are all in the Line Islands: *Bidens kiribatiensis*, a species in the worldwide genus *Bidens*, which belongs to the daisy family (*Asteraceae*), is endemic to Starbuck island, in the Line Islands, and there were two bird species on Kiritimati, *Acrocephalus aequinoctialis*, the Kiritimati Reed-warbler; and *Prosobonia cancellata*, the Christmas Sandpiper (but this is now extinct).

Chapter 1: The Islands

- To survive, the Tungaru people had to evolve strategies to deal with perennially acute shortages of potable water, and crop failures in times of drought.

The next few Chapters trace how this apparently inhospitable environment came to support what was one of the densest populations of pre-contact Oceania.

Chapter 1: The Islands

Further Reading

1. **Reconnaissance Geology Of The Gilbert Group, Western Kiribati,** by Bruce Richmond, published by the SOPAC Technical Secretariat, May 1993
2. **Climate and Meteorology of the Gilbert Islands,** by Marie Hélène Sachet, published in the Atoll Research Bulletin 60, 1957
3. **Atoll Archaeology in the Pacific**, by Dr Frank R. Thomas
4. **Reducing the Risk of Disasters and Climate Variability in the Pacific Islands - Republic of Kiribati Country Assessment**, published by the World Bank and others at https://sustainabledevelopment.un.org/content/documents/1220kiribatiDisaster.pdf
5. **Gilbertese astronomy and astronomical observances**, by Arthur Grimble, Journal of the Polynesian Society, Volume 40, 1931
6. **Kiribati Fisheries Bibliography**, by Robert Gillett, Mose Pelasio, and Elizabeth Kirschner, published by the FAO, November 1991
7. **FAO Species Identification Guide for Fishery Purposes - The Living Marine Resources of the Western Central Pacific,** edited by Kent E. Carpenter and Volker H. Niem, FAO, Rome, 1998 (in 3 volumes)
8. **Social Principles Underlying Traditional Inshore Fishery Management Systems in the Pacific Basin**, by Kenneth Ruddle, published in Marine Resource Economics, Volume 5, 1988
9. **Report on the Gilbert Islands: Some Aspects of Human Ecology,** by René L. A. Catala, published in Atoll Research Bulletin 59, 1957
10. **The Material Culture of Kiribati,** by Gerd Koch (translated by Guy Slatter), published by the Institute of Pacific Studies, University of the South Pacific, 1986
11. **Ciguatera and Other Marine Poisoning in the Gilbert Islands** by M. J. Cooper, Contribution No. 214, Hawaii Marine Laboratory, University of Hawaii, 1963
12. **Plants of Kiribati: A Listing and Analysis of Vernacular Names** by R.R. Thaman, published in Atoll Research Bulletin 296, 1987
13. **Kiribati Agroforestry: Trees, People and the Atoll Environment** by R.R. Thaman, published in Atoll Research Bulletin 333, 1990
14. **Ornithology of the Marshall and Gilbert Islands** by A. Binion Amerson Jr. published in Atoll Research Bulletin 127, 1969
15. **Wikipedia entries** on: Co-ordinates of Kiribati; El Nino and La Nina events; Coral lenses.

Chapter 2.

SETTLEMENT

Competing theories of origins

It has been said that *'debates concerning the source regions, directions and dates for the human colonisation of the Pacific have provided exasperation and no little entertainment for scholars since the golden days of eighteenth century exploration'*.

Assessments as to when, and by whom, Tungaru was first settled have been variously based on: oral histories; physical anthropology; sailing capabilities; linguistics; genetic analysis; and archaeological discoveries - roughly in that order, over the 250 years or so since those eighteenth century explorations.

Dates assigned to the first settlement of Tungaru vary by a span of more than 6,000 years: from as early as 5,000 BCE, to as late as 1,300 CE. Places from which they migrated to the Gilbert islands archipelago have been similarly and variously described: as an original creation in situ, or in Samoa; eastwards migration from Indonesia, across Palau and the Caroline Islands and down through the Marshall Islands; north-eastwards from the Solomon islands; north-westwards from Vanuatu; and even westwards from South America [7].

This Chapter seeks to navigate through the competing theories, and reach a tentative conclusion.

Oral histories

On every island, certain families kept traditions about the creation of their world. Stories varied from family to family and island to island; most ascribe the opening up of the world and the heavens to Nareau the Creator, a spider, although some traditions prefer Tabakea, a turtle [8]. The location of the first

---

[7] Not including the (now officially abandoned) former Mormon proposition that Polynesians and Micronesians were lost tribes of Israel.

[8] I have not included an account of the creation stories here. One version may readily be found at http://www.janeresture.com/micronesia_myths/kiribati.htm ; another is set out in *Aspects of History; Pattern of Islands* has a version; and there is a fourth version in *Tabiteua Kiribati* (see Further Reading).

Chapter 2: Settlement

land varies: in some cases it is Tamoa (Samoa), in others the island of Beru in the Gilberts, and in yet others the island of Tarawa. The Tabiteuea people claimed that their island was the first to be created at *Takoronga i Nano* and that the tree called *Te Ueanikai* (tree of Kings) was grown there; and Butaritari and Aranuka people also claim the first land [9].

Nareau was also said to have created the I-Matang world, a land of white-skinned spirits, and sent *Nareau the Wise* to care for it; and the *Batabata* or *Be'e'roro* world, the land of black-skinned spirits, to which he sent *Nareau Te Kikinto* (Nareau the Cunning). Nareau the Creator ruled that on no account should the white and black-skinned people migrate to each other's lands. If they did, much trouble would occur. The Gilbert Islands were Nareau the Creator's world, and this was where he remained.

The following account of settlement is based on oral histories of Tungaru, as interpreted by Arthur Grimble. He wrote this in 1923, at the height of the fashion for *euhemerism*, an approach to the interpretation of mythology in which such accounts were presumed to have originated from real historical events: the classic modern work of euhemerism, *The Golden Bough*, had been published fifteen or so years earlier. Euhemerism states that historical accounts become myths as they seek to explain the natural world; that they may then become exaggerated or distorted in the retelling; but that there still remains a kernel of historic truth [10].

Grimble wrote:

> *'According to the evidence of tradition, which is to a great extent substantiated by an examination of the social organisation, there formerly lived in the Gilbert Islands (and probably also in the Marshalls to the north and the Ellice Group to the south) a small black skinned, large*

---

[9] It is perhaps worth pointing out that Samoa and Beru were, successively in later times, the sources of 'elite' invaders of other Gilbert islands, which could mean that origins were sited in their lands in order to confer legitimacy to these invaders, as has been shown to have happened in other cultures.

[10] I would not wish however to discount euhemerism, as do many modern commentators, especially the influential Noam Chomsky. For example, the Irish oral histories always but controversially placed their origins in Spain rather than in the supposed Celtic homeland on the Danube; and genetic analysis has now shown that they were quite right to do so.

Chapter 2: Settlement

eared, flat-nosed race much addicted to magic, whose society was divided into exogamous moieties, and whose system of descent was matrilineal. The deities of this people seem to have been the spider and the turtle; they also appear to have conserved some socio-religious memories of a creature called Te Kekeneu, which from its description as a "lizard as long as two men" was probably a crocodile or other saurian.

'It is impossible to say when the peace of these people was first disturbed by invaders, or how long they had been in occupation before that epoch. But it is certain that in very early times they were overrun by a people from the west.

'The physical type of the immigrants was utterly different from that of the autochthones. They were of great stature, red-skinned (i.e. light brown) with bushy hair standing high on the head and curled at the ends. They seemed to have been tremendous fighters but in their struggle with the spider folk were handicapped by their ignorance and horror of magic. They practised the cult of the ancestor, in conjunction with the preservation of skulls; had probably been kava drinkers; and possessed a social organisation based upon totemic exogamous clans in which descent was patrilineal. […] It is extremely likely that, like the majority of migrant races in Oceania, they brought no women with them and so had to take wives from the spider-folk.

'In the fusion of religious beliefs and the modifications of social organisation that followed the immigration and settlement, it is certain that the matrilineal spider-folk left many traces of their system embedded in that of the patrilineal invaders.

'Of the brown-skinned sea-folk it seems that only a fraction stayed to win a foothold in the Gilberts; the majority […] pushed down to Savaii and Upolu of Samoa.

'During this period of settlement, there seems to have been a considerable amount of intercourse between the Samoan immigrants and their kinsmen in the Gilberts. Canoe voyages are described in detail by tradition. Then came the cataclysm. In the language of tradition, "the tree of Samoa, the ancestor, was broken, and its people were scattered over the islands of the sea" […] as a result of a family quarrel. What we do know is that the flight took place and that a horde of fugitives came back northwards…'

Chapter 2: Settlement

Until quite recently most observers of Kiribati [11] would probably have accepted some variant of this account. However, in the past two or three decades it has been severely challenged, for the reasons set out later in this chapter.

According to his daughter Rosemary, Arthur Grimble later in life widened this theory:

> *'They [the Gilbertese] had a natural dignity and taste which set them apart from others. It suggested descent from some great civilisation of the past .... He was convinced that they came from the west, at any rate and was impressed by repeated references in their myths to a fair-skinned breed of giants, who made great voyages across the Pacific .... There were many migrations, at least four from the west that we know about, and perhaps many more. He never questioned the proposition that rafts from Peru could have reached the Gilbert Islands, bringing new cultures with different traditions'.*

Indeed he eventually tried to tie in links to ancient Egypt and Babylon!

Physical anthropology

As early as 1799, J. Wilson – a very early missionary – had suggested the same origins as Grimble: that a *'darker race'* had been the original inhabitants over New Holland (Australia) and New Guinea, the islands adjacent to New Guinea, as well as those of *'Solomon, Santa Cruz, New Caledonia, the chief part of the New Hebrides, and the group called Feje'*. These people soon became known as Melanesians and the people to the east and south of them, of *'lighter race'*, as the Polynesians and Micronesians. These, he was confident, *'have been traced to the coasts of the great Asiatic islands and Borneo, and from thence to the peninsula of Malacca'*. These observations – leaving aside the now doubtfully valid concept of 'race' - have also been largely discredited over the past two decades, as have the three designations of the islanders as coherent genetic or cultural groups.

Early physical anthropology moved on to analysis of both cranial and cephalic measurements; and later to analysis of blood groups. The Gilbertese appear

---

[11] Including myself. It is similar to the Anglo-Saxon 'wipe out' theory of 'dark age' Britain, on which I was brought up, but which archaeological and genetic evidence have now shown to be very doubtful.

Chapter 2: Settlement

largely to have been spared the former of these, although some measurements were made in the 1920s and 1930s (when the main concern of researchers seems to have been that of trying to link the measurements of the 'primitive' Pacific islanders to those of Africans, with which they had little success). Later on, after WWII, research into the inherited blood diseases anticipated genetic research: in the process of establishing the link between sickle cell anaemia, thalassaemia and malaria, many samples of blood were collected around the Pacific. In both 1953 and 1961, extensive samples were taken in the Gilbert Islands by visiting teams who reported on blood groups, serum genetic factors, and haemoglobins. Whilst confirming the prevalence of Type A blood groups, however, these studies (which were in any case concerned with combatting disease, not with researching from where the I Tungaru came) do not appear to have found any useful pointers as to origins.

The current consensus about the settlement of Oceania

More extensive genetic research on Pacific Islanders started in the 1970s. Since then, it has been well established that, between 50,000 (some say earlier) and 30,000 years ago, Australoid and Papuan hunting and gathering groups were able to cross sea gaps up to 70 km. wide. There were several potential routes through the Philippines and Indonesia, to Australia, New Guinea, the Bismarck Archipelago, and to the Northern Solomon Islands as far as San Christobal.

Of these, only the Timor to Australia route (thought to have been taken by those who went to Australia) meant leaving the sight of land from source to destination.

From the San Christobal to the Santa Cruz islands there is a water crossing of 300 km. These early settlers evidently did not possess the sailing technologies to cross that gap and to spread further; and sea levels were rising steadily, eventually drowning both the Sunda and Sahul sub-continents which had emerged at the Last Glacial Maximum, about 24,500 B.C.E.

The - current - majority view of scholars about the much later spread of the quite separate Austronesian cultures is summarised below.

Austronesian horticultural populations with advanced voyaging technology, originating in Taiwan rather than the straits of Malacca, entered the Western Pacific (but not Australia) after 3000 BCE, and over the next three millennia reached the far corners of the Pacific, including Tungaru. They had various southern Mongoloid physical characteristics (*phenotypes*), including '*sundadont*' dental patterns.

In 2016, one of the most extensive DNA analyses yet carried out resulted in a new finding as to how the Austronesian language family spread across such a large but genetically diverse region. The conclusion was that most of the modern people of Indonesia, Malaysia, Philippines and Madagascar are genetically not related to Taiwanese or Polynesian people; they are instead mostly pre-Austronesians who have adopted the Austronesians' language.

The current hypothesis is that there was quite a small-scale migration '*Out of Taiwan*' into Sundaland and the Philippines, whose people mixed into the local population. The language shift suggests that these newly arriving Taiwanese were an elite group – possibly connected to a new religion, or with technical or other cultural superiority.

The Austronesian-speaking peoples may thus now be grouped into two *genetically* but not *linguistically* distinct groups:

- The Sunda or Malay group, consisting of most people in Indonesia, Malaysia, the southern Philippines, other parts of the southeast Asian mainland, and Madagascar
- The Taiwanese - Polynesian group, consisting of aboriginal people in Taiwan, the northern Philippines, Polynesia, Micronesia, and historically also in southern China.

On their way to Oceania, these Austronesians mixed with the existing Melanesian populations; although the speed of the '*express train to Polynesia*', which posits that humans moved rapidly through Melanesia to Oceania with very little mixing, is still a matter for debate. Some continue to argue for a '*slow boat*': that the movement was much more disjointed, occurring over an extended period, and involving different Melanesian populations, and varied levels of genetic mixing.

In 2016, for example, DNA analysis of four Lapita skeletons from cemeteries on Teouma and Talasiu (in northern Vanuatu) showed that, when compared against modern populations, these ancient samples are genetically closest to the Ami and Atayal people from Taiwan, and the Kankanaey people from the northern Philippines. They have little DNA similarity with modern Papuans. According to Matthew Spriggs (Professor of Archaeology at ANU), the

Chapter 2: Settlement

ancient population at Teouma came 'straight out of Taiwan and perhaps the northern Philippines'.

As they travelled into the further reaches of Oceania, these people gradually abandoned the Lapita pottery culture and other aspects of what I call below 'the Austronesian Package' that they had brought with them, as they settled islands with no suitable clays for pottery or soils for all their trees and crops. As we shall see in Chapter 7, by the time they had reached the Gilbert Islands, they had perforce shed many aspects of such an 'Austronesian package' - but they had also invented new techniques, such as the cutting of toddy from the coconut tree to provide the vitamin C that is largely unobtainable from other local resources there.

The northern and central Pacific area now defined as Micronesia ('small islands') was initially settled from at least five different sources, beginning about 3,500 years ago with the settlement of the Marianas, almost certainly directly from the northern Philippines. This involved an ocean crossing of some 2,300 km. – the longest in human history to that date - and jettisoning of aspects of the original Austronesian culture such as rice and millet growing. A second wave of immigrants came to the Marianas about 1,000 years ago, with associated megalithic architecture.

Secondly, Austronesians colonised Palau about 3,000 years ago, most likely from a source in the southern Philippines or Indonesia.

Both these Marianas and Palau settlements are associated with Western Malayo-Polynesian languages, rather than Oceanic languages (see below).

The third set of settlements centred on Yap, in the Caroline Islands. These people probably came northwards from island Melanesia, and have a relatively high admixture of Melanesian genes compared to other Micronesian populations both westwards and eastwards.

Fourthly, another movement of people, almost certainly originating in what are now called the Banks Islands in northern Vanuatu, are thought to have colonised the most easterly volcanic islands in Micronesia around 2000 years ago: firstly Kosrae, and then Pohnpei and Chuuk, all in the Caroline Islands. It is thought that people spread out from this group into atolls in the Marshall islands (where archaeological evidence of people also dates to about 2000 years ago) and the Gilbert islands; and they were thus the most likely first

Chapter 2: Settlement

inhabitants of Tungaru. (However a minority view is that the Marshalls and Gilberts were settled first).

Lastly (not shown on map below), there was 'back filling' of (mostly small atoll) islands in both Micronesia and Melanesia from Polynesian islands far to the east - which had been settled from a jumping-off point in the Solomon Islands by a quite different route, via Fiji and then Samoa. How far this may also have resulted in some early intermixing with the founder Micronesian/Melanesian population in Tungaru (as opposed to the immigration of Polynesians from Samoa and Tonga to the Gilberts much later) does not seem to have been researched [12].

There also seems to have been some 'back-filling' by Micronesians as well, for example to the Ninigo Islands near Manus, off the coast of New Guinea, almost completing a circle back to the spot through which their ancestors had passed maybe 1,500 years previously.

One source can now definitively be discounted: there was no contribution to Pacific Island genes from South America. Romantic as Thor Heyerdahl's 1952 voyage was, DNA evidence is conclusive that Amerindians were not ancestors to the Polynesians or Micronesians.

It is more likely that the *kumara* (sweet potato) - which is undoubtedly of South American origin but is widely grown in Oceania (although not much in Kiribati) - was brought back by voyagers ranging out of the Pacific islands to South America. A 2007 study examined chicken bones in Arauco Province, Chile, radiocarbon-dated to between 1304 and 1424, well before the documented arrival of the Spanish. DNA sequences were exact matches to those of chickens from the same period in American Samoa and Tonga.

Oceania-to-America contact is however still hotly disputed.

The map on the next page thus summarises the current consensus as to how Micronesia was originally settled, both from the west, and from the southeast, and then from further east.

---

[12] So far as I have been able to discover

Chapter 2: Settlement

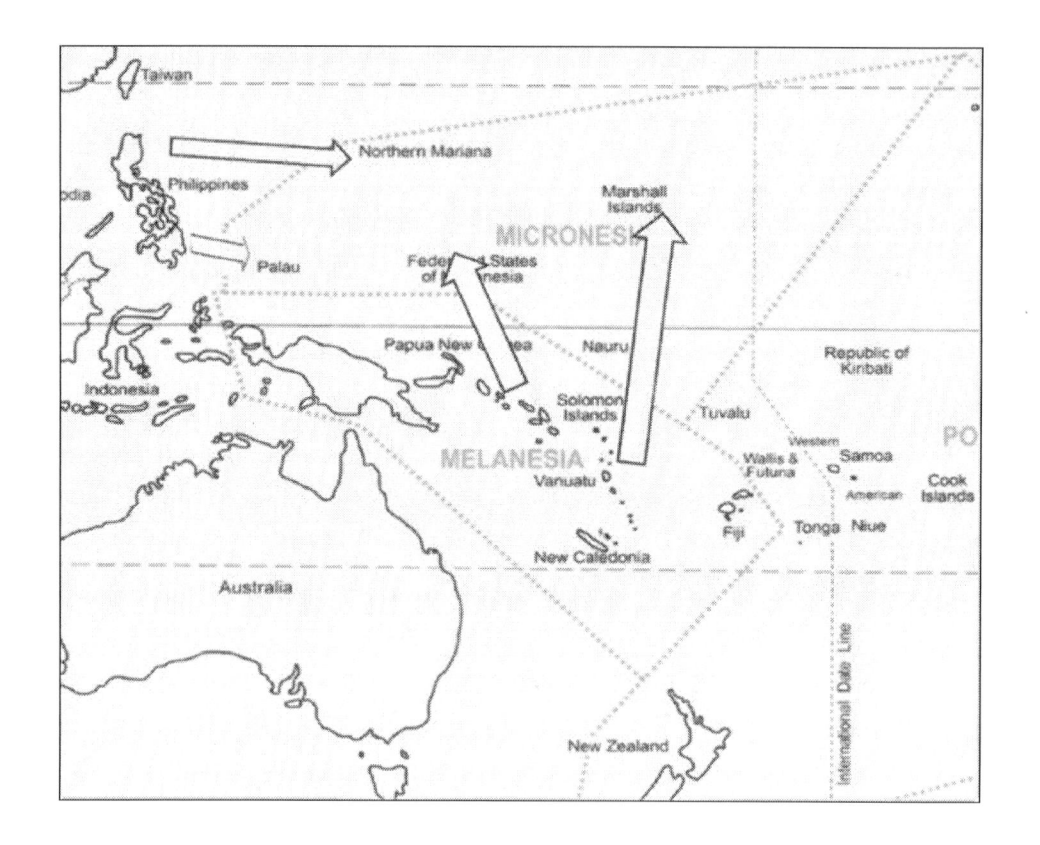

Sailing capabilities

Oceanic sea-going craft of the type used in the Pacific are thought first to have been developed in the Taiwanese straits, or in South China. They were certainly an early development of Austronesian culture: the archetype was the multihull sailing boat known as the *proa*, which is still common in the Philippines and Indonesia. *Proas* consist of two parallel hulls, usually of unequal length, sailed so that one hull is kept to windward, and the other to leeward. This means that it is necessary to 'shunt' to reverse direction when tacking.

Variants of this design have been an essential feature of oceanic life since its outset. Their construction varies according to the available material: in Melanesia, and much of Polynesia (including Tuvalu), where large trees are available, they were made from a dug-out canoe hollowed out of the trunk of the tree, although with a double hull or an outrigger. In Tungaru, where suitable trees were not available, construction methods were by necessity different (see page 114 in Chapter 7).

Chapter 2: Settlement

The I Tungaru people employed a range of techniques for navigation: stars, movement of ocean currents and wave patterns, the air and sea interference patterns caused by islands and atolls, the flight of birds, winds and the weather. Their point of reference was the *mwaneaba*.

Navigators regarded the night-sky as a vast roof: the *uma ni borau*, which signifies literally, 'roof of voyaging'. The terminology of their astronomy and navigation follows from this fundamental idea. The eastern horizon is called *te tatanga ni mainiku* (the roof-plate of east) and the western, in a similar manner, *te tatanga ni maeao* (the roof-plate of west). The meridian is *te taubuki*, the ridge-pole.

The roof is supported by imaginary rafters (*oka*), three on the eastern slope and three to correspond on the west. The apex of the middle pair is held to be at the point where the star Rigel crosses the meridian. These middle rafters represent the Gilbertese celestial equator. A navigator thus sat in imagination beneath this framework, in which the stars themselves form the ever-shifting thatch.

Trainee navigators learnt this celestial framework in relation to a *mwaneaba*, long before they actually went out to the night sky and to sea so they could be trained in the other techniques described below; and their mental conception of a voyage was always that they stayed stationary, while the sea moved round them.

Between five and ten stars were typically needed for observation over a night's journey. The navigator Teeta, who took David Lewis on a journey through the Gilbert Islands in the 1960s, in reply to a question as to whether one always steered by the star in front explained that *'we may use one to the side or astern for steering because from it we can tell the direction equally well as from one in front'*.

The star course might allow for currents in the ocean. Abera of Nikunau, another informant of David Lewis, distinguished two different star routes between Beru and Nikunau, and also Beru and Onotoa: one for normal conditions and one for when the north-going current was unusually strong.

On any substantial voyage star navigation must be supplemented by other means, as the stars will be invisible for half the voyage. David Lewis comments that 'in practice the navigator is naturally checking his bearings all the time from the swells and more temporarily by the wind, as well as the

Chapter 2: Settlement

sun... holding course by swells seems always to be a matter more of feel than sight'.

Nearer to landfall, techniques for 'expanding' the size of the target were an integral part of navigation: *'the idea applies in two situations. In the first, an isolated atoll is appreciated as being surrounded, far beyond sight range, by a zone of land indicators. In the second, the gaps between the islands of a group are bridged by the overlapping zones around individual islands, so that the whole archipelago becomes a target for landfall. Both applications depend on the observation of land signs such as homing birds, clouds, or wave patterns'*.

Teeta is quoted by David Lewis as saying that 'if I were heading for somewhere far away I would go in the general direction and then look for signs of land'. Teeta for example knew of a course that would bring him to 'somewhere in the Marshall Islands' where he was confident of making a landfall by these subsidiary methods.

The activities of noddies, terns, and other birds not only betray the presence of shoals of fish; their regular and consistent excursions from islets to fishing-grounds, especially in the early morning and evening, provided a valuable guide as to the whereabouts of land up to twenty miles away, twice the sight range of an atoll. Frigate birds range even further, up to 75 miles.

However, observation of cloud patterns was probably even more important to the I Tungaru people. About 15 miles from land it is possible to distinguish colours and brightness in the clouds that stand over land, which are quite different to those over the sea [13].

There are effects when an atoll obtrudes into, and disturbs, the even run of ocean swells. To quote Abera again: 'If you are in a canoe bound from Onotoa to Tabiteuea you feel it as a slow heave that rolls the canoe a little from the port side. This swell [*nao bangaki*] can be detected all over the seas'.

Finally, there are navigational stones on certain islands to indicate the direction in which to set off. Thirteen such stones, Te atibu ni Borau, at Arorae were described by Vic Ward in 1946, which provide such directions for Banaba, Nikunau, Beru, Tamana, and 'Orona' – an island in the Phoenix Group, although H. E. Maude insisted that this island was unknown to the I

---

[13] During my time travelling around the Gilberts, even I learned to interpret at least the obvious ones!

Chapter 2: Settlement

Tungaru people and actually constituted a second set of directions to Tamana, some 50 miles away [14]. These directions allowed for both swells and drift.

Similar stones at Butaritari point towards the island of Mili in the Marshalls, some 165 miles northwards. It is possible there were once more such stones, but that like the ancient shrines the Missionaries had them incorporated into foundations for churches (Chapter 8.)

I return below to the issue as to how far these techniques were useful on exploring voyages into the *unknown*, rather than just ensuring that the navigator could follow already traversed routes.

Language

I Kiribati is an Austronesian language, and thus is part of one of the two largest language families in the world, the other being the Niger–Congo language group.

Austronesian is divided into several primary branches, all but one of which are confined to Taiwan: all Austronesian languages *outside* Taiwan belong to just one branch, Malayo-Polynesian.

The two great migrations were described above, firstly of Malayo-Polynesians across the Philippines, Indonesia, and Melanesia (and over to Madagascar) who were genetically distinct but who had adopted Austronesian languages; and secondly that of a further sub-group of more directly Taiwanese genetic descent, and speaking what are known as the *Oceanic languages,* across parts of Melanesia, the whole of Polynesia and most of Micronesia. Palau and the Marianas, although conventionally classified as part of Micronesia, speak non-Oceanic, although still Austronesian, languages - and are thus part of the first group.

The Micronesian branch of Oceanic consists of Kosraean, Nauruan, and nineteen 'central Micronesian' languages, seventeen of them grouped together into a Chuukic-Ponapeic set, with Marshallese fairly closely, and I Kiribati less closely, related to this seventeen.

---

[14] These stones are the ones ascribed to extra-terrestrial beings, the 'astronaut gods', by Erich Von Daniken in his 1981 book *'The Stones of Kiribati'*. This book probably contains more elementary factual errors about Kiribati than any other I have come across, against quite a lot of competition.

Although linguists can spot these relationships, I Kiribati is not mutually intelligible with any other language. The language spoken in Micronesia shows greater homogeneity in the western part of this set of languages, while there is greater diversity to the east (of which the Gilbert archipelago is the extreme edge). It has thus been suggested, but is not generally accepted, that the Marshalls and Tungaru were settled from eastern Melanesia *before* the rest of Micronesia, about 3000 years ago.

Such homogeneity could however have arisen from 'founder effects' (the loss of variation that occurs when a new population is established by a very small number of individuals from a larger population).

How long it takes for a group of people to develop their own language has been said to be *'a question linguists don't want to answer'*. One rule of thumb is that two languages are 'separate' if they share only 80% of a core 100 words; it has been (reluctantly) suggested that, while the time needed for this degree of separation to take place with populations isolated from each is highly variable, it is *'probably between 500 and 1000 years'*.

If this is the case, and the I Kiribati came to Tungaru from Vanuatu, via Kosrae, then there would need to have elapsed between 1,000 and 2,000 years for its language to shift not once but twice: from Kosraen to proto - central Micronesian, and from that to I Kiribati. The earliest known settlements on Kosrae date to about 2700 BCE, so these estimates would be consistent with the emergence of I Tungaru as a separate language about the beginning of the Common Era.

The structure of I Kiribati

Two striking characteristics of Oceanic languages are:

- Affixation (use of prefixes and suffixes to form or to modify words)
- Reduplication (repetition of all or part of a word, such as *nako* (walk) and *nakonako* (run) so as to form new words.

Oceanic languages also have relatively small phonemic inventories (phonemes are the smallest units of sound that can differentiate meaning), so that a sentence typically has few but frequent sounds.

The LMS Grammar (1900) comments: 'it is doubtful whether in a Gilbertese ear two vowels are ever united as to form what in European tongues is termed

Chapter 2: Settlement

a diphthong, that is, the coalition of two vowels into one sound ... the mellifluous manner in which adjoining vowels are enunciated is most marked' [15].

Grammatically, I Kiribati seems to have been influenced by the Papuan languages of northern New Guinea. However this influence seems more likely to stem through proto-Micronesian developed on the way from Taiwan, rather than directly from Grimble's aboriginal Melanesians.

There are also loan words from Polynesian languages that most likely arrived with the Samoan invasions of around 1400 CE (see page 35 below). These seem more of Tongan derivation than Samoan, supporting the hypothesis that although the incoming migrants to Tungaru had come from Samoa and were traditionally referred to as Samoan in oral histories, they were actually from the Tu'i Tonga dynasty of mixed Tongan and Samoan heritage. Such loan words include *moa* (chicken), *baurua* (ocean going canoe) and *rongorongo* (news).

The written form of the language was conceived by the Congregationalist Missionary Rev. Hiram Bingham (see pages 143 - 144 in Chapter 8). He distinguished five vowels as in English (each of which has both a short, and a long, expression); but only eight consonants. Being a good Victorian, he 'rationalised' their order: so that the I Kiribati alphabet is declaimed as: 'a, e, i, o, u, m, n, ng, b, k, r, t and w'.

One of these consonants represents the nasal sound '*ng*' (as in the English *sing*) and is written as such.

The Reid Cowell Grammar (1950) states that *'none of the last five [consonants of the alphabet] can end a word'*; and overall, he notes only six examples of consonantal pairing: *m* doubled; *m* with *n, b, k, r, t* and *w*; *n* doubled; *n* with *r* and *t*; *ng* with *k*; *bw*; and *kw*. It was also Hiram Bingham who rendered the phoneme spelled as '*s*' in English as '*ti*', as in the English words 'nation' or

---

[15] Which is why, to the untutored European ear, I Kiribati speech seems so vowel-heavy. Holding these vowels for a precise length of time for a particular word (mellifluously or otherwise) is essential when speaking I Kiribati. As I know from many personal experiences, getting a vowel length even slightly wrong means that one has probably said a completely different word to that intended.

Chapter 2: Settlement

'station' [16]. There is a well-known, though apocryphal, story that the reason for this was that the 's' stamps in his printing set were lost overboard when he landed in the Gilberts. A second slightly different orthography was later developed by the Roman Catholic Mission, although the two have now been standardised; and in the 1980s another set of changes has been made (e.g. *maneaba* is now correctly *mwaneaba*) [17].

Another feature of the language is the many ways of counting:
- *ua*: general classifier, used for common objects, as well as for periods of time. It is the classifier used for 'general' counting
- *man*: animate things (people, animals, birds, insects and most fish, except very large ones, which use -ai)
- *kai*: trees, shrubs, land sections and fish-hooks
- *bai*: teeth, timbers, fingers, and other objects of elongated shape (such as sticks or by extension, bottles)
- *waa*: canoes
- *baa*: leaves, and by extension flat objects such as sheets of paper.

Archaeology

The Micronesian islands were described in the early 20th century as 'stepping stones from western Indonesia to Polynesia'.

Grimble for example writes that:

> *'Of the brown skinned sea-folk that came from the west* [18] *it seems that only a fraction stayed to win a foothold in the Gilberts; the majority of what must have been a mighty swarm turned southwards down the chain of islands sailed coastwise through the Ellice group, took Rotuma in its stride, and pushed forward to Savaii and Upola of Samoa. This is not an imaginary itinerary. It is shown by the evidence of tradition and genealogy.'*

---

[16] Thus inadvertently making the country name of Kiribati, some 150 years later, the most mispronounced in the world!

[17] I have used the 'old' spellings for contemporaneous quotations in this book

[18] i.e. the west as viewed *from* the Gilberts – if, as Grimble confidently asserts, their origins were the island of Bouru, now part of Indonesia, their journey *to* the Gilberts was eastwards, not westwards!

Chapter 2: Settlement

This view has been discounted since the Lapita culture (which is mostly defined in terms of pottery) was discovered in 1952, in excavations on New Caledonia. In the six decades since 1952, more than two hundred Lapita sites have been uncovered. They range over some 4,000 km: from the Bismarck Archipelago, along coastal and island Melanesia, and then over to Fiji and Tonga, with the eastern limit (so far) in Samoa; but with extensions of Lapita-derived pottery also northwards into the Caroline islands in Micronesia.

In fact, while the Melanesian and Polynesian sites were being uncovered in the latter half of the 20th century, Micronesia was rather set aside in the active study of prehistoric dispersals. This changed with the discovery of Lapita-derived pottery in Fefan, in Chuuk, in the late 1970s: *'significant quantities of a sand-tempered mostly plain earthenware ... associated with this pottery was an impressive range of shell artefacts, including adzes, chisels, discs, pendants, and probable fishhook fragments manufactured from* Tridacna, Comus, Cassis *and other shell taxa'*.

In 2004 it was said that:

> 'On the high volcanic islands of Truk [now rendered as Chuuk], Pohnpei and Kosrae where potting clay was available, they continued to practice their ceramic arts, although these would later decline and be abandoned as they were in Polynesia. As people moved off the high islands and colonised the neighbouring coral atolls they faced a new set of environmental and ecological challenges, including a complete lack of clay and stone resources. However the sophisticated shell manufacturing technology ... readily enabled these adaptations to atoll conditions'.

Archaeological work began earlier in the Marshall Islands than in the Gilberts, and more than 40 sites have been investigated in them. Excavations of giant taro pits on Maleolap and Ujae have shown that there have been human settlements for more than 2000 years. In the Gilberts, no reported excavations were conducted before 1983, when brief surface surveys were made on Makin, Butaritari, Tarawa and Abemama. Since then, more detailed work has been undertaken on Makin (which confirmed the presence of dogs some 1600 years ago); and work in 1988 concluded in relation to digs on Tarawa and Tamana in that year (mainly of fishing gear) that:

> *'excavations on Makin, Tamana and Vaitupu [in Tuvalu] have led us to postulate that Makin has closer parallels in the Marshalls and the*

Chapter 2: Settlement

> *Carolines to the west than Tamana, whereas Tamana has a closer historical relationship with Polynesia than Makin'.*

However the earliest dates for settlement in the Gilberts come from a 1999 dig on Nikunau, of two earth ovens. Charred pandanus keys from these ovens were radiocarbon dated to about 2000 years ago, or around the beginning of the Common Era. Archaeological research carried out on North Tarawa in 2010 and 2012 yielded evidence of human activity between the third and seventh centuries CE.

Genetic evidence to date

Techniques such as *Polymerase Chain Reaction* were not developed until still later, in the 1980s; since then, geneticists have for the first time been able to trace migrations through DNA, and particularly the statistical distribution of Asian-Melanesian ancestry amongst Micronesians.

Mitochondrial DNA evidence—passed down exclusively from female ancestors — tends to support the '*express-train*' theory; but the Y-chromosome, or male, evidence at least to some extent supports a slow-boat process (note that this is the exact opposite of Grimble's assertion above, that the spider-folk were the founder female ancestors, and the males fairer-skinned invaders who intermarried with them).

The closest detailed analyses to Kiribati [19] have been conducted on the people of Nauru, and indicate contributions from south-east Asia of 65%, and from Melanesia of 30%. A rare blood group that originates in the Sepik region of New Guinea, Gerbich negative, is also widespread in Nauru.

Possible first settlements: conclusions

The evidence suggests therefore that:

> *'Micronesians are a distinct hybrid of the island South-East Asian and Melanesian gene pools. However it should be remembered that because Micronesians appear to have been relatively recent arrivals in their islands (in the last 2000-3500 years) a prior migration of pre-Polynesians might have left little genetic trace in present-day Micronesia.'*

---

[19] That I have been able to find

Chapter 2: Settlement

The fishhooks recovered on Tamana are conceivably such a trace.

Another question is the extent to which linguistic analysis might support the Grimble hypothesis, well-based as it was on oral histories, that the I Tungaru people were a mixed population, and thus possibly created a creole language. It has been said that new 'creole' languages are *'most commonly born of the mixing of two peoples with incompatible languages ... The pattern is that one generation starts to use a pidgin language to aid communication ... The original languages persist in everyday use within linguistically and socially separate communities. The next generation develops the pidgin language into a creole. This evolves rapidly. Words gain new meanings. Clashing grammatical rules get ironed out. As the creole gains expressive power, and because everyone is speaking it, the original languages fade away.'*

One might speculate that such a language arose from Austronesian - speaking migrants from Kosrae, and then direct arrivals with Taiwanese genes similar to those whose bones were excavated at Teouma in the Banks Islands. However this has not been tested and it remains just that: pure speculation.

Radiocarbon dates have fixed the approximate:

- Dates at which potentially inhabitable islands emerged in the Gilbert archipelago (Chapter 1): this is about 2000 BCE, although islands were still forming for 1500 years or so after that date
- Earliest *yet known* evidence of humans: this is about the turn of the Common Era.

We cannot know whether the first people to land were purposeful explorers, refugees from wars or overpopulated areas in Melanesia, or if they simply arrived by accident (although the last is doubtful); nor whether there was one founding group, or many.

We do know that navigating into the unknown was not as chancy a business as might be thought, both because of the techniques for 'expanding' the size of the target described above, which in effect meant that the whole archipelago became the target, rather the individual atolls; but also, as it has separately been argued, because Oceanic peoples maximised their survival chances for exploratory voyages by heading into what has been called the *safe bearing for exploration* (SBE).

By heading *into* the prevailing wind on outward, exploratory journeys, explorers would have a much better chance of a safe return from searches

Chapter 2: Settlement

which failed to find habitable land. Thus, rather than colonisation moving outward in all directions from a central point, voyages were directed by this SBE. A recent computer simulation around such a theory considered ten canoes leaving the Reef islands (in the Banks Islands group in Vanuatu). It resulted in seven finding the Marshall archipelago, two, the Gilberts archipelago, and one reaching Banaba – so possibly all these were colonised directly from Vanuatu, at least in part.

We cannot be sure of the extent to which the initial Tungaru populations were formed from independent groups of settlers although this both seems very likely, and would be in accord with oral traditions; and perhaps also accounts for the archaeological differences between Makin and Tamana (page 29 above).

It does not however seem probable from the genetic evidence that the first people were the pure Melanesian 'spider-folk' of Grimble's account: and they certainly did not arrive from the direction that he posits. It seems more likely that there was some mixture of Austronesian and Melanesian genes along the way from Taiwan; but that this mixture might have been in different proportions for different founder groups. The extraordinarily wide definition in Tungaru society of what constitutes incest (page 45) [20] might possibly reflect experience of a founder population that had experienced trouble from early inbreeding.

The islands, although then not capable of permanent habitation, must have been settled within about a millennium of their emergence from the sea. Permanent habitation required a process of transforming the land from what was probably mostly Guettarda - Pisonia forest, with some Pandanus species, to the predominant coconut groves and Cyrtosperma pits of today.

We cannot be sure either whether the settlement process was that of a totally 'transported landscape', with all the subsistence items brought directly from Vanuatu, or at least from a neighbouring 'high' island (in the case of the Gilberts, Kosrae) and planted on cleared ground; by the creation of a 'habitus' by manipulation of the native vegetation to cause erosion and the progradation of the shoreline, with the population living almost entirely off

---

[20] In fact stricter than in any other society for which I have been able to find rules.

Chapter 2: Settlement

marine resources in the interim while this developed; or by 'seeding' of the islands by exploratory voyages prior to full settlement. All three have been proposed.

It seems safe to conclude, at least tentatively, that the very first settlers in Tungaru probably had a similar genetic make-up to the current population of Nauru, but that a modern day detailed analysis of the I Kiribati population would show a Polynesian component (absent in Nauru) which the *Tongafiti* refugees from Samoa, themselves of partly Tongan ancestry, introduced some 25 or so generations ago, as described below [21].

What we can be sure of is that when Europeans arrived in the early 19th century, the population had become unusually homogenous because of centuries of further mixing, as described in the remainder of this Chapter.

Contacts with other parts of the Pacific before 1800

Micronesia

Traffic between the Caroline Islands and more westerly parts of Micronesia is well attested, with the island of Yap playing a major role, most famously involving the large money discs quarried from Palau and Guam. The pre-contact presence in Tungaru of the seeded breadfruit *Artocarpus mariannensis* (which is endemic to the Mariana Islands and Guam) is evidence of contact across to Tungaru; but there is no way of knowing how frequent this was, by what precise route it came, or whether it involved migration (and back – migration) of people. As an example of the latter, the Pohnpei Sounmaraki clan, according to their traditions, came originally from Marakei in Kiribati; and people of the Auainano family from Abaiang are said have a common ancestry with the Kabua family of the Marshalls.

There is indeed much evidence of contact between the Marshall islands and Tungaru (especially the two northernmost islands of Butaritari and Makin). *Artocarpus mariannensis* must have come by this route. Butaritari tradition tells of a *uea* named Rairaueana travelling to Bukiroro in the Marshall islands,

---

[21] For once the standard conclusion of most research pieces, that *'more research is needed'*, seems justified.

Chapter 2: Settlement

which H. E. Maude identified as Mili; and that Rairaueana's nephew Kakiaba subsequently became *uea* of an island called Nakiroro in the Marshalls. David Lewis was also informed of a sea mark by Teeta (who had learned of it from his grandfather), called *te maabubu*, which is some 400 km. north of Butaritari and where *'the voyager runs into a belt of low visibility which indicates that he is in the latitude of Taaruri [Jaluit] and must run west for two or three days before he can make land'*.

The Wilkes expedition noted of Butaritari that:

> *'their canoes are larger and better built than those of the southern islands, and made of different wood; and they are better supplied with masts and paddles, but still of nearly the same shape: the side of the canoe opposite to the out-rigger was much less curved ... resembling more the flying proa of the Ladrone [Mariana] Islands'.*

These canoes may have been used for voyages northwards and westwards.

Polynesia

By the 12th century CE, the dynasty of Tongan kings who were named the Tu'i Tonga exercised authority across the Pacific from Niuē and Samoa, as far as Tikopia, southwest of the Solomon Islands. They ruled these nations for more than 400 years, causing some historians to refer to a 'Tongan Empire', although it was probably more of *'a network of interacting navigators, chiefs, and adventurers'*. Distinctive pottery and Tapa cloth designs also show that the Tongans had travelled to the far reaches of Micronesia, as well as to Fiji and Hawaii; so Tongans and Samoans may have established an early foothold in Tungaru as well.

Both Grimble and Sabatier maintain that contact between Tungaru and Samoa was continuous from early times. Sabatier writes:

> *'The Samoan islands had been inhabited for more than two thousand years...in the sixth century [CE] a second wave of migration took place, when the Tongafiti arrived...they landed at Upolu in fifty canoes and challenged the inhabitants, who were forced to seek refuge in the forest .... While Samoa suffered under the yoke imposed by the Tongafiti, the king Talaifeii [mentioned in the family tree of Ti'u-Tonga] had all the people assembled for the task of building a huge terrace ... the Tongans were attacked on all sides ... the Gilbertese have symbolised this defeat in*

Chapter 2: Settlement

> *their tale of the overturned tree: they have retained two distinct memories: an idea of happiness and plenty on a large and very fertile island and also that of a family quarrel which destroyed the people's happiness and meant that some had to go through the risks of migration ... that they headed north when they made their flight was because they knew the islands were inhabited by a people with whom they had always maintained relations ... the Polynesians had been to the Gilberts and had left groups of settlers there'* [22].

The Samoan wars were known in Tungaru as *Uruakin Kain Tiku-aba*, '*the breaking of the tree of the resting place of lands*'. Genealogies given to H. E. Maude in the 1930s for the coming of Tematawarebwe from Samoa to Beru imply a date for the migration of about 1400 CE, based on a reckoning of 25 years per generation. According to these genealogies Tematawarebwe was the leader of the Samoans: he landed at the southern end of Beru, with his parents, two of his brothers, and a number of followers.

Beru was already inhabited by the descendants of Tabuariki and Nainginouati, but they were few in number. The three groups amicably intermarried, and Tematawarebwe set up the first *mwaneaba* in Tungaru, as a copy of the one left behind in Samoa; it is even said to have incorporated timber brought from the original. The mwaneaba also became the *nen te boti*, part of the essential structure of I Tungaru society (see Chapter 3).

Other named refugees from Samoa settled on other islands: for example Nei Matennang on Tarawa, and Akau and his daughter Nei Beia on South Tabiteuea.

The I Tungaru people themselves later ranged southwards to Tuvalu – the distance from Arorae to the northernmost island in Tuvalu, Nanumea, is just under 300 km. There are records of invasions of both Nuitao and Nui. According to Nui tradition, that island was invaded by three waves of warriors from Tungaru: firstly from Tabiteuea, in a *baurua* called Toantebuka, led by Teroko; then from Nonouti, with an expedition led by a female navigator called Nei Ruruobu, and her husband Ten Tinti; and a third from

---

[22] Samoan history describes how the 15th Tui Tonga, Talakaifaiki, became a paramount Chief in Savaii. His Chiefdom in Savaii was short-lived, for he was defeated and expelled from Samoa by Tuna and Fata, which lead to the creation of a new title and dynasty known as Malietoa.

Chapter 2: Settlement

Beru, led by Ten Navei and his wife Nei Miango. These invaders led to the formation of three mixed Micronesian/Polynesian families on the island, and the adoption of the I Tungaru language in Nui. When these invasions took place is uncertain, although Maude considered that they may all have been by refugees displaced by Kaitu of Beru (see below), which would date them as being about 1650 CE.

When Captain Cook visited Tonga in 1777, his navigator Anderson recorded the names of 95 islands known to them, of which three are definitely (and others possibly) in Tungaru (e.g. *Tavala / Tarawa*).

As well as intentional voyaging, there are many instances of drifts by fishing canoes lost off Kiribati. Fishermen sometimes survived months of drifting, which might take them westwards as far as Papua New Guinea, north to the Marshall and Caroline Islands, or (less frequently) eastwards as far as Samoa [23].

Creation of a homogenous society: redistribution of genes and land in the centuries after first settlement

It was from the *mwaneaba*, at Tebontebike on Beru, that the warriors Kaitu and Uakeia set out, in the mid to late 17th century, to conquer many of the Gilbert islands.

There had been prior migrations within Tungaru: for example, Tamana is said to have been first settled by refugees from drought in Banaba; and Onotoa by the giants *Toa ake Onoman* from North Tarawa.

The Beru invaders' 17th century campaign is however described by Sabatier *'most famous by virtue of its size and its consequences …. Kaitu, the instigator, was an enterprising fellow who had his way because of his energy and his presence. As for Uakeia, he was steeped in the occult and was both strategist and soothsayer'*. McClure adds that:

> *'Kaitu is reputed to have been of such immense stature that he commonly went into battle carrying a man on each shoulder. These fought from their perches as from a fighting top, and when their giant supporter became weary they held open his eyes …*

---

[23] However, so far as I am aware, there are no modern recorded instances of drifts of people, rather than of timber, **to** Kiribati.

Chapter 2: Settlement

> *'Uakeia had a dog named Tebuti – n – ang to which he was devotedly attached. This animal was inordinately fond of fish. So his master invariably took as his spoils on a conquered island the part that provided the richest fishing grounds'.*

They assembled a fleet of 37 war canoes and an army of about 600 men; the names of a number of women who accompanied them are also recorded. After passing Onotoa without landing, they landed on south Tabiteuea, the population of which fled north. Uakeia set out a plan: they erected standing stones between 10 and 15 feet high on the island of Te Aboaera, which Nicolas Hamann (in whose time they were still there) wrote *'looked from a distance like ghosts'*. The next morning, returning to fight, the Tabiteueans mistook the stones for giant warriors and fled, many of them drowning. Only two northern villages were spared, because the grandfather and uncles of one of the Beru invaders lived there.

The fleet then sailed on to Nonouti where Queen Nei Tapiria welcomed them to her residence of *Uma n te Wenei*. Kaitu slept with her and gave her a *'splendid ornament that she wore during festivities in his honour'*; her villages were spared. However, magicians elsewhere in Nonouti were more effective and repelled the Beru invaders through their magic; so they moved hastily on to Abemama, spreading panic as they went. According to Sabatier, they then occupied Kuria, Aranuka, Abemama, Maiana, Tarawa and Abaiang. The army stopped at Marakei, after challengers from Butaritari came to meet them at Taratai on North Tarawa.

Kaitu returned south, but his dynasty survived: the last *uea* of Tarawa, Matang, had the title *Kaitu n Tarawa* in recognition of his heritage. After Kaitu's departure the original people of Tarawa rose against the invaders, starting a cycle of ten civil wars which were only ended by HMS Royalist, more than two centuries later.

Captain Davis' Log reports:

> *'I then drew up a Treaty of Peace which was signed by the King and the 14 Chiefs ... they all appeared glad for this excuse to end the war, for the island is in a most impoverished state. After the Treaty was signed they all sat down to a hearty meal...'*

Chapter 2: Settlement

About the same time, Banaba was invaded, also from Beru, by a party led by Nei Angi-ni-maeo (indeed Maude considered she and her party may themselves have been refugees from Kaitu's wars).

In Abemama, a new and different kind of dynasty came to power in the early nineteenth century. The giant warrior Tatabo had led the opposition to an invading army from Tarawa in about 1780, and his family had become gradually dominant over Abemama society. His grandson became the *uea*, Tem Baiteke, who was not a traditional warrior but became involved in trade with the newly arrived Europeans, and bought firearms from them. He laid waste to and annexed the neighbouring islands of Kuria and Aranuka. He was also responsible for an overnight massacre of 17 European castaways and traders across his domains, who he had decided were exploiting him. In 1878, he was succeeded by his son Tem Binoka, whose magic and whose guns were feared in equal parts. In 1883, Binoka opportunistically chartered the *Kate McGregor*, in order to transport 100 of his warriors to Nonouti. (This conquest was rescinded by HMS Dart a few months later).

R L Stevenson wrote of him in 1889, two years before he died:

> *'There is only one great personage in the Gilberts: Tembinok' [sic] of Apemama; solely conspicuous, the hero of song, the butt of gossip. Through the rest of the group the Kings are slain or fallen in tutelage: Tembinok' alone remains, the last tyrant, the last vestige of a dead society ... there is only one white on Apemama, and he on sufferance, living far from court, and hearkening and watching his conduct like a mouse in a cat's ear ... he is not only the sole ruler, he is the sole merchant of his triple kingdom ... he is greedy of things new and foreign ... of the number of the king's wives I have no guess; and but a loose idea of their function.'*

From Stevenson's account Tem Binoka evidently also spoke some English.

These examples are but a small sample of the endemic warfare that characterised Tungaru. The means by which this warfare was carried out before and immediately after the introduction of firearms are described in Chapter 6. As the victors of these wars normally took over the womenfolk of the losers, the islands became thoroughly interconnected; many families across the Gilberts still trace their ancestry back to Beru.

The strict prohibitions on incest also encouraged marriage across islands. Thus, although governance varied between the 'chiefly' and the 'republican'

Chapter 2: Settlement

islands, as described in the next Chapter, the culture and language became to a high degree homogenous (with a few differences in the two most northerly islands of Butaritari and Makin, and on Banaba); although each family zealously guarded its own secret knowledge: traditions, magic, cultivation and fishing methods, and technology.

Chapter 2: Settlement

Further Reading

1. **The Global Prehistory of Human Migration**, edited by Peter Bellwood, published by Wiley Blackwell, 2015
2. **The Colonization of the Pacific: A Genetic Trail** edited by Adrian V.S. Hill and Susan W. Serjeantson, published by Oxford Science Publications Clarendon Press, 1989
3. **Kiribati: Aspects of History,** multiple authorship, published by the Institute of Pacific Studies and the Ministry of Education, Kiribati, 1979
4. **Tabiteua Kiribati,** by Guigone Camus, published by the Fondation Culturelle Musée Barbier, 2014
5. **The Lapita Peoples** by P V Kirch, published by Blackwell, 1997
6. **Health Survey of the Gilbert and Ellice Islands** by S.M. Lambert, of the Rockefeller Foundation, published by the Government Printer Suva, 1924
7. **We The Navigators**, by David Lewis, published by The Griffin Press 1972
8. **Fast Trains, Slow Boats, And The Ancestry Of The Polynesian Islanders**, by Stephen Oppenheimer and Martin Richards, published by Science Progress, 2001
9. **Resolving the Ancestry of Austronesian-speaking populations**, multiple authors, published in Human Genetics, 2016
10. **Driving Factors In The Colonization Of Oceania: Developing Island-Level Statistical Models To Test Competing Hypotheses** by Adrian V. Bell, Thomas E. Currie, Geoffrey Irwin, and Christopher Bradbury, published in American Antiquity, 2015
11. **Traditional Micronesian Societies, Adaptation, Integration, and Political Organization**, by Glenn Petersen published by the University Of Hawai'i Press, 2011
12. **Gilbertese Grammar**, published by the London Missionary Society, 1900
13. **The Structure of Gilbertese,** by Reid Cowell, published by the Rongorongo Press, 1951
14. **Narrative of the United States Exploring Expedition During the Years 1838, 1839, 1840, 1841, 1842** (Chapter II, Vol 5) by Charles Wilkes, published in Philadelphia by Lea and Blanchard 1845
15. **Astride the Equator,** translated by Ursula Nixon from **Sous l'équateur de Pacifique** by Ernest Sabatier, Oxford University Press, 1977
16. **Evolution of the Gilbertese Boti,** by H.E. Maude, first published by the Polynesian Society 1963, reprinted by the Institute of Pacific Studies, University of the South Pacific, 1977
17. **The Archaeology of Micronesia** by Dr. Paul Rainbird, published by Cambridge World Archaeology, 2004
18. **Historical Ecology in Kiribati: Linking Past with Present** by Dr. Frank R. Thomas, published in Pacific Science, 2009

19. **'Sustainable Archaeology' and Landscape Transformation in Eastern Micronesia** by Dr Frank R. Thomas, paper presented at the Samoa Conference III: Opportunities and challenges for a sustainable cultural and natural environment, 2014
20. **Tungaru Traditions**, edited by H. C. and H.E. Maude, Institute of Pacific Studies, University of the South Pacific, 1994
21. **Tuvalu – A History**, multiple authors, published jointly by the Institute of Pacific Studies and Extension Services and the Ministry of Social Services, Government of Tuvalu, 1983
22. **The Proceedings of HMS Royalist,** by Captain E. H. M. Davis, mimeograph published by the Tungavalu Society, 1976
23. **Nicolas Hamann and the Material Culture of the Gilbert Islands (Kiribati),** by Professor J. M. Massing
24. **Land-Travel And Seafaring: A Frivolous Record Of Twenty Years Wanderings** by H. R. McClure, published by Hutchinson & Co., 1925
25. **The Dynasty Of Abemama** by R. G. Roberts, published in Journal of the Polynesian Society, Volume 62, 1953
26. **In The South Seas** by R. L. Stevenson, republished by The Hogarth Press 1987 (first published by Chatto and Windus 1896)

Chapter 3.

SOCIETY

Framework

I Tungaru society lived within a strict framework, defined by *aia mwaan ikawai* - the 'customs of the ancients'. This covered all aspects of life, from daily social behaviours, to marriageability of prospective spouses, to land disputes. Disrespectful behaviours, as well as the breaking of social norms, could be severely punished. Only the 'chiefly' families in the northern Gilberts could to some extent disregard custom (e.g. against marriage between cousins), or dispense justice across whole islands; and their power was circumscribed.

Justice within a *kaainga* (family group – see below) was exercised by *te batua* (or *te ikawei*), who was generally the oldest male, working in concert with other *unimane* (old men) [24]. He might simply reprimand an offender, or in extreme cases he could expel them from the *kaainga*. Each *te batua* would also represent his *kaainga* in dealings with other *kaainga*, which might involve civil matters such as marriages and adoptions, minor disputes over land or other rights, or negotiations to acquire the services of specialists. (Serious disputes more often led to warfare than to arbitration). Punishments included death by suffocation (either in water, or under pandanus mats); banishment (sometimes by being cast adrift, but more usually by enforcing a move of the offender to another district); confiscation of land or of a valuable object such as a canoe; and enslavement. Crimes such as murder, rape and adultery could be compensated for by the handing over of a piece of land; but theft was considered the most heinous crime of all and was not condoned under any circumstances [25].

---

[24] And, but behind the scenes, the *unaine* (old women) of the *kaainga*

[25] In this, by some curious incidence of parallel evolution, there are many similarities between I Tungaru and ancient Welsh law. Notable features of both included the collective responsibility of kindreds for their members; the *gavelkind* inheritance of land among all descendants (although in Wales, unlike Tungaru, only male ones); a system of blood money (*galanas*); slavery and serfdom; inability of foreigners to acquire status in society; and the very lax treatment of divorce and legitimacy that

Chapter 3: Society

Personal discipline was also strict. This incident is taken from '*Broken Atoms*' by E. C. Eliot (an early Resident Commissioner of the Gilbert and Ellice Islands):

> *'During a native dance a young blood was audibly 'windy'. Many young girls were present including his betrothed. He was so ashamed that he left the meeting. The next day he was found dead.*
>
> *'The method of his death shows the pluck and endurance of these people. He had sharpened a stake which he had firmly fixed in the ground, and sat on it with such force that the sharpened end was embedded deep in his vitals.'*

Many observers have remarked on the rigid sense of equality in I Kiribati society, although it now seems to be eroding (Chapter 24). John Smith, for example, in his Valedictory Despatch as Governor in 1978, recorded his conclusion from several years' residency that:

> *'The community moves forward as a whole. The person who steps out of line is pulled back ... houses in a village are all traditional, until it seems that everyone has started to build in permanent materials ... no one seems interested in politics and then, as in the recent general election, there is a massive turnout and every indication of an understanding and discriminating electorate. It is the entire community that is literate, not just an educated elite.'*

As will be seen below, however, although there was in *material* terms little inequality – for economic reasons, it will be argued in Chapter 8 – it would be wrong to think that traditional society, before European contact, had no *social* inequality.

Organisation: *kaainga*

The basic unit of society was the *kaainga*. This comprised some 20 to 100 people from three or four generations of closely related families. They shared a piece of land, on which they built their houses (*mwenga*): access to this land, which usually ran right across the islet on which it was located and onto the adjacent ocean and lagoon-side reefs, was restricted to members of the *kaainga*. These settlements were not (as in the 20th century) clustered into villages, but

---

once scandalised the non-native clergy of Wales almost as much as it did the British and French Missionaries in Kiribati.

Chapter 3: Society

were spread along the islands. (Multi – *kaainga* villages were a later innovation, firstly of the missionaries, and later of the colonialists).

The *kaainga* 'hamlet' also typically included a *mwaneaba* (in the north; in the southern islands, *mwaneabas* were more commonly shared across a district of several *kaainga*); a communal kitchen; one or more storehouses; and a 'bleaching house' in which young girls were prepared for marriage. Each nuclear family then had its sleeping quarters, traditionally raised well above the ground (unlike their modern day equivalents) as a protection from attack - and often with a higher floor for storage away from rats, as well as the one for sleeping on. In the *kaainga* land there would also be a *baangota* for worship of whichever deities the *kaainga* favoured (see Chapter 4). When numbers became too large, subsidiary *kaainga (kawa)* might be established nearby; while these operated as separate entities, they would acknowledge the supremacy of the original.

Many *kaainga* – or parts of – were fenced. The Rev. George Pearson visited Beru in 1855 and

> *'noticed a high stone wall that encompassed several houses. I saw only women and children in the yard or houses. I asked if I might go inside the enclosure, my guide said no … no man dared on the penalty of his life to enter. This wall was about six feet high and made of the recent formation of coral stone, so it was bleached very white and looked beautiful as the bright sun shone upon it.'*

It had been because of his entering such an enclosure on Tabiteuea that the unfortunate John Anderson, of the Wilkes Expedition, became the first named European to die in Tungaru. The Tabitueans still remember his killer as Teaeki, whose wife (or daughter) Anderson had molested. As well as defensive stone walls, the *tani kaiwa* (sorcerers) operated behind walls within the *kaainga* for reasons of secrecy.

Each *kaainga* was – with very limited exceptions – self-sufficient, being reliant on its own resources of land and sea. While ceremonial exchanges of food might be made, for example at weddings, there was no concept of 'trading' between different *kaainga*.

Chapter 3: Society

Organisation – *te utu*

The *people* of the *kaainga*, as opposed to the physical place, were known as *te utu*; as they married or otherwise moved out, they remained members of *te utu* but not *te kaainga*. (*Utu* is often translated as 'clan' but 'extended family' is probably a better description). Members of an *utu*, whether resident in the same *kaainga* or not, expected to assist and be assisted by each other in activities beyond the scope of a nuclear family, both for social occasions such as feasts and investment activities such as canoe building, fishing excursions and land improvement. Sabatier describes the structure of *te utu* as follows:

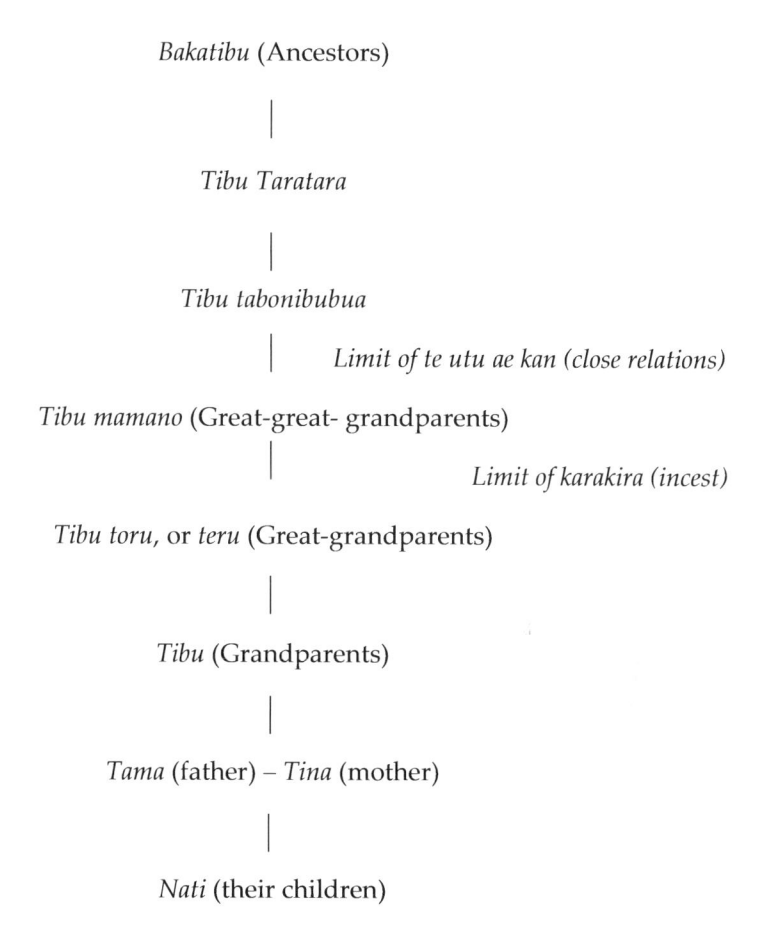

Bakatibu (Ancestors)
|
Tibu Taratara
|
Tibu tabonibubua
| *Limit of te utu ae kan (close relations)*
Tibu mamano (Great-great- grandparents)
| *Limit of karakira (incest)*
Tibu toru, or *teru* (Great-grandparents)
|
Tibu (Grandparents)
|
Tama (father) – *Tina* (mother)
|
Nati (their children)

Relationships tended to become dormant if members of *te utu* did not live in the same area, especially once they had passed the boundary of *te utu ae kan*; and indeed statistically, it is almost certain that every I Kiribati person shares

Chapter 3: Society

at least one common ancestor [26]. However relationships might be revived if a member subsequently became co-located with other *utu* members, or, for example, if they wished to *bubuti* them (see pages 56 - 57 below).

Land and reef ownership

In Tungaru, inheritance and land ownership was *ambilineal*; that is, an individual belonged to both their father's and mother's descent groups and both men and women owned land in their own right. (Most societies around the world are wholly either matrilineal or patrilineal) [27].

While the *kaainga* itself was the property of the overall landholding group, and held communally, all other land *(buakonikai)* was divided into individual plots (although sometimes siblings might jointly own property). There also were separate property rights for *babai* pits, fish traps, and fishing areas; and for intellectual property (i.e. secret family knowledge, material or magical), which might sometimes form part of an inheritance in lieu of land.

People could acquire property rights other than by inheritance, as gifts in appreciation of favours, for adoption or care-taking, or through *tinaba* (see below). Land might also be bestowed for services such as healing. T*e aba n nenebo* was land transferred as compensation for the committing of a crime.

Systems could be complicated in 'chiefly' areas. In Butaritari and Makin *'lands and pits ... have traditionally been owned by groups of kinsmen, and their possession has involved moral obligations, both within the owning group and towards the donors of the property [which is] ...normally inherited jointly by all the children ... the heirs constitute a corporation for the use and disposal of the property, and often for other purposes as well. For example, the land-owning descent group was formerly responsible for offences committed by any of its members'.*

---

[26] All Europeans do, and moreover, according to the Yale statistician Joseph Chang, one who lived at the surprisingly recent date of 1400 CE.

[27] Many areas of the Pacific have traditionally been matrilineal, particularly across the west and north: for example the Trobriand Islands, Hawaii, Palau, the Marianas, the Maori people and much of Melanesia and the Australian aborigines were traditionally matrilineal; by contrast parts of Vanua Levu in Fiji, Tokelau, Tikopia, and some islands in the Marshalls, Vanuatu and the Solomons were patrilineal. There are other instances of ambilineal societies in Polynesia, but they are less common.

Chapter 3: Society

The complex social stratification of Butaritari and Makin also meant that 'aristocratic' families in those islands shared ownership or sometimes *usufruct* of a piece of land with those lower in the hierarchy. Butaritari and Makin were ruled by a *Uea* who traditionally functioned as the apex of both the political and kinship structures of the two islands. This meant, firstly, that tribute of *babai* and other goods was regularly payable to the *Uea*; and secondly, that aristocrats had 'superior' rights to the estates of their associated commoners, although their relations with the latter were patterned after those existing amongst kinsmen.

Under the 19th century Binoka dynasty in Abemama and its two satellite islands Kuria and Aranuka, much land was diverted to the direct ownership of the *Uea* [28] by enforced 'gifts'. However, this had little to do with *aia man ikawai,* and more to do with the guns through which Binoka enforced his rule.

Until the Lands Commissions run by the British colonial authorities, there were mechanisms to avoid the splitting of plots into smaller and smaller holdings (warfare being the most obvious, but it might be simple neglect of land by owners who lived on other islands). One unintended consequence of formalising land tenure was its ossification into very small plots: in the mid-1970s, there was one extreme example where a piece of land less than one acre (0.4 hectares) in extent was found to be divided into 72 individual plots.

Land had a special significance, way beyond its economic value. It was the source of individual self-worth; it was a continuance of the ancestors and their customs; it was simply where they *belonged*.

Whatever the rights and wrongs of the Banaban case for separation from Kiribati there is no doubt of the sincerity of their argument, or that those from other I Kiribati islands would not have similar sentiments:

> *'Living on Banaba is the dream of every Banaban – young and old. Every Banaban elder quotes their desire to die and be buried on their homeland. They do not care about the hardships faced living amongst the ruins and not enough coconut trees or pandanus to make their traditional housing. For them Banaba is home, the only place in the world that they can say they really belong.'*

---

[28] As became apparent when the Coconut Replanting Scheme (see pages 329-330) was implemented on the three islands.

Chapter 3: Society

Marriage and adoption in Tungaru society

I Tungaru society practised both *polygyny* and *polyandry*, and forms of both group marriage and of 'licensed adultery' (*eiriki* and *tinaba*) that have few parallels in other societies. Adoption was very common. There was also a recognised class of women known as *nikiranroro*, (literally meaning, *'left behind their generation')* who remained unmarried after most of those of their age had done so, but who had become sexually active.

Laws against incest were particularly strict. In Tungaru society a man or woman was prohibited from marrying any individual with whom they trace common descent from any ancestor up to and including the third generation (see the *te utu* chart above). This prohibition is expressed by the maxim *e ewe te karoro* ('the fourth generation goes free'). It was also not permitted to marry someone of the same *'boti'*.

Girls were generally married soon after puberty, usually to men in their 20s, who had undergone the lengthy process of becoming *rorobuaka* – a warrior, during which they were not allowed to mix with women, even their own mothers. Marriages might have been arranged amongst *kaaingas* long before, even at or before their birth.

Marriage negotiations would be conducted by parents or close relations, often with an eye for the likely inheritance of the prospective partner. The negotiation would have less chance of success if the boy came from a family of lower class, or was the youngest of many sons and therefore unlikely to inherit much land.

Virginity among brides was demanded and there was thus considerable control over the social behaviour of young women. The wedding ceremony was celebrated with a large feast attended by members of both *kaainga*, and generally the wife would thereafter live with her husband's *kaainga:* although she might return to her parents' *kaainga* during pregnancy.

Divorce could be initiated by either party and was not uncommon. Adultery was punished through disfigurement of the offending party, often by biting off their nose.

Chapter 3: Society

Reports by early visitors about the incidence of polygamy vary. The Wilkes Expedition in 1841 reported that on Butaritari:

> *'Polygamy is common amongst them; and Wood* [a Scots beachcomber who had lived on Butaritari for seven years] *stated that some of the principal chiefs and landholders have from twenty to fifty wives; the king even exceeded this number; while the poorer classes and slaves are doomed to perpetual celibacy…. Polygamy …is allowed to any extent, and limited by the ability of the person to support his wives'.*

However other sources claim that other than in chiefly families, one wife was the norm. The host on Beru of the Rev. Pierson in 1855 had four wives. Customs thus seem to have varied: on some islands, when a man married the oldest daughter of a family her younger sisters also became his consorts after reaching puberty. These younger sisters were called *taua ni kai* (usually translated as concubines). Or a wife might select just one of her sisters, or a first cousin, to become a 'second' wife and to help with household tasks.

By contrast, my wife's great-great grandmother was simultaneously married to two brothers, which although less common seems to have been an accepted practice.

The custom of *tibutibu*, formal adoption, was common. This was often triggered by the desire of a middle-aged individual to obtain a protector and companion for their old age: one who will eventually gather food, cut toddy, nurse them in sickness, and look after their interests generally. Adoption especially provided for the needs of childless couples, who would then have someone to whom they could transmit their knowledge of arts and crafts, magic, and the traditions and genealogy of the family, as well as to look after them in old age. In the southern islands no objection was raised to a child being adopted by someone unrelated, but in the northern islands the adopter was normally an uncle, aunt, or grandparent. An adoptive contract was frequently entered into to cement or inaugurate a friendship between the adopter and the real parents of the adopted, since by custom no enmity should henceforward exist between these parties.

Orphans were always looked after by some member of the extended family, but there was not usually any formal adoption of the orphan and the typical land-gifts —*te aba n tibu*—was not normally given. In exceptional cases, however, when those who looked after the orphan had grown particularly

Chapter 3: Society

fond of the adoptee, he or she might have been formally adopted on reaching the age of puberty.

An adopted person was, by exception, able to elect to belong either to the *kaainga* of his real father or that of his adopter. Such a child would however not only be prevented from marrying within the prohibited degrees (see above) as traced through his biological parents, but also within the corresponding degrees as – notionally - traced through his adopting parents.

Organisation: *mwaneaba*

As set down in Chapter 2, the whole *mwaneaba* system, and with it the associated *boti*, is claimed to be from the original *mwaneaba* of Tabontebike on the island of Beru, which was based on those built in Samoa. In some accounts the system is said to have been spread to other islands by Kaitu and Uakeia, in about 1650 CE (page 29), but this seems doubtful and on other islands there were different explanations.

This characteristic style of *mwaneaba* on Beru varies only in detail on the neighbouring islands of Nonouti and Onotoa; but in the more northerly islands local political factors (such as the rise of the Binoka dynasty on Abemama) or the centuries of civil war on Tarawa, as described in that Chapter, resulted in modification [29]; while the small size of the two most southerly islands of Tamana and Arorae resulted in only partial adoption of the *mwaneaba / boti* systems. On Butaritari and Makin there were only four *boti*, as opposed to up to 25 or more in the southern Gilberts.

The *mwaneabas* themselves, as physical structures, are the 'cathedrals of Tungaru'. H E Maude, in his introduction to his 1980 monograph *The Gilbertese Maneaba* [sic], writes:

> *'The western shore of a Gilbert island appears to the approaching voyager as a long line of green coconut palms broken at interval by a cleared area on which stands a large pandanus-thatched roof, resting on short coral or sometimes wooden pillars ... this large building is the district maneaba: the focus of the whole social life of the community; in it were held all discussions concerning peace or war or any of the other innumerable concerns affecting the common weal; it was the Law Court, where*

---

[29] Or were different all along – see the next footnote

Chapter 3: Society

> *offenders against customary norms were tried, and disputes heard and arbitrated by the Old Men; and the centre for the many ceremonies and feasts of a formal character, as well as the more dignified community recreations and dances.*
>
> *'The maneaba was all that to the Gilbertese, and much more: the traditional club-house of the aged; a* pied à terre *for the stranger; and a sanctuary for those in flight.*
>
> *'All behaviour under its roof had to be seemly, decorous, and in strict conformity with custom, lest the maneaba be* matauninga *(offended) and the culprit* maraia *(accursed)'.*

Maude's chief informant was Tem Mautake, born about 1880 in the village of Buariki, on north Tarawa. He was a member of the *boti* Maerua who were traditionally possessors of the lore and practicalities of *mwaneaba* construction; he and his father claimed to be the last who knew the complete lore, including the all-important rituals, ceremonies and incantations. These had been given at a time immemorial to his ancestor Bue, a 'hero' who was born of the union of the Sun, and a human woman Nei Matamona [30].

It seems there were three basic types of *mwaneaba*: Tabontebike, Maungatabu, and Tabiang (this last also from Beru). Each of the styles was moreover divided into sub-types.

They differ in the ratio of length and breadth of construction, the *boti*-plan, and the privileges and duties of individual *boti*. Details of the scoping of the building, preparation of materials, and construction methods (as well as of the ceremonies that must accompany these) are set out in *The Gilbertese Maneaba*.

Organisation: *boti*

One important function of the *mwaneaba* was that of *te nen te boti* (the container of the boti). The literal meaning of boti has been described as: *'a place in the mwaneaba reserved for the members of a clan'* but figuratively:

> *'Far more than a place of social festivities or a hall of debate, it was a tabernacle of ancestors in the male line: a sort of social map, where a man's group or clan could be recognised the moment he took his seat, his totem*

---

[30] A quite different story to that above from Samoa / Beru; in this rendition the most traditional type of Mwaneaba is thus the *Maungatabu* design found on Tarawa.

> *and his ascendants known, and his ceremonial duties or privileges discovered'*

At the creation of a new *mwaneaba*, *boti* could be formed or reconfigured by partition; by conquest; by fission; and by invitation or consent. H. E. Maude's monograph *The Evolution of the Gilbertese Boti* gives detailed examples. The number and to some extent functions of individual *boti* again varied between islands, and even sites on the same island.

Allocation of an individual's *boti* was strictly patrilineal. It could however pass through a female line: if, for example, *'a man dies with only female issue the eldest daughter becomes head of the* utu. *If her father's branch was the senior in the clan she was recognised as the head of the clan but took no active part in clan ritual and could not speak in the* mwaneaba. *Her place in ceremonial was taken by her father's brother. Her own son, however, will become head of the clan or utu and on arriving at age will take over his duties from his grandfather's brother ... the woman is said to be the* kawai *(path) for passing on her father's* boti *to her son'*.

H. E. Maude discusses at length the inherent contradictions between the ambilineal nature of *te utu* (and thus land ownership), and the patrilineal nature of *te boti*: 'how this complete variance between the inheritance of *boti* and *kaainga* rights, and *buakonikai* rights, arose we may never know but the Gilbertese have long taken it for granted'.

Maude speculates that the patrilineal system associated with *boti* arrived with the Samoan invasion, with the original ambilineal land tenure systems being maintained through the inhabitants with whom they intermarried. This view is consistent with that of Grimble (p. 13), although he judged that the discrepancy arose much earlier.

Boti were also associated with a wide variety of *atua* (totemic objects): these are discussed in the next Chapter.

Social stratification

There seem to have been in early times up to five social classes (the following list is based on Abemama):

- At the top of the apex was *Te Uea*, a hereditary King (or, as it seems from oral histories, sometimes Queen). His (or her) children (including

Chapter 3: Society

the eldest child if this was female), and their grandchildren, formed a class known as *Ba n uea* or *utu n uea*
- Next in importance was a group of freemen, ancestors of whom either pleased in some way the *Uea* at the time, or excelled themselves in battle. They were known as *inaomata*: their title was hereditary
- Freemen, in a class known as *aomata*
- Persons who, while landless, were free to work for whom they pleased, to come and go at will, and who were known as *rang*
- Slaves, known as *toro* (*kawa* on Butaritari and Makin) who were the lowest of all in the scale. They were landless and were compelled by custom to live upon the lands of those who had enslaved them, and to work in return for nothing but the food those lands might produce.

As always, there are variations of this structure between islands.

Those who owned no land in Kiribati were, by local definition, *toro*. Arthur Grimble (knowingly or not) alluded to this when he recorded what his predecessor E. C. Eliot had said to him in 1913: *'You may walk around the villages satisfied you're a hell of a fellow, while all the time they're thinking what a mannerless young pup you are'* [31].

Strangers who arrived on an island who were unable to substantiate their position in a *boti* in the *mwaneaba* were also considered to be slaves, and any property of theirs forfeit; this was, not surprisingly, the cause of early misunderstandings when Europeans first arrived in the Gilberts.

How widespread this stratification on all islands across the Gilberts Group and Banaba was (before the Beru invasion described in the previous Chapter) is uncertain, as is the extent to which this invasion created a new 'ideology' of governance.

What is certain is that it was replaced in the southern islands with a 'republican' system, whereby authority was collectively maintained by the heads of each *kaainga*, meeting in a district *mwaneaba*, and taking decisions by consensus amongst the elders.

---

[31] Once I became aware of the technical status of Imatang in Kiribati as slaves, it explained much about how they regarded us. However, the I Kiribati draw a very fine distinction between those Imatang who are clearly trying to be good-mannered by their own lights, and the many Europeans who do not think good manners and politeness toward 'natives' to be of the slightest importance.

Chapter 3: Society

John Pitchford notes of modern Tabiteuan society:

> *'Tabiteuea means literally 'the land of no leader'. It is very difficult for anyone who has not lived there ... to believe to what degree of egalitarianism this was taken, nor how everyone was king in his own right.'*

The Wilkes Expedition a century and a half earlier had however *thought* they were encountering chiefs on Tabiteuea (they list a 'chief's' name for each of fourteen 'towns'), although they did comment:

> *'An old man soon made his appearance, whose deportment, and that of the crowd, pointed him out as the chief. He had, apparently, little actual authority...'*

(This rather begs the question whether early visitors saw 'chiefs' because they could not envisage that there were none).

What does seem certain is that civil wars meant that no domination of one *kaainga* by another, or institution of kingship, was permanent - at least until guns allowed the chiefly dynasties of Butaritari/Makin, Abaiang, and Abemama/Kuria/Aranuka to consolidate in the late 19th century; that these in turn were short-lived was due to the arrival soon after of the British navy.

Specialists

Each *kaainga* was basically self-sufficient, and, as noted above, there was no trading between them. Within the everyday tasks of the *kaainga*, however, roles were differentiated by sex, and to some extent by age. To quote the Wilkes Expedition again:

> *'All the hard work is performed by men, whose employment consists in building the houses and canoes, catching fish, collecting and bringing home the produce of their plantations, and attending to the cultivation of the taro, in which the women assist only by weeding of the ground.*
>
> *'The employment of females is almost exclusively confined to in-door occupations ... such as cooking and preparing food, braiding mats etc., and they seem to have exclusive control over the house.*

Chapter 3: Society

> *'The work of both sexes is however very light, and the greater proportion of their time is spent in pastimes.'* [32]

Despite the complete absence of Adam Smith-like 'pin factories' in Tungaru, certain tasks were nevertheless undertaken by specialists. These were sometimes from a particular *boti*; although every family jealously guarded its own knowledge. The principal specialisms, the secrets of which were carefully guarded, included:

- Mwaneaba construction (the responsibility of the *boti* Maerua)
- Maintenance of oral traditions concerning history and custom (the responsibility of the *boti* Karangoa n Uea)
- Canoe building
- Healing
- Tattooing
- Navigation
- Sorcery.

Generally, payment for services was through the maintenance and feeding of the specialist and his family whilst he was engaged on the task in question (building a canoe, for example, might take several months). Gerd Koch, writing in the 1960s, notes that:

> *'Unless a man is able to build a canoe himself he will ask an experienced man (tiakaba), preferably one of his relations, to make one for him and will reward the builder with food and presents. The building of a canoe is undertaken with a considerable degree of secrecy'.*

In a few cases – for example healing – a piece of land might be donated for services rendered. On Banaba, for example, should someone dislocate an arm or leg, a piece of land called *te aba n riring* was payable to the bonesetter.

The status of women

As has been seen in this and the previous Chapter, women in pre-contact I Tungaru society were not the equals of men in everything.

---

[32] This account surely underestimates the role of women fishing, particularly the collection of seafood in the lagoon, and torch fishing by night.

Chapter 3: Society

However, they:

- Owned property in their own right
- Could be *Ueas*. (Nei Arirei was recognised as Uea at Abaiang as late as the 1950s, much to the amazement of the colonial government)
- Could learn specialist skills such as navigation, and lead ocean voyages
- Could initiate divorce
- Had control of households
- Were economically active
- Participated in warfare.

They had admittedly little choice of marriage partner, but then neither did the men; both were subject to stringent social control, especially when young and unmarried.

Only in the patriarchal *boti* and *mwaneaba* aspects of society were they formally excluded, although rights would pass through them, from their fathers to their sons.

Early visitors also observed their status as exceptional. The Wilkes Expedition commented that: *'More consideration is awarded to the female sex than has been observed in any of the other groups* [of islands visited by the Expedition]'. Captain Davis recorded the same in 1892: *'women in the Gilbert Group are well treated by the men'*.

Arguably, under the joint influence of two of the most patriarchal of institutions ever devised - the Christian Churches and the Colonial Service - women's status went into a decline in the 20th century from which it is only now beginning to recover.

Summary: the family as society

This Chapter has outlined the importance of family as the basis of I Tungaru society, in its three overlapping, but still separate, aspects: *kaainga, utu and boti*. There was no sense of island solidarity, and even less was there a sense of I Tungaru nationhood.

Arthur Grimble's *From Birth to Death in the Gilbert Islands* sets out in detail the many roles played by aunts, uncles and grandparents at key stages of a

Chapter 3: Society

person's life; and the reciprocal roles that an individual had in caring for these in later life.

Members of the family were expected to help each other. The custom of *bubuti* in particular has been the subject of much comment (usually disapproving) ever since the Wilkes Expedition. E. C. Elliot, who had much sympathy for the I Kiribati, writes (a little inaccurately) in *Broken Atoms*:

> *'What is counted as really disgraceful is theft. This is the rarest of crimes and the unforgivable sin. Its infrequence was due to the native custom of 'bubugeeing' [sic], an ugly word but pronounced as spelt .... To 'bubugee' was to ask for something which could not be refused – provided of course that the family from whom the loan was asked had more than enough for themselves. For example let us suppose that a family lost all their canoes in a storm; they could it is true build new ones, but this would take time. They would approach some well-to-do family and ask for a temporary gift. This was native custom and the loan would not be refused. Land alone could never be 'bubugeed'. Land meant everything: money very little. Money came and went; land remained. It was the one inalienable possession in a changing world. Ill luck might follow the family that borrowed too much. Years might elapse before the borrower could repay the loan. How old Micawber would have loved the Gilbert Islands!*

> *'No record was kept but the debt would never be forgotten. It might be the case of the sins of the fathers, for a son or grandson must pay. No interest accumulated, and the debt might be repaid in kind or by manual work. Time is a European failing: time meant nothing to the islanders. Why then should the return be greater than the loan? Mincing Lane should note!*

In fact, at least in modern times, the custom of *bubuti* is rather more restricted. It applies only to fellow members of the *utu*, and is not as formally reciprocal across generations as this quotation implies [33].

---

[33] In the 1970s a Gilbertese friend of mine had saved for years to buy a motor cycle, which his uncle promptly bubuti'd. Although he complied with the request, this incident was widely felt to be an abuse of the system and led to a degree of censorship of the uncle.

Chapter 3: Society

By contrast, I Tungaru people could be quite indifferent to the fate of non-family members. H. E. Maude recounts:

> *'On one occasion ... a man mentioned in my presence that on crossing the lagoon an hour before he had passed a woman endeavouring to swim to the shore with her baby (evidently her canoe had sunk); and he expressed the opinion that she would never make it. When asked why he had not stopped to pick her up his reply was, to all except me, perfectly reasonable:* tiaki kain au utu *(she was not a member of my utu)'* [34].

---

[34] I should record that my reviewer Teburoro Tito expresses doubt as to whether Maude had correctly understood this incident, which he does not think characteristic of I Kiribati society even in old times. He notes that a similar story is contained in a song from Tauma village, in Tabiteuea, *Ti mwananga mai Tauma*, in which the woman and child are saved after being teased.

Chapter 3: Society

Further Reading

1. **Narrative of the United States Exploring Expedition During the Years 1838, 1839, 1840, 1841, 1842** (Chapter II, Vol 5) by Charles Wilkes, published in Philadelphia by Lea and Blanchard, 1845
2. **Broken Atoms,** by E. C. Eliot, published by Geoffrey Bles, 1938
3. **The Story of Karangoa,** narrated by an *unimane* of the Boti Karnagoa n Uea on Nikunau in 1934, transcribed by Tione Baraka, translated by G. H. Eastman, edited, annotated and revised by H.E. Maude, published by the Institute of Pacific Studies 1991
4. **Rank and Ramage in the Northern Gilberts,** by B. Lambert, PhD Thesis, University of California, 1963
5. **Astride the Equator,** translated by Ursula Nixon from **Sous l'équateur de Pacifique** by Ernest Sabatier, Oxford University Press 1977
6. **Evolution of the Gilbertese Boti,** by H.E. Maude, first published by the Polynesian Society 1963, reprinted by the Institute of Pacific Studies, University of the South Pacific, 1977
7. **The Gilbertese Maneaba,** by H. E. Maude, Institute of Pacific Studies, University of the South Pacific, 1980
8. **Migrations, Myth, and Magic From The Gilbert Islands**, writings by Arthur Grimble edited by Rosemary Grimble (this includes *From Birth to Death in the Gilbert Islands)*, Routledge & Kegan Paul, 1972
9. **Tabiteua Kiribati,** by Guigone Camus, published by the Fondation Culturelle Musée Barbier, 2014
10. **The Material Culture of Kiribati,** by Gerd Koch (translated by Guy Slatter), published by the Institute of Pacific Studies, University of the South Pacific, 1986
11. **Social Changes In The Southern Gilbert Islands, 1938-1964,** by Henry P Lundsgaarde, Published by Department of Anthropology, University of Oregon, Eugene, 1967
12. **Kiribati: Aspects of History**, multiple authors and editors, published jointly by the Institute of Pacific Studies and the Ministry of Education, Training, and Culture, 1979
13. **An Island In The Autumn,** by John Smith, Librario Publishing Ltd., 2011
14. **The Last District Officer**, by John Pitchford, Librario Publishing Ltd., 2013

Chapter 4.

RELIGION AND MAGIC

The I Tungaru pantheon

The I Tungaru pantheon deserves to be placed on a par with those of Olympus or Asgard of European tradition, or of the *Vedas* and *Upanishads* of South Asia. A full description would require a book in itself. Amongst the stories about the gods are comparable stories to all of these about their roles: of actors in natural phenomena, of the tricks they played on each other, of acts of divine interference with humans, and of the procreation of *heroes* (*anti ma aomata* - children of mixed parentage, gods and humans). There are shape-changers, giants, dwarves, and people who live under the sea or the land. There are many parallel worlds to that which the I Tungaru inhabited, both paradises and hells; and voyage to the west after death.

The core pantheon consisted of more than 40 commonly named deities (*te anti*): these included creator gods, father/son gods at odds with each other, gods fashioned from the body parts of other gods, and gods fashioned from inanimate objects. How many is difficult to know: in the story '*Korata and the Anti*' (included in *Tungaru Traditions*) Anetiba of Nui recounted a tale involving '*an assembly of* anti *so large, it was impossible to count their number ... perhaps there were as many as two or three million of them*'.

There are also less cosmic (and on a day-to-day basis, perhaps more important), 'household' deities. Ritual incantation, divination, use of special language [35], and acts of propitiation all played important roles in everyday

---

[35] The former islet in the Tarawa lagoon was known as '*Bikeman*' (bird island) when one was on land but as '*Te aba ni uea*' (the King's island) when one was at sea. In the 1980s my wife and I (with our young children) were sailing down at night from Tearinibai, near the top of northern Tarawa, to the south, in a canoe piloted by one of my brothers-in-law, and with my wife's mother also on board. Commenting towards the end of this (to me) cramped and uncomfortable journey of several hours, and as we were passing the islet, I referred to it as 'Bikeman'. Immediately my mother-in-law froze, and she dressed me down severely (the only time that I remember her not being tolerant of my ignorance of custom and proper behaviour). She insisted that I immediately throw a packet of cigarettes into the lagoon as propitiation. A few

Chapter 4: Religion and Magic

life. Each family had its own 'totems' which determined, for example, what they might eat. On each island, there were 'holy' areas of special spiritual significance – Nuatabu on north Tarawa, and Eita on south Tarawa, for example.

Care of ancestors was important, and continued communication between them and the living was common. Belief in sorcery was universal; and the use of magical rituals and incantations was essential to nearly all aspects of life, from everyday activities such as fishing, to fundamental ones of love and war.

Family trees also distinguish between *Te Anti* (Gods), *anti ma aomata* (semi-divine heroes) and *aomata* (ordinary people). Traditions, genealogies, and stories vary from island to island, and from family to family; and because they are secret to each family, may not have been accurately (or indeed, and as a deliberate act, fully) transmitted to the Europeans who have collected them, notably Hamann, Sabatier, Grimble, Reid Cowell and Maude.

As Sabatier wrote *'all we can do is make a fumbling attempt to clarify the maze of their beliefs and practices'*; and in a general history such as this it is impossible to do more than give a flavour. It is likely that more parts of the maze remain unwritten, and are still preserved only as oral traditions.

Te Anti - the gods

The deities of the Tungaru people included those shown below, with their associated 'essences', totems, and whether they were associated with particular boti. Some of *te anti* did not have totems. This table has been compiled from several sources, and is unlikely either to be complete or wholly accurate [36]:

	Name	Essence	Totem (s)	Boti with which associated
1.	Na Atibu	Stone		
2.	Nareau		Spider	

---

moments later, the canoe was violently rocked from side to side by three enormous waves, but was not over-turned. We had merely been given a severe warning.

[36] Another, only partly overlapping, list of the *anti* and other mythological beings known in Tewai, on South Tabiteuea has been compiled by Guigone Camus (see Further Reading)

Chapter 4: Religion and Magic

3.	Tabakea		Te ibi tree, turtle, te Kekenu (crocodile), toddy	
4.	Tabuariki	Thunder	Shark	Karangoa n Uea, Karangoa Raereke, Uman Taburimai, Te Katanrake, Uman Taburimai ae meang, Te Kaotirama, Te Bakoa n Uea, Inaki ni Bakoa, Nei Abinoa, Niku Tengetenge, Rautetia, Karumaetoa, Te Nguingui, Te Inakin Akawa.
5.	Auriaria	Light	Rat, cockerel, tern, giant clam, pandanus tree	Umani Kamauri
6.	Nei Tituabine		Sting ray, cockroach, tropic bird, te ntaraai (a creeping plant), beche-de-mer	Keaki, Kaburara
7.	Nei Temaiti			Te Kokona, Katanaki
8.	Nei Moa Aine		Hen	Keaki Rangirang, Bakarawa
9.	Nei Ati		Bonito, octopus, garfish	
10.	Bue and Rirongo	Sun and moon	Rock cod, porpoise	Ababou

Chapter 4: Religion and Magic

11.	Taburimai		Sandsnipe, trevally
12.	Tabakeaantari			Benuakura
13.	Te Baiku			Birimo
14..	Uka	Moving air	
15.	Karitoro	Energy	
16.	Riki	Procreation	Eel
17.	Kanaweawe	Dimension	
18.	Naotanai			Te O
19.	Nabawe	Antiquity	
20.	Ngkoangkoa	Time	
21.	Te Kai	Healing		Nei Ati Meang
22.	Teweia		Kanawa tree
23.	Nei Tevenei		Comet, meteor, porpoise's head
24.	Kaobunang		
25.	Kaoioti	Healing	
26.	Te Rakunene	Caster of spells for women	
27.	Te Batuku		
28.	Nei Teiti	Lightning	
29.	Nei Tenaotari		
30.	Nei Tereitaburi		
31.	Nei Karua	Caster of spells for men	
32.	Nei Kika		Octopus
33.	Te Korongutungutu		
34.	Tabuae te Baobao		
35.	Te Titune or Buatoronteaba		
36.	Na Rabenuwai	Healing (especially of madness)	Oval white shells
37.	Rurubene		
38.	Ningoningo		
39.	Taitai	Speech	
40.	Teinamati		
41.	Temamang		

Chapter 4: Religion and Magic

Another important element of the core mythology was the tree *Te Kaintikuaba*, made from Na Atibu's spine, although this is variously sited in different family traditions: in Samoa, in Tarawa, in Beru, in Aranuka, and elsewhere [37].

There have been attempts to ascribe an Austronesian origin to the 'essence' gods, and a Melanesian one to the 'totemic' gods. It seems more complicated than this. Sabatier comments:

> *'The Gilbertese do have a rational streak and they expect their Anti to prove their existence and their power through manifestations. They want to see and touch them, so the Anti have to take on bodily form... Each Spirit-ancestor, then, has a creature – or sometimes even two: one for land and one for the sea'.*

Early accounts emphasise the worship of *Tabuariki*, which is consistent with the large number of *boti* associated with him in the table above. The Wilkes Expedition recorded that:

> *'He is their most popular god, and is considered by some the greatest. About two-thirds of the natives acknowledge him as their tutelary deity. The rest do not acknowledge him but have other deities: and some worship the souls of their departed ancestors, or certain birds, fishes and animals. A female deity is the object of adoration to very many. She is called Itivini, [sic; more accurately, Nei Tituabine] is reputed to be of a cruel disposition, and all the little children who die are supposed to be killed and eaten by her. The natives always refuse to eat the animals, fish, etc., worshipped by them but will readily catch them that others may partake of the food.'*

Explaining natural phenomena

There are many stories that explain natural phenomena. I have retold this one as an example [38]. It shows that the I Tungaru gods were viewed by the

---

[37] From the dismembering of this, other lands were created (including Matang, from where the Europeans were deemed to come; hence their modern designation as I-matang).

[38] So far as I know it has not been published in English before: my wife and brother-in-law received this story from her mother's cousin Timon Taaita from Nuatabu (the last of his generation), just before he died in 2014. It had also been recorded by Natan

Chapter 4: Religion and Magic

Gilbertese as earthy, as opposed to the often expressed European view of them as dour. Nareau evidently behaved as outrageously any Greek or Scandanavian god.

> *Tabuariki (thunder) and his wife Nei Teiti (lightning) lived in their kaainga, Tooribwa, in Nuatabu, North Tarawa. Tabuariki was friendly with Nareau, who often came to visit them; they often, too, had a competition as to who could produce the tastiest food. On one occasion Nareau brought a pudding he had hollowed out, into which he had placed one of his own turds. Tabuariki ate until he came to the middle of the fruit and realised what was there. Nareau had tried on similar stunts before, but he and Tabuariki had always made up afterwards, but now he proceeded to chase Nareau off: but Nareau hid in a crab shell, and when Tabuariki put his hand into the shell Nareau lacerated his right hand so that it became deformed and useless.*

> *'Nareau then tricked Nei Teiti. He hid buried under her coconut grater, and from where he was hidden, he made a hole upwards for his cock. As she used the grater, she felt it and was pleasured. But Tabuariki reacted: "What are you doing? What is happening with your grater? Why are you breathing heavily? Is there something between you and Nareau?"*

> *'He chased after her; and ever since, he has continued to chase her. But before, when he made thunder with his right hand, it boomed at the same time as the lightning; but now, he has to use his left hand, and there is a pause before the boom.*

> *'Thus first, in a storm, do you see Nei Teiti, but only later do you hear Tabuariki.'*

Te Anti Ma Aomata

Sabatier was of the view that 'the anti are those spirits who have the power to change into men ... te anti ma aomata (spirits and at the same time people) on the other hand are the Ancestors or Heroes who become anti only after their death'. A traditional family tree would contain both.

Itonga, who has kindly supplied me with a transcript. This, however, is a retelling of a tale sometimes difficult to follow in Timon's account, and is not a straight translation.

Chapter 4: Religion and Magic

The convoluted relations between *te anti* and men are illustrated by the case of Taburimai (whose totem, as listed above, was the sand snipe):

> *'The first offspring of Bakoa and his wife, Nei Nguiriki, were all fishes. Later were born the man Taburimai, and his brother Teanoi, 'the hammer-headed shark'. Because Taburimai had a different shape, the fish children were ashamed and plotted his death. Teanoi warned Bakoa and he sent Taburimai away on the back of the shark brother. Having landed the threatened man on the island of Samoa, Teanoi gained the sky and became a star.*
>
> *'Taburimai stayed on earth, sailed among the islands, and married a woman. Their son was the adventurous Te-ariki-n-tarawa, who claimed uekera, the sacred tree that reached to heaven, and took to wife Ne Te-reere, the tree goddess. From their union came Kirata-n-te-rerei, 'the most beautiful of men', the founder ancestor, whose handsomeness was enough to beget children without meeting a woman'.*

More stories about Kirata and the mother of his child (who lived underground) are related in *Tungaru Traditions*.

Maude notes that:

> *'It is not unusual in genealogical tables to find a line drawn across the page with beside it the annotation* karikin aomata *(the issue of men) indicating that all names following are those of historical persons'*.

The daily practice of religion

In Tungaru society, there were no separate priestly classes, nor communal churches, although there were *ibonga* (sorcerers and sorceresses) who in some circumstances were the only ones permitted to enter the sacred family enclosures (*baangota*) and carry out ceremonies.

As we have seen above, the relative importance of the various deities varied from household to household, and certain deities were favoured by particular *boti*. Often a single spirit would be the principal object of worship, but others might be invoked for more specialised functions, such as fishing or warfare.

Members of the *kaainga* other than the *ibonga* might become helpers (and apprentices): they would gather together with the *ibonga* early in morning and

Chapter 4: Religion and Magic

evening and at certain phases of the moon, to make offerings of special foods (and later, of tobacco).

Numerous shrines were observed on Arorae by Samuel James Whitmee of the London Missionary Society in 1871:

> *'Nearly every house had either a small circle or a small square* [te nikawewe] *fenced off with large stones set in the earth. In the centre of this square or circle a large stone was placed on end, and the floor of the enclosed space was neatly spread with broken coral and fire shells.'*

George Turner of the London Missionary Society wrote about the worship of Tabuariki, also on Arorae, in 1884:

> *'In his temple there lay a great clam shell, thirty inches by eighteen, filled with water. All who brought offerings and came to pray dipped their hands before sitting down, in token of their desire, on account of these offerings, to be clean and free from illness or other expressions of the wrath of Tapuariki [sic]'*

Turner also noted that: *'In their houses they had sacred stocks or small pillars of wood, four or five feet high, as the representatives of household gods, and on these they poured oil and laid before them offerings of cocoa-nuts and fish'*.

Holy places

There were also special although unenclosed areas which were regarded as holy, and where no trees or plants were to be cut (although they might contain babai pits, as is the case at Nuatabu on North Tarawa).

One of the best known is that of *Te Aba n Anti* in a clearing in the bush on Eita on south Tarawa. Important visitors to South Tarawa must, as soon as they arrive, visit the *mwaneaba* at Eita to be greeted there by the elders [39].

---

[39] John Smith records that he and his wife were taken there by Reuben Uatioa, the Leader of Government Business (page 264) - straight from the airport - when he arrived to become Governor of the Gilbert Islands in 1973. Sadly the mwaneaba is now roofless, because builders with the magical knowledge necessary to re-roof it are no longer resident in or available to the village, and no one else dares.

Chapter 4: Religion and Magic

A stone clearing nearby bears the name *Te Aba Ni Maneka* (the Rock of Footprints). It is situated about 400 yards from the lagoon side of the island and some 100 yards from the reef side.

It contains the footprints of giants. The largest footprint is said to be that of Tabuariki (see above), who, according to the old men of Eita, was born and grew up on Tarawa. He was so tall that he could pick the nuts from the coconut trees without climbing; and he was renowned as a fisherman, being particularly noted for his exploits in roaming Tarawa Lagoon on foot, fishing as he went, especially in the vicinity of Bikeman Island.

This particular footprint is said to be his left foot— *'it sinks a good inch into the solid rock, a coral limestone, has 12 toes and measures 3 ft. 9 in. across the toes and 4 ft. 6 in. from the toe to heel —its counterpart, the right foot, is reported to be near the village of Tekaranga on Maiana, the next island some 20 miles to the southwest of Tarawa'*.

Close alongside the large indentation presumed to have been made by Tabuariki is a smaller one attributed to Nei Teiti, his wife (see above). This is her right foot (history does not relate the whereabouts of her left foot).

Nuatabu, an islet on north Tarawa, also contains several assemblies of significance:

- Another large stone shrine dedicated to Tabuariki, and a smaller one to Nei Teiti
- A place where seven giants lived, before they departed for Onotoa
- A 'ghost' *mwaneaba* (*Te Kamaraia* – the cursed land) which was the seat of the *uea* Nei Karabung. According to tradition, she subsisted on a diet only of human brains.

There is also on north Tarawa still existing the shrine of *Beia Mwa Tekaai*, just north of Buariki, which can be visited by permission of the family who guard it. This consists of a bare circle, with a clam shell in the middle. Any living creature that enters the circle (even a bird above it) will allegedly be struck dead [40]. Also at Buariki, there is a piece of land called *te umwa-n-anti*, where, according according to local traditions, the *anti* from all over Tungaru gathered to meet. Still further north, there is a shrine to Nei Temakua on the lagoon side of Naa, near the tip of the atoll.

---

[40] I for one have not wanted to put this to the test...

Chapter 4: Religion and Magic

Holy places exist also on other islands; for example footprints of either Tabuariki or Teweia occur also on Beru.

The *katabwanin* is a tradition unique to Marakei; first time visitors need to pay their respects to the four *anti* of Marakei, travelling anticlockwise, before any other activities. Offerings at the shrines of Nei Reei, Nei Rotebenua, Nei Tangangau and Nei Nantekimam must be made.

Magic

To quote Sabatier again, *'from religion we move quite imperceptibly to magic'*. There were two distinct kinds of magic: *te kawai* and *te tabunea*. *Te kawai* was purely ritual, for example, the lighting of a fire of twigs laid in a circle surrounded by a square, in the preparations of a poet to compose a new song. *Te tabunea* was the incantation, generally combined with a ritual - and equally important, one being powerless without the other. Arthur Grimble was obsessed with spells and rituals; records of many of them are scattered through his published work.

It is difficult to overstate the importance of magic even in quite everyday activity, let alone investment activities such as *mwaneaba* or canoe building.

If things went wrong, it was because some part of the formula had been omitted or wrongly expressed, rather than because of lack of skill on the part of person undertaking the task in question.

Sorcery

Private spells were supplemented by those of sorcerers. This magic could be either offensive or protective. The most sinister form of magic was called *te wawi* - the death magic - but there were experts also in the promotion of healing, success in love, dancing prowess, and weather management, amongst others.

Grimble gives an example of offensive magic:

> *'Food and cooking-fires were formerly much used in connection with the sinister form of magic called te wawi — the death-magic — which, though sternly prohibited by British law, is without any doubt still occasionally practised. A man is held to be particularly vulnerable through the embers or ashes of a fire upon which his fish is being broiled, and will keep a sharp look-out upon any individual not of his own household who approaches*

Chapter 4: Religion and Magic

while cooking is under way. The method of the magician is to possess himself covertly of a handful of ashes, or a few morsels of charred wood, before the food is taken from the fire, and retire with them to a dark corner. Setting them upon the ground before him as he sits, he stirs the fragments slowly, in a counter-clockwise direction, with a piece of the riblet of a shrivelled coconut-pinnule, muttering to himself the following formula:

Ewara-n ai-ni kana-na:	The stabbing of the fire of his food:
Boa-rio, boa-rake,	Strike westwards, strike eastwards,
Boa-mate, boa-tabwe!	Strike death, strike rending apart!
A bung kanoa-n-nano-na:	His bowels give birth (i.e., begin to labour):
A bung, ao a rai, ao a mate, ao a tabwenaua. Maama-ia, bekebeke-ia!	They give birth, and they are over-turned and they are dead, and they are rent apart. Their shame, their unease!
Raira ato-na!	Overturn his liver!
E a tia, b'e a mate-o-o!	It is done, for he is dead-o-o!
Kokon-na ... konie-e-e!	Strangle him ...!
Kokon-na ... konae-e-e!	Strangle him ...!

'The section of the formula beginning with the words 'A bung kanoa-n-nano-na' and ending with the last line is repeated a second and a third time; after which the magician stabs the ashes and leaves his riblet of coconut-leaf standing upright in their midst.

'It is claimed that, if the man against whom the ritual is directed eat of the food cooked in the cursed fire, he will soon begin to vomit, after which he will be seized with stomach-cramps and die within three days. His companions will feel no ill effects, as 'their pictures have not stood in the heart of the sorcerer' during his performance of the spell.'

Chapter 4: Religion and Magic

By contrast, here is Sabatier on a report of protective healing magic:

> 'She [a sorceress] had come back from Fiji where she had been initiated into the practices of Na Rubenuwai ... the patient lay covered by a mat, a roof over him, but no walls around him. The surrounding crowd of people could see everything. Her attendant lit a big fire and beside it she placed a coconut leaf torch, a gourd full of sea water and a pipe filled with tobacco. She withdrew some distance ... from a bag she took six white shells. She put three down on the mat and balanced the other three on top of them ... next she asked for her pipe. Her companion lit it and gave it to her. Then, very swiftly, she emptied the contents of the pipe into her hand and swallowed them. Then she asked for a burning chip of wood ... and swallowed it. Then it was time to take up the gourd of sea water which was emptied as if it was a glass of fresh water. Then she stood up, took the torch, lit it, and danced around the patient, singing in a strange language and scattering the sparks from the torch onto the sick man's mat. When she had done this she said 'that's it, the young man is cured'. Just then the patient got up and said 'I'm better' ... she went calmly off to bed ... rather proud of being successful'.

The journey after death

Although the *worship* of ancestors is common in Polynesia, in Tungaru society the relationship seems to have been primarily one more of *reverence and respect*. However early accounts differ; and the drawings of ancestor stones that have come down to us do show that they *look* very like the deity shrines, the *baangota*.

As with the *anti*, people expected to continue to communicate with their ancestors after they had died. Thus death was treated seriously, but was not final.

For three nights following a death, a ceremony called *bo maki* was performed to encourage the soul of the dead to leave for the afterlife. The body would be anointed with scented oil, wrapped in a new sleeping mat, and kept for three to nine days. A female relation (*te tia tabe atu*) would then hold the dead person's head in her lap, and then the body would be buried, face upwards, covered with a screen made of coconut leaf, and then a mat. This was filled in with sand and its limits demarcated with a rectangle of small white coral stones.

Chapter 4: Religion and Magic

After the successful completion of *bo maki*, the spirit of the deceased commenced an arduous journey to paradise. He or she first had safely to pass on their way westwards to the land of the dead the *Nei Karamakuna*, a bird-headed woman (see page 78); and *Na Ubwebwe*, the Old Man of the Cats-cradle (see page 87). He or she was then caught in the netting strand of *Nakaa*, guardian of the entrance to paradise, and entertained for three days upon the *'food of spirits'* before being allowed to join the great company of the ancestors.

During that period the ghost was tested by availability of the fruit of an inexhaustible tree, the fish of an inexhaustible lake, and the water of an inexhaustible well, owned by *Nakaa*. The well had no name, being simply called *te Maniba*, the term for the ordinary well. Upon arrival the ghost was sent to draw water to wash their feet and slake their thirst. The lake was called by the name *Neineaba*; it was believed to be of great expanse, and fringed with immense shoals not more than ankle deep. *Neineaba* was situated *'in the middle of Bouru'* due north of the coastal place called *Manra*, where *Nakaa* lived; it contained a single fish, the *mon-n-taai* (mon-of-the-sun), of a brilliant red-gold colour. The *mon-n-taai*, once caught in the net of a ghost, was immediately replaced in the lake by another. The belief was that if the ghost could abstain for three days from eating either the flesh of this fish or the fruit of *Nakaa's* tree, and from drinking the water of the well, they would be free to return to their body in the land of the living; but if being hungry and thirsty after the long journey, they could not resist the temptation of food and drink, they would be forever bound to *Nakaa* on Bouru.

In any case, back in the land of the living, the Wilkes expedition noted that:

> *'The skulls of their ancestors are carefully preserved by their family, and held in great reverence. When they desire to invoke their spirits, these skulls are taken down, wreathed with leaves, laid on a new mat, anointed with oil, and presented with food'.*

Grimble writes:

> *'After several years, the skull was again buried with the skeleton ... around this a small white shingled enclosure was demarcated by a low curb of trimmed coral, and the place became a sort of shrine'* [41].

---

[41] My parents-in-law both died on South Tarawa and were temporarily buried in our family plot there, as had been the body of their son Tonga, who predeceased them. In 2015, on the occasion of my wife and myself visiting Kiribati, and thus all the

Chapter 4: Religion and Magic

Later, the grave might be opened again to *'appropriate a bone or two for the manufacture of fish hooks, thatching tools ... when the teeth dropped out they would be kept and the canines used for making dancing necklaces'* – or tattooing instruments (p. 64).

In the early twentieth century ancestor stones were recorded by Nicolas Hamann. He photographed the *uea* Kauabanga II on Nonouti next to the memorial of his ancestor Te Ikae.

Hamann also made drawings of the ancestor stone of Te Maiawa on Maiana (before using it as the cornerstone of the Roman Catholic church that he built!); and also the stones on the tomb of the ancestor of the Ten Tabaua family in Tekaranga on that island.

Many of the ancestor stones were destroyed under the influence of Missionaries, and others were uprooted by the Japanese and Americans in WWII. Few remain today.

---

surviving siblings being present, all three sets of bones were exhumed and transported to their 'proper' burial place at *Tebonobono* near Tearinibai on North Tarawa. The bones were dug up, carefully washed, and taken up there to be laid to rest beside several previous generations, in exactly the way described by Grimble.

Chapter 4: Religion and Magic

Further Reading

1. http://www.janeresture.com/micronesia_myths/kiribati.htm
2. **Narrative of the United States Exploring Expedition During the Years 1838, 1839, 1840, 1841, 1842** (Chapter II, Vol 5) by Charles Wilkes, published in Philadelphia by Lea and Blanchard, 1845
3. **The Migrations of a Pandanus People: As traced from a preliminary study of Food, Food-traditions, and Food Rituals in the Gilbert Islands** by Arthur Grimble, Supplement to the Journal of the Polynesian Society, 1933
4. **Astride the Equator,** translated by Ursula Nixon from **Sous l'équateur de Pacifique** by Ernest Sabatier, Oxford University Press 1977
5. **Migrations, Myth, and Magic From The Gilbert Islands**, writings by Arthur Grimble edited by Rosemary Grimble (this includes *From Birth to Death in the Gilbert Islands)*, Routledge & Kegan Paul, 1972
6. **Tabiteua Kiribati,** by Guigone Camus, published by the Fondation Culturelle Musée Barbier, 2014
7. **Evolution of the Gilbertese Boti,** by H.E. Maude, first published by the Polynesian Society 1963, reprinted by the Institute of Pacific Studies, University of the South Pacific, 1977
8. **Tungaru Traditions**, edited by H. C. and H.E. Maude, Institute of Pacific Studies, University of the South Pacific, 1994
9. **The Footprints Of Tarawa** By I. G. Turbott, published in the Journal of the Polynesian Society, 1949
10. **Ancestor Stones and Megalithic Structures in the Gilbert Islands (Kiribati)** lecture to the Pacific Arts Association – Europe, by Professor J M Massing, 2005
11. **Kiribati: Aspects of History,** multiple authors and editors, published jointly by the Institute of Pacific Studies and the Ministry of Education, Training, and Culture, 1979

Chapter 5.

ARTS, CRAFTS, COMPETITIONS AND GAMES

Artistic traditions

Art in Tungaru was abstract: there was no tradition of representational art, like that found in Polynesia and Melanesia, or other parts of Micronesia such as Palau.

Nor did the Tungaru people make musical instruments; the accompaniment to their songs and dances was by rhythmic clapping of their hands or else by slapping, either their bodies, or rolled up mats (and later, wooden boxes). Their singing, by contrast, was highly sophisticated polyphony: that is, it comprised two (or often more) simultaneous lines of independent melody.

Pandanus woven decorations (for example on mats) are also abstract in nature: Koch recorded more than 50 different patterns still being made in the 1960s on Nonouti and Onotoa.

In the dance, however, many of the movements were consciously based on observation of birds – especially the frigate bird - and fishes, or sometimes the actions of everyday activities, such as taking the husk off a coconut.

In traditional arts, songs and games, competition filled Tungaru. It permeated their games and their dances. As always, magic played an important role. It has been said that although they were *'ostensibly a contest of singing and dancing,* kaunikai *(formal dance competitions) were actually competitions between bodies of knowledge'* [42].

Dress and Ornaments

It is clear from the early accounts that Tungaru people generally went about their daily tasks naked, except possibly wearing a sun hat, fashioned from either coconut or pandanus leaves, when fishing. Women might wear a very short skirt (*te riri*) made from sedge (*maunei*) or coconut leaf pinnules attached to a sennit belt – although they would discard even this when fishing (and in

---

[42] In this they differed markedly from *'te maiu ni Imatang'* sports, where it was important (until recently) that no-one was perceived to 'win'.

Chapter 5: Arts, Crafts, Competitions And Games

any case, as the Wilkes report delicately put it, the *riri 'serves no purposes of decency'*).

At festivities, men wore pandanus mats (*te be*) from the waist downwards. The Wilkes report again:

> *'Some load the waist with heavy strings of beads; others adorn the neck with rows of shells, and sometimes with one or two large whale's teeth, while others again have small rows of the latter across the back. Almost all wear a great many human teeth on the arms and round the neck; these are taken from their slain enemies; for after killing a man, the first object with them is to knock out his teeth, for the purpose of obtaining them for ornaments....*[43]

> *'The natives are very fond of ornamenting themselves: in the lobes of their ears they wear strings of small leaves of the mangrove, and the pith of a large species of Scaevola, which is common in the low islands. This pith is cut into strips and put up into a long roll; a wreath of which surrounds the neck, and to which a white ovula-shell, or a large whale's tooth, hangs suspended on their breast ... long strips of beads or braided hair are worn around the body, at times a hundred fathoms in length, which serve to fasten the mat. The hair for this purpose is taken from the female slaves, and is braided into a string about the size of a packthread. The beads are manufactured by the old men who are beyond doing any other labour, and are of the size of a small button-mould; they are made of cocoa-nut and shell, and strung alternatively black and white, being ground down to a uniform size and fitted together for the purpose...*

> *'They also besmear the face and body with cocoa-nut oil and some daub each cheek with fine white sand, and blacken their eyebrows and beards with charcoal. The hair is oiled and combed out with a pointed stick, and stands out from the head, forming an ornament which they esteem as very becoming.*

> *'The women wear their usual dress and a few ornaments, but about the decorations of their persons they are very attentive and scrupulous.'*

It is not clear whether the phrase 'usual dress' here refers to the kinds of grass skirt now worn for various types of dance (see below); or that women wore

---

[43] One of my wife's Tarawa ancestors allegedly had such had a necklace, of 82 teeth, one from each person he had killed in battle.

everyday *te riri* at these occasions. No mention, either, is made in the early accounts of the now common *kaue*, floral garlands, although these were common by the early 20th century and were presumably worn pre-contact as well.

Durable ornaments were regarded as family property and guarded in the *kaainga,* and worn by family members only at feasts or dances. A well-dressed dancer might wear:

- A headdress, of which there were many kinds
- A necklace (*te bunna*) with a pendant (*te ntabo*)
- A chest ornament (*te karaebari*)
- A sash (*te ririko*)
- Two ornamental belts: (*te katau and te taona n riri*)
- A dancing skirt (*te karoro*)
- Armbands such as *te etete* for some types of dance.

There were many kinds of necklace: Koch lists *te bunna, te karoro, te mae, te nuota,* and *te mae te nuota* as well as several kinds of pendant (which are often worn to look as if they are suspended from the necklace); and various designs of *te karaebari,* the diagonally-worn chest ornament.

Types of belt included:

- *Te katau*, made from closely-lying round discs of coconut shell strung on a cord
- *Te taona n riri*, a belt of two strips of pandanus leaves with a third strip wrapped diagonally around them, and completed by the addition of a coconut fibre cord with small shells attached
- *Te tumara*, a dancing belt consisting of *te tumara* shells threaded onto a thick woven cord through a single hole
- *Te bare*, a belt made again with two strips of pandanus leaves with a third strip wrapped diagonally around them (but thinner than the *taona*)
- *Te kamakorokoro*, made from strips of pandanus doubled over and twisted onto a cord of hair to look like teeth, closely hanging together and pointing sharply upwards and downwards.

Chapter 5: Arts, Crafts, Competitions And Games

Ceremonial ornaments

As well as dance necklaces, a variety of ceremonial ornaments, with various other purposes, are recorded. Nicolas Hamann in particular noted more than 100 such bespoke 'works of art' that he had seen, and himself collected some especially elaborate pieces:

- An ornament made from fibres with tortoise shell, an egg shell, a mother-of-pearl ornament and feathers, which rested on the shoulders of a member of only four families in Tabiteuea. (This is now in the museum at Leipzig in Germany)
- *Te uba are te nikabono* – a chest ornament, rounded and polished, made from the bottom of a cone shell. In the Te Baiteke family of Aranuka, it could only be worn by a virgin of exceptional beauty; when she married, *te unimane* chose a successor to wear it. It was used for defensive purposes: if a war canoe was spied off shore, the young woman in whose charge it then was put on her *uba,* and other magical objects round her neck, and led the population to the shore to oppose the enemy
- *Te mae are te nikabono* which was worn by the *Uea* Te Moaniba on Maiana. He wore it during celebrations such as dances, kite-flying displays, and canoe races. Those who did not show sufficient respect by bowing to it were excluded from the competitions
- *Te mae are te tawatawa* which was made for Matang, the *Uea* of Tarawa, when he thought he was not being accorded sufficient respect. He collected their *tawatawa* (hooks for fishing skipjack) and incorporated the shanks into the necklace. Again, when Matang wore it, his subjects had to bow down and touch the ground with their foreheads. This necklace – in Hamann's museum in Lorraine - was sadly destroyed in WWII.

Tattoos

In tradition, when a man or woman died and their spirit was voyaging to the lands in the west the path was blocked by *Nei Karamakuna*. She had a face like a bird; she pecked out all the tattoo marks on the person and ate them. Should the man or woman not have tattoos, *Nei Karamakuna* pecked out their eyes and ate those instead; they had to proceed on their way blinded, and live so in the afterlife. There was thus a strong incentive to become tattooed.

Chapter 5: Arts, Crafts, Competitions And Games

The tattooing instrument was called *te wii n taitai*, and marks it made *taitai*. The handle was made of *tarine* wood (the wild almond), and the points of sharpened turtle shell (or in the case below, human bone; fish bones are also recorded). When tattooing, the *wii n taitai* was normally hit with a piece of *te ba* (midrib of the coconut frond), the hammer being termed *te kai n oro*. The turtle shell was cut with a large *te batino* (sea urchin) which had previously been sharpened by rubbing it against a stone from the reef known as *ena*.

The tattooing 'ink' was made from the ashes of the coconut known as *te wae*, which has no kernel; this was mixed with salt water, or occasionally fresh water.

Arthur Grimble described his experience of being tattooed with the 'mark of the serpent' when he was adopted into the *boti* Karangoa n uea:

> *'I went to Tekirei's mwenga on a day appointed ... only he and Mautake-Meake, with two girls of fifteen or sixteen, dressed in minute kilts of leaf, were there to receive me. The girls ranged themselves on either side of me as soon as Tekirei brought them forward, and stood silent, holding my arms against their small bosoms ... as we stood so, Tekirei showed me the tattooing comb. It was a flat splinter of bone a quarter of an inch broad and an inch and a half long, beautifully fashioned at one end into a row of five needle-sharp teeth. 'I made this' he said 'from the shin-bone of my grandfather'...*

> *'He went on to explain how the comb was to be mounted for use in the position of an adze-blade at the end of a little wooden handle: 'first I dip it in the dye, then I set it in this handle. I can hold it firmly so, down upon the flesh that is to be tattooed. And then, so that the teeth may be driven into the flesh, I say 'strike' and Mautake strikes down upon the back of the handle' with [...] the ivory like eighteen inch spear of a spear-fish, the thick end of which was to serve as a mallet...*

> *'Tekirei and Mautake first drew guide lines on my arms with stretched strings, which they dipped in their tattooing dye and pressed down on the skin, to leave transfer marks ... they began on my right arm ... Mautake struck. The teeth bit deep. Tekerie pulled them out again, dipped them afresh in the dye, laid them in place again immediately above their first five punctures ... and Mautake struck once more. So it went on... half an hour saw the first line finished. Then they returned to the bottom and*

began on the second line. As soon as that was done, they went over to the left arm and dealt with that...

'*Custom dictated that it was my duty to Tekirei to show no shameful sign of suffering ... if there were groans to be groaned, the tender companions of my pain were there to emit them on my behalf, which they did at exactly the right moments ...* [for the second and third rounds of the tattoo] *... the synchronised stings of five hornets could not have improved on the smart of it ...* [the two young girls] *responded with a scream of mortal agony... their screams for me were syncopated by gusts of delirious sobbing as the fiery comb crawled in its merciless way to a finish*'.

The shape of the tattoos was either a single, or a double, straight line with feathers going out on either side, sometimes straight and sometimes bent. Some of the designs were:

- *te atu ni kua*: four feathered lines from the shoulder blades to the top of the thigh, ending on the back of the thighs
- *te kana ni kua*: extending from where the *atu ni kua* leaves off to the top of the ankle, going down the side of the thighs and legs
- *te manoku ni wae*: extending from the back of the ankle, straight up the back of the leg and thigh to the top of the buttock
- *te moa ni wae*: extending from the chest above the breasts to half way down the thighs. Only the ends at the thighs are known as *te moa ni wae*, the continuation upwards being called *te kua n nanoa*
- *te kua n en an* or *te moani kua* is the continuation upwards of *te atu ni kua*
- *te kuan nanoa*: continuation of the *te moa ni wae* upwards
- *ten anon nange*: on the inside of each thigh
- *te uba*: up the shin bone of each leg, starting at the top of the ankle and going over the knee to the top of the thigh.

A man might also have three or four lines running up his foot from his toes to below the ankle; although there was always a gap at the ankle. The face might also be tattooed; and if the man was bald, the top of his head as well. He might have a necklace line tattooed around his neck. Women were also tattooed. They had no *ten anon nange* but instead a line around their legs at the bottom of their *riri* and known as *te korea n riri*. A well-tattooed man or woman (as opposed to Grimble's rather token tattoos) was termed *aekia*, and if he or she were tattooed all over, as *bonotia*.

Chapter 5: Arts, Crafts, Competitions And Games

Weaving patterns

Woven mats were used in Tungaru as clothing (*te be*), for sitting on (*te roba*), and for sleeping on (several types including *te kie ni matu*, *te wewene*, and *te kie n ataei*). Specially woven mats were produced for important life events: birth, puberty, marriage and eventually for the dead.

Women wove them from pandanus strips, with known varieties producing different coloured leaves, although the darkest shades were obtained by dyeing with an infusion of the leaves of Clerodendron inerme (*te inato*) and Scaevola sericea (*te mao*).

Koch (writing in the 1960s) comments that '*nowadays at least there are no particular rights attached to the use of individual patterns ... usually a main pattern is woven into the mats together with a variable second pattern. Individual mats have several patterns...*' He lists more than 50 such patterns, some with colourful names such as *kauniman* (battle of the animals), or *roata n ni* (centipede on the coconut palm).

Traditional fans (*te iriba*), were not, according to Koch, decorated: those now produced as handicrafts, often with brightly coloured imported dyes, were not a part of Tungaru culture.

Song

Polyphony - as practised in I Kiribati arrangements of music - has a wide, if uneven, distribution among the peoples of the world, mostly in sub-Saharan Africa, Eastern Europe and Oceania. It is now believed that use of polyphony in traditional Oceanic music predates its emergence in European 'classical' music (which took place in the late Middle Ages); although some writings about the Pacific assert that the Tungaru people learned it from missionaries in the late 19th century.

The oldest type of song is probably the *katake*. This is a chant in praise of ancestors and is often expressed in rich (and now archaic) language with vivid images and great poetic imagination. It is sung on a high keening note, frequently as a duet with a fine sense of rhythm. The duettists deliberately employ the device of discords drawing together in close harmony to resolve finally on clear and powerful notes in coincidence with the climacterics of the verse. The sung phrases are long sustained; considerable skill is required to render them properly.

Chapter 5: Arts, Crafts, Competitions And Games

The *ruoia* song groups (see below) have their own songs, the most common being the *'te bino'*. This is a seated dance. The performers adopt a trident form, the leader being seated at the point of the central spear. The song shows a more developed melodic line than that of the *katake* but also uses the device of deliberate discord resolving into organ-like harmonies. The dance movements are limited to head and hands with an occasional turning of the torso, and are most precisely linked to the words and music. No instruments are used, the rhythms being marked by hand-claps of spectators.

Songs were also important in aspects of everyday life: for example a toddy cutter aloft would always sing loudly to show that he is not spying on those below, but at his legitimate work.

Music in Tungaru was composed by *te kainikamaen,* with an ability that is said to pass from father to son, but who as individuals received their songs from magic: through the ether, as it were. Composers might, nevertheless, write songs on demand, as well as creating songs of their own accord. The composer would dictate the various polyphonic melodies to be combined, and allocate them to them to members of a group called *te rurubene,* an *ad hoc* gathering of volunteers who wished to participate in the work; they then sang the work in its various parts to the composer, after which it became public and could be sung by anyone: at this point, the song was considered blessed (*mamiraki*).

More modern songs are often love-themed, but there are also competitive, religious, children's, patriotic, war and wedding and even songs about contemporary events [44]. Here, as an example, is a translation of a well-known song called *Teiraken te Man,* which was composed in 1939 by Tekaiti Moote. A women from Banaba, Nei Tabeta, laments that her lover, Iete, must return home from Banaba to his own island, Maiana.

> *'You spread your wings; and where will you fly to?*
> *Where will you touch down, on the branch of a tree?*
> *Get ready to fly, and to never return*
> *To go back to your land that you love*

---

[44] One of my favourites of this last category is about the Apollo XI mission, that landed the lunar module Eagle on the moon in 1969; and how, while they were on the Moon, the astronauts met *Nei Nibarara* , the *anti* who in I Tungaru tradition lives, and cooks *kaimaimai,* there.

Chapter 5: Arts, Crafts, Competitions And Games

Chorus for verses 1 and 2

You, flower of my tree
Where will you fly to?
Where will you stop now?
You go and will never return.

When I hear the sound of your cries
They fill me with sadness
They will always make me remember
Those dreams that eluded me

My friends, remember this song
For I follow the flock of birds
Flying above Maiana
So far away from my home

Chorus for verse 3

I am Nei Tabeta
Where will you fly to?
Where will you stop now?
You go and will never return.

Dance

I Tungaru dancing was described thus by Fanny Stevenson on her visit in 1889:

> *'The conductor gave the cue, and all the dancers, waving their arms, swaying their bodies, and clapping their breasts in perfect time, opened with an introductory. The performers remained seated, except two, and once three, and twice a single soloist… there was a pause in the introductory, and then the real business of the opera – for it was no less – began; an opera where every singer was an accomplished actor. The leading man, in an impassioned ecstasy which possessed him from head to foot, seemed transfigured; once it was as if a strong wind had swept over the stage – their arms, their feathered fingers thrilling with an*

emotion that shook my nerves as well: heads and bodies followed like a field of grain before a gust.

'My blood came hot and cold, tears pricked my eyes, my head whirled, I felt an almost irresistible impulse to join the dancers ... at no time was there the least sign of the ugly indecency of the eastern islands [i.e. Polynesia]. *All was poetry pure and simple.*

'The music itself was as complicated as our own, though constructed on an entirely different basis...'

As Fanny Stevenson recognised, dances in Tungaru were not just a form of entertainment; nor were they merely an opportunity to display the beauty, skilfulness, and often sheer endurance (and thus sometimes the marriageability) of the dancers. Individual dances might reflect many things: tributes to particular *anti*, celebration of the unification of two *kaainga*, the telling of stories, and so on. But they were also highly competitive: *'people seethed with antagonism and tensions as the rivals, ritually strengthened and protected, faced each other'.*

They are unique amongst Pacific nations in their formality; their emphasis on carefully controlled movements in the outstretched arms of the dancers; and the sudden birdlike movements of the head of the participants [45]. Dances were taken extremely seriously: smiling whilst dancing was considered very vulgar, although tears, hysterical outbursts, or signs of ecstasy (*angin te maie*), were not only acceptable but common.

There were several main styles, with differences in the movements, the costume worn, the gender of the dancer or dancers, the number of dancers, and whether there is accompanying percussion:

- *Te bino*: one of the oldest forms of dance, performed by dancers sitting cross-legged, with a mat spread over their legs, and with a chorus of men singing behind them
- *Te ruoia*: another old form of dance, where the dancer or dancers stand in front of a chorus of singers. Performances of *te ruoia* usually consist of three verses, sung with an increasing tempo. Within the *rouia* there

---

[45] There are several semi-professional Pacific Islander dance groups currently operating in the UK. As one of them recently said to me, 'we do dances from throughout the Pacific, except those of Kiribati. They are simply too difficult'

were three genres – *te kemai* (usually performed by men), and *te kabuti* (performed only by woman): the third genre was only performed on Abemama where it was greatly stylised and called *te wa ni banga*

- *Te kaimatoa*: this is probably the most widely practised dance in contemporary Kiribati. It means literally *'the dance of strength'*. This dance tests the dancer's physical endurance to stretch out their arms for long periods, but also the dancer's emotional resilience, as the music and rhythm arouse intense feeling. The *kaimatoa* can be performed by men, women or children

- *Te buki*: a form of dance which is thought to be relatively modern, and to have originated in the northern islands of the Gilbert group, although it is now widely danced in all islands. The dance is only performed by women; it requires the dancer to wear a thick and heavy coconut frond skirt made of the boiled and softened pinneals of coconut leaf (*te kakoko*). The skirt can weigh up to ten kilograms and is generally shin length. As in other forms of Pacific dance such as the Tahitian *hura, te buki* dance emphasises movement of the hips, as if the torso and hips were disconnected. The torso and shoulders are kept as motionless as possible, while the movement of the hips resembles that of water

- *Te tirere*: this usually performed by a group of ten to twenty dancers, lined up in pairs. Each dancer has a short stick which is struck against that of the pair, in time with the accompanying song, thereby creating a strong rhythm

- *Te rebwe*: dances performed by men, with clapping and step footing, which emphasise war and fighting movements.

Training to be a good dancer began at an early age. My wife [46] relates:

'When I was eleven, in 1963, I was living with my parents on Makin, where my father worked as a Dresser for the Medical Department.

'With two other girls, I was entered into a kaunikai (dance contest). Our teacher was Na Rakobu, an old man of perhaps 45 years, and an inheritor of musical tradition (tia kainikamaen). He put us under strict discipline, and we practised for weeks at Te Maie Tera Te Mamaie (A

---

[46] Who was 'classically' trained in dance styles, and who has coached the younger generations in the UK. She has most recently performed the same dance in October 2017, at the British Museum in London.

Chapter 5: Arts, Crafts, Competitions And Games

variant of Te kaimatoa, *or as it was called in Tarawa,* Te Kai Ni Meang).

'*Part of the discipline was that we were forbidden to eat fish: the main part of our diet.*

'*I am sorry to say that shortly before the event, we three stole some cooked fish and ate it. We were soon discovered and were severely chastised by Na Rokobu.*

'*He made us drink an expiating potion just before we danced, which was disgusting; but whether through this and our skill, or perhaps because one of my fellow dancers was banuea (from the royal family of Butaritari), we still won the competition*'.

The potion may have been made by employing the *karuoia* magic as described in *The Journal of the Polynesian Society* (see Further Reading below under *Ruoia - a Gilbertese dance*).

Dancing was severely restricted during the early colonial period, indeed forbidden at times, firstly by the churches, and then by the government: but despite this, and unlike many other aspects of traditional I Tungaru life, it has survived into the modern period, if not intact, at least as a living part of the culture of Kiribati.

Other amusements

There was a wide variety of other games, contests, and amusements.

Making string figures

In their seminal paper on string figures, H. C. and H. E. Maude comment:

'*Even a cursory acquaintanceship with the Gilbertese must reveal the exceptional extent to which they are addicted to the making of cats-cradles. Like their other games, string-figures will suddenly, and for no ascertainable reason, become the fashion on an island, and young and old may be seen sitting in the communal meeting-house or in their homes weaving intricate designs with a speed and dexterity which shows their long familiarity with the art*'.

The generic name for string-figures in the Northern Gilberts is *wau*, while in the Southern islands it is *tai*. The former is probably a purely Gilbertese term and is the only one given in Bingham's Dictionary, while the latter is very likely a Polynesian loanword.

The *anti ma aomata* Na Ubwebwe (the Old Man of the Cats-cradle) was essentially the father of string-figures. Shortly after meeting *Nei Karamakuna* a dead person on their westward voyage will meet *Na Ubwebwe*; he will display the series of string-figures collectively called by his name. The ghost is bound to name correctly the figure of the series called *te Ubwebwe*, whenever it appears. If he fails, he will be either strangled in the string or else impaled by the old man's staff, and die forever.

Grimble comments that:

> *'The being Na Ubwebwe is represented as a stunted, black, curly-haired person; he appears in a servile capacity in some versions of the Creation Myth, and is believed by some to have invented the string-figure and displayed it for the first time while heaven was being separated from the earth.'*

While, however, *Na Ubwebwe* is, in Gilbertese myth, invariably connected with the making of string-figures, Nareau the Trickster (see page 50) was also adept at making cats-cradles and in particular, string-catches and tricks.

The general method of making a cats-cradle is referred to as *karika-na* and each of the fingers has a special name: *tabotabo* being the index finger, *kiremkirem* the middle finger, *tongabiri* the ring finger, *ukirere* the little finger, and *ukinaba* the thumb. A large number of the Gilbertese figures represent *maniba* (wells) in some form or other.

Kites

Kite-flying may have been first invented in insular Southeast Asia by Austronesians (and later borrowed by the Chinese); certainly the use of kites in prehistoric Oceania was widespread. Kite-flying was practiced for a variety of reasons: fishing, meteorology, and navigation, as well as for recreation and competitions. In the Indonesian islands, simple kites were basically made from large leaves; but kites from remote Oceania were more complex in their shape, design, and construction methods. They also tended to be more of a high-aspect ratio (greater width to height ratio), represented as birds, and associated with religious and ceremonial purposes.

Chapter 5: Arts, Crafts, Competitions And Games

The first written reference to kites in Tungaru comes from *Hawaiian Games*, by Stewart Culin, which was published in 1899. He comments in this that Gilbert Islanders from the 'Kingsmill Group' are *'said to make fine kites of pandanus'* which had been *'reduced to half of its thickness'*. The generic name for an I Tungaru kite is *utuao*. H. E. Maude lists eight different named types, which were associated with particular *boti*. Gerd Koch gives details of kite construction and use: *'the old men still recall that after the appropriate spell had been uttered the utuao would take to the air near the cult places and then climb to a height of 30-90 m. above them ... the largest kites are said to have been several metres long and to have been carried at both ends and in the middle bunches of slit pieces of pandanus leaves (hanging on long cords) to stabilise their flight.'*

Games

These were many and varied:

- Martial arts, similar to ju-jitsu, but also disarming those with clubs
- Wrestling (*te kaunrabwata*)
- Stone throwing (*te katua*)
- Model canoe racing (for adults)
- A complicated stick game called *te bwerera*
- Various ball games (the ball (*ano*) being a cube of various sizes, woven from coconut fronds): *warebwi, bwebwe, boiri, oreano*
- Toys, such as windmills and simpler kinds of model canoe racing
- Cock fights, and fights between captured wild birds (see p. 160)
- *Kauniben* (fighting with nuts); *kaunibwatua* (fish fighting) and *uniwaka* (self defence)

Descriptions of each are in *The Material Culture of Kiribati* (see Further Reading below).

Chapter 5: Arts, Crafts, Competitions And Games

Further Reading

1. **Narrative of the United States Exploring Expedition During the Years 1838, 1839, 1840, 1841, 1842** (Chapter II, Vol 5) by Charles Wilkes, published in Philadelphia by Lea and Blanchard, 1845
2. **The Material Culture of Kiribati,** by Gerd Koch (translated by Guy Slatter), published by the Institute of Pacific Studies, University of the South Pacific, 1986
3. **The Migrations of a Pandanus People: As traced from a preliminary study of Food, Food-traditions, and Food Rituals in the Gilbert Islands,** by Arthur Grimble, Supplement to the Journal of the Polynesian Society, 1933
4. http://www.janeresture.com/oceania_tattoos/kiribati.htm
5. **A Pattern of Islands,** by Arthur Grimble, published by John Murray, 1952
6. **The Concise Garland Encyclopaedia of World Music Vol I,** edited by Koskoff et al, published by Blackwells 2008
7. **A Gilbertese Song,** by P. B. Laxton, published in the Journal of the Polynesian Society, 1953
8. **"Ruoia" A Gilbertese Dance,** by P. B. Laxton And Te Kautu Kamoriki, Illustrations by Dr. C. H. Pietsch, Posed by Ten Tibwe Of Maiana, published in The Journal of the Polynesian Society, 1953
9. **In The South Seas,** by R L Stevenson, first published in 1896, republished by Penguin Books 1998
10. **String-Figures From the Gilbert Islands,** by H. C. and H. E. Maude, Supplement to the Journal of the Polynesian Society, 1936

Chapter 6.

WARFARE

Causes, incidence, consequences

Almost the first thing that the Wilkes Expedition's report says of 'Drummond's Island', that is, Tabiteuea, is this:

> 'The arms and legs of a large proportion of the natives exhibited numerous scars, many of which were still unhealed. These have been made with sharks' teeth swords... they were evidently in the habit of having severe conflicts with each other, and war seems to be one of the principal employments of this people...'

> 'They had invented a kind of armour which was almost an effectual defence against their weapons, and accounted at one for their arms and legs being the only part where scars were seen...'

The expedition reported on recent evidence of warfare on all the islands visited, except on Butaritari and Makin where the ruling dynasty had managed to preserve peace for perhaps a century, and where weapons and armour were absent in the 1840s (without apparently inviting an invasion from neighbouring islands!). However, traditions suggest that wars had in earlier times been endemic there as well.

Wars arose from:

- Feuds between individual *kaainga* on the same islands, arising for example from refusal to honour a crime by payment of *te aba n nenebo*
- Wider civil wars within an atoll, notably the more than 200-year cycle of wars on Tarawa that were only ended by the arrival of the British in 1892
- Deliberate invasions which set out from one island to conquer others. Earlier Chapters have listed that of Kaitu and Uakeia in the 17th century, the invasion of Abemama from Tarawa about 1780, and the subsequent invasions of Kuria, Aranuka and Nonouti from Abemama; but there are accounts of others.

Chapter 6: Warfare

Another form of war was a formal challenges between champions. Each *kaainga* would have such a champion.

Training for warfare

Sabatier details the rigorous training and ceremonies that destined a young boy to be a *rorobuaka*, that is, a warrior. At the age of about 12, his hair was cut with a shark tooth and he was made to live alone on the east side of the island in a specially constructed hut, apart from his *kaainga*, and apart especially from female company (being forbidden even to see his mother).

Further details of these and subsequent ceremonies were also recorded by Grimble.

> *'When ... he was considered ready for the succession of trying ordeals called collectively* te kanna ni mane *...[he was allowed] an increase in rations ... his hair had been allowed to grow untouched so that by the time* te kanna ni mane *era arrived he was the owner of a plentiful mop. When the star* Rimwi-maata *appeared above the eastern horizon at sunset the elders of his family appointed a day for the cutting of his hair'*

This ceremony, known as *te kaura* (the scorching), involved him sitting staring unblinking into a large fire while his father again cut his hair with a shark's tooth. This completed, the second part, *te kabue-ari* (burning of the eyebrows), began. Sparks from a burning dry coconut leaf were fanned onto him and allowed to burn on his head and shoulders; he was not allowed to flinch or wipe his eyes. These two ceremonies were repeated once he had recovered, about two months later.

At dawn on the fourth moon he underwent an even more testing ceremony: *te ati ni kana*. Again, he must sit on a stone close to the hottest fire that could be kindled. He drank a potion of fresh water, sea water and coconut oil stirred by a sting ray barb: this was to give him courage for the rest of his life. His father then proceeded to lacerate his skull with a shark's tooth until blood streamed over his face. He must then continue to sit on the stone without fainting or showing any distress, until sunset. This ordeal was repeated for three successive months.

This life continued until he had undergone several years – enough for the thatch on his hut to rot - of carrying out hard labour and physical tests under the direction of his grandfather and uncles. There were also many endurance tests he had to undergo to *'strengthen him against all testing situations for the rest of his life'* – including no doubt the inconvenience of his armour, which, together with his weapons, was being made for him at the same time.

Once the thatch on his hut on the east side of the island had rotted, he was escorted back to his family. A dance was performed in his honour, and he was endowed with the title *rorobuaka*. Very often, he would be married to his long betrothed fiancée shortly after.

Armour

The armour consisted of:

- *Teotana*: trousers made of coir twine (sinnet)
- *Tetuta*: a tunic made of sinnet
- *Tetana* : a coat made of plaited coir twine with a high back piece to protect the head, worn over the *Tetuta*
- *Tekatibana*: a band of woven coir twine, or dried ray skin, from 7 to 10 inches broad, worn round the body and over the abdomen as a protection from spears
- *Tebarantauti*: helmet made of the inflated porcupine (puffer) fish skin
- *Tebaratekora*: a close-fitting skull cap of plaited sinnet to protect the head from blows.

Weapons

The names of weapons and their manner of use varied considerably, according to George Murdock, who in 1923 published in the *Journal of the Polynesian Society* this (edited) description of those with which he was familiar in the central Gilberts:

1. *Teunun* (shark's tooth spear), from 12 to 18 feet long. Used in tribal warfare and in family and other feuds resulting in fighting. As a rule in tribal war the spearman was attended by a henchman armed with a *Taumañgaria* or *Teie*. The henchman generally preceded the spearman, engaging the henchman of their opponents' spearman. The spearmen then themselves became engaged fighting side by side with their attendants, who assisted them by catching or fending off the spears by their weapons. The vulnerable parts of the body exposed were the arms, legs, armpits, between the legs, the face and throat. On breaking or discarding the spears, the spearsmen and their attendants used their

Chapter 6: Warfare

Tembo (sword club) or *Toañgea* (shark's tooth sword club) to finish the encounter (usually fatally).

2. *Temaran* and *Taboua* (long, smooth spears), from 12 to 18 feet long, made of coconut wood, 1¼' to 1½' in diameter in the centre and tapering to a fine sharp point at each end, which was used in the same manner as the shark's tooth spear, but which could be used both in front and rear.
3. *Te Tembo* or *Batiraku* (sword club, either round or with four sharp edges), some 2 feet 6 inches to 3 feet long, was used in infighting and hand-to-hand encounters.
4. *Tetoanea* or *Tewinnarei* (shark's tooth sword club), 2 feet 6 inches to 3 feet long, was also used in infighting.
5. *Tetaumanaria* (branched spear), 14 to 18 feet long. Used by the attendants of spearsmen who engaged one another, and also assisted the spearsmen by catching or fending off the spears with the branches. The staff, like nearly all Gilbert Islands weapons, is made of old, well-seasoned coconut wood, and the branches of a hard wood *tenea*, resembling *Ti*-tree. The points of the branches were sharp, and together with the sharp point of the spear, were used as a weapon.
6. *Teie* (branched spear), 12 to 14 feet long. Made of the same woods and used in like manner as the *Tetaumanaria*.
7. *Tekoromatan* (throwing stick), 3 feet to 3 feet 6 inches long, which was made of coconut wood or mangrove, and pointed sharp at each end. This was used for throwing.
8. *Tebakabota* (sting-ray spear), 4 to 5 feet long. Made of coconut or mangrove wood, with the serrated bones of the weapon of the sting-ray tied in a cluster on the end and used as a spear. The bones were also burnt, on occasion, to make them brittle and break in the flesh
9. *Tetara* (barbed spear), 7 to 9 feet long. Made of coconut wood, with the barbs cut out of the wood, sometimes made of mangrove; and used both as a throwing spear, and in hand-to-hand encounters
10. *Teauabubuti* (double-ended spear), up to 14 feet long. Made of hardwood, coconut or mangrove, with a sinnet line from end to end near the point, and travelling loosely in a loop of sinnet held in the left hand. It could be used both in front and rear
11. *Teronikiri* (lasso rope and stick), 2 feet long. Made of hardwood, with a strong coir sinnet line fastened to the centre. Used to lasso the arms or legs. Murdock comments that *'A turn of the line is taken round the*

Chapter 6: Warfare

arms or legs to the wood which is then twisted as in a "Spanish windlass," rendering the victim helpless'

12. *Tebutu* (cutting or scratching weapon), from 4 to 6 inches long, with from one to four shark's teeth fastened to it, and string of coir sinnet arranged as a loop to put one or more fingers through. Used by the women to cut and disfigure each other when quarrelling from jealousy or other causes.
13. *Tebana*: knuckle duster made of sinnet, woven or plaited hard, especially on the knuckles.

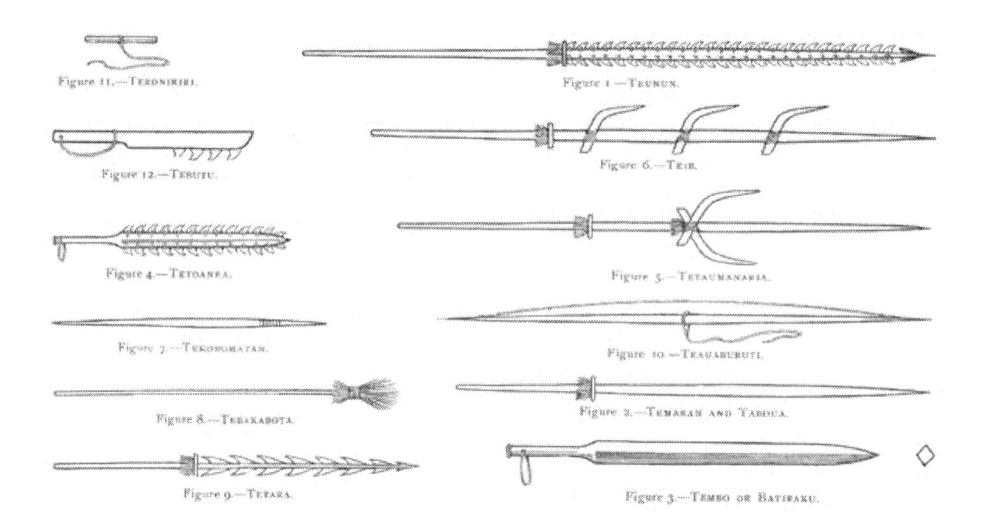

Source: Journal of the Polynesian Society 1923

The conduct of war

The conduct of war was described by Paul Hambruch, an early German ethnologist whose observations were primarily made on Nauru and Banaba, but are equally applicable to the low islands of Tungaru; he published an account in 1915.

Combats were strictly regulated. The place and time were agreed between the old men of the *kaainga* involved, and the *kaainga* would prepare weapons and equipment. Emissaries might be sent out to drum up support from other members of the *kaainga's utu*, from other islands if necessary.

Nei Teraabuki, an *anti* who was particularly associated with warfare, would be propitiated with special offerings.

Chapter 6: Warfare

Hambruch describes the rituals and incantations used while dressing for battle, as well as those associated with the combat itself, the aim being to render the fighters invincible. First the body was carefully oiled with coconut oil and covered with freshly cut leaves to protect the skin from friction. Over these the warrior wore his trousers, jacket and armour, fastened by strings and a belt. He then put on his helmet. Each fighter also wore short cut-and-thrust- weapons in his belt. The ensemble also included shell ornaments which were credited with warding off magic from the opponent. All this dressing was done with the aid of an *ibonga*, whose spells Hambruch collected.

The actual combat was ritualistic as well.

Brother Urswald, an early missionary, whose informant was a former warrior from Abaiang, Te Kakiaman, described in a letter how on the day of the combat the protagonists would advance in close ranks. In front were the women of the *kaainga* (except young girls and nursing mothers). They were armed with weapons about 30 cm. long (*ui n aine*) set with sharks' teeth. Behind the women were the main body of fighters, especially the spearmen, while adolescents and older men stood behind with slings and throwing stones.

Skirmishes began with the women, who aimed to scratch the faces and chests of their opponents. Brother Urswald recounts that 'they did not often kill each other but inflicted serious wounds that would heal only slowly and left great scars… they only left the fight when exhausted, having lost hair and flesh … providing a feast for the local crabs'.

Then came the male fighters and their rear-guard, fighting with long lances. The older men engaged in combat also with clubs.

This battle lasted until defeat for one side, or nightfall. Only when one party was defeated – and if no settlement could be reached – did the combat become a general mêlée. If nightfall arrived first, the elders of the two groups would try to negotiate an end to hostilities. If no agreement could be reached, the combat would be delayed while armour and weapons (and wounds) were repaired; then it would be resumed. According to Te Kakiaman, in a really bitter struggle the whole adult population of a kaainga might be destroyed, and its children enslaved.

Chapter 6: Warfare

Further Reading

1. **Narrative of the United States Exploring Expedition During the Years 1838, 1839, 1840, 1841, 1842** (Chapter II, Vol 5) by Charles Wilkes, published in Philadelphia by Lea and Blanchard, 1845
2. **Gilbert Islands Weapons and Armour,** by G M Murdoch, Journal of the Polynesian Society, Volume 32 Number 127, 1923, at http://www.jps.auckland.ac.nz/browse.php
3. **Astride the Equator,** translated by Ursula Nixon from **Sous l'équateur de Pacifique** by Ernest Sabatier, Oxford University Press 1977
4. **Migrations, Myth, and Magic From The Gilbert Islands**, writings by Arthur Grimble edited by Rosemary Grimble (this includes *From Birth to Death in the Gilbert Islands*), Routledge & Kegan Paul, 1972
5. **In Arms and Armour. Battles in the Gilbert Islands** by Professor J M Massing, based on a talk given to the Stuttgart meeting of the Pacific Arts Association Europe in 2001.

Chapter 7.

MATERIAL CULTURE, TECHNOLOGY AND THE TRADITIONAL ECONOMY

Adaptation of the 'Austronesian package' to local circumstances

The ultimate Southeast Asian origin of what is now known as the Lapita complex, which originated from the Austronesians in Taiwan or southern China some 5,000 to 6,000 years ago, was set out in Chapter 2.

In Taiwan and southern China, and also the northern Philippines, people cultivated rice and millet, and engaged in hunting; but were also heavily reliant on marine shells and fish. Long-distance trade of obsidian, adzes and favourable adze source rock and shells was practiced.

Those who migrated further southwards seem to have been 'elite' invaders with a 'package' of crops, pottery, language and technologies (and some think, religious beliefs). As they left the Philippines and reached the Pacific islands, they perforce abandoned elements of the package: firstly, cereal crops - in favour of horticulture based on both root crops and tree crops, most importantly taro and yam, coconuts, bananas and varieties of breadfruit. Fishing and mollusc gathering remained important. Domesticated animals still consisted of pigs, dogs and chickens, as in Taiwan.

Lapita pottery is found from the Admiralty Islands eastwards as far as Samoa, and Lapita-derived pottery in the Caroline Islands. There were successive styles, but essentially these were similar to the "red slip" pottery of Taiwan. None has yet been found in Kiribati.

Of all the Lapita food sources, the first settlers of Tungaru managed to establish just eight food plants and one domestic animal, the dog (although rats came along for the ride too!); and they had to modify the tools and technologies they brought to their new islands.

In addition to edible cultivars of *te kaina* (Pandanus tectorius) the aboriginal introductions to the Gilberts include the other major staple food crops: *te ni* or coconut (Cocos nucifera) – though some think this preceded humans - *te*

Chapter 7: Material Culture, Technology and the Traditional Economy

babai or giant swamp taro (Cyrtosperma chamissonis), and two breadfruit species, both called *te mai* (Artocarpus altilis and Artocarpus mariannensis, plus a hybrid of the two). All these crops have a diversity of named cultivars.

It is thought that the pandanus preceded human occupation of the Gilbert islands, and that it had already colonised them from drift seeds when the first people arrived. The first populations must have used pandanus as a basic plant food until the coconut palms they had (probably) brought with them were sufficient in number to supply their needs; and pandanus was always important, especially in the drier southern islands where growing breadfruit was problematical.

Other aboriginal introductions include the formerly more important *te makemake* or Polynesian arrowroot, now a 'famine food' plant; the occasionally cultivated *te taororo* or taro (Colocasia esculenta); *te iam* or yam (Dioscorea spp.), which although having a name derived from the English name, was reportedly present at the time of European contact; and *te kabe*, now planted mainly as an ornamental.

Now commonly grown crops such as papaya and bananas have been introduced since European contact, as are now widely grown ornamental plants such as hibiscus and frangipani; although it has been suggested that a pre-contact cultivar of banana, *te touru*, (no longer present) may have been cultivated.

The settlers definitely brought dogs and rats; but opinion is divided as to whether the they brought chickens (*te moa*) with them. 'Moa' is thought to be a Tongan loanword so possibly they were introduced by refugees from Samoa, in about 1400 CE. The Wilkes expedition noted the 'fowls' at Utiroa in Tabiteuea, but Hiram Bingham found none on Abaiang a decade or so later. Chickens were certainly widespread by the early 20th century, although according to Grimble, they were then only eaten on Butaritari and Makin. Wild jungle fowl are now encountered in thick undergrowth on most islands; these can fly considerable distances, and roost in the tops of coconut trees.

There is however a consensus that pigs were another part of the Austronesian package which was left behind in Melanesia, and were not introduced into the Gilberts until brought there by Europeans.

Grimble, in *The Migrations of a Pandanus People As traced from a preliminary study of Food, Food-traditions, and Food-rituals in the Gilbert Islands,* describes a

Chapter 7: Material Culture, Technology and the Traditional Economy

folk memory of what seems to be betel-nut chewing, another part of the Austronesian package that did not survive the journey:

> 'According to the old man Taakeuta, of Marakei Island, the substance traditionally known as te renga was the food of ancestors (bakatibu) in "the line of lands in the west" called by the inclusive name of Te Bu-kiroro or Te Bongiroro. Quoting the same authority, who is backed by other old men of Marakei, Abaiang and Tarawa—all in the Northern Gilberts— "te renga was a food which made the mouth red when it was eaten." There is a tradition in Taakeuta's social group, and also extant upon the island of Abaiang, that this substance was not taken alone, being chewed (kantaki) with the leaf of a certain tree....[There seems to be] an immediate identification of this substance with the betel-mixture (areca-nut, betel-leaf, lime), which is, of course, still commonly chewed in the far western Pacific and Indonesia.
>
> 'The question which naturally arises, if the Gilbertese forefathers had the betel-chewing habit, is why their descendants have not persisted in the practice until to-day. This is fairly answered by the physical conditions of the Gilbert Group, whereof the almost purely coralline soil will support only two food-trees—the pandanus and the coconut-palm. If the areca-palm ever was introduced into these atolls, it could not well have outlasted the first generation of settlement. As the betel-chewing habit must thus have been involuntarily abandoned at an early epoch of the race-history, the memory preserved of the ancestral practice is remarkably precise [47].

Of the aquatic mammals, both porpoises and whales provided 'meat feasts'. The former were famously 'summoned' to the beaches; the latter were not hunted - but when they were naturally beached, they were cut up and eaten. Taboos and magic applied here too [48]. Turtles were also taken, although there were probably more taboos around this resource than any other.

---

[47] And perhaps explains why the Tungaru people took so rapidly and enthusiastically to chewing tobacco – see Chapter 8.

[48] A whale was washed up at Abaokoro on Tarawa on the day my mother-in-law died in 2010, just opposite what had been her kitchen. The two events were widely thought to be connected – her whale had come to carry her away to the west.

Chapter 7: Material Culture, Technology and the Traditional Economy

Of the species of wild bird present in Tungaru only five were considered edible, and unlike the practice in many islands in Polynesia (including neighbouring Tuvalu) they played little part in the traditional diet. Eggs were also not eaten [49].

Domestic animals

The early settlers introduced two species of terrestrial mammal: the dog (*te kiri*, which is not ancestral to most of the dogs now in Kiribati - they are descended from dogs (*te kamea*) introduced by Europeans in the 20th century); and the Polynesian rat (*te kimoa*, Rattus exulans).

Dogs appear to have been both a food source, and well-regarded companions (see page 37). Cats, however, were a European introduction.

Tame frigate birds (*Fregata minor palmerstoni*) were once quite common, although less so today; they were usually kept on elevated perches on the windward side. The Banabans (and Nauruans) were especially keen on having these birds as pets, but the practice existed on other islands as well. In order to tame the birds, the I Tungaru used special diets, such as a particular species of small fish, or the boiled abdomens of hermit crabs. Others, when feeding the bird, added some of their personal hair-oil to the food and rubbed some of this oil on its bill so that the bird would recognise its keeper.

Fish and molluscs in Tungaru culture

It is only because the sea, the lagoon, and the eastern reef are all major sources of food that the Gilbert Islands ever became habitable at all.

The Tungaru people were, unsurprisingly, experts in the exploitation of marine resources. Perhaps the proof of this is contained in a study of the outlier Polynesian people of Kapingamarangi, in the Caroline Islands, of whom it has been said: *'they speak the purest Polynesian, except when fishing, when they speak Gilbertese'.*

So far as daily diet is concerned, the gathering of clams, sea crabs and worms were as important as fishing, often more so during the *Nei Auti* season when

---

[49] As late as the 1970s old people would regard the consumption of an egg with the same revulsion that a European might express if they saw someone eat a slug!

fishing was often seriously hindered by adverse winds. This was all the more so in pre-contact times, when canoes were a relatively rare resource.

There were many traditional ways in which fish were captured: more than 50 different methods have been recorded (see below). Unlike in Polynesia, there was no class of 'master fishermen'. Each family had its own methods, which were regarded as secret to that family. Most I Kiribati traditionally recognised and ate between 80 and 100 species of fish; and even today, the FAO estimates that Kiribati has the highest *per capita* consumption of fish of any nation in the world.

Taboos applied to certain fishes, and also to turtles, to the members of the particular clans who traced their descent from the divine forms of these creatures, rather than to the general population (Grimble makes much of these, as will have been evident in Chapter 4). However the I Kiribati do not eat some species that are considered as food in other parts of the Pacific (and I have no explanation as to why) - for example, *holothuria* (sea cucumbers, not an ancestral totem), although widespread in the Gilbert Islands, were not part of the traditional diet (despite being considered a delicacy in Samoa).

Each island had its own rules about fishing; when to fish, how to fish and where to fish, and what should be done before, during and after each fishing expedition.

Very local knowledge of fish was also of vital importance. There are a number of different ways in which reef fish especially may be poisonous. Some fish are naturally poisonous; puffers for instance are always toxic. Some species of fish can be poisonous at certain seasons. A third type of poisoning is found where some fish are poisonous to eat when they are caught on certain reefs or parts of a reef, and yet when caught on other parts of the same reef, or on nearby reefs, are perfectly safe to eat. Fourthly, toxicity goes in cycles, and seems to be catalysed when metal is deposited on the reef, as happened to the local Betio fisheries after the Battle of Tarawa in WWII.

The most common type of poisoning is known as *ciguatera*, which is caused by a toxin made by some types of dinoflagellates (a form of marine plankton) such as *Gambierdiscus toxicus*. These dinoflagellates adhere to coral, algae and seaweed, where they are eaten by herbivorous fish, which in turn are eaten by larger carnivorous fish like barracudas, and omnivorous fish like basses and mullet.

Poison thus gets concentrated as it goes up the food chain. Moray eels (*Muraenidae*), red snapper (*Lutjanus bohar*), and surgeonfish (notably *C. striatus* and *Acanthurus lineatus*) are the most infected, but poisonous sharks, crabs, molluscs, and turtles are also encountered. Ciguatera poisoning (which is often fatal) is regarded as an occupational hazard, especially by those who have lived all their lives in a toxic area.

Some fishing techniques

There were myriad ways in which fish were caught, each having its own set of tools, techniques (and magic). They ranged from catching fish or octopus with the bare hands, encircling fish, spearing, catching with a noose and stick, baskets and frame nets, drag nets, traps made from Pemphis wood and sennit, eel traps, hook fishing in both lagoon and open sea, bottom fishing, trolling using mother-of-pearl hooks, shark fishing with large wooden hooks, and rattles and clubs (described in detail by Koch in *The Material Culture of Kiribati*, and by Roniti Teiwaki in *Management of Marine Resources in Kiribati* - see Further Reading at the end of the Chapter). I focus here on just a few examples.

The hunting of some species such as moray eels was the preserve of certain families, who specialised in making the traps (*te u*) in which they were caught. These eels were an important 'famine' food. Hunting of the octopus, by contrast, was widespread [50].

Fish traps were a primary means of catching large numbers of especially bone fish *(te ikari)*. These Albula species are found in tropical areas around the world but were more important as food, at least in those Gilbert Islands with appropriate lagoon habitats, than in any other culture; in the 1930s Sabatier estimated *te ikari* accounted for half the fish consumed on a typical lagoon island. Their abundance was due to an exceptionally high reproduction rate.

---

[50] Although I have not yet met an I Kiribati person who recognises the technique for catching octopus as described in Grimble's *Pattern of Islands*, with himself in a leading role.

Chapter 7: Material Culture, Technology and the Traditional Economy

The I Tungaru fished for at least two species of *te ikari*: *Albula vulpes* and *Albula glossodonta* (in the latter of which the infamous bones, from which the species gets its English name, are less prominent) [51].

Bonefish returning to the lagoon after spawning at sea were captured in rockfish traps (*te ma*) built specifically for that purpose, at strategic spots on the outer-reef flats. These were made from piles of coral limestone about 1 m. high, with a corridor typically some 40 to 50m long, of ever decreasing width, running out eventually with a dead end.

In 1957 Catala reported:

> *'It is indeed exactly at the moment of the full moon that they approach the shore and that a great number of them get caught inside the traps without being incited to escape by the ebbing tide. Unlike mullet caught in this way, they do not jump over the walls; or when they try to do so it is too late. The fishermen are around the trap spearing them. The women carry them to the shore where the sharing is done in the shade of the coconut trees between the owner (of the trap) and the close relations and friends, a portion being left for the people who helped catch or carry the fish. . . . .The haul will vary in importance each month. We were fortunate enough to attend one of these distributions at the full moon of August. While not a record, the catch was nevertheless one of the best for the year, totalling over two thousand fish for one trap only. Only four hundred had been caught the preceding month, which was considered a very low figure. The weights we recorded gave a total of 45 pounds for twenty fish, taken at random. The largest weighed 4.5 lbs.'*

As well as fish traps, milkfish (*te baneawa*, Chanos chanos) were maintained in specially constructed inland ponds. Milkfish was favoured due to its fat content as well as its taste.

Traps were not used in the southern Gilberts, where many islands have no lagoon in any case. The constant surf around reef islands such as Nikunau, Tamana and Arorae required fishermen to have particular expertise in facing

---

[51] Although the Kiribati fisheries chart in my possession, which was produced by the Ministry of Natural Resource Development in the 1980s, identifies *te ikari* as a third species, Albula Neoguiniaica. It seems that the taxonomy of the Albula genus continues to evolve as scientists decide that there are more species around the world than was once thought.

waves, often of six to ten feet, as they cross the reef when leaving or returning to the island.

Shoals of bonito were tracked by following black noddy birds; both feed on surface-swimming squid. Several canoes would put out to sea, each armed with a rod made from Guettarda wood about 2m long, to which was attached a line made from sennit and human hair. A bonito lure (*te kaneati*) was fastened to this; no bait was necessary. As the bonito went into a feeding frenzy [52], the rod was placed over the stern and the glittering lure dragged behind the canoe. As soon as a fish took the lure, it was hoisted aboard, and the lure thrown out again. On a good day, as many as 50 bonito might be taken by a single canoe.

The lures were made from mother-of-pearl (*te baeao*, Pinctada marginifera), except on Banaba where stalactites were used. The hooks were made from coconut shell, human bone, or sometimes the spine of a porcupine fish (*te tauti*, comprising a range of species in the family Diodontidae) [53].

Other techniques are described in Further Reading.

Agroforestry in Tungaru culture

Although, or perhaps because, many of the useful food crops in Tungaru were introduced by human settlers, *'forestry, agriculture, housing, medicine and the production of a wide range of materials goods were not compartmentalised into 'sectors'; rather they were generally part of integrated agroforestry systems or strategies tailored to the environmental and societal needs of each island ecosystem'*.

The pandanus and its uses

It is a matter for debate whether the pandanus (*te kaina*) or the coconut (*te ni*) was most fundamental to I Tungaru society.

---

[52] I remember the sight of maybe half a square mile of sea erupting with fish as both entrancing and exciting, although sadly it seems less common now than it was 40 years ago

[53] My father-in-law was a skilled maker of lures, as well as of eel traps, and we are lucky to have a collection of both of those that he gave to us.

Chapter 7: Material Culture, Technology and the Traditional Economy

The I Tungaru recognised many cultivars of *Pandanus tectorious* (Sabatier lists 259 of them). Pandanus grows on very poor and thin soil – even more so than the coconut. As the various cultivars were grown for specific purposes, they were usually propagated by cuttings rather than seed, and were often mulched with the leaves of *te uri* tree (Guettarda speciosa), itself probably more widespread in the past than it is now.

The fleshy part of the ripe fruits was a very important part of the diet especially in the south, where breadfruit were often absent: the fruits might be consumed raw, or prepared and included in other dishes such as *te tangauri, te tuae,* and *te karababa*. Equally important was the role of preserved pandanus fruit as a voyaging and also famine food, when drought struck and coconuts ceased to provide (see below); and the pandanus drupes also provided medicines, toothbrushes, perfumes and many other useful objects.

Pandanus leaves were laboriously processed and used for a wide range of plaited ware, from thatch to finely woven mats, hats, sails, kites, and baskets for growing *babai* (and in the 20th century, as cigarette wrappings).

Pandanus wood was the principal building material, and many cultivars were selected for this purpose. They provided the poles for house and mwaneaba construction (*te boua*), and the aerial roots might be split to make walls (*te kaibara*); and the thatch of pandanus leaves covered the roof.

The coconut and its uses

The Tungaru people recognised some sixteen different cultivars of coconut, divided firstly into those where the mesosperm (the husk of the nut) is edible (*te bunia*), or non-edible (*te ni*), the latter term also being used for coconuts in general.

Some of these cultivars were favoured for their juicy flesh, others the quality and sweetness of the toddy, some for the quality of their fronds, coir, or wood; and still others for their drought resistance, tolerance of salinity, susceptibility to occasional tidal surges, or ability to withstand the very occasional fires.

In the I Tungaru diet, coconuts were the major source of dietary fats, as well as contributing some iron, fibre, and other nutrients - and above all else, vitamin C: virtually the only source of this vitamin in the traditional diet. Coconut toddy (*te karewe*) techniques were indeed a necessary condition for permanent healthy settlement of the Gilbert islands - although perhaps surprisingly, they never spread to many other places in Oceania (only a few parts of the Caroline Islands, and most likely brought to those by I Tungaru migrants).

Toddy is the sap extracted from the coconut-blossom before the hard spathe which contains it has burst. The tip of the spathe is cut off, exposing an inch or two of compressed unopened blossom; the spathe is then bound around with string, in the manner of a cricket-bat handle, upward from the base to the cut-off end. A section of the exposed blossom is shaved off, and the toddy oozes from the cut surface; the spathe is pulled down, so that it protrudes horizontally from the tree, and lashed in that position; a coconut-shell suspended below the tip catches the sweet liquid, which is guided into its mouth by a funnel of leaf. A leaf-shield prevents the intrusion of insects.

Numerous schools of toddy-cutting exist, nearly every family group having its own technique. The methods of binding the spathe are particularly varied, and the flow of sap depends very much upon the skill with which this operation is performed (and of course use of the correct magic).

The collecting-shell is changed twice (sometimes three times) a day, and on each occasion a fine wafer of the exposed bloom is sliced away, to stimulate a fresh discharge of sap. As cutting progresses, the binding of the spathe is gradually unwound, so that further lengths of the contained blossom may be exposed as necessity arises.

Toddy cutting is usually performed just after sunrise and just before sunset, but some toddy-experts favour an intermediate operation at midday. A skilled cutter can obtain more than two pints of sap from a single spathe in twenty-four hours.

In the I Kiribati language there are at least seventeen recognised stages in the development of a coconut fruit [54].

---

[54] As always, there are many names for those things which are important – like the cliché of Inuit names for types of snow (although the Sami people of northern Europe have, apparently, twice as many names for types of snow and ice as the Inuit, more than 180 of them).

Chapter 7: Material Culture, Technology and the Traditional Economy

The generic name of the nut is *te uaa-n-ni*, but each stage of growth was distinguished by a particular term:

1. *Te nimoimoi* is the name of the nut from the time of its first appearance until the water begins to develop
2. *Te onobua* contains water, but as yet no flesh, save a little gelatinous deposit (*marai*) at the distal end
3. *Te matari* has a gelatinous deposit covering the whole interior of the shell. This is held to be the best food for infants, and is given with good results even to babies in arms
4. *Te moimoto* is the drinking-nut, wherein the marai has begun to form itself into a soft, milky-white flesh. The husk is still green and sappy
5. *Te bukimaere* (the end-striped). The flesh is now thoroughly firm, and fit to be the food of adolescents. The distal end of the husk begins to crinkle and turn a reddish-brown
6. *E tangi ni kimoa*. If shaken close to the ear, the nut gurgles a little, as the water is beginning to absorb. The water is considered to be at its best at this stage; the flesh is still food for adolescents
7. *Te aamakai* is the nut of which the husk is nearly all turned a greenish and reddish-brown
8. *Te ben* is the ripe nut, of which the flesh has reached its maximum thickness. The flesh is adult's food; the husk is brown; but the fruit has not yet fallen from the tree
9. *Te moi* is the freshly-fallen nut. At this stage, the water begins to dry up quickly, and the sweet spongy substance called *te bebe* takes its place.
10. *Te ranimauna*. The nut is dry inside.
11. *Te maeke*. The flesh begins to become oily. During this and the next three stages it is considered at its best for food purposes when eaten raw
12. *Te bobo*. The flesh begins to turn a yellowish-brown
13. *E tawaa* (ripe) or *e uraura* (red). The flesh is brown throughout
14. *E tenatena* (it clings or sticks). The flesh is leathery, and no longer breaks off crisply when bitten; it is now held in particular esteem by the aged on account of its sweet oily flavour
15. *E nananga nako* . The flesh is easily separated from the shell, but begins to taste rancid.
16. *Te boka* or *te bokakua*. The flesh becomes pitted

Chapter 7: Material Culture, Technology and the Traditional Economy

17. *Te momoka*. The flesh becomes spongy as the pitting increases, and eventually turns a dirty greyish-black.

At the *moi* stage above, the nut begins to sprout. If opened at this stage, it is seen to be pushing out a tender white shoot; this is called *te buro*. If it is planted the tree goes through more stages before becoming a full-grown tree. When the first bloom (*ari*) appears, the *ni* is said to be *ribaiai* (coming into first flower); when it begins to bear nuts, it is called *kati-ririeta*.

Coconut shells were used as containers, especially for toddy; mugs; and for cooking, both as fast-burning wood and (when filled with water or oil) for simmering items such as fish livers and roes, on charcoal.

The leaves (*te ba*) of the coconut also had many uses: the fronds were woven into everything from rough mats (*te kabanin*) to finely woven hats (*te kakoko*); used as torches; provided thatch for canoe and copra sheds (*te bareaka*); and were the material for everyday kinds of skirt (*te riri*). The dried midribs of the fronds were used as both floors for houses (*te bwia*) and walls, as well as in the construction of thatches (*te rau*).

The other critical use of the coconut was for production of sennit, the string or rope which was the substitute on Tungaru for nails, screws and other fastenings. This again needed extensive processing:

> '*A youth from the family climbs a coconut palm, the nuts of which have elongated husks* (te benu) [...] *One of the men of the family removes the husks from the nuts* [...] *These are placed in a basket which at low tide is taken to the lagoon where it is buried by the women in shallow water not far from the shore and weighted down with stones and old coconut fronds. After two or three months the women retrieve the husks, which have now rotted in the sea water* [...] *The woman who is intending to undertake the production of string next places bundles of fibres on something hard and beats them with a mallet* [...] *From the flattened bundles the woman shakes off the crumbly substance from between the fibres and then spreads them in the sun to dry* [...] *When she is ready she takes a few fibres from a bundle and using the thumb and index finger of both hands she rolls these into small strands* (binoka). *Once she has a good supply of them she begins to roll them into a cord. She does this by rolling together two*

overlapping binoka *on her right thigh using the palm of her right hand, each time joining a further* binoka *to the projecting one.'* [55]

Coconut wood was difficult to cut and shape with the tools available to pre-contact society; and was, for example, too heavy for construction. It was however hardened and used for the shafts of weapons.

Te bwabai (Cyrtosperma chamissionis)

The genus Cyrtosperma is most prominent in New Guinea; it is the only one in the Araceae family (colloquially known as 'arums', and the edible roots as 'aroids') which grows east of Wallace's line. It was thus a part of the Austronesian package which must have been picked up in New Guinea, after the Taiwanese migrants had left Asia for Oceania.

In Tungaru the main species was the Cyrtosperma chamissionis (*te bwabai*), which was cultivated in pits dug down to the water lens. The aroids needed sophisticated systems for mulching and fertilisation. These pits can cover surprisingly large areas and are a conspicuous part of the landscape, especially where the islands are comparatively wide. They were evidently more important in the past than at present (indeed, today, many pits have been abandoned).

Excavation of *bwabai* pits must have been a formidable task for the early settlers: they had to dig through at least 1.5m of hard conglomerate and limestone to reach the freshwater lens; some pits were as much as 3m deep.

The shoot might be planted into baskets of pandanus or coconut leaves, into a fertilized medium; alternatively mulch might be administered to the plants when planted directly into the pit. Young shoots were planted in holes about 0.3m deep in the bottom of the pit and mulched and fertilized with black topsoil (*te bon, te iarauri,* or *te ianuri*). Leaves were mixed with black topsoil and plant waste, particularly old pandanus leaves and coconut refuse, and occasionally ground pumice (*te uuan*). The mixture was then applied, either green or dried, to the basket or placed in the pit near the plant.

---

[55] In the 1970s we experimented with an 'intermediate technology' string-making machine to mechanise this process. However, the I Kiribati claimed that the string was too weak to use because it had not absorbed, and been strengthened by, the requisite sweat from the thigh; so the experiment was deemed a failure!

The leaves used for fertilization and mulching were: *te kaura* (Sida fallax), *te uri* (Guettarda speciosa), *te ren* (Tournefortia araentea), *te mai* (Artocarpus spp.), *te wao* (Boerhavia repens); and to a lesser extent, species such as *te kaura ni Banaba* (Wollastonia biflora), *kanawa* (Cordia subcordata), and *kiaou* (Triumfetta procumbens). The introduced Hibiscus tiliaceus was added to the mix in the 20th century.

Te bwabai were daily food in the Northern Gilberts; and important to produce for feasts and other ceremonial occasions on all islands. My wife remembers three varieties from her childhood:

- *Te ikaraoi*, which had the highest prestige and would not be harvested until it had grown to a large size [56]. It, particularly, was reserved for special occasions
- *Te katutu*, a much smaller variety which was used as an everyday food
- *Te imaiaki*, which was intermediate between the other two (and rare – she thinks it may have only been grown on Marakei).

Te mai (Breadfruit)

The next most commonly cultivated tree in Tungaru was *te mai*, the breadfruit. The typical eastern Melanesian - Polynesian seedless breadfruit, *Artocarpus altilis*, is thought to be a domesticated form of the wild species *Artocarpus camansi*. This is endemic to New Guinea; like *te bwabai*, it was thus picked up by the Austronesians *en route* to Oceania. This form of breadfruit was carried northward by early settlers into eastern Micronesia.

At some point it hybridized with the far western Marianas' endemic species *dugdug*, the seeded *Artocarpus mariannensis*. This hybrid produced many varieties that particularly thrived on the Micronesian atolls.

In the Caroline islands, it has been argued that the increased availability of easily grown food arising from the hybrid led to a *'breadfruit revolution'*; and that this led both to the successful establishment of an island-wide Pohnpeian chiefdom by the Saudeleur, and also to population increases on the neighbouring atolls, and also across the Marshall islands. Tungaru was at

---

[56] Which meant that they were extremely woody and completely tasteless, and required strong jaws to eat. Young ikaraoi are delicious but it was and still is regarded as wasteful to consume them (a bit like vegetable marrows in village England!)

most on the fringes of this revolution, although they did acquire the hybrids from the Marshalls [57]:

Breadfruit only became a staple part of the diet in Butaritari and Makin. It was present in the other northern islands and the central Gilberts; but was cultivable in decreasing frequency further south: they were the first trees to die in droughts. Breadfruit was prepared in a number of ways, and also preserved by being dried. The technique of long-term preservation of breadfruit fermented in pits (which was a famine food in the Carolines after hurricane damage to their trees) does not, however, appear to have been part of the Tungaru material culture. The trees are nowadays dominant around villages. Breadfruit wood was valued to make outriggers and fishing floats, and it also had medicinal uses.

Other forest crops

The only other tree cultivated as a food crop in Tungaru was *te bero*, a type of fig.

Important indigenous trees or tree-like species, which are integral and widespread components of the Kiribati agroforestry system, include *Scaevola sericea, Guettarda speciosa, Tournefortia arpentea, Sida fallax, Morinda citrifolia, Clerodendrum inerme, Premna serratifolia, Pemphis acidula,* and *Dodonea viscosa*. Also of importance were the mangrove species *Rhizophora mucronata, Bruguiera gymnorhiza,* and *Lumnitzera littorea*.

All of these species have traditional uses as wood, for mulching crops, as medicines, and others. Some of the Austronesian-introduced crops became gradually neglected, and some vegetable foods were only eaten in times of famine (see below).

Storage of food: fugitive, voyaging and famine foods

Products such as desiccated pandanus fruit (*te kabubu*) were carefully hoarded in times of plenty, so as to provide food in periods of drought. They were also kept in stock as the 'food of fugitives' (e.g. those conquered in battle, who might have to flee rapidly if they were not to be killed or enslaved – see

---

[57] There is a tale of the seeds being smuggled from Mili 'inside the women's vaginas' after the Marshallese refused to allow them to be exported

Chapter 7: Material Culture, Technology and the Traditional Economy

Chapter 6). *Te kabubu* was also the 'food of voyagers', the principal sustenance of those undertaking long sea voyages.

It was a sweet powder, of the consistency of sawdust, to be mixed with water. Extraordinary care had to be taken to expel moisture in the manufacture of this food, as the durability of the finished article depends wholly upon the degree of desiccation achieved. When packed for storage in tubular containers of pandanus leaf (called *iria*) it would, if securely tamped down, keep for at least two years.

Another emergency diet was the over-ripe fruit of the *non* (Morinda citrifolia). This was used as a stimulant by fishermen; it was said to be hot and comforting to a tired body. A cultivar of *non, te non-nabanaba* was particularly prized because of the large size of its fruit.

The Tungaru people also dried and salted fish, both for everyday consumption but also to keep for times of famine [58]. On Abemama, for example, people would wait for the seasonal transverse between ocean and lagoon of large shoals of the Sharpjaw Bonefish (*te ikari*, Albula Neoguiniaica) which were caught and salted in very large quantities. Dried eel was also a reserve food, especially prized for its high fat content.

There were also some varieties of shallow-water invertebrates and algae which were not eaten by choice, but reserved for consumption during times of hardship when fish were unavailable in sufficient quantities and as a form of "social security" for old people and other disadvantaged who could not fish.

Kamaimai, the treacly product obtained by boiling and reboiling of toddy (*kareve*) which in consistency varies from a state of liquidity comparable to that of olive-oil to the solidity of caramel (depending on how many times it was repeatedly boiled) might keep for several months [59].

---

[58] I was given a piece of salt fish on Onotoa in 1972 that my host proudly said he had laid down in the early 1950s!

[59] Although my wife remarks that in her childhood it was in practice seldom kept for very long; and of course the supply of toddy was not reliable in times of drought either, which limited use of *kamaimai* as a famine food. In the droughts of the early 1970s, for example, a survey on Abemama showed that nearly 60% of coconut trees had ceased to bear.

Chapter 7: Material Culture, Technology and the Traditional Economy

Some vegetable foods were eaten in times of drought, when not only the ordinary agroforestry plants, but all kinds of fish, became scarce: *te mtea* (purslane or turtle grass, Portulaca australis), *te wao* (several Boerhavia species), and *te boi* (purslane, of several other Portulaca and Sesuvium species). In normal times these would be scorned.

However none of these storage methods were necessarily enough.

Banaba was especially prone to drought, as it is a high island with no water lens. The problems with water were described by the Resident Commissioner E.C. Eliot:

> *'In two successive years during my residence the rainfall was under ten inches. Cloud would approach the island only to be broken up by the blast of heat sent up from the coral and the phosphate. No rain would fall directly on the island unless there was a really heavy storm, or if it came in the early morning after the hours of night had somewhat cooled the island ...*

> *'The phosphate deposit was very porous. The rain that fell percolated through to ... subterranean caves and collected in rocky basins a hundred feet or more below the surface. The caves were very hot ...[which] made it more comfortable for the women whose job it was to collect water to slip off their clothes outside the caves and enter naked...[there was] an old Banaban law that death should be the penalty for any man found in the caves or hiding near the entrances'.*

An account in the Missionary Herald in 1887 similarly describes women making a *'twenty minute crawl into a subterranean passage by the light of a torch and there the water is muddy and limited'*. Water was in that year rationed to one coconut shell-full per household per day. An earlier three-year drought, starting in 1873, had been even worse: over three quarters of the population died and so did almost all of the trees; many of those who survived left the island on passing ships – many taken to Hawaii, some to Kosrae - to escape the drought; and only some of these were able to return, often years later.

Conditions in the rest of Tungaru were not as extreme as this, but the southern islands were prone to drought also and there were memories of older people voluntarily starving themselves to death on Tamana and Arorae at these times, in order that the limited food might be shared amongst the others.

Only Butaritari and Makin escaped drought entirely.

Chapter 7: Material Culture, Technology and the Traditional Economy

Technology, tools, and techniques

Given the resources available to them, and the absence of trading opportunities to extend the range of those resources, the sophistication of I Tungaru technology and techniques is remarkable.

Modification of Austronesian tools for atoll resources

Tools and technologies required modification by the early settlers.

Pottery-making was not possible owing to lack of suitable clays, and was replaced by using coconut shells as containers, by basket making, and by the ingenious earth oven designs described later in this Chapter.

Stone and obsidian tools were also unavailable. They were replaced, somewhere along the way to Tungaru, by axes and adzes whose blades were made from saltwater clams of the *Tridacna* genus; they were sharpened with pumice stones that had floated to the shore. Sting ray skin was used for files, and (see previous Chapters) sharks' teeth as cutting implements. The Tungaru people also shaped wood while it was still growing on the tree, for example to make large fishhooks.

It seems likely that the first settlers had arrived in dug-out ocean-going *proas*, but this technology also needed modification, because of the absence of suitable timber. Tungaru canoes were based, not on dug-outs, but on the joining together of planks of wood with glue, which were then tied together using coconut fibre. To become a boat owner thus first required the acquisition of a supply of timber [60]. Given that trees in the Gilbert Islands generally grow both knotty and crooked, only a single plank could usually be made from a single trunk. Pandanus, coconut and mangrove provided suitable raw materials for boats, and breadfruit wood material for outriggers.

There were three types of canoe. The design of the largest, *te baurua*, which could be up to 30 metres in length, is considered to have been '*the most sophisticated of all the Austronesian sailing vessels*'. These canoes had the same

---

[60] Occasionally large trees are washed up by storms, having floated at least 2000 km from a 'high' island to the west, and sometimes even drifting eastwards from the west coast of America. I remember seeing about a dozen such trees on the very northern tip of Tabiteuea in 1973, but I was assured that such bonanzas were rare events.

Chapter 7: Material Culture, Technology and the Traditional Economy

or greater carrying capacity as Captain Cook's ships. In the times of oral history, they were mainly used for warriors to invade other islands.

The other two designs were for fishing canoes, and for racing canoes [61].

The triangular sail was originally woven from strips of oiled pandanus leaves (although they were laborious to make, these had the advantage that they dried very quickly compared to the modern day sails made of canvas). The boat is always sailed with the outrigger wind-wards. It is steered with a paddle fashioned from a single piece of wood. The paddle is tied to a special rest on the stern of the boat. Paddles used for propulsion were built up from two pieces of wood. Equipment was completed by a bailer and a pierced big chunk of coral to serve as an anchor.

In spite of those limitations the I Tungaru people developed the fastest sail-powered boats of the world, at least before 20th century engineering technology and materials [62]. Given the right wind and sea conditions, these boats can easily reach a speed of 20 knots.

An example of technical sophistication: the earth oven

Chapter 3 noted the sophistication of building techniques, especially those involved in *mwaneaba* construction; and Chapter 6 those of weapon design. I have chosen to focus below on an every-day but remarkably sophisticated piece of technology, the earth oven.

The word *umuna* means 'cook in a covered hearth'. The process of cooking by this method is called *te umum*, the hearth itself being referred to as *te ai-n-umum* (the fire-to-cook).

A shallow depression about 10 inches deep and 20-24 inches in diameter was first scooped in the sand. This was lined in the way shown in the diagram on the next page (drawn by Arthur Grimble, on whose writings this section is based).

---

[61] The latter of which I suspect arose after imported wooden planks became available, when canoes became much easier to construct, and thus became a lesser investment of resources

[62] Again, we are indebted to Arthur Grimble for a detailed description of construction methods – see Further Reading.

Chapter 7: Material Culture, Technology and the Traditional Economy

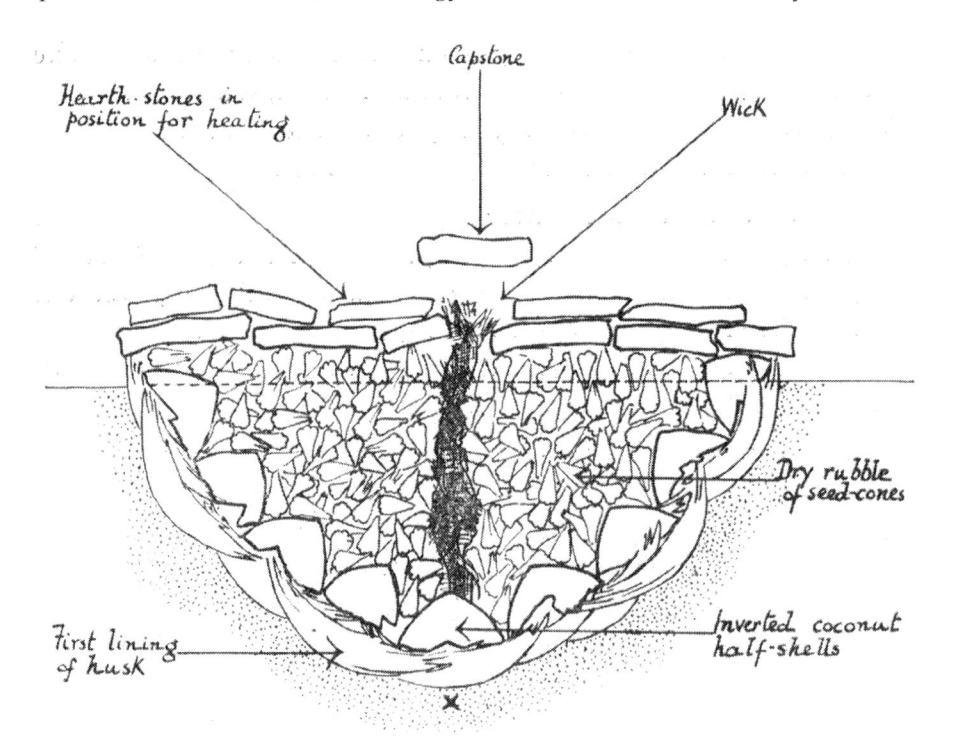

Diagram A. Gilbertese cooking-hearth (Section 2)
The cross marks the position in which the cockle or sea-snail shells are laid in the Katura or Nabanaba ovens.

Grimble writes that there was:

> 'a layer (sometimes a double layer) of segments of coconut-husk, quite dry and each about four inches broad in the middle. Upon the husk is laid a stratum of coconut half-shells, mouths downward, as pictured. As a top-dressing over the coconut-shells is thrown in a filling of small dry rubbish, generally composed of the chewed and discarded seed-cones of the pandanus-fruit. In the centre of the filling is scooped a hole, right down to the level of the coconut-shells, and this is filled in with a wick of te ing, the fibrous material which grows at the base of the coconut-leaf. The whole is then covered with a double layer of stones, preferably flat or flattish, each about as big as a man's hand.

> 'The wick of te ing having been lit, it is covered with a capstone, and the flame descends into the fuel. The fire is allowed to burn itself clear, the stones settling down as the fuel is consumed. When the stones are red-hot, and neither flame nor smoke issue from the interstices between them,

Chapter 7: Material Culture, Technology and the Traditional Economy

they are spread out in a single layer so that they form a pavement in the depression. The hearth is now ready for cooking.

'Before the food is laid upon the hot stones, a little fence of stones or green husk is raised around the lip of the hearth. This serves to keep clear of stray sparks the mat with which the oven is to be covered.

'The food having been put into the oven, an old mat is laid over it, totally concealing the hearth. For most foods, except fish, babai, and pandanus-fruit, steam is used in the process of cooking; one edge of the mat is lifted, and about half a pint of water is poured on the outer edge of the hot stones; the mat is quickly pressed down again and the process repeated on all four sides. The act of pouring in water is technically called teboka-na. *When this is complete, the edges of the mat are buried in sand and the oven left to do its work.*

'According to the nature of the food, it may be set direct upon the hot stones, or kept clear of them by "keels" of green coconut-husk or midrib laid across the pavement of the hearth. For steam-cooking, each kind of food has its particular form of jacket. The pudding called buatoro *has a* nira *(winding) of babai-leaf, while that known as* tangana *has a* baabaa *(plaited basket) of coconut-leaf. A fish, cooked dry, is enclosed in a spiral winding of coconut-pinnules, knotted at head and tail, called a* bara *(hat).*

'The dimensions of an oven depend entirely upon the amount of food to be cooked. That which I have described and pictured is of the size appropriate to the daily need of a single household of three or four people, and is of the type known as te bora teuana *(the single layer). This name refers to the single strata of husk and coconut-shells respectively with which the bottom is lined; a larger oven generally contains two layers of each sort of fuel, laid alternately, and is called* te bora uoua *(the double layer). Four strata of husk and four of coconut-shell are the most I have seen. In no case is there more than a single filling of small rubble.*

'A particularly deep and narrow form of steam-cooking oven is called te ai-ni-Kiroro *(the fire of Kiroro) or simply te Kiroro. The mechanical arrangement of fuel in this type of hearth is different in no detail from that already described, but the depth of the pit prepared for the fire is so great in relation to its diameter that the sides are precipitous, and the hearth-stones eventually lie at the bottom of an almost straight shaft. This is one of the commonest forms of oven, being used when great quantities*

Chapter 7: Material Culture, Technology and the Traditional Economy

of food are to be cooked. It is stated to be "the fire of olden time," which is to say, a type long known to the Gilbertese ancestors who immigrated [sic] *from Samoa some 22-25 generations ago.*

'An oven called te katura, *which I have seen only in the Northern Gilberts, is also used for steam-cooking. Its form is identical with that pictured, the highly technical difference being that a* katura *(smooth cockle) shell is set in the centre of the hearth before the first lining of husk is laid. But the method of producing steam distinguishes this oven very clearly from other types. The water used for the purpose is not introduced in four places, nor is it poured direct upon the hot stones; it is carefully directed through a single hole in the centre of the covering mat, with the object of saturating the food under treatment before it drips upon the hearth-stones and is turned into steam. A fundamentally different mechanical conception of cooking is thus involved.*

'The katura *oven, together with the shell-fish of the same name, is said on Tarawa to have been introduced by an ancestress called Nei Katura, who came from a very distant western land named Onouna. Local tradition is rich in allusions to Onouna, and evidence from all sources seems to indicate that a stream of immigrants came thence into the Gilbert Group about 25 generations ago.*

'An oven called te ai-n-Nabanaba—*the oven of* Nabanaba —*is precisely the same in construction and principle as the* katura *oven; but whereas a smooth cockle-shell is set in the centre of the katura hearth, a* nimataanin (Nerita plicata) *shell is laid in that bearing the name of* Nabanaba. *This is the only difference between the two. The land of* Nabanaba *is famous in Gilbertese tradition as the western home of an ancestress named* Nei Tekanuea, *who married into a family of Tarawa Island about 27 generations ago, and became the grandmother of an illustrious local high chief named* Kirataa....

'Te ruanuna *is the name of an oven used for dry*— i.e., *steamless*— *cooking. Its mechanism is similar to that of the ordinary steam-hearth pictured, but the covering mat is entirely buried in sand as soon as it is put into position. The natives state that the object of burying the mat is to prevent the free ingress of air and thus to control the heat of the oven, which might otherwise scorch the food in the absence of steam'.*

Chapter 7: Material Culture, Technology and the Traditional Economy

The economics of traditional society

The I Tungaru economy differed in a number of quite fundamental respects from those found in the original homeland in Taiwan, in Southeast Asia, in Melanesia, and even in other parts of Micronesia.

I Tungaru society is one of the very few in the world that never felt the need to invent even the *idea* of money. It:

- Was not populated by profit-seeking *economic man*; indeed it was innocent of any concept of 'market', 'unit of account', or even 'price'
- Had no commerce
- Had very little economic division of labour, other than within the *kaainga* and *utu* which were self-sufficient to a high degree
- Did not produce durable economic surpluses (including erection of large monuments)
- Did not take risks with technology or agricultural practice
- Did not value individual entrepreneurship, or those who economically 'got out of line'.

Even in the 21st century, none of these concepts have really taken root in modern I Kiribati society. I shall argue in Part 3 that this is why many well-meaning initiatives by outside economists and businessmen since the early 1970s have failed to deliver the benefits expected from them. They were (and still are) all predicated on behaviours absent from local society.

If any Western economic concept is useful, it is that of *satisficing* (see below).

I Tungaru society did however provide 'safety net' systems for:

- Personal insurance
- Welfare
- Redistribution.

The absence of the concepts of 'money' or 'market'

'Money' was classically defined in the 1920s, by J. M. Keynes, as having three aspects, as a:

- Medium of exchange
- Measure and store of value
- Unit of account.

Chapter 7: Material Culture, Technology and the Traditional Economy

Many commodities have been used across the world as a *medium of exchange* supporting markets and trade in a more efficient manner than barter: cows, bags of corn, metals, and *cash* (Chinese paper money).

Money was widely used, pre-contact, in other parts of Oceania. Shells were - and still are - used as a means of exchange, and commerce has existed in PNG for centuries between inland and coastal communities. It was facilitated by shell money; as late as 1882, local trade in the Solomon Islands as well was carried on by means of a coinage of shell beads, made from small shells which were laboriously ground down to the required size by the women. The shells were worked into strips of decorated cloth whose value reflected the time spent creating them [63].

On the island of East New Britain, shell currency is in fact still legal tender and it can be exchanged for the modern currency Kina. Glass and ceramic bead money (*oudud*) also played a significant role in an exchange economy in Palau. Closer to Tungaru, there appears to have been a system of exchange based on sea shells on Kosrae, although little is known about how it operated.

The Yapese have for centuries used stone money *(rai)* for the second of Keynes' categories, as a *store of value*. The sparkling rock is a form of crystalline calcite that is found primarily in the walls of limestone caverns on Palau, some five days' sailing from Yap; and also on Guam. Transporting the larger pieces of stone money from coast to village was an even more arduous task, greatly increasing its value. This monetary system relied on an oral history of ownership: this simply involved agreeing that the ownership had changed. No physical movement of the stone was required. *Rai* stones were used in rare social transactions, such as marriage, inheritance, political deals, sign of an alliance, or (in history) ransom of the battle dead.

It might be argued that in Tungaru, land and other property rights were akin to a store of value; however, although these might be given away as a *reward* (not an exchange) for services, or be valued in a prospective marriage partner, they were never bartered; and they are best seen as significant in cultural rather than in material terms. There was no 'market' in land, any more than there were markets for anything else produced in Tungaru; nor were there

---

[63] This is remarkably similar to the Proof-of-Work System used in Bitcoin Mining, only that that was developed some ten to thirty thousand years later!

even cultural barter-like norms about 'units of exchange'. Nor could precious land be subject to '*bubuti*'.

As the Wilkes report put it, for possessions other than land:

> *'They never buy or sell, but if any person desires an article which another has, he asks for it, and if not too valuable and esteemed, is seldom refused: it is the general understanding that such favours are to be returned, and that the request should only be made by persons who can afford to do so.'*

In Part 2 of the book, I shall argue that the absence of these ideas, coupled with lack of knowledge of the rest of the world, was responsible for the apparent readiness of the Gilbert islanders to be exploited by Europeans, and their apparent passivity when they were confronted with manifestly one-sided arrangements. This was not just at Banaba (Chapter 10). For example, among the early whaler-traders in the Gilberts was Captain Ichabod Handy of Fairhaven, Massachusetts, master and principal owner of the barque *Belle*, who commenced oil trading at Abaiang in 1849. The Missionary George Pierson noted:

> *'While we were on the island we saw the Captain buying oil, it was measured in a bucket that measured three and a half gallons, for this full he paid one and a quarter pounds of poor tobacco, which cost thirteen cents a lb. making seventeen cents for three and a half gallons of oil for which he will get three dollars and a half.*

> *'The trade was clearly worthwhile when oil fetching a dollar a gallon could be obtained for about 5 cents' worth of trade goods; Handy readily admitted that he could afford to give 50 cents a gallon for the oil and still make a good net return on the deal'.*

The Gilbertese as 'satisficers'

In economics, satisficing is a behaviour which *'attempts to achieve at least some minimum level of a particular variable, but which does not necessarily maximise its value. The most common application of the concept in economics postulates that producers treat profit not as a goal to be maximized, but as a constraint'*. This contrasts with conventional economic thinking which posits that firms and individuals are motivated by *'profit maximisation, i.e. the short run or long run process which determines the price and output level that returns the greatest profit'*.

Chapter 7: Material Culture, Technology and the Traditional Economy

In terms of village life in Kiribati, dependent on a mix of non-market subsistence activity and cash income, income may be taken as a proxy for profit – as they were, and still are essentially price takers, for example for their copra.

Once his or her perceived needs – for taxes, for school fees, for tools, and perhaps for a few luxuries - have been met it is quite rational economic behaviour – however odd it may seem to a *profit maximiser* - for a *satisficer* simply not to produce any more, even if additional saleable things are abundantly available for the same level of effort.

The *satisficer* simply trades off their time, and the quantity of material goods consumed by them, at a different level. The economic jargon for this is that *'they have a divergent indifference curve'* from a typical European or Chinese person. (An indifference curve is the trade-off between various points showing different combinations of two 'goods' - in this case money and leisure - which are of equal utility to the consumer).

The contrast between these two views has caused much confusion between those concerned with 'development' in Kiribati, and those who live in traditional ways. It has fuelled accusations from many outsiders that the Gilbertese are somehow 'lazy' (see for example pages 228, 329, 389, 409 and 500).

Systems for insurance and redistribution

Although there were no systems for commerce or exchange in Tungaru, there were systems for *insurance, welfare* and *redistribution*.

Chapter 3 described how the *kaainga* functioned as a largely self-sufficient unit of production. Meal preparation often (though not always) took place at the level of the *kaainga* rather than the household, in a communal kitchen, with individual households often taking turns to prepare and cook the food.

Some food-sharing may be regarded partly as insurance and a safeguard against the failure of an individual *kaainga*'s daily foraging. Wilkes again:

> *'Another custom is remarkable: when a fisherman arrives with a well loaded canoe, his neighbours assemble around him selecting and taking away such as they please, leaving the owner nothing in return but the satisfaction of knowing that on a similar occasion he has a like privilege*

> *to help himself. Custom has so far sanctioned this habit that, according to Kirby, they have no term to designate a poor man.'*

On a wider scale, *te utu* also functioned as a potential welfare system and provided a safety net for the orphaned; to provide for old age; and, through *bubuti*, those who had suffered temporary economic dislocation, for example through natural disasters. Adoption (page 38) provided for family obligations where lines were in danger of dying out.

On chiefly islands, there were tribute systems. Lambert describes that of Butaritari:

> *' The lands at the disposal of the High Chief produced sufficient food to fill the daily needs of his residential group, making it possible for him to redistribute most of the 'tribute' that he received from his subjects …the right to receive large amounts of food from descent groups and villages was traditionally the principal symbol of his status. The people showed their recognition of his legitimate authority (or that of his heir) by bringing him these gifts and they could, in effect, deprive him of his position by withholding their tribute or by transferring it to one of his kinsmen.*

> *'The High Chief for his part assured himself of the goodwill of his subjects by being generous and fair in redistributing the food they brought…. People from outside Butaritari town were feasted in the High Chief's compound when they turned over their tribute to him, and received a generous present of* cyrtosperma *when they left for home'.*

Tribute systems thus had no real *economic* impact.

Summary: Tungaru on the eve of first contact with Europeans

The foremost impression of early visitors to Tungaru was that of a society where material wants could be satisfied, under normal conditions, by a few hours' labour a day.

Merrie Tungaru it was not, but it was a society in which:

- There were effective welfare systems, so no-one went uncared for; but this required that they accept considerable social control from their family groups

Chapter 7: Material Culture, Technology and the Traditional Economy

- The status of women was higher than in most societies, and more so than it became in the 20th century
- There was time and leisure for a wide range of crafts, songs, dances, games and competitions
- Technology had probably evolved as far as it could, given the resources locally available and the absence of trade or commerce externally
- Governance over many of the islands was collective, leading to risk aversion and decision-making by consensus; even in the chiefly islands, the powers of the *Ueas* were circumscribed by custom
- There were few serious diseases.

On the other hand:

- Individuals who 'stepped out of line' were subject to severe societal disapproval and sanction
- Slavery was practised, and strangers regarded as 'prey'
- Poisoning from fish or molluscs was an occupational hazard, and quite often fatal
- Drought caused great hardship on Banaba and the southern Gilbert Islands, as did very rare cyclones
- Warfare was endemic, and could wipe out entire families.

Richard Randell, a trader resident on Butaritari, claimed in the 1860s that the inhabitants of Tungaru numbered between 50,000 and 54,000; and even higher estimates were recorded by the United States Exploring Expedition in the early 1840s, where figures of 60,000 and 85,000 are cited. However, it is likely that these were overstated for a number of reasons, and that a more probable figure is between 31,000 and 35,000.

Even so, population densities in Tungaru were amongst, if not the most, dense in the Pacific.

Chapter 7: Material Culture, Technology and the Traditional Economy

Further Reading

1. **Kiribati Agroforestry: Trees, People and the Atoll Environment** by R. R. Thaman, Atoll research Bulletin No. 333, 1990
2. **The Archaeology of Micronesia** by Paul Rainbird, published by the Cambridge University Press, 2004
3. **Traditional Micronesian Societies** by Glenn Petersen, published by the University of Hawaii Press, 2009
4. **Narrative of the United States Exploring Expedition During the Years 1838, 1839, 1840, 1841, 1842** (Chapter II, Vol 5) by Charles Wilkes, published in Philadelphia by Lea and Blanchard, 1845
5. **Astride the Equator,** translated by Ursula Nixon from **Sous l'équateur de Pacifique** by Ernest Sabatier, Oxford University Press 1977
6. **Migrations, Myth, and Magic From The Gilbert Islands**, writings by Arthur Grimble edited by Rosemary Grimble (this includes *From Birth to Death in the Gilbert Islands)*, Routledge & Kegan Paul, 1972
7. **The Material Culture of Kiribati,** by Gerd Koch (translated by Guy Slatter), published by the Institute of Pacific Studies, University of the South Pacific, 1986
8. **Social Changes In The Southern Gilbert Islands, 1938-1964,** by Henry P Lundsgaarde, Published by Department of Anthropology, University of Oregon, Eugene, 1967
9. **Management of Marine Resources in Kiribati**, by Roniti Teiwaki, published by the Atoll Research Unit, 1988
10. **Canoes in the Gilbert Islands**, by Arthur Grimble, published in the Journal of the Royal Anthropological Institute, 1924
11. **The Migrations of a Pandanus People: As traced from a preliminary study of Food, Food-traditions, and Food Rituals in the Gilbert Islands,** by Arthur Grimble, Supplement to the Journal of the Polynesian Society, 1933
12. **Tungaru Traditions**, edited by H. C. and H.E. Maude, Institute of Pacific Studies, University of the South Pacific, 1994
13. **Broken Atoms,** by E. C. Eliot, published by Geoffrey Bles, 1938
14. **Ciguatera and Other Marine Poisoning in the Gilbert Islands** by M. J. Cooper, Contribution No. 214, Hawaii Marine Laboratory, University of Hawaii, 1963
15. http://www.maritima-et-mechanika.org/maritime/models/gilbert/gilbertcanoe.html
16. **The Book of Banaba**: From the Maude and Grimble Papers, and Published Works By Sir Arthur Francis Grimble
17. **Historical Ecology in Kiribati: Linking Past with Present** by Dr Frank R. Thomas, published in Pacific Science, 2009

Chapter 7: Material Culture, Technology and the Traditional Economy

18. **'Sustainable Archaeology' and Landscape Transformation in Eastern Micronesia** by Dr Frank R. Thomas, paper presented at the Samoa Conference III: Opportunities and challenges for a sustainable cultural and natural environment, 2014
19. **Rank and Ramage in the Northern Gilbert Islands** by B Lambert, published by University Microfilms, 1963
20. **Kiribati: Aspects of History,** multiple authors and editors, published jointly by the Institute of Pacific Studies and the Ministry of Education, Training, and Culture, 1979
21. **Population Estimates For Kiribati And Tuvalu, 1850–1900: Review And Speculation by** Richard Bedford, Barrie Macdonald and Doug Munro, published in the Journal of the Polynesian Society 1980

Chapter 8.

EARLY CONTACT WITH EUROPEANS

Sightings and first contact

The very first sighting of the Gilberts archipelago by Europeans is believed to have taken place in 1537, when Hernando de Grijalva's vessel *San Juan* sighted (probably) Nonouti, Marakei and Abaiang.

The islands were then left alone until 1606, when Pedro Fernandes de Quiros in the vessel *San Pablo* sighted either Makin or Butaritari.

The third known sighting, and first recorded contact, was by Commodore John Byron of HM ships *Dolphin* and *Tamar*. Contact took place at sea off the island of Nikunau (the visitors did not apparently land there).

The voyage by Captains Gilbert and Marshall which eventually gave them and their nearest northerly neighbour their names took place in 1788, when the British vessels *Charlotte* and *Scarborough* passed through the 'Gilberts', and then the 'Marshalls', *en route* from Australia to Canton. This again seems to have resulted in some limited contact, but not landings.

The American James Cary in the *Rose* visited Tamana and possibly other islands in 1804.

The French captain Louis Duperrey was the first to map the whole Gilbert Islands archipelago. He commanded *La Coquille* on its circumnavigation of the earth between 1822 and 1825.

Originally, the southern islands were called the Kingsmill Group, the central Gilberts Simpson's Group, and the northern islands the Scarborough Islands The islands were formally named the Gilbert Islands by Adam Johann von Krusenstern, a Baltic German admiral of the Czar [64].

---

[64] Their sighting, naming and mapping was thus altogether a very international effort. The irony - in that the I Tungaru language had no 'g' or 'l' phonemes, and that the combination of two consonants 'rt' also had no place in the structure of the language (hence the transliteration of 'Gilbert' into 'Kiribati') - was completely lost on those bestowing these names.

Chapter 8: Early Contact With Europeans

There are two lists for the 'discovery' of the individual 17 islands: one by Andrew Sharp, and the other by H E Maude.

Early voyagers also gave each island one or more 'European' names, by which they were referred to in 19th Century charts. Where I have been able to track them down, these are recorded below (this list may not record all the names by which they were at one time known).

Island	Sharp	Maude	European Name(s)
Makin	1606 (Quiros)		Buen Viaje, Little Makin (Makin meang)
Butaritari	1537 (Grijalva)	1606 (Quiros)	Makin, Pitt Island, Taritari Island, Touching Island.
Marakei	1537 (Grijalva)	1824 (Deperrey)	Matthew's Island
Abaiang	1788 (Gilbert and Marshall)	1788 (Gilbert and Marshall)	Charlotte Island
Tarawa	1788 (Gilbert and Marshall)	1788 (Gilbert and Marshall)	Knox Island
Maiana	1788 (Gilbert and Marshall)	1804 (Patterson)	Hall's Island
Kuria	1788 (Gilbert and Marshall)	1788 (Gilbert and Marshall)	Woodle Island
Aranuka	1788 (Gilbert and Marshall)	1788 (Gilbert and Marshall)	Henderville Island
Abemama	1788 (Gilbert and Marshall)	1799 (Bishop)	Simpson's Island, Harbottle Island, Hopper Island
Nonouti	1537 (Grijalva)	1799 (Bishop)	Bishop's Island, Sydenham Island. Blaney's Island
Tabiteuea	1765 (Byron)	1799 (Bishop)	Drummond's Island

Onotoa	1826 (Clerk)	1826 (Clerk)	Rotch Island, Maria Island, Eliza Island
Beru	1826 (Clerk)	1826 (Clerk)	Francis Island, Peroat, Peru Island, Sunday Island
Nikunau	1826 (Clerk)	1765 (Byron)	Byron Island
Tamana	1804 (Cary)	1804 (Cary)	Phoebe Island
Arorae	1809 (Patterson)	1809 (Patterson)	Hope Island, Hurd Island
Banaba	1801 (Gardner)	1801 (Gardner)	Ocean Island

Most of these 'European' names were quickly abandoned, except for the name Ocean Island, which was still in common usage in the 1970s (being the preferred name for Banaba of the British Phosphate Commission).

Before the whalers, contacts did not involve commerce, which (page 121) was a concept anyway unknown to the I Tungaru people. Byron tried unsuccessfully to obtain coconuts; but Gilbert in 1788 managed to exchange a mirror, a bottle and a few nails for some 'necklaces'; and in 1804 Cary bartered hoop iron for 'beads' (presumably also shell necklaces).

Whalers

In the 1700s, American colonists had begun to develop an industrial scale whale fishery (the term "*fishery*" was used despite the fact that the whale is a mammal, not a fish). Islanders from Nantucket, who had taken to whaling because their soil was too poor for farming, killed their first sperm whale in 1712. This, their favoured species of whale, was highly prized as it had the blubber and bone and also a unique substance called spermaceti, a waxy oil found in the massive head. The gigantic carcasses of this and other whale species were chopped and boiled down and turned into products, later including the fine oil needed to lubricate increasingly advanced machine tools. Their bones were additionally used to make a wide variety of consumer goods.

Although American vessels dominated offshore whaling in the 19th century, substantial numbers of British and French whaling ships were active as well. In the early 19th century the American whaling industry was in its most

Chapter 8: Early Contact With Europeans

malignant phase, spreading literally to the ends of the earth. Almost half of the 80 species of cetaceans (whales, dolphins and porpoises), were present in the Central Pacific Ocean: the valuable (to the whalers) species were rapidly hunted to the brink of extinction. Logbooks show that in the Pacific at least 30,000 sperm whales were killed: although the true number is probably much higher, because not all whalers kept accurate records, and because many whales were harpooned but escaped. Although sperm whales were the prime target for the early whalers, several thousand baleen whales, mainly humpbacks, were also taken.

This hunting has had a lasting impact. Right whales in the North Pacific and around New Zealand were mostly exterminated within a decade. Even today, two hundred years later, sperm whales are rarely reported from previously busy Pacific island whaling grounds, including round Kiribati: the whaling industry around the southern Gilbert islands and Banaba was not long lived.

At its height in the 1840s, there were more than 600 American vessels operating in the industry. In the Gilberts, Barrie Macdonald estimates that:

> *'In the 1840s and 1850s Ocean Island, Nikunau, Tamana and Arorae were visited at least weekly during the season, and the sight of three or four vessels lying 'off and on' was not unusual'.*

However, many captains were loath to approach some of the islands at all, not only owing to their being badly charted, but because the I Tungaru regarded all strangers, whether they came by canoe or by ship, as 'prey'. In the central Gilberts especially, they would cut off, plunder, and (if provoked) kill any vessel's crew that got into their hands. Nonouti had a particular reputation in this respect, and there were attacks or attempted attacks on the crews of the *Columbia* (1846), *Triton* (1848), *Flying Fox* (1850) and *Charles W. Morgan* (1851).

By the 1870s, however, the valuable whales had been more or less been exterminated, and the visits by whalers ceased.

During this time the *'world's oldest profession'* [65] became the first form of Gilbertese commerce.

---

[65] Although the origin of this phrase was later, in a story by Rudyard Kipling which was published in 1888.

Chapter 8: Early Contact With Europeans

The I Tungaru women were noted for their beauty; *Nikiranroro* (page 48 above) were shipped out to the vessels and received, in return for their services, metal pieces (barrel hoops were especially prized), rope, and tobacco.

The last-named became an addiction and the first-ever 'means of exchange':

> *'Their chief desire was to obtain tobacco, of which they were extravagantly fond; it was their constant request, and whilst in their canoes alongside, the cry was constantly 'tebake'. It was not begged as a gift; for what appeared to be singular enough for Pacific Islanders they seemed to have no idea of receiving a gratuity; but instantly made a return of something for whatever was given them. So eager were they after it, that when one had put a piece in his mouth, other would seize him, and actually force it out with their fingers.'*

Trading transactions soon began to use heads of plug tobacco; and as Commander Blake found in the Carolines, *'the only purpose to which they would apply a dollar or any other coin was to make a hole in it and fasten it round their necks'*.

In addition to the services of the *nikiranroro*, coconuts became part of the trade, as well as what the Europeans called 'molasses' (*kaimaimai*), sennit, 'broom stuff', and increasingly, handicrafts which the sailors could sell as curios on their return home [66]. By the 1850s, the Tungaru people had taken to rearing chicken and could supply as many as 200 to a ship. The whalers also introduced pigs for the first time, and tried goats, ducks and other animals, even horses, none of whom survived on the diet available to them [67].

During this early time, there were far fewer visits to the central and northern Gilberts. When Hiram Bingham arrived on Abaiang in 1857, for example, there were no chickens or pigs (although there were dogs). The people of the northern Gilberts principally coveted iron, of which they had by then certainly learned the utility.

---

[66] Hopefully there will soon be an inventory of I Kiribati artefacts in British museums – one is in preparation. There are surprisingly many, although few are on permanent display.

[67] Although my wife recalls both ducks and domestic pigeons on Makin in the early 1960s.

Chapter 8: Early Contact With Europeans

The visit by the Wilkes Expedition in 1841

The significance of the Wilkes Expedition's report for this history is that it is the first detailed published survey of pre-contact Tungaru.

The *United States Exploring Expedition* (to give it its official name) was an exploring and surveying expedition of the Pacific Ocean and surrounding lands which was officially conducted by the United States between 1838 and 1842. Its report has been one of the primary sources of Part 1 of this history, and excerpts have informed earlier Chapters. The expedition is sometimes called the "*U.S. Ex. Ex.*", but more often the *Wilkes Expedition* in honour of its commanding officer, United States Navy Lieutenant Charles Wilkes.

Its voyage through the Gilbert islands, though, was actually a minor side line from the main expedition, and one in which Wilkes himself personally played no part. In April 1841, *USS Peacock*, under Lieutenant William L. Hudson, and *USS Flying Fish*, first surveyed Drummond's Island, which was newly named for an American of the expedition. Lieutenant Hudson had heard from a member of his crew that a ship had wrecked off the island, and that the crew had been massacred by the Gilbertese. A woman and her child were said to have been the only survivors, so Hudson decided to land a small force of marines and sailors, under William M. Walker, to search the island. She and the child were not found.

This, the first contact with the I Tungaru people to be written up in detail – although not by that date an unusual contact, evidently by a long way - was fraught by misunderstandings. From the start the Wilkes Expedition was at odds with I Tungaru custom in relation to strangers.

This is their interpretation:

> *'All the party on shore were much incommoded with the rudeness of the natives, who did all in their power to pilfer from them; and if their attention were diverted for a moment the hands of a native were felt in their pockets. When detected, they would hold up their hands with open palms and laugh'.*

The I Tungaru interpretation (had it existed) might have gone more along the following lines:

> *'The strangers from* Matang *arrived in our islands. We entertained them and gave them food, which they accepted; but with extreme bad manners,*

> *they refused to be anointed with oil when we honoured them with it. They were unable to account for their descent, or, when asked, to establish from which* boti *they came.*
>
> *'In accordance with our custom they therefore became our slaves, and their property became ours. We proceeded to claim it'.*

A modern account states:

> *'Initially, the 'natives' were peaceful and the Americans were able to explore the island without results. It was when the party was returning to their ship that Hudson noticed a member of his crew was missing. After making another search, the man was not found and the natives began arming themselves.*
>
> *'Lieutenant Walker returned his force to the ship, to converse with Hudson, who ordered Walker to return to shore and demand the return of the sailor. Walker then re-boarded his boats with his landing party and headed to shore. Walker shouted his demand and the natives charged for him, forcing the boats to turn back to the ships.*
>
> *'It was decided on the next day that the Americans would bombard the hostiles and land again. While doing this, a force of around 700 Gilbertese warriors opposed the American assault, but were defeated after a long battle. No Americans were hurt, but twelve natives were killed and others were wounded, and two villages were completely destroyed'.*

As the I Tungaru saw it, there had been a gross violation of law by the missing sailor Anderson. He had transgressed custom and he had been killed in accordance with custom: the same treatment would have been dealt out to any I Tungaru person who had done the same. So the American searches and destruction of Utiroa was simply an unjustified act of war against them.

However, despite many further cultural misunderstandings, the Wilkes Expedition's visits to other islands were more peaceful, and have been referred to in earlier Chapters.

Early residents and visitors

The Wilkes Expedition repatriated two beachcombers: an Irishman, John Kirby, on Kuria, who had deserted from a whaling ship three years earlier;

Chapter 8: Early Contact With Europeans

and a Scot, Robert Wood, who had at his own request been landed from the whaler *Janie* of London on Butaritari, seven years earlier.

Although they had been stripped of their possessions, both men maintained that *'the natives had always treated them kindly'*; Kirby had a wife and daughter, who he promptly proceeded to abandon (his wife *'showed much concern and wished to accompany him ...* [on departure] *the natives all left the ship much gratified except Kirby's wife who continued to be somewhat downhearted'*)

These two are thus the first known Europeans to live in the Gilberts, although there were a few others known to be living with the I Tungaru at that time who the Wilkes Expedition did not meet. In 1835 there were said to be three European beachcombers living on Butaritari, a Hawaiian on Tabiteuea, and no doubt a few on other islands. By 1841 there were at least 16 Europeans; and from then on their numbers increased rapidly, to a total estimated by H E Maude as being at least 50 by the 1860s.

Traders

The person most associated with early trading (as opposed to whaling) was Captain Trainer, an Englishman by birth, who made several voyages to Tungaru over a number of years. An account of one of these voyages was made by a whaling surgeon, Dr. John Coulter, who travelled in 1835 as a passenger on board the 200 ton brigantine *Hound*. The *Hound*, which carried a crew of 16, was owned and operated by Trainer himself.

Its trading operations in Tungaru were well organised. The vessel was armed with four small carronades, a long brass nine-pounder and small arms for the crew; and boarding nets were turned up on arrival at each island, with a special watch set to prevent any unauthorised person coming on board. Trading hours were strictly from 10 a.m. to 6 p.m., during which period a flag was flown from the mast-head as an indication to the natives ashore. At such times, *'although great numbers of natives were round the vessel, some through curiosity, others to trade, and the noise was great, as the nettings were raised only on one side at the gangway, all was conducted on board in a very orderly manner'*.

It is clear that the I Tungaru were by 1835 already accustomed to trading visits, for they had accumulated stocks of both bêche-de-mer and tortoise-shell (then more accurately called turtle-shell), which they exchanged for tobacco, hoop-iron, clay pipes and various *'trifling articles of small value'*. At Abemama a regular bêche-de-mer station was already in operation, with sheds for curing and drying built on the edge of the reef.

The first *resident* traders to commence operations were Richard Randell and George Durant, who set up their trading establishment on Butaritari in March 1844, shortly after the Wilkes Expedition had called there. Unusually, there is a documented I Kiribati tradition of their arrival:

> *'From one visiting vessel a man whom the people called Koakoa* [Randell's local name which means 'the sharp one' – see below], *and who informed them that he came from Parramatta, was left ashore at the small island of Tikurere in the Butaritari lagoon and here opened a trading store. For copra he traded such things as rifles and ammunition, food, cannons, whisky, gin and rum. There was, thereafter, much drunkenness and fighting and many people were killed. The cannons, some of which were quite big, were used for making a noise and frightening people.'*

Randell was to remain on Butaritari for a quarter of a century. He gained the confidence of the *Uea*, Te Itimaroroa, and the islanders; and was soon fluent in their language.

Maude suggests that he and Durant were initially operating on a very small scale, collecting coconut oil for sale to visiting whaler-traders in return for tobacco and muskets. Without capital they could not make use of trading vessels; so in 1850 Randell visited Australia and secured financial backing, by entering into partnership with Charles Smith. Smith was well connected with the mercantile business world through his association with Fotheringham, a founder of the Marine Insurance Company, and with the important firm of Flower, Salting and Company, which had just appointed him the manager of their whaling fleet. Two schooners, the *Chieftain* (77 tons) and *Supply* (127 tons), were immediately assigned to the Gilberts trade. Randell returned to Butaritari in the former in August, 1851, while Smith followed, on board the latter, two months later.

While Randell managed the island trading side of the undertaking, and Smith the Sydney end, Hugh Fairclough became the third and final partner and was made shipping manager. He acquired a financial interest in the business, which became Smith, Randell and Fairclough.

Prospecting missionaries from Hawaii were astonished to discover the Union Jack flying over a busy trading station with 14 European employees, and facilities for the watering, provisioning and repair of visiting ships, as well as store houses for a growing entrepôt trade.

Between 1851 and 1866 Fairclough made more than 20 round voyages between Australia and the Gilbert Islands. In the earlier years cargo from Sydney consisted almost entirely of kegs and boxes of plug tobacco, in sticks (or heads), an occasional case of hardware, empty oil casks or 'shooks' to make such casks, and some provisions (beef, flour and biscuits) and spirits (usually rum and geneva) for the traders.

As time went on, however, the value of tobacco began to depreciate, and traders found that that a knife would purchase more than several heads of tobacco. The only export of any consequence, for which these were exchanged, was coconut oil; though small quantities of bêche-de-mer, tortoise-shell and coir were shipped from time to time as a sideline.

Randell was determined to expand his trading operations throughout the Gilberts archipelago, and apparently visited every island. Life for his traders (then termed oil agents) was precarious: they were left on the beach to fend for themselves with nothing except a supply of empty casks and a case of tobacco to buy the oil to fill them with (as well as for their own food and shelter), so their life must have been hard in the extreme. Indeed on Abemama, when Captain Terry landed to collect oil in February, 1851, he found that all of the agents had been killed on the orders of the *Uea*, Tem Baiteke. The *Uea* thereafter kept the entire trade of the central Gilberts, including that of his tributary islands of Kuria and Aranuka, in his own hands.

Nevertheless Randell continued to appoint European traders on other islands as his agents: James McCarthy and Benjamin Graham on Abaiang, and John Walch and John Desman on Tarawa; while in May, 1852, "Tommy" was landed to commence trading on Maiana, and George Adams and Henry Green on Tabiteuea.

The routine of trade consisted of the landing of relief traders, trade and empty casks, and the embarking of time-expired traders and oil in casks (at Tarawa and Abaiang these were rafted to the ship).

Chapter 8: Early Contact With Europeans

On one tour, for example, 252 casks of oil were collected, with a full 100 gallons bought at Abemama. The *Uea* there, Baiteke, did not allow traders (see above); he never visited ships or dealt with Europeans directly but only through intermediaries, who were at first his brother and brother-in-law; and later his son and heir-apparent, Binoka.

The architect of this trade, Randell himself, was quiet, temperate in his habits and devout: the antithesis of the stereotype of the island trader [68]. As he told Hiram Bingham, he was *'desirous of doing good'*. The missionary literature contains many references to information provided by him on the customs, beliefs, political systems, and material culture of the Gilbertese, and they reveal a person genuinely and sympathetically interested in the people amongst whom he lived.

According to Hiram Bingham's fellow missionary Dr. Gulick:

> *'He never hesitated to condemn the wrongs done to them by unscrupulous traders and recruiters,* 'who had not only robbed them at times of their produce, but had also taken away many of their young men and women by force' ... *judging from only one of the many horrible stories that Captain Randell told me about the barbarous treatment which these islanders had received in former years, it is surprising that thereafter they did not murder every white man who landed on their shores'.*

H E Maude comments:

> *'The Gilbertese .... treated Randell with a respect and affection which few other Europeans have possessed. To them he was the first white man to be accounted, and treated with the deference due to, one of their own unimane ... Perhaps their ultimate accolade, which again few other Europeans have received, was to be called not by his European name but by the Gilbertese name Teng Koakoa (the sharp one)'* [69]

---

[68] Although he did adopt at least some local customs in that he had, simultaneously, four wives; and Durant is said to have had a 'harem' on Makin.

[69] But, so far as I have been able to discover, and unlike many families today who proudly claim descent from early Europeans, no descendants claim his legacy in Kiribati

Chapter 8: Early Contact With Europeans

The resident traders whom Randell began to introduce in the 1860s would, according to Maude, have:

> *'agreed with the advice of Theodore Weber, the Samoa – based Godeffroy's manager, that it was essential to*: 'have a woman of your own, no matter what island you take her from; for a trader without a wife is a man in eternal hot water'; *but these marriages were often lasting unions; and it was increasingly the wife who tended to conform to European customs and indeed was often an invaluable assistant in his trading affairs'.*

Several of the later men who started trading in Randell's employ lived all their lives in the islands and became persons of substance and authority. Robert Corrie, the best-known of all, commenced trading on Maiana in 1860. *'Quiet, spectacled Bob Corrie, of wild Maiana, who can twist them round his little finger without an angry word'*, was building and running schools at his own expense before the arrival of the mission teachers. Offered the governorship of Maiana by Tem Binoka and recommended as British Vice-Consul for the Gilberts in 1886, Corrie lived to act as the official interpreter for Captain Davis on the establishment of the Protectorate in 1892.

James Lowther, who chose Nonouti, the most unpromising island of all, for his home in 1865, also lived on into the 1890s, despite an environment of war, murder, drunkenness and theft; as did Robert Randolph of Abaiang: *'a man of tremendous nerve and resolution'*.

It was Randolph who in 1869 put an end to the continual pilfering of property at Bingham's mission headquarters by refusing to purchase any further oil until everything stolen had been restored.

In 1868, Thomas Redfern had taken over from Waters as Randell's representative at Onotoa, where he lived for many years, and he founded a notable island family. Another prominent resident of Abemama at the end of the 19th century, and one who became Tem Binoka's Agent, was George Murdock. After the death of Binoka, Murdock joined the new colonial adminstration; but he also founded a family that continues in Kiribati to this day.

After Randell's retirement and return to Australia in 1870, most of his traders set themselves up independently, as well as becoming *'the respected advisers of the emergent island governments of the immediate pre-Protectorate days'*.

Chapter 8: Early Contact With Europeans

Once Randell had shown the way, the possibilities of the new coconut oil trade came to be noticed by Smith's main competitor in the whaling industry, the Sydney ship-owner Robert Towns. After several false starts, he began to trade in a minor way in the 1850s. With one exception, however, (named Stanbury), Towns's agents seem to have been all beachcombers: a Frenchman (but named John Cook) on Tabiteuea, and Tarpaulin Jack (or John) and his associate Bob from Sydney on Nonouti; to these were added a second beachcomber at Tabiteuea, together with a refractory seaman who had deserted the *Louisa*, while an unsuccessful attempt was made to persuade yet a third, by the name of Richard Anson (or Hanson), to serve as agent on Tamana. These were not trustworthy men, and the business was not profitable.

Towns thus took a break from both coconut oil and the Gilberts until 10 years later, when one of his whaling masters, Captain Michael Eury, persuaded him to fit out the barque *Caernarvon* as a whaler-trader, a class of vessel by then virtually extinct in the Pacific. Eury left Sydney in March, 1865, and in September established trading stations on Butaritari and Makin, and by 1867 on Marakei, Abaiang, Tarawa, and Maiana, as well as in the Marshalls.

Eury knew the Gilberts well and was a capable businessman, while his one-third financial interest in the venture ensured his loyalty to Towns. Despite setbacks the enterprise survived the death of Towns in 1873, and even took over the remains of Macdonald, Smith and Company's business the following year. It was still prospering modestly when coconut oil was superseded by the copra trade in the 1880s.

Blackbirders and labour recruiters

In 1847 Benjamin Boyd – who had started life as a stockbroker in London - commenced the Pacific labour trade by sending the *Portenia* and *Velocity* to the Loyalty Islands, New Hebrides, Rotuma and the Southern Gilberts to recruit labourers for his estates in New South Wales; they only succeeded in obtaining 22 recruits in the Gilbert Group (17 from Tamana and five from Arorae) - but it was a prelude to what was to come. Boyd's venture proved a failure as most of the labourers deserted from their employment, found their way to Sydney, and were eventually repatriated.

In the 1850s French recruiters were active; some people from Kiribati were taken to Reunion, others probably to New Caledonia.

Chapter 8: Early Contact With Europeans

'Blackbirding' in the Gilberts began on a serious scale in the 1860s. The depredations there were not on the scale of those elsewhere, including the neighbouring Ellice islands, but they contributed to a drop in population in the last quarter of the 19th century.

In 1863 the *Ellen Elizabeth*, under a Captain Muller, left South America to recruit for the Peruvian indentured labour trade. At the time there was a drought in the southern Gilberts and recruits came from Nonouti, Tabiteuea, Tamana and Arorae; they were in part voluntarily recruited through 'fallacious' promises - but also though kidnapping, by sailing away with any islanders who came aboard *Ellen Elizabeth*, either in the hope of pilfering or trading, or simply out of curiosity. The *Ellen Elizabeth* took 161 Gilbertese to Peru.

They had a bad and stormy journey to Peru, which took five months. The 'recruits' had to pump water continuously, and 33 of them died of overwork and cold, as well as mistreatment: *'one of the greatest pleasures of the captain was to cover the women with tar, pull their hair, and have them beaten by seamen'*. Then, when they arrived, Captain Muller was refused permission to land them as licences to recruit and employ Pacific Islanders had been withdrawn. He eventually disembarked the 110 survivors on Penrhyn in the Cook Islands, where their descendants still live.

After this episode, recruiting for employment in Fiji (1864–1895), Tahiti (1867–1885), Samoa (1867–1895), Hawaii (1877–1887), Mexico (1891), Guatemala (1892) and Queensland (1895) ensured that there was a fairly consistent circular movement of people away from and back to their islands, albeit sometimes for decades. For example about 700 Gilbertese were recruited for plantation work in Tahiti between 1867 and 1872, some of whom were not repatriated until well into the 20th century.

Although described as 'recruiting' the operation was in fact often straightforward kidnapping: the mate of the Tahitian barque *Moaroa*, for instance, describes how on Beru *'they had great sport in the bush catching them and making them fast'*, and again how on Arorae *'thirty-eight young women were all made fast by the hair of their head and led into the boat'*. The Gilbertese and Marshallese women were particularly sought after for their good looks: *'they fetch at the Fiji Islands twenty pounds a head, and are much more profitable to the slavers than the men'*. Abductions at Maiana and Tabiteuea in 1873 show that at least one of the Fiji recruiters, Carl, was as capable of kidnapping as his

Chapter 8: Early Contact With Europeans

confrères from Peru or Tahiti, although generally the Fiji trade was more humanely conducted than that of Peru.

Between January 1870 and December 1875 at least 27 recruiting vessels visited, and over 900 I Tungaru signed on for terms of three to five years in Fiji. Over the next 20 years a further 35 voyages obtained more than 1,000 recruits. The high point in this migration coincided with drought conditions in southern Tungaru. In 1878 and 1883, particularly dry years, over 200 were taken. The main sources of recruits between 1875 and 1895 were Beru and Tabiteuea, where over 350 and 200 respectively are known to have worked in Fiji. Nikunau, Onotoa and Arorae provided between 100 and 150 over the same period while Abaiang, Maiana, Abemama, Nonouti and Tamana provided less than 100 each. The only other year in which adult migration to Fiji exceeded 100 was in 1891, when more than 50 left Tabiteuea.

Tungaru was also a major recruiting area for German planters in Samoa. Over 1,500 people from Kiribati were recruited during the 1870s, the vast majority of whom worked on the plantations of J. C. Godeffroy & Son. From 1881 to 1884, however, German recruiting in Kiribati almost ceased (as a result of Godeffroys' decision to seek plantation workers instead from Melanesia); but during the mid-1880s recruiting in Tungaru resumed and became a significant back-up to labour supplies from elsewhere.

This trade was one of the reasons that Germany pressed the British Government to declare a Protectorate over the area (which fell within Britain's sphere of interest as defined by the Anglo-German Agreement of 1886); the Germans feared encroachment by Americans. However, labour recruitment became subject to much closer regulation under the new British administration and the Germans found that *'without the whip, the imprisonment and irons they cannot get the same work out of the Gilbert Islanders as before'*. In the decade after declaration of the Protectorate only about 200 were indentured for employment in Samoa. On the basis of what is known about German recruitment and employment of Pacific Islanders, it would seem that overall, about 2,500 Gilbertese worked in Samoa between 1867 and 1895.

Between 1877 and 1887 some 1,500 adults and 300 children went to Hawaii. Although a prime intention in seeking labour in the south Pacific was to stimulate recovery of a declining Hawaiian population, and despite conditions of employment and wages being decidedly superior there than elsewhere, most I Tungaru still preferred to go home after their three years.

Chapter 8: Early Contact With Europeans

The final episodes in long-distance overseas labour migration involved two short-lived destinations during the 1890s. Between 1890 and 1892 about 1,000 adults were recruited for work in Central America. Three ships were involved — the *Helen W. Almy* in 1890 (300 recruits), the *Tahiti* in 1891 (300 recruits, 100 children) and the *Montserrat in 1892* (400 recruits). The *Tahiti*, bound for Mexico, capsized with total loss of life off the southern California coast. The *Montserrat* took its recruits to Guatemala; but in 1896, it repatriated 203 adults from its own recruiting. Of the remaining recruits, 39 adults were re-engaged, 68 were reported as dead, and 5 had settled in Mexico. The fate of the others is unknown.

The final, and short-lived, movement was to Australia. Although a few migrants made their own way to Queensland during the 1880s and early 1890s, formal recruiting for this area from Kiribati did not commence until 1895. In that year the *May* recruited 62 males and 11 females, and the *Lochiel* 104 males and 13 females — a total of 190, of whom 165 were from the Gilbert islands. The Queensland trade was halted after these two voyages by the Western Pacific High Commission.

Soon after the declaration of the Protectorate, opportunities for employment on Banaba and Nauru, combined with the 'museum' policy of the successive Resident Commissioners up to WWII, meant that recruitment for service overseas more or less ceased until the Marine Training School revived the idea of extensive overseas employment in the 1960s.

As the article *Population Estimates For Kiribati and Tuvalu, 1850–1900: Review and Speculation* (of which this section has mainly been a digest) concludes:

> *'To sum up, the effects of overseas labour migration on the nature of population change were not the same throughout Kiribati. Normally the number of persons leaving a given island in any one year did not exceed 100. Because almost as many women as men left to work elsewhere, the sex ratios of island populations were not distorted to the extent they were in other parts of the Pacific. Age composition was certainly affected but in most cases the majority of adults were only temporarily absent. The loss to potential population increase caused by labour migration was not nearly as great as has sometimes been claimed'.*

Chapter 8: Early Contact With Europeans

Missionaries

Protestant missionaries, sent by the *American Board of Commissioners for Foreign Missions,* first arrived in northern Tungaru in 1857; and Congregationalist missionaries from the London Missionary Society (LMS) arrived in the south in 1870 [70]. Together with the Ellice the latter were known as the North-West Outstations of the Samoan mission. Banaba (and Nauru) were brought into the LMS sphere between 1916 and 1919, although missionary residence on these islands was sporadic and relied heavily on the native South Seas ministry. In fact (other than Rev. and Mrs. Bingham) much of the work of conversion in the Gilberts was entrusted to Hawaiians and Samoans3, with occasional visits from European supervisors. In 1917 the American Mission left, and the LMS became responsible for supervision of all the islands, which had by then started to appoint their own Gilbertese clergy as well as relying on Samoan pastors.

The first Roman Catholics - missionaries of the Sacred Heart – came in response to pleas from I Tungaru who had been converted to that faith whilst working in Tahiti. They left France in 1888 and arrived at the island of Nonouti in May of that year. The Sacred Heart Priests and Brothers were soon joined by nuns from both France and Australia; and the Roman Catholic mission remained a much larger, expatriate-led, Church throughout the 'Gilbert and Ellice Islands' era, which is the subject of Part 2 of this book.

The two churches had different styles and approaches; but were each convinced that they should have exclusivity. Indeed they were united only in their dislike of, and rivalry with, each other: from reading the early accounts, it is difficult to avoid the impression that they regarded 'conversion' of those of the opposite Christian faith as being of even greater importance than the baptism of the 'heathens'.

Many of these missionaries (but especially, it must be said, the Protestants) had also come, not to understand and work with local customs - but to obliterate them. Their object was to replace the indigenous culture with a carbon copy of themselves. Here is an extract from the Revd. Hiram Bingham at the outset of his mission to the Micronesians (the reason it does not mention

---

[70] The Protestant Churches basically had a 'no competition' agreement in the Pacific. Thus, Anglican missionaries were most active in Melanesia; Methodists in Fiji and Tonga; and Congregationalists in Samoa, the Ellice Islands, and the Gilberts.

Chapter 8: Early Contact With Europeans

their 'wickedness' in relation to matters of sex is explained by its intended audience, pious American children!):

> *'You know, of course, that before the missionaries visited them they had no books; neither could they read or write, so dark were their minds; but, alas, their hearts were darker still. The unconverted Micronesians are all liars. The fathers lie, the mothers lie, and the children lie. Indeed, they seem just as ready to deceive as to speak the truth.*
>
> *'They are much disposed to steal, moreover. They steal from one another, from the ships which visit them, and frequently from missionaries who live among them. In their way they are very covetous. They know very little about nice houses, railroads, bank-stocks, fine horses, and fine clothes; but they are greedy of fishhooks, tobacco, plane-irons, large knives, scented oils, and beads.*
>
> *'They often treat their women with great cruelty, beating them, stabbing them, making slaves of them. The little children, for the most part, have much kindness shown to them; but I am sorry to say that they do not honor [sic] their fathers and their mothers. And I will add that very little respect is paid to old people ... they are very passionate and revengeful. Hence they are much given to fighting and killing one another. A great many murders are committed every year.*
>
> *'The Micronesians can hardly be called idolaters; that is, they do not bow 'down to wood and stone;' but they are heathen nevertheless, and they worship false gods. I think we might call them 'spiritualists.' They believe there are a great many spirits which have to do with them. They set up stones in honor [sic] of them, and often make offerings of food to them; for they are much afraid of them. Some persons profess to hold intercourse with these spirits.'*

Anyone who has read earlier Chapters of this book will recognise that this statement is a mess of prejudices, not an accurate reflection of I Tungaru society; and Bingham was positively *sympathetic* towards the Gilbertese compared to many of the other missionaries. However his progress was slow, and his converts limited. The Samoan-led LMS pastors in the Southern Gilberts had greater success.

Efforts at conversion also led to some unsavoury incidents, such as the slaughter of a good proportion of the unconverted of Tabiteuea by converts

Chapter 8: Early Contact With Europeans

led by their Hawaiian pastors Kapui and Nanim, in 1868. It also resulted in Church–imposed disciplines on the population (see p. 124 below), and their collection into villages, where they could be more readily supervised. These processes, which were subsequently reinforced and extended by the colonial government had profound effects on Gilbertese daily life.

The naturalist Charles Morris Woodward visited the Gilberts in 1884, when he found the LMS Pastors in control of much of the economic life of the islands where they were dominant, as well as the spiritual. He found that on Nikunau the pastor had bought wood from New Zealand from funds donated by his flock, which he proceeded to have made into canoes, which he then rented out for his own personal benefit. Another 'despotic' missionary fined locals for misdemeanours at the exorbitant rate of ten bags of copra worth £2 each.

Woodward wrote that:

> *'The people have blind faith in them and whatever they tell them they think must be right and the promise of eternal punishment if their commands are not obeyed'.*

By 1894, two years into the era of the Protectorate, the Catholic inventory of converts numbered 5,300, all but a handful on six Southern islands (but not the two most southern, Tamana and Arorae); and on Makin. There is no comparable figure available for the Protestant Churches.

Captain Davis presciently reported in 1892 that: *'the pay and cost of maintenance of the Native Missionaries and the Subscription to the Mission – are a heavy drain on the Natives. They charge for books ...* [and levy fines] *for trivial breaches of Church discipline ... if matters are not placed on a better footing in the English and American Missions, it would not surprise me if in a few years the whole population became Roman Catholics'* – because the priests also allowed at least some dancing and singing, permitted tobacco, and did not engage in trade.

'Heathens' would however have then been still a significant part of the population – estimated at a third of the population as late as 1931, when the first thorough Census of the Gilbert and Ellice Islands Colony (GEIC), as it had by then become, was conducted.

Chapter 8: Early Contact With Europeans

Anthropologists

Anthropology was a development of the 'comparative' methods developed in the earlier 19th century. The first of the explicitly anthropological societies, the *Société d'Anthropologie de Paris*, met for the first time in Paris in 1859, although *The Ethnological Society of London* had been founded in 1843 as an offshoot of the *Aborigines' Protection Society* – an anti-slavery organisation.

The Pacific has been one of the most researched regions for traditional anthropology, and the earliest studies of the Gilberts were primarily by German researchers whose main focus was the colonies awarded to Germany in 1886. Augustin Krämer, a naval surgeon turned anthropologist, visited nine Gilbert islands in 1897; his book *Hawaii, Ostmikronesien und Samoa* was first published in 1906, and has recently been re-printed. Paul Hambruch was another an early German ethnologist researching primarily on Banaba, who published an account in 1915 [71].

The Royal Navy

The gradual (and mostly reluctant) extension of British power over the Pacific islands is traced in the next Chapter. In 1872 the British Parliament passed the *Pacific Islanders Protection Act*, which inter alia made removal of labourers without their consent a felony; and extended jurisdiction of the government based in Fiji to any British subjects in the islands. The task of enforcing the new Act was given to the Royal Navy, as it quickly became apparent that the 1872 Act was only effective when a warship appeared offshore. Naval captains were made Deputy Commissioners and in March 1881 the *Emerald* was sent to Micronesia, the first formal expression of imperial authority. Another Act, *The Pacific Islanders Act* of 1882, empowered naval officers to judge offences against (as well as by) British subjects, if necessary by acts of war (several villages in the Solomons were bombarded; but the threat of the Navy's guns always sufficed to bring Gilbertese to heel). They were drawn into the many complaints about the behaviour of the missionaries, as well as the traders.

This tale comes from a book called *Rodman The Boatsteerer And Other Stories* by Louis Becke, an Australian Pacific trader, short-story writer and novelist who

---

[71] Few of the German works have been translated into English and they are an underused source of information on Tungaru - as I have no command of German, certainly by myself.

Chapter 8: Early Contact With Europeans

died in 1913. I include it in full (without apology, as the book has been out of print for many decades) because it seems perfectly to encapsulate the relations between the Gilbertese and Europeans in the last free-wheeling years, before the Protectorate was declared, and the role of naval officers. It highlights the precarious life of the traders; the arbitrary nature of justice from visiting naval vessels; the disdain of the Gilbertese (recorded elsewhere as well) for the British method of execution by hanging; the presence of an early *'kamea'*; and, not least, the concerted attempt by the people of Abaiang twice to substitute a slave for the miscreant, who was of high rank.

> *'Years ago, in the days when the "highly irregular proceedings," as naval officers termed them in their official reports, of the Brig Carl and other British ships engaged in the trade which some large-minded people have vouched for as being "absolutely above reproach," attracted some attention from the British Government towards the doings of the gentlemanly scoundrels engaged therein, the people of Sydney used to talk proudly of the fleet of gunboats which, constructed by the New South Wales Government for the Admiralty, were built to "patrol the various recruiting grounds of the Fijian and Queensland planters and place the labour-traffic under the most rigid supervision." The remark quoted above was then, as it is now, quite a hackneyed one, much used by the gallant officers who commanded the one-gun-one-rocket-tube craft aforementioned. Likewise, the "highly irregular proceedings" were a naval synonym for some of the bloodiest slaving outrages ever perpetrated, but which, however, never came to light beyond being alluded to as "unreliable and un-authenticated statements by discharged and drunken seamen who had no proper documentary evidence to support their assertions."*

> *'The Australian slave-suppressing vessels were not a success. In the first place, they could not sail much faster than a mud-dredge. Poor Bob Randolph, the trader, of the Gilbert and Kingsmill Groups, employed as pilot and interpreter on board, once remarked to the officer commanding one of these wonderful tubs which for four days had been thrashing her way against the south-east trades in a heroic endeavour to get inside Tarawa Lagoon, distant ten miles (and could not do it), that "these here schooners ought to be rigged as fore-and-afters and called 'four-and-halfters; for I'll be hanged if this thing can do more than four and a half knots, even in half a gale of wind, all sail set and a*

Chapter 8: Early Contact With Europeans

smooth sea." But if the "four-and-halfters," as they were thenceforth designated in the Western Pacific, were useless in regard to suppressing the villainies and slaughter that then attended the labour trade, there was one instance in which one of the schooners and her captain did some good by avenging as cruel a murder as was ever perpetrated in equatorial Oceania.

'One Jack Keyes was a trader on the island of Apiang [sic], one of the Gilbert Group, recently annexed by Great Britain. He was very old, very quiet in his manner, and about the last kind of man one would expect to see earning his living as a trader among the excitable, intractable native race which inhabit the Line Islands. His fellow-trader, Bob Randolph, a man of tremendous nerve and resolution, only maintained his prestige among the Apiang natives by the wonderful control he had learnt to exercise over a naturally fiery temper and by taking care, when knocking down any especially insulting native "buck," never to draw blood, and always to laugh. And the people of Apiang thought much of Te Matân Bob, as much as the inhabitants of the whole group—from Arorai in the south to Makin in the north—do to this day of quiet, spectacled Bob Corrie, of wild Maiana, who can twist them round his little finger without an angry word. Perhaps poor Keyes, being a notoriously inoffensive man, might have died a natural death in due time, but for one fatal mistake he made; and that was in bringing a young wife to the island.

'A white woman was a rarity in the Line Islands. Certainly the Boston mission ship, Morning Star, in trying to establish the "Gospel according to Bosting—no ile or dollars, no missn'ry," as Jim Garstang, of Drummond's Island, used to observe, had once brought a lady soul-saver of somewhat matured charms to the island, but her advent into the Apiang moniap or town hall, carrying an abnormally large white umbrella and wearing a white solar topee with a green turban, and blue goggles, had had the effect of scaring the assembled councillors away across to the weather-side of the narrow island, whence none returned until the terrifying apparition had gone back to the ship.

'But this white woman who poor old Keyes married and brought with him was different, and the Apiang native, like all the rest of the world, is susceptible to female charms; and her appearance at the doorway of the old trader's house was ever hailed with an excited and admiring chorus of "Te boom te matân! Te boom te matân!" (The white man's wife.)

Chapter 8: Early Contact With Europeans

But none were rude or offensive to her, although the young men especially were by no means chary of insulting the old man, who never carried a pistol in his belt.

'*One of these young men was unnecessarily intrusive. He would enter the trader's house on any available pretext, and the old man noticed that he would let his savage eyes rest upon his wife's figure in a way there was no mistaking. Not daring to tackle the brawny savage, whose chest, arms, and back were one mass of corrugations resulting from wounds inflicted by sharks' teeth spears and swords in many encounters, old Jack one day quietly intimated to his visitor that he was not welcome and told him to "get." The savage, with sullen hate gleaming from cruel eyes that looked out from the mat of coarse, black hair, which, cut away in a fringe over his forehead, fell upon his shoulders, rose slowly and went out.*

'*Early next morning old Keyes was going over to Randolph's house, probably to speak of the occurrence of the previous day, when his wife called him and said that someone was at the door waiting to buy tobacco. "What have you to sell?" called out the old man. "Te moe motu" (young drinking-coconuts), was the answer, and the old man, not recognising the voice as that of his visitor of the day before, went unsuspectingly to take them from the native's hand, when the latter, placing a horse-pistol to the trader's heart, shot him dead, with the savage exclamation— "Now your wife is mine!"*

'*The poor woman fled to Bob Randolph for safety, and, dreading to remain on the island, went away in a schooner to her home in New Zealand. Nearly a year passed, and then a man-of-war came and endeavoured to capture the murderer; but in vain, for the captain would not use force; and "talk" and vague threats the natives only laughed at. So the ship steamed away; and then the natives began to threaten Randolph, and talk meaningly to each other about his store being full of te pakea and te rom (tobacco and gin). A long, uneasy six months passed, and then the little "four-and-halfter" Renard, Commander ——— sailed into Apiang lagoon, and the naval officer told Randolph he had come to get the man and try him for the murder.*

'*The commander first warped his vessel in as near as possible to the crowded village, and moored her with due regard to the effectiveness of*

Chapter 8: Early Contact With Europeans

his one big gun. Then, with Randolph as interpreter, negotiations commenced.

'*The old men of the village were saucy; the young men wanted a fight and demanded one. Randolph did his part well. He pointed out to the old men that unless they gave the man up, the long gun on the ship would destroy every house and canoe on the island, even if no one were killed. That meant much to them, whereas one man's life was but little. But, first, the natives tried cunning. One and then another wretched slave was caught and bound and taken off to the naval officer as the murderer, only to be scornfully rejected by Randolph and the captain. Then the officer's patience was exhausted. If the man who murdered Keyes was not surrendered in an hour he would open fire, and also hang some of the chiefs then detained on board as hostages.*

'*Randolph's gloomy face quickened their fears. This captain could neither be frightened nor fooled. In half an hour the slayer of the trader was brought on board. The old men admitted their attempt at deception, but pleaded that the murderer was a man of influence, and they would rather the two others (who were absolutely innocent) were hanged than this one; but their suggestion was not acted upon. The trial was just and fair, but short, and then Randolph urged the captain to have the man executed on shore by being shot. It would impress the people more than hanging him on board. And hanging they regarded as a silly way of killing a man.*

'*The naval officer had no relish for work of this nature, and when Randolph told him that the natives had consented to execute the prisoner in his (Randolph's) presence (and the captain's presence also if necessary) he, no doubt, felt glad. Bob Randolph then became M.C., and gave his instructions to the old men.*

'*The whole village assembled in front of Randolph's to see the show. An old carronade lying in the corner of the copra house was dragged out, cleaned, and loaded with a heavy blank charge. Then the prisoner, sullen and defiant to the last, but wondering at the carronade, was lashed with his back to the muzzle, and, at a signal from one of the old men, a firestick was applied to the gun. A roar, a rush of fragments through the air, and all was finished.*

'*Bob Randolph's fox-terrier was the only creature that seemed to trouble about making any search for the remnants of the body. Half an hour*

Chapter 8: Early Contact With Europeans

afterwards, as Bob was at supper, he came in and deposited a gory lump of horror at his master's feet.

Summary: guns, germs, steel – but also Gospels

In 1892, when the Gilbert Islands became a British Protectorate, the indigenous population was estimated to number 26,400 (plus some 3,100 in the Ellice Islands, to which they had just been joined). In Chapter 7, I concluded that there had been a population of between 31,000 and 35,000 in the Gilberts in 1850 (page 124).

It seems, therefore, that there had been a significant but not catastrophic drop in the population of Tungaru, of some four to five thousand, in the last quarter of the 19th century. In this respect they fared rather better than many societies had done after first contact.

The impact of guns

As part of the declaration of the Protectorate in 1892, naval officers rounded up and confiscated all the guns they could find. The numbers are phenomenal: more than 600, of which 300 were confiscated on Tarawa alone (it being in the throes of civil war).

These had made the traditional armour useless.

Sabatier records their first use on Abaiang. His account is based on that included in H. R. McClure's *Land-Travel And Seafaring: A Frivolous Record Of Twenty Years Wanderings*, which was published in 1925.

> *'A runaway from Abaiang became friendly with a white man from Tarawa, who had a gun.*
>
> *'Suddenly he decided to make use of this powerful aid to get his revenge. He took the white man and some friends in his expedition. Off they went to Abaiang on a launch. They rowed in close to land. Abaiang's warriors were there to prevent a landing. Suddenly one of them was wrenched out of the ranks. He had been standing there, spear in hand, and yet now there he was, well set up, but arching his body in pain. The others thought that this was odd. There had been smoke over there, a cracking noise, and there was their comrade on the ground.* 'It's a trick played on us by the spirits' *they decided.* 'This place isn't favourable. We'll go and fight somewhere else'.

Chapter 8: Early Contact With Europeans

'They moved further away. The launch followed along the shoreline. Once again the warriors ranged themselves in battle formation. The man with the gun had only to calmly choose the largest target as victim and reload his weapon when he wished. The same scene was replayed farther on.

'The Abaiang warriors eventually realised that it wasn't safe to stand along the shore opposite this tube that smoked, made a cracking noise, and sent death to them. After these first emotions, interest focused entirely on ways of obtaining and using similar magic.'

After 1892, however, guns disappeared from society; and have never been replaced. Except for a very few incidents described in Parts 2 and 3 (pages 363, 393 and 403) Kiribati has not been troubled by internal strife since then.

The impact of germs

Throughout history, isolation has spared communities from epidemics and pandemics. However, this led to decreased 'herd' immunity, and when a deadly pathogen was re-introduced after a long time, there were no immune individuals remaining. As a result, it has, for example, been estimated that up to 95% of the pre-contact population of the Americas died of introduced diseases - many long before they encountered an actual European.

In Fiji, measles killed more than 40,000 people in 1875, reportedly after Ratu Cakobau and his two sons returned from Australia, where they had contracted the disease.

The first explorers frequently commented on the good health of the inhabitants of Tungaru.

Alien diseases were indeed introduced from the earliest years of interaction with Europeans, but there is no oral or written record of group-wide population decline as a result of epidemics. Undoubtedly diseases caused sickness and discomfort among residents on certain islands at different times, especially after the 1870s when people began to return after periods of employment in other countries. A report from 1923 identifies leprosy, TB, Yaws, and scabies as having *'been introduced some 60 years earlier'*, i.e. about that time, from Samoa, Fiji, and Rotuma.

Sabatier records an outbreak of measles, complicated by dysentery, on Nonouti in 1889 which resulted in 140 fatalities. Yet such references in

Chapter 8: Early Contact With Europeans

mission records to large numbers of deaths due to epidemics before 1900 are rare.

The impact of steel

Particulars of the cargo of the brig *Tyra* during a trading voyage through the Gilberts in 1866, which have survived, show that the variety of trade goods then being imported had evolved from tobacco (although this is still first on the list!):

> *"The commodities for barter were of a great variety. The bulkier consisted of tobacco, pipes, powder, shot, old flintlock muskets, revolvers, tower rifles, guns and carriages, calico in bales, turkey red handkerchiefs, axes, knives, etc. Besides these articles, but of lighter bulk, were beads, needles, scissors, thread, small looking-glasses, combs, fish-hooks and lines, soap, umbrellas, tin pots, pans, and many others too numerous to mention."*

The new imports profoundly modified I Tungaru technology: within a couple of decades the clam shell adze, the coral file and rasp, the wooden digging stick and many other artefacts of local manufacture were in process of disappearing, except as curiosities. They were replaced by metal tools and utensils which enormously reduced the labour of constructing a *babai* pit, fish pond, or canoe, of preparing food or drawing water, of house building, fishing, or toddy cutting; or indeed for undertaking almost any process.

The impact of the Missions

The missions had material as well as religious impact. They:

- Began the process of concentrating the people to villages containing multiple unrelated families, rather than their *kaainga*
- Replaced the (minimal) dress with *'that aesthetic and hygienic abomination of the Pacific, the Mother Hubbard'*
- Solicited a variable but significant contribution of cash from their congregations – one estimate is that about 20% of people's cash incomes were donated, a double tithe
- Reinforced a few traditional social codes of behaviour, but also introduced many new ones, by for example, banning infant betrothal, polygyny, the *eiriki* custom and even *bubuti* – in fact anything that was considered to be objectionable from a European perspective, such as allowing pigs to run free

Chapter 8: Early Contact With Europeans

- In Protestant areas, banned dancing and singing (other than of hymns) altogether as *'lewd and indecent'*; in Roman Catholic ones, severely regulated the practice
- In the far south, turned the *mwaneaba* system into a tool of the LMS Pastor; elsewhere began the (now widespread) establishment of sectarian rather than neighbourhood *mwaneabas*
- Became the only route through which the Gilbertese could acquire literacy.

All of these practices began before the establishment of the Protectorate, but many were supported and reinforced, even extended, by early Resident Commissioners.

Father Sabatier, who had at least studied and understood the Gilbertese very well, concludes the first part of his book *Sous l'équateur de Pacifique* with this approving statement:

> *'The younger generation have only known the new order of things and they view the past more with pity than regret. They take the same sort of interest in their ancestors as our French students might take in the ancient Gauls ... the young people are amazed at those Europeans who ask them absurd questions about Stone Age men simply so they can show off by holding forth about them'.*

He was wrong. I Tungaru culture was resilient, as we will see in Parts 2 and 3.

Chapter 8: Early Contact With Europeans

Further Reading

1. **The Discovery of the Pacific Islands** by Andrew Sharp, published by Oxford University Press, 1960
2. **Post-Spanish Discoveries in the Central Pacific** by H E Maude, published in the Journal of the Polynesian Society, 1959
3. **An account of the voyages undertaken by the order of His Present Majesty for making discoveries in the Southern Hemisphere, and successively performed by Commodore Byron, Captain Wallis, Captain Carteret, and Captain Cook, in the Dolphin, the Swallow and the Endeavour**, by John Hawkesworth, published by the Office of the Admiralty and Marine Affairs, 1773
4. **A Directory for the Navigation of the Pacific Ocean, with Descriptions of its Coasts, Islands, etc.,** by A. G. Findlay, republished by the Cambridge University Press, 2013
5. **Cinderellas of the Empire,** by Dr Barrie Macdonald, published by the Institute of Pacific Studies, 2001
6. **The Coconut Oil Trade Of The Gilbert Islands, by** H. E. Maude and Ida Leeson, Journal of the Polynesian Society, 1965
7. **Slavers Paradise** by H E Maude, published by the Institute of Pacific Studies, 1981
8. **The Cargo of the Montserrat: Gilbertese Labor in Guatemalan Coffee, 1890-1908** by David McCreery and Doug Munro, published in The Americas, Vol. 49, No. 3, 1993
9. **Kiribati: Aspects of History,** multiple authors and editors, published jointly by the Institute of Pacific Studies and the Ministry of Education, Training, and Culture, 1979
10. **Population Estimates For Kiribati And Tuvalu, 1850–1900: Review And Speculation by** Richard Bedford, Barrie Macdonald and Doug Munro, published in the Journal of the Polynesian Society 1980
11. **Rodman The Boatsteerer And Other Stories**, by Louis Becke, published by Unwin, 1898
12. **Dr. Augustin Krämer: a German ethnologist in the Pacific**, by Sven Mönter, published PhD Thesis 2010
13. **Hawaii, Ostmikronesien und Samoa; meine zweite Südseereise**, by Dr. Augustin Krämer, **first** published in 1906 and republished by the Nabu Press, 2013
14. **Guns, Germs, and Steel**, by Jared Diamond, published by Jonathon Cape, 1997
15. **Story of the Morning Star - The Children's Missionary Vessel** by Reverend Hiram Bingham, Jr., published by the American Board Missionary House, 1866
16. **The Naturalist and His 'Beautiful Islands',** by D. R. Lawrence, published by the ANU Press 2014
17. **Astride the Equator,** translated by Ursula Nixon from **Sous l'équateur de Pacifique** by Ernest Sabatier, Oxford University Press 1977

Chapter 8: Early Contact With Europeans

18. **Land-Travel And Seafaring: A Frivolous Record Of Twenty Years Wanderings** by H. R. McClure, published by Hutchinson & Co., 1925
19. **Fragments of Empire: A History of the Western Pacific High Commission 1877 – 1914**, by Deryck Scarr, published by C Hurst & Co, 1967
20. **Winding Up The British Empire in the Pacific Islands,** by W. David McIntyre, published by the Oxford University Press, 2014
21. **Health Survey of the Gilbert and Ellice Islands** by S.M. Lambert, of the Rockefeller Foundation, published by the Government Printer, Suva, 1924

PART 2

GILBERT AND ELLICE ISLANDS

Chapter 9.

PROTECTORATE TO COLONY 1892 - 1916

European claims to Oceania

Successive waves of European explorers crossed the Pacific from the 16th century: some set off from the west coast of South America, and some went eastwards from bases in the Indian Ocean. Between Magellan's pioneering voyage in 1565 and the beginning of the 19th century, the Pacific was transversed many times by Spanish, Dutch, English and French, and later American and German ships. They came in search of 'spice islands' like those they had already discovered to the west of New Guinea; to find the 'terra Australis' that the ancient Greeks had long ago predicted must exist in the Southern Hemisphere so as to 'balance' the earth; to further scientific studies, such as observation of eclipses; and because both Britain and France had more ships and captains than they needed for operational naval purposes after the naval arms race of the Seven Years' War, which had ended in 1763 (exploration was a way to employ them).

Eventually, although not in the Gilbert Islands, the British and their Australasian offshoots sought places in which to plant English settlers abroad, in support of the project described in *'The Expansion of England'* - a hugely influential book by the Cambridge historian Sir John Robert Seeley, which was published in 1893, building on Darwinian ideas: and which moulded the outlook of a generation.

By the year 1800:

- The Spanish East Indies had existed for more than two centuries: it principally comprised the Philippines, but also encompassed Palau, the Mariana Islands, and the Caroline Islands, all administered from Acapulco and later Manila. Guam and the Northern Mariana Islands were actually the only real outposts in the Pacific Ocean, as a resting stop for the galleons trekking between Acapulco and Manila; control of the other islands was nominal, and an early Spanish attempt to establish a colony in the Solomon islands was a failure

- The Dutch East India Company (VOC) in Batavia, in a 1660 treaty, had recognised the Sultanate of Tidore's supremacy over the Papuan people (although the Sultan did not appear to exercise much actual control on the island of New Guinea, as opposed to trading with them, this Treaty became the basis of the subsequent 19th century Dutch and eventually Indonesian claims to the island)
- The English had colonised Botany Bay as a place to which to transport the convicts that had previously been sent to the American colonies, which were by then independent and no longer willing to take them; in 1788, Captain Arthur Phillip's commission as Governor of New South Wales was extended to include New Zealand
- Whaling fleets had started to fan out through the Pacific (Chapter 8)
- The London Missionary Society had been in existence for five years, and it had established its first Pacific mission in Tahiti in 1797 (although the Roman Catholic Church would not arrive in Oceania for another 25 years).
- All of the island groups, if not yet all the individual islands, had been visited by exploring ships, and mapping was taking place.

The first 'British colony' in the Pacific was actually the settlement of Pitcairn by the Bounty mutineers in 1790. More official expansion was done tardily and reluctantly, and owed much more to expansionist ambitions of the colonists in Australia and New Zealand than any desire on the part of Britain to take over lands which were seen as profitless, and which were not near any vital sea route (although there was some fear of rival metropolitan powers seizing good harbours).

There was a humanitarian concern, in Britain at least, to 'protect' the islanders.

There was equally - if not more importantly, at least to the British Government - a desire to prevent the cost of wars similar to those into which Britain had been sucked by the privately organised settlers in New Zealand. These wars, at the peak of hostilities in the 1860s, necessitated the deployment of more than 18,000 British troops, supported by artillery, cavalry and local militia – against only about 4,000 Māori warriors. When Hawaii (already disrupted by missionaries and American adventurers) was briefly declared, at the request of its rulers, to be a British possession in 1843, the government in London had repudiated the arrangements.

Chapter 9: Protectorate to Colony 1892 - 1916

The French took possession of parts of Polynesia in the 1840s, and of New Caledonia in 1853. In 1856 the U.S. Congress passed *The Guano Islands Act*, which enabled citizens of the United States to take possession of any previously unclaimed islands containing guano deposits. More than 100 islands were claimed for the United States under this Act, including several of the Line and Phoenix Islands which subsequently became part of the GEIC; and also several of the Ellice Islands. US claims to several islands within the borders of present day Kiribati were only finally withdrawn in 1980.

The US established consulates in Fiji in 1844 (the British not until 1858), and Samoa in 1856.

The map below was published in 1859, and still shows most of the islands in the central ocean, including Tungaru, as not being under the control of any European power, except perhaps a tentacle to Butaritari.

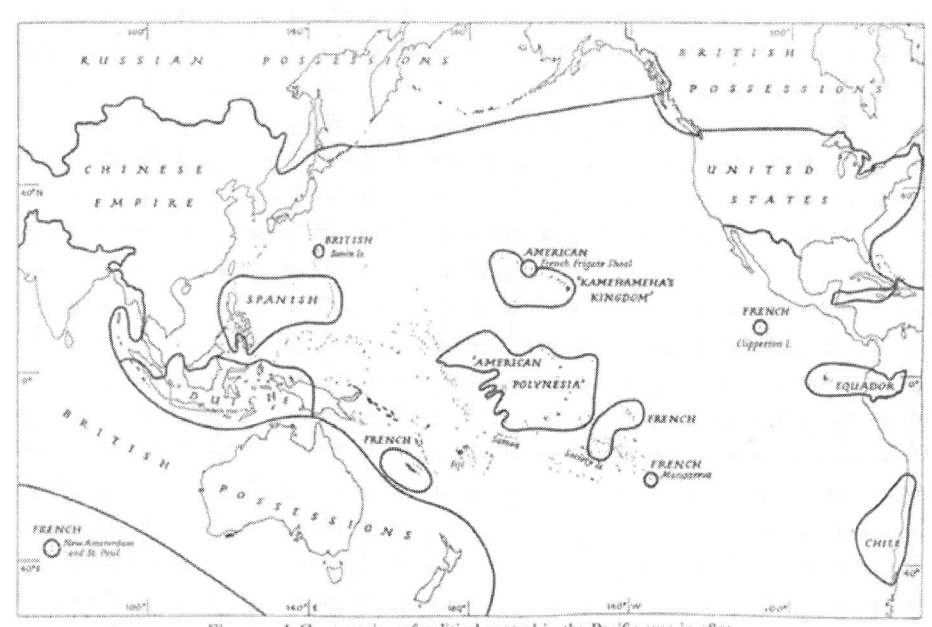

Fig. 92. A German view of political control in the Pacific area in 1859

In Fiji, in the mid - 19th century, private interests had begun seriously to disturb the balance of power between local rulers in a manner similar to that of New Zealand. An offer to cede sovereignty by the chief of the island of Bau was repudiated by Britain in 1863; but the rise in the price of cotton during the US Civil War, and the brief Fiji gold rush in the 1870s, led to a large influx of adventurers and would-be settlers who demanded annexation. The deed

Chapter 9: Protectorate to Colony 1892 - 1916

of Cession was eventually signed in 1873 [72]; and was this time accepted by Britain.

Despite calls from interests in both Australia and New Zealand, both private and governmental, the Colonial Office refused to consider further formal acquisitions in the region after that of Fiji. The British Parliament did however in 1872 pass the *Pacific Islanders Protection Act*; and in 1882, *The Pacific Islanders Act*.

The situation came to a head in the 1880s, as the newly unified German Empire began to look for its *'place in the sun'*. Germany enthusiastically sought out the last unclaimed territories in both Africa and the Pacific, including the Samoan Islands (albeit disputed with the US) and the unexplored north-east quarter of New Guinea, with its adjacent islands. Germany bought the Caroline Islands and the Northern Mariana Islands, other than Guam, from Spain. Palau, at the time considered part of the Carolines, was also occupied by them.

Whatever the wishes of the local 'Whites' (as they had started to describe themselves), and unlike in Africa (where more substantial commercial interests were at stake), the metropolitan European powers were however anxious not to fall out with each other over *'a few unprofitable islands'*. In 1884, therefore, they came to an agreement as to *'spheres of influence'*, whereby: Samoa was divided between the US and Germany; the island of New Guinea was divided between Holland, Germany and Britain; and Germany acquired, supposedly, all of Micronesia other than Guam. Hawaii, Guam, and various Line Islands became US possessions. French sovereignty over New Caledonia, the Wallis and Futuna Islands, and 'French' Polynesia was confirmed, as was British influence over the Solomons, Fiji, Tonga and several other smaller Polynesian island groups, including the Ellice Islands. The New Hebrides became a shared British-French Condominium.

In 1886, the British Empire and the German Empire made two further and formal bilateral declarations about the spheres of interest:

---

[72] According to the 1930 History of Britain *'1066 and All That'*, the annexation was one of the loyal attempts to amuse the Queen, which had led to a wave of *Justifiable Wars* and *Subsequent Annexations*. None of these had amused her. When news was brought to the Queen that the Fiji Islands had been annexed *'by the desire of the inhabitants'*, however, *'Her Majesty's lip was observed to tremble'*...

Chapter 9: Protectorate to Colony 1892 - 1916

- *Declaration between the Governments of Great Britain and the German Empire relating to the Demarcation of the British and German Spheres of Influence in the Western Pacific; April 6, 1886*
- *Declaration between the Governments of Great Britain and the German Empire relating to the Reciprocal Freedom of Trade and Commerce in the British and German Possessions and Protectorates in the Western Pacific; April 10, 1886.*

The declaration was valid for the area between the 15th parallel of north latitude and the 30th parallel of south latitude, and between the 165th meridian of longitude west and the 130th meridian of longitude east. The border between the spheres of interest started near Mitre Rock in North East New Guinea, on the 8th parallel of south latitude, and then followed a zig-zagging set of seven points with defined longitudes and latitudes. The area to the north and west of this line was to be a German, and the area in the south and east a British, *'sphere of influence'*. (The islands of Samoa, Tonga and Niue were excluded, as were *'areas under control of other Great Powers'*).

It was through these declarations that the Gilbert Islands, although a part of Micronesia (which it had been agreed in principle would become German) were finally allocated to the British [73].

The creation of the Western Pacific High Commission

The Foreign Office in Britain quickly thereafter recognised the need for an extended consular system in the Pacific, as from *'the very fact of our assumption of the Sovereignty of the Fijis'*, they forecast, there would be an *'increased demand for labour ... Abuses are certain to arise'*. At the same time the Colonial Office was subject to increasing Australasian pressure to adopt a comprehensive, and for them preferably annexationist, policy for the islands.

---

[73] Either this was simply an accidental mistake in the drawing of these lines across the Ocean, or, more probably, it had not yet been realised by the 'Great Powers' that the I Tungaru people were Micronesian rather than Polynesian – the Illustrated London News account of their annexation (page 169 below) certainly describes them as 'Polynesians'; and even in E. C. Eliot's book *Broken Atoms*, which was published in 1938 (although it was based on his experiences of the GEIC more than 20 years earlier), he states quite categorically that the Gilbertese *'are pure Polynesians, as distinct from the Melanesians and Micronesians'*.

Chapter 9: Protectorate to Colony 1892 - 1916

This resulted in the creation of a Western Pacific High Commission, located in Fiji but separate from its administration. The first Governor of Fiji and High Commissioner, Sir Arthur Hamilton-Gordon, was (at least until he stood to make a fortune from Banaba, see Chapter 10) personally much more sympathetic to the islanders than he was to the 'Whites'; he strongly argued that he should also assume the mantle of *'Her Majesty's Principal Consul or Consul General to the Islands of the South Pacific ... with such Vice-Consuls as may be required by the extent of the area to be supervised and by the nature of the duties to be discharged'*.

After an extensive bureaucratic tussle between departments in Britain, it was agreed that Gordon would be *both* a High Commissioner reporting to the Colonial Office *and* a Consul-General reporting to the Foreign Office; the terms of his remit were finally promulgated in 1878. They were sufficiently vague to be subject to conflicting interpretations; but it *was* explicit that the High Commissioner did not have jurisdiction over either non-British traders and recruiters, or islanders. The Pacific Islanders Protection Act of 1872 had expressly denied any intention to *'derogate from the rights of the tribes or people'*. Disputes with islanders were to be dealt with as a matter of acts of war between *'sovereign nations'*, thus also involving the Admiralty in the tussle (since it fell to the Australian Squadron of the Royal Navy to conduct these acts of war).

Most of these bureaucratic struggles, by good fortune, passed by the affairs of the Tungaru people, unlike in some other territories.

Towards the end of the 1880s, however, pressures arose to establish actual control of the islands that the Anglo-German Agreement of 1886 had allocated to Britain.

In February 1888, Sir John Bates Thurston, who had already served Fiji in a variety of capacities (including as Premier of the Kingdom of Viti before the islands were ceded to the United Kingdom) succeeded as Governor of Fiji and High Commissioner for the Western Pacific. Thurston was an unusual character who had, *inter alia*, been a mate on a vessel in the Gilberts in the 1860s (see p. 133), and had also spent eighteen months stranded in a Samoan village after a shipwreck. In his eleven years as High Commissioner he was to have a profound effect on the way that the new protectorates in the Solomons, Ellice, and Gilberts were administered by the High Commission.

Chapter 9: Protectorate to Colony 1892 - 1916

In 1889, Thurston recommended to the Colonial Office the establishment of a new deputy High Commissioner to be responsible, inter alia, for the Gilbert Islands and the Ellice Islands (this person was to be based at Makira in the Solomon Islands). This idea was ignored.

In 1891 the German Foreign Office itself urged Britain to declare a Protectorate; and implicitly threatened that they would themselves do so, despite the 1886 Declarations, if it was necessary to stop the Americans from establishing a Treaty with the King of Butaritari, which they believed was imminent [74]. The Germans were concerned that the U. S. would cut off Gilbertese recruitment for their plantations in Samoa (page 115) in favour of Hawaii.

The Colonial Office at first demurred, but then realised that there would be a violent reaction from Australasia if they let the Germans go ahead; and concluded that:

> *'Tearing up the settlement with Germany which grew out of the intrusion of Germany into New Guinea cannot for a moment be entertained. The Australasian Colonies would look upon it as a breach of faith portending surrender in all directions to Foreign Powers'.*

They were especially concerned that the French might take the opportunity of British redrawing of the 1884 agreements to seize the Solomon Islands, which would have caused an even bigger outcry in Australia.

The Foreign Office's concurrence with this view was also based on considerations of higher matters: they were anxious to have German support against the French objections to the continued British presence in Egypt, for which the declaration of the Gilbert Islands Protectorate would be a *quid-pro-quo*.

---

[74] The US had appointed Adolph Rick as its official Commercial Agent at Butaritari on May 25, 1888, in order to protect U.S. trade in the region. Rick did in fact try to persuade the *Uea* (who he had taken on a trip to San Francisco) to reject the British flag in favour of America, but in the end he had little support for this from his own Government, who also thought the Gilberts unprofitable.

Chapter 9: Protectorate to Colony 1892 - 1916

Declaration of the Protectorate

In January 1892 the Admiralty was thus requested to raise the British flag over the Gilbert Islands, and in September of that year the request was extended to include the Ellice Islands as well [75]. Captain Davis, R.N., of *H.M.S. Royalist* was sent through a secret memo in April of that year from the Commander-in-Chief, H.M. Ships in Australia, to carry out the mission.

Davis set off from Suva on the 13th of May and arrived at Tabiteuea (by way of Nukulaelae and Vaitupu in the Ellice islands) on the 24th of May, when he *'dressed ship in honour of the Anniversary of Her Majesty's birthday, and at noon fired a Royal Salute'*.

He intended first to visit Abemama, which, with Butaritari, was viewed as having a government with whom to negotiate. Lying off the island, he sent a letter to the King on the 25th May to announce his purpose; but first he needed to go to Maiana, to pick up *'the best and most trustworthy Interpreter in the Group'*, Bob Corrie, who had personally been recommended to him by Thurston.

At noon on the 27th May, Captain Davis reported that:

> *'At noon that day I proceeded in a boat with a party of seamen and marines for the King's village which is 6 or 7 miles across the lagoon from Entrance Island and not visible from the ship. Having ascertained from Mr Corrie and other traders on Islands with which I had communicated that they were unaware that any Foreign Power laid claim to the Gilbert Group, I, in compliance with your secret memo of April 22nd 1892, explained my mission to the King and his council in the Maniaba [sic] or Meeting House in the presence of some 300 or 400 natives and having read the Proclamation declaring a British Protectorate over the Gilbert Group from that date, I hoisted the Union Jack on the King's Flagstaff with the customary honours […]*

---

[75] However, Foreign and Colonial Offices *did not consult the Treasury beforehand*. There is a wonderful file in the British National Archive in Kew, with the Treasury vociferously objecting to the acquisition of these *'worthless islands'* and only very reluctantly accepting them in the end, with the proviso that they *'should never cost Her Majesty's Government one penny'*.

Chapter 9: Protectorate to Colony 1892 - 1916

> *'I handed the Proclamation to the King to be kept in his charge and in the Missionary's care, I left a notice for the information of Traders concerning the prohibition of the sale of arms etc. and supplying of intoxicating liquors to natives […]*
>
> *'That particular constitution of the Gilbert Islands with no less than 13 different Governments, necessitated in my opinion a repetition in the other 12 islands of the ceremony performed at Apamama [sic].'*

The *Illustrated London News* added to this sparse account some months later, on 10th September 1892 (together with sketches made by an 'Officer of HMS Royalist'):

> *'The natives were very much pleased at being placed under the protection of Queen Victoria, and asked many questions about England … the formal annexation of these islands which could not be effectually controlled by the British High Commissioner residing in distant Fiji, will certainly be beneficial to the natives, affording them protection from kidnapping and various other lawless outrages too easily practised in such remote parts of the world'.*

In fact, Captain Davis reported that their chief enquiry and concern about Queen Victoria was whether (unlike the missionaries) she would allow them to sing and dance.

HMS *Royalist* duly visited the other twelve islands (Kuria/Aranuka and Makin, being considered dependencies of Abemama and Butaritari respectively, were not visited until later) and performed the same ceremony.

Captain Davis demanded on each island that all firearms should be collected and made available to him on his return. He also adjudicated on disputes between the Gilbertese and Traders, fining several of the latter as well as demanding better treatment of them by the *Ueas* of the northern islands, from whom he also collected fines levied two years earlier by HMS *Miranda*. He intercepted the *Monserrat* at Abaiang, which was recruiting labour for plantations in Guatemala; he disapproved but as he had *'no orders to prevent it I should not disallow it'*. At Abaiang he also insisted that the *Uea* try one Tantarabe for the murder of Ah Sam, a British subject (he himself having no jurisdiction, as the murder had preceded the Protectorate); the Uea and his council finding Tantarabe guilty, he was shot in Captain Davis' presence. In

Tabiteuea he finally expelled the Hawaiian missionary Kapui, who had been responsible for the massacre of pagans ten years previously (page 118).

By 18th June he was able to discharge Bob Corrie back at Maiana, his primary mission completed. He then took a side trip to the Marshall Islands, where he visited the German Imperial Commissioner, returning to the Gilberts on 3rd July with the intention of taking away all the firearms which he had ordered to be collected, as well as to judge further disputes between traders and islanders, and a few missionaries. In some cases (notably Tarawa) this entailed his marines undertaking house-to-house searches for guns which had been hidden away. *HMS Royalist* continued to visit and revisit islands (each twice and some three times) in the Gilberts until 27th July; and then left to call at several of the Ellice Islands, arriving back in Fiji in early August.

Davis' actions were an odd mix of strict legalities and arbitrary judgements; but his account is remarkable both for its acuity and its thoroughness. He subsequently wrote a detailed description of each island, on which I have drawn in subsequent Chapters.

Administrative convenience: joining of the Ellice Islands to the Gilberts

Technically a British Protectorate, such as that just declared was *'a territory which was not formally annexed: but in which, by treaty, grant or other lawful means, the British Crown had ultimate power and jurisdiction'*. It fell to the High Commissioner in Fiji to work out what in practice this meant for the newly acquired Gilbert Islands, bearing in mind the stricture of HM Treasury that this new possession must not *'cost Her Majesty's Government one penny'*.

Once the Protectorate had been declared (and one also over the Ellice Islands on 10th September, by Captain HWS Gibson on *HMS Curacoa*), Sir John Thurston started a protracted correspondence with the Colonial Office and Treasury in Britain on the nature and cost of its administration. He was eventually given permission to appoint a Resident at a salary of £500 a year, so long as this sum and all expenses were covered from local revenue. The Resident was to rely on trading vessels and Royal Navy patrols to get about exercising his new responsibilities, as no official money was forthcoming for his transport.

Chapter 9: Protectorate to Colony 1892 - 1916

Thurston was also empowered to negotiate 'treaties' under which the island governments would give the Resident jurisdiction over all Europeans living in the two groups, Ellice and Gilbert. In 1892 Thurston appointed Charles Swayne (a Stipendary Magistrate in Fiji, and an old friend) as Resident for the Ellice; but he resolved himself to revisit the Gilberts, which he had last seen some thirty years earlier, in part to appoint local tax collectors. He gave this interview to the *Auckland Star* during a brief visit to New Zealand beforehand:

> *'Sir John stated that one of his objects in coming to Auckland was to recuperate before going in May next via Fiji to the Gilbert and Ellice Groups for the purpose of establishing a settled form of administration, and arranging for a regular connection between these islands and Fiji. The islands are about twenty in number, and consequently it will take a good deal of labour in visiting them all. Sir John intends to establish Courts of Law there and hopes to elaborate some plan for the more perfect commercial development of the islands, and for the amelioration of the condition of the people'.*

In Australia, *The Queenslander* put the purpose of the trip more succinctly:

> *'[Where] no white trader's services were available some influential nigger was installed to collect the one dollar per adult male that was meant to support the British administration of the islands'.*

On this trip, Thurston privately lamented the changes he observed in the Gilberts since his voyage to them on the *James* thirty years before [76]. He blamed the *'rotten pestilential civilisation ... [changing] old time cleanliness to modern mongrel civilisation and dirt'*. He also changed his view to one where the Gilberts and the Ellice should be administered as a single entity (previously he had recommended that the Ellice be joined to Rotuma); and extended Swayne's remit to cover the Gilberts.

---

[76] Thus becoming the first of many Europeans to hark back to better days and happier people in the 'real Gilberts' of their youth, a charge to which I must also hold up my hand!

Chapter 9: Protectorate to Colony 1892 - 1916

The Ellice Islands

The Ellice Islands (now Tuvalu) comprise three reef islands and six true atolls spread out between the latitude of 5° to 10° south and longitude of 176° to 180°, to the south of the Gilberts. They were even smaller: the total land area of Tuvalu is only 26 square kilometres (10 sq. mi).

The eight permanently inhabited islands (a ninth, Niulakita, was only sporadically inhabited) had been settled from Samoa and Tonga (possibly by way of Tokelau and the Wallis and Futuna Islands) and spoke a mutually intelligible Polynesian language. Before European contact the islands had periodically been raided from Tungaru, but only on the island of Nui had substantial intermarriage taken place. Thus, although to the incoming administrators they seemed superficially similar to the Gilbertese, the Ellice islanders had a number of significant differences, both traditionally, and in adoption of 'western' traits in the 19th century.

The most significant of these were:
- The islanders were undoubted 'pure' Polynesians, except on Nui; their language was not mutually intelligible with that spoken by the Gilbertese
- Populations were much smaller – the overall population at the time of contact was less than 3,000; numbers were traditionally kept down through abortion and infanticide (although there is some evidence that the numbers had once been higher)
- The climate was similar to that of the Gilberts, but the Ellice islands were more likely to suffer from occasional hurricanes; further, the Ellice were wetter and generally more fertile than the Gilberts, permitting for example the cultivation of taro (*pulaka, Calladium esculentum*) as a staple crop rather than *bwabai*. *Pulaka* cultivation had high status. Bigger trees also meant that their canoes were paddle-driven dug-outs rather than built to the Gilbertese design
- They were equally dependent on marine resources from the reefs as in the Gilberts, but wild birds were also an important source of protein. Deep-sea fishing was generally of lesser importance, but fleets would go out periodically to catch flying fish (of the family *Beloniformes*) and sometimes bonito

- Society was economically as well as socially stratified: *'those of higher birth had to ensure they had more possessions than the ordinary people'*, and commoners acted as servants
- The economy was different: specific families had tasks and skills which they traditionally performed on behalf of their island community as a whole, rather than the much less differentiated activities of the *kaaingas* in the Gilberts
- Governance was traditionally by *aliki*, hereditary chiefs, although by the time of the Protectorate their power had in large part passed to Samoan LMS Pastors, who in places vigorously exploited their position for personal economic gain. The Roman Catholic church never gained a foothold in the Ellice, so there was religious conformity across the group
- Blackbirding and the labour trade had had a proportionately greater impact on the Ellice, especially in the southernmost islands.

The Ellice people were soon regarded by incoming European administrators as more *'receptive'* than the Gilbertese to western influences. At a time when it was still acceptable to use such language, the official Gilbert and Ellice Islands report to the UK Parliament for 1916 declared:

'The Gilbert islander is not a model domestic servant; his talents are adapted to sterner conditions. Though he is faithful and shows much desire to please, his forgetfulness and lack of method seldom prove amenable to teaching. As a policeman under conditions of strict discipline, he shines: without unremitting 'nursing' he is a failure.

'The Ellice boy... makes a better house servant. He is quicker to learn than a Gilbert islander ... as a personal servant he is ready, hard-working and retentive, but too often dishonest. Cases of dishonesty among Gilbertese houseboys are exceedingly rare'.

Although later less openly expressed, such views persisted; and even in the 1950s such official reports would commend the *'adaptability'* of the Ellice people, by perceived contrast with the Gilbertese who were categorised as resistant *'to the effects of white civilisation'* [77].

---

[77] The Ellice islanders certainly came strongly to believe that most, if not all, Europeans secretly favoured them over the Gilbertese – see note on page 348 below.

Chapter 9: Protectorate to Colony 1892 - 1916

For better or worse, the Ellice were to be joined to the Gilberts for the next eighty-two years; but for the first fifty of those years, a strict quarantine was maintained between the two groups, for medical reasons. The only real pre-WW II contact between the two peoples took place on Tarawa and Banaba, in the colonial HQ and the phosphate workings.

Establishment of systems for indirect rule

Thurston modelled the administration of the new Protectorate largely on what was already in place. This - above all else - met the criterion of cheapness, and in particular it required fewer Colonial officials: as has been seen above, economy was – again above all else - to be the watchword of the new administration. Thus:

> 'It ...appeared my duty to avail myself of such organisation as the natives, with the aid of Missionaries, had themselves set up, and to improve it from time to time as the people advanced in civilisation and as other circumstances would permit'.

He thus made the (in some cases, supposed) *Uea* of each island in the northern Gilberts (down to Abemama) responsible for good order, with the assistance of *kaubure*, who were councillors elected from each *mwaneaba* district. In the southern Gilberts, this duty was given to the *kaubure* alone.

Magistrates, Scribes, and police were appointed on each island. The Scribe was responsible for the 'Island Fund', into which all taxes and fines were payable.

For the Gilbertese and Ellice islanders there was thus to be no concept of an overarching, rather than Island, government; but in 1894 a unified set of *Native Laws of the Gilbert Islands Protectorate* was issued by the High Commissioner's Office. It was based on a codified and then rationalised set of traditional customs prepared by Charles Swayne, the first Resident Commissioner. A separate but similar document was prepared for the Ellice Islands.

A capitation tax was to be paid – not in money, but in copra - by the islanders, and various taxes were imposed on European residents and on trading vessels. These were intended to produce a more than sufficient income to meet the expenses of the Protectorate government.

Chapter 9: Protectorate to Colony 1892 - 1916

The first Resident Commissioners

Charles Swayne

Charles Swayne had spent more than 20 years as a Magistrate at Lomaloma and then in Lau in Fiji before being seconded to the Protectorate, where he spent the next few years in a peripatetic way, moving from island to island by whatever commercial or naval vessels he could find and often having to go from one island to another via Suva or Sydney.

Initially, he had two sets of problems:

- Drought in the southern Gilberts made collection of the new capitation tax impossible without causing enormous additional hardship; the costs of the Protectorate would thus need to be (and were) borne by the High Commission
- Claims from traders, especially on Butaritari, the local headquarters of all four commercial firms with interests in the Pacific: Wightman Brothers and Crawford & Co. of San Francisco; the Jaluit Gesellschaft based in the Marshall Islands; and On Chong & Co. of Sydney. These had tempted the Gilbertese into a 'clip' system whereby goods were advanced - on credit - in return for a lien on stated coconut groves, usually at a profit of several hundred percent for the traders.

The latter situation was resolved by placing a *tabu* on sales of copra until enough had been collected to settle claims allowed by the Resident; the former just reinforced the suspicions of the Colonial Office and Treasury that acquisition of the Gilberts had been an error.

Swayne also found that the democratic traditions of the Southern Gilberts were so strong that the *kaubure* were reluctant to appoint Magistrates. He thus proceeded to break the 'indirect rule' system at its outset, by appointing the Magistrates himself.

He also deported the *Ueas* of both Marakei and Tarawa, to Fiji and Rotuma respectively, for insufficient zeal in keeping order.

Two years later, the drought had eased and the capitation taxes had made the Protectorate able to pay for itself; in 1895 a decision was taken to erect a Residency at Betio, on Tarawa. The following year Swayne was succeeded by a new Resident Commissioner, W. Telfer Campbell, who was to remain in the Protectorate until 1909.

William Telfer Campbell

Campbell was an aggressive autocrat, intolerant of the slightest opposition; and an unrelenting Orangeman, who had started his career in the Royal Irish Constabulary. It was on his watch that large quantities of high grade mineral phosphate were discovered on Nauru and Banaba (see below) and there is a suspicion that he was - at the least - complicit in the unequal bargain made for its exploitation.

Campbell was twice the subject of official enquiries into high-handedness, brutality, and the use of forced labour. In 1901 complaints began to reach England of misgovernment in the Gilbert Islands. The matter was mentioned several times in the Press, was the subject of questions in Parliament, but was temporarily set at rest by the promise of an inquiry by the Colonial Office: but, according to *Modern Buccaneers in the West Pacific*: *'All, however, the Colonial Office appears to have done was to request the incriminated officials to send in a confidential report on themselves and to accept this as a complete answer and refutation of the charges'*.

Complaints continued from missionaries, other Europeans and natives, concerning W. Telfer Campbell's *'conduct of affairs legislative, administrative, and judicial; in particular of the great amount of forced labour exacted from the Gilbert Islanders, the cutting down of their food trees for timber, the unjust imprisonments, the numerous floggings, the unfair system of taxation, the taking away of land from natives, the seizure of foodstuffs for taxes even in the time of famine, and the suffering, sickness, and death which this conduct brought about. The Aborigines Protection Society and others brought further pressure to bear till at length the Colonial Office instructed the High Commissioner, Sir E. im Thurn* [Governor of Fiji 1904–1910], *to attend in person and hold an inquiry in this part of his jurisdiction'*.

This visit also absolved Campbell (but the Colonial Office refused to publish it). According to the New Era account 'News from the Islands, indeed, shows that his Excellency's visit of inquiry was farcical, that he had shielded Mr. Campbell and his officials, and had really refused to hold investigation into their conduct'.

Yet another enquiry was conducted in 1909, by Arthur Mahaffy. This came about because members of Parliament in the UK had had:

Chapter 9: Protectorate to Colony 1892 - 1916

'Their attention drawn to the wrongs in the Gilberts, and by certain signs of interest it appeared that an adjournment of the House might be moved to raise the matter. The Colonial Office did not altogether ignore the agitation; for, before the year 1908 had closed Mr. Campbell and some of his officials were removed from the Gilberts. Not only so, but a secret edict against the flogging and ill-treatment of natives was evidently sent out, and a further direct tax which Mr. Campbell, in order to increase the Revenue, had proposed to place on the already overtaxed cocoanuts of the natives, was cancelled.

'The private company, however, was not required to contribute out of its immense profits on the phosphates; the money was taken from the Imperial Exchequer. The Lords Commissioners of the Treasury were approached and they agreed that the small royalty on the phosphates paid to the Imperial Exchequer should, after April 1, 1909 be credited to the Gilbert Protectorate Funds.

'Declining an independent investigation and retaining all the Inquiry in its own hands, the Colonial Office in the beginning of 1909 sent down the Assistant High Commissioner, Mr. Mahaffy, to the Gilberts. The principal complaints had been made against the Resident Commissioner, Mr. W. Telfer Campbell, the Assistant Resident Commissioner, Mr. Cogswell, and an official not on the regular staff, a Mr. Murdoch [sic]. Mr. Campbell and Mr. Cogswell had just been removed from the group, but Mr. Murdoch was still there and was taken round by Mr. Mahaffy to assist him in his inspection.

'Strangely enough Mr. Mahaffy himself had also personal reasons for wishing the truth suppressed ; for he had commenced his career in the Colonial Service as a junior official under Mr. W. Telfer Campbell in the Gilberts; and before being on duty a year had involved himself in an affair about a reprieved native, who was shot. It is this Mr. Mahaffy, however, whose general report on the Gilberts has been published in a White Paper by the Colonial Office as an official refutation of specific charges which the Colonial Office has never yet been able to show any attempt properly to investigate.'

In fact, from reading the White Paper it is clear that the first concern of Mahaffy was not the conduct of Campbell - but the finances of the Protectorate. He was accompanied around the GEIP by a Mr. Best who had

Chapter 9: Protectorate to Colony 1892 - 1916

been one of the earliest appointments to the Protectorate - as an Accountant. Mahaffy reported that Best had found *'that in no single instance was any deficiency in the money detected, a circumstance which, I submit, redounds greatly to the credit of the natives concerned. The fact is more remarkable in view of the very short and irregular visits of inspection which have been possible under the Protectorate Government ... since the proclamation of the Protectorate, I very much doubt whether any Government official has ever spent twenty-four hours in one visit to any island in that Group* [78]*'*.

The White Paper continues with effusive praise of Campbell:

> *'It would be difficult to praise too highly the work done by the late Resident Commissioner ... the islands are kept in the most perfect order; trees are constantly being planted, land reclaimed, and the wants of the natives are ministered to by every means which the physical peculiarities of these extraordinary islands render possible .... I have not heard a single complaint against the incidence of taxation ... the poorly paid uneducated official does his duty well and truly and in the case of those who have charge of considerable amounts of money with an honesty as remarkable as it is wholly admirable'.*

The issues of brutality, floggings and forced labour are simply not mentioned.

Campbell had been transferred to Tonga, where he quickly fell out with the King and was forced to *'withdraw from service in the Pacific'*. (He resurfaced two years later in Africa, as Governor of The Gambia).

Cinderellas of the Empire concludes that:

> *'Swayne laid the foundations for colonial rule; his successor, William Telfer Campbell, constructed upon them an edifice of control that remained virtually untouched until the 1930s'.*

This edifice, and its implications for the Gilbertese people, is the subject of Chapter 11.

---

[78] Mahaffy notes elsewhere that no government official at all had visited the Ellice islands in the previous eight years.

Arthur William Mahaffy

Mahaffy was another Irishman, born in Howth, and educated at both Trinity College Dublin and Oxford. After a career in the British Army, he joined the Western Pacific High Commission and in 1909 became Acting Resident Commissioner, when he was also responsible for investigating the conduct of Campbell. In 1910 he was appointed as Assistant to the Western Pacific High Commissioner. He eventually became administrator of Dominica.

John Quayle-Dickson

Having served with distinction as an Intelligence Officer during the Boer War, Quayle-Dickson assumed a number of important roles in the field of Native Affairs in South Africa. He was the Resident Commissioner in the Gilbert and Ellice Islands Protectorate between 1909 and 1913, when he was removed and demoted to Colonial Secretary of the Falkland Islands.

Considered a *'haughty old man from the Veldt'* by some, he struggled to strike a balance between giving genuine support and technical advice to the local Banaban inhabitants concerning the new interest in phosphate mining taking place on the island, and promoting the commercial interests of the Crown and other agents. This balanced view caused much displeasure to the British Phosphate Company and the Colonial Office. After being dismissed also from the Falkland Islands [79], he became Sub-Commandant of the Great War P.O.W. & Aliens Detention Camp at Knockaloe, in the Isle of Man.

While Dickson has received some strong criticism (especially in '*Cinderellas of the Empire*') for administrative failures and extravagance, he does appear to have had unusually progressive attitudes towards assisting and protecting the long-term natural and economic interests of the local inhabitants.

In '*Consuming Ocean Island*' K. M. Teaiwa writes that both Dickson and his successor E. C. Elliott had *'challenged the British government and the Company on what they saw as a very raw deal for Banabans.'*

---

[79] I have a suspicion that Quayle-Dickson was the 'Correspondent' of the New Age Journal article (see further Reading) and that this was also suspected by the Colonial Office and was the cause of his demise in the Falklands.

Chapter 9: Protectorate to Colony 1892 - 1916

Edward Carlyon Eliot [80]

Compared to the establishment figures who had preceded him, Eliot was something of a rolling stone. His brother was Charles Eliot, who was Commissioner for British East Africa and later British Ambassador to Japan; but Edward had in turns been a 'cowboy', and then a railway employee, in Argentina and Uruguay; an overseer at a sugar plantation, and then a junior official in Guyana – where he became assistant to the Government's *Protector of the Indians* and acquired a reputation for being *'good at negotiating with natives'*. This experience resulted in his next three posts: in the Gold Coast, Tobago, and eventually the Gilbert and Ellice islands.

He was to spend seven years in the Pacific, including the period of the First World War, and oversaw the change of the Gilbert and Islands from Protectorate to Colony. He was then sent to Uganda, and finally as Administrator to Dominica, where he spent eight happy years and was still courageous enough to take up the cause of the original inhabitants of the island, the Caribs, against the 'Whites' and the Colonial Office!

Transition to Colony

A Protectorate (see above) was *legally* defined as a state, with its own sovereignty (or in the Gilberts 14 states) but *under the protection of another country*. A Colony was a territory *governed* by another country; and crucially for the Pacific Phosphate Company, had no independent sovereignty. Originally British colonies had been ruled directly by the Colonial Office in London; others were ruled indirectly through local rulers supervised by British 'advisers', who worked behind the scenes and could exercise a veto power. At the turn of the 20th century, many of the West African colonies (the system had been pioneered in Nigeria) were ruled indirectly. As the British Prime minister Lord Salisbury had explained the idea in 1890:

> *'The condition of a protected dependency is more acceptable to the half civilized races, and more suitable for them than direct dominion. It is cheaper, simpler, less wounding to their self-esteem, gives them more career as public officials, and spares of unnecessary contact with white men'.*

---

[80] In my view Eliot was one of the best of the British people to rule the Gilberts, and it is sad that this has so seldom been acknowledged in the sources. It is time he was appreciated.

Chapter 9: Protectorate to Colony 1892 - 1916

The motive of the Colonial Office for changing the status of the Gilbert and Ellice Islands was primarily that the Banabans - by now very wary of the Pacific Phosphate Company - were refusing to grant further leases to the Company, but could not legally be coerced into doing so, since in strict legal terms Banaba was still an independent nation.

It had also become 'convenient' further to extend the boundaries of the territory to include the Union Islands (now Tokelau).

Broken Atoms describes the transition:

> 'If the outside world took any interest in the matter during a world war – which is indeed doubtful – they might have seen a very small paragraph in the Times that "at the special request of the natives of the Gilbert, Ellice and Union Groups His Majesty had been graciously pleased to transform these Groups into the Colony of the Gilbert and Ellice Islands".
>
> 'Needless to say the natives had not the foggiest idea of the difference between the terms "Protectorate" and "Colony", neither had they in any way suggested the change of status ... "at the special request" is as humorous as many of our diplomatic modes of progression'.

The Union and Line Islands

The then called Union Islands (originally, and now, called Tokelau) consist of three tropical coral atolls (Atafu, Nukunonu and Fakaofo), with a combined land area of 10 km2 (4 sq. mi). Tokelau lies north of Samoa, east of Tuvalu, and south of the Phoenix Islands.

They had been declared a British Protectorate in 1889. The population was (then) very small, as the atolls had been almost completely depopulated by Peruvian-based blackbirders.

They were not long combined with the GEIC; Tokelau was removed and placed under the jurisdiction of the Governor-General of New Zealand just nine years later, in 1925. [81]

Three islands of the Northern Line Islands were also at this time included within the new colony: those then known as Washington and Fanning (added

---

[81] A District Officer had been posted there for three years after 1916, but the GEIC had little bandwidth to take much interest in the Tokelau Islands and they were largely left to their own devices over the period.

Chapter 9: Protectorate to Colony 1892 - 1916

in 1916); and Christmas Island (added in 1919). None of the three had any indigenous inhabitants. In 1902 Fanning had become an important wireless station between Canada and Australia, a part of the 'All Red Line'; and was the only part of the GEIC to see action in WWI when the cable was briefly cut by a German raid.

Chapter 9: Protectorate to Colony 1892 - 1916

Further Reading

1. **Fragments of Empire: A History of the Western Pacific High Commission 1877 – 1914**, by Deryck Scarr, published by C Hurst & Co, 1967
2. **Winding Up The British Empire in the Pacific Islands,** by W. David McIntyre, published by the Oxford University Press, 2014
3. **The Proceedings of HMS Royalist**, mimeograph published by the Tungavalu Society, 1976
4. **The Illustrated London News**, 10 September 1892
5. **Tuvalu – a History,** edited by Hugh Laracy, published by the Institute of Pacific Studies and Ministry of Social Services, Government of Tuvalu, 1983
6. **The Material Culture of Tuvalu**, by Gerd Koch, originally published in German in 1961, translated by Guy Slatter and republished by the Institute of Pacific Studies, 1981
7. **Tungaru Traditions**, edited by H. C. and H.E. Maude, Institute of Pacific Studies, University of the South Pacific, 1994
8. **Report of Mr Arthur Mahaffy: Visit to the Gilbert and Ellice Islands 1909**, presented to both Houses of Parliament by Command of His Majesty and published by HM Stationery Office, 1910
9. **Modern Buccaneers in the West Pacific**, by a Correspondent, published by New Age Magazine, 1913.
10. **Broken Atoms,** by E. C. Eliot, published by Geoffrey Bles, 1938
11. **Kiribati: Aspects of History,** multiple authors and editors, published jointly by the Institute of Pacific Studies and the Ministry of Education, Training, and Culture, 1979
12. **Cinderellas of the Empire**, by Dr. Barrie Macdonald, published by the Institute of Pacific Studies, 1982

Chapter 10.

THE PACIFIC PHOSPHATE COMPANY 1902 - 1920

The discovery of phosphate deposits

A detailed story about what is actually a chapter of accidents, which resulted in the Pacific Phosphate Company's enormous dividends, is set out in *'The Phosphateers'* (see Further Reading below).

To modern eyes, and to at least some at the time, none of the self-described 'Christian Gentlemen' involved come out well: the whole enterprise was based on blatant violations of the eighth, ninth and tenth Commandments to which they professed to adhere [82]. It involved serious conflicts of public and private interests, even by contemporary standards.

Nevertheless, it needs to be set in the context of the time:

- In the *Descent of Man* (published in 1871) Darwin had applied natural selection to humanity, that the *'highest races and the lowest savages'* differ in *'moral disposition ... and in intellect'*. Darwin went on to argue that *'From the remotest times successful tribes have supplanted other tribes. ... At the present day civilised nations are everywhere supplanting barbarous nations'*. This view became common currency in Europe and the US in the late 19th century and early 20th century
- It was widely believed that these *'inferior'* races were giving way to their *'superiors'* (a view bolstered by the decline in Pacific populations from disease and blackbirding); and that there would be *'a steady advance of the sturdy Anglo-Saxon'* leading eventually to the Pacific becoming *'a White Man's Lake'*, the original Pacific Islanders gradually dying out. The Europeans' role was to *'smooth the pillow'* as they vanished away
- It followed that there was nothing morally wrong in the appropriation of their natural resources. The owners of the Pacific Phosphate Company were of the opinion that it was generous of them to provide

---

[82] These are the commandments that: *'thou shalt not steal'*; *'thou shalt not bear false witness'*; and *'thou shalt not covet ... anything that is thy neighbour's'*.

the '*natives*' with any benefit at all, arguing that the '*phosphate in its natural state was of no value to them*'.

Early official as well as private reports took continued decline and the eventual extinction of the indigenous inhabitants for granted.

Arthur Mahaffy, as Acting Resident Commissioner in 1909, first flagged up that Banaba would eventually become uninhabitable and that provision would at some point have to be made either for rehabilitation, or else resettlement; but Lord Stanmore was of the view that as the mining might continue for a century or more, the Banabans would long since by then have become extinct; William Lever thought that the sooner, the better.

The Pacific Islands Company

The original company involved was called the *Pacific Islands Company*. It had numerous interests, from general trading in several territories including the Gilberts, to plantations in the Solomons and elsewhere (including Caroline Island), to the collection of low-grade phosphate deposits on Baker and some of the other Line Islands.

The Banaba and Nauru phosphate story starts with the discovery by Albert Ellis, in 1899, that a souvenir doorstep of 'fossilised wood' from Nauru was nearly 80% high grade phosphate; and his guess that the same was probably true of the then 'unprotected' island of Banaba. It progresses through the by-chance meeting with Telfer Campbell and his wife while they were on Christmas leave in Australia; continues with the frankly deceitful manoeuvring to prevent the German rulers of Nauru realising the value of their assets; and concludes with the rescuing of what looked to be a failed enterprise, by the equally by-chance meeting (on a ship between Sydney and San Francisco) between a Director of the company and a millionaire Lancashire Grocer, William Lever, who was in a position to provide emergency finance.

Throughout, the Company deliberately lied to the Colonial Office about both the amounts of the phosphate on Banaba, and also about the price they received for a ton of it when landed at Sydney. (The Colonial Office conveniently claimed that it was 'unable' to check the veracity of the figures; and repeated questions in the UK Parliament were simply fobbed off).

Chapter 10: The Pacific Phosphate Company 1902 - 1920

The two most important Directors of this Company were John T. Arundel; and the Chairman Lord Stanmore, as Arthur Hamilton-Gordon had become in 1893, after his retirement from the Western Pacific High Commission. These two were the main protagonists in the acquisition of Banaba, and in negotiating with the German company that controlled the licences to mine in Nauru. Amongst other influential shareholders was Sir George Wyndham Herbert, who had been until the turn of the century Permanent Under-Secretary at the Colonial Office; he was later joined on the Board of the Pacific Phosphate Company by other former senior Colonial Office officials, as they retired from Office, right up to the demise of the Company in 1920.

The original Treaty

Albert Ellis was dispatched to acquire rights on Banaba; he set out in May 1900. At the time there were neither traders nor Missionaries there, so he dealt only with the Banabans themselves, through an Ellice Islands interpreter. The Agreement he signed with the 'King' is set out below.

'Ocean Island, May 3rd, 1900

'An agreement made this day between the Pacific Islands Company, Limited, of London, England, and of Sydney, hereinafter called the 'said Company' and the undersigned King and natives of Ocean Island (Paanopa) for and on behalf of the entire population of Ocean Island hereinafter called the 'said natives' of the other part –

1. *The said natives concede to the said Company the sole right to raise and ship all the rock and alluvial phosphate on Ocean Island for and on account of the said Company.*
2. *The said natives agree that the said Company shall have the right to erect buildings, lay tram lines, make roads, build jetties and shipping places or make any other arrangements necessary for the working of the phosphate deposits, also to bring labourers from other countries for the purpose of carrying on the aforesaid work.*
3. *The said Company agrees not to remove any alluvial phosphate from where cocoanut or other fruit trees or plants cultivated by the said natives are growing but to have the right to remove any non-fruit*

> *bearing trees which may interfere with the working of the phosphate deposits.*
> 4. *The said Company agrees to keep a store or stores on Ocean Island where the said natives may buy stores at prices current in the Gilbert Group and shall purchase for the said natives cocoanuts, fruits, vegetables, fish, etc. at prices in the Gilbert Group, the said natives agreeing that the said Company shall have the sole right to keep stores or trading stations on Ocean Island.*
> 5. *In consideration of the foregoing privileges, the said Company agrees to pay the natives at a rate of fifty pounds (£50) per annum, or trade to that value, at prices current in the Gilbert Group, payable half yearly.*
> 6. *This agreement to be in force for a term of nine hundred and ninety nine years (999) years.*
>
> *Witness to all signatures   THE PACIFIC ISLANDS COMPANY LIMITED*
>
> *J. MAKINSON   per Albert F. Ellis*
>
> *TEMATI King of Ocean Island   His X mark   Witness: E Riakim*
>
> *KARIATABEWA Chief   His X mark   Witness: E Riakim'*

Translation between Ellis and Temati and Kariatabewa (neither of whom could read nor write) had been conducted by Temori, from the island of Nui. Temori could not read well either, so could only retail the general import of the Agreement; for example, the period of 999 years had been rendered in translation as *'after my death'*.

It was not until five days later that Ellis (who had been wondering if he had been *'excessively generous'*) came to the realisation that the so-called 'King' was nothing of the sort; that there was no concept of commonly-owned land; and most importantly, that the land he wished to buy or lease was not the 'King's property' to dispose of at will, but was composed of innumerable privately owned plots in the Tungaru ambilineal manner (see Chapter 3).

Chapter 10: The Pacific Phosphate Company 1902 - 1920

Extension of the Protectorate to Banaba

The legal status of the Agreement he had signed (under British law, let alone under Banaban custom) was also unclear.

Although Banaba lay within the British 'Sphere of Influence' it had not been declared to be part of the Protectorate in 1892, and was legally an independent state. Thus, when the British Chairman of the company (Lord Stanmore) applied to the Secretary of State for the Colonies for a sole grant to raise and export phosphate, his statement that *'Ocean Island was under the Crown'* was simply not correct.

It thus became a matter of urgency - for the Company - that Britain extend the Protectorate to cover Banaba, as well as the Gilberts and the Ellice. This was delayed, partly due to lack of enthusiasm on the part of the Western Pacific High Commission for an extra burden on their meagre resources; and partly due to the simple lack of an available naval vessel: the Australian Squadron was too busy on ceremonial duties connected to the establishment of the Commonwealth of Australia *'to waste coal at 30/- a ton to humour a private individual'*.

Eventually, the objections of the High Commissioner were overruled by the Colonial Office (again under the influence of Lord Stanmore and Sir George Herbert); and on 28th September 1901 Captain R G O Tupper of *HMS Pylades* formally confirmed both the extension of the jurisdiction of the Resident Commissioner of the Gilbert and Ellice Islands to Banaba; and, perhaps more importantly, the Company's monopoly.

A new lease or licence had been drawn up and signed at the Colonial Office on August 13th, 1901 (before the declaration; and without Banaban representation). By this fresh agreement the company were bound to pay £50 per annum in rent to the end of 1905 and afterwards, in lieu of rent, 6d. per ton royalty on all the phosphate shipped. After the year 1905 by the terms of the licence granted by the Colonial Office, the payment of royalty in lieu of rent commenced, and this royalty went to the Imperial exchequer; the Banabans and the Gilberts Treasury receiving nothing at all until 1909, when the royalty payment was switched to the colonial government.

At the same time Lord Stanmore had completed his negotiations with the German interests. In 1902 PIC was merged with Jaluit Gesellschaft of Hamburg to form the Pacific Phosphate Company ('PPC') to engage in phosphate mining in both Nauru and Banaba. The Germans took one third of the seats on the Board, and also took over PIC's trading interests in the Gilberts. At the same time Stanmore and his colleagues persuaded the Colonial Office to extend the exclusive license it had granted (of 21 years) to 99 years. In this negotiation, the Company deliberately understated, by estimates ranging from half to a tenth, the anticipated value of the phosphate.

An article in the *New Age Magazine*, published in 1913 and entitled '*Modern Buccaneers in the West Pacific. By a Correspondent*' provides a highly charged but apparently accurate exposé of the extent to which the Colonial Office allowed the Pacific Phosphate Company, many of whose Directors were recently retired officials and colonial servants, to obtain a benefit of an estimated then £40 million (in today's values, about £500 million or AUD$750 million) - whilst paying a pittance to the Banabans, and nothing at all to the government of the Protectorate:

> '*The revenue of the Gilberts should have been derived from the phosphates. The whole sum would have been the merest fraction of the immense profits made from exporting them. Unfortunately these phosphates, many tens of millions sterling in value, were, with the exception of a trifling royalty to the Imperial Exchequer, presented by the Colonial Office as a free gift to an Influential private company, some of whose members had held high positions in the Colonial Office Service! The Gilbert Islands Treasury itself received not one penny piece from the phosphates, the whole of the revenue being practically raised directly or indirectly from the cocoanuts, the principal food of the natives*'.

The initial workings on Banaba

On Banaba, Ellis had meanwhile continued to negotiate the deal he had signed with the 'King'. The day after signing this Agreement, he and Mr Naylor put up a flagpole and raised a red ensign, assisted by Temati.

It soon became apparent that people in the other villages were aggrieved. A week later, after he had belatedly realised that land was held in individual plots by the inhabitants of several distinct villages, and was not communal (as he had supposed), he held a meeting with Temati and about 50 *unimane* from the other villages. Ellis proclaimed that '*everyone would be able to engage in the new kind of trade*'; and that all who assisted in collection and delivery of

Chapter 10: The Pacific Phosphate Company 1902 - 1920

phosphate rock for shipping would be paid at the rate of eight shillings a ton [83]).

This meeting also agreed that:

- The Company would bring in its own Indentured Labour (although, at the behest of the Banabans, not from Samoa or the Solomon Islands, nor were there to be any Roman Catholics)
- No guns would be offered for sale, also at the insistence of the Banabans
- No 'white men' other than Company employees would be permitted to live on the island, at the insistence of Ellis.

With the initially enthusiastic help of the Banabans, free-standing bits of phosphate (for example, those that had been assembled into walls) began to be taken to the shore that very week, while Ellis and Naylor surveyed the island in more detail. Ellis sent a letter to a colleague:

> *'This island is a wonderful place – there are millions of tons here – more than will be worked out in our lifetimes. There are such great advantages about it that I really believe when we get into full swing – it may take two years - we should be able to ship 20 or 30,000 yearly'.*

He also sent off for the Company's team on Baker Island to abandon it and join him.

The first shipments started to Australia and New Zealand, where the supply of phosphate was to play, over the next 75 years, a critical role in the biological transformation of these nations to outposts of temperate Northern Hemisphere flora - and to their economic development as rich nations.

Disaster struck a few months later in July 1901, when the *Moonstone* sank with 2270 tons of phosphate on board. Progress in putting in place the infrastructure required to scale up to Ellis's planned amounts was also slower than anticipated; and in 1902 especially (when there was unusually heavy rainfall) severe problems were experienced in keeping the phosphate dry, which reduced its value.

The Company began to experience cash flow problems, and Arundel and Stanmore commissioned Mr Danvers Power, of Sydney, to undertake an

---

[83] Paid in trade goods provided by the Company, on which it made a large profit

independent metallurgical engineering assessment in order to drum up further financial support. Power came up with the surprisingly precise figure of 12, 867, 035 tons as the amount that the Company could expect to extract from Banaba; he put the equivalent Nauruan figure at forty-one million tons.

Stanmore managed to get Jaluit Gesellschaft to agree a delay of six months in the merger of their two enterprises but wrote to Arundel: *'if the new company is not speedily established I do not see how we can keep afloat after the New Year'*. However, in November, Arundel met Sir William Lever on board a ship from Sydney to San Francisco: *'an angel who, in twenty-four hours, changed the whole situation'*. Sir William immediately invested £25,000 of his own money, and arranged for his company Lever Brothers to acquire the PIC's coconut plantations in the Pacific, for another £25,000.

This cash injection enabled the new Pacific Phosphate Company to get its operation going, and the Company began to prosper. It was able to pay to its shareholders a dividend of 25% in 1904, 30% in 1906, and no less than 50% in 1907 and 1908. In all, between 1900 and 1913, the company made profits for its shareholders of more than £1,750,000 (in today's values about £200 million, or AUD $ 350 million). It paid, for their trees, land and phosphate, less than £10,000 to the Banaban landowners; and to the Protectorate Government, nothing at all until 1909, when the royalty payment was switched from the Imperial Treasury to the Protectorate Government.

Questions, however, continued to be asked in Parliament, *'and the Secretary of State for the Colonies, though forced to admit that the licence was wrongfully obtained, would not cancel it - pleaded he could not do so'*. He did negotiate with the company to have the royalty doubled. The company agreed that from 1913, instead of 6d., it would pay 1 shilling on every ton of phosphate exported from Ocean Island. This was still, however, as the *New Age Magazine* article commented, *'a mere trifling payment out of the immense profits made on the sale of these phosphates'*.

The Banabans' perception of the deal

It did not take very long for the Banabans to recognise the one-sided nature of the bargain they had made; the ruthlessness with which it was enforced; and the contrast between the luxurious lifestyle of the European phosphate workers and their own existence.

Chapter 10: The Pacific Phosphate Company 1902 - 1920

The Company had at first removed surface rocks and isolated pockets of phosphate in barren areas; but as early as 1903 the Assistant Resident Commissioner R H Cogswell reported problems, in that the Company regarded only thickly cultivated groves as coming within the definition of lands where *'other fruit trees or plants cultivated by the said natives are growing'*. Even Campbell remonstrated:

> *'It is stated in your agreement that no damage is to be done to food producing trees. I regret to find that this has not been observed; excavating up to the butts of trees, cutting and exposing their roots, is a distinct injury'.*

Ellis, on the other hand, maintained on behalf of the Company that:

> *'The patches of Pandanus and Cocoanuts away from the village are very badly cultivated or not at all, owing to the inherent laziness of the natives ...*
>
> *'There is ample room for planting thousands of coconuts in localities right away from the mining areas, not that I think they will ever do much good, unless some magic wand is waved, which will transform the Banabans into an industrious population .... It is ... useless to rely on the Banabans for working at the pinnacles or anything else which requires much exertion...'*

In 1905, Alfred Gaze, the General Manager of the Company, visiting Banaba, complained of the 'lengthy and troublesome negotiations with the natives as to land leases. No one had contemplated the difficulty that had arisen in securing lands and the consequent trouble in obtaining ground for the extension of the settlements and the phosphate fields ... the new house being put up for... [Ellis' brother George]... had to be placed in a different position to that originally intended because an obstinate old woman refused to grant a lease'.

By 1909 Ellis at least was honest enough to admit that:

> *'Though the King of Ocean Island and subsequently all the Four representative chiefs agreed to our working the island under an annual payment of 50 pounds per annum [sic], they didn't for a minute think it would be possible to export so much Phosphate as we have been doing, and therefore require so much land ... If we were to limit our payments to the 50 pounds per annum the Oceans Islanders (and others as well)*

Chapter 10: The Pacific Phosphate Company 1902 - 1920

could with some truth say that we took advantage of their ignorance and bound them down by a hard and fast agreement when they had no adequate idea what they were letting themselves in for'.

By that year, the 450 or so Banabans shared their island with more than 1000 Pacific island labourers; 400 Japanese; about 80 Europeans; and a contingent of Fijian police.

Mary Hunt, who joined her husband there in 1906, recorded:

'Two extremes of life mix on Ocean Island. On one hand are primitive dwellings of the native Banabans, Banaba being the native name, a few pandanus posts supporting a palm leaf thatched roof with a few mats spread on the ground, and in striking contrast the comfortable dwellings of the European residents with the electric power for driving machinery and supplying light and ice, a good telephone service, recreation rooms, libraries, locomotives and large steamers at anchor, in fact in a small way all the bustling activity of civilisation'.

Included in these after 1906 was the house for the Resident Commissioner, as it had been decided that he would move from Tarawa, so as to be on the spot to help obtain leases. The Residency was built by the Company to Telfer Campbell's own design (albeit at the Protectorate's expense). However, Campbell had barely occupied it when he was removed in 1908 [84].

Campbell was replaced by Mahaffy as Acting Resident Commissioner for six months, and then by two Resident Commissioners, John Quayle-Dickson and Edward Eliot, who were to prove rather less accommodating to the Company; both of their careers were broken by it.

Quayle-Dickson quickly realised that the Company's methods were aimed solely at the extraction of the richest parts of the phosphate, regardless of both the short term damage to Banaban crops, and the long-term damage to their

---

[84] Ellis himself was to remain as General Manager on Ocean Island (as the company insisted on calling Banaba right up to 1979) until 1911. This did not end his involvement: he continued as a Manager in the Company until it became the British Phosphate Commission, and was for thirty years the first Commissioner for New Zealand, from 1921 to 1951. He was eventually knighted, and lived long enough to give a – typically patronising - speech to the newly arrived Banabans on Rabi.

financial interests. He proposed that a Trust be set up for the Banabans as he was hesitant about simply increasing their income, given that the Company would then find ways to defraud them of the benefit. He also refused to register any more leases; proposed that the mining should be reorganised from the most profitable to contiguous plots, which could then be rehabilitated; insisted that the Company should not mutilate trees and then claim them to be non-bearing, and therefore disposable; and recommended to the Colonial Office that more should be paid to the Banabans for the leases. In the meantime the Banabans had come to a position where they flatly refused to lease any more land, under any circumstances.

Quayle-Dickson had reckoned without the continuing influence of Lord Stanmore and his nephew Lord Balfour, who had become a major shareholder; or the determination of William Lever that the Company stand firm and *'not agree to the slightest item of our rights on the island'*. When Quayle-Dickson went on leave to the UK in 1911, he was sacked and 'offered' the Falkland Islands position.

In 1912 the Sydney Morning Herald reported:

> *'The Ocean islander saw his lands and only means of existence gradually disappearing leaving, instead of his palm and pandanus groves, worked out quarries. Foreseeing the inevitable end, the natives some time ago definitely refused to sell any more lands. A public meeting was held to discuss the matter with the native owners. The natives unanimously refused to sell any more land, declaring that the lands, and the palm and pandanus trees thereon were all that they had, and they asked what they should do when the big steamers had carried away all their habitable land. There the matter stands awaiting adjustment at home* [i.e. the UK].

> *'Naturally some think the native owners are right, yet it is inconceivable that less than 500 Ocean-island born natives can be allowed to prevent the mining and export of a product of such immense value to the rest of mankind. The question is under the authorities' consideration at present and the outcome is uncertain.'*

The authorities had in fact chosen a new Resident Commissioner, Edward Eliot, in the hope that he could resolve the situation. In his autobiography *'Broken Atoms'*, Eliot describes how in 1913, after accepting the post, he had a long interview with a Mr. Johnson, Chief Clerk of the Colonial Office:

Chapter 10: The Pacific Phosphate Company 1902 - 1920

> *'He told me I had been selected for two important and rather delicate tasks. Were I to carry them through with success I should receive substantial promotion and (here he put his hand above his heart) some further sign of His Majesty's approval. He went on to explain ... [that] the natives of [Ocean] island had refused to let the company have any more land for their operations ...*
>
> *'The second part of "my special work" was to change the "Protectorate" of the Gilbert and Ellice Islands into a "Colony"'.*

Broken Atoms continues:

> *'Shortly after we reached Suva the Company's steamer arrived from Ocean Island to meet us. The steamer was a chartered German vessel, and the Company's Manager [Cleeve Edwards] was on board. The Manager was anything but persona grata with the natives of the island so it would have been difficult for the Company to have made a more stupid, short-sighted or tactless arrangement. To crown everything the Manager, who was our host, asked me if I was empowered to enforce the surrender of the land which his Company required. "Certainly not" I replied, nettled, "my instructions from the Government at home are to use my best endeavours to persuade the natives to agree to the surrender of the land your company needs." To this the Manager replied "Well, then you might just as well have stayed in England!" '*

Relations did not improve, even when Eliot had persuaded some of the Banabans to lease further land (using the argument that the phosphate had no value to them where it was, but also by gaining their trust):

> *'After I had obtained the further land which the Company needed for their operations, I pressed them to improve the housing conditions of the Gilbert and Ellice labourers. The local Manager of the Company told me in my own house, and before my wife, that if I tried to force them to spend what they considered unnecessary money, the Company would call on the Colonial Office to remove me as they had removed my predecessor.'*

Eliot had in fact struck a significantly better bargain for the Banabans. The new terms were that the Company should pay between £40 and £60 an acre, in defined areas, the price to be fixed by the Resident Commissioner (this was more than double the prices proposed by the Company). In addition to the 6d. per ton paid to the GEIP Government, another sixpence was to be paid into a Trust Fund, the interest from which would be paid to the Banabans or used for their benefit (a sum of £ 4734 was to be paid into the Fund immediately). Owners of leased land could continue to use it until it was mined. The Company could exchange leases already held outside the mining area for similar blocks inside. Other clauses in the agreement made it obligatory for the Company to sell trade goods at uniform prices to all inhabitants regardless of nationality (which they subverted – see page 323); and to sell fresh water to each Banaban at the rate of one gallon a day, for three farthings.

The new agreement was signed on 28th November 1913.

Eliot declined to return to the Colony – as it had then become – whilst on leave in England in 1920, when he had a rather different interview:

> *'My natives there would ask me certain questions which I was not in a position to explain satisfactorily without further explanation. The Under-Secretary [of the Colonies] replied that he did not wish to hear the questions. So I said I was not prepared to return ... Sir A answered that it was unnecessary for me to resign and that an appointment would be found for me elsewhere. I left the Colonial Office with the realisation that my career was at an end but that the authorities were anxious to keep me in harness to muzzle me'.*

The replacement of the Company by the BPC

However, it appeared that by 1914 Eliot (and others) had caused enough doubt and Parliamentary interest to persuade the British Government to consider changing the basis on which the operation had been built: that is, the Indentures issued by the Colonial Office.

However, events were overtaken by the outbreak of war between Britain and Germany; and the issue was parked for the duration of hostilities.

In the Pacific, the Ocean island operation continued to function; but the Company was instructed by the Colonial Office to hold no further communication with Nauru, which had in any event been put under martial law by the German authorities (since British subjects outnumbered Germans by two to one). On 3rd November 1914, three months after the start of the war, the Australians captured Nauru and took the German workforce as prisoners to Australia. Charlie Workman (the Chief of Police in the GEIP) was installed as Administrator.

Meanwhile, in the UK, the German shareholdings in the Company had been confiscated. They were purchased from the Public Trustee by the Elder Dempster shipping company.

At the end of WWI, Australia made a bid to take over all the territories of the Western Pacific High Commission, together with Nauru, and to incorporate them into the Commonwealth of Australia (New Zealand was to get Western Samoa). However, strong objections were made by New Zealand (for whom access to phosphate was an important political issue); and it was they who came up with the idea of a three-power commission.

In the summer of 1919 the Prime Ministers of both countries were in London pressing their claims. On 27th June (over the vociferous objections of the Company – but Lord Stanmore had died, and with him much influence over the British Government) it was agreed that a Mandate for Nauru would be held *'by the Empire'*; and, in 1920, that the Ocean Island mining should become, with that on Nauru, a *'non-profit'* enterprise held by Britain, Australia and New Zealand in the proportions 42:42:16.

After some haggling, the Directors of the Pacific Phosphate Company were bought off for £3.5 million.

Thus the British Phosphate Commission (answerable to three Commissioners, one appointed by each of the three governments) came into existence. The BPC was to outlive the deposits on both Banaba and Nauru, and was eventually wound up in 1981.

Chapter 10: The Pacific Phosphate Company 1902 - 1920

Further Reading

1. **The Phosphateers**, by Maslyn Williams and Dr Barrie Macdonald, published by the Melbourne University Press 1985
2. **Report of Mr Arthur Mahaffy: Visit to the Gilbert and Ellice Islands 1909**, presented to both Houses of Parliament by Command of His Majesty and published by HM Stationary Office, 1910
3. **Modern Buccaneers in the West Pacific**, by a Correspondent, published by New Age Magazine, 1913.
4. **Broken Atoms,** by E. C. Eliot, published by Geoffrey Bles, 1938
5. **Consuming Ocean Island,** by Katerina Martina Teaiwa, published by the Indiana University Press, 2015
6. **Cinderellas of the Empire,** by Dr. Barrie Macdonald, published by the Institute of Pacific Studies, 2001
7. **Disconcerting Issue, Meaning and Struggle in a Resettled Pacific Community**, by Martin G Silverman, published by the University of Chicago Press, 1971
8. **The Book of Banaba,** by H C and H E Maude, published by the Institute of Pacific Studies, 1994

Chapter 11.

THE EDIFICE OF CONTROL: 1916 – 1941

Competing authorities

Part 1 of this book has described how, from the very first advent of Europeans 100 years before, the boundary had begun to change between two rival concepts of living: *'Te maiu ni Kiribati'* and *'Te maiu ni Imatang'*. At the risk of some simplification, I have defined these as follows:

- *'Te maiu ni Kiribati' (things pertaining to the Gilbertese way of life)*, as described in Part 1 of this book, were characterised by: family as society (Chapter 3); intense competitiveness between bodies of knowledge, including magical knowledge across activities, and reliance on indigenous deities (Chapters 4 and 5); settlement of serious disputes through warfare (Chapter 6); and a material culture based on the limited range of natural resources, with no concept of either markets, or money (Chapter 7). As we have seen in Chapter 8, a range of technical innovations were incorporated into *'Te maiu ni Kiribati'* in the late nineteenth century, notably metal tools; and to a limited extent, concepts of trade and exchange, although not fully of 'pricing'. Concepts of justice also, though, shifted quite early: from being interpersonal (or inter-familial), to overarching laws and regulations
- *'Te maiu ni Imatang' (things pertaining to Europeans)* refers to concepts, technologies, and imports which, by contrast, were essentially ephemeral and if needs be could be 'done without'. If necessary (and this did become necessary during the Japanese occupation) society could in this period still function effectively without external inputs.

In the 50 years after the declaration of the Protectorate, the boundaries continued to shift (as indeed they are still doing in the 21st Century):

- Warfare was effectively abolished (and was gratefully recognised as having been abolished). Land (which to their credit, the colonial authorities refused to allow to be alienated) began to be surveyed and catalogued by a series of British Lands

Chapter 11: The Edifice of Control 1916 - 1941

   Commissioners; and disputes to be governed by Courts rather than conflict
- While the basic material culture for the majority of Gilbertese did not change significantly, additional new resources did become embedded into daily life. Two examples are imported planks for canoe making, and sewing machines for making clothes. Imported foodstuffs, however, remained rare luxuries except for the Banabans who gradually abandoned traditional in favour of usually tinned Australian foodstuffs
- Housing based on *kaainga* was replaced by multi-kaainga villages built to a standard design (see below), and a central District *mwaneaba* increasingly gave way, on islands where the two competed, to separate 'confessional' *mwaneabas* for Roman Catholic and Protestants
- Christian converts, although at most two-thirds of the population at this time, began to assert 'Mission' values and to subvert the authority of the *Unimane*. At the same time at least some of the government-appointed officials began to subvert traditional authority in favour of the precepts of District Officers
- The status of women declined; they were effectively excluded from all formal forms of governance, from religious leadership, and from employment, although not wholly from education
- More generally, the execution of justice moved and was perceived to move from that of *direct compensation* on a personal or family level, from the perpetrator to the aggrieved: to that of *law made and enforced by a national government* in the form of fines and imprisonment, and ultimately capital punishment by hanging (a form of death which the Gilbertese despised).

From the Gilbertese villager's point of view, governance was, up to WWII and beyond, an act of balancing three competing sources of authority: colonial, Mission, and traditional [85].

Commercial interests had little influence on the Protectorate and Colony, except on Banaba, where the BPC, despite formally being a 'governmental' organisation, continued to put its commercial aims first. The phosphate operation became the principal source of employment outside of the poorly

---

[85] Fortunately there was never a 'White settler' interest to placate

Chapter 11: The Edifice of Control 1916 - 1941

paid 'native government' posts, and the continuing subsistence activities that sustained the vast bulk of the population.

The BPC wholly replaced the external labour recruiting of the 19th century; and virtually no Gilbertese had opportunity to travel abroad. As the generation that had done so died off, the Gilbertese were effectively cut off from any knowledge of the outside world or importation of ideas other than ones retailed to them by missionaries or colonial officials.

This Chapter describes and examines the *'edifice of control'* [86] established by Telfer Campbell, and built upon by his successors, notably by Arthur Grimble; and how it had only gradually eroded before the Japanese invasion in 1942.

Government Authority

Government authority, both colonial and 'native', became more and more prescriptive over even trivial aspects of daily life (such as picking up dead leaves, or visiting a latrine); it is estimated that in any year of the 1930s, three quarters of adults at some time fell foul of, and were fined or imprisoned for, breaches of the uniform 'regulations' then imposed at national level, including in the Ellice Islands.

These regulations, that came to dominate everyday village life (at least when they were enforced), were a mix of what the colonial administrators thought local customs to be, for example canoe and fishing rights; and *Imatang* norms for matters such as polygyny or divorce where these customs were different from their own or Church norms.

Creation of 'planned' villages

The first such change, that was clearly imposed (but seems to have moved surprisingly quickly from *'Te maiu ni Imatang'* to *'Te maiu ni Kiribati'*) was that it no longer became possible for Gilbertese to live with their *kaainga*, or on traditional sites. New settlements, decreed by the British, compelled unrelated families to live beside each other in 'planned' communities [87].

---

[86] As Dr Barrie Macdonald has so aptly described it.

[87] The 'garden city' movement had been initiated in the United Kingdom in 1898, by Sir Ebenezer Howard, and may have influenced the Colonial authorities; however,

Chapter 11: The Edifice of Control 1916 - 1941

In 1910, Mahaffy's report commented that:

> 'The greatest difference which I noted after my 13 years' absence from the Protectorate was the excellent housing accommodation on almost all the islands of the Gilberts Group. A system of extraordinary uniformity has been developed and the best types of native houses have been finally evolved after a series of experiments which may have been somewhat exasperating to the natives but which have undoubtedly resulted in their general good. The villages are kept in admirable order and the roads are scrupulously clean'.

In 1923, S.M. Lambert of the Rockefeller Foundation commented that:

> 'With Government control houses were collected into ordered villages along the lagoon shores. These houses were built on an improved plan with eaves some six feet from the ground; they have open sides and raised floors of coconut mid-ribs. Attached to each of these sleeping houses is a cook and eating house, a store house, and a bathing shed. There must be a space four fathoms long between each building.'

These villages, and associated roads, were built through the instituting of a corvée – the obligation to provide unpaid compulsory labour - for between 52 and 78 days' work each year; which under Campbell could be extended to up to four days a week or even more if imposed as a collective punishment.

Free labour was used to build houses for the native government officials, put up walls around island prisons, make roads and line them with stones, and for the raising of prominent flagpoles. Later, public works programmes such as causeways and bridges were seen as of greater benefit to the community [88].

---

they were building on existing Mission initiatives to replace family with confessional living arrangements.

[88] Such systems had been favoured in many historical economies, especially for those in which barter was more common than cash. The corvée in fact lasted (in modified form) until the beginning of the 1960s, when it was abolished under pressure from the International Labour Organisation; but replaced by island taxation that was arguably more irksome to the population than had been supplying their labour directly.

Chapter 11: The Edifice of Control 1916 - 1941

Such arrangements were a necessary condition for subsequent regulation of the villagers, as described below. *Aspects of History* concluded:

> 'Asked now whether they objected to the new living style, many old Gilbertese say they did not, firstly because the Resident Commissioner said it was to be done, and secondly because they found the change to be to their advantage. There were the advantages of a quicker assembly for social purposes and also they could now live on land which was not their own and to which traditionally they had no entitlement'.

The 'Native' Administration

Most day-to-day control was exercised by the 'native' administration.

In 1910, Mahaffy described how Swain and Thurston's system of 'native government' had evolved under the centralising instincts of Campbell:

> 'In islands where there is a hereditary high chief he is usually recognised and he commonly sits as president of the 'Bowi' [court] or island parliament.
>
> 'The next official of importance is the magistrate who is usually picked as the most intelligent native whose services can be secured. He is assisted by the 'scribe' whose duty it is to keep all the island books in order, and this is no light task. The books comprise cash book, court book, land register, registers of births, deaths and marriages, and the tax accounts. On the whole these books are kept well and generally quite up to date.
>
> 'The other native Government officials are a chief policeman, village policemen (usually one or two for each village), a gaoler, and a wardress to look after the prisoners (male and female), and finally, and only in recent times, a hospital orderly who takes charge of the native patients in the island hospital, dispenses the drugs, and always resides or should reside close outside the hospital fence.
>
> 'The natives detailed above are all paid from the land tax – which is now the only form of taxation paid by the natives.
>
> 'There remain the unpaid members of the native parliament, who are for the most part content to remain unpaid when the fact is explained to them that in England membership of Parliament was formerly held to be so great an honour that payment was never thought of. These are the Kaubure: 'advisers' or 'talking men'.

Chapter 11: The Edifice of Control 1916 - 1941

The Kaubures met each month with the Magistrate to *'administer the law or formulate new regulations'*.

It is clear, however, that even after Campbell's departure, the 'independence' of the native administration, although in theory near absolute, was in practice nominal. Mahaffy says of the Kaubures:

> *'In former days they were usually chosen from among the older natives and were a somewhat argumentative lot although they were loyal enough once convinced; and they certainly had a considerable amount of authority with the natives who have the respect of a primitive people for the opinion of the 'Old Men'.*

> *'The Kaubure are now recruited from among the younger men who may be supposed to be more progressive, less dilatory, and less wedded to ancient customs and methods, but who are certainly less interesting and have less authority among the people. It is I fancy a rare thing for any of the modern Kaubure to differ from the opinion of the European Government Officer, or, if he differs, to have the courage of his opinions and the ability to explain and maintain them.'*

Telfer Campbell had also deliberately undermined the *Uea*: in 1907 he was able to claim that *'the office of Uea or High Chief of an island has been abolished'*, although his claim was premature.

The Gilbertese had their own assessment of the genuineness of self-rule: *'E taku te kamitina'* (*'the Commissioner has decreed'*).

The Colonial Administration

Until the Second World War, the 'central' government of the GEIC – located on Ocean Island after 1908 - was very small. In Eliot's time it comprised just seven posts: the Resident Commissioner, an Assistant Commissioner, a Chief of Police, a Postmaster/Customs Officer, a Clerk, a Cadet (Arthur Grimble), and the all-important Treasurer. They were supplemented by five District Officers (DOs), four in the Gilberts and one in the Ellice Islands; and after WWI by a Senior Colonial Medical Officer and two educationalists.

The Colony Police force consisted of some 70 armed Police (mostly on Banaba) together with about 250 unarmed village policemen.

A colonial officer started as a Cadet, undergoing training (whilst filling whatever other jobs had been left unfilled by leave or transfer); he was then

Chapter 11: The Edifice of Control 1916 - 1941

normally promoted to be an Assistant District Officer after two years of successful probation - and after passing a set of examinations. Critically, these included language exams: until the late 1960s all DOs (District Officers) became fluent in Gilbertese. Later in his career he would fill posts at Headquarters between spells in the field. Specialists - other than the doctors and educationalists - only became sub-branches of the colonial service in fields such as Public Works, Agriculture, or Marine (and thus separate career paths) in the late 1930s.

The DO was the link between the colonial government and the people of his district, and acted as the supervisor of the native administration.

Eric Bevington, who became DO Southern Gilberts in the early 1930s, wrote of his arrival on Beru:

> *'I was next in line of men who, to them [the Gilbertese] represented the King [of England]. This attitude was by no means unique to the Gilbertese. Few native peoples ... could envisage the entity that was called Government. They knew nothing of 'establishment'. To them the Empire was governed by the King and the local District Officer was the direct representative of the King, and they could not doubt for a moment that he had direct access to the King. They were quite sure the King had personally selected their DO and sent him to them....*

> *'The District Officer in those days was Jack of All Trades, and master probably of none. He was alone in his District, unarmed and proud to be unarmed. Whatever came to hand had to be done ... The DO was magistrate, health officer, the public works department, agricultural officer, chief jailer, and if necessary hangman. He was also accountant, postmaster, and general representative of the people to the government, and of the government to the people...*

> *'Funds were always extremely limited and never sufficient for the task ...each year the DO received a volume called the Estimates, showing exactly how much money had been allocated to each purpose in each District... he is personally responsible and can be called upon to refund [any over-expenditure under any purpose, even if funds for other purposes have not been expended]. Detailed accounting was required, and vouchers for every penny spent'.*

Chapter 11: The Edifice of Control 1916 - 1941

Harry Maude, appointed as Acting Colony Treasurer soon after his arrival as a Cadet in 1929, wrote to his mother that 'Jack of All Trades' applied equally at headquarters:

'The more I think of this service, the more I laugh – it's exactly like a comic opera out here. I've never had an ounce of training in Treasury work and practice in my life and yet here I am running both the Treasury Departments of the whole Colony'.

In his work the District Officer was also driven by regulations – Maude lists 67 different forms which he was regularly supposed to fill in when he became one.

Administration of Justice

This account of the 'Old Men of Buota' and Anton Meyer was collected by Tabunawati Tokoa in October 1949, on behalf of the then Resident Commissioner John Peel.

It illustrates the arbitrary way in which Telfer Campbell operated:

'This event happened long ago when the British Government was just setting her feet on Tarawa, there was only one murder case occurred on Tarawa in the village of Buota in which a Chinaman trader settled. The trader's name is not known. [It was Ah Sing].

'In this village there was a man called Kabotau who set a trap on the beach on the weatherside to catch small birds – a variety of snipe or sand piper. He hid himself inland amongst bushes. This kind of bird was kept for a popular game amongst the villagers of Buota for they liked to see the birds fighting. While this man was hiding in the bushes gazing at his loop he was surprised to see the birds near his trap flying away as if they were frightened away. Kabotou looked about the beach and he saw two women called Nei Roro and another. These women were returning from fishing not knowing anything about the trap they were disturbing. Kabotau got very annoyed because he has been there very long and none of the birds was caught so he chased the women with the intention to kill them both. Nei Roro was the first to be caught so Kabotau brought her down onto a rock and lift another rock and dropped it on her. He then ran after the other woman called Nei Tetou but she was lucky to be in the village before Kabotau caught her. None of them belonged to Kabotau.

Chapter 11: The Edifice of Control 1916 - 1941

'News of the murder was spread and came to the ears of Mr. Campbell the first Government Officer to settle and also was the Resident Commissioner. So a canoe loaded with policemen was sent up to Buota to investigate and bring the murderer back to Betio. The policemen tried all means to get the murderer but the villagers seemed to know nothing about it. When the policemen knew that the murderer could not be found out, they ordered the whole village to go to Betio. (This is why an additional boat of the Chinaman trader was lent – not Meyer's). The whole village got to Betio and they were forced to construct a half mile wharf from the beach out into the deep water in the lagoon as their punishment.

'They were compelled to work hard at day time like prisoners and free in the evening. At night they used to play cards in the 'maneaba' with the policemen also. One group was talking for being unfairly punished for a single person's crime. They sensibly decided to blame one youth who was Nei Tetou's son-in-law (the murder's company). This made Nei Tetou reveal the right murderer. While the talk in this group of card players was increasing the Senior Member of the policemen enquired and said 'What's going on?'. These men replied 'That man is the murderer' pointing at Nei Tetou's son-in-law. The Senior Policeman ordered the accused to be tied up and be put in goal. Nei Tetou having seen this, she yelled out saying 'Oh no it is not him. It is really Kabotau, I saw him when he killed my companion Nei Roro.' Now Nei Tetou's son-in-law was immediately released from the hand-cubs [sic] and so was the villagers of Buota from wharf construction, and Kabotau was tied up and everyone was ordered to return to Buota including Kabotau. The Government officers at that time and the police force went to Buota with the people.

'At Buota, Kabotau was tied to a pandanus tree and was shot in front of all the villagers. This took place where himself, Kabotau, did the killing. This action frightened the people and made them think that if they did the killing, the same would be done to them also'.

Neville Chapman (a former supercargo who had often visited the Gilberts in the early 1900s) wrote in February 1950 that the last bit of this account, the summary shooting, was inaccurate; and that a gallows was ordered from Australia which *'was landed on 4th or 5th May 1903 out of the 'Ysabel' at Tarawa'*. He said that Kabotau's execution by hanging was then supervised by the

207

Assistant Commissioner, Bob Cogswell. In that case Kabotau spent some time on death row, which is consistent with the need described below to get the Western Pacific High Commissioner to confirm the death sentence, as was required under Colonial Regulations.

The system of native administration in relation to justice in the early 20th century was further described by E. C. Eliot:

> 'In each island there was a native Magistrate. He was not necessarily the chief of the island, and a number of councillors [Kaubure, see below] sat with him in court as advisers. There was no limit to the sentence they could impose. The Commissioner or any District Officer acting in his name could, however, vary or reduce sentences of imprisonment or corporal punishment. So it can be seen that nominally the native courts had full jurisdiction, but actually the Commissioner and his deputies had control. The prisons too were under white supervision.
>
> 'Trials for murder were somewhat differently arranged. The District Officer sat with and 'helped' the native magistrate to see that the evidence was correctly taken and recorded. The evidence was then referred to the Chief Judicial Commissioner in Fiji by the Resident Commissioner, who then appended his own observation on the case. There was neither wireless nor cable in the Gilberts in those days [89]. A whole year might go by while the unhappy prisoner awaited a decision on his case....
>
> 'There was a proper 'death house' at Tarawa, a model of Newgate. It had been erected by one of my predecessors [see above]. I found that by having the three policemen to whom the task was entrusted perfectly trained in their several duties, the condemned man could be 'turned off' within thirty seconds of entering the building. In fact the native parson remonstrated with me for not giving him sufficient time to speed the fleeting soul.'

The Resident Commissioners at this time

Pen portraits of the Resident Commissioners up to the time of Eliot were set out on pages 175 to 180 above.

---

[89] A wireless station was eventually installed on Banaba in 1916

Chapter 11: The Edifice of Control 1916 - 1941

After Eliot had declined to return in 1920, the Resident Commissioners up to the time of the Japanese invasion were:

- **Thomas Dundas Hope Bruce**, who acted uneventfully from May 1920 to May 1921. He was a former Resident Magistrate of Jamaica and was re-appointed to that post after leaving
- **Herbert Reginald McClure**, who had been a naval cadet in China and then a senior district commissioner in Kenya, served for five years between 1921 and 1 Jan 1926, when he died in office during a trip to Australia. His main achievements were in education and medicine
- **Arthur Francis Grimble**, who was Resident Commissioner between 1926 and 1933, after service in the Gilberts since 1914. This book is not the place for a detailed appraisal of Grimble, the best known of all the Resident Commissioners, and through his 1950s radio broadcasts and book *Pattern of Islands*, the progenitor of many people's impressions of the islands. He is frankly a conundrum. His romantic attachment to the Gilbertese is undoubted; his early anthropological works (mostly unpublished until after his death) preserved knowledge that might well have otherwise been lost; but his applications for academic posts in Anthropology were turned down. Maude wrote to his mother that after he and his wife arrived in 1929, Grimble '*ignored everyone else and talked anthropology by the hour, it's quite embarrassing*'. Barrie Macdonald notes that his '*vehement identification with the traditional Gilbertese, his lyrical defences of dancing, the fact that he had dancing marks tattooed on his arms ... and his intransigent attitude towards the Mission hardly made him an impartial observer*'. He jealously guarded his position as the '*expert*' on matters Gilbertese, and after he became Resident Commissioner in 1926 refused to relinquish the post of Lands Commissioner; he would not allow DOs to deal with land matters except under his personal supervision, even although he seldom left Ocean island after that date. Above all, Grimble '*constantly acted as if the islanders were children in need of firm patriarchal control ... although he was fond of Gilbertese on an individual, personal basis, he had a somewhat jaundiced view of their collective capacity*'. Hence the 1930 Regulations (pages 216 - 220). Finally, it was Grimble who was prepared to enforce the BPC and Colonial Office's will against the Banabans, rather than to sacrifice his own career as Quayle Dickson and Edward Eliot had done.

- **Charles A. Swinbourne** was briefly Acting Resident Commissioner in 1933
- **Jack Charles Barley**, who was in office from 18 Oct 1933 until 1938. Barley had been a first-class cricketer in his youth and subsequently District Officer at Tulagi in the Solomon Islands. He was made the scapegoat for the disastrous renegotiation of tax arrangements with the BPC, but he was one of the least authoritarian Commissioners of them all, and started (under the influence of his younger colleagues, led by H E Maude), to dismantle the 1930 Regulations. He became a heavy drinker, however, and was eventually removed from office
- **Ronald Garvey** served as Acting Resident Commissioner of the Gilbert and Ellice Islands colony in 1938-1940, after being a District Officer in the Solomons for six years. He subsequently became Resident Commissioner in the New Hebrides, and after the war served in Africa and the Caribbean. He returned to the Pacific as Governor of Fiji from 1952, where he demonstrated his considerable public relations skills, until his retirement in 1958. In retirement he became Lieutenant Governor of the Isle of Man.

Mission Authority

The Missions, who had arrived in the Gilberts before the colonialists, and who had in many places become accustomed to untrammelled authority, thus had an uneasy relationship with the government from its outset.

Although their power was less absolute than in the Ellice Islands, this observation from a scientist visiting Funafuti in 1897 applied at least to the southern Gilberts also:

> *'The natives were rather astonished to see us shake off our working garb but we advised them to put on their best clothes too, because as we put it, "Man o War, plenty big boss" but they laughed and said "No, Missionali Big Boss'.*

Early relations were not helped by the strong personal antipathy of Telfer Campbell (with his Northern Irish background) to Roman Catholicism; although his relations with the Protestants were in fact little better. According to a Mission teacher, Campbell *'wrote in the sand with his cane, thus, two holes, one as Earth, one as Heaven. The roads of both Protestants and Catholics he represents as curved lines, but his road is a straight one'.*

Chapter 11: The Edifice of Control 1916 - 1941

From his first visit to the Gilberts in 1888, and after taking up residence on Beru in 1900, William Goward led the Protestant Mission. He was responsible for replacing the often exploitative Samoans in the Ellice and southern Gilberts with indigenous pastors, but he vied for influence in the south with Campbell.

In 1913 he was replaced by the more conciliatory George Eastman, who had transferred from the Cook Islands (and by then Campbell had in any case gone); relations with the government became more constructive.

In 1917 the LMS replaced the American Board of Missions in the northern Gilberts. Hubert Arnold took over the Abaiang Mission, and also localised it, by phasing out Hawaiian pastors (although their replacements in the Northern Gilberts continued to be trained by the Americans at Kosrae). In 1922 Eastman was joined by Wilfred Levett, a Lay Accountant, who was a mainstay of the Church until his death in 1940; another long-term missionary of note was Emily May Pateman, who taught at the girl's school and was a collector of Gilbertese customs, art forms and stories, many which she printed in their Press.

With the exceptions on Beru and Abaiang, the Protestant Church was from about 1920 run entirely by Gilbertese, and is described in an LMS pamphlet as follows:

> *'The care of the villages is largely in the hands of the pastor-teachers. Once a year the Missionary from Beru or Abaiang visits the islands to check the schoolwork of the pastor and to consider his church problems ... unlike the Ellice Islands, there are not many villages in the Gilbert Islands wholly Christian or wholly Protestant, and the pastor is confronted with many difficulties. Frequently the visit of the John Williams will be the only contact with the outside world throughout the year.*
>
> *'The headquarters of the work is the central training institution at Rongorongo on the island of Beru. Here in an area of just over 35 acres, about 300 people live as a community consisting of theological students (with their wives and children) and the boys and girls who attend the different schools within the mission compound. There is a printing press, an electric plant* [Rongorongo functioned as a transmitting station from the 1930s], *a dispensary and an infant welfare centre, a trading store, a carpenter's shop and a boat building centre ... education starts*

Chapter 11: The Edifice of Control 1916 - 1941

with a beginner's class and leads through to a teacher and theological training institute'.

Many Gilbertese pastors appreciated the technical skills they acquired at Beru as much (or more than) the theology they learned there. Although they had no leadership roles in the Church, the LMS Mission did educate girls as well as boys.

By contrast, the Roman Catholic Church was much better financed and resourced, but remained very much dominated by expatriates. The Bishops and Priests and Lay Brothers were French, Swiss and German; although growing numbers of Irish-Australians replaced the original, French, nuns [90]. *Astride the Equator* contains a detailed description of the struggles of the Church against Protestantism and, with a seemingly lesser degree of enthusiasm, to convert non-Christians.

While choice of which church to join was governed by many things – residence, other members of the *utu*, and political allegiance (there was most rivalry on those islands such as Nonouti and Tabiteuea which in Tungaru days had been least united), an important factor – as Captain Davis had predicted in 1892 – was the respective attitudes of the two churches toward singing and dancing [91].

Goward – despite boasting that in eighteen years he had never personally *witnessed* a 'native' dance – was utterly convinced that dancing was the cause of *'sorcery, drunkenness, and violence – a sign of heathen decadence to be swept away'*. On the other hand the Sacred Heart Missionaries, whilst by no means fully approving, were prepared at least to tolerate some dancing.

Thus, by 1934 the number of Roman Catholics had increased (by Sabatier's estimation) to 12,249 while the Protestants numbered some 7,878 – although 1,197 brave souls were still prepared to assert their adherence to pre-Christian

---

[90] But Sister Clementine, who had arrived as a young nun from France in 1891, was still active eighty years later and at the age of almost 100 when I arrived in the Gilberts in 1971. She had only returned to France once.

[91] Religion also seems to have played a surprisingly small role in the choice of marriage partners

Chapter 11: The Edifice of Control 1916 - 1941

deities [92]. The Roman Catholics had by then come to dominate in the Northern Gilberts, especially Makin and Butaritari; but had made few inroads in the four southernmost islands [93].

Religion became an influence on the native administration of some islands. There was harassment of minority groups, refusal to accept Magistrates and Chief Kaubures of the opposite faith, and frequent allegation of partial tax assessments and court decisions. Missions often made excessive demands for exemption of their teachers and catechists from the corvée. Only in one instance, in 1930 on Onotoa, did religious fervour erupt into pitched battle and murder; but there were other instances of church burning and destruction of property.

The *Unimane* had support against the Missions as well from Arthur Grimble, when he assumed the office of Resident Commisioner between 1926 and 1933. He was not personally hostile to the missionaries (as Campbell had been) but saw himself as the defender of tradition (despite being the author of the 1930 Regulations, most of which were dubiously traditional):

> *'The Gilbert Islands owe much to Protestants and Catholics alike. But the intolerance of some of the early teachers of both churches too often frustrated the kind work of their fellows. Their indiscriminate hate of everything pagan uprooted by the way much that was beautiful and useful'*

The three-way tug of authority is illustrated a few pages later in *Pattern of Islands*:

> *'Walking one day on the ocean side of Tarawa, I had chanced on a box-shaped arrangement of coral slabs …. No skull was inside but a heap of*

---

[92] My wife's paternal grandmother, who died in 1970, remained defiantly pagan until the end of her days, but she was by then unusual

[93] In fact after several ugly incidents, especially at Arorae, the Government in 1936 passed the Closed Districts Ordinance under which permits were required for non-Gilbertese to land there or on Tamana, and in the Ellice Group, on which the Sacred Heart Mission had also long had designs. As late as 1973, the first sight to which I was led on arriving on Tamana was a large stone on which had been inscribed: 'Only The Protestant Religion Allowed'

> *two-shilling pieces, perhaps thirty or forty of them ...* [Grimble was told] *"It is a thing made by the villagers for a certain old man called Tabanea .... Whole villages sought his protective spells ....Tabanea sends a message before him when he is about to pass through a village and the people bring gifts of money...*
>
> *"But, Mautake, this thing must be stopped at once ... the man's levying a kind of tax on the villagers"...*
>
> *"And the Missionaries? The missionaries bring us their prayers and their schools and ask for gifts in return ... does the Government accuse the missionaries of levying a tax on us? ... if the Government or Missionaries could give them something to keep their hearts alive night and day as the magic of kindness does, perhaps they could be happy without Tabanea and his like ... but if you cannot give them an equal thing in return you will kill their hearts"'.*

It was in fact not the assembling, but the dismantling, of control that triggered rare public disagreements between government and the Missions. When it was suggested in 1935 that compulsory settlement in villages be rescinded, Eastman sent out a circular letter:

> *'Another difficulty that threatens very seriously to hamper our work is that Government by a complete reversal of policy is deliberately breaking up the villages and encouraging the people to go off and build shacks anywhere they like on their own lands in the bush. The result is that the attendance of the people at Sunday services and of children at school is seriously interfered with and our work is definitely rendered more difficult.'*

At the same time the Sacred Heart Priest Fr. Choblet was very publicly objecting to tolerance of traditional dress for children and young women. He erected a large bill board on Beru with pictures of soberly clad people and the legend: *'This is how the Church would like people to be clothed'* on one side; and on the other side, a picture from *La Vie Parisienne* of a naked (French) couple

Chapter 11: The Edifice of Control 1916 - 1941

and the legend *'This is how Mr and Mrs Maude would like the people to be clothed'*.[94]

Mission authority rested on:

- The fact that they had become established in society before the Protectorate had done so
- Their ability to sustain the fervour of their flocks, which varied from island to island and time to time (Sabatier, for example, when boasting of the numbers of converts to the Roman Catholic church, always lists alongside the numbers of backsliders, as he saw them, both to paganism and to Protestantism)
- Proximity and sheer numbers: priests, pastors and nuns, and the catechists lived on the islands and were thus much more visible to the ordinary Gilbertese villager than the rarely-visiting colonial officials
- Control of education.

The comment in *'The Covenant Makers'* that *'when it came to the crunch, the colonial government was always going to win'* seems correct about *'Te maiu ni Imatang'* matters; but it is doubtful whether the government had the same *moral* authority as the Churches – except, perhaps, in relation to dancing.

Traditional Authority

It was in fact the *Unimane* (and the *Ueas*) who continued to have the most *moral* authority; but as time went on (and despite occasional attempts to revive it – see page 232) - their formal authority was more and more hemmed in.

Customary law survived in many contexts. Despite Campbell's boasts (page 159) the *Uea* on Makin, Butaritari, Abaiang and Abemama/Kuria/Aranuka were frequently able to subvert their native governments, and ensure that members of their family were appointed to official positions. *Mwaneaba* systems continued to function in the southern Gilberts.

---

[94] The reaction of the 'people' to this spat is not recorded – nor has it been explained quite why the copy of *La Vie Parisienne*, a racy contemporary French publication, was in Fr. Choblet's possession!

Chapter 11: The Edifice of Control 1916 - 1941

Cinderellas of the Empire concludes that overall:

> *'There was a general adherence to a deeply rooted body of custom upon which alien laws and religious beliefs had made only a superficial impact'.*

When the District Officer was present his authority was undisputed; when he left, prosecutions and conviction rates in the Island Courts more than halved.

The 1930 Regulations also took away the power of the *Bowi* to make their own laws in accordance with their perceived needs and local traditions; and a factor in the reaction against them was the recognition by the 'reformers' amongst the DOs (Maude, MacDonald, Cartwright and others) of increasing reluctance on the part of officials to enforce regulations that had no basis in custom.

The regulations of 1930

The *'Regulations for the Good Order and Cleanliness of the Gilbert and Ellice Islands'* are described on the cover as having been *'made by the Native Magistrates and Kaubure'* and *'approved by District Officers on behalf of the Resident Commissioner under Section 15 (1) of Part I of the Schedule of the Native Laws Ordinance No. 2 of 1917'*. As the particular Resident Commissioner who was responsible for that Ordinance, Edward Eliot, might well have put it in *Broken Atoms*, they were nothing of the sort. They were the brainchild of Arthur Grimble, and reflected his own take on customary law, and his own moral attitudes and controlling nature. They were to be the high tide of paternalism and Grimble's 'museum policy'. It is illuminating that by contrast with these Regulations taking up 34 pages, the Penal Code of the GEIC, addressing truly criminal behaviour, comprised just three.

The Regulations were grouped into 45 headings. The table below contains an analysis of their cultural origin [95] as well as illustrating their extraordinary scope. By my estimation, some 70% of these rules had no basis in traditional (pre-contact) society, and only about 10% could be said to be more relevant to Mission values than colonial ones. They did partly reflect some acquired post-

---

[95] I appreciate that this is my own, doubtless subjective, assessment though aided by my wife

Chapter 11: The Edifice of Control 1916 - 1941

contact values which by 1930 had become *'Te maiu ni Kiribati'* [96]; but (by my estimate again) only about 15% would have been recognised in Tungaru custom. They also took no account whatever of differences in customs between islands – still less the distinct culture of the Ellice Islands, of which Grimble had no personal experience.

Breaches of the Regulations carried either fines or imprisonment. Fines were stipulated against each, and varied between 1 shilling and ten shillings. However, few were able to pay sums of this magnitude and the prisons were very often full. Imprisonment was considered as a *'Te maiu ni Imatang'* matter and carried no social stigma amongst the Gilbertese: indeed it was regarded as being more in the nature of a holiday from village life [97].

Heading	Number of rules*	Of which primarily based on:			
		'Tungaru' values	Church values	Colonial values	Uncertain
Adoption	1	1			
Bathing	4	2		2	
Bowi (Courts)	1			1	
Bubuti	1			1	
Burials	2		1	1	
Canoes and Fishing	5			5	
Children	2	1			1
Communal Works	13	2		11	
Cleaning	8			8	
Cruelty and Neglect	5	2		3	
Cultivation	2			2	

---

[96] My wife thinks that in her childhood in the 1950s about half of them would have been regarded as reasonable aspirations for daily communal living and, if ignored, village disapproval.

[97] I recall being told by Rosemary Peel of the surprise in the late 1940s when it was discovered that one prisoner was not the person who had been sentenced; the imposter explained that it was not 'convenient' for her friend to go to prison just at this time, so she had volunteered to stand in for her.

Chapter 11: The Edifice of Control 1916 - 1941

Dancing	13		6	7	
Danger	*				
Defecating	*				
Dogs	1			1	
Feasts	5			5	
Fires	1			1	
Food	1	1			
Fowls	1			1	
Games	1		1		
Government Stations	1			1	
Knives	3	1		2	
Land and Trees	3	3			
Latrines	4	2		2	
Hospitals and Sickness	4	1		3	
Houses	7	2		5	
Husband and Wife	1			1	
Meetings	1			1	
Mosquitoes	1	1			
Obstruction and Nuisance	5	1		4	
Obstruction of Officers	1				1
Pigs	3	1		2	
Prisons	1	1			
Religion	2		2		
Schools	3		3		
Smoking	2			2	
Spitting	*				
Strangers	3	1		2	
Toddy	2	1		1	
Trading Stations and Trade	2			2	
Travelling	4	2		2	
Urinating	*				
Vehicles	3			3	
Villages	4	1		3	
Wells	4	2		2	

Chapter 11: The Edifice of Control 1916 - 1941

| Total number of Regulations | 141 | 29 | 13 | 87 | 2 |

*   excluding cross-references

After Grimble left in 1933, pressure to reform and liberalise the regulations was applied to his successor, Jack Barley, by younger and mostly more educated District Officers. Although the person responsible, MacDonald, continued to work on a new set, progress was slow and Barley's interest spasmodic.

In the event it fell to Harry Maude to go over the head of the Resident Commissioner: in 1935 he gave a copy of the Regulations to Camilla Wedgwood, an anthropologist working on Nauru whose father was a Labour MP in Britain. Col. Josiah Wedgwood, who had previously championed colonial subjects in India and Africa, found them *'utterly repugnant to all British ideas of justice'* and confronted the Secretary of State for the Colonies with the threat that he would begin a campaign by reading the regulations out in Parliament. This was enough to make the Colonial Office demand action from the Western Pacific High Commission, and a full revision was prepared by MacDonald, Armstrong and Maude, *'together with carefully selected representatives of the Gilbertese race'*, under Barley's chairmanship [98].

It was also agreed that Maude should visit each island and consult the native administrations; this nearly backfired as on the first islands visited the native governments demanded that far from being liberalised, the regulations should be made still more severe. It was only when he summoned a meeting of the whole *mwaneaba* that the feeling of the villagers came out:

> *'An uproar of protest from the people pointing out the iniquity of the regulations, their unbalanced character, their lack of point in some cases and their result in making ordinary men and women into gaol-birds.* [99]*'*

---

[98] There was an awkward moment when Barley looked at Maude and declared *'who the hell could have told the authorities in London about these damned regulations?'*

[99] Perhaps I should point out that this was Maude's own description of the results of these meetings.

Chapter 11: The Edifice of Control 1916 - 1941

In 1939 The Western Pacific High Commissioner Sir Harry Luke paid a visit to the Gilberts and also the Ellice. He recorded in his diary:

> *'We have on board the prints of the new regulations, which we are distributing to the islands as we go along. These have just been passed in modification of the old ones, some of which were of a ferociously grandmotherly nature ... I rather regret the disappearance of this one, now merged in a more general provision: "It is an offense for any person with intent to deceive the public to raise the cry of Sail Ho in the absence of any ship"...*
>
> *'[The Regulations] would have been more suitable as by-laws for the next world. Had they been implicitly obeyed the natives would have been too good to be true ... in the new Regulations the curfew has been lifted and various other restrictions on human activities removed, and I don't suppose the morals of the islands will be any the worse for it.'*

The disjunction between the native government officials and the *mwaneabas* convinced Maude that a new system of local government was required; in the event this had to wait until after the Japanese invasion and American occupation (Chapter 13), when Maude had himself become Resident Commissioner.

The acceptance of expatriate authority 1892 to 1941

Just as - in an earlier era – the missionary Dr Gulick had expressed surprise that the Gilbertese did not *'murder every white man who landed on their shores'*, it might surprise the modern reader as to just why the Gilbertese seem so meekly to have succumbed to arbitrary expressions of power in the early period of the Protectorate, and to the draconian controls of the Colony in the later period. It seems at odds both with their warlike past, and their society of proudly independent individuals. Indeed according to many of those who have written autobiographies of those years, they became renowned in the colonial service as being intensely 'loyal' to the King and Empire (and by extension, to the representatives of these locally).

Although it was said that Campbell dared not visit Beru without a gunboat at his back, there was in this period only ever one incident of physical violence offered to a colonial officer, and that had been severely provoked. As Eric Bevington pointed out, District Officers and other visitors were *'always*

Chapter 11: The Edifice of Control 1916 - 1941

unarmed and proud to be unarmed', unlike the situation in many other parts of the Empire [100].

The translation of the status of the *Imatang*, from slaves whose property was forfeit, to accepted supervisors, was some mix of many things:

- The initial tradition of social control by the *kaainga* and *mwaneaba* systems, of which the rules of the Missions and government were to some extent mere extensions
- The early prohibition of alienation of their most prized possession, their land, to foreigners. This made irrelevant the principal causes of conflict in Africa, and indeed elsewhere in the Pacific (although it does not apply to the Banabans after 1908)
- An appreciation of the benefits of *Imatang*-imposed peace; and a realisation that they had no effective riposte to the 'gunboats' (life might be cheap, but loss of possessions to gunfire was not)
- Later, a similar appreciation of *Imatang* 'deep sleep' operations, injections to treat yaws, and medicine generally
- The fact that money played no part in traditional society, so it passed them by that the one-sided financial arrangements imposed on them were exploitative (again, with Banaba excepted)
- A widespread belief that traditional weapons of magic and sorcery were simply ineffective against *Imatang*.

Additionally, in every society, there are people who wish to become petty tyrants - and Gilbertese society was no exception. By substituting appointment of native government officials for their election by the local communities as instituted by Swayne, the colonial authorities created opportunities for such *'men who may be supposed to be more progressive, less dilatory, and less wedded to ancient customs and methods'*. Some of the edifice was created by them, not their rulers (as evidenced by their reaction to the proposals to liberalise the 1930 Regulations).

Nor were all the *unimane* cowed. When the Western Pacific High Commissioner Sir Murchison Fletcher visited Nikunau in 1931, he was rather

---

[100] I still have my Grandmother's ivory handled revolver, an 'honour gun' which was standard issue to British wives in India in the 1920s; and can remember the tales of my aunt about her compulsory training in the use of guns in Kenya in the 1950s.

taken aback, after making his set speech on the advantages and freedoms brought to the island by British rule, to receive the response from one old man:

> *'You have told a wonderful story. I thought I was listening to a fairy tale. This isn't the Gilbert Islands that I know, and I have lived here all my life'.*

The Gilbertese also became experts in 'gaming' colonial administrators, and refused to be overawed. Herbert McClure tells against himself the time when the speaker (i.e. himself, in a *mwaneaba*):

> *'... reached his peroration. It was of some length and dealt principally with administrative processes in South Africa where the Commissioner had previously served. These reminiscences were probably of great interest, but the interpreter, with a deep knowledge of human nature, thought otherwise. He thought in fact that the audience whose attention had obviously began to wander, had reached its limit of endurance. Most reprehensively, therefore, he transated his master's words as follows:* "The Old Man says" *he interpreted* " that he is very pleased with me and that he wished you to bring a dozen bottles of sour toddy" *(a most pernicious, intoxicating and utterly prohibited drink)* "to my house tonight, that I might have a little refreshment. Those are his words".*

> *'In this manner the meeting concluded in an atmosphere of universal satisfaction. The Commissioner felt he had made an impression. The audience was spared a recital of experiences ... Friday* [as the interpreter was known] *could look forward with reasonable certainty to a convivial evening...'*

Similarly, for some reason known only to Grimble, divorce (under custom, easy) became only permitted under a court constituted by a District Officer. The full ramifications of British law were applied and *'a large and cunning set of blue forms in a large tear out book was devised'*. This led to a widespread belief that the procedure *required* a would-be divorcee to commit adultery (having invited observers to satisfy the court); and then to serve a three-month prison sentence for that crime, adultery being thus punishable under the 1930 Regulations. Once the sentence had been served, the divorce could proceed. Several autobiographies of this period single out how the divorce process in particular *'became, tediously and inevitably, a farce'*.

Chapter 11: The Edifice of Control 1916 - 1941

Ultimately, the 'edifice of control' was thus just another '*Te maiu ni Imatang*' thing to be worked around.

I would argue also that it was the sheer proximity of the Gilbertese and their British rulers that enabled them to rub along together – it was a very different situation to many more developed parts of the Empire, with their settlements, clubs, crowds of servants, and separate living arrangements. In the Gilberts at that time, an expatriate outside Banaba or Tarawa was, if lucky, accompanied by his wife, but was more often alone. His food might be supplemented by some tinned goods, but his material living standards were not really so different from those of his charges. If he did not socialise with Gilbertese and learn their language, there was no one else living nearby with whom to maintain human contact.

As Eric Bevington recorded overhearing as he lay in the *mwaneaba* on Beru, the Gilbertese harboured few illusions about their colonial overseers:

> *"Is he asleep?"*
>
> *"Yes, this one sleeps well"*
>
> *"Strange people, aren't they, these Imatang"?*
>
> *"What makes you say that?"*
>
> *"Well – they're so clever, and so helpless ... they can put you to sleep and cut your body open, and you live. They have these little talking boxes and you can hear voices miles across the ocean. They can make engines which move ships into the teeth of the wind.*
>
> *"But what good does that do them? They are rotten fishermen, they cannot climb a coconut palm to cut toddy and get nuts. If they lived here alone, they'd be dead in no time".*

Chapter 11: The Edifice of Control 1916 - 1941

Further Reading

1. **Report of Mr Arthur Mahaffy: Visit to the Gilbert and Ellice Islands 1909**, presented to both Houses of Parliament by Command of His Majesty and published by HM Stationary Office, 1910
2. **Broken Atoms,** by E. C. Eliot, published by Geoffrey Bles, 1938
3. **Private Papers** of Sir John Peel, Resident Commissioner Gilbert and Ellice Islands 1948-1950 (unpublished)
4. **Health Survey of the Gilbert and Ellice Islands** by S.M. Lambert, of the Rockefeller Foundation, published by the Government Printer Suva, 1924
5. **From A South Seas Diary**, by Sir Harry Luke, published by Nicholson and Watson, 1945
6. **Astride the Equator,** translated by Ursula Nixon from **Sous l'équateur de Pacifique** by Ernest Sabatier, Oxford University Press, 1977
7. **She Sailed On "John Williams III",** pamphlet published by the London Missionary Society (undated, but immediately post WWII)
8. **The South Seas Look Ahead,** by P Knightly, published by the Livingstone Press, 1947
9. **Footsteps in the Sea: Christianity in Oceania to World War II,** by John Garrett, published by the Institute of Pacific Studies, 1992
10. **The Covenant Makers: Island Missionaries in the Pacific,** edited by Doug Munroe and Andrew Thornley, published by the Pacific Theological College, Suva, 1997
11. **Grimble: The Myth and the Man** by Dr. Barrie Macdonald, published in **Pacific Islands Portraits Vol. 2** (edited by D. Scarr), ANU Press, 1979
12. **Cinderellas of the Empire,** by Dr. Barrie Macdonald, published by the Institute of Pacific Studies, 1982
13. **Where Our Hearts Still Lie – A Life of Harry and Honor Maude In The Pacific Islands,** by Susan Woodburn, published by Crawford House Publishing, 2003
14. **The Things We Do For England – If Only England Knew**, by Eric Bevington, published by the Laverham Press, 1990
15. **Land Travel And Sea Faring: A Frivolous Record Of Twenty Years Wanderings** by H. R. McClure, published by Hutchinson & Co., 1925
16. **A Pattern of Islands,** by Arthur Grimble, published by John Murray, 1952
17. **Regulations for the Good Order and Cleanliness of the Gilbert and Ellice Islands,** published by His Britannic Majesty's High Commission for the Western Pacific, 1930

Chapter 12.

THE ECONOMY 1916 - 1942

The village economy

Subsistence

The vast bulk of Gilbertese families continued to grow and consume their own food from their lands, and from the reef and ocean as described in Chapter 7, but aided by the technical innovations described in Chapter 8.

The 1923 Health Survey commented:

> *'Except during periods of long drought food supplies are ample'*

but immediately followed this observation with the bafflingly contradictory statement that:

> *'The scarcity of food in the Gilberts and the constant effort on the part of both men and women which is necessary to obtain and prepare it is one of the great reasons of their resistance to the effects of white civilisation. For these, the Pacific Islands poorest in natural gifts, are alone in having maintained a dense population after years of contact with white men and their customs.*
>
> *'The Ellices [sic] are richer in soil and its products, life is less strenuous and here we have the familiar picture of a slowly declining race'* [101]

The cash economy never took hold with regard to daily living, at least until the 1960s [102]. H E Maude wrote of his time living on Tamana in 1936:

> *'I could get very little fish to eat, although I paid a good price for it. On alluding to my troubles in the council house an old man got up and*

---

[101] This seems to be saying that the Gilbertese were healthier because they had stuck to their traditional diet rather than switching to imported foods, which in the view of most modern commentators is quite correct.

[102] And still had not for the most part when I first went to the Gilberts in the 1970s

informed me with some heat that unless I gave up my revolting habit of paying for things, he supposed that I would starve.

'I gave it up; and the fish never failed. But one should not conclude from this that by adhering to their customs the European can live like a king, for nothing. I had to give a series of feasts to the island which cost me double what I would have had to pay for my fish'.

The Lands Commissions

What did concern villagers, however, was the backlog in dealing with disputes over the ownership of land, which could no longer be resolved solely by negotiations amongst the *unimane*, or through warfare. Disputes had essentially been frozen since 1892, which was particularly problematical on Tarawa where the civil wars being fought over over land had been abruptly halted. It was not until nearly thirty years later that Edward Eliot's administration passed an Ordinance, in 1919, which aimed at ensuring the settlement of disputes *'in accordance with customary law'*.

This Ordinance provided the legal standing for the Native Lands Commission. To begin with, the position of Native Lands Commissioner was either left vacant, or the incumbent was seconded to other departments; but in 1922 Arthur Grimble assumed the post and began serious work. There were then 76,000 outstanding disputes, distributed amongst a population of some 27,000.

The Lands Commissions drew up 'Lands Registers': registers of land owners, under whose names were listed the lands for which they (and usually other people) were registered as the proprietor. Each landowner had one or more pages in the register for any particular island, showing from whom the land was acquired (normally a forebear) together with its size, Lands Court case number and any encumbrances. The Lands Commissions did not use cadastral surveys but the location of coral stone boundaries, which as they were movable were often challenged in the Lands Courts.

It must be said that lands disputes were for the Gilbertese almost an art form. Grimble commented:

'I should be sorry if it were gathered that the Gilbert native was an unreliable person in all his dealings. He is not so ... [but] land is his passion and in dealings therewith he is a changed being whose chief characteristics are an amazing untruthfulness and supreme cupidity'.

An alternative view, and perhaps a more measured one, is that, in the words of Henry Lundsgaarde:

> *'Although English colonial law is responsible for almost insisting on the two-party litigant and third party authority judicial pattern, it has not been difficult for the Gilbertese to dissociate individual action from social or collective action. Gilbertese ideology is quite striking in its general postulate of individualism within a general framework of co-operation ... [there was a] ... peculiar mixture of a Western Court sitting and Gilbertese conceptions of fairness and justice'.*

In other words, the Gilbertese gamed the colonial administration, as they did so often.

As time went on, however, and the population rose, the Lands Commissions began to produce genuine evidence of pressure on land resources, especially in the Southern Gilberts, resulting in the Phoenix Islands Resettlement Scheme. This is described below. The Lands Commission was active until the 1950s (other than during WWII) until it was merged into the District Administration in 1954.

Cash crops and imported goods

Until the early nineteenth century interior lighting in Europe and the United States was provided by candles made from either wax or tallow: the wax was expensive, the tallow had an unpleasant smell. Experiments by Michel Eugène Chevreul, a French chemist, made possible the employment of other burnable fats. Spermaceti from whales could be used for candles, and this helped to fuel the Pacific sperm whaling industry (Chapter 7). Continued researches created a market for another Pacific product: coconut oil.

In 1829, J. Soames took out a patent for separating coconut oil into solid and liquid constituents; and by 1840 it was being used for soap and candle manufacture. However, the trade, like the whaling, was short lived: it was supplemented, and then superseded, by trade in copra. Between 1867 and 1869 Theodor Weber, the newly appointed agent in Apia for the German firm of J. C. Godeffroy and Son of Hamburg, experimented with the shipment of copra instead of oil; and copra came to replace oil completely as the main export in the 1870s. J. C. Godeffroy (later Jaluit Gesellschaft) established a store at Butaritari from its headquarters in the Marshall Islands, and the first copra was shipped from the Gilberts in 1872. In 1892 Captain Davis estimated

Chapter 12: The Economy 1916 - 1942

that about 3500 tons were exported per year from the Gilberts Group. (The only other exportable commodities from the Gilberts were small amounts of shark's fin and bêche-de-mer).

In the Gilberts copra remained the cash crop of individual villagers, although Mahaffy's White Paper about the Gilberts group, published in 1910 following his tour of the Protectorate, expressed the hope that:

> *'The continued decrease of the native population will at no very distant date permit the leasing of comparatively large tracts of land on many of the islands which should make extremely valuable cocoanut plantations'.*

There was reluctance in some islands to part with their surplus coconuts in the form of copra (Maude estimates that between 40% and 90% of coconuts were consumed locally, although this was dependent on both island population density and drought, which varied from island to island and time to time. Often, the Gilbertese – being satisficers rather than 'economic men' (see pages 121 - 122) preferred to let the surplus rot).

5lbs (2.3 Kg.) of copra paid, in kind, the capitation tax to the government (which took the risk of price changes); payments to the Missionaries were several times as much, especially in Protestant areas where it was compulsory to own Bibles and Hymn Books, as well as clothes. After these levies, Maude estimates that an average household at this time earned, from copra, less than £1 per year to spend in the store for their own consumption [103].

Grimble described the contents of Anton Meyer's store on Tarawa in about 1920:

> *'Anton kept a marvellous assortment of [goods] beyond the ordinary run of prints and tobacco, sailcloth and fishing gear, sheath-knives and tools, sewing cotton and kerosene that ranked as village necessities. He was particularly strong on Chinese silks, mouth organs and perfumery. The last two made very acceptable presents for village friends.'*

Captain Davis had remarked in 1892 that *'the export of copra might be greatly increased, if spare land were cultivated and trees were more uniformly planted'*; and as more cash goods became available, and the price the villagers received improved, copra production did rise: up to 6,000 tons per year were being exported from the Gilberts, at least in non-drought years, just before WWII.

---

[103] So it is not surprising that prison sentences were preferred to fines.

Prices also fluctuated: they were high between 1900 and 1914, stable during WWI, but fell back immediately after; then after reaching a peak price again in 1926, fell by as much as 90% during the Great Depression of the 1930s.

As regards other cash income, village policemen were paid £6 a year, and on each island the Chief Kaubure, Chief of Police and the Scribe were paid £12. Employment on Banaba also provided the wherewithal to acquire store goods, especially capital items.

Commerce

Trading companies

At the outset of the colonial era, the copra trade and imports were mostly in the hands of small individual traders, although some of these were agents of larger concerns. They were an international lot. Norman Chatfield, who had been the Supercargo on the trading ship 'Ysabel', records in a letter to the Resident Commissioner John Peel in 1949, that:

> *'When I first went to Tarawa in 1902, there were quite a number of traders there. Starting up north from Betio, we first came to the Catholic Mission Station, then to a chinaman's Station* [Ah Chew], *then to Meyer, a German trader, then another chinaman* [Ah Sing], *then Captain Kustell* [American], *then to Anton Kowarra* [actually Anton Kavaro, an Austrian], *then Peter Grant, an old Irishman, then Francis J. Lodge the New Zealander who said he was the only white man in the Group and who wrote to the Prime Minister of Australia, Mr Deakin, complaining that I would not take his copra; and lastly a trader called Russian Tom, an old Russian with a hole in his side which he said was made by an old copper bullet fired by an English Soldier in the Battle of Balaclava'.*

He wrote also that Peter Grant had an Irish wife and two daughters, one of whom later caused a scandal by *'getting into trouble with a native'*.

As time went on, however, these small and undercapitalised individual traders were squeezed out by larger companies: On Chong and Burns Philp (South Sea) Ltd. (based in Sydney); Jaluit Gesellschaft, based in the Marshall Islands; and after WWI, the Japanese Company, Nanyo Boyeki Kaisha, that had replaced Jaluit Gesellschaft. This last was only permitted to trade in

Chapter 12: The Economy 1916 - 1942

Butaritari and Makin, although it consistently but unsuccessfully tried to persuade the colonial authorities to let it expand to the rest of the group [104].

By the 1930s shipping had become more regular and both Burns Philp and On Chong ran their own inter-island vessels. On Chong was eventually bought out by W R Carpenter and this company and Burns Philp continued to trade until the Japanese invasion.

Although these two companies were less exploitative than the early pre-Protectorate traders, the Gilbertese and Ellice islanders were beginning to become more savvy, and less inclined passively to accept prices given to them by the traders.

A co-operative movement was established first in 1926, by Mr D. G. Kennedy, the European schoolmaster at Vaitupu in the Ellice group. The first retail society, the Vaitupu *'fusi'*, was a notable success and by 1931 had imported the first motor lorries in the Colony to collect coconuts, which had doubled the production of copra on that island. The co-operative movement (although not the motor lorries) caught on rapidly throughout the Gilberts group and by 1934 there were 34 societies (known as the *'boboti'*), operating on every island except Tamana. The general pattern of the co-operative societies was much the same: they existed to buy trade goods from, and sell copra to, one or both of the European wholesale firms, and their profits were made from a difference of about 10% between the wholesale price at which they purchased their trade goods and the retail price at which they sold them to their members; and a similar difference of ten shillings a ton between their copra buying and selling rates. The principal, and usually the only paid, officer of the societies was the Scribe (a name which was later changed to Manager) who kept five standard books: the Membership, Cash, Copra, and Store Books, and the Members' Pass-Books in which each transaction with a member was recorded. Entrance fees and Membership Subscriptions were quite steep: they ranged from five shillings to £1.

The Societies were usually controlled by a Committee consisting of from two to ten members elected by each hundred members of the Society. These Committees served for periods varying between three months and a year and were in turn subject to the decisions of the General Meeting, held at least twice a year, at which the books, store balance and copra stock were examined and

---

[104] The British assumed – correctly – that the company was also involved in espionage

all matters connected with the welfare of the society were discussed and voted on. In the early days there was often a President as well, who represented the society in dealings with European trading companies or the government, but it was found in practice that his duties were increasingly assumed by the Manager or the Chairman of the Committee and the position gradually fell into abeyance.

The co-operative movement had to fight against difficulties from the very start. Prominent among these was the fact that the societies had no option but to buy from and sell to the two European commercial companies, who had a price-fixing arrangement which made them, in effect, a single monopoly. The commercial rivalry between the two companies was nevertheless sufficient to prevent either of them from boycotting the co-operative societies; and so, by playing one firm against the other, the co-operatives were able to increase their own strength. By the time of the outbreak of war with Japan, there was not one European or Chinese trader left in either the Gilbert or Ellice Islands, other than a few salaried managers of the Companies' main branches. When the Gilbert Islands were occupied by the Japanese all trade ceased and so – temporarily – did the societies; after WWII they were revived and became even more dominant in commerce.

The British Phosphate Commission

The BPC may have taken over from the Pacific Phosphate Company, and have become a governmental body, but it did not change its spots: the same attitudes, and mostly the same personnel, persisted.

An example of this was the discriminating 'dual pricing' system in the BPC store (which had a monopoly on the island under the 1900 agreement). 'Natives' and Chinese were charged about twice as much for the same item as Europeans (and, while they were still employed on the island, as honorary Europeans, the Japanese).

Edward Eliot records that:

> 'Before Captain Dickson, my predecessor, was removed from Office he had reported to Downing Street the unfairness of the 'two-price' system. The Colonial Office had requested the Company to change the system and to sell to all at one price. Plainly, the only fair thing to do would have been to reduce the native prices considerably and to have increased slightly the price to the whites sufficient to make a reasonable profit. This the

Company had not the least intention of doing. It did lip-service to the Colonial Office. It made considerable reductions in the native price only on things the natives seldom if ever bought. It raised the white man's price to only slightly below the old native rate on all articles much in demand by natives...

'The Company told their employees that all their purchases would be made on the 'book system'. A discount would be allowed to bring the prices down to exactly what they were before. The same concession was made to the priests and sisters. The Manager then had the impudence to offer us officials the same 'book terms'. I replied that on instructions from the Colonial Office I had already told the natives that there would be one price for whites and natives alike and that we could not entertain for one moment his offer of any reduction. The Manager then told me that his Directors in London had obtained the sanction of the Colonial Office to his offer. I reported this conversation to the Colonial Office ... I never received an answer'.

That was in the days of the Company, and after their scourge Eliot left in 1920 the old dual pricing system seems to have been quietly re-established by the BPC (and accepted by the then officials, who were clearly less principled than Eliot). It came under attack again in the early 1930s: when it was abolished for the second time, the BPC simply raised the wages of white staff to compensate, about which the government could do nothing.

The phosphate operation

After Eliot had persuaded the Banabans to grant the leases in 1913 there were a few years of comparative quiet while these were exploited (the BPC was also internally preoccupied, with each of the three Commissioners, and also the management of BPC, jostling for control). Japanese labourers were replaced by Chinese recruited in Hong Kong; the total labour force of between 1200 and 1500 had fluctuating numbers of Gilbertese, Ellice and Chinese through the 1920s and 1930s.

In 1925 there were clashes between the Chinese and Gilbertese. An investigation by the Secretary to the Western Pacific High Commission found that the BPC had ignored most of the labour regulations applicable and that the GEIC Government had largely abdicated responsibility for their enforcement. As a result rigorous segregation was enforced between the two

Chapter 12: The Economy 1916 - 1942

communities, and token efforts made to enforce the regulations; but there were further disturbances in 1931 [105].

In 1927 BPC started to agitate for the acquisition of more land, but negotiations stalled over the Banabans' demands for better terms. The Banabans stood their ground, even after receiving this missive on 5th August 1928:

'To the People of Buakonikai Village.

'Greetings. You understand that the Resident Commissioner cannot again discuss with you at present as you have shamed his Important Chief, the Chief of the Empire, when he was fully aware of your views and your strong request to him and he had granted your request and restrained his anger and restored the old rate to you – yet you threw away and trampled upon his kindnesses to you. The Chief has given up and so has his servant the Resident Commissioner because you have offended him by rejecting his kindnesses to you. Because of this I am not writing to you in my capacity as Resident Commissioner but I will put my views to you as from your long standing friend Mr Grimble who is truly your father who has aggrieved you during this frightening day which is pressing upon you when you must choose LIFE or DEATH. I will explain my above statement.

'POINTS FOR LIFE. If you sign the Agreement here is the life: (1) your offence in shaming the Important Chief will be forgiven and you will not be punished (2) the area of land to be taken is well known, that is only 150 acres that will be part of the Agreement (3) The amount of money to be received will be properly understood and the Company will be bound to pay you, that will be part of the Agreement

'POINTS FOR DEATH. If you do not sign the Agreement:- (1) Do you think that your lands will not go? Do not be blind. Your land will be compulsorily acquired for the Empire. If there is no Agreement then who will know the area of the lands to be taken? If there is no Agreement where will the mining stop? If there is no Agreement what lands will remain unmined? I tell you the truth – if there is no Agreement the limits of the compulsorily acquired lands on Ocean Island will not be known (2) And

---

[105] In both instances of riots, to be fair, Grimble showed considerable personal courage; in 1925 he had had a tooth knocked out when a stone was thrown at him

> your land will be compulsorily acquired at any old price. How many pence per ton? I do not know. It will not be 10 ½ d. [The amount then being offered]. How many pounds per acre? I do not know. It will not be £150. Far from it. What price will be paid for coconut trees cut down outside the area? I know well that it will remain at only £1. Mining will be indiscriminate on your lands and the money you receive will also be indiscriminate. And what will happen to your children and your grandchildren if your lands are chopped up by mining and you have no money in the Bank? Therefore because of my great sympathy for you I must ask you to consider what I have said now that the day has come when you must choose LIFE or DEATH. There is nothing more to say. If you choose suicide then I am very sorry for you but what more can I do for you as I have done all I can. I am your loving friend and father ARTHUR GRIMBLE.
>
> P.S. You will be called to the signing of the Agreement by the Resident Commissioner on Tuesday next the 7th August and if everyone signs the Banabans will not be punished for shaming the Important Chief and their serious misconduct will be forgiven. If the Agreement is not signed consideration will be given to punishing the Banabans. And the destruction of Buakonikai Village must also be considered to make room for mining if there is no Agreement'.

By now the Banabans were sophisticated enough to know the value of their product, and they also knew that these were empty threats under the deal which Eliot had negotiated; so the British Government was forced to enact Mining Ordinance No. 4 of 1928, to permit compulsory acquisition of land on Banaba. This also - for the first time - gave the Banaban landowners only surface rights to their land, the underlying phosphate now being deemed to be the property of the Crown. The High Commissioner Sir Murchison Fletcher informed them that:

> 'With regard to land it was the rule generally that the surface belongs to the owner; and any minerals under the land belong to the Government, which can do what it pleases with them. The surface owners did not plant the minerals nor were they responsible for them, therefore they belonged to the Crown' [106]

---

[106] Such a policy would have been news to e.g. the owners of coal mines in Britain at the time. Only the 'Mines Royal' - gold and silver – then belonged to the Crown under

Chapter 12: The Economy 1916 - 1942

The Colonial Office took the view that *'as regards under-surface rights investigations [107] have shown that insofar as the Banabans had any clear idea of such rights at all they were held ... by groups who did not necessarily hold the surface rights'* and that therefore *'in any further discussions with the Banabans there should be no admission that rights in phosphate deposits not already surrendered belong to individual Banabans claiming surface land rather than to the community as a whole'*.

Early in 1931 150 additional acres of land were compulsorily taken over and leased to the BPC.

Payments to the Banabans

The other preoccupation of the High Commissioner and the GEIC Government was that they should hold and control all payments in trust for the Banabans, whereas the latter wanted direct distribution to the landowners involved.

A brief, again written by Grimble, suggested the following principles:

1. *It is agreed that in the administration of Banaban trust moneys, the general benefit of the community should be the chief object sought; the direct payment of large income to individual natives should be avoided if possible.*
2. *Nevertheless the right of individual Banabans to receive certain payment from common funds was conferred by contract in 1913 and must be recognised in any new plan of administration adopted.*
3. *Deference is also due to native custom, Banaban usage unequivocally admits to the right of the individual to hold land; the land has now been compulsorily converted into money, but this fact cannot nullify the landowners' inherited right of individual enjoyment.*
4. *A scheme of administration is required which while based upon communal principles preserves a proper regard for individual enjoyment.*

A long-running negotiation with the Banabans on this issue was not finally concluded until 1937, when a compromise Annuities Agreement was signed by all the Banabans other than Rotan and his family (the largest landowners). Their annuities were held in trust.

English Law. Even the Colonial Office did comment - internally to itself - that this statement was unwarranted!

[107] That is, an assertion by Grimble!

Chapter 12: The Economy 1916 - 1942

In 1940 the 1931 concessions were coming to an end of being mined out, and Mr A. H. Gaze, the General Manager of the BPC, approached the landowners with proposals for further acquisitions. Negotiations about these were overtaken by WWII, and parked until 1946, by which time the Banabans had moved to Rabi, in Fiji.

The Government and the BPC

At the same time, the long-running argument over the extent to which mining revenues should contribute to the overall welfare of the GEIC (and to government expenditure in particular) was re-opened (see below). Sir Arthur Richards and Sir Harry Luke, Western Pacific High Commissioners in the late 1930s, tried to establish some degree of government control over the BPC, but with mixed success.

Both urged that the Resident Commissioner and the GEIC Headquarters be moved from Banaba, where they would be less susceptible to BPC bullying, and not so dependent on it for their daily living needs. Sir Luke commented after his visit in 1939:

> *'Why the natives are as patient and loyal as they are I cannot understand, for I have never encountered an Administration that does less for its ressortissants ... I realise that to move the headquarters will involve a considerable outlay, but there is little doubt in my mind, any more than there was in the minds of* [his predecessors] *Fletcher and Richards, that the administration can only emerge from its present nerveless and paralysed condition when the change has been made'.*

Government Finances

Initially, the British had established Island Funds: but as these began to build up substantial amounts, covetous eyes were turned on them. In 1908 the Colonial Office, to avoid paying for a Protectorate ship, suggested that the Island Funds pay instead as the ship would be *'clearly for the benefit of the natives'*; in 1914 the Funds were absorbed into the budget and in 1917 all revenues were assumed by the Colony Government, and island administration funded by it instead of locally.

In fact, such was the parsimony of the administration that when the disastrous (for the Colony) deal was made with the BPC (see below), there were accumulated reserves of more than £100,000 – nearly two years' expenditure.

Revenue came from capitation taxes, import duties (including on machinery imported by the BPC) and duties on tobacco and alcohol, as well from the ever-increasing incidence of fines as the Island Regulations were tightened.

The BPC had turned its attention to another long-term aim soon after gaining the right to compulsorily acquire land: reducing the amount it paid into Colony funds. In 1934 the British Commissioner Arthur Gaye and the BPC Manager Gaze took advantage of the simultaneous presence in Suva of themselves, the Western Pacific High Commissioner Sir Murchison Fletcher, and a sick Grimble, recently departed from the GEIC, to negotiate a new arrangement.

Under this the Commissioners would no longer pay a whole range of taxes, licenses and import duties (they would continue to pay the 6d. per ton royalty charged under the original agreement made with the Pacific Phosphate Company). Instead the BPC would undertake to make up the balance between the Colony's other income (derived mainly from taxes on the copra trade and duties on liquor and tobacco) and the official estimate of each year's expenditure. This sum was to be annually agreed between the Resident Commissioner and the Ocean Island Manager, with no changes to be agreed by a higher British Government entity without consultation with the BPC's three Commissioners [108]. This agreement was to run for five years.

From the GEIC viewpoint, the deal was a disaster. The BPC ended up paying significantly less than they had before taxation was commuted. Also, because they no longer had to pay a capitation tax for Chinese labourers, these were to a degree substituted for Gilbertese and Ellice Islanders which led to lower cash employment and income locally.

Predictably, the BPC also took their oversight of the Colony budget as a mandate to challenge *any* expenditure outside of keeping law and order on Banaba (even the principle of there being a Colony vessel was disputed).

They were especially and vehemently opposed to any expenditure on native education, the '*pale imitation of European education*' which had been established by the Australian Administrator on Nauru being seen by them as '*an ill-considered policy on native questions*' which '*would lead to difficulties in the not too distant future*'.

---

[108] The principle having been established, exemption from taxation by the GEIC for the BPC and its employees was to last right up to Independence in 1979.

Although he had not been responsible for its negotiation, J. C. Barley took most of the blame: he was described as *'somewhat afraid of the Phosphate Commission and determined to be their most humble obedient servant'*. Both Sir Arthur Richards and Sir Harry Luke tried to establish some paramountcy over the BPC during their tenures of the Western Pacific High Commission, but with mixed success: Richards did manage to get an additional £10,000 a year added to the budget, but the situation was not resolved before the outbreak of WWII.

Social Services

Parsimony meant that services beside 'administration' and law and order were almost non-existent before WWII, other than medicine and education.

Medicine

The most appreciated were medical services. A native medical school had been started at the Colonial Hospital, Suva, in 1884 where a three years' course of training was given to Fijian youths selected after competitive examination; access to this school was extended to other parts of the Western Pacific High Commission as they became part of its remit. By 1923 there were in the GEIC a senior native medical practitioner (NMP) and three native medical practitioners who had graduated from the School, as well as 42 native dressers, who were locally trained. They were under the supervision of a single British Senior Colonial Medical Officer.

There were by then also 28 local hospitals as well as a central hospital on Tarawa, and a leper colony (leprosy had been introduced from Tahiti) under either an NMP or a Dresser. An earlier TB epidemic had by then largely been contained, but yaws was still common. Filiarisis was common in the Ellice Islands, but rare in the Gilberts. The BPC also operated a hospital on Banaba.

Eric Bevington writes of the Medical Practitioners in the 1930s:

> *'At each headquarters there was a Native Medical practitioner: these were the products of the magnificent Central Medical School ... it is hard to speak too highly of this school and its products. The local schools were creamed off for the most promising boys... from the earliest days the highest standards of medical ethics were required and the four years course ended with the award of certificates and a public taking of the*

Hippocratic Oath. The qualification was not then technically a registerable one.

'Medicine was in fact one of the prime tools of administration and of pacification'.

Education

By contrast, education was left to the Missions to provide; and moreover, within the GEIC Government, its purpose was hotly debated (although the 1930 Regulations made attendance at Mission schools compulsory for all children of primary school age, including those of the remaining 'pagan' families).

The spread of literacy had been led by the Protestants. Even Sabatier wrote that *'if we compare the tactics of the Protestants with those of the Catholics in their battle in the Gilberts, we can see a prepared and carefully organised campaign of one hand and on the other an attack motivated by eager improvisations ... indeed the Protestant Minister in the islands is little more than a headmaster with a vague leaning towards being a lay preacher'*. The Rongorongo school on Beru was described on page 164 above, and that on Abaiang was similar. The equivalent Roman Catholic institution at Manoku was set up some 30 years later, in 1914, and was more explicitly religious in tone, being focused on training (male) catechists. It was not thought desirable by either of the two Missions for pupils to learn English. In 1913, with the arrival of Eliot, the Government instituted a grant of £75 p.a. to each of the three schools.

However the government and to a lesser extent the BPC were by now developing a demand for clerks and interpreters with a knowledge of the English language; and so the colony opened the King George Vth School, at Bairiki in Tarawa, in May 1922 - and a similar school was set up in the Ellice Islands in 1924.

The nature and purpose of these two schools quickly became a matter for strong disagreement: the headmasters of the two schools, F.G.L. Holland and D.G. Kennedy, wanted to teach academic subjects and use English as the medium of instruction; but to the Resident Commissioner - by now Herbert McClure - the GEIC was *'unique in its isolation and lack of potentialities'* and therefore education in English was *'utterly unnecessary, if not fraught with actual danger'*. This view prevailed; and in 1926, when the first KGV graduates were due to enter Government service, Grimble questioned whether there was a need to educate another cohort for many years, when the new recruits would need to be replaced. After the new financial dispensation agreed with the BPC in 1934 spending on education again came under sustained attack:

> *'All academic instruction should now be abandoned and a revised syllabus, having in view every need and limitation of village life, should be adopted.'*

The Missions tended to agree: they were dissatisfied with the secular nature of KGV and the Ellice School, and the subsequent unwillingness of its graduates to accept church discipline. This debate was to continue after WWII, and even, albeit framed in different language, after Independence.

Nevertheless most Gilbertese and Ellice islanders were literate in their own language by the end of the 1920s. The Ellice School – further from these influences and with strong leadership from Kennedy - also played an important role in the revival of Ellice as a written and church language (as opposed to the Samoan used by the LMS Mission there before the 1920s); and this school produced an outstanding crop of academically-qualified graduates for the post-war government.

Population growth and 'the need for a new homeland'

The first official census in the GEIC was overseen by Harry Maude in 1931. The total population of the Gilbert Islands was then counted as 26,416; and of the Ellice Islands, 3,994. The Census did not cover Banaba, or the Phoenix and Line Islands, which would have added perhaps 1,000 more.

It had become apparent that the confident predictions of the BPC - and of early colonial officials such as Mahaffy - that the Pacific Islanders were a doomed population were false; and that in fact the population was well on the way to recovering its pre-contact levels. Further, the traditional limitations on fertility had been mostly declared illegal; the Missions encouraged children (Sabatier noted with particular satisfaction that the Roman Catholic were outbreeding the LMS congregations); and infant mortality had fallen with the advent of medical services. Instances of land hunger in the Southern Gilberts were becoming apparent from the Lands Commission.

The 'received wisdom' of the colonial authorities – although not that of the Missions - thus turned completely around. The idea that the Gilbert and Ellice Islands were 'overpopulated', and that the 'surplus' population needed to be transplanted elsewhere, took firm root in official thinking, indeed sometimes dominated it, right up to the time of Independence in 1979. The location of the 'new homeland' was variously identified – it was firstly in the Phoenix Islands, and then Fiji, although the Western Pacific High Commissioner Sir Arthur Richards favoured Christmas Island (Kiritimati) [109]. He wrote in 1937:

'There can be no question that the resumption [sic] of Christmas Island must be the ultimate solution of the Gilbertese population problem, as I forsee for it a marvellous future as the new home of the Gilbertese race'.

The Phoenix Islands

The Phoenix Islands or Rawaki are a group of eight atolls and two submerged coral reefs, lying in the central Pacific Ocean east of the Gilbert Islands and west of the Line Islands: they include Kanton (formerly Canton), Enderbury, Rawaki (formerly Phoenix), Manra (formerly Sydney), Birnie, McKean, Nikumaroro (formerly Gardner), and Orona (formerly Hull).

Archaeological sites have been discovered on Manra and Orona, which suggest two distinct groups of early settlers, one from eastern Polynesia, and one from Micronesia; but when Europeans arrived, the islands had been abandoned and were unpopulated. Spasmodic attempts to establish coconut plantations took place in the late 19th and early 20th century, as well as gathering of low-grade phosphate by the Pacific Islands Company (see page 143) and others. Rawaki was overrun by rabbits, left behind at some point by a passing ship, who shared burrows with gannets (see p. 358).

Nikumaroro may have been the landing site and later the graves of Amelia Earhart and her navigator, who disappeared a few months before the colonists arrived in 1937, during an attempt to make a circumnavigation of the globe by air; although the evidence as to whether the skeleton and detritus that the colonists found there was hers is disputed.

The Phoenix Islands were incorporated by Britain into the GEIC in 1937 with a view to their settlement (see below); but they had also been claimed by the United States under the Guano Islands Act. In 1938 the United States formally claimed sovereignty over Kanton and Enderbury, and in 1939 the two

---

[109] The area of Kiritimati (the largest of any coral atoll) is equivalent to that of the Gilbert Islands archipelago, so that *ceteris paribus* it had the potential to take half its population. Kiritimati now has a population of a little over 5,000.

countries agreed to exercise joint control over the two islands for 50 years, as the Canton and Enderbury Islands condominium.

Pan American World Airways (Pan Am) arrived on Kanton on 18 May 1939, to build facilities for their New Zealand flying boat service. The service commenced on 12 July 1940 with the Boeing 314 Clipper. On 4 December 1941, the Pacific Clipper departed Kanton for New Caledonia as the final civilian flight before the USA joined the war, and a military airstrip was operated in WWII. In November 1946, Pan Am resumed service to Hawaii, Australia and New Zealand via Kanton with Douglas DC-4 aircraft. British Commonwealth Pacific Airlines (BCPA), Australia's first trans-Pacific airline, also served the island via a co-operative agreement with Australian National Airways.

In 1960 a tracking station for the Mercury programme was built on Kanton, which operated until 1965. The last commercial flight was in November 1965; after the opening of a new airport in Auckland, Pan Am's Boeing 707s flew directly to there from Hawaii. Kanton's airport remained operational as an emergency landing field for some years afterwards.

The U.S. Air Force and the U.S. Space and Missile Systems Organization continued to use the island for missile-tracking operations until 1976 [110]. That year marked the end of the American presence; the airfield was abandoned and all U.S. personnel were removed. The British closed their post office, ending their permanent presence on Kanton as well. After the closure of the Phoenix Islands Settlement Scheme in 1963 (see below) the islands other than Kanton were more or less abandoned completely until 1974, when a GEIC vessel visited each to assess their developmental potential (then considered to be none).

They were then largely left to nature again, although a token government presence was established after Independence (when the US finally relinquished their claims to the Group). Kanton became, and still remains, the only island in the Group which is permanently inhabited.

The Phoenix Islands Settlement Scheme

The Phoenix Islands Settlement Scheme was begun in 1938; it was the last attempt at human colonisation within the British Empire. The scheme was the

---

[110] I remember being indignant at being ordered to falsify the 1973 GEIC Census, to pretend that there were no Americans there.

Chapter 12: The Economy 1916 - 1942

brainchild of Harry Maude although it was enthusiastically approved by Sir Harry Luke in Suva. The intent was to reduce overpopulation in the southern Gilbert Islands by developing three atolls in the Phoenix Islands archipelago. The three atolls, Sydney, Hull and Gardner were renamed in Gilbertese as Manra Island, Orona Atoll and Nikumaroro respectively. An explicit secondary goal was to enhance the British presence in the western Pacific in response to American claims under the Guano Islands Act (see above).

A report written by H. E. Maude estimated that when planted with suitable trees, Orona could sustain a population of 1,100, Manra 900, Nikumaroro 1,100 and Kanton 1,200 (in total, the equivalent of nearly 20% of the overall population of the Gilberts). By 1940 a total of 727 residents had been settled, excluding temporary military and airport personnel.

The settlement scheme was almost immediately hampered by the onset of World War II, the islands' subsequent isolation, and the death on Nikumaroro in 1941 of the District Officer in charge, Gerald Gallagher, who had been the mainstay of the settlement for its first four years. After 1945, the three settlements continued to struggle with supply problems, limited markets for copra, and drought.

The Resident Commssioner, High Commissioner, and British government determined in 1963 that the settlement could not be self-sustaining and evacuated the settlers to the Solomon Islands [111].

---

[111] It is difficult, when reading the file today, to avoid the impression that these droughts were no worse than those regularly experienced in the Southern Gilberts, and that the administration unnecessarily panicked about the situation. The file also contains some racially charged language by the then Western High Commissioner, by the 1960s relocated to the Solomon Islands, that the Protectorate there needed the services of the Gilbertese as government clerks - since they were so much more *'intelligent'* than the Solomon Islanders; and that they would be useful as labourers for Lever Brothers' plantations as well.

Given the current Phoenix Islands Protected Area and its importance for marine preservation, it was however (in the words of *'1066 And All That'*) probably a *'Good Thing'* that the settlement failed when it did.

Chapter 12: The Economy 1916 - 1942

Further Reading

1. **Cinderellas of the Empire,** by Dr. Barrie Macdonald, published by the Institute of Pacific Studies, 1982
2. **The Phosphateers**, by Maslyn Williams and Dr. Barrie Macdonald, published by the Melbourne University Press 1985
3. **Report of Mr Arthur Mahaffy: Visit to the Gilbert and Ellice Islands 1909**, presented to both Houses of Parliament by Command of His Majesty and published by HM Stationary Office, 1910
4. **Broken Atoms,** by E. C. Eliot, published by Geoffrey Bles, 1938
5. **Health Survey of the Gilbert and Ellice Islands** by S.M. Lambert, of the Rockefeller Foundation, published by the Government Printer Suva, 1924
6. **Where Our Hearts Still Lie – A Life of Harry and Honor Maude In The Pacific Islands,** by Susan Woodburn, published by Crawford House Publishing, 2003
7. **The Things We Do For England – If Only England Knew**, by Eric Bevington, published by the Laverham Press, 1990
8. **Of Islands and Men,** by H E Maude, published by the Oxford University Press, 1968
9. **Social Changes In The Southern Gilbert Islands, 1938-1964,** by Henry P Lundsgaarde, Published by Department of Anthropology, University of Oregon, Eugene, 1967
10. **Co-operatives and Development**, by Patrick Develtere, published by the University of Saskatchewan (not dated but recent)
11. **The Co-operative Movement in the Gilbert and Ellice Islands,** paper delivered by H.E. Maude at the South Pacific Commission, SPC Technical Paper No 1, 1949
12. **A Pattern of Islands,** by Arthur Grimble, published by John Murray, 1952
13. **The Strategy and Etiology of Gilbertese Property Disputes**, by Henry P Lundsgaarde, reprinted from American Anthropologist, Volume 70 No. 1, 1968
14. **Transactions in Gilbertese Law and Justice,** by Henry P Lundsgaarde, published in The Journal of the Polynesian Socitety, Volume 82 No. 2 June 1974
15. **From A South Seas Diary,** by Sir Harry Luke, published by Nicholson and Watson, 1945
16. **Astride the Equator**, translated by Ursula Nixon from Sous l'équateur de Pacifique by Ernest Sabatier, Oxford University Press, 1977
17. **Files in the British National Archives**
18. **United Nations Decolonisation Reports**

Chapter 13.

JAPANESE, AMERICANS, AND AFTERMATH OF WWII

The coming of foreign wars

A League of Nations mandate had been given to the Empire of Japan following World War I. The South Pacific Mandate consisted of all the islands in the northern Pacific Ocean that had been part of German New Guinea. The Imperial Japanese Navy initially divided the territory into five naval districts, including one based at Jaluit Atoll in the Marshalls; later, rule was nominally by civilians, but the Governor was usually an Admiral in the Japanese Navy. The major significance of the territory to the Empire of Japan was its strategic location, which dominated sea lanes across the Pacific Ocean and provided convenient provisioning locations for sailing vessels in need of water, fresh fruit, vegetables and meat. The territory also provided important coaling stations for steam-powered vessels.

Their Pacific possessions became an integral although minor part of *The Greater East Asia Co-Prosperity Sphere*, an imperial concept created and promulgated for Asian populations occupied by the Empire of Japan during 1930–1945. The Sphere ostensibly promoted the cultural and economic unity of Northeast Asians, Southeast Asians, South Asians and Oceanians and had the declared intention to create a self-sufficient *'bloc of Asian nations led by the Japanese and free of Western powers'*. The long-term plan included Japanese control of much of India and East Asia, and the settlement, by two million Japanese, of Australasia as well as all the islands in the Pacific.

The Sphere was in theory based on the concept of equality, and *'Asia for the Asiatics'*; but in practice the rights and status of the indigenous populations, including those of the Micronesians, differed markedly from those of Japanese imperial subjects [112]. Employment prospects for Micronesians were restricted,

---

[112] Although when I went to the Mandate countries in the late 1970s, on an UNDP project, I did meet some elderly Micronesians who compared the Japanese (and especially their technical education) favourably to the Americans, for whom it had become a UN Trust Territory after 1945: so it is not a wholly black and white issue.

with unequal labour conditions and pay. Japanese settlers also started to arrive in large numbers and land was confiscated for them to settle on. It is estimated that the largest towns in the Marshall Islands, Jaluit and Jabor, had about a thousand Japanese each; and even in the most isolated atolls there were a few Japanese individuals.

In the 1920s people of German-Marshallese descent began to arrive in the Gilberts; the Japanese had been making their lives in the Marshalls increasingly difficult, even compared to ordinary Marshallese. Many settled at Butaritari, which had long had trading links to the German territories to the north and was also to where the Roman Catholic Headquarters had moved in 1900; and was from 1925 the location of a boarding school for Marshallese and part-Marshallese under Brother Engelhardt.

German-Marshallese families such as the Narruhns, Reihers, Schutzes, Mullers, Von Reymond and Brechtefelds had become established in the Gilberts – and had mostly intermarried with Gilbertese - by 1940. Despite some initial distrust of their potential German sympathies, many of these families were to play prominent roles in support of the Americans in WWII; and several are still prominent in I Kiribati society.

Eric Bevington, newly transferred from Beru to Tarawa in 1940, recorded:

> *'Each month a Japanese trading vessel used to visit from the Marshall Islands to the north ... stories began to come in of visits by the super-cargo of the Japanese vessel to remote villages: stories of liberation from the White Man, of a Greater East Asia Co-Prosperity Sphere ... the Gilbertese knew well how their fellow Micronesians were treated by their Japanese 'Protectors' under the League of Nations Mandate ... as soon as the vessel had gone* [they reported] *every word to me. This in turn I would sift, analyse and send off a resumé in cipher.'*

Part of the message was that the Gilbert Islands would be incorporated into the Greater East Asia Co-Prosperity Sphere within days of war breaking out: in the event, this incorporation took place on 9th December 1941, two days after Japan declared war on America.

Sir Harry Luke's book (see Further Reading) has a chapter about the coming of world war to the Pacific. On Empire Day in 1940 he noted:

> *'Among the most striking individual gifts was one from the Banabans of Ocean Island, who number no more than 400 adults and 750 souls*

Chapter 13: Japanese, Americans, and Aftermath Of WWII

altogether ... They sent me a W/T message through the Resident Commissioner that they were placing £10,000 at the disposal of His Majesty's Government as a contribution to British War Funds'.

Until 1941 the main worry of the Western Pacific High Commission had been of activity by German warships (Japan had not then entered the war). Four days before the official declaration of war, troops from New Zealand were secretly dispatched to guard the submarine cable station on Tabueran (then Fanning Island). They arrived early in September 1939, and stayed for nearly five – in the end quite uneventful - years. As it turned out, the German warships were active, rather, off Banaba and Nauru where they sank several phosphate ships anchored off the shore, and successfully bombarded installations on Nauru.

In July 1941 twenty-two volunteers from the New Zealand Army 8th Brigade Group, and fifteen radio operators from the New Zealand Post and Telegraph Department, departed from Suva on the *RCS Viti* for coast-watching duties (to spot German ships) in the Gilbert and Ellice Islands. At about the same time, the Bairiki Wireless Training School was set up at KGV to train local people to assist these New Zealand staff. The New Zealand operators were paid a premium salary of £300 a year (although it was vigorously denied that this comprised 'danger money'); the Gilbertese were paid £18 a year. None of these NZ coast-watchers ever saw a German raider, and all were captured by the Japanese, with those in the northern Gilberts sent as prisoners to Japan, and those in the Gilberts south of Tarawa eventually executed after the Carlson Raid (see below).

At this time also Australia and New Zealand evacuated dependents of British Phosphate Commission employees from Banaba.

In December 1941 orders were sent out from the Resident Commissioner Ronald Garvey (who had recently replaced Barley) that all the European women and children in the Gilberts as well were to be evacuated to Fiji via Beru, on the *John Williams*. On the way back to Tarawa from Beru, where they had been collected by the Fiji Navy, Eric Bevington was in sight of land when *'the first sound from Tarawa was a morse key being bashed hard, giving over and over again the L.L.L.L. signal denoting an enemy landing'*. It was Willie Schutz. He continued until he was physically restrained by the Japanese [113]. The *Kiakia*

---

[113] Willie escaped, along with 28 others, in February the following year. After evading the Japanese, two separate sets of escapees managed to reach Nonouti, where they

turned around and took Bevington and some 20 Gilbertese who were on board to Fiji, without being detected by the Japanese.

Occupation of the Northern Gilberts

On December 8th, a Japanese flying boat had dropped six bombs on the Government Headquarters on Banaba; and on the following day Japanese troops occupied Makin, Butaritari, Abaiang and Marakei; and visited, but did not then occupy, Tarawa. Japanese landing parties rounded up the European population in the northern Gilberts, and informed them that no one might leave without the permission of the naval commander. The District Officer on Butaritari and all the coastwatchers north of Maiana were then taken to Japan and spent the war as prisoners; but two parties on Tarawa managed to escape on boats which the Japanese had damaged, but which had been repaired by William Reiher (see footnote).

At the outbreak of WWII, there were two Japanese people resident on Butaritari, both of whom had married Gilbertese; but they had for some time also been active spies for Japan, making reports by radio to Jaluit. The senior of them, Kanzaki, is credited after the occupation both with protecting Gilbertese women from molestation, and more generally with trying to create a peaceful co-existence between occupied and occupiers.

The Gilbertese on Butaritari indeed had few problems at first. The Japanese garrison was small and fitted in with island life. Father Guichard and Brother Engelhardt (French and German respectively) – and 22 Nuns in various places - also lived largely untroubled.

Robuti of Ukiangang recorded that:

> 'The Japanese bought eggs, pawpaw, drinking coconuts, breadfruit with cigarettes. They lived like Gilbertese, even ate babai'.

The main Japanese activity was to enlarge the King's Wharf to make it a suitable base for their flying boats. Many people on Butaritari who lived near

---

were picked up by *MV Degei*, coming up from Fiji. Willie spent the rest of the war serving in the Fiji Navy.

the King's Wharf moved out to remoter parts of the atoll and had little interaction with the occupiers [114].

The Carlson Raid and its consequences

Not all the remaining Gilbert Islands were at first occupied: the Free French cruiser *Triomphant* was able to evacuate the remaining Europeans and Chinese from Banaba in February 1942; although it was explicitly decided by the Prime Minister of NZ and the Western Pacific High Commissioner, meeting in Auckland, not to evacuate the coast-watchers south of Tarawa (who could then have been collected at relatively low risk) because *'the very reason for which they had been sent to the islands had come into existence'*.

The situation catalysed in August 1942, when the submarines USS *Nautilus* and USS *Argonaut* landed two companies of the Marine 2nd Raider Battalion on Butaritari, under Lieutenant Colonel Evans Carlson and Major James Roosevelt (son of President Roosevelt). The Marines wiped out the Japanese garrison, and the *Nautilus* sank a freighter and a patrol boat, before the force withdrew.

Although this action was judged by the Americans to have been a success, it had consequences, and it undoubtedly brought greater attention to the Gilberts from the Japanese high command. The Japanese reaction was to:

- Bomb the village of Keuea, some 15 km. to the north of the action of the raid, killing 48 quite innocent and uninvolved Gilbertese (including 10 children), and injuring another 30. It has never been clear why they did this, nor why Keuea was selected: it was possibly as a general reprisal for assistance perceived to have been given by the Gilbertese to the Americans during the raid, or it may have been because it was thought that some U.S. Marines were still there. *Aspects of History* suggests that the intent was to bomb Butaritari village and Keuea was simply selected in error
- Behead the nine American Marines who had been left behind on Butaritari (although not at Keuea), after taking them to the Marshall Islands

---

[114] One side effect of the war was the end of government-imposed restrictions as to where people could live. They were not re-imposed after the war; but by then village as opposed to *kaainga* living had become established as *'te maiu ni Kiribati'*; and few people moved out of villages until the 1970s.

- Kill also, mostly by beheading, all the remaining 22 Europeans (other than the Roman Catholic missionaries) who were in their custody in the Gilberts. The remaining NZ coastwatchers, members of the Administration who had chosen to remain, and the LMS missionary Alfred Sadd, who had done the same, were killed
- Occupy Banaba, Nauru and Abemama (see below)
- Start the fortification of Betio.

The fortification of Betio

The establishment of a redoubt on Betio started in September 1942, when more than 1100 Japanese and Koreans were landed there. Gilbertese labourers were conscripted to work on the project. It became a formidable bastion with gun emplacements, bunkers, a barricade wall along the lagoon of coconut logs wired together, and a network of trenches to allow troops to move unseen from place to place; as well, there were three airstrips.

The Japanese had closed the KGV school, but used many of the senior boys to act as interpreters, or for construction work. They were provided with a special 'student' armband and were generally treated better than other labourers. Ironically, in view of present day dietary habits in Kiribati, they complained of having to live off rice [115]:

> 'Some of the officers were very rough to the Japanese but not to us ... Gilbertese were taken as labourers, no pay only food ... the food was always rice, rice in the morning, rice at noon, rice in the evening ... we were divided into three teams, 60 of us, one party collecting stone from the Ocean reef for construction work, some cleaning the land, digging holes, etc.'

Ordinary workers had less happy memories. Taberannang Teuaba of North Tarawa recorded that:

> 'We couldn't refuse because we were afraid of the Japanese. Our work was carrying rocks, digging holes, constructing the airfield. It was heavy

---

[115] On Christmas Island in 1942 Harry Maude reported the equal dissatisfaction of the Gilbertese there, who were being fed by the Americans. On asking them what they had had for lunch that day, he was told: *'Roast turkey followed by chocolate ice cream. How can you eat such stuff as that? What we want is our big ships biscuits and tins of bully beef'*.

work ... we were beaten if not working hard enough. There was no pay and the food was only a handful of rice ... [we] left our families, worked hard with little food.'

The American invasion

In October 1942, American forces occupied the Ellice Islands (partly to forestall an expected Japanese invasion there). They constructed airfields on Funafuti, Nukufetau and Nanumea as their base of operations against the Japanese in the Gilbert and Marshall Islands. The United States Seventh Air Force established its forward headquarters base on Funafuti, and in November of that year American bombers from Funafuti began bombing Tarawa in preparation for the amphibious landing. The Americans also occupied Christmas Island, and several others in the Line and Phoenix groups.

The Ellice islanders were thus the first to experience the cultural shock that was later to hit the Gilberts: unlike the *Palangi* (European people) they had met until then, these new people seemed to have unlimited goods and resources. Neli Lefuka, who subsequently settled in Fiji, recalled how he and friends:

'...Went around the island to look at all the trucks and big machines. I had seen trucks on Ocean Island but nothing like that. And all the time the planes were taking off and landing from the airfield the Americans had built. We had no idea about war. We thought that only some people would come to the islands to fight and then go back to America, or Germany, or England.

'But the real war looked different: from one end of the island to the other there were landing boats, big guns, boxes, trucks, cargo, foodstuff. That made me think that a war is a very difficult thing'.

'The Americans were really very good to us. Whenever the boys wanted something I went to Colonel Hicks and asked him, and he always said, "O.K., you can have it." That's why we worked very hard, even on Sundays. The boys didn't want to work on Sunday, but I told them, "This is wartime, mind you! In wartime you work, day and night, hurricane time or not, until the job is done. So forget about Sunday until you are back in Vaitupu." When I explained that, they agreed to work also on Sunday'.

Chapter 13: Japanese, Americans, and Aftermath Of WWII

At the peak, more than 350 aircraft and several thousand US personnel were based in the Ellice. Many of the lagoon passages were mined, while those used by the larger ships at Funafuti were cleared of coral heads. Irving Johnson, a US engineer, recorded:

> 'In the northern end of the lagoon we found a coral castle right out of fairyland. My weirdest dreams had never pictured anything like its caves, tunnels, verandas and grottoes, all decorated in extravagant colour schemes. In these rooms lived brilliant tropical fish, so tame they could almost be petted ... Before we set off the explosives, I had every man of the diving party go down to see this wonderland.
>
> 'What a shame that military necessity compelled us to wreck it'.

Operation Galvanic

Operation Galvanic, the U.S. invasion of the Gilbert Islands, began with a massive airborne and naval bombardment on 17th November 1943. The land Battle of Tarawa was fought on 20–23 November 1943. On November 22nd American forces also landed on Butaritari and Abemama. Nearly 6,400 Japanese, Koreans, and Americans died [116]. There was only one Japanese survivor, and a handful of Koreans [117].

Although altogether about 780 Gilbertese and Ellice islanders lost their lives during WWII (the largest number being on Banaba, see below, as well as the 48 Butaritari people killed at Keuea, see above) they were mostly bystanders

---

[116] The Sacred Heart nuns had a lucky escape. Sister Estelle, still living on Tarawa in the 1970s, described to me how the Japanese had planned to kill them on North Tarawa, as soon as the Americans arrived. Their officers had discussed this plan without realising that their Gilbertese waiter had secretly learned enough Japanese to listen in. The Gilbertese managed to smuggle all the nuns off the island in canoes that night, and hid them in the bush on Marakei until it was safe to emerge again.

[117] John Smith recalls: *'we invited the Japanese back* [in the 1970s] *to hold a Shintu service and dedicate a memorial garden on Betio. The party included the only Japanese survivor from the battle who missed it by chance having been sent to Guam just a day or so before the invasion. He was well known to the I Kiribati because he had been in charge of purchasing local food supplies, behaved well and was well liked. Beretitara* [then Chief of Police] *and others rushed up to him and spoke warmly of him'*. Two Koreans on Butaritari hid in the mangrove swamps there and were only finally captured two years later.

Chapter 13: Japanese, Americans, and Aftermath Of WWII

during the actual Operation Galvanic fighting [118]. There were only a few casualties there.

Unfortunately local advice was not always heeded in American planning. Major Holland, who had lived on Tarawa for 20 years before the war as headmaster of KGV, had before the invasion strongly advised against the date selected for the landings, which coincided with a neap tide at Betio:

> '*Admiral Hill spoke at length, and most interestingly at that, on the natural phenomena that affected tides. He added that while not wishing to doubt my word* [that there would be insufficient water on the date selected for the landing craft to reach the shore] *he still expected there would be about 4 feet of water on the reef at Betio; and referred finally to his luck, which had never deserted him.*
>
> '*Newspapers afterwards reported that a sudden wind lowered the water over the reefs, grounding the landing boats and forcing the marines to wade the last 800 yards to the beach. In plain terms, there was no 'sudden wind' nor any other abnormality* [just the predicted neap tide, leaving less than two feet of water].'

A few Gilbertese (mostly, but not all, part-Europeans) who had been outside the Gilberts during the war had also been embedded into the American forces as intelligence officers; and they, during and after the landings, became interpreters. Others joined them as the Americans moved up Tarawa: Frank Highland at Eita gave much valuable information about the numbers and dispositions of the Japanese on North Tarawa; when they arrived at Tabiteuea islet D C I Wernham, a British Administrative Officer who had returned with the US invaders, was delighted to see the Medical Practitioner Tutu Tekanene unharmed, and introduced Colonel Murray to him. Tutu arranged canoe transport over the deep passage there; he remained with Col. Murray as an interpreter, and ministered to the wounded when they eventually encountered the Japanese on Naa.

Colonel Colley, the Division Intelligence Officer, acknowledged in a set of interviews about the battle made in 1953, on its 10th anniversary, that '*no division had ever gone into combat better informed of the enemy than ours*'.

---

[118] For this reason I have not included a detailed description in this book of any of the 1943 battles. (For two such accounts, see Further Reading)

Chapter 13: Japanese, Americans, and Aftermath Of WWII

Return of the British Administration

Lt. Col. Vivian Fox-Strangways and Major F. G. L. Holland went ashore under heavy fire on the second day of the Battle of Tarawa. The British wanted to reclaim possession as soon as possible to forestall moves by the US to dispute ownership of the islands to which they had claims, if not (as feared by the Foreign Office) the whole of the four archipelagos that made up the GEIC.

Vivian Fox-Strangways had been based at Funafuti since his appointment as Resident Commissioner in 1941, after previous service in Nigeria. He held a British Army Commission and (as a Major) had briefly organised a local defence force in the Solomon Islands before the Japanese arrived there. Frank Pasefika remembered him as a 'hands-on' administrator:

'On the day after I flew away from Funafuti on 20th September, 1942, a ship came into the lagoon which Fox-Strangways thought might be a Japanese ship. He ordered the police to take him in a canoe from the back of the island to Funafala, a small village at the southwestern tip of the island about ten miles away. It was revealed afterwards that it was an American ship which had been crippled in a sea battle in the Solomon Islands and it had come to Funafuti to seek shelter.'

Alexander Grantham became Western Pacific High Commissioner in 1945 and paid a visit to Tarawa soon after. He records that:

'The task of the Resident Commissioner Vivian Fox-Strangways was not an easy one. War requirements were still paramount but they must not be allowed to press hardly on the natives. At the same time the Colony needed to be put on its feet again ... although he wore only badges of a Colonel – the Gilberts and the Solomons being fighting areas, the civil officers held military rank – he was held in respect by American officers of higher rank'

Fox-Strangways (who *Time Magazine* said - rather less respectfully - had brought with him only *'a Union Jack and a spare pair of underpants'*) was quick to form a Gilbert and Ellice Islands Labour Corps, firmly under British control. New Zealand provided officers and NCOs, and the men were to be trained to defend themselves as well as to provide services. The Labour Corps HQ was set up at Abaokoro; the Corps personnel quickly became known as *'bootless soldiers'*, since they wore a smart uniform and were known for their spit and polish, as well as their ability to march in step - but, as they always had, they went barefoot. By the end of 1943 the Corps numbered 652, and it peaked in January 1945 at 1524 men. Another 400 Gilbertese went to the Solomons to act as stevedores for the Americans, and 140 Ellice posts were retained at Funafuti. The authorities – native, British and American – attempted to keep any Gilbertese who were not employed away from the US camps, with mixed success. Equally, the American soldiers were forbidden to visit Gilbertese villages (this was enforced quite efficiently on Tarawa but seemingly less so on Butaritari and especially on Abemama – see below). Visits to neighbouring islands were also banned.

The Native Governments on the islands not affected by direct occupation had largely continued over the two-year period. The National Geographic Magazine reported of Marakei:

> *'The normal government had gone on functioning. When [British] officials came back, they find the people presenting few problems for official action other than those which have arisen from necessary neglect and lack of supplies.*
>
> *'Marakei suffered mainly from lack of medicines. Arabrine and sulfa drugs supplied by the United States forces have since saved many youngsters. Though the Japanese had hindered the villagers little, they had done nothing to help them.'*

Gradually, US troops began to leave: the garrison on Fanning in 1944, on Canton in 1946, in the Gilberts in January 1948, and on Christmas Island in October of that year. The airfields were decommissioned in 1945.

Banaba

After taking the Gilberts, the US forces moved rapidly on to the Marshall islands. It was decided to let the Japanese occupiers of Banaba and Nauru *'wither on the vine'*, and they were not retaken (by Australian troops) until August 21st, 1945, more than a week after Japan had surrendered.

Experiences on both these islands had been much worse than in the Gilberts: they were brutal in the extreme. The officer in charge on Banaba was Lieutenant-Commander Suzuki Naoomi, eventually hanged as a War Criminal in 1946.

Before the Japanese arrived BPC demolition gangs had blown up most of the infrastructure on 10 December 1941. They then sat and waited. The BPC

Manager pleaded that food would run out, which triggered the visit to Nauru and Banaba by *Le Triomphant* in January 1942. Some 823 people (591 of them Chinese) were crowded onto the ship and arrived in Brisbane. They left behind, on Banaba, 713 Gilbertese and Ellice islanders and their families; the Acting Resident Commissioner; a radio officer; two BPC staff who elected to stay; the Catholic Priest and Brother; and of course all the Banabans. (There were also 149 Gilbertese on Nauru when it was occupied by the Japanese).

To these were added five hundred Japanese troops and 50 Korean labourers. They built anti-landing-craft barriers, electric fences, and fox-holes; but made no attempt to restart the phosphate operation: Nauru *'had become simply a significant link to Japan's defence system* (with a new airstrip), *with Ocean Island as an outrider'*.

Life under the Japanese occupation

Food did indeed run out, and all six of the Europeans died of malnutrition (or by some accounts, were either bayonetted or deliberately mutilated in the hospital). The lepers and their families were taken away and killed as encumbrances.

Strict regulations were enforced on the others. Three Banabans and several Gilbertese were executed for breaking them. Nabetari – the sole survivor of a group of seven who eventually tried to escape by canoe – described life on Banaba at this time [119]:

> *'The Japanese made the Gilbertese fish for them. This was not without its hazards as a poor catch was rewarded with a beating while two Gilbertese who had caught a tuna and secreted it were found out and shot.*
>
> *'As the war continued and the Japanese suffered defeats, they adopted a two-pronged and nonsensical policy towards the Gilbertese. They taught them the use of fire-arms so they could help resist any invasion of the island and they treated them with ever less consideration. For not bowing to a Japanese or not bowing satisfactorily a beating with a rifle butt was common and any breaking of the curfews was punished by shooting.*

---

[119] The actual words are not his, but a recounting of them made by the European Chief of Police to Ian Butler a few years later and included by him in his book *Ghost Stories And Other Island Tales* (see Further Reading).

Chapter 13: Japanese, Americans, and Aftermath Of WWII

> *Floggings were also administered. A Gilbertese was chosen to administer these. He used a cat – a stout stick with six knotted cords bound on the end. The cords were stiff and tarry and the knots gave them weight. A dozen lashes turned a back into mincemeat. One Gilbertese who refused to lash a friend was beaten with rifle butts until his head was pulped.'*

Two people were deliberately electrocuted solely in order to test the efficacy of the fences:

> *'Two Banabans, one called Kauaba and the other Tabuia were prisoners. They were taken to test the power of the electricity and were electrified on the other side of the island ... When the first one went to test the electricity, Kauaba, the electricity wasn't turned on and he got through alive, so the Japanese shot him dead. The other man, Tabuia met the power of the electricity and was electrocuted and burnt instantly. Until they saw that the whole of his body had been burnt they turned off the power. No one knows where these people were buried.'*

As well, a number of young girls were raped:

> *'An interpreter named Taninta who was a Japanese civilian brought over from the Carolines, used to go around the native villages and gather native girls and forcing them to go and be violated by Japanese officers'.*

Eventually, the Japanese moved all but 143 of the Gilbertese and Banabans, in batches, to Tarawa [120], Nauru, Ponape and Kosrae. Some of those sent to Nauru were later further moved to Chuuk, along with most of the Nauruans.

The ones left behind were to fish and cultivate for the occupiers. At the end of the war, and after they had surrendered, the Japanese troops on Banaba murdered the islanders remaining on Banaba, apparently so they could not give testimony about the occupation. Only one man, Kabunare Koura, survived the massacre (and did indeed give the testimony that resulted in successful prosecution of several Japanese for war crimes):

> *'I was with one from Tabiteauea, Ueaititi, Taeka, Irome, Terara from Abaiang and some others. We were seated on the sand and asked, where do you come from, how old are you, but they lied. They actually were*

---

[120] One batch included my future father-in-law, then a young man of about 15, who before the war had been staying on Banaba with his sister and her husband.

preparing the people they were going to kill. ... the Japanese started to tie our hands, one time, two times and I gave my hands. We were taken to the sea shore and they put up a very high barb wire. We felt homesick, but what can we do, the time is up. I was trying to concentrate to get onto the other life, if there is another life. They will have to shoot their own targets, so I slid down facing the sea and in the middle of the rock. There is nothing I can see and the other guy fell down, and I moved up, and I was poked by the bayonet. I stood up facing the sea and Tarawa with the rock underneath and one who is bigger and taller than me, and the shooting stopped. My ears exploded, and it was after 5 p.m. and I pulled away thinking that I was shot, and I thought that I was going to die later.

'The wave started to break on me, and I was surprised because my eyes were tied. My companions never talked because they were dead, and the Japanese were talking. 'Leave them for the sea will kill them and we will come back for them tomorrow morning.' I was going to lay down for a while longer not knowing if there was a Japanese guard, and for a while I twisted my body and tried to free my hand. Then I climbed up the cliff to see if anybody was there. I went back to check and see my friends, but they were all dead. About midnight I went to one of the caves and I was surprised to see some of their bodies inside the cave. And that is where sorrow came in. The next morning I heard the Japanese yell, 'Here!' I waited awhile and then came a boat. It was filled up with the people from Tabwewa and the big canoes were put into the water. So, they took the dead bodies from off the shore and loaded them onto the Japanese boat. While they were doing this, I left and went away. I tried to get away but the barbed wire blocked my way, so I tried to break my way through. I injured my hands ... on reaching the third wire I was fortunate not to touch it, for if I had touched it I could have died'.

After Kabunare's miraculous escape, he hid for almost two months in the pinnacles and caves until he finally realised that the island was safely under the control of the Australian occupation force.

Chapter 13: Japanese, Americans, and Aftermath Of WWII

The BPC during WWII

The Phosphateers reports how the BPC, for its part, had spent the war: promoting the idea that the administration of Nauru and Banaba be combined under solely Australian sovereignty, so as to relieve the Phosphate Commissioners of any responsibility for the GEIC; arguing that none of the exiled Banabans be allowed back to their homeland, but be sent directly to Rabi in Fiji (which had, in 1942, been bought by their trust fund); and stressing the need for *'up to date mechanisation and minimum labour'* in the design of a rehabilitated phosphate operation. They failed in the first of these endeavours; and only partially succeeded with the third. With the second, they were only too successful.

Settlement of the Banabans on Rabi

The Banabans ended the war widely dispersed: some 250 on Kosrae, 346 on Nauru, and 107 on Tarawa. The Banabans were persuaded that their homeland had at least temporarily been rendered uninhabitable and agreed to a direct transfer of the refugees to the island of Rabi in Fiji, which had some 10 times the area of Banaba, as well as lush vegetation and no shortage of water.

On 14 December 1945, 703 Banabans together with about 300 Gilbertese and a few Ellice islanders arrived at Rabi on the BPC ship *MV Triona*.

The island failed to meet expectations. Life began inauspiciously: there were no houses, no canoes, and no gardens. It was the hurricane season. Tent floors soon became covered in mud, and they had to sleep on army stretchers. The school had neither books, paper, nor pencils. There was no doctor available, and few medicines. The staple crop was cassava, to which they were not used, and the fish were of different varieties to those in the central Pacific; some proved to be poisonous. Markin Corrie, now a Banaban elder, was a young 15-year old at the time, and recalled how during their first night in Rabi, resident cows came down to graze in the area where the tents had been erected. In the darkness, the cattle duly trampled the tarpaulin structures, razing several of them to the ground. The Banabans had never seen a cow before and were terrified.

Initially, the Fiji Government would not allow them off Rabi. Several Banabans died of pneumonia and 'flu. Conditions slowly improved over the next two years (the trial period to which they had agreed in 1945); especially

Chapter 13: Japanese, Americans, and Aftermath Of WWII

after Holland had replaced Kennedy (who had not only fallen out in a big way with the Banaban leaders, but had also taken to drink) as the Banaban Welfare Officer on Rabi.

Consuming Ocean Island sums up their dilemma:

> *'The Banabans, devastated by the war, irritated at being treated like children by both the Company and the Colonial Office, and alarmed that they were so far away from their home island, proceeded to make a number of key choices on Rabi. In 1947, by a majority decision [270 to 48], they voted to remain on Rabi, after a return trip to Ocean Island during which land boundaries were marked and further leases were granted.*
>
> *'According to one story, a man on this trip met Nei Tituabine ... who proclaimed "So you Banabans are not dead after all" and proceeded to follow them back to Rabi.'*

Twenty years later, egged on by foreigners (some of whom took large sums of money from them for dubious financial and legal advice) the story had changed. The BBC was by then claiming that they had been *'rounded up'* and sent to Fiji against their will, and that through neglect *'a race of skilled and crafty fishermen had diminished into a race of tin openers'*. The 'Banaban issue' came to pre-occupy the GEIC and British Governments in the run-up to Independence.

'Spoiling of the Natives'

When the Americans arrived on Tarawa, the Gilbertese were in many cases barely surviving - with not enough food to sustain them, and no access to imported medicines. Toward the end of the Japanese occupation, fishing had been banned and other food commandeered by the Japanese Navy. Immediately after the American invasion, Fox-Strangways recorded that:

> *'When we first arrived on Tarawa atoll it had been given an extremely thorough going-over by the assault forces. Batio [sic] island had been sprinkled with 2,000 pound bombs and 15 inch shells and so forth ... small wonder that such of the fish as were not concussed or blown out of the water decided it was healthier elsewhere; for a while the lagoon was practically empty of fish life, nor were there as many fish showing off the reef as there generally are ... while the islanders, who depend very largely*

> *on fish for their sustenance, were being so well fed on Navy and Marine rations that they could hardly have cared less.'*

North Tarawa (to which the population of the south of the atoll had relocated, and which had also received refugees from Banaba) was particularly short of food; other parts of Tarawa – especially Betio – no longer had a stick of vegetation on them. Overall, it is estimated that about 60,000 coconut trees were destroyed by the two sets of invaders during and soon after the hostilities.

The Americans distributed rations and medical supplies, as well as the tobacco which so many Gilbertese had craved during the occupation [121]. As one islander put it, *'We fed the Japanese; the Americans fed us'*. In addition to a similar shock to those on Funafuti at the sheer scale of material goods that the Americans brought with them (see above), the Gilbertese soon discovered that the GIs were generous; and they became keen to trade with, or to work for them. Urgent tasks included, firstly, burial of the dead, and soon after, American construction projects. Labour was needed to support the US forces in laundry, mess, and other such duties as well as general labouring.

The import of (to the Gilbertese) unimaginable quantities of goods continued. In February 1945 the National Geographic Magazine reported that:

> *'Men stationed here now live in thatched houses and canvas tents and enjoy the luxury of electric lights and running-water showers. True, the water in which they bathe and wash their clothes is brackish, but it is purified. No longer do they dip it in fetid wells or coral rock holes ...'*

> *'Our army forces stationed on Makin* [Butaritari] *protest that life is rather dull now. Nurses with whom I talked in the hospital say they have but little to do ... but planes perpetually roar about the runway and most men seem to be busy'.*

Orders placed locally by the Americans were often large: for example, one in 1945 was for 31,000 bundles of thatch and 30,250 *te ba*, and then another 500,000 bundles of thatch for use in the now conquered Marshall Islands. The GIs also had an inexhaustible demand for handicrafts, and paid good prices for these; and many women and girls were employed as laundresses.

---

[121] There is a story that the first tobacco brought to Nikunau after the war was so greedily smoked that several of the *unimane* became unconscious from it

Chapter 13: Japanese, Americans, and Aftermath Of WWII

As Fox-Strangways wrote in 1944, the British were at a disadvantage:

> *'Especially when the food he distributes (and himself eats) the money, with which he pays the natives, and the road and water transport on which he depends, all hail from America ... [it is] easy to persuade the natives ... that they would be better off under the flag which flies over such rich resources'.*

Resources were not however the only consideration: the Americans simply had a different attitude. Whereas the British were paternalistic (and at worst, treated the Gilbertese as if they were children), the Americans were more prepared to regard them as equals. Secondly, the Americans were convinced that Gilbertese lucky enough to be employed by them should receive 'equal pay for equal work' to themselves, regardless of the long-term ability of the island economy to sustain such rates of pay [122].

On the other hand, the Americans could be culturally insensitive in ways that the British administrators (at least up to that time) seldom were: at Abemama, on being told that local custom did not allow dancing on Sundays, the answer was 'inform them that the island commander **orders** the dance'. On Abemama two of the Marines went AWOL for several months, apparently tempted by two young women, 'Nada' [123] and Buna, who had been themselves hiding from the Japanese at the northern tip of the island.

In 1944 various villagers in Tarawa started to suggest that they would be better off remaining US possessions, and Nabeina Village in North Tarawa drafted a petition to that effect, which was presented to the U S Commander by some 200 people from several parts of North Tarawa. They were rebuffed, and 30 of them briefly imprisoned by the British. There was similar unrest on Butaritari, with the Gilbertese wishing to negotiate directly with the Americans over pay and conditions rather than to be obliged to do so through the British administration, with demands for the US to take over the running

---

[122] I found exactly the same attitude amongst the Americans in the 1970s, when I did consultancy work for the UN in the then US Trust Territories. Application of this policy had caused tremendous distortions in the economy. There was a total contrast between the District centres and the rest of the islands: air-conditioners, buildings of imported materials, and tarmac roads gave way abruptly at their boundaries to Micronesian villages which had not changed since the 19th century.

[123] As spelled in my (American) source; it should probably have been Nata

Chapter 13: Japanese, Americans, and Aftermath Of WWII

of the Labour Corps. Again, nothing came of this; although the US commander in this case did forward their wishes to Washington, there was no reply.

Alexander Grantham summed up the difference in outlook:

> *'That the natives were not downtrodden and oppressed by the British Colonialists must have come as a surprise to some of the Americans. They voiced criticism, both fair and unfair, and I recollect a very young District Officer telling me that an American Officer had chided him at the absence of a Parliament and of substantially built schools and hospitals, and ended with the question: "What have you done for these people?" To which the District Officer replied "We have left them alone" – a very good answer.*
>
> *'There is no parliament or legislative council. That may come in time, but much of the administration is in the hands of local councils and appointed native officials under the supervision of the administrative officers – a replica of the indirect rule of Nigeria. The Council members, particularly in the Gilberts, are not afraid of speaking their minds, not even to the High Commissioner, as I know from experience; whilst to erect elaborate schools and hospitals would not only be unsuitable, but would be unkind as well, for they would be far above what the islanders have in their own homes.*
>
> *'None the less, I would agree that in pre-war days not enough was done...'*

The bottle had indeed been opened, even if the genie took some time fully to escape it (Chapter 14). War years spent in Fiji had been formative for future leaders such as Reuben Uatioa; and never again would the Gilbertese be as wholly unaware as they had been in the fifty years before 1942 of what went on in the outside world.

American claims to the Line and Phoenix Islands

The two northernmost Line Islands, Washington and Fanning (now Teraina and Tabuaeran) were incorporated into the GEIC in 1916; and Christmas (now Kiritimati) Island in 1919. The Phoenix Islands were formally annexed in 1938 (p. 188 above).

Chapter 13: Japanese, Americans, and Aftermath Of WWII

After WWII, it appeared that the US, looking for places to test nuclear weapons, might actively dispute ownership in all or some of these islands (they also had claims to some of the Ellice islands). In the event, the only real incident took place in 1952 (see p. 206 below).

There was also a slightly bizarre suggestion in the late 1940s (apparently emanating from the British Ambassador in Washington) that Tarawa, or at least Betio, should be given to the US in memory of the battle that had taken place there. This fortunately never got off the ground.

Teraina and Tabueran (Washington and Fanning) Islands

Both islands were discovered by Captain Fanning and claimed for the United States under the Guano Islands Act of 1856. Guano was never mined or exported to any notable extent, however; their humid climate prevents the formation of substantial deposits. Teraina was annexed by Britain in 1889 and Tabueran in 1888.

Both islands had been visited by Polynesians in the past (probably from the Cook Islands), but had never been permanently inhabited.

Teraina in particular possesses a unique ecosystem, including lush forests and a fresh-water lake.

A deep opening was blasted at Tabueran, thereafter called the English Channel, on the west side of the atoll. The island hosted a station on the Trans-Pacific Cable between Canada and Australia, a part of the All Red Line, beginning in 1902, and was the only part of the GEIC to see action during WWI.

The Burns Philip Copra Company operated plantations on the islands after the Second World War. At various times, contract labourers were brought from Manihiki, Tahiti, and the Gilbert Islands to work the coconut plantations.

Kiritimati

Kiritimati has the greatest land area of any coral atoll in the world, about 388 square kilometres (150 square miles); its lagoon is roughly the same size. The atoll comprises about 50% of the total land area of Kiribati.

At Western discovery, Kiritimati was uninhabited. As on other Line Islands, there may have been at times a temporary population, most probably Polynesian traders and settlers, who would have found the island a useful

Chapter 13: Japanese, Americans, and Aftermath Of WWII

replenishing station on the long voyages from the Society Islands to Hawai'i - perhaps as early as 400 C E. This trade route was apparently used with some regularity by 1000 C E.

Kiritimati was discovered by the Spanish expedition of Hernando de Grijalva in 1537, which charted it under the name Acea. Captain James Cook visited it on the Christmas Eve of 1777. It was later claimed by the United States under the Guano Islands Act of 1856, though little actual mining of guano took place.

Permanent settlement organised by various European people started by 1882, and it was inhabited by workers in coconut plantations and fishermen; but, due to an extreme drought which killed off tens of thousands of coconut palms, the island was once again abandoned between 1905 and 1912. Later, a French Priest, Father Emmanuel Rougier, leased the island: between 1917 and 1939 and he caused the planting of some 800,000 coconut trees there. Kiritimati was occupied by the Americans during WWII, to prevent the Japanese from constructing an airbase that would have disrupted the main Hawaii-to-Australia supply route.

In December 1960 (after Operation Grapple, see below), the British colonial authorities gazetted Kiritimati as a bird sanctuary under the "*Gilbert and Ellice Island Colony Wild Birds Protection Ordinance*" of 1938. The flora and the fauna consist of taxa adapted to drought. Terrestrial fauna are scant; there are no native land mammals and now only one endemic land bird – Kiribati's reed-warbler, the *bokikokiko* (*Acrocephalus aequinoctialis*). More than 35 other bird species, some migratory, have been recorded.

The incident of the USS Missouri

After the burial of the proposals to purchase Christmas, Washington and Fanning Islands for resettlement in the 1946 *Ten Year Plan of Reconstruction*, it was initially concluded by the Resident Commissioner Bernacchi that the Line Islands were '*uneconomic*' and that '*the idea of colonisation by Gilbertese from the more crowded parts of the Colony must be abandoned*'.

Bernacchi also doubted whether a District Officer '*can have received adequate training and possess sufficient experience to enable him to conduct the business of the coconut plantations*'. He then suggested the islands be given to the Americans. However, his attitude changed when he received a Top Secret telegram from the British Ambassador in Washington, to the effect that the USS Missouri had been reported to be on its way to Christmas Island to raise the US flag there.

Chapter 13: Japanese, Americans, and Aftermath Of WWII

Ian Butler (see Further Reading) records Bernacchi's reaction:

'Within 24 hours he had:

- *Declared the Gilbert and Ellice Islands to be in a state of emergency and ordered all officers to assume duties in accordance with the security plan*
- *Organised the censorship of letters and closed wireless stations to private messages*
- *Set up a Committee to study the seizure of enemy property (i.e. the property of American Missionaries)*
- *Commandeered the Tungaru, the only ship in port (preparing to sail to Suva to have her deck plates replaced)*
- *Mobilised the Gilbert and Islands Armed Constabulary and put forty members of it in an expeditionary force under the command of a District Officer who had been a Major in the Parachute Regiment* [124]*, with powers of detachment commander*
- *Issued battle orders to the expeditionary force …*
- *Despatched the expeditionary force … at 9 knots to Christmas Island on the Tungaru'…*

'I do not know but doubt whether the Colonial Office heard of this matter'.

They did, as the file has now been declassified and is in the British National Archive.

The *Tungaru* arrived at Christmas Island less than 24 hours before the *USS Missouri*. There are conflicting accounts of what then transpired. Douglas Freegard [125] maintained that the sight of the Constabulary armed with their WWI (or earlier) 303 rifles, neatly paraded on the quayside, resulted in the

---

[124] This was Douglas Freegard, who when I first arrived on Tarawa some two decades later had become Financial Secretary, and the person to whom I reported. Despite the fact that, like so many colonial officers, he was a 'functioning alcoholic' and chain smoker (he drank at least a bottle of whiskey every day, and often more; and I once counted seven cigarettes simultaneously lit and spread around various ash-trays in his office), I remember him as probably the most intelligent, supportive - and above all totally honest - of any of the managers to whom I have been subject in my career, then or since.

[125] At least when describing the incident to me. There is also a notable Gilbertese song recording the incident in these terms.

Chapter 13: Japanese, Americans, and Aftermath Of WWII

Americans backing down. Ian Butler maintains that the Americans never intended to infringe British Sovereignty in the first place, but were just revisiting the scene of wartime bases; while Vic Ward's memoir says that they had come to land two American oncologists. The official file merely states that the incident was amicably resolved.

Eric Bailey's account is most likely to be accurate:

> *'The United States wished to set up a Government Fishery and Wild Life Establishment... the Secretary of State for the Colonies had instructed that he wished every reasonable assistance and facility to be given... the party devoted their energies to helping the four-man scientific team in their search for tuna bait, poison fish and the setting up of water thermographs and other weather recording instruments'* [126].

In the event, all US claims to islands in Kiribati were finally withdrawn under the Treaty of Tarawa signed in 1980.

The final foreign interventions: Operations Grapple and Dominic

The final chapter in the impact of foreign wars on the GEIC took place when WWII had been over for a decade, and the Axis powers had given way as an adversary to the Soviet Union.

Operation Grapple was the name of four series of British and American nuclear weapons tests, of both early atomic bombs and hydrogen bombs, carried out in 1957 and 1958 at Malden Island and Kiritimati (then spelled Christmas) Island. They were an essential part of the British hydrogen bomb programme. Kiritimati had been chosen as a base after both the Australian and New Zealand governments had refused permission to use their territories (some first tests had been undertaken in Australia), or their off-shore islands, as sites for the testing. However, an Operation Grapple planning meeting was of the view that 'only very slight health hazard to people would arise, and that only to primitive peoples.'

In all there were 33 U.K. and U.S. nuclear weapons tests in and around Kiribati between 1957 and 1962. The 1.8-megaton Grapple X test on Nov. 8, 1957 in particular produced an unexpectedly severe shockwave that 'demolished

---

[126] So much for *euhemerism* (see page 15), at least as practised by Imatang.

buildings, equipment and infrastructure.' Rain following the 2.8-megaton Grapple Y test, on April 28, 1958, dispersed fallout over the island and on ships offshore. The tests also killed and maimed wildlife and damaged vegetation. An official report by U.S. military observers of the 1957 Grapple X test recorded visiting the south-eastern point of Christmas Island after the explosion: 'Timber and debris thrown up onto the beach were burning with a great deal of flame. ... Birds were observed to have their feathers burnt off, to the extent that they could not fly. Dead fish were reported to have washed ashore.'

Although part of the GEIC, Kiritimati had no indigenous population; but at that time about 260 Gilbertese lived on the island.

Teeua Tetoa, a child during the British nuclear weapons tests, recorded her experience of gathering on the tennis courts in her village in the middle of the night. *'The people were really afraid'*. The British authorities gave them blankets and some eye protection, *'but not enough glasses for everyone.'* When the countdown began, everyone was instructed to hide under the blankets and cover their eyes. *'The babies were crying because they don't like the blanket and some kids ran away from their families and their eyes were blinded because the light was so strong'*. The blast was very hot and so loud that *'people tried to put their fingers in their ears.'*

As well as the resident Gilbertese, some 43,000 military and civilian personnel from the United Kingdom, New Zealand, the United States and Fiji participated (more than the then population of the GEIC). Many suffer from the long-term impacts of the tests, experiencing higher rates of cancer, particularly thyroid cancer, due to exposure to radiation; the Operation Grapple veterans still pursue claims of injuries resulting from the tests. The District Officer at the time, Dudley Cook, also died from cancer three decades later.

The United States conducted 22 further nuclear detonations as part of Operation Dominic in 1962.

Chapter 13: Japanese, Americans, and Aftermath Of WWII

Further Reading

1. **Asia In The Pacific Islands – Replacing The West**, by R G Crocombe, published by IPS Publications, University of the South Pacific, 2007
2. **The Things We Do For England – If Only England Knew**, by Eric Bevington, published by the Laverham Press, 1990
3. **From A South Seas Diary,** by Sir Harry Luke, published by Nicholson and Watson, 1945
4. **Gilbert Islands in WWII,** by Peter McQuarrie, published by the Masalai Press, 2012
5. **Neli Lefuka's War Years In Funafuti,** from **Logs in the Currents of the Sea**, published by the Australian National University Press, Canberra, 1978
6. **Gilbert Islands in WWII,** by Peter McQuarrie, published by Masalai Press, 2012
7. **Tarawa – The Dramatic Story Of One Of The Most Devastating Battles In Marine History,** by Tom Bailey, published by Monarch Books, 1962
8. **Tarawa – The Story Of A Battle,** by Robert Sherrod, published by the Admiral Nimitz Foundation, 1993
9. **War Finds Its Way To Gilbert Islands,** by Sir Arthur Grimble, published in the The National Geographic Magazine, February 1945
10. **Gilbert Islands In The Wake of Battle,** by W Robert Moore, published in The National Geographic Magazine, February 1945
11. **Via Ports: From Hong Kong to Hong Kong**, by Alexander Grantham, published by the Hong Kong University Press, 2012
12. **Wandering Fisherman,** by V. Fox-Strangways, published by Arthur Barker, 1955
13. **Cinderellas of the Empire,** by Dr. Barrie Macdonald, published by the Institute of Pacific Studies, 1982
14. **Kiribati: Aspects of History,** multiple authors and editors, published jointly by the Institute of Pacific Studies and the Ministry of Education, Training, and Culture, 1979
15. **Consuming Ocean Island,** by Katerina Martina Teaiwa, published by the Indiana University Press, 2015
16. **Ghost Stories and Other Island Tales,** by I E Butler, self-published by Tom Butler, 2015
17. **Report tabled in the Maneaba Ni Maungatabu**, in November 1996, of a Committee appointed by the Kiribati government to investigate the death, injury, damage and other atrocities which happened in Kiribati during the World War II
18. **Captain Ward – Pacific Navigator,** by Roddy Cordon, published by Cordon and Wood, 1995

Chapter 13: Japanese, Americans, and Aftermath Of WWII

19. **The Christmas Island Story,** by Eric Bailey, published by Stacey International, 1977
20. **Grappling With The Bomb – Britain's Pacific H Bomb Tests,** published by the ANU Press 2017
21. **Files in the British National Archives**

Chapter 14.

SEPARATE EXISTENCES 1950 - 70

Post-war Policy Developments

Post-war settlements utterly changed the institutional context of Empire and colonialism:

- In 1945, the United Nations replaced the moribund League of Nations. At its founding, the UN had 51 member states (there are now 193)
- In 1947 India and Ceylon (now Sri Lanka) achieved an equivalent status, as Dominions, to the so-called 'white nations' of Canada, Australia, South Africa and New Zealand – and they then broke the Empire mould by becoming Republics
- The Empire itself soon became the Commonwealth of Nations constituted by the London Declaration in 1949, which formally recognised member states as "free and equal".

The scene had been set for the dismantling of Empire, and the ending of colonial status: even if perceptions of this change took a long time to percolate into the Pacific (unlike for example Ghana, which became independent in just 4 years; for Kiribati, the process was to take another 35).

For a long time after 1950 [127], little changed in the mindsets of either colonialisers or colonised: and neither MacMillan's *'Winds of change blowing through this continent* [i.e. Africa]' speech in 1960, nor the announcement of British withdrawal from East of Suez in 1968, suggested to most expatriates in the GEIC, or indeed to many of the islanders, that Britain would ever leave the Pacific [128].

---

[127] John Smith comments: *'I am very aware of this because it was the year I joined the colonial service. On my arrival in Nigeria in 1951 (the year in which the first elections were to be held) the governor asked me how long I thought I had got. I told him a certain 5 Years, a possible 10 and a lucky 15. His response was to say that I had a full career ahead of me'.*

[128] It was the Australians who first realised that withdrawal from East of Suez also implied withdrawal from 'west of Panama'.

Chapter 14: Separate Existences 1950 - 1970

The issue of security, defined in military terms, dominated thinking about statehood in the cold war era and the early days of decolonisation – with New Zealand then often held out as the 'minimum' size of state that should be considered viable. Many – including initially the UN Secretary General and the Commonwealth Secretariat - thought that *'the line would have to be drawn somewhere'*, but it never was; and by the time most of the Pacific countries were along the path to constitutional change the 'big powers' had pretty much accepted the concept of micro-states, and that they would have to learn to live with them.

The second important change was in attitudes in the metropolitan countries towards the idea of 'development'. Development (and its counterpart, 'underdevelopment') was the subject of much debate after the Second World War. There are numerous definitions of the concept [129]; most emphasise some mix of *'improvements in economic, social and political aspects of a society as a whole - including its culture, social activities, security and political institutions as well as the material living standards of its people'*. It ceased to be acceptable to western opinion, however, to argue as Mitchell and (to some extent) Maude did in the late 1940s (see below), that 'underdeveloped' societies should be deliberately left alone [130].

With the idea of development went the concept of 'aid'. During the 1950s the United Nations began to adapt its institutions to take on 'developmental' functions. It already had technical expertise within its specialised agencies, but it also devised a mechanism to channel financial resources. In 1957, therefore, it established a *'Special Fund to support the growth of infrastructure and industrialisation'*. This was later to be transformed into the United Nations Development Programme (UNDP).

The third change in geopolitical context occurred in 1961, when the UN established the *Special Committee on the Situation with regard to the*

---

[129] In 1971 the Planning Office was advised to employ the I Kiribati word *'karikirake'* (lit. 'make to happen to get bigger quickly') to use as a translation of the term. Unfortunately, we did not realise that a decade before this term had been used in the Civil Service as a translation for 'promotion' [of an individual]. This caused much confusion amongst the Gilbertese at the time!

[130] Until recently, when the pendulum has swung back, for some, to a belief that 'tribal societies' in the Amazon basin or the Sentinel islands should simply be left alone.

Chapter 14: Separate Existences 1950 - 1970

Implementation of the Declaration on the Granting of Independence to Colonial Countries and Peoples. It also passed a *Declaration on the Granting of Independence to Colonial Countries and Peoples* which stated that all people have a right to self-determination; and proclaimed that colonialism *'should be brought to a speedy and unconditional end'*.

The Committee of Twenty-Four, as it became known, became a constant goad for the colonial powers. Fear of 'looking bad' at the UN increasingly influenced British policy towards its Pacific possessions.

The future of the Colony: changing perspectives

Immediately after WWII, however, the whole structure of the Gilbert and Ellice Islands as a separate colony was being questioned, and it was suggested that the GEIC should revert from colonial status to that of a 'Native Territory'.

The Western Pacific High Commissioner from 1942, Sir Philip Mitchell, had spent most of his career in District Administration in Tanganyika and was unwilling to see the GEIC as anything other than a local government. (He was not the only one to take this view, as will be evident later in this Chapter). He proposed that the GEIC be incorporated into Fiji. This proposal was essentially driven by his assessment that an unmodified colony would cost some £100,000 a year to run; whilst its revenue, with phosphate revenue disrupted, would be unlikely to exceed £20,000.

Mitchell's 'solution' was to propose the transfer of most administrative, financial and technical responsibilities to the islanders themselves as soon as this could be achieved. A very small expatriate staff was to supervise education and local governments; they would be appointed on secondment from the Fiji, or the general Colonial, Administrative Service. There would be no permanent headquarters or other British base in the islands. A 'sea-borne' group would visit. A native legislative authority was vaguely outlined in the proposals and Mitchell conceded that a native executive authority capable of taking over responsibility for groups of islands, and *'perhaps eventually for all the Colony'*, would have to be devised.

The idea of an elective authority for the colony as a whole, rather than for each individual island, was actually a significant new element; although it was so vague and futuristic not to be alarming, as the time-frame for it was ten to twenty years in the future.

Mitchell was refreshingly blunt, in that his intent was to enable the British Government to discharge its perceived obligations as rapidly as could be done before getting out of the islands, leaving the Gilbertese and their 'Native Territory' with a subsistence economy and in almost complete isolation. This was in many ways the logical culmination of the 'Museum' policy of Grimble, but without his paternalism and control freakery.

Mitchell expressed his aims honestly, but his objective was - in practice - implicit in all the subsequent (mostly secret at the time) reviews of the next thirty years. All of these reports are full of circumlocution (the 1955 statement about the Gilbert and Ellice Islands, for example, hoped that they would, *'while obtaining a sufficiency of the benefits which Western civilisation had to offer, at the same time keep the best features of their own way of life'*); but they essentially repeat the objectives that Mitchell had set out. Successive Whitehall enquiries about the future of smaller dependencies were: Attlee's *Smaller Territories Enquiry* (1949-51); the *Statehood paper* referred to the *Ministerial Colonial Policy Review* in 1955; MacMillan's *Audit of Empire* (1957-60); the Pacific Future Policy Committee (1961-62); the *Lady Margaret Hall Conference* (1965); the *Programme Analysis and Review on the Future of the Dependent Territories* (1973); and finally, the policy of *'Accelerated Decolonisation'* adopted in 1975 [131].

Between the 1950s and 1970s, both UN and UK opinion increasingly began to favour 'development', rather than to the leaving of subsistence societies to their own devices which had been implicit not only in Mitchell's proposals but also in Maude's (Maude at that time simply wanted to extend traditional societies to other, previously uninhabited, islands). Most of these Whitehall reports, however, after a parade of statistics, put the Gilbert and Ellice Islands into a *'will never have a viable enough economy to sustain independence'* box. Only the last, the *'Accelerated Decolonisation'* policy (adopted by the Callaghan government just four years before Kiribati Independence) accepted the prospect as a reality.

In October 1944 Mitchell's proposals were published, with the approval of the Colonial Office. He then rather abruptly departed to become Governor of Kenya.

---

[131] Details of the deliberations of all of these are contained in David McIntyre's *Winding Up The British Empire In The Pacific Islands* – see Further Reading. Notably, they are concerned almost exclusively with the costs and benefits to Britain of having colonies – and very little with the long-term prospects of the colonialised peoples.

Chapter 14: Separate Existences 1950 - 1970

It was left to Harry Maude to pick up the pieces; and in 1945, whilst at the Western Pacific High Commission in Suva, he produced his own *Memorandum on Land Settlement Post-War Policy*. Whilst he paid lip service to the Mitchell proposals, many of them went against his own views, especially that of transferring responsibility for the settlement of land disputes to the locally elected island councils, as against separate land courts consisting of the magistrate and *kaubure* and native members of the Lands Commission, as provided for in the draft Native Governments Ordinance he had produced in 1941. Implementation of this had been deferred because of the war. Maude had had also a long-held conviction of the need for migration and colonisation of new islands because of 'over-population', while Mitchell had had reservations about migration possibilities. Maude also thought that the idea of European supervisors on short-term contracts who would have no knowledge of local customs, and who would have to communicate entirely through interpreters, was not likely to lead to an improved administration.

Maude as Resident Commissioner

In 1946 Maude somewhat reluctantly accepted the post of Resident Commissioner in the GEIC. However uncertain he was (and it was principally his wife Honor who persuaded him it was his duty to return) it was a very popular choice amongst both islanders and expatriates.

As well as completing the replacement of military by civilian government, and phasing out the American presence, he faced a number of issues which had been 'parked' because of the war:

- Re-organisation of local government and lands work
- Re-establishing a Headquarters on Tarawa (not, incidentally, Maude's own choice of islands for this, see below)
- Establishment of better communications, including wireless stations on every inhabited island
- Replacement of the functions of the pre-war trading companies who had decided not to return to the Gilberts, by a Government Trade Scheme
- The continuing debate as to whether the Gilberts were overpopulated, and thus, the urgency attached to resettlement of Gilbertese in other islands
- The continuing debate about the nature, purpose and extent of Gilbertese and Ellice education.

Chapter 14: Separate Existences 1950 - 1970

To deal with such issues, the colonial government had expanded very considerably: Maude had a European staff of more than 60, of whom some 20 were graduates, as opposed to the pre-war establishment of fewer than a dozen. Salaries in the Pacific Colonial Service had been raised to equal those paid in Africa, and Maude complained that *'hordes of African careerists'* were swamping those with a genuine interest in the Pacific islanders.

In 1946, a *Ten Year Plan of Reconstruction* was published, the centrepiece of which was a proposal to purchase Christmas, Washington and Fanning Islands for resettlement. The Plan was designed to take advantage of the abandonment of the long standing policy that colonies must pay their own way: a Colonial Development and Welfare Act was passed in 1940, and extended in five-year re-enactments thereafter. For the first time, external funds became available. The proposed expenditure of the Plan included $270,000 for purchase and settlement of Christmas, Washington and Fanning Islands, $900,000 for reconstruction of infrastructure destroyed during the war, $600,000 for expansion of sea transport and communication facilities; and $360,000 for social services, including $76,000 for a reconstituted Lands Commission, to which, following Maude's own priorities, considerable importance was attached.

Shortly after, in 1947, the Maudes went on long-overdue leave. From the boat to England, Harry wrote enthusiastically to Grimble:

> *'We have a terrific 15-year plan [sic] getting into full swing in the G. & E. I.C and aim to have the whole show in local hands before it is finished. You would scarcely recognise the Colony now, with its wireless station on every inhabited island (by the end of this year), its little fleet of ships plying in and out of Tarawa, its Savings Banks, employment scheme, co-operatives of all descriptions and all the trimmings of a modern administration. We are trying to speed up the rate at which we are able to hand over the administration to the people themselves, and have over 50 Gilbertese and Ellice Islanders now at various secondary schools and training institutions in Fiji ... As the founder of 'Lands Settlements, you will be interested to hear that we have at length [sic] started to tackle lands seriously, with five full-time European Lands Officers and a determination to settle every dispute within seven years by straight-out lands settlement coupled with a colonisation programme designed to relieve population pressure ... Next year we hope to have got headquarters removed to Abemama, when it is intended to inaugurate the*

Chapter 14: Separate Existences 1950 - 1970

> new 'Council of Representatives' consisting of 40 elected members from various islands in the four groups .... '

While they were in the UK, however, the new Lands Commissioner B. C. Cartland (who had come on transfer from Nigeria) published a report strongly arguing that the Gilberts were not overpopulated and that the 'problem' was one of distribution of land, and acceptance of local custom rather than encouragement of the commercialisation of land. Cartland argued that systematic replanting and use of 'waste' land, together with population transfers within the group and development of a 'market' in land would be less costly than resettlement to other islands thousands of miles away. He commented: *'nor has there been any serious attempt to assess the effect of customary land law on the distribution of land and its development. There is just blind faith that if the ancient land customs ... is [sic] rigidly adhered to all will come well'.*

This was perhaps the first – but certainly not the last – clash between 'technocratic' and 'ethnological' visions of development within the GEIC administration (the BPC of course had always taken the 'technocratic' approach). Cartland saw land in financial terms; Maude in cultural terms.

Maude resigned from the Colonial Service in early 1948, disillusioned by being, as he saw it, sabotaged by his staff; but also because of advice from doctors that his health would not stand a return to the Gilberts. He was not then to know it, but he had a long and distinguished future ahead, not as an administrator, but as an academic specialising in Pacific customs and history; and he and Honor Maude came to be held in great respect for their role in recording Tungaru traditions. (He was one of very few ex-colonial officers to receive an official invitation to the Kiribati independence celebrations in 1979).

Cartland's report had killed the prospect of the Colonial Office supporting the main item in the *Reconstruction Plan*. Other parts, such as the 'Council of Representatives', the educational vision, and the placing of Headquarters on Abemama, soon followed ideas of resettlement into oblivion. The 1941 Native Government Ordinance, which retained the prominence of the Native Magistrates, but which Maude had intended to reform, was put into effect unmodified.

In effect, after Maude's departure, the colony went into stasis for nearly 20 years.

Chapter 14: Separate Existences 1950 - 1970

Resumption of phosphate operations

At the end of the war the Banaban's Welfare Officers and other Colonial officials were explicitly forbidden to give them advice by a directive from the Western Pacific High Commissioner, Sir Alexander Grantham. (Grantham even forbad an official going on leave privately and unofficially to take £70 to a lawyer in Australia to represent them).

The Banabans were left to negotiate terms with the BPC by themselves. They agreed to a fee of £200 per acre for land on the plateau and £65 for the lower-yielding fringing land. It was estimated by the BPC that future payments (other than the royalties) would, as mining proceeded, amount to £82,900.

The BPC recommenced shipments of phosphate in July 1946, although it was not until 1950 that production again ran at pre-war levels. This level of production however invalidated Mitchell's assumptions about the ability of the GEIC to pay its own way. By the early 1950s, the GEIC budget was actually running a surplus.

Becoming a conventional Colony

In December 1948, the prospective new Resident Commissioner, John Peel, then British Resident on Brunei, received the following letter from David Wernham, who had transferred from the GEIC a few years before.

Kuala Belait

Brunei

'Dear Peel

'So you're going to the Gilbert Islands or at least may do so. I would say lucky fellow although a move from the luxurious living of Malaya or even of Brunei to the arid islands of the G. and E. would not suit everyone. With the exception of Ocean Island where the British Phosphate Commission have a staff of about 100 Europeans (mostly Australians) the islands of the Gilbert and Ellice Islands are sans clubs, sans cinemas, sans shops, sans everything.

Chapter 14: Separate Existences 1950 - 1970

'I left most of my books in Kuala Lumpur and am sending you the only two I have here. Keesing's book is excellent, if you have time to read it, although some of his statements about the ability of the Gilbertese to govern themselves and run co-operative societies with success are over optimistic. They are probably inspired by Maude who is even more inclined than I am to see the Gilbertese through rose coloured glasses.

'With the books I am sending a few snaps of the G. and E. Clothing is not as rare among the natives as these photographs would seem to indicate although on some of the more remote islands a short grass skirt is the daily dress of the bulk of the population. I should like to have these books and snaps back when you have finished with them but there is no hurry for them.

'Yours sincerely

'D C I Wernham'

The Peels stayed only for about three years: John Peel had been separated from his family during the war, as a Japanese POW; and had two small post-war children, as well as two pre-war daughters at boarding schools in England. He did not take kindly to the Colonial Office refusing to pay for these to visit over their summer holidays. In 1950 he resigned, returned permanently to the UK, and became a Conservative MP.

Writing in 1949 to Norman Chatfield (who had first visited the Gilberts in 1902) he commented:

'Those who knew Tarawa before the war say that the people here have been spoilt by the Americans and to some extent this is probably true, but they seem to be settling down again after the inevitable disturbances of the war years and I am finding them a very pleasant and loyal people'.

In the Peels' time the Colony settled into what was probably nearer to a 'conventional' British colonial set-up than at any time beforehand: and it was a pattern that continued under his successors Michael Bernacchi and Val Andersen. Bernacchi started a deliberate concentration of institutions onto South Tarawa (see below), seemingly in part because he thought the Europeans would be happier and could be provided with more amenities if they were all living together (although his own controlling nature must also have played a part in this design). Colonial life for Europeans developed into

Chapter 14: Separate Existences 1950 - 1970

something nearer that experienced in a 'conventional' colony: Clubs for men, coffee mornings for wives, tennis courts, a monthy newsletter, cinema showings, and other paraphernalia of expatriate communities (even if the GEIC largely remained *'sans shops'*) [132].

Separate lives

Reading through contemporary accounts, the extent to which different groups simply did not interact is striking. Those of part-European descent were caught in the middle; but for ordinary Gilbertese and Ellice Islanders as well there were increasingly institutionalised divides, of religion, and between the Gilbertese and the Ellice, as well as between them and their - increasingly remote - colonial rulers; and crucially, as the Bernacchi centralisation was realised, between Tarawa and the 'outer islands'.

A census had been held in 1947, revealing a total of some 36,000. It broke down the various ethnic groups ('races' in the terminology of the time) into:

Micronesian	29,923
Polynesian	5,066
'Racially-mixed natives'	523
Europeans	304
Chinese	142[133]
Others (mostly Fijian)	42

This represented an increase of nearly 10,000 over the previous census in 1931.

At this time there were only 24 Gilbertese in the Ellice islands, and 169 Ellice in the Gilberts.

---

[132] As another comment on the community that then developed, when I was about to go out to Tarawa in 1971, Sir John Peel (as he had then become) took me quietly aside to impart an important piece of advice. It was this: *'at all costs avoid the advances of bored married European women'*.

[133] 140 of whom were from Hong Kong and temporary residents on Banaba working for the BPC

Chapter 14: Separate Existences 1950 - 1970

The Programme for the King's Birthday in 1949

As an example of how official events were organised, John Peel's papers include those for the planning of the King's Birthday (at that time the principal formal event of the year) in 1949. As they arrived guests were segregated into categories, 'Natives', 'Staff', 'European Staff' and (native) Schoolchildren. The official party then arrived for a formal inspection and salute, as the Union Jack was broken out and the National Anthem (of Britain) sung. Separate songs then were sung by the Protestant Choir, the Catholic Choir and the Ellice Choir, followed by a performance by Gilbertese dancers.

A speech was made by the Tarawa Native Magistrate on behalf of Island Governments, translated by Tutu Tekanene, and then another on behalf of Civil Servants at Bairiki, Betio and Abaokoro. 'His Honour' (the Resident Commissioner) then replied, mentioning *'two events of considerable importance'*: the first was the birth *'of a son to HRH Princess Elizabeth'* and the second was *'the affliction which His Majesty has suffered as a direct result of the unremitting strain and hard work of his services to Great Britain and The Empire'*. The speech concluded with the aspiration: *'let each one of us strive to the utmost of our power to be worthy of a great King'*. There was no mention in the speech of the colony at all, only a passing reference to the King's interest in his overseas subjects.

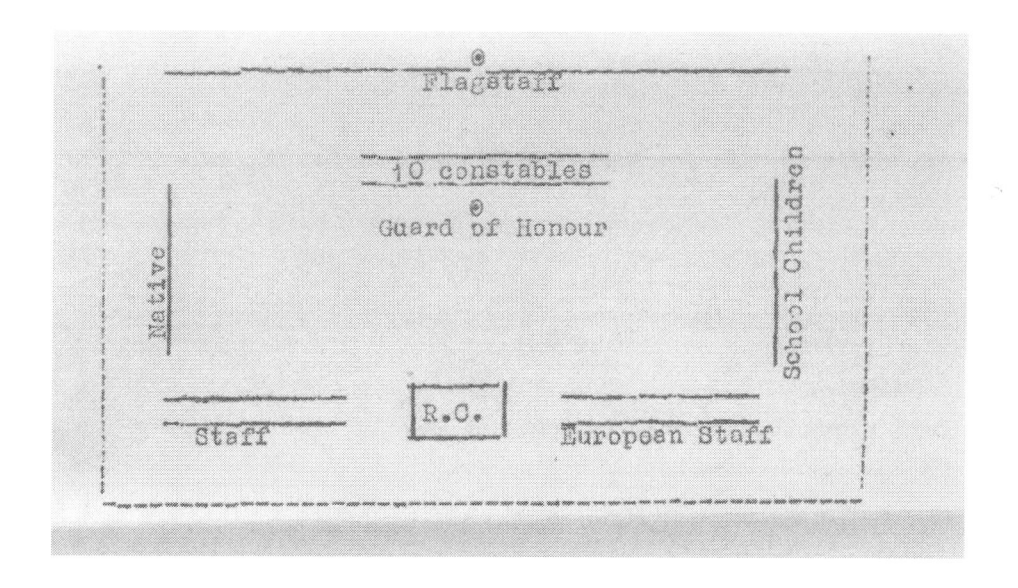

King's Birthday 1949: the Parade

Chapter 14: Separate Existences 1950 - 1970

After Sports and an afternoon reception at the Residency, involving about 20 of the European staff and five Gilbertese and Ellice, the events concluded with an Ellice *fatele* (dance) and a final rendition of *God Save the King*.

There was a similar programme to celebrate the Peels' departure, with again the Catholics, Ellice and Protestants separately delivering especially composed songs [134].

The Europeans

What became known as the 'African influence' had started under the Maudes:

> 'On one notable occasion, a deputation approached Honor because they were concerned at the apparent intention of the senior medical officer to marry a Gilbertese woman. Where, they asked, would she be seated at

---

[134] Which are, to my modern ears, somewhat reminiscent of those composed some years later in honour of Chairman Mao. For example the Catholics hoped that

On Your Way to where
It is Far Away
We wish you remember us
Do not forget us all

The Ellice sang:

T'is a farewell song for you
My master whom I had served for years
Heartedly wishing you
A lucky journey

And the Protestants concluded:

The trip is being prepared
To travel away
The trip of our Resident Commissioner
He is going on leave
Oh! Goodbye with love
Oh! Mr Peel goodbye with love
His Righteous hand over you
He will be with you wherever you go
Oh! Mr Peel Goodbye GOODBYE.

When I showed the papers to my wife, however, I was amazed to find that she could immediately sing all three songs, as when Bernacchi left they had simply substituted his name and she had been in one of the choirs; so they did clearly have resonance with the people who sang them.

Chapter 14: Separate Existences 1950 - 1970

official dinners if this happened because if she were to be accorded the usual recognition of a European wife they would refuse to attend.

'Her eyes blazing, Honor advised them that as the wife of a senior official the woman would be seated on the Resident Commissioner's right, and that she was obliged to them for making their position clear, as it would save her the trouble of sending them an invitation'.

Bernacchi a few years later insisted that houses and gardens in his vicinity be kept immaculate. Bairiki became known as 'God's little acre' (Bernacchi himself called it the 'Flagship'). He had an intense dislike of earth ovens (see p. 115 - 118) in the Gilbertese village there, and if he came upon one during his evening inspections he would kick it into pieces.

A sense of rigid hierarchy developed, more akin to that of the African and Caribbean colonies than to the small and relatively informal government community which had been based on Banaba before the war. Fewer and fewer of the new arrivals took the time to learn Gilbertese or Ellice languages.

The Resident Commissioner, at the apex of this structure, now reported to a High Commissioner based at Honiara in the Solomon Islands, to where (after splitting the responsibilities from those of the Governor of Fiji) the Western Pacific High Commission had been moved.

Ian Butler's memoir of the early 1950s (see Further Reading) describes the community of expatriates on Tarawa:

'Bairiki was the seat of the Resident Commissioner and senior civil servants. It was small, shady and quiet with a neat village of Gilbertese and an assortment of Government personnel, all aware of their hierarchical ranking in terms of the official order of precedence.

'Betio was in almost every way the opposite. It was large, two square miles, it was hot owing to the remains of an American airstrip down its middle and it was noisy with a shifting population of Gilbertese and the excitement and vices that go with ports and boats, as well as having a landrover, a car and two lorries. It was also divided in its loyalties. The District Commissoner was top in terms of the Government pecking order but in terms of power the Manager of the Wholesale Society was preeminent, having under his command money, ships, and a well-stocked store. There were also, beholden to neither the Government nor the Wholesale Society for employment, independent traders and artisans'

Chapter 14: Separate Existences 1950 - 1970

'Both islets had clubs which were the nuclei of communal social life. The Bairiki Club was owned by the Government ... the sole patrons were civil servants clothed white from shirt to shoes, drinking in the evening with their peers, to many of whom they had spent the day writing letters...

'The Betio club was the opposite in life and character and in no way being the stereotyped Club of Colonial novels, being neither stuffy nor racially exclusive. The only criterion for membership was to be a lawful drinker and have the money to pay for your alcohol'.

A few pages later he describes the Secretariat on Bairiki:

'The Secretariat was head office for the Colony. It was of pre-war construction and of entirely Gilbertese materials except for the floor and without a perpendicular or straight wall inside or out ... the interior was gloomy with a grey mould on the walls and exposed timbers soaring to the roof. There were no ceilings and no glass in the square openings which served as windows. Under such a window in the west wall I acquired a desk (where behind my back I could hear the lagoon lapping at high tide), a pile of files, and some advice from the departing incumbent: "If you get an old file out make sure there is not a scorpion in it and keep the whites happy and you will be alright".

'If the first piece of advice was practical the second struck me as cynical but proved only too true. There were thirty-nine white families on Tarawa and they and their affairs took up far more time and money than the affairs of five to six hundred local staff'.

Families who wanted to experience Kiribati culture rather than to advance their careers in the Colonial Service, like Dick and Peggy Turpin (who arrived in the Gilberts in 1950), were glad to escape Bairiki for the Districts [135]. Nancy Phelan reports of her stay with this family on Tabiteuea:

'Utiroa village was a pretty place ... there was not a great deal of it. Dick's Offices, the courthouse, and mwaneaba tapering off to the long neat rows of houses with raised platform floors and coconut venetian blinds, and on the other side an enclosure surrounded by whitewashed

---

[135] They were instructed to take food with them sufficient for a year, in case of disruption of shipping.

> *coral walls over which two largish wooden buildings could be seen. These visible structures were the upper parts of Her Majesty's prison'....*
>
> *'It was a peaceful world. People were busy but no one was in a hurry... each morning I made it my business to ride Peggy's bike up and down the white road to the village ....'*

However, Colonial Regulations still bore down, even on such free spirits. *The Resident Commissioner's Orders (1951)* (see Further Reading) contains 78 pages of minutely detailed instructions for officials, which attempted to prescribe how District Officers and other officials were to approach (and account for) every conceivable aspect of their work.

Cinderellas of the Empire aptly sums up Bernacchi's period in office in the 1950s, and how officials both blurred and accentuated the separate existences:

> *'The fact that the Colony embraced two distinct peoples had little effect on policy formulation in the 1950s; there was South Tarawa, the centre of Government, and there were the outer islands.*
>
> *'Nor could the outer-islanders travel to Tarawa to see, or share in, the benefits of development. South Tarawa was effectively closed to all except for those (with their families) who owned land on the island or who were employed by the Government. Unrestricted movement and uncontrolled urbanisation were not in Bernacchi's scheme for his Colony'.*

The Islanders

For most Gilbertese, the war years quickly receded into the background; my wife, growing up in the 1950s and 60s, says they were seldom mentioned. The War had been firmly parked as a *'Te maiu ni imatang'* matter; only bits of Marston Matting and other American equipment recycled as pigpens remained as visible reminders, except on Betio with its big guns, rusting AMTRAKS on the reef, and occasional finds of unexploded bombs and bodies. The airfields that the Japanese and Americans had put in place were deliberately degraded and replanted with coconuts.

In the years immediately after the war, there was relative prosperity: the UK, desperately short of oils, guaranteed copra prices for ten years until 1957 - copra now fetched £27 per ton, as opposed to £3 before the war. The elimination of the outside trading companies in favour of the co-operatives and Wholesale Society meant that these prices did benefit the producers, as

Chapter 14: Separate Existences 1950 - 1970

well as retaining for villagers the profits that middlemen had previously made on imports. On the other hand, the pre-war copra poll taxes were replaced by monetised copra export taxes and taxes on land.

There were also increased employment possibilities: in the civil service, the phosphate operations, and the co-operatives; but not overseas until the late 1960s, unless those who were relocated to the Solomons from the Phoenix Islands in 1963 are counted amongst these numbers.

However, there was an effect from the interruption of Gilbertese education in the war, whereas that of the Ellice had continued: an increasing proportion of the more senior jobs went to Ellice Islanders, who were in any case seen by many Europeans as 'more adaptable' (i.e. apparently open to European ideas and direction). Most of the local civil servants (other than those posted to what were now becoming known as 'the outer islands') were based at Abaokoro, the base of the 'native administration'.

For the first time, as the Civil Service expanded in the 1950s and 60s, Gilbertese and Ellice Islanders were beginning to live and work in significant numbers near each other – but the Ellice had their own separate housing, just north of Abaokoro.

Part Europeans

Part Europeans (and part Chinese) occupied an anomalous position at this time. Their official status as set out in Colonial Reports was that '[for] *any person wholly or partly of Micronesian, Polynesian or Melanesian descent there is legal provision for declaring persons of mixed descent to be non-native, but the authority is rarely invoked*'.

Ian Butler, however, suggests that it was merely another set of overcomplicated rules to be gamed:

> '*Alcohol was forbidden to a native unless he had a permit and a native in terms of the Native Status Ordinance was defined as a "person wholly of Micronesian, Polynesian or Melanesian descent" unless he was domiciled in Fiji.*' [136]

---

[136] Fijians (of whom there were a number working in the government) were thus allowed to drink.

Chapter 14: Separate Existences 1950 - 1970

> '[Being declared a non-Native], *while it eased access to alcohol could severely affect your matrimonial life ... divorce for a non-Native was a business for the High Court and intimidatingly expensive. Against this with native status a divorce could be obtained "if the temperaments of the parties to the marriage are incompatible"... as a non-Native could ask to be re-declared as a native some richer Gilbertese hopped from one to the other and appeared or disappeared from the club with the ebb and flow of matrimonial fortunes and alcoholic or social needs'.*

Some of the major part-European families originated from early traders in the 19th century (Chapter 8); and others from the German - Marshallese families who had emigrated to escape Japanese rule in Micronesia in the early 20th century.

As well, there were (and are still) a number of part-Chinese families. The first known trader, Ah Sam, is recorded in 1883. The numbers grew: in the 1930s On Chong's Headquarters on Butaritari employed more than 50 Chinese staff with their own clubhouse and with food, wine and opium specially imported for their use. All of these staff, almost without exception, married Gilbertese: for example, William Kum On who was the On Chong agent on Tabiteua, or Kwong Choy, the agent on Nikunau. Other prominent families stem from Zhang Jinqi, or Jong Kum Kee as he became known in the Gilberts, who was born in Guangdong county in China and initially worked on On Chong vessels in the first years of the 20th century; and also the Tong family: Tong Tin Hai was first employed on Fanning Island by Cable and Wireless and moved to Tarawa after the war. (See the article by Bill Wilmott in Further Reading for details of these and other families). By 1947, there were only 7 Chinese – born people in the GEIC, other than those temporarily employed on Banaba by the BPC; and mixed descent people, as one respondent told Wilmott, *'tend to stress our I Kiribati side'*.

Both they and the part-Europeans had, from the Gilbertese perspective, been thus largely absorbed into general society well before Independence. After the war, when copra sales had been taken over by the co-operatives, they set up most of the private sector businesses on Tarawa; and so, while they numbered less than 2% of the population, they dominated what non-government commerce there was.

Chapter 14: Separate Existences 1950 - 1970

The Churches

The immediate post-war years saw the arrival of two more denominations: the Seventh Day Adventists and the Ba'hai' faith. The Church of God of South Carolina arrived a few years later.

Seventh Day Adventist church worker John T. Howse began the Gilbert and Ellice Islands Mission in 1947. He arrived via the church's mission boat, the *Fetu Ao*, or the "*Day Dawn*". The mission's first church was organised in 1954. The next year a school began and in 1957, a boarding high school was established on Abemama.

`Abdu'l-Bahá, then head of the religion, had first decreed that Bahá'ís should take the religion to the Gilbert Islands in 1916; but the first missionaries – who were an American husband and wife team called Roy and Elena Fernie - arrived on Abaiang in 1954. They encountered serious opposition from the other missions, and after Roy had made some injudicious comparisons between British and American styles of colonialism, he was deported a year later; his wife remained. Their first Gilbertese convert was banished to Tabiteuea, his home island. However within the year the Fernies had established a community of more than 200 Bahá'ís, and a Bahá'í Local Spiritual Assembly; and by 1963 there were 14 assemblies and a total congregation of 571.

In the meantime the two established Roman Catholic and Protestant Missions began to pick up their ministries and associated schools after the wartime disruption. Competition continued fiercely and there was little or no co-operation between them.

Ian Butler recorded:

> '*Catholic and Protestant Missionaries were generally on very bad terms ... each sect only wished good for its own following and slighted the opposition at every chance...*
>
> '*For the Government it was difficult to steer a middle course. The Catholic bishop ... seemed delighted to cause the maximum inconvenience to the administration by reporting any supposed wrong to Rome where it was relayed to London and back to the Western Pacific...*

Chapter 14: Separate Existences 1950 - 1970

> *'Against this, all touring officers held the Australian Catholic nuns, stationed in pairs on the islands, in the highest regard and made a point of calling on them ... they were exceptionally kind and good women'.*
>
> The expatriate Protestant missionaries *'mostly lived lives of the most intense loneliness...'* which, unlike some of the Roman Catholic Priests, they were not willing to mellow with alcohol [137].

As part of the Bernacchi centralisation, the Protestant Mission Headquarters moved to Tarawa; and in 1968, the first general assembly of the Gilbert Islands Protestant Church established it as an autonomous church (the name being further changed to the Kiribati Protestant Church at the time of Independence). In the 1960s, the London Missionary Society decided to withdraw from delivery of primary education (they had earlier consolidated their two secondary schools onto Beru); and government schools began to take over primary as well as secondary education.

The Roman Catholic Mission moved its headquarters twice: from Butaritari, where it had been before the war, to Tabiteuea; and then, with all the rest of the colony institutions, to Tarawa (where it has remained since). In 1966, its status was elevated from a Vicariate to become the Diocese of Tarawa (in 1978, the name changed to the Diocese of Tarawa, Nauru and Funafuti). It also began to 'localise': in 1950, Bishop Octave-Marie Terrienne founded an indigenous congregation called the Sisters of St. Therese; and in 1960, several Gilbertese novitiates joined the Daughters of Our Lady of the Sacred Heart, and were sent to study at the sisters' Australian novitiate; they joined the (mostly Australian) community of nuns on their return. Bishop Terienne was succeeded by Bishop Guichet in 1961; and the first Gilbertese Bishop, Bishop Mea, in turn succeeded in 1978, just before Independence.

The Gilbertese – or some of them – were evidently as ready to 'game' the churches as they were the government. In the background, the old religion still played a part. Nancy Phelan describes a meeting with Tutu Tekanene [138], who had been one of the first Gilbertese to be sent to the Medical School in

---

[137] In the 1970s Bishop Guichet (who was much friendlier to government officials such as myself) freely admitted to me that arranging for supplies of drink to get to his dispersed clergy was one of his major preoccupations.

[138] See page 253 and 281.

Fiji, and who in the 1950s had become a senior doctor and much trusted surgeon. He was regarded as one of the most 'Europeanised' of the Gilbertese: for example, he was one of the few to frequent the Residency as a guest. Tutu had in fact been an LMS Deacon when he was serving in the Ellice Islands, but when he returned to the Gilberts had re-joined the Catholic Church.

> *'For all his flirtations with the Christian Church Tutu had not lost his head. He had preserved a proper impartiality on the subject of religion which was based on sound common sense. This became clear when he began to talk about Gilbertese gods and mythological heroes. "You are a Christian now, aren't you, Tutu?" I said. "Oh yes" he said "we're all Christians now". "But what about the old gods? Are they dead?"*
>
> *'He looked astonished. "The Gilbertese gods?" he said. "Of course not – they are not dead at all". "Do the Gilbertese believe in them?". "Of course".*

Similarly, my wife remembers from her childhood the occasion when a Roman Catholic Catechist on North Tarawa, in order to show that the *anti* no longer had power, had deliberately gone to the *tenikawewe* at Nuatabu to cut building materials on land he owned there. On his return he fell into a deep sleep in which, through a dream, he was ordered in no uncertain terms to return them. He was sufficiently frightened by this dream to do so, but *te anti* were not satisfied; he was dead within a week.

The first steps of constitutional change

Constitutional change was slow to arrive; and as more Asian and African countries (and a few in the Caribbean) became independent, their experiences were (sometimes deliberately) ignored.

There was change also in the UK during this period: the Colonial Office was abolished in 1968, when its political functions were assumed by the Foreign and Commonwealth Office; but enhanced developmental functions became the remit of the newly-formed Ministry of Overseas Development.

The Lands Commission

One of the few parts of Maude's legacy that survived his resignation as Resident Commissioner was the Lands Commission, which was funded from

Colonial Development and Welfare funds from 1946 onwards. Between 1920 and the WWII this had only managed partial surveys on nine islands, but between its resuscitation after the war and 1953, it determined and registered nearly all lands, working with the *unimane*. The 1952 - 53 Colonial Report acknowledged that *'much of the work of the Commission, particularly in adjudication, is thrown unto the local elders of the islands, who afterwards form the core of Land Courts which will control all future transfers of land and will maintain the registers'*.

Sorting of land issues, some of which dated back to the declaration of the Protectorate some sixty years earlier, was undoubtedly a major achievement of the immediate post-war period.

In 1954 lands work became again absorbed into District Administration [139].

Native Government

By contrast, Maude's proposed Council of Representatives was buried, and there was little evolution of the Native Governments. These continued to operate under the 1941 Ordinance.

Islands continued to be controlled by the Native Magistrate, although in his capacity as an executive authority he was *'helped'* by an Island Council *'on which there is a freely elected minority'*. In the Magistrate's judiciary capacity he was advised by elected *kaubure*. The idea that all local officials should be elected had of course been long defunct in practice, but now the island officials – Magistrate, Chief Kaubure, Island Scribe (later Secretary) and Chief of Police were all formally appointed by the Colony Government (as it had started to describe itself).

In the 1950s, *kaubures*:

> *'Although elected by the village communities for three year periods, are subject to confirmation by the District Officers who seek the advice of the Councils in exercising this authority. The councils beside being legislative bodies with fairly extensive authority but subject to a right to veto reserved to the Resident Commissioner, may appoint their own police, confirmation of the appointments being subject to the District Officer's approval. They may also dismiss police and* kaubure *by a*

---

[139] Although Lands Courts Appeals from these 1950s adjudications (as well as later ones) still surface today

> *majority vote, and may indict any of the senior officials except the Magistrate, suspend them from duty, and refer the matter to the District Officer for final decision'.*

This description (from the *Colonial Report for 1952 and 1953*) continues with commendable honesty:

> *'They have as yet no financial authority and this has led to their having little real control over the island's affairs'.*

Such authority began in 1955 and was gradually extended.

The corvée system for communal works was also reconstituted after the war and continued for another twenty years, albeit reduced from 52 to 24 days' labour *per annum*.

Constitutional advances of the 1950s and 1960s

The very first 'national' institution to involve islanders was set up by the Colonial Government in 1952, sixty years after the islands formally came under British rule. The Native Magistrates Conference took place each year until 1956, and - for the very first time - brought representatives of every island to a single venue. It was initially as much a training event as a means of consulting native governments, but it was recognised from the outset as something on which to build.

In 1956, it evolved into a Colony Conference, the first of which was held on Marakei in that year, and which continued to be held every two years until 1963. The Colony Conference involved all Chief Magistrates, eight regional representatives elected by Island Councils, three Mission Representatives, and three civil servants. They became a forum in which island problems and grievances could be aired, and government departments could disseminate information. The expatriates however then left, and delegates were left to discuss matters (although they had no power, other than persuasion, to influence either executive or legislative matters).

In 1963, after Bernacchi's retirement, a new Resident Commissioner, a New Zealander, Val Andersen, transferred to the GEIC after service in the Royal Navy and some 15 years' colonial service in the Solomon Islands.

Andersen initially set in train what had by then become the conventional path for Colonies. By Order in Council in London, he was given an Executive Council and an Advisory Council, both of which he could override at will, but both of which had provision for a minority of 'non-officials'. The Advisory council in practice became a forum in which all proposed legislation was discussed.

Andersen, however, while he thought that the Executive and Advisory Councils gave a useful introduction to representative government, was worried both that they did not give a voice to the 'outer' islands; and also that they were too complex a system for such a small population. Like Mitchell in 1946, he was attracted to local government models as a way forward, specifically to the idea of a single Council combining both Legislative and Executive functions (this idea had also attracted interest more widely as a means of governing small territories, at the Lady Margaret Hall conference in 1965). Andersen also began to give thought to the eventual destination of the Gilbertese and Ellice, although he did not really extend this beyond lists of options.

He proposed that an elected House of Representatives be constituted mainly to be chosen by universal suffrage, which would become a forum for public debate to a new 'Governing Council' consisting of five appointed officials, and five elected Members of the new House - the latter group led by a 'chief elected member' and containing one Ellice Island representative. The Governing Council was to have both executive and legislative responsibilities.

Andersen considered that:

> *'The general effect of these proposals is to secure direct representation of the main islands in the House of Representatives which can exercise effective influence on the unofficial element in the Governing Council'*

Although approved and put into practice in 1967, this new system did not prove durable or satisfying to the islanders. *Aspects of History* quotes one of its members:

> *'We have advised Government what the people wanted us to do for them. Because they cannot see any correction, nor explanation of their problems, they naturally lost confidence in us and feel that we cannot do our job, and of course are useless in the House. They regard us as nothing more than Government rubber-stamps'.*

Chapter 14: Separate Existences 1950 - 1970

Reuben Uatioa [140], who had by now clearly emerged as the most prominent Gilbertese politician, was keen to move forwards to self-government (and to break the subservience of the GEIC to the Western Pacific High Commission). Discussions about another move forwards thus began almost immediately. Moreover by 1969 the atmosphere had changed significantly, in part influenced by Nauru's achievement of full independence in 1968. The acting Resident Commissioner reported to London that *'Reuben and a few other ambitious persons are vigorously and impatiently seeking for more power for elected members and a bigger say in the affairs of the country'* [141]

Although they were described by the then High Commissioner as *'a compromise between Reuben Uatioa's desire for independence or at least immediate self-government, and the majority of the unofficial members, and most officials, who would turn the clock back if they could'*, the next set of constitutional arrangements – separate Executive and Legislative Councils with some (minority) official representation, but without any concept of collective responsibility – were actually another reversion to the conventional pattern followed by other colonies. This next step was approved by order-in-council in 1970.

Reuben Uatioa became Leader of Government Business and four other members of the Executive Council (one an Ellice Islander) became responsible

---

[140] Reuben Uatioa was the son of LMS employees and was born on Onotoa, although he was *kain* Nonouti. He attended the Hiram Bingham High School on Beru. He became a wireless operator and spent WWII in the Fiji Navy, and after the war joined the meteorological service there. He returned to the Gilberts in 1950 and became Colony Information Officer in 1955. He became active in politics in the early 1950s, first in the 'Tungaru association' and then as founder of the Gilbertese National Party. In 1967 he was elected member for South Tarawa, and became Leader of Government Business in 1970.

As a personal note, Reuben was one of the few politicians of any nationality that I have worked with over my 50-year career for whom I have profound admiration: his pursuit of influence and power was driven by principle, not by ego; and it is sad that he died in 1977, before independence had been achieved. One of his later public appearances was at Rotee's and my wedding in October 1975, when he gave a most gracious speech.

[141] Reuben was a close friend of Hammer De Roburt who had led the Nauruan Independence movement and who became the first President of Nauru; and he was a frequent visitor to Reuben's house on Tarawa.

for Social Services, Natural Resources, Communications, and Works and Utilities. The Assistant Resident Commissioner (Internal affairs and Civil Service management), the Financial Secretary, and the Attorney-General – all expatriates - remained on the Executive Council with analogous sets of responsibilities.

The Gilbert and Ellice Islands were detached from the Western Pacific High Commission in October 1971 under the new Resident Commissioner, Sir John Field, who at that time became the first Governor, reporting directly to Whitehall.

The end of 'Native Government'

Between his first and second settlements at a national level, Andersen also re-organised local government. In 1966, a new Ordinance replaced Native Governments with elected Island Councils.

The venerable office of Native Magistrate, instituted by Swayne some seventy years earlier, was finally done away with. Scribes were replaced by Island Executive Officers, who were part of the mainstream civil service rather than a separate cadre. Kaubures became Island Councillors, their appointments no longer subject to approval by District Officers.

The Island Courts were also at this time split from Island Government; three members chosen by the Resident Commissioner were to be appointed, with severely reduced powers.

Responsibilities for the salaries of most teachers, post office officials, police and medical staff were transferred to the central government, although island councils were given responsibilities for maintenance of both island and central government buildings.

Finally, the corvée was abolished (partly because of international pressure via Britain, from the ILO); but it was replaced by local taxation. Communal works became the responsibility of village wardens (who were promptly renamed *kaubure*). Cash taxation was bitterly resented, and failed to produce enough revenue for any substantive programme of works. It was partly replaced by 'voluntary' labour; where this related to *Te maiu ni Kiribati* matters such as replacing thatch on a *mwaneaba*, such labour was forthcoming; where it related to *maiu ni Imatang* matters – and government buildings were emphatically assigned to this category – it was not. In 1969, a clause in the ILO's conventions was found which permitted compulsory labour for *'minor communal services'*, and most councils rapidly passed by-laws to permit this.

Island Councils were not established for South Tarawa until the 1970s.

Thus, under the guise of greater democracy, many of the functions of the Native Governments (and their financing) were in practice transferred to the colony government.

Abandonment of the Phoenix Islands settlements

In 1963, Andersen agreed to the evacuation of the Phoenix Islands settlements and B C Cartland was sent to survey the places in the Solomon Islands to which they were to be transferred.

He wrote of one of the sites where they were to be deployed:

> *'The Titiana site, although excellent for administrative purposes, has been found to have three defects from the Gilbertese point of view. It has insufficient coconuts, the fishing is below average, and, being surrounded by jungle-clad hills, it has a depressing effect on settlers from coral atolls.'*

It was, of course, the 'administrative 'argument that won the day, and to Titiana they went.

The subsequent success of the resettled Gilbertese in the Solomon Islands relative to that of the indigenous people (which rather mirrored that of the Ellice back in the GEIC) became an issue there at the time of their Independence in 1978, although not one for this book.

Tensions for the next decade

The Gilbert and Ellice islands went into their final decade as a colony with a number of tensions emerging.

Firstly, there were local politicians who were increasingly willing to challenge colonial norms; and in 1971, the first batch of three graduates educated in New Zealand returned. The number of graduates rose steadily during the decade, following the establishment of the University of the South Pacific in Fiji in 1968. These graduates were equipped with language skills, qualifications and - above all - the confidence to challenge expatriate assumptions and paternalism.

Secondly, there was increasing unease between the Gilbertese and the Ellice peoples (although only the elites met). The Ellice realised (perhaps fully for the first time) that they were a minority, whilst the Gilbertese increasingly resented the Ellice dominance of senior public service posts. In 1965 Reuben Uatioa had set up a Gilbertese National Party and the colonial government (few of whose members now spoke Gilbertese) took some time to realise what he was broadcasting on the Party's behalf over the radio. This tension eventually led the two communities to separate completely, though by then the initiative was mostly from the Ellice side (Chapter 17).

Thirdly, the ability of newly independent Nauru both to tackle the exploitation of phosphate by the BPC solely for the benefit of Australia and New Zealand, and to challenge the apartheid nature of its occupation there, provided leverage to both the Gilbertese and the colonial authorities finally to mitigate, at least partly, the unequal terms that the BPC had exploited since 1920; but the next decade was also to open up tensions between the Banabans and other Gilbertese, which came to dominate the Independence negotiations (Chapter 17).

Fourthly, the old problem of competing authorities resurfaced. The reorganisation of local government had never really taken root and was regarded as a set of *'changes made at the whim of the Government, or more specifically, its European administrators'*. The *Reitaki* movement on Nonouti – which was an attempt in the late 1960s by the *unimane* of the island to take Andersen's new forms of local government seriously, but to use them to reassert their traditional authority - was seen to have failed through the combined, and quite ruthless, efforts of the District Administration (threatening imprisonment) and the Churches (threatening excommunication) to suppress it.

It became easier to consider local government as just a *Te maiu ni Imatang* matter to be 'gamed' in the manner that the Gilbertese had so many times applied to foreign impositions. John Pitchford reports of Tabiteuea:

> *'I was there when the nomination of councillors was made. The mwaneaba speaker produced a handful of* te kora *(coconut string). Lots were drawn (te tau timoi) and the representatives to a new island council were nominated on this basis. Woe betides anyone who stood in opposition.*
>
> *'The main thing was to accommodate the wishes of Her Majesty the Queen's emissary, and this had been achieved with dignity. Everyone*

Chapter 14: Separate Existences 1950 - 1970

> *knew that despite all assaults through the ages, the island had always been ruled through the* unimane *in mwaneaba areas and would continue to be so. This was just the latest Imatang aberration to go along with'.*

Fifthly, the whole disconnect between Tarawa and the rest of the Gilberts, with virtually all Government 'development' spending going to the former, was becoming increasingly visible: although the pressures that this might have caused, if Andersen had not loosened Bernacchi's controls on internal migration, were eased by people moving to the urban areas. The issue of the dominance of Tarawa was however to feed the Ellice secession movement.

Sixthly, as employment grew on Tarawa, trade unionism began to emerge amongst urban workers and became increasingly vocal. The historical role of trades unions as vehicles for opposition and independence movements in the Caribbean, and to a lesser extent in Africa, caused their emergence on Tarawa to alarm all three establishments: the new politicians, the colonial authorities, and the UK.

Less obviously visible (and not queried by many at the time) was the way in which, during the 'stasis' period since the war, the direct *social* control exercised by Grimble and his successors before WWII had given way to a no less complete domination of *economic* life by expatriate administrators on Tarawa. Examples have been given in this Chapter, and more are to be found in Chapter 15. The consequence was that prices for housing, works, and marine transport (as well as for copra, through manipulation of the stabilisation fund) were more the result of administrative fiat than objective commercial assessment, let alone market forces and competition. As a result, by 1970 the economy was riddled with hidden subsidies and distortions, mostly to the benefit of public sector employees [142].

---

[142] I would not want to suggest that they were deliberately designed as such; it was more a matter of an uninformed judgement as to what seemed a 'fair' price, which was set without regard to any underlying cost structure. The use of government 'supply' accounting methods made it impossible to determine the latter in any case.

Chapter 14: Separate Existences 1950 - 1970

Further Reading

1. **Winding Up The British Empire In The Pacific Islands,** by W David McIntyre, published by the Oxford University Press, 2014
2. **Kiribati: Aspects of History,** multiple authors and editors, published jointly by the Institute of Pacific Studies and the Ministry of Education, Training, and Culture, 1979
3. **Where Our Hearts Still Lie – A Life of Harry and Honor Maude In The Pacific Islands,** by Susan Woodburn, published by Crawford House Publishing, 2003
4. **Post-War Development Proposals for the Gilbert and Ellice Islands Colony** by Susan Woodburn, from The Defining Years - Pacific Islands, 1945-65, edited by Brij V. Lal, published by the History Research School of Pacific and Asian Studies, Australian National University, 2005
5. **The Strategy and Etiology of Gilbertese Property Disputes**, by Henry P Lundsgaarde, reprinted from American Anthropologist, Volume 70 No. 1, 1968
6. **Transactions in Gilbertese Law and Justice**, by Henry P Lundsgaarde, published in The Journal of the Polynesian Socitety, Volume 82 No. 2 June 1974
7. **Cinderellas of the Empire,** by Dr. Barrie Macdonald, published by the Institute of Pacific Studies, 1982
8. **Private Papers** of Sir John Peel, Resident Commissioner, Gilbert and Ellice Islands 1948-1950 (unpublished)
9. **Ghost Stories and Other Island Tales,** by I E Butler, self-published by Tom Butler, 2015
10. **Atoll Holiday,** by Nancy Phelan, published by Angus & Robertson, 1958
11. **Resident Commissioner's Orders (1951)** obtainable at http://eap.bl.uk/archive-file/EAP110-1-1-3-7#?c=0&m=0&s=0&cv=3&xywh=-238%2C0%2C3738%2C2447
12. **The Chinese Communities in the Smaller Islands of the South Pacific,** by Bill Wilmott, published by the MacMillan Brown Centre for Pacific Studies, 2007
13. **Colonial Reports: Gilbert and Ellice Islands Colony and the Southern and Central Line Islands 1952 and 1953**, published by HMSO, 1954
14. **Captain Ward – Pacific Navigator,** by Roddy Cordon, published by Cordon and Wood, 1995
15. **The Church In The South Seas: Looking Towards Reconstruction,** by Norman Goodall, the Livingstone Press, 1943
16. **History of the Diocese of Tarawa and Nauru,** at http://pacificunion.mscmission.org/who-we-are/history-diocese-of-tarawa-and-nauru
17. **Seven Years Island Hopping,** by Roddy Cordon, published by Cordon and Wood, 1995
18. **Te Reitaki N Nonouti – A Survival of Traditional Authority in the Gilbert Islands,** by Dr Barrie Macdonald, published in the Journal of Pacific History, 1972

Chapter 14: Separate Existences 1950 - 1970

19. **Kiribati: Aspects of History,** multiple authors and editors, published jointly by the Institute of Pacific Studies and the Ministry of Education, Training, and Culture, 1979
20. **The Last District Officer,** by John Pitchford, published by Librario, 2013
21. **Files in the British National Archives**

Chapter 15.

CENTRALISATION ONTO TARAWA 1946 - 1970

Balancing the budget

Contrary to Mitchell's assessment (p. 272), and although the numbers of expatriates and thus the cost of the colonial Government rose sharply after the war, there was a budgetary surplus by 1953 of more than £30,000. A surplus continued over much of the 1950s, although during the 1960s surpluses became rarer as recurrent expenditure rose for education and other social services, including outlays on heavily subsidised public-sector housing for civil servants.

In 1956 the government set up a Revenue Equalisation Reserve Fund (RERF) [143] to invest surpluses, against the day that the phosphate would be exhausted and royalties ended.

Attempts were periodically made by colonial officials (and since Independence a few politicians) to 'raid' the funds for pet projects that aid donors would not fund; but the RERF has been generally preserved - not only before but also since Independence - and still plays a major role today in preserving the financial stability of Kiribati.

In 1970 the value of the fund was approximately AUD $ 1.5 million.

Revenue from Phosphate Royalties

The pricing policy of the BPC was, in the 1950s, questioned for the first time. The Colonial Office in the UK queried especially whether the difference between the world price of phosphate, and that at which it was sold in Australia and New Zealand ('at cost'), was not akin to a 'profit' which should be taxed.

Gaze (visiting London) regretted that '*the general attitude of officials* [in Britain] *was not at all helpful from our point of view*'. He eventually in 1953 conceded roughly a doubling of payments to the GEIC Government, despite describing

---

[143] In effect what is now known as a Sovereign Wealth Fund; arguably the world's first.

Chapter 15: Centralisation Onto Tarawa 1946 - 1970

it as *'forcibly increased taxation for the benefit of the whole Colony, not on merits but because we have some money ... [it] seems like highway robbery'*.

In these negotiations, the Colonial Office laid down an important marker for the future:

> *'It would not be proper for the Government [of the UK] as administering authority to conclude with itself as partner in the Commission an agreement by which the Ocean Island phosphate deposits were available to the Commission on terms unrelated to those which would be given to any other mining concern'*.

The new agreement made with the BPC nevertheless confirmed the largely tax-free status that the Commissioners and their employees had enjoyed since 1931. They were given exemption from the majority of fees, licences and income tax, and from *'payment of import duties on imports on which the British preferential rate of duty is levied'*. They were to pay the difference between preferential and general rates of import duty on goods not subject to the British preferential rate (not many).

In return, the Commissioners agreed to pay to the Government:

- An annual payment of £40,000
- A tax of 6 shillings per ton on all phosphate exported from the GEIC
- A supplementary payment of 3 shillings and 9 pence per ton on all phosphates exported in excess of 212,500 tons, in any financial year.

These resulted in payments [144] of £63, 581 in 1951; these increased, as the operation continued to build up, to £115, 000 in 1953.

In 1955, moreover, Bernacchi returned to the charge: his first proposal, that the BPC 'buy out' all future taxation through a lump sum payment into the RERF got nowhere; and instead the Colonial Office sought to increase the taxation to 17s 6d a ton, still a rate *'substantially below those prevailing in comparable colonial mining ventures'*.

By then, the three Commissioners, no longer bound together by the idea of 'Empire', had ceased to act in concert and had, in effect, become representatives of their respective governments (and both Ellis and Gaze had

---

[144] Somewhat coyly described as 'Miscellaneous Revenue from Property' in the Government's Accounts

Chapter 15: Centralisation Onto Tarawa 1946 - 1970

died). After government to government haggling, a compromise of 14 shillings was arrived at – but only for three years.

In 1959 negotiations restarted, with the new BPC General Manager as just an observer. This time round, the Colonial Office insisted that the negotiation be conducted on the basis of a world price for phosphate, and not minimum costs for Australian and NZ farmers. The world price was estimated at 122 shillings 7 $1/2$ d per ton and a proposed tax on this would have upped it to 28 shillings and 6d. (the price then being paid in Australia and New Zealand was 41sh 6d). Despite shrill protests from the BPC itself, horse trading between the three governments arrived at a figure of 21 shillings per ton for three years, and 23 shillings thereafter.

More trouble was in store: the Banabans, stuck on Rabi, began to realise how much better off the Nauru people, who had returned to their island after the war, had become. They began to use information published by the UN and Australian Government to agitate for an increase in the 1 sh 3d received per ton by them. The Commissioners did agree to contribute funds to a housing project on Rabi.

Desire by both Australia and NZ to increase the rate of extraction of phosphate in order to accommodate demand from their farming communities led to a further set of negotiations in 1963. The Nauruans, by then determined on both full independence and their own control of the phosphate industry as basic principles, to which they added a total rejection of long-standing Australian proposals to resettle them, achieved the goal of a world price as the basis for future sales. Hammer de Roburt appeared before the UN Trusteeship Council in 1966 and made these arguments forcefully, and the Australian Government in 1967 finally conceded that they could not delink independence and ownership and control of the phosphate operation. It became accepted that the BPC had no future role on the island.

In the meantime, negotiations over Banaba had started in 1965, coinciding with renewed agitation by the Banabans on Rabi. At the insistence of the UK, a Technical Advisory Group was set up and reported (for the first time) on the actual cost structure of the BPC operation on Banaba. Much to the horror of the BPC, the findings of this report were published and became available not only to the three governments but also the Gilbertese and the Banabans. The Advisory group concluded that the BPC could well afford to increase its payments to both the GEIC and to the Banabans.

The principles applied to Nauru were now applied also to Banaba. In 1967 it was agreed that the 'world price' would be paid; that the Commissioners could retain the 'costs of production'; and that the UK Government would be responsible for splitting the 'net proceeds' between the GEIC and the Banaban community. It was also agreed that the rate of extraction would be increased from 300,000 tons per year to 450,000.

The Banabans, having boycotted the 1967 financial negotiations, in 1968 took their case directly to the UN Trusteeship Council, demanding also independence for themselves *outside* the GEIC. In 1971 they issued writs against the Commissioners and UK Government.

Re-establishing a Headquarters on Tarawa

The *Ten Year Plan of Reconstruction* had included a provision for $900,000 for reconstruction of infrastructure destroyed during the war. This was very largely spent on facilities at Tarawa (Maude's proposal to re-establish the headquarters on Abemama, which had much more unused land available, was quickly dropped). Progress was, however, painfully slow in the early years.

By the end of 1953 the relocation of KGV secondary school from Abemama to Tarawa had been completed, and three houses built for expatriate staff; but the annual report for that year states that '*the full team of supervisory staff which is to construct the Colony headquarters ... had not arrived by the end of 1953*' (a full seven years after the Reconstruction Plan had been launched!). Under the new Resident Commissioner, Michael Bernacchi, the pace stepped up; but facilities for administrators (including imported materials housing for them) had the highest priority. No more was to be spent on education, and very little on medical services until the late 1950s when the main hospital was, like everything else built by Bernacchi, re-located to South Tarawa.

By the middle of the decade, attention turned to improving the harbour and shipping facilities; and, at the end of the decade, to the establishment of a secondary school for girls (named Elaine Bernacchi School (EBS) after the Resident Commissioner's wife); and to a teacher training facility. The girl's school had been promised to Funafuti, but it was again added to the buildings on South Tarawa.

Five Year Development Plans (in fact, shopping lists of projects) produced in 1955 and 1959 more or less ignored productive sectors (there was only a token coconut improvement scheme; and a proposal by the South Pacific Commission to establish an atoll agricultural research station, following on from the Catala Report, was turned down). This attitude reflected Bernacchi's fixed view (in which he was supported by successive High Commissioners in Honiara) that there were simply no avenues for 'development' in an atoll environment, and that no effort therefore needed to be put into any new form of productive activity.

His successor Andersen brought a new outlook in relation to education (especially the teaching of English), and on provision of social services on South Tarawa (although centralisation continued unabated under Andersen). These initiatives were taken to require more expatriates (and more building of houses for them to live in).

Andersen also took a different view about funding than that of his predecessors:

> *'We must plan for what we think the Colony really needs and then look around for funds, materials and bodies – in other words let us not tailor our planning to our funds but plan for what we need and then scratch for the funds'.*

One way to scratch for funds was to use all the phosphate revenues on current services: so, during most of the 1960s, no payments were made into the RERF; it became moribund.

Andersen realised that control of movement within the GEIC was no longer acceptable to UK public opinion; and as a result the population of Tarawa began to expand rapidly. A Census in 1968 showed that there were 10,600 people there, an increase of nearly 50% over 1963. South Tarawa had by then become three built-up centres: Betio, with District Administration, Telecommunications and Marine (as well as the Wholesale Society and what little commercial activity remained in private sector hands); Bairiki, with senior civil servants and the Public Works Department, as well as a new Parliamentary building; and Bikenibeu, with education and medical services, as well as new departments such as Agriculture. By 1970 more than 100 expatriates were employed by the government, double the numbers of a decade earlier.

It was, however, changes in the UK's outlook towards development, and new interest in the economic advancement of even the smallest territories which had resulted in the creation of the Ministry of Overseas Development in Whitehall, that drove new policies, and resulted in the Mooring Report (see below).

Replacement of the functions of the pre-war trading companies

In 1945, the small group of colonial officials preparing for the post-war administration of the GEIC (including Maude) written a memorandum to the effect that:

> *'The pre-war commercial system of virtual monopoly coupled with duplicated overhead costs was not the best possible from the point of view of the native population. The enormous expense of maintaining two separate shipping services, duplicate European and native staffs and two series of trading stores resulted in the consumer having to pay higher prices for his imported goods, while at the same time the benefits of free commercial competition could be negatived by buying and selling price agreements.*
>
> *'The solution to our way of thinking lay in concentrating all wholesale commercial activity in a Government-run Trading Organisation which would work entirely through the island retail co-operatives'.*

Such a scheme was included in Maude's 1945 memorandum on Post-War Reorganisation and Administrative Policy and was largely implemented, although not in the way Maude had intended, being subjected to control by the administration rather than being a way for the Gilbertese to acquire commercial expertise (see below). A Government Trade Scheme was set up with a loan from the British Government. It was, however:

> *'Very much a Government Department, staffed by Government Officers from the Treasury, one of the first proposals made to me being that revenue vouchers in triplicate should be made by every over-the-counter purchaser ... it seemed clear that we had far too little commercial experience to enable us to buy, with any hope of success, the goods the societies required from all over the world with nearly every item in short supply'.*

The company Morris Hedstrom were thus appointed as buying agents, a commercial manager was appointed, and two vessels, the *Tungaru* and *Tuvalu*, were bought in 1947.

Maude had intended that the co-operative societies provide *'the training in economic principles which co-operation gives to the ordinary native in the village… co-operation achieves the democratic management of economic and commercial activities… political advancement towards self-government is not enough, in fact it may prove a definite handicap unless it is balanced by corresponding advance in the economic and cultural spheres'*.

However, as implemented, the Trade Scheme has been described as *'nowhere connected in the minds of the islanders with their former co-operatives'*. It became another *'Te maiu ni Imatang'* set-up.

Gradually, the true societies were reconstituted. The largest was the *Tangitang*, managed by Paul Schutz, which covered six islands and had its own transport. By 1950, working co-operatives had been set up on most of the inhabited islands; and in 1955 the Government Trade Scheme was superseded by the Wholesale Society, which also took over the copra trade, which until then had been run by the District Administration.

Other than a very few small private stores on Tarawa and the BPC's store on Banaba, the co-operatives and the Wholesale Society thus soon established their own post-war monopoly over commerce. This monopoly was then quickly placed under the thumb of the central government: Bernacchi established a *Committee of Control* [sic] with himself as Chairman, which consisted of equal numbers of co-operative staff and Government officials (both groups virtually all expatriate). Thus, at least temporarily, Maude's original intent was stifled. Paul Schutz soon found himself prosecuted for mismanagement and fraud: but he was acquitted by the court.

However, over time the *boboti* and *fusi* crossed the line between *'Te maiu ni Kiribati'* and *'Te maiu ni Imatang'*, as Maude had intended. *Aspects of History* commented in 1979:

> *'Almost every household belongs to a village co-operative and each member receives an annual bonus in proportion to the volume of copra sales and store purchases. Those households without membership normally buy and sell on the account of a close relative who is a member. The people seem happy and contented with the co-operative movement. They have annual*

meetings where they discuss problems and development. It belongs to them and they are well served by it'.

Transport

External transport in the early 1950s consisted of:

- Phosphate ships plying between Banaba, Nauru, Australia and NZ. There were about six per month arriving and departing from Banaba
- Cargo ships ex-UK about every six months, and annually in the Line Islands, which shipped copra direct to Britain
- Annual recruiting voyages on behalf of the BPC and Fanning island plantations
- Cargo ships from Fiji and Canada which supplied Cable and Wireless on Fanning two or three times a year
- 'Very occasional' fishing vessels and yachts.

Internally, the government had taken over transport from the pre-war trading companies. There were three wooden vessels, the *Nareau*, the *Kiakia*, and the *Maureen*. The Wholesale Society operated *Tungaru* and *Tuvalu* primarily to collect copra (although these could be, and were, commandeered at will by the government); and a copra vessel in the Ellice Islands, *Te Matapula*.

Internal transport prices for these vessels were fixed by administrative fiat rather than commercial judgement; and by the start of the 1970s shipping subsidies (albeit hidden in the Supply Estimates rather than acknowledged) were consuming a significant proportion of GDP.

The Missions also operated vessels *Santa Teretia* (Roman Catholics), *Fetu Ao* (Seventh Day Adventists), and *John Williams VI* (which was not resident and operated once or twice yearly cruises). The Tangitang Co-operative had its own vessel *Te Aratoba*.

Air services (other than the flights through Canton) were confined to occasional visits by NZ Air Force flying boats stationed in Fiji. Although the 1953 Report remarks that *'these do not normally provide any passenger or cargo facilities'* this policy was relaxed at some point; many Europeans who grew up on Tarawa remember them as ferrying schoolchildren up for their summer holidays in the 1960s. A more conventional air service recommenced in 1967, when the airstrip at Bonriki was reopened and Fiji Airways commenced turbo-prop flights from Fiji to Tarawa via a refurbished grass airstrip at Funafuti (the very early flights stayed there overnight). At the same time airstrips were built at Butaritari, Abemama and North Tabiteuea, and flights to them using Heron aircraft were also operated by Fiji Airways.

In 1953 there were nearly 50 licensed vehicles in the GEIC (other than on Banaba, where there were 87) – but very few in private hands. The numbers scarcely increased over the next two decades. People got around by bicycle or canoe - or by foot.

Employment

In the early 1950s employment opportunities for Gilbertese and Ellice were confined to:

- The phosphate operations on Banaba and Nauru, which employed nearly 1300 (with 1660 dependents); and an unspecified number (but fewer) on Nauru
- Copra plantations in the Line Islands (245)
- Cable and Wireless on Fanning, and Pan American Airways on Canton (25 and 80 respectively)
- Government employees (about 450) and Native Government (just over 500). Projects employed a few more as labourers (e.g. 50 for the construction of KGV buildings) [145].

Private sector employment was then negligible. Pan American's operations ended in 1965, but in the late 1960s the Marine Training School was opened (see below) and significant numbers of young men began to work worldwide in the German Merchant Marine.

Until the 1960s women were simply not employed in any capacity other than domestic service, but as they graduated from EBS (established in 1959, see above) women did become eligible for clerical and support roles within the Civil Service, as nurses, and – later - as teachers.

---

[145] These figures are taken from Colonial Reports which make no mention of Mission employment, but this must have accounted for additional opportunities, including those for teachers. In addition expatriates employed some Gilbertese and Ellice men and women as domestic and laundry staff, as well as nursemaids.

Chapter 15: Centralisation Onto Tarawa 1946 - 1970

The Phosphate Operations

Although the BPC had planned during WWII to mechanise more of the operations at Nauru and Banaba:

> *'Phosphate raising was mostly a hand operation: labourers, working under a task system, either loaded ships attached to cableways stretching between the work-face and rail-points, or where the terrain made it practicable, shovelled the phosphate directly into small 'cars' (each holding about a ton of wet phosphate) which ran on a narrow gauge railway network. When the phosphate proved too hard for a pick and shovel operation, blasting was necessary'.*

In late 1948, first the Australian labour force, and then the Gilbertese and Ellice one (the Ellice mostly employed as 'boatmen' rather than general labourers) went on strike for higher wages. The Australians were quickly given higher wages; the Gilbertese and Ellice were simply sent back to their islands, and the BPC recruited in Hong Kong instead.

Ellis hoped that *'some sort of punishment will be meted out to those who have thus broken their agreement with such serious effects to our operation'* but the GEIC District Officer was more inclined to blame:

> *'American Soldiers, Whites, Hawaiians, Chinese and Negroes all of whom, not too particular about basic truth, were anxious to boast of equality, to point out the wages current in America, and which they consider the right of every man, were fabulous compared to the pay of the Gilbertese and to establish in the local mind the erroneous impression that they were being harshly exploited.'*

The European women on Banaba felt especially hard done by because of the strike as, *'deprived of house labour, the full burden of house cleaning, cooking and laundry work had to be done by them'*. With typical insensitivity the BPC agreed to replace 'houseboys' by 'housegirls' but recruited these solely from the Ellice (viewed as less likely to strike): this became another factor in the developing discord between the two GEIC communities. The strikes did have some impact on BPC attitudes: Gaze wrote that *'we are in post-war times and it behoves us to keep a step forward rather than behind if we are to achieve results equal to pre-war in these more difficult and uncertain days'*. Wages for the next generation of recruits were raised to equate to those paid to Chinese, although they were still a fraction of the wages paid to Australians.

There was another, more serious, strike in 1961 led by Tito Teburoro [146]. The root cause of this was rude and bullying European supervisors, but the BPC did admit that *'we have been prone to allocate Gilbert and Ellice islanders to jobs which the Chinese dislike and for years we have got away with it'*. The BPC had also by now discovered that educated islanders such as Toalipi Lauti and Naboua Ratieta (later Prime Minister of Tuvalu and Chief Minister of the Gilberts respectively) could be useful as 'liaison and labour officers'; and even be trusted with junior management positions.

The BPC also accepted formation of Workers' Committees and a formal negotiation process at this time. However, right up to the end of phosphate operations in 1979, the communities on Banaba remained largely segregated.

The Marine Training Centre

An emergency aboard a Hamburg Süd ship in 1964 led to the founding of a Marine Training Centre on Betio.

A crew member who had been injured needed urgent help. In the ensuing rescue operation, the local fishermen displayed great nautical prowess. The captain enthusiastically reported these skills to the head office in Hamburg. This gave rise to the idea of fostering the enormous nautical potential of the Kiribati and training them as qualified seafarers.

This employment took off in the 1970s and has now for fifty years been a major source of employment for, and remittances sent to, Gilbertese families. Remittances from seafarers were estimated at AUD $ 250,000 in 1971 (although it was thought that this figure, based on telegraphic money transfers, was an underestimate) and still run nowadays at about AUD$ 12 million p.a.

Education

The war had simply postponed the 1920s and 30s debate within the Administration about the extent, purpose and nature of education for Gilbertese and Ellice. This was a genuine debate. Some argued that education was every person's birthright, and pointed to the hunger of local people for it. On the other hand, there was understandable fear that people would be

---

[146] Who was to become a prominent MP in later years (and was the father of the third I Kiribati Beretitenti, Teburoro Tito).

Chapter 15: Centralisation Onto Tarawa 1946 - 1970

'educated out of their environment', and that education would simply make young people despise village life without properly equipping them for anything else.

Policy oscillated between these two viewpoints. In 1945, it had been agreed that a rapid expansion of education was required in order to sustain Mitchell's 'Native Territory'. As a short-term measure, nearly 100 Gilbertese and Ellice were sent away for education in Fiji and New Zealand between 1945 and 1950. This was a mixed success, as many lacked the basic command of English to benefit. Approval was also given for a co-operative venture with the Missions to establish a Teacher Training college.

Mitchell's successor Sir Robert Stanley (the first Western Pacific High Commissioner to be based in Honiara) then argued, as Grimble had done, for selective education only for civil service needs; and although he did rebuild KGV and was the founder of EBS, Bernacchi had much the same view. He halted the programme of sending boys overseas and encouraged a narrow curriculum.

Policy changed yet again under Andersen (despite continued questioning by the High Commission in Honiara). A new education policy was adopted in 1965, prompted in part by the decision of the LMS to withdraw from primary education, and partly in response to a visit by the British Government Education Adviser the year before. Andersen especially emphasised the importance of English language teaching [147], and reintroduced the idea of sending a few of the brightest pupils away for education in New Zealand, to attend boarding school there, and then to take degrees. (Two future Beretitenti – Ieremia Tabai and Anote Tong – were beneficiaries of this policy). As part of this new policy, girls [148] were also enrolled in the first mixed-sex

---

[147] This led to a surreal moment for me in 1973. I was visiting South Tabiteuea and paid a visit to the Primary School. To my amazement, the young children were being taught – in English – about the correct names for male and female ferrets. The nearest ferret must have been several thousand miles away, and the prospect of the Tabiteueans ever encountering one was extremely remote. (N.B. Male ferrets are called *hobs*; female ferrets are *jills*.)

[148] My wife was one of this class, and thus, for example, was taught scientific subjects rather than the 'needleworking' and 'domestic economy' that the girls at EBS had learned before.

classes between the two government secondary schools, EBS and KGV, with, for the first time, a common curriculum.

Andersen also hoped that use of English as a *lingua franca* amongst both Gilbertese and Ellice might defuse tensions between the two communities: although in practice Ellice on Tarawa soon learned Gilbertese.

Primary Education

Basic literacy (in the vernacular) was widespread in the GEIC from a surprisingly early date, compared to other colonies [149].

Primary education had, from its outset to before WWII, been mostly left to the Missions, although it was partly funded by the government. As well as the LMS schools, a few government schools were set up after 1946, controlled by the Native Governments, but the Roman Catholics dominated: by 1958 they had established a primary school at the District centre of every Gilbert island (except Tamana and Arorae) which were staffed by expatriate nuns and teachers from the mission's own training school. Village schools (mostly run by Island Councils) persisted where the population was Protestant, or locations were too remote for attendance at the Roman Catholic schools (although children could board at these).

The Education Adviser brought in by Andersen in 1964 found that there were 255 different Primary Schools, but that between them there were only 95 qualified teachers. A period of major consolidation followed, by amalgamating LMS and Island Council schools and making grants available both to them and to the Roman Catholic schools; nearly a third of Colonial Development and Welfare funds obtained in the 1960s went to educational facilities.

As part of Andersen's 1965 reforms English became the medium of instruction for a standard six-year course of primary education; this was extended to nine years in 1970. A fully unified national primary education service eventually came into being in 1977, when the Catholic schools were also absorbed.

---

[149] Education had been compulsory under Grimble's 1930 Regulations, and only a few remaining pagan families – who did not want their children's beliefs contaminated by the Missionaries - did not value education.

Chapter 15: Centralisation Onto Tarawa 1946 - 1970

Secondary Education

Mission secondary schools were consolidated after the war onto Abaiang and North Tarawa (Roman Catholic), Beru (LMS/GPC) and Abemama (Seventh Day Adventists); these co-existed with the two government-run Boarding Schools at KGV and EBS, both on South Tarawa. The Ellice Secondary School on Vaitupu (Motufoua) also continued, as it had throughout the war years. They all gradually became co-educational, other than St Joseph's at Abaiang (which had originally been established to train boys for the Priesthood).

Collectively, these schools (all of which were both fee-paying and selective), took in about 200 children per year, for a five year course, from as many as 3000 applicants. Secondary education was thus highly restricted. English was again the medium of instruction, over a five-year period, leading to 'O' level standards. KGV and EBS in particular were run very much along British lines, with uniforms, neat dormitories, prefects, and strict discipline. The EBS headmistress Miss Charlton insisted on specially ordered cutlery, cups and saucers, and plates so the *'girls would learn to eat properly'* [150].

Greater access to tertiary education became possible with the founding of the regional University of the South Pacific in 1968.

Medical Services

By contrast with Education, Medical Services were a model of improved standards achieved at relatively modest cost (albeit they still accounted for nearly a fifth of the annual budget). The Fiji Medical School continued to train highly regarded new doctors, and there was a lesser reliance on expatriates than in other parts of the Administration. The 'dressers' operated efficiently as 'barefoot doctors' on those islands without Medical Practitioners.

My wife describes the role of her father as a dresser in the early 1960s:

> *'My father was successively posted as a dresser to Nonouti, Marakei, Makin, to North Tarawa, and then Abaiang, taking his growing family (ten of us survived to adulthood) with him to each of them. On these islands we saw a visiting ship maybe four or five times a year, and that*

---

[150] And food. My wife remembers at EBS being served corn flakes, porridge, and the like, imported at vast expense. She and her fellow pupils did not like and would not eat them, and they ended up being fed to the pigs – probably the most expensive pig swill in the world (and, according to her, resulting in the fattest pigs on the island).

was our only contact with the outside world. He was paid £3 per month, and we were provided with food mostly by our in-patients (although we were also able to live off relatives' land on Makin and Abaiang).

'My father's role was to treat common ailments; to provide medicines and injections; do simple operations (including amputations, toothpulling, setting broken bones and sewing up of wounds); and to recognise more serious problems to report to headquarters via the wireless. As supplies of medicine were erratic, they had to be looked after with care. The most common drugs I remember were penicillin, iodine, aspirin, and gentian violet. As a child, I often used to help him to make up medications (it wouldn't be allowed nowadays).

'My mother was a traditional healer and also an expert mid-wife, so they made a team'.

The main hospital at Abaokoro was rebuilt on South Tarawa in 1956, and in the early 1960s a programme of nursing training was instituted. Nurses began to be a feature of island life, working alongside the Medical Practitioners and Dressers.

Housing

With increasing numbers of expatriates came increasing demands for housing.

The GEIC Government had passed an Ordinance just after WWII that made it mandatory for any employer whose staff *'could not return home at the end of their day's work'* to provide housing for them (the Ordinance did not actually however define what 'home' was, and whether, for example, someone who had a permanent civil service appointment was still legally domiciled at their home island, even if they had no intention of living there again).

Housing (increasingly constructed of imported materials – concrete blocks and corrugated iron roofs for larger houses, Masonite for the workers' houses) thus became a major part of expenditure, although the government was always in serious breach of its legal obligations; in practice it housed only about one-third of its local civil servants, as well as all the steadily increasing number of expatriates.

The rents charged became another source of massive 'hidden subsidy': the imputed rent for 'E' grade Masonite buildings for lower-grade government employees, for those who had a house, exceeded the salary they were paid – but the actual rent demanded was a small fraction of this. Higher grades of houses were rented out by the government below the costs of their maintenance, let alone repayment of their construction cost.

Housing policy and its associated subsidies thus became a contentious issue in the 1970s.

Coconut replanting and other agricultural development

A Department of Agriculture was finally set up in the mid-1960s, focussed primarily on research into methods which it was hoped would improve yields of copra, in particular through 'scientific' spacing of coconut trees, together with the discouragement of burning to clear bush, and rat control.

Coconut replanting schemes became the main focus of the 1970-72 Development Plan (see Chapter 16).

The Mooring Report

In 1967, the newly constituted Ministry of Overseas Development, its mind concentrated by the realisation that the end of phosphate mining was little more than a decade away, and that the level of social expenditure had expanded beyond the long-term capacity of the post-phosphate economy, commissioned a Socio-Economic Survey. The survey team spent two months in the GEIC at the end of that year, led by Sir George Mooring, a former Financial Secretary of Nigeria. It was a watershed in attitudes towards development.

Although the report has been described as 'impressionistic' its endorsement of a complete change of direction was clear:

> *'The tightness in the current financial position means that it will not be possible to spend development funds on any substantial expansion of services, or the infrastructure, unless this contributes to production and thereby provides extra funds to meet the increased recurrent expenditure which will be involved....*
>
> *'The expenditure which seems particularly necessary, to encourage increased production, is primarily on agricultural investigation and improvement and also on fisheries and the possibilities of industrial development ...*

Chapter 15: Centralisation Onto Tarawa 1946 - 1970

> *'In particular we would suggest – while recognising that as the administrative and commercial centre of the territory the position of South Tarawa is unique - ... [that it is undesirable to have]* a concentration of 'infrastructure of roads, buildings etc. which is too far in advance of that in any of the other islands'.

The Mooring Report also believed that the concentration of virtually all economic activity, other than subsistence and copra growing, into the hands of government administrators was dysfunctional. Neither traditional government accounting methods, nor expecting colonial administrative staff to undertake management of commercial functions (in which the Report included the Marine Department, and the Public Works Department, to whom housing had been entrusted) were up to the tasks involved. Mooring recommended the establishment of a Development Corporation with a different management attitude, and the substitution of commercial accounting for Supply Estimates.

Finally, the Mooring Report recognised that administrative staff had neither the expertise nor the capacity to produce or to implement any plan that was more sophisticated than an unconnected list of projects. As a stop-gap a Regional Development Planning Unit was put in place (covering, principally, the Solomons and New Hebrides but also the GEIC), and this three-person team (comprising two economists and one financial expert) produced the first comprehensive Development Plan, for 1970 – 72. A longer-term plan, to set up a National Economic Planning Office, was approved.

The two decades of stasis were about to be replaced by a decade of accelerated changes. As Naboua Raticta said in the new Parliament of 1970:

> *'This plan should have been written 20 years ago, or at least 10 years.'*

Chapter 15: Centralisation Onto Tarawa 1946 - 1970

Further Reading

1. **Colonial Reports: Gilbert and Ellice Islands Colony and the Southern and Central Line Islands 1952 and 1953**, published by HMSO, 1954
2. **The Co-operative Movement in the Gilbert and Ellice Islands,** paper delivered by H.E. Maude at the South Pacific Commission, SPC Technical Paper No 1, 1949
3. **Kiribati: Aspects of History,** multiple authors and editors, published jointly by the Institute of Pacific Studies and the Ministry of Education, Training, and Culture, 1979
4. **The Phosphateers**, by Maslyn Williams and Dr. Barrie Macdonald, published by the Melbourne University Press 1985
5. **Cinderellas of the Empire,** by Dr. Barrie Macdonald, published by the Institute of Pacific Studies, 1982
6. **50 years of the Marine Training Centre Tarawa: A half century of seafarer training in the South Pacific** at https://www.hamburgsud-line.com › sustainability_1 › contentpage_35
7. **Atoll Agriculture In The Gilbert and Ellice Islands,** by C A Small, published the Department of Agriculture, 1972
8. **Mooring Report,** published by the Ministry of Overseas Development, 1968
9. **Development Plans 1947, 1955, 1959, 1965, 1970-72**
10. **National Accounts 1972-74**, by M R Walsh and G Quince, published by the Ministry of Finance, Gilbert Islands, 1976

Chapter 16.

THE QUEST FOR A MODERN ECONOMY [151]

The coming storm

In 1970 the new Resident Commissioner Sir John Field warned the House of Representatives that a *'violent economic storm'* was approaching. In the spirit of the Mooring Report, he recommended *'belt tightening'* to make economic self-sufficiency possible; he promoted the new Development Plan, that sought to maintain the then current living standards through agriculture, fishing, and enhanced education (including training sailors to work on foreign ships and send home remittances); and encouraged family planning.

Reuben Uatioa, newly installed as Leader of Government Business, whilst accepting these aims, pressed also for more development on the outer islands, and empowerment of local councils; for more local people to be trained and hired for development projects; for more government ordinances to be translated into indigenous languages; and for faster constitutional progress. He urged greater unity in addressing the needs of the people, as well as a more extensive internal air service, and more overseas scholarships. He argued that it was mainly *Imatang* on Tarawa whose living was being improved, not least by building houses too *'fancy'* for local needs.

First analyses of the macro-economy

The Mooring Report had made the first estimates of the National Income of the GEIC, with what were little more than informed 'guesstimates' for the years 1963 and 1966. Slightly more researched figures were produced for 1968 and 1970 by the Regional Development Unit; and a comprehensive set of

---

[151] As will be evident from the list of sources, in this and the next Chapter we are dealing with *'participative history'*, as I was myself deeply involved in many of the issues and actions during this time, and personally wrote some of the development-related documents; and I provided as well the information and analysis on which many others were based. I hope that my reviewers have helped me to remove most of the inevitable bias and selective memory, but it is right to warn readers of this book that some refighting of old battles may remain – for which I of course accept full responsibility.

National Accounts was produced in 1976 by the National Economic Planning Office, covering the years 1972 to 1974.

These showed that per capita Gross Domestic Product in the early part of the decade was around US$ 300; but rose rapidly with phosphate prices, to more than double that amount in mid-decade, making the Gilbert Islands technically into a 'middle-income' country. However, a high proportion of GDP was then being invested abroad in the Revenue Equalisation Reserve Fund; if only the direct contribution of phosphate, let alone its multiplier effects, was excluded these per capita figures fall by 40%. Estimates of GDP in parts of the Gilberts other than Tarawa were not produced but would have shown much lower levels. Nevertheless, as the politicians who were starting to travel abroad in Asia and Africa came to realise, the Gilbertese lived in relative plenty compared to large parts of the less developed world. About a fifth of private consumption by value (but more than half by quantity) was estimated to be through non-monetary (i.e. subsistence) production [152].

The statistics also quantified the imbalances that had steadily developed since WWII, as described in previous Chapters, and how skewed income distribution had become:

- The dominance of phosphate mining, as a proportion of nominal GDP, of exports, and as a source of government revenue: 51%, 95% and by mid-decade more than 90% respectively
- The dominance of the government in all aspects of the non-subsistence economy
- Within the government sector, the high proportion of spending on South Tarawa, as described in Chapter 15
- The significant drain on the economy of 'hidden' subsidies (see below).

The 'violent economic storm' thus included the certainty of losing half the national product and income; the likelihood of a severe shortfall of funding for public services; and an almost complete lack of viable plans for a modern economy, to support the rapidly growing population.

---

[152] Although this was based on some heroic interpretations of sparse data.

Chapter 16: The Quest For A Modern Economy

Development Planning during the decade

In the 1970s the idea of 'development planning' was at its apogee, and it was mandated for all British territories (albeit not much promoted in Britain itself). A seminar held in 1973 at the University of the South Pacific, which included amongst its number most of the then local practitioners of the art, showed '*a clear acceptance of a reasonable degree of planning*'; but expressed much doubt about the '*narrow range of skills, ideas, and beliefs*' of its practitioners, and its '*disproportionate emphasis on money and goods*'.

The first 'integrated' Development Plan was produced by the Regional Planning unit. This covered the period 1970 – 1973. Its three main themes were: expansion of copra production; increased emphasis on secondary education, in order to speed up the localisation of posts held by expatriates; and building up of the Marine Training School, to increase the numbers of seamen on overseas ships, and thus the flow of remittances.

Its successor, the 1973-76 Development Plan (the 'Third Plan'), which was based on better statistics and more detailed analysis than those available to the Regional Unit, put Sir John Field's 1970 analysis even more starkly:

> '*The future is dominated by a steadily rising population, the impending exhaustion of Ocean Island phosphates, and doubts about the existence of local resources for long-term self-reliance.... Great emphasis has been given to agriculture and fisheries programmes, in search of new sources of income to initiate a closing of the 'phosphate gap'; but no tangible results have been achieved so far.*
>
> '*The development objective is to attain a degree of economic independence .... Even a moderate level of self-sufficiency, after phosphates are exhausted, can only come from the fullest exploitation of the resources of the sea; the greatest possible development of agricultural production; extending the early gains of family planning into a lasting reduction in family size; and more determined efforts to control consumption, personal and national...*'

The Plan recognised a number of pre-requisites and constraints:

- The need for political oversight and local engagement, as well as technocratic development proposals

Chapter 16: The Quest For A Modern Economy

- The urgent need to grow the *capacity* to carry though investments and to manage the effects of policy changes
- Wholesale changes to the accounting and resources management systems, to make them more transparent
- The absence of a financial sector
- The need (in all of the above) to balance local management and employment against the need for 'experts' to appraise the technical and economic feasibility of changes

This plan also gave a higher priority to reduction of the rate of increase of the population, by encouraging and supporting family planning.

These early Development Plans perforce accepted that the private sector would not be the engine of change in the then foreseeable future; and they comprised, essentially, a set of public-sector programmes.

However, from the viewpoint of ordinary citizens, and especially villagers on 'outer islands', these – essentially technocratic - plans often seemed as remote and foreign as had been the reorganisation of Local Government the decade before (Chapter 15) [153]. Indeed a major constraint on rural development proposals arose from the experience the Gilbertese had had when tilapia fish (*Oreochromis mossanbicus*) had been introduced to their milkfish ponds.

In East Africa tilapia species are widely harvested and are an important source of protein. Tilapia fisheries were an initiative by the South Pacific Commission, which were based on wildly optimistic assumptions taken from Africa.

In 1963, with the best of motives, the SPC Fisheries adviser had travelled widely through the whole Pacific region, including the Gilbert Islands and some of the Line Islands, to introduce tilapia fingerlings into milkfish ponds, apparently oblivious to any idea of piloting their introduction in a new environment. Unfortunately, these tilapia not only failed to grow to an edible

---

[153] I vividly remember trying in 1973 to explain to an audience of *unimane* on Abemama how copra prices fluctuated in accordance with world trends in supply and demand, and how this explained why they had recently fallen. My exposition, although politely received, was a total failure: everyone in the *mwaneaba* **knew** that the price had gone down at some whim of the government; and I had feedback that although they had no doubt that I was sincere, I must be mistaken. Decades of projection of supposed administrative power had been only too successful!

Chapter 16: The Quest For A Modern Economy

size but both outbred and preyed upon the milkfish fingerlings, thereby rendering the ponds useless. Efforts then to dislodge the tilapia using poison, explosives and bull-dozing of ponds were ineffective: they are still there. The *physical* effect was thus to reduce the amount of protein.

However the *psychological* effect was even deeper: to engender a deep suspicion in the minds of villagers of any proposed '*Imatang*' innovation that might impact on their way of life. Programmes based on the 'conventional' development theories of the time, such as the intended transformation of traditional agro-forestry to coconut monoculture (see below), were to be viewed by them (as it has turned out, also quite rightly) with grave suspicion.

Although the newly appointed planners of the early 1970s were aware of the need for an alternative approach to village development, it proved very difficult to come up with a successful one. For example, an 'intermediate technologies' programme was tried on Tabiteuea, but its products were almost universally rejected: the only innovation that had any success was the bicycle trailers that are still made and used today [154]. Another early action of the new Planning Office was to commission a Rural Socio-Economic Survey to research ways in which the wider engagement of rural people with the modern economy could be fostered – see Chapter 19 for its results.

The innovative approach taken to the encouragement of family planning, by contrast, harnessed village enthusiasm and was highly successful (see below). Remittances from sailors who had graduated from the Marine Training School also contributed a significant amount of household income, especially to the rural economy (see below); and long periods spent working away from home had become part of the expected life experience of young men.

The other drawback of 1970s planning was its tendency suddenly to focus on a 'big project', not to create employment and income, but to replace the phosphate revenue which funded public services. In the 1970 – 72 Plan this role was ascribed to copra production; later, to fisheries programmes; and enthusiasm for more off-beat developments, such as brine shrimp, tourism,

---

[154] I grew a variety of vegetables on Tarawa for my own consumption, using an ingenious 'intermediate technology' hydroponics system. I Kiribati people would often admire these vegetables, but very few of them were then willing to taste them: it has taken another generation before most I Kiribati would accept any vegetable other than onions (and the occasional potato) as an edible foodstuff.

Chapter 16: The Quest For A Modern Economy

aquaculture, and even mining of deep-sea manganese nodules, waxed and waned.

None had borne fruit by the end of the decade.

Building implementation capacity

The early Development Plans also struggled to implement the strategy laid down. There were a number of reasons for this but the root cause was a simple lack of trained and motivated people before and just after independence (Chapter 18). Other constraints included:

- The difficulty of identifying viable economic opportunities in a country with so few natural resources, so little fresh water, such complicated and expensive logistics, and with no tradition of commerce or entrepreneurship
- That the government was trying to compress into a decade what should have begun many years earlier, given the basic lack of knowledge, statistics and research
- Although there were exceptions, many overseas 'experts' brought in to supplement local skills took little or no account of local conditions; their reports, more often than not, were not capable of implementation [155]
- Although the diversification of aid donors over the decade was in some ways beneficial, each had their own set of procedures and bureaucracy which complicated access to their projects
- Limits on crucial inputs: for example, there was only a single digger on Tarawa. Most projects needed this at some stage [156]
- Controversy over the principal agent of implementation of reforms, the Development Authority.

---

[155] I could write at great length about this; my letters to my parents are full of complaints of the disruption that shepherding 'experts' around caused to the Planning Office. By all accounts, the problem persists to this day.

[156] So the personal preferences of the middle – level engineer who was responsible for scheduling this piece of plant effectively controlled the order in which projects went forward, whatever the nominal priorities of the Development Committee and the Planning Office.

Chapter 16: The Quest For A Modern Economy

The Development Authority (GEIDA, later GIDA)

The Development Authority (as the Development Corporation recommended by the Mooring Report (p. 246) came to be known) came into existence on 1st January 1972. It brought into a single management structure the Wholesale Society, the Public Works Department, and most of the Marine Division. In addition to running these activities along commercial lines, its remit was to foster economic development through development of new commercial opportunities, where appropriate in partnership with private sector partners.

The Authority was wholly owned by the government, which retained the right to direct it on matters of public interest; but this was also subject to the new and crucial stipulation that '*if such directions result in financial loss to the Authority, the Government is required to underwrite such a loss from* [its] *revenues*'. The intention was that the Authority be both funded by long-term loans, and profit-making, although all such profits would legally accrue to the government who had to approve their re-investment.

The Authority inherited all the assets of the Wholesale Society and, with a few minor exceptions, the government's shipping, engineering plant and vehicle assets.

As there were no accumulated funds for asset replacement (previous government accounting methods made no provision for this), it was agreed that British aid funds would provide for their replacements - and that such assets would only come onto the Authority's books *when* replaced. It was recognised that '*a marked increase in local costs will occur as assets are replaced and [capital] charges introduced*'. New accounting systems were to be developed; to this effect a Basic Works Services Agreement (and a number of subsidiary agreements) were put in place during 1972.

On 1st January 1973, the Co-operative Federation took over wholesale trading operations from the Authority, again with assets provided without rent or land charges. It was intended that these assets (most of which, such as the warehouses, were near the end of their economic life) be returned to GEIDA when the Federation had built new ones elsewhere.

GEIDA immediately became the largest employer in the country, with some 1800 staff employed on similar terms to those they had had before, including housing provision; this number was 30% more than expected as it transpired that the Public Works Department had actually employed, through various accounting devices, many more people than it had declared to the planners.

Exposing the 'hidden subsidies'

The 1973-76 Development Plan estimated for the first time the full extent of the 'hidden subsidies' in the supply accounts that the government had built up during the previous two decades (see Chapter 15):

- In 1972, direct losses in the shipping operation were more than AUD $ 300,000. If capital charges were added to this, the subsidy for marine operations was estimated at AUD$ 427,000
- Rents for government-provided housing recovered only about 10% of the economic costs, which were of the order of AUD $ 6 million when capital costs were taken into account - of which 95% had been expended on South Tarawa
- Public utilities (electricity, water supply and sanitation – all effectively confined to South Tarawa) were, in the case of electricity, set to cover operating costs with no provision for the cost of capital (for what is inherently a heavy capital user); and water and sewerage were provided free to the employees of the government and GEIDA, and at a nominal cost to others. It was estimated that direct water costs on South Tarawa were AUD$ 90,000; but several hundred thousand dollars additional capital investment was needed even to provide 2 gallons/per capita/per day for the projected 1980 population (the original target had been five times that amount)
- Costs of refuse disposal were also met directly by the government and GEIDA on behalf of their employees.

In all, such direct and hidden subsidies – almost entirely for the benefit of those who lived on South Tarawa, and greatest by value (especially housing) for expatriates - accounted for nearly 10% of national income.

Exposing them was not popular with their beneficiaries, and the operation of the Development Authority was constantly undermined by administrators, especially those from the 'African tendency'; *Cinderellas of the Empire* describes it as a *'monster'*.

However, unlike the incubus of the old system, it became a *visible* monster [157], as the parliamentary question and answer in 1973 set out below made abundantly clear. The question concerned the price of a bag of cement. The answer:

> *'The F O B price Suva is $1.28 per bag, the freight from Suva to Tarawa is $1.94, the freight levy* [158] *is 60 cents, lighterage is 40 cents, and the insurance is another 5 cents. The landed cost is thus $4.27 and on this there is a 33 1/3 mark-up to cover the costs of the Supply Division and a contribution towards GEIDA Headquarters costs, giving a cost of $5.69 less a discount to Government giving a price of $5.31 per bag of cement in store'*

While this might seem *'a very unreasonable and frightening price'* it was one which was no longer invisible within an overall PWD supply estimate, and showed where costs should have suggested greater use of local materials rather than imports, as well as where organisation and staff numbers needed critical examination – for example those of the Marine and Supply Divisions, and the GEIDA HQ, which the Authority had inherited from the Wholesale Society and Government Departments that it had replaced.

The 1976 Review of the Authority

In 1976, there was a partial reversal of policy. A Committee of Inquiry recommended a return of some functions to the government, and the transfer of others to separately constituted utilities, for example a separate Shipping Agency. Efforts were also made to encourage private sector provision of construction and shipping services. Effective management of state-owned

---

[157] In 1971 I recall discussing the concept of commercial accounting systems with the then Head of the Public Works Department. Did I realise, he asked, how often he was able to use the PWD's resources to make life easier for 'expatriate ladies' – why, only last week he had quietly had two garages built for senior wives. Under the new regime, they would have to pay for them! Sadly, there was no meeting of minds with those who had run the old regime; but it was no wonder they disliked the new one.

[158] The purpose of the freight levy was to equalise prices across the territory by levying a tax on all imports arriving at Tarawa. The costs of further shipment to 'outer islands' were then reclaimable, so that the bag of cement cost the same on say Beru, as it did on Tarawa. This levy – an early brainchild of the National Economic Planning Office – was one of the few government schemes attempting to slow down urban migration.

enterprises (SOEs) has been a recurring problem for Kiribati up to the present day.

Agriculture and fisheries: the failure of 'conventional' development thinking

After decades of neglect, agriculture and fisheries programmes began in earnest during the decade; but they took considerable time to have impact. It is only since the present day Law of the Sea institutional infrastructure and regional agreements were put in place in the 1980s and 1990s that fisheries licensing, in particular, has been able to provide funds and to a limited extent employment.

The Coconut replanting schemes

The 1970 - 73 Plan placed coconut replanting and enhanced copra production at its centre. Incorporating as they did a set of 'western' assumptions, these schemes were an object lesson for the future. Their design very much reflected conventional European foresters' thinking of the time. It was based on:

- Consolidation of landholdings into plantations, with a 'scientific' planting of a coconut mono-culture, and all undergrowth cleared
- Introduction of new varieties of 'high-yielding' coconut seedlings from Malaysia and elsewhere
- An assumption that growers would strive to maximise production from their new plantations
- Projections of continued strong world demand for the high-quality sun-dried copra produced in the islands.

Atoll Agriculture, published as a guide for agricultural staff in 1972, stated confidently that:

> 'the practice of underplanting ... does not work well under atoll conditions ... to get a palm to grow reasonably quickly it must be planted in the open... to get the best yields from coconuts it is necessary to plant selected seedlings at the correct spacing and in a hole filled with rotting organic matter ... an alternative method of planting ... is planting in polythene plastic bags ... it is essential that the land should be cleared of adult palms and bush before making the plantation ... the old palms

should be felled or where this is not possible, poisoned .... The circle around each palm should be weeded.'

By the middle of the decade, about 3,400 acres of land had been replanted. However, as *Aspects of History* commented at the time:

'Coconut schemes met with some success, but for most of those who offered land, money was the main attraction, rather than a desire to have their land improved. Perhaps these schemes might have been more successful if the people had been consulted and better instructed at the planning stage. The people did not like to see their old productive trees being cut down, knowing they would have to wait some years for produce from the new trees. Had there been some compromise by leaving the trees still producing, confining the replanting to areas where the trees were sparse and past producing, the schemes might have been more welcome'.

The (implicit) assumption in the 1970 – 73 Plan that villagers would behave like profit-seeking entrepreneurs and seek to maximise production was equally erroneous. No analysis of the correlation between rainfall and production (with various assumptions about lags), or between prices and production, ever showed any statistical validity. However, mysterious spikes in production occurred regularly: it took some time for the planners to realise that these took place when the island concerned undertook a communal project (usually a new church). The satisficers were at work again (pages 121 - 122); the actual production of copra was always well below the potential [159].

The Fisheries Programmes

The Coconut Replanting Schemes were at least followed through consistently during the decade; fisheries programmes were not, but they were equally unsuccessful.

A Fisheries Department was set up in 1970 (for the first time). This entered into an agreement with Van Camp, a US tuna processing company based in American Samoa, to conduct a survey of tuna resources and also bait fish. This confirmed that there were ample supplies of yellowfin and skipjack (in

---

[159] From the hindsight of 40 years on, it has moreover become apparent that these 'scientifically planted monocultures' actually have lower productivity than those where traditional mixed agro-forestry continues.

fact it has now long been established that that of Kiribati is the most productive tuna fishing Exclusive Economic Zone in the western and central Pacific; but in the early 1970s not only did such zones not exist, but there were then no accessible data at all on what foreign vessels caught around the islands).

The survey also showed that bait fish – essential to the pole-and-line catching methods of the time - were not available in Gilbertese lagoons in sufficient quantities to sustain a large-scale industry. When the survey vessels were sunk at Funafuti in 1972 by Hurricane Bebe, Van Camp thus withdrew.

A new plan was then drawn up to develop an artisanal industry based on locally owned dories (a type of small fishing boat), together with aquaculture of bait fish. Although this industry would have been far superior in developmental terms to a foreign-based operation, being both locally owned and employment-intensive, it is clear with hindsight that Kiribati did not possess the entrepreneurial, logistical or managerial capacity to run it. The strategy was abandoned in 1974. By contrast the aquaculture project supported by UNDP was relatively successful in culturing bait – but without an industry to buy its products, it had no future.

What these projects did demonstrate was the expertise of I Kiribati fishermen, which was eventually, after Independence, put to good use.

Next, reliance was put on replication of the (successful) Joint Venture developed by the new Governor, John Smith, in his previous position as Financial Secretary in the Solomon Islands. He brought in the company concerned with the Solomons fishery, Taiyo, and discussions continued with them for some years without ever reaching a conclusion [160].

In 1978, a further project was undertaken with British aid: acquisition of a Japanese pole - and – line vessel to be operated by Kiribati in competition with foreign companies. This project also faltered. In 1979, therefore, another attempt was made to interest foreign companies; this time using purse-seining technology rather than pole-and line. A UNDP funded consultancy identified

---

[160] I confess that at the time I was of the private opinion that Taiyo were operating more out of respect for John Smith than from genuine interest, although lack of bait resources and fresh water were real and continuing differences from conditions in the Solomons.

a consortium and a Memorandum of Agreement was signed with Castle-Cooke, the US third largest tuna fishing company; but this too never took place as the consortium ran into financial difficulties.

There was a parallel strategy in the Line Islands: development of an industry based on aquaculture of *Artemia salina* (brine shrimp) on Kiritimati Island, promoted by the Development Authority, appeared to be promising. A series of existing ponds were modified, and brine shrimp raised and marketed successfully on a small scale. Yields of 8,400-14,400 kg/ha per year (comparable to the yields projected for commercial raising of lobsters or shrimp) were forecast, which at mid-1970s prices and demand patterns for fish-food, were achieved - which, if scaled up successfully, would have yielded significant profits. However, the price of brine shrimp plummeted after a similar (but much lower cost) operation was developed in Brazil, and the scheme was abandoned as unprofitable in 1978. The ponds were subsequently re-used for production of milk-fish (*Chanos chanos*) for export to Hawaii, but this industry eventually also succumbed owing to transport problems.

The judgement contained in *Management of Marine Resources in Kiribati*, by Roniti Teiwaki [161] aptly sums up the decade of fisheries programmes:

> '*After more than a decade of frustration - from the Van Camp survey in 1971 to the abortive Castle-Cooke and Martinez purse-seining proposal in 1982 – Kiribati was still without an established tuna fishery, despite the vast amount of capital invested and time expended by both British and I Kiribati officials*'.

The Family Planning Programme: the success of unconventional thinking

Family Planning programmes had started soon after the Mooring Report in 1968 and were initially very successful in their objective of family limitation and spacing. In 1972 it was reported that:

> '*Over one third of the female population between 15 and 44 years have adopted and are continuing to use modern contraception … this rate of acceptance is unusual in predominantly rural, subsistence oriented*

---

[161] Himself involved throughout the decade, as Minister for Finance, and then of Natural Resources.

> societies ... [the Gilbert Islands] *may have set a precedent. It may have little to learn from the experiences of other countries and is left to plough a lone course in the next stage...'*

This success was largely due to an innovative use of a radio-based educational programme, including especially a traditional medium: a song contest (see Chapter 5). It was also due to sustained effort: tutors, nurses, dressers, and radio announcers all were pressed into forming a 'radio repertory company'; women's sections provided plays and items devoted to family planning; and a half-hour series of weekly feature programmes on family planning would be supported by daily radio spots, news items, and contributions to current affairs programmes.

Its principal designer, John Pitchford, recorded that:

> *'I launched a nation-wide family planning song competition with the promise that every one of over 200 Gilbertese and Ellice villages would be visited by me with a Uher recording machine to ensure standardisation ... there was hardly a village that had not composed at least one song. The quality and educational / motivational sense of the lyrics as well as the music was excellent, infinitely better than any of those propagandist / educationalists I had been studying in London could ever possibly have imagined, and all 100 percent home grown!'*

Unfortunately, however, as personnel changed, the programme lost impetus; by the end of the decade the numbers of women using secure contraception methods had dropped back to less than a fifth of the target audience. There have been periodic efforts to revive the programme since Independence, but never again have they been as successful as in those few years.

Marine Training and the growth of remittance income

The Marine Training School continued to equip significant cohorts of young men, and by the mid-1970s there were more than 650 of its graduates working abroad at any one time. The 1973 – 76 Development Plan estimated that remittances had, by 1970, already overtaken returns from copra production and handicrafts as the principal source of cash income in rural areas, and accounted for 40% of such income. Spread as they were across all islands, they also contributed greatly to poverty reduction. Demand for Gilbertese seamen remained high, so they were also viewed as the most promising growth area for employment.

Chapter 16: The Quest For A Modern Economy

The Plan commented:

> *'The importance attached to remittances appears to be reflected in the readiness of families to send younger members away for long periods to ensure a continued flow of cash regardless of the strains this produces in the society'.*

The Rural Socio-Economic Survey also commented at length on how overseas employment was perceived (see Chapter 19).

Creating an infrastructure for Independence

With spending on salaries some 15 times greater on South Tarawa than the rest of the country (other than Banaba), and service provision on a scale unthinkable elsewhere, the 1973 – 76 Development Plan accepted that *'the decision to move into town appears logical and attractive'*.

The 1973 Census showed that nearly a third of the overall population had by then made this choice. The subsequent need for investment on South Tarawa in urban facilities of water, sewerage, waste disposal and roads (including the Betio-Bairiki Causeway) was constantly urged as pressing; as was housing for the increased numbers of expatriates considered to be required for these programmes. Despite attempts to exercise tight control, a third of public sector capital spending over the decade had to be diverted to building physical infrastructure in this urban area. Even so, an outbreak of cholera in 1978 – blamed on lack of investment in clean water systems - led to much introspection and pressure to divert even more capacity to Tarawa.

By contrast, the network of 'Outer Island' airfields – which was expanded during the decade to provide for air travel to every island in the Gilberts archipelago [162] – did provide major benefits to rural citizens, as well as simplifying the logistics of providing services (such as specialist medical services).

Financial infrastructure

The Australian pound had been introduced as the legal currency in 1914; it continued to be the main source of exchange until decimalisation and

---

[162] The economic case for which was my final piece of work before I left the Gilberts.

replacement by Australian dollars in 1966. For a brief period in 1942, local banknotes were issued under the authority of the Gilbert and Ellice Islands Government and were locally produced; but after the wartime emergency had passed, these notes were discontinued and then gradually phased out.

In 1966, the then new dollars became the official currency of the Gilbert and Ellice islands, replacing the pound notes. It was decided in the planning for Independence to continue use of this currency, rather than to incur the costs of setting up a Central Bank and attempting to run a local monetary policy; and this arrangement has continued to the present day. A set of Kiribati coins were introduced in 1979, directly pegged to the Australian dollar and others were produced at intervals in the 1980s and early 1990s. Kiribati has not issued local coinage since 1992.

An external Australian commercial bank commenced central and retail banking operations in 1970, taking over some functions previously performed by the Government's Treasury Department, such as the Savings Bank.

The decade also saw the establishment of several important public sector economic institutions for the future. A National Loans Board was established to help expand the functions and scope of private enterprise, and it funded a number of small developments (not all long-lasting); as well as (for the first time) loan funding for private housing. A National Provident Fund was established in 1977 to provide a (compulsory) retirement savings mechanism for those in employment: both employees and employers were to pay monthly contributions to the Fund, and these contributions started to be credited into the individual contributors' accounts to which interest was added annually, to give them a lump sum on retirement. The fund replaced the former Government pension and gratuity scheme, which had applied to civil servants only. Plans were made for a Kiribati Insurance Corporation, which was established shortly after Independence, in 1981. The National Loans Board evolved into a Development Bank at this time also.

In addition to these formal institutions, a loose network of 'village banks' (*mronron*) served as an informal banking sector.

Chapter 16: The Quest For A Modern Economy

An unplanned development: the rise in Phosphate prices

OPEC rose to international prominence during this decade, as its member countries took control of their domestic petroleum industries and acquired a major say in the pricing of crude oil on world markets. On two occasions, oil prices rose steeply in a volatile market, firstly, one triggered by the Arab oil embargo in 1973; and then after the outbreak of the Iranian Revolution in 1979.

On Tarawa, the first of these resulted in severe petrol rationing, and shortages of fuel oil.

However, OPEC inspired another Arab country. At that time, Morocco controlled nearly half of the world's rock phosphate deposits; and while '*in the 1970s you could get phosphate for $4 … one day they just decided to raise the price to $20*'. The price of BPC's phosphate increased from US$ 14 per ton to US$63 in the mid-1970s.

As a result of the careful husbanding of this windfall, the value of the Revenue Equalisation Reserve Fund grew from its original A$556,000 in 1956, and just $1.5 million in 1970, to $69 million by 1979. The people of Kiribati had become, for once, not *collateral damage* from world events, but *collateral beneficiaries* - of an action over which they (or for that matter, the British Government) had neither control nor influence. Had this happened earlier, the principle of world prices would not have applied to phosphate mined by the BPC, and the Gilberts would not have benefitted. Had it happened later, it would not have helped. Phosphate deposits elsewhere became viable, and the peak in prices in the 1970s were followed by a period of much lower prices that lasted several decades after Independence.

For all the efforts made, the 'quest for a modern economy' was thus, despite changed attitudes, little more successful than that of King Arthur's Knights for the Holy Grail. Without the actions of the Sultan of Morocco, Kiribati would have faced an even more difficult future than that described in Chapter 18.

Chapter 16: The Quest For A Modern Economy

Further Reading

1. **Seminar on Development Planning**: Various authors, published in Pacific Perspective, the Journal of the South Pacific Social Sciences Association Vol. 2 No. 2 and No.3, 1973 and 1974
2. **Kiribati: Aspects of History,** multiple authors and editors, published jointly by the Institute of Pacific Studies and the Ministry of Education, Training, and Culture, 1979
3. **Mooring Report,** published by the Ministry of Overseas Development, 1968
4. **Development Plan 1970-72**, published by the Government Printing Division 1970
5. **Third Development Plan 1973-76** published by the Government Printing Division 1973
6. **Development Plan 1973-76 First Annual Review,** published by the Government Printing Division 1974
7. **Fourth Development Plan 1979 - 82,** published by the Government Printing Division 1978
8. **National Accounts 1972-74** by M R Walsh and G Quince, published by the Government Printing Division 1977
9. **Atoll Agriculture In The Gilbert and Ellice Islands,** by C A Small, published the Department of Agriculture, 1972
10. **An Island In The Autumn,** by John Smith, Librario Publishing Ltd., 2011
11. **The Christmas Island Story**, by Eric Bailey, Stacey International, 1977
12. **Management of Marine Resources in Kiribati**, by Roniti Teiwaki, published by the University of the South Pacific, 1988
13. **Reproductive Health and Family Planning in the Pacific: Current Situation and the Way Forward** by Sun-Hee Lee, published by United Nations Population Fund, Country Support Team for the South Pacific., 1995
14. **The Last District Officer,** by John Pitchford, published by Librario, 2013
15. **Cinderellas of the Empire,** by Dr Barrie Macdonald, published by the Institute of Pacific Studies, 1982
16. **Cessation of Phosphate Operations at Banaba: Termination Plan**, internal document of the British Phosphate Commission, 1978
17. **King Of Rock**, by Devon Pendleton, article published in Forbes Magazine, 2009
18. **Files in the British National Archives**

Chapter 17.

THE ROAD TO POLITICAL INDEPENDENCE 1968 – 1979

The working of the 1970 Constitution

The Mooring Report of 1968, and the arrival of Sir John Field to replace the retiring Val Andersen in 1970, signalled a wholly new direction.

Sir John's arrival coincided with a new constitution (as described in page 294 above). The working of this constitution and design of its two successors, collectively the transition from colonial administrators to Gilbertese, elected, control of affairs, owed a great deal to Reuben Uatioa, who had put aside his former nationalism and consciously presided, as Leader of Government Business, over the GEIC as a whole; and his close working with the new Resident Commissioner (soon to become Governor) [163].

Sir John had served most of his career in Nigeria, before becoming Governor firstly of the British Cameroons, and then of St Helena. Although he and Lady Field were derided by many of the new expatriates as 'colonial relics' – and they did retain customs such as dining in full black tie, despite the heat at the Residency (there was no air conditioning in those days) [164] – he very early on gained the respect of the Gilbertese through his age, his demeanour, his wry sense of humour, and not least, his soft-spoken good manners [165].

---

[163] I can recall Reuben telling me that Sir John was the first Resident Commissioner he fully trusted.

[164] As well as being the only person I have ever met whose lunchtime drink was gin and iced water, laced with a pickled onion!

[165] He also knew *exactly* what went on in his colony, despite appearing remote from it. My wife recalls a terrifying (for her) episode when, as a 18-year-old, she became the clerk and PA for the Attorney-General's Office. The occupant of that post, and his Higher Executive Officer, would respectively consume large quantities of beer and sour toddy every lunchtime; and they then spent the afternoons lying across their desks, sleeping off the results. Her task at this time was to make excuses for their being too busy to take calls, and to fend off any visitors. One day, after fobbing off

The 1970 Constitution came into effect after an election in March 1971. Other than Reuben Uatioa and Sione Tui Kleis, most of the former members of the Governing Council failed to be returned. New members included several former Civil Servants, four presidents of Island Councils, and the first woman to be elected (Tekarei Russell, a teacher).

At the legislative level, the new arrangements saw a higher standard of debate; but the members of the Executive Council felt they were struggling to assert any authority over expatriate Heads of Departments. Pressure quickly built to move on again: constitutional progress, Reuben said, was only happening *'because we, the people of this colony, are pushing for it. No doubt about that.'*

A Select Committee was appointed in December 1972 and approved a further advance in December 1973. By that time, moreover, the issue of Separation of the Ellice had reached the stage whereby most Gilbertese members regarded new arrangements as pertaining to the Gilberts only, and, protests of the Ellice Islanders notwithstanding, approved a new Constitution.

The 1974 and 1976 Constitutions

In 1974, *The Gilbert and Ellice Islands Order* thus introduced the last intermediate stage before Internal Self-Government, which was followed by achievement of that status after only two years.

Numbers of ex-officio members in the House of Assembly were reduced to three (the Chief Secretary, the Attorney-General, and the Financial Secretary); 21 elected representatives were to elect a Chief Minister. In theory the Governor appointed another six ministers after consulting the Chief Minister, but in practice was not going to oppose his choice.

The Governor nevertheless continued to preside over both the House of Assembly and Council of Ministers, as well as holding reserve powers over defence, security, finance and external affairs.

Reuben himself was not to take the GEIC forward. An election was held in 1974, and, badly weakened by a nine-day strike just before the election (see below), he failed to be re-elected.

---

telephone calls from his office three times, she was horrified to find Sir John himself at the door, insisting that she unlock it and let him into the office…

Chapter 17: The Road To Political Independence 1970 – 1979

I wrote to my parents at the time:

> 'General election last Thursday: poor old Reuben got thrown out on S Tarawa, very sad personally as his own real ambition was to be Chief Minister and then to retire. Both the candidates who did get elected [166] offered to stand down in his favour, but he wouldn't let them...

> 'Chief Minister will probably be Naboua ... He is not at all popular with many of the Gilbertese, but the only other credible candidate is Ellice (Toalipi [167])...

> 'Generally the elections have produced a lot of young, well educated, articulate and probably radical members, plus a few like Tito [Teburoro] to restore the balance ... As well as Roniti [Teiwaki], one other graduate (Ieremia [Tabai]), 25, NZ graduate [was] elected for Nonouti ... Four pastors (same as last time) but three of them very young. No fewer than 10/28 members are ex-school teachers. So the House should be a bit more lively than the Legislative Council was'.

The 1974 government successfully took the Gilbert Islands through the process of separation from the Ellice, and bore the brunt of the negotiations with the Banabans (both described below); and as soon as the former was out the way (but delayed by two months because of representations from the Banabans, supported by Fiji) the Gilberts moved on to internal self-government.

In practice, the next, 1976, Constitution embodied only a minor and incremental set of institutional changes: officials other than the Attorney General were no longer members of either the executive or legislature; the Governor ceased to attend meetings of the Council of Ministers; the position of Chief Secretary was abolished; and there was to be a Minister of Finance. However, the removal of appointed staff from formal participation in Cabinet meetings had a profound psychological effect: discussion was, for example, increasingly in Gilbertese rather than English.

These years also saw a marked transition in senior advisers: most of the generation of Colonial Administrators who had joined the Western Pacific

---

[166] Abete Merang (the BKATM Union Leader) and Tekarei Russell

[167] Who became the first Prime Minister of Tuvalu (see below)

High Commission in the late 1940s and early 1950s had now come to the age of retirement. Some posts, including some which had previously been filled by Ellice islanders, were filled by Gilbertese on promotion. Many, however, were filled by new expatriate recruits who had served in their previous careers in both colonial and independent African countries. Some of these, such as Sir John Field's successor as Governor, John Smith, and John Pitchford, brought in to run the Family Planning Campaign, brought new perspectives with them, and were prepared to adapt to the different Pacific culture [168]; but there was also a new '*African tendency*' in the senior ranks of government who thought that independence in the Pacific would soon result, as it had so often in Africa, in one-party rule and 'Presidents-for-Life'. Many of these new expatriates felt quite happy to facilitate such an outcome.

Political issues

The debate about the future of the economy and the role within it of the new Development Authority continued at a political level through the 1970s; this debate was discussed in the previous Chapter.

The style of the new Government

The new Ministers were quickly captured by office. *Cinderellas of the Empire* comments that:

> '*The Ministers, in their anxiety to show that they had taken over the powers of the often aloof expatriates, began to behave rather like them. Some were criticised for seeming to relish the exercise of power, for their salaries, the official houses, their lifestyle and for their expectation and ready acceptance of … preferential treatment…*'

---

[168] John Smith wrote in his Valedictory Despatch to the Foreign Secretary in Britain that '*fortunately for these people* [the Gilbertese] *they usually have quite as much influence upon those who administer them as the reverse… because those of us on the ground have been few and remote from the normal influences of our own society we have the more easily absorbed local attitudes and, of course, prejudices…* [until recently] *I would have had to confess that in the Atolls I had met my match*'. John Pitchford also consciously recognised what a change the Gilbertese were: '*So, so different from the exuberant Bantu … breakers on the reef called to me – forget Africa, a new life, a new philosophy*'.

Chapter 17: The Road To Political Independence 1970 – 1979

As I wrote to my parents in the same sentiment (which I shared with most amongst the younger and educated Gilbertese, and as they learned of it from opposition members, equally the *unimane* on outer islands):

> '*An enormous car has just arrived for the Chief Minister – not of course his idea but that of a generous bureaucracy. Really I think the expatriates here* want *the place to become like an African country … the price of phosphate has doubled and is likely to go up again in the near future so it's almost certain that this country will achieve economic independence … but it all seems a bit pointless when the elite just suck up the revenue for their own comfort…*'

Despite Naboua's managing to co-opt one potential opponent, Roniti Teiwaki, to become the first Minister of Finance, the Government struggled to maintain its authority - and it had an increasingly vocal opposition. Opposition grew [169]; and between 1974 and 1976, the government maintained its majority on occasions only because the three remaining 'Officials' were required to vote for it. Some proposed legislation, for example a Bill to grant the Chief Minister powers to dismiss any elected Island Councillor, or the whole Council, at will, and also to pass any island bye-law he wished, had to be withdrawn as the government's own supporters refused to vote for it.

It was easier where the government could take administrative action, for example to attempt to control the news. The Information and Broadcasting Department had been nurtured by secondees from the BBC, who had also been very successful in its localisation (which, unlike that of most Departments, was almost complete by the mid-1970s). The tone and content of editions of the '*Atoll Pioneer*' (as the '*Colony Information Notes*' had been renamed in 1972), a weekly newspaper, distributed free of charge, altered significantly; and contrary opinions such as those of Union members (see below) were simply banned from the airwaves.

The '*cult of the leader*' was promoted, with headlines such as 'Our Leader Off Tomorrow for NZ'. Large photographs of Naboua appeared frequently on its front page. In November 1976 it was front page news in the Atoll Pioneer that the first-ever visit to Tarawa by an interior designer was to be made, in order to design a special guest house wing for the Chief Minister's house; far from

---

[169] And, to be fair, doubts in the minds of at least some of Naboua's Ministers.

impressing the public, this did not go down well with the egalitarian Gilbertese culture.

Several members of the Information and Broadcasting Department were dismissed for objecting to have to toe a 'government' line, rather than exercise the independence they had learned from the BBC secondees.

What the '*African tendency*' did not however realise was that, far from building up Naboua as 'the leader' in the minds of the Gilbertese through these actions, they were actually digging his political grave. [170]

Trade Unions

Meanwhile, a rival 'national' force arose, in the labour movement. The largest union was the BKATM (*Botaki ni Karikarikean Aroia Taan Makuri*), which in 1972 combined the public employees association and staff in the Wholesale Society. Strikes – some for pay, some for less justifiable reasons such as that demanding the sacking of supervisors – became a regular feature of life on Tarawa.

The government accused strikers of holding the country for ransom, of disrupting communications, and of destroying public property - and outer islanders often agreed. Intelligence reports (now declassified) in the British National Archive sought to blame outsiders in NZ and elsewhere for *'encouraging industrial action for little or no cause'*. In actuality, however, the emerging national elite were often themselves the cause. I wrote to my parents on June 26th 1974:

> *'Strike bound again! The Government unclassified workers have gone out, which is not desperate – applies to telephone operators, messengers, etc. However there is a General Strike on Monday which will affect everything ... Direct result of the Ministers' salaries – the reason given is that the Ministers can get double at one go, then so can everyone else. Plus a wildly inflationary increase given last week to the wharfies, which has encouraged them...'*

---

[170] What I have never fully understood is why Naboua, who was a highly intelligent person, did not appreciate this. But his rejection after the 1978 election was clearly a shock, and although he did manage to become a candidate again in the first election after Independence, in 1982, he won few votes. When I saw him in the early 1980s he had visibly shrunk, to be an aged man; and he died not long after.

Chapter 17: The Road To Political Independence 1970 – 1979

But the Union was not blind to evidence. On 4th July I followed that letter up with this:

> *'Strike was averted as the Union leader said that if they could be shown figures as to why the country couldn't afford the pay increases demanded they would be more prepared to listen – so I spent half the night preparing a case and sat in with Ministers producing endless statistics with [sic] the meeting with the Union Executive.'*

They had fewer and fewer chances with evidence. As Naboua's term in office progressed, more restrictive legislation was brought in, to permit the Minister at will to declare any strike illegal, and indeed automatically making strikes illegal for a wide range of activities.

Opposition leaders in the House of Assembly (including the future president, Ieremia Tabai) meanwhile built followings among union members. Ironically it was he, after he had assumed office, who had to have the final show-down.

The Defence Force

Partly because of these spats with the Unions, and partly to support the image of the 'leader', Naboua was persuaded that he needed a Defence Force. He wrote later (after failing to become President) that his intent was to create:

> *'A disciplined group of people, peace-time soldiers, to undertake projects such as the construction of airfields … and to help the Island Councils in their various construction programmes … and of course a defence force would provide us with an insurance against acts of violence. The Banabans, for example, are not going to go away …* [171]

John Smith describes how he was able to defuse what he could see was a highly unpopular proposal amongst most Gilbertese:

> *'Defence was my concern and a reserved subject … I also had no wish to antagonise the Chief Minister. I suggested he bring a paper to the Council of Ministers. He won the day… My approach was to keep things moving, but slowly, because I sensed that the Chief Minister did not have much*

---

[171] From 'late night' conversations with Naboua at the time, however, it was clear to many of us that it was not really the Banabans, but the Unions and indeed any form of post-independence opposition that were in his sights.

> *real support at grass roots and even some ministers were beginning to express mild opposition ...*
>
> *'Fortunately we had not got too far before the pre-Independence general election took place in 1978. The defence force became a major election issue...'*

This experience inspired Article 126 of the Kiribati Constitution, such that Kiribati is unusual amongst States in that it does not permit armed forces [172]. Article 126 states:

> *'No disciplined force shall be established other than the Kiribati Police, the Prison Service, the Marine Protection Service and the Marine Training School'.*

Boundaries of the emerging new state

As well as internal issues, there were three 'boundary' issues to be resolved before Independence. The most pressing was that of the Ellice.

Discontent in the Ellice Islands

The discontent of the Ellice came fully into the open in March 1970, in the context of the debate on the next constitution. This, it was pointed out, for the first time gave the Gilbertese a majority over the combined muster of Ellice representatives and 'Officials'.

The constitution was changed in an attempt to mollify the Ellice: it was to embody the principle that each island, however small, should return a member to the new house (so that on average an Ellice member represented 724 residents, as opposed to nearly 2,400 in the Gilberts). One seat on the five-member Executive Council was also to be reserved for an Ellice.

Sione Tui Kleis had emerged as the most vocal exponent of separation and he was, in fact, the only existing Ellice representative to be returned at the March 1971 Election, having continued to stand out against the new Constitution in highly charged language (such as claiming that the Gilbertese were planning *'suppression, annihilation and enslavement'* of the Ellice); he was supported by

---

[172] Costa Rica being the most cited example, but there are 22 such countries worldwide, including Iceland and Mauritius as well as several small states in the Caribbean, Pacific and Europe.

Chapter 17: The Road To Political Independence 1970 – 1979

seven other MPs who were strongly English-speaking, and it was soon clear that the issue could no longer be ignored.

In December 1971 all but one of these newly elected Members tabled a motion in the Legislative Council calling for separation, and asking for Gilbertese support (which they got).

In 1971 the newly formed Planning Office had produced a paper on the *Economic Implications of Ellice Separation*, which Sir John Field built on to use as a discussion document for a tour of all the Ellice Islands in May 1972 [173].

These papers quantified the situation:

- Ellice Islanders were at the 1968 Census 13.9% of the overall population
- In the Civil Service as a whole, excluding expatriates, they occupied 27% of posts; but more than half of the most senior posts staffed by islanders were occupied by Ellice islanders, including a large percentage of doctors
- In the newly-formed GEIDA, 29% of staff were Ellice, with an even greater preponderance of senior posts than in the Civil Service [174]
- They had 27% of the pupils at KGV/EBS and 18% of the Teacher Training College, together with 19% of overseas scholarships
- 18% of seamen in employment were Ellice
- No fewer than 31% of those employed by the BPC were Ellice.

On the other hand, very little of government expenditure was in the Ellice [175]: about AUD $ 170,000 (of which medical services were by far the largest component, nearly a third, followed by Posts and Telecommunications).

It was also estimated that government revenue from the Ellice Islands was about AUD $ 83,000. The paper contained a first estimate for the costs of a

---

[173] Accompanied by myself, the author of the Planning Office Paper.

[174] The English Head of the Public Works Department in the late 1960s (the PWD had contributed a high proportion of GEIDA staff) had been shamelessly and vocally biased toward Ellice people; and he consistently promoted them over the heads of Gilbertese as foremen, and into higher positions.

[175] Although it was not different from that in the Gilbert Islands other than Tarawa

separate Ellice government, and of the economic and financial impact on a separate Gilberts.

Thus, while the Ellice Islanders were making more than proportionate use of the opportunities available to them, they had to migrate to the Gilberts (either Tarawa or Banaba) in order to do so. This in turn led to worries amongst the remaining Ellice that their culture and language was being diluted, especially owing to relatively frequent intermarriage with Gilbertese, the children of which unions tended to grow up in the Gilberts. This was undoubtedly the main driving force for separation.

In Sir John's tour of all the Ellice Islands, he was left in little doubt that sentiment in the islands there was by now very strongly in favour of separation, and that they wished for this as quickly as it could be put in place. In October 1972 the Parliamentary Undersecretary for the UK Foreign and Commonwealth Office (FCO) Anthony Kershaw visited and was given the same message.

The Monson Report

The instinct of the FCO was to continue to play for time; the very public situation of Anguilla in the West Indies, and its refusal to stay joined to St Kitts and Nevis, was still being played out; and they had no desire for a similar situation to emerge in the Pacific. In December 1972, they thus appointed Sir Leslie Monson (just retired as a Deputy Secretary at the FCO, but with many years' experience at the Colonial Office) to produce another report. He was joined by a former Financial Secretary from Tanganyika [176]. After consultation with both Ellice and Gilbertese members on Tarawa, Sir Leslie also toured each Ellice Island, as well as holding a three-day meeting with island–wide representatives assembled on Vaitupu.

The consultations were held in the *Maneapas* in the traditional manner and were open to all (and were widely attended), although in practice few other than old men, Pastors and Councillors spoke. Proceedings were in the Ellice language throughout and translated for the benefit of the visitors. Few consultations in the history of the Empire can have had this degree of openness.

---

[176] And, again, myself, as notetaker and fact-finder-in-chief

Chapter 17: The Road To Political Independence 1970 – 1979

Proposals put forward by the Ellice representatives followed a philosophy that the assets of the GEIC should be divided 'equally', which they interpreted as being a 50:50 split, despite the disparity in numbers of the population.

They therefore proposed at Vaitupu that:

- The Reserve Fund be equally divided with the new Ellice Government receiving half the amount
- The Ellice should receive - in cash - half the value of all capital grants received from the UK since Colonial Welfare and Development funds had become available in the late 1940s
- The shipping fleet be equally divided
- A separate Marine Training School be set up in the Ellice, again with a transfer of 50% of all past expenditure on the school at Tarawa being given as a cash gift to the Ellice
- Christmas Island (as representing half the land area of the GEIC) be given exclusively to the Ellice, and to form part of their territory.

In addition, a large number of allegations were made as to Gilbertese 'inferiority' in terms of innate characteristics such as treatment of their women, and supposed violence [177]; and active current discrimination by them against the Ellice people was alleged, although no evidence was produced.

Sir Leslie's Report found these demands unreasonable, and the claims of discrimination to be unproven. His Report, that *'to sever would be to cripple'*, was uncompromising:

> *'If the reaction of the Gilbertese leaders was to relax the very praiseworthy restraint they are now exercising, the cost to British funds in the years ahead could be greatly increased ... separation would improve the financial position of a Gilbert Islands Government and should assist it in achieving financial viability ... the political leaders of the Gilbertese have*

---

[177] Repeated in even more forthright and racially charged terms in informal evening sessions. It was very clear that all of the Ellice present confidently expected agreement and sympathy, from us expatriates, and from the British Government, with their viewpoint. It seemed to me, moreover, that the Ellice had taken at face value expatriate protestations over the years about Britain's 'children' who would always be given favours - while the Gilbertese (rightly) took such statements with very large pinches of salt.

Chapter 17: The Road To Political Independence 1970 – 1979

> *not been responsible for the separatist movement, have taken a statesmanlike attitude in the face of it, and their constituents should not be penalised because of any of its results…'*

It is clear from this passage [178] that his motivation was not to try to 'frighten' the Ellice by restricting the division of assets to them to one ship (as is suggested in both *Cinderellas of Empire* and *Winding Up The British Empire in the Pacific*). Rather, Sir Leslie had been impressed by the determination of the Gilbertese to achieve a viable economy; and thought that separation should not be the cause of failure in this aim. Nor was it in Britain's interests, in his view, to have two unviable territories, when by leaving the Reserve Fund wholly with the Gilbertese, Britain might avoid this in at least one case.

Despite his assessment that they themselves would become worse off economically, socially, and financially, he nevertheless supported the Ellice political objectives.

His principal recommendation was:

> *'So much controversy has already been generated by the separation issue and continues to be so generated, that it could not be expected to lie dormant…the spokesmen of the separationalists have assumed that in the last resort the British Government will be guided by their wishes … I consider that a dictat by the British Government would now be too late to quash the separatist movement … I recommend therefore that the British Government should formally state that provided it is satisfied that majority Ellice opinion supports the separation of the Ellice from the Gilbert Islands, it will be ready to take the necessary action to put the separation into effect'.*

Whatever the FCO had expected by the dispatching of Sir Leslie to the Ellice, it was not this. Their first reaction was to make sure that no-one in the GEIC, other than the Acting Governor John Hunter (and even that reluctantly, suspect as he was for thinking separation was a *'foregone conclusion'*) ever saw the report [179]. As their second reaction, John Nichols, Head of the Pacific

---

[178] And from my own recollections of discussions with Sir Leslie at the time

[179] It was indeed never published, and has only recently become available in the British National Archive. Evidently in 1973 no one, either in the FCO or the GEIC, realised that I - then on leave in the UK, but due to return – had been asked by Sir Leslie privately to comment on the draft, and knew precisely what was

Department, wrote that a *'separate Ellice Colony could only be a financial, economic and administrative nonsense ... '*. Their reaction, thirdly, was simply to reject the report.

The newly appointed successor to Sir John Field, John Smith, was asked for confidential advice as to whether separation might at least be delayed; but John Smith was quick to realise that *'we cannot now apply the brakes in order to come to a stop, without a nasty skid'*. In the summer of 1973, the British Government also held discussions with Reuben Uatioa (in London for heart surgery) and came to the conclusion that an announcement could not be delayed beyond the Parliamentary Session in November of that year. It gradually became clear in Whitehall that, however unwelcome it was to them, separation could not be stopped.

On 13th November, Sir Alec Douglas-Home, then Foreign Secretary, gave the final approval:

> *'There are a lot of nonsenses in this world and I suppose we must connive at another. But the cost is deplorable & I think we should say that if they must go their silly ways, they must bear much more of the charge.'*

A simple announcement that separation would be the subject of a referendum, and if approved by that, would go ahead, was made in the Legislative Council on 27th November.

The referendum

The referendum went ahead in a week straddling August and September 1974, island by island (including the Ellice on Tarawa and Banaba), on a rolling basis. It was organised by Eric Bailey, who had initially been recruited to run the 1973 GEIC Census.

In a huge reversal of previous UK policy, the Committee of 24 was invited to observe the process, and three observers (together with four UN Staff) arrived in August 1974 for this purpose. At the end of their visit they recorded that the Ellice people had voted by 3,799 to 293 in favour of separation; but also that there was widespread dissatisfaction there with the terms offered by the British Government, rather than the 'equal' split for which they had asked.

---

recommended; so I was in a strange position for a few months. But I did keep silence, as was my duty under the *Official Secrets Act!*

Chapter 17: The Road To Political Independence 1970 – 1979

The visitors commended the way in which the referendum had been conducted.

The Ellice islanders themselves were somewhat bemused by the process, as they regarded the referendum as very much redundant: separation was already *'tausi'* (taken care of). They had already made their views known twice in the *maneapas*; they had never heard of the Committee of 24; and they were confused by questions about human rights *'designed to draw out details of exploitation they may have suffered under British colonial rule'*.

They equally bemused the UN visitors, by asking why Britain was now throwing aside the *'children it had succoured for so many years'*.

The birth of Tuvalu

In November 1974 a Separation Committee comprising the eight Ellice members of the House of Assembly was set up under the Deputy Governor Tom Layng. This decided the name of the new colony – Tuvalu; the form of government; and what institutions would be needed. Despite the predominance of Tarawa being a major complaint before separation, a proposal for a low-cost government [180], to be achieved by splitting the new government into eight parts and locating one on each island (so that they could be fed, housed, and sewage locally [181]) was very quickly brushed aside by this Committee; and plans began to replicate everything that had been centralised onto Tarawa, on a smaller scale, onto Funafuti - other than the secondary school, which was to remain on Vaitupu. An intervention by a senior visiting official from the Ministry of Overseas Development, strongly objecting to his Ministry being asked to provide aid for expensive houses for the returning Civil Servants, did result in a new housing policy to be based on loans and self-builds, but that was all.

A formal Separation Conference was held in March 1975, attended by British officials, chaired by John Smith, with attendees: Tom Layng, eight Ellice members, and six Gilbertese led by Naboua Ratieta. This agreed citizenship issues, the structure of the new government, the transfer of the ship *Nivanga*,

---

[180] Prepared by Eric Bailey and myself

[181] The savings in administration and infrastructure to be spent on a flying boat air service operating twice weekly between islands.

Chapter 17: The Road To Political Independence 1970 – 1979

and the expansion of Motufoua; and finally, timing. Other than another last attempt by the Ellice representatives to gain some islands from the Gilberts, quickly rebuffed, it was surprisingly non-contentious.

Tuvalu came into existence on 1 October 1975. Tom Layng became its first (and last) Commissioner. Three years later, to the day, Tuvalu became independent – nine months ahead of Kiribati [182].

The Banaban Issue

No sooner had the issue of separation for the Ellice been settled, however, when that of the Banabans began in earnest.

By the 1970s they had been living on Rabi for a generation. Like the Nauruans, they had all but abandoned their traditional diet and lived off *'tinned salmon and strawberry jam'*. When the FCO Minister Ted Rowlands visited in 1975 he described Rabi as looking like a refugee camp, despite its permanent houses, piped water, electricity and pool tables – all unknown to Gilbertese villagers.

Unlike for the Nauruans, however, the royalties accruing to the Banabans were not enough to buy Cadillacs for villagers, nor to run an airline for the convenience of the Banaban leaders.

The Banabans, having boycotted the 1967 negotiations on phosphate, appeared before the Committee of 24 in June 1968, but were firmly opposed there by Reuben Uatioa, appearing on behalf of the GEIC Government. They received only general sympathy, and an attempt in 1971 to divide the BPC Commissioners by holding separate talks with the Commissioners of Australia and New Zealand failed. Rebuffed also there, they sued for compensation: Case No. 1 against the BPC was for breach of replanting requirements, for which they sought AUD $ 21,389,793; and Case No. 2 against the British Government from whom they sought AUD $ 100 million for breach of its fiduciary duty towards them.

---

[182] Perhaps I should record my private view in 1974, that the Ellice people had made an enormous strategic mistake. I wrote to my parents at the time: *'The Ellice conference finished yesterday. I feel sorry for them. There has been absolutely no imagination or learning from experience and they are setting up what I'm certain will be a miserable sort of place – particularly Funafuti which is likely to become the worst slum in the Pacific'*. With the hindsight of more than 40 years, I was wrong; Tuvalu has had ups and downs, but has survived successfully as an Independent State.

Chapter 17: The Road To Political Independence 1970 – 1979

As well as the legal case, the Banabans had lined up many supporters in the UK, and employed professional advisers to promote their cause. They had a network of supporters at Westminster led by Sir Bernard Braine, a maverick right-wing backbencher MP renowned for championing of 'causes', and the source of many parliamentary questions on their behalf. A *Justice For The Banabans* campaign was orchestrated by the PR advisers who had worked for the Biafrans during the Nigerian Civil War. In 1974, their former legal counsel Lord Ilwyn Jones was appointed Lord Chancellor in the incoming Labour Government. The Banabans also received vocal support from a number of well-known 'celebrities' and other public figures, skilfully tapping into the mood of post-colonial guilt in the UK.

The Minister responsible, Joan Lestor, instructed civil servants to *'look again'* at the issue of Banaban separation *before* the granting of internal self-government to the Gilberts [183].

The Gilberts government, now with Naboua Ratieta as Chief Minister after their own 1974 election (see above), had therefore a political fight on their hands (in the Court cases, they were bystanders).

The High Court cases

The hearing before the Chancery Division of the High Court began on 8th April 1975 and set a record in legal history: it lasted for 206 days and cost the Banabans £750,000 in legal fees alone. It required site visits by the Judge, Sir Robert Megarry. Ten thousand pages of documents were presented.

The Judgment itself took five days to deliver, from 29th November 1976. Megarry concluded that *'stripped of all that is false or misleading or intemperate, their claims have a central core of genuine grievance'*. However, as a matter of law he dismissed the case against the Crown, on the technical grounds that, in a strictly legal sense, there had been no breach of Britain's fiduciary duty. In the action against the BPC, he allowed charges at the rate of only AUD $ 75 an acre, largely on the grounds that it was not the BPC, but the Pacific Phosphate Company, that had given the original pledge to reinstate lands destroyed by mining.

---

[183] Later, after leaving office, Joan Lestor became Patron of the *Justice For The Banabans* campaign.

Chapter 17: The Road To Political Independence 1970 – 1979

He concluded:

> *'I think a Judge ought to direct attention to what he considered to be a wrong that he can't right, and leave it to the Crown to do what it considered to be proper'.*

In other words, he returned the problem from the Courts to the politicians.

The British Government appointed R. N. Posnett to report. After visiting Banaba, Tarawa, and Rabi, Posnett recommended an ex-gratia payment of AUD $ 10 million to the Banabans; on the separation issue, Posnett concluded that the *'Banaban case fails to establish grounds for departing from the long established policy that the wishes of the people of the territory as a whole should be the guide'.*

In *An Island In The Autumn* John Smith (who bore much of the brunt of Banaba's re-emergence as *'a skeleton in the colonial cupboard'* in the UK) writes of this time:

> *'Banaba soon dominated all my dealings with the Foreign and Commonwealth Office, frequently demanding re-assessment of priorities, delaying constitutional progress, and absorbing time that could have been more profitably allocated. The Banaban cause was taken up by all manner of organisations and individuals and I received a steady stream of resolutions and protests from Churches, Trades Unions, Student Unions, not only from the United Kingdom but also from Australia and New Zealand as well, all of which required my attention. Parliamentary and public interest kept forcing Banaba to the top of the agenda but that was not where either the Gilbertese or I felt it should be. There was a country to be governed and a people to be helped toward Independence.*

> *'Reporting on a visit he paid us, Mr Henry Stanley, Assistant Undersecretary in the FCO, commented that we all seemed to treat the Banaban issue as a tiresome distraction. It was fair comment. The Banabans were far away in Fiji and their leaders always endeavoured to deal with London, which they frequently visited, rather than Tarawa … not once did they address me directly either in person or by letter'* [184].

---

[184] Although, to be fair, given the treatment they had received from past Resident and High Commissioners, this is perhaps understandable.

Chapter 17: The Road To Political Independence 1970 – 1979

The Banabans' political case

Central to their political case was the Banabans' proposition that they were a separate nation from the Gilbertese. This was despite their speaking essentially the same language (differences were no greater than those between Northern and Southern Gilbert islands); their having the same gods and culture; and their many shared historical links with islands in Tungaru, such as the colonisation by them of Tamana, and the Beru invasion of Banaba in the seventeenth century [185]. There were some accepted minor cultural differences, particularly in relation to the status of women – for example, on Banaba women were traditionally allowed to speak in the *mwaneaba*; and men would often move to their wife's village after marriage which, although not unknown, was less common elsewhere in Tungaru. Equally wide cultural variants could be found across the Gilbert archipelago; and it was less than 20 years since the first-ever pan-GEIC meeting. As we have seen in Part 1, and until halfway through the 20th century – the 1950s - there had been no concept of a 'Gilbertese' nation, only of individual islands.

In any case many, if not most, Banabans were by the 1970s of mixed descent with other Gilbertese: in the 1967 Census, 67% of the population of Rabi were either born in a Gilbert Island other than Banaba, or had at least one parent so born. However, on Rabi the definition of who was allowed a voice was tightening; many citizens who had lived or been born there since 1947 were now cut out of debate:

> *'If a Gilbertese or other non-Banaban, even one who is married to a Banaban, wishes to speak in a public meeting, he or she will most likely be silenced ... Gilbertese on Rabi are usually barred from actively participating in any position of responsibility or leadership.'*

Most scholars and observers in the Pacific – including Maude, who had eventually been brought into the Court cases as an interpreter – did not (and would still not today) accept the proposition that there was a Banaban nation or culture separate from other Gilbertese: the most Maude, for example, would allow as an analogy was the difference between Cornwall and England.

---

[185] As we saw in Part 1, there was no shared sense of nationality in Tungaru, in fact barely a sense of even island solidarity. Society was family-based.

Chapter 17: The Road To Political Independence 1970 – 1979

Their other claims of the Council of Elders at this time were that:

- They had been forcibly included in the Gilbert Islands against their will (for the history of this see Chapter 10)
- They had never been governed by Gilbertese
- The Ellice Islands had been allowed to separate
- The whole phosphate income should accrue to them.

They thus refused to negotiate directly with the elected government of the Gilbert Islands until October 1975, when the then Prime Minister of Fiji, Ratu Mara, chaired a meeting on Tarawa that agreed to keep separate the issues of compensation (where the Gilbertese fully supported Banaban aims) and Independence. This agreement was not honoured, and the Banabans again began to link the two: especially after losing their case against the British Government (see above).

Further meetings were held in 1977 at which the Gilbertese government offered a referendum of the people of the Gilberts and Rabi, following claims in the media that the bulk of the Gilbertese supported the Banaban claims and only their politicians did not. The Banaban Council of Elders initially agreed to this but their 'advisers' were clearly not willing to put it to the test, so they reneged on the agreement shortly after. The Banabans again threatened that they would block the move of the Gilbert Islands Government to internal self-government, which had been agreed with Britain as 1st November 1977; their lawyers produced an Opinion arguing that the British Government could not proceed. Ratu Mara also abandoned any pretence of neutrality and began openly to support the Banabans.

In the meantime the Gilbertese were beginning to lose patience with Fiji (that the Fiji Trades Unions blocked flights to Tarawa for a month in solidarity with the Banabans did not help). When Britain announced a delay to self-government in October, John Smith had to report to London that *'I have never before seen Ministers so united, so talkative, and so angry. The Chief Minister was actually shaking with rage during several hours of discussion … We have made them feel weak, ashamed and friendless'*. The next month Naboua spoke in favour of a motion in the House of Assembly that *'as a result of the intervention of another country, Her Majesty's Government has seen fit to delay the operation of the Order granting self-Government'* and seeking an assurance that *'neither the country concerned nor any other body will be allowed to intervene further in the affairs of the Gilbert Islands'*.

Another meeting was held in 1978 (see below), but the British Government continued to procrastinate until the final showdown came, at the very last available moment, at the independence negotiations (also see below).

United States Claims to the Phoenix and Line Islands

The third territorial issue in the run-up to Independence was the residual US claims to eighteen GEIC islands - in the Phoenix and Line Groups and four of the Ellice Islands. Despite an initial FCO view that they should *'let sleeping dogs lie'*, the British Embassy in Washington was able to advise that US interest in the islands had waned since WWII. This issue therefore proved rather more tractable than those of the Ellice and Banabans; and after the Independence of Kiribati and Tuvalu the US was content formally to renounce the claims.

Accelerated decolonisation 1975 – 1979

The debate initiated by the Conservative Prime Minister Edward Heath in 1973, through his PAR (Policy Analysis and Review) of the costs and benefits to the UK of the remaining dependencies, had meandered on for more than two years. It was finally brought to a conclusion through the 'death warrant' despatch signed by Labour Prime Minister Callaghan in June 1975.

This announced a policy of 'accelerated decolonisation':

> *'Their continued dependence involves a significant political cost; it means we are liable to take the rap for locally engendered crises, and accept international criticism for 'colonialism' … our political and economic relations with countries which have territorial claims against them are impaired; and we may have to accept defence commitments which we might otherwise be able to get rid of; we may be required to divert to them administrative and financial resources from tasks much more important to the UK itself'.*

The Gilberts was in this despatch finally classified by the UK as a country whose dependence on Britain should be ended, and that within five years.

The Constitutional Convention of 1977

John Smith's experiences in Nigeria had convinced him that the conventional route to a 'Westminster' Constitution (often complete with wigs and maces) was not sensible. His reaction to the 'death warrant' was thus to devise both a widespread education programme about options, and also to convene in the

Chapter 17: The Road To Political Independence 1970 – 1979

Gilberts a Constitutional Conference involving a wide range of interests. In both of these he was assisted by Professor David Murray of the University of the South Pacific, who in late 1976 ran a series of seminars to consider alternatives to a 'Westminster' model, as well as the applicability of it to Gilbertese circumstances. At the same time, John Smith gave a series of radio talks covering the same ground.

Despite some opposition from Naboua as Chief Minister – he later accused the Governor of *'benevolent manipulation'* (and with definite opposition from the 'African tendency', several of whom complained directly to the FCO [186]) - the Convention met in April and May 1977. It comprised some 160 members: the House of Assembly representatives, Presidents of Island and Town Councils, representatives of the *unimane*, co-operative societies, churches, Trades Unions, Womens' Clubs and senior civil servants and Development Authority staff. Professor Murray was on hand to answer questions, but other than that, there were no expatriates present. The Convention also met in public, in the South Tarawa Council mwaneaba.

As with Ellice separation, the Convention thus followed a process which was unique for a British Colony.

It decided to work to a list of 52 questions that John Smith had assembled as the basis of his radio talks. The recommendations it came up with followed the Westminster models in some respects, but others were modified to follow Gilbertese customs and to reflect their colonial experiences (positive and negative). It made a number of recommendations, the most important of which are set out below.

All inhabited islands (the Line Islands for the first time) were to be represented in a *Mwaneaba ni Maungatabu* (Supreme Mwaneaba) of twenty-three constituencies. Rather than a 'first past the post' electoral system, there would be two rounds of elections for each of these (unless a candidate won more than 50% of the vote in the first round), with weaker candidates eliminated in the second round.

The government was to be headed by a unique blend of the concepts of Prime Minister and President: the Beretitenti (President) had first to win a seat in the Mwaneaba, and then be selected by its members to be a candidate (along with up to three others) for a nationwide popular ballot. Once elected, the

---

[186] Their complaints are now in the British National Archives

Chapter 17: The Road To Political Independence 1970 – 1979

Beretitenti was then to choose Cabinet Ministers from amongst the members, on the Westminster model.

Other bespoke features of the proposed political structure were that:

- A speaker was to be elected (by MPs) from outside the Mwaneaba, rather than be one of its members
- All members other than the Beretitenti were to be subject to recall by a petition of his or her constituents
- If the government lost a vote of no confidence, the Mwaneaba was automatically to be dissolved and new elections were to be held. In the meantime, a Council of State would assume executive functions.

The last of these provisions has proved particularly useful in maintaining political stability in Kiribati, and has prevented successive Beretitenti being able to 'buy' votes after losing a no confidence measure (as has frequently happened elsewhere in the Pacific); also, the prospect of facing the electorate has usefully made members pause before bringing down the government of the day.

The Convention also agreed:

- That the Gilberts should not change its name (e.g. back to Tungaru), but that the 'Kiribati' form of this would apply after Independence
- Kiribati would be a Republic. HM The Queen would be acknowledged but as the Head of the Commonwealth, which Kiribati would join [187].

This Constitution was amended by the Election of Beretitenti (Amendment) Act 1980, which provided that where the President comes from a single member constituency, a bye election must be held to replace him or her so that constituents have a member who can represent them effectively and, if necessary, criticise the government. From time to time, a Constitutional amendment to allow for dual nationality (at present forbidden) to

---

[187] This was partly because of the perceived additional costs of setting up a Governor-General (which would have to be borne by local finances), but also because the Convention thought that a Prime Minister and a Governor-General might well end up in opposition to, and interfering with, each other. That situation had just visibly occurred at the climax of the 1975 Australian constitutional crisis, with the dismissal of the PM Gough Whitlam by the Governor-General Sir John Kerr.

Chapter 17: The Road To Political Independence 1970 – 1979

accommodate the growing I Kiribati diaspora, has been discussed, but not yet implemented.

The 1978 election

The last election before Independence was held in February 1978. There was a turnout of 81% in the first round of voting, and 78% in the second. The most divisive issue was that of the Defence Force, and there was an entry of younger and able civil servants, mostly to express their opposition to the previous government. Eight members of the previous House (including one Minister) lost their seats.

Although technically the new House could then have selected a new Chief Minister from amongst their number, they unanimously chose to uphold the spirit of the Constitutional Convention; and they selected four of their number to be candidates for Chief Minister. Most of the new members were also united in their determination that Naboua (who had been re-elected for Marakei) should not himself be a candidate.

The four candidates were Ieremia Tabai, Babera Kirata, Roniti Teiwaki, and Toamati Iuta. Ieremia, who had circumvented the radio ban by tirelessly touring the outer islands to speak in *mwaneabas*, and whose preference for a simple lifestyle and traditional values were well known [188], emerged as a clear 'anti-establishment' winner. He scored twice as many votes as any other candidate, and an absolute majority of those cast; and notably, garnered support from both Protestants and Roman Catholics, as well as from all parts of the Gilberts.

He immediately took his three Presidential rivals into the Cabinet as Ministers, as well as two of the most prominent Trade Union leaders, who had also been elected as Members. His government was to be one of national unity.

The Independence negotiations

As soon as Ieremia Tabai was established as Chief Minister, he flew to London and Washington, in June 1978, to discuss future financial aid, the Banaba issue, and the US claims.

---

[188] As Beretitenti, he continued to cut his own toddy and could frequently be seen bicycling around Tarawa without a Police guard, and shirtless.

Chapter 17: The Road To Political Independence 1970 – 1979

He:

> *'Spoke bluntly of the economic predicament. His country faced bankruptcy when phosphate income ceased, but it was not sensible to go forward to independence on a programme of cutting services ... a financial package had to be completed prior to the pre-independence constitutional package.'*

The FCO had in fact already agreed with the Ministry of Overseas Development that the existing policy, whereby reserves (in this case the Revenue Equalisation Reserve Fund) must be emptied before any budgetary aid kicked in, would have to be modified.

The FCO's main concern was the Banaban issue. As it happened, the Banabans were by then in serious financial difficulties themselves, owing to mismanagement of their finances and various commercial enterprises. They had ousted the Rotan family from the Council; and were minded to accept the ex-gratia payment offered by Britain four years earlier. But they were still making stipulations that they would only accept it subject to separation of Banaba, that the whole must be paid to the Rabi Council to dispose of as they saw fit, and that the Gilberts should cease to have the right to tax phosphate revenue. At a meeting in Suva on 29 September 1978, where agreement to budgetary aid - without the Gilberts having to first expend their reserves - was finally offered, Ieremia Tabai yet stood firm that Banaba could have no special status after Independence. In October he followed this with a telegram laying down the Gilbert islands' Government's *'absolute right to proceed with independence with its territory intact'* although he was willing to confirm the safeguards agreed in 1975.

Goronwy-Roberts warned the Foreign Secretary that the impending meeting was *'likely to be the most difficult pre-independence conference that we have held for a Pacific territory'*. It was held between 21 November and 7 December 1978. The Banabans refused to accept a status as observers and brought Sir Bernard Braine, and their Fijian lawyer K C Ramrakha with them. After they repeated their demand for separation before Independence, the negotiations were suspended for a week. On 28th November the British Government finally came off the fence. The boundaries of the new state were to be *'as at present constituted'*. At this point the Banabans and their advisers walked out, Sir Bernard Braine pausing only to spit in the face of the Gilbert Government's own constitutional adviser, David Murray, as he left.

Chapter 17: The Road To Political Independence 1970 – 1979

The new Constitution – based closely on that agreed at the Constitutional Convention held on Tarawa the year before – was then quickly agreed, including the assurances made since 1975 to the Banabans as to their rights in Kiribati, and for their representation in the Kiribati parliament. As well as incorporating Chapters on Fundamental Rights, Citizenship, the Judiciary, and Banaba and the Banabans, the Constitution differed from the Convention only in introducing term limits for the Beretitenti; making provision for a Vice-President; limiting the number of Ministers to ten; and exempting all Ministers from recall provisions. The Attorney-General remained as a sole ex-Officio member of the Government, appointed by the Beretitenti [189].

The negotiators also agreed a financial settlement:

- Development aid of AUD $ 15.5 m for four years
- Special financial assistance of AUD $ 9.1 m to meet agreed budget deficits
- Continuing technical co-operation
- Additional support in case of emergencies or natural disasters.

The handover

There was more drama to come. The Kiribati Bill was introduced into the House of Lords in February 1979, and in the same month 154 Banabans (most of whom had just become unemployed as a result of the Banabans' business enterprises collapsing) decided on a symbolic 'invasion' of Banaba, unfortunately taking petrol bombs with them. Following the dispatch of police units from Tarawa, some 35 of them were arrested and then convicted of arson.

In March 1979 the Callaghan Government in Britain (after its 'winter of discontent') collapsed, and with it the Kiribati Bill. Invitations had already been sent out for Independence on 12 July, yet the UK election was in progress and the new government would not take office until mid-May.

In the meantime Ieremia Tabai was persuaded to meet the Banaban leaders one last time, and did so in Suva again under the (partisan) Chairmanship of Ratu Mara; *'although no one in London was expecting a substantial result ... talks should take place because if they did not, the Banaba lobby will be able to misrepresent the reasons'*.

---

[189] At this time there were no qualified lawyers of Gilbertese nationality.

Chapter 17: The Road To Political Independence 1970 – 1979

During the election period Goronwy-Roberts – unable by British conventions to raise the matter officially - had 'happened' to meet his Conservative counterparts at a party and explained the urgency to them; the Kiribati Bill thus had the distinction of being the first piece of legislation passed by the incoming government of Mrs Thatcher. Despite Sir Bernard Braine and several other's best efforts, and the tabling of several amendments to the Bill for Banaba to be excluded from Kiribati, it successfully passed through Parliament with a majority of 108 to 16. Royal Assent was given on 11 June 1979, leaving just a month to Independence Day itself.

Princess Anne represented the Queen on Tarawa; and Princess Margaret at a ceremony at Westminster Abbey in Britain. On 12 July, the former went to the stadium at Bairiki to read a message from HM The Queen, and to hand over the instruments of independence to President Tabai.

Writing shortly before the event, the authors of *Aspects of History* admitted some mixed feelings about the future:

> *'Our Independence is only meaningful to us [when] we have it in our own Gilbertese way, te katei ni Kiribati. Only the future will reveal the reality of Independence. Whether good or bad, we will have to face it .... Despite the disruptive forces we have experienced during the past two centuries, our katei ni Kiribati has remained intact. We have arrived at the present changed, but still strong in our sense of Gilbertese identity.'*

Chapter 17: The Road To Political Independence 1970 – 1979

Further Reading

1. **Winding Up The British Empire In The Pacific Islands,** by W David McIntyre, published by the Oxford University Press, 2014
2. **The Economic Implications of Ellice Separation**, written as **Planning Office Paper No. 1**, by M R Walsh (not published, but presumably in the Kiribati archives), 1971
3. **Report by Sir Leslie Monson,** 1973, never published but now declassified and in the British National Archive
4. **Handwritten notes of Sir Leslie Monson's visit,** by M R Walsh (unpublished, 1972)
5. **Private papers of Eric Bailey,** who supervised the Ellice Separation Referendum (unpublished, dated between 1972 and 1974)
6. **Secession In The Defence Of Identity – the Making of Tuvalu,** by Dr Barrie Macdonald, published in Pacific Viewpoint, May 1975
7. **Cinderellas of the Empire,** by Dr Barrie Macdonald, published by the Institute of Pacific Studies, 1982
8. **An Island In The Autumn,** by John Smith, Librario Publishing Ltd., 2011
9. **Consuming Ocean Island,** by Katerina Martina Teaiwa, published by the Indiana University Press, 2015
10. **Ocean Island (Banaba)** published by the GEIC Government 1975
11. **Go Tell It To The Judge – but Tell It True** issued on behalf of the Government of the Gilbert Islands 1977
12. **Banaba and The Gilbert Islands – A Factual Summary** issued on behalf of the Government of the Gilbert Islands 1979
13. **Report of the Constitutional Convention,** published by the Government Printer, 1977
14. **The Kiribati Constitution** published as The Kiribati Independence Order 1979, HMSO, 1979
15. **The Last District Officer,** by John Pitchford, published by Librario, 2013
16. **Kiribati: Aspects of History,** multiple authors and editors, published jointly by the Institute of Pacific Studies and the Ministry of Education, Training, and Culture, 1979
17. **Letters sent to his parents between 1971 and 1975,** by M R Walsh (unpublished)
18. **Atoll Pioneer newspapers from 1971 to 1979,** published weekly by the Information and Broadcasting Department
19. **Files in the British National Archives**
20. **United Nations Decolonisation Reports**

PART 3
THE REPUBLIC OF KIRIBATI

Chapter 18.

THE NEWLY INDEPENDENT COUNTRY

Kiribati in 1979

Kiribati was neither the first 'micro-state', nor the smallest, to become independent. It was perhaps one of the poorest, as measured in terms of monetisation and GDP. It had but recently emerged via the British Government's 'death warrant' despatch of 1975, from lists of territories that *'were deemed too small, too weak in resources, and too remote to be Sovereign States'*.

This Chapter describes the critical differences between the colony of the Gilbert Islands and the new Sovereign State of Kiribati – politically, economically, and in terms of new obligations arising from its reassumption of sovereignty. The next Chapter, *Village and Urban Societies at Independence*, addresses more subjective issues: how people saw these differences, and how the issues raised in this Chapter were seen to impact on their lives; and how they then saw the future.

Chapters 20-22 then continue a mainly chronological story, covering the first four Beretitenti; although occasionally it has seemed more informative to follow a topic so that a single section considers through an issue over the whole period from independence up to 2019 (e.g. defence, the influence of the Missions, pollution of Tarawa lagoon, corruption), rather than to split it between Chapters. Chapter 23 reviews the emergence of an I Kiribati diaspora, and Chapter 24 concludes the book with a discussion of issues for Kiribati into the future.

Viability of the new nation

The 1983 – 86 Development Plan contained an early section which posed a fundamental question, one to which few other newly independent governments would have owned up. It was entitled, simply: *'Is Kiribati Viable'*?

Chapter 18: The Newly Independent Country

This Plan set out an even more apocalyptic assessment than that of the 1973-76 Development Plan (p. 250 above):

> 'The difficulties inherent in the task of stabilising the population at a level that can be supported by the resources of the country are considerable and must not be underestimated; but the task must be attempted and must succeed if the territory is to avoid increasing poverty and overcrowding and in the long run the danger of under-nutrition and even starvation.
>
> 'Even under the most favourable conditions, no person in Kiribati is going to survive on what would amount to less than half an acre of available agricultural land, which is all that will be available at the end of the century. Child malnutrition, surely one of the most valid indicators of the effects of development, is now common in both urban and rural areas – it was hardly known ten years ago...
>
> 'Nor may we be too confident that aid from overseas will relieve the situation when it becomes unsupportable ... donors are more likely to direct aid to countries where the millions are suffering, rather than a few hundreds in remote places ...

It concluded that *'Kiribati has unique problems requiring original solutions which may only be worked out within Kiribati'*.

The leaders of the new nation displayed a defiant attitude about 'viability' from the outset. Ieremia Tabai was sure that the I Kiribati people were *'better poor but free'*. In an interview with NZ radio (recorded some years later, after his term of office) he said:

> *'I understand that in this world you do not have permanent friends, just permanent interests. It was no longer in the interests of the British to hang around here ... We accept that and we know that we have to be on our own, and just do what we can afford.*
>
> *'That belief influenced a lot of my thinking when I came to Government and the words I used a lot were self-reliance'.*

He had a popular mandate to implement such a policy; and, even more importantly, a legitimacy that the colonial government had never had. The transition over which the Tabai and successive governments presided, as described over the next few Chapters, was rightly described by the IMF some two decades later as *'remarkable'*.

Chapter 18: The Newly Independent Country

From the perspective of today, forty years on, it is clear that Kiribati *has* been a viable country: although climate change, the issue that has now come to dominate much discussion of its future, was, at the time of independence, neither recognised nor mentioned.

The population

The 1978 Census showed that the population had increased some 8% over the five years since the previous Census, and was growing at a rate of about 2.2% per annum. The early reductions in the birth rate from the family planning campaign had not been sustained. The total population on independence day was estimated at some 56,000.

Of this population nearly one-third were by then resident on South Tarawa, up from just over 20% a decade earlier.

The urban area then comprised three main centres: Betio (with a population of 7,600); Bairiki, with associated 'labour lines' (public sector housing) on neighbouring Nanikai; and Bikenibeu. Between these, there were smaller clusters around the principal Missions, but generally the areas between villages along South Tarawa were still without houses, as was Temaiku (although the bund reclaiming land there was already in place). Most of Bonriki was occupied, as it is now, by the airport. The Defence Force had been placed on Buota, and after its abandonment some Government Departments were located there.

The preponderance of Tarawa in terms of the population and economy was not itself an issue unique to Kiribati. In fact, Tarawa was about halfway down a list of Pacific island capitals when they were ranked by the percentage of the overall population clustered in the capital city; and both the remaining US and French colonies at that time exhibited similar characteristics of urban subsidy (in fact the capitals of the Districts of the US Trust Territories had even more distorted economies [190]). The density of population on Tarawa was, for example, almost identical with that at Majuro, the capital of the Marshalls.

What Tarawa did not then have was the safety valve of emigration to a metropolitan country, which characterised many of the ex-NZ dependencies

---

[190] As I had realised when I did a consultancy study of them on behalf of UNDAT in 1976.

Chapter 18: The Newly Independent Country

(there, emigration from rural areas to the capital was often a half-way house towards emigration to New Zealand itself).

The economic background

Between 1979 and 1981 (the first year in which phosphate was completely absent from the national accounts), real GDP (at 1980 prices) shrank from AUD$ 43.1 million to AUD$ 21.3 million – more than 50%.

The Development Plan commented that:

> 'Per capita GDP in the case of Kiribati is a poor socio-economic indicator because of the geographical distribution of economic activity … a typical outer island with a population of about 2,000 will generally have no more than 100 persons permanently employed. These are mainly employees of central and local government or of religious organisations, the private sector on the outer islands remaining very small … the average per capita figure masks large variations in distribution'

Nevertheless, the economy still presented all the problems foreseen in previous Plans, ever since the Mooring Report had identified them in 1968. Despite much effort and money, very few had been mitigated over the final decade of colonial rule, and then usually not because of governmental, nor British, action (they were rather due to the price of phosphate as determined by Morocco, and to the establishment of the Marine Training School by German companies).

The phosphate boom of the 1970s had also resulted in a substantial surplus on the balance of trade: it accounted for more than 85% of exports by value. Immediately after Independence exports fell from some AUD $18 million to less than AUD$ 3.6 million, leading to a trade deficit in 1982 of some AUD$ 16 million.

Similarly the government moved into a deficit (before drawing on the Reserve Fund, or the temporary budgetary support promised by Britain as part of the independence settlement), of some AUD$ 8.75 million in 1982.

Sources and extent of external aid

External aid also financed the bulk of capital and development expenditure [191]. The capacity to absorb aid funds had been steadily expanding (expenditure funded by aid rose from AUD$ 3.5 million in 1977 to AUD$ 13.7 million in 1983).

As well as the UK, Asian Development Bank and UN aid that had been available to the Gilbert and Ellice Islands, Australia and New Zealand had become more active as Independence approached, and Independence made Kiribati eligible for participation in the then European Economic Community's Programme Lomé II. Japanese aid to fisheries programmes, as well as technical assistance, also began after 1979.

Whilst the diversification of donors was welcome, the Development Plan noted that *'the variety of donors involved with Kiribati each has its own policy and system, which Kiribati Planners and others must accept and work with'*. A first Development Coordinating Meeting of Donors was held in 1985, and these have continued since.

The Revenue Equalisation Reserve Fund

As part of the 1979 Independence Financial Settlement Kiribati had been forced to concede that 50% of any income exceeding AUD$ 5 million in any year would be offset against UK Budgetary aid (and this in fact happened twice). The government therefore adopted initially a strategy of minimising income from the fund, in favour of its capital growth; only after the cessation of budgetary aid after 1986 did a more balanced strategy emerge.

Impressive growth in the value of the fund did continue: by 1989, ten years after independence, it had grown from AUD$ 69.3 million to more than AUD$ 200 million, despite average draw-downs in the previous five years of around AUD$ 5 million annually. Despite the rapid inflation of this decade (and the appreciation of the Australian dollar against the currencies in which the Fund was invested) this represented considerable real growth.

---

[191] When I worked in the National Economic Planning Office I always appreciated the irony of filling in a 'Capital Aid Project' application each year which had the title 'Recurrent Costs of Family Planning'. Donors did take a realistic view at that time of what constituted 'development' expenditure (in fact probably more so then than now).

The educational, employment and manpower background

Kiribati had achieved virtually 100% coverage of primary education at Independence (unlike many developing countries at the time). A 1980 survey showed that 90% of I Kiribati then aged between 15 and 55+ could read and write in their mother tongue, and also do simple arithmetic. At that time also nearly 30% were proficient in reading and writing in basic English.

However, at higher levels, educational statistics showed a very similar variation, imbalance and dominance by the public sector as was the case with GDP. Overall, the government employed 82% of those educated to tertiary level, 79% of those educated to secondary level, and 51% of those who had completed primary education. The private sector employed only 5% of graduates and 4% of those educated to secondary school level.

The 1983-86 Development Plan commented that:

> *'The most significant motivating factor that encourages Kain Kiribati to pursue academic education and to come to Tarawa is the search for paid employment. This is because the cash economy is thought to be easier, offers better return for labour and more security than the rural subsistence life supplemented by copra sales. The largest influx to Tarawa from the outer islands occurs among young men aged 20 to 29. The ratio of population of working age to employment opportunities has declined and this gap is widening.'*

At the level of graduate jobs, however, although numbers were by now beginning to fall, the government still relied to an unhealthy extent on expatriate manpower, with the additional expense that that entailed. The number of students successfully completing their courses (especially in subjects such as engineering, law and medicine) was also still below demand.

Overseas employment

The main source of overseas employment continued to be seamen who had graduated from the Marine Training School. About 120 new seamen were being trained each year. At Independence it was estimated that about AUD$ 2.25 million annually was remitted or brought back to Kiribati by them, out of their total earnings of some AUD$ 3.5 million.

The 1983-86 Development Plan commented that *'at present all trainees passing successfully through the school are able to find employment'*, although it warned that other Pacific countries were setting up similar facilities which would in the future compete. There were then few other opportunities for employment abroad, other than some plantation jobs in the then New Hebrides and limited continued employment in the phosphate operation on Nauru.

The decentralisation debate, and reorganisation of governance

A study had been commissioned in 1978 of the costs and benefits of a conscious policy of 'decentralisation'. It identified a number of options:

- Relocation of all or most of the central government to another island
- Relocation of parts of the central government to other islands
- Delegation of more decision-making to District Officers, and to the Northern Line islands
- Keeping the government on South Tarawa, but introduce 'better urban management'
- Transferring powers and functions from the central government to Island Councils and Urban Councils.

Perhaps surprisingly, this report considered continued urbanism to be desirable, rather than reprehensible; and it argued strongly in favour of the status quo, together with 'better urban management' and transfer of powers and functions from central to local urban government.

That set of policies did not however accord with the priorities of the new government. After considerable debate, and a somewhat inconclusive consultation exercise comprising more than 150 island and village meetings, a 'decentralisation' package was put together, designed to achieve a better standard of living and quality of life on the outer islands. John Pitchford, who had moved from running the successful family planning campaign and joined the administration, was then given the task of planning a comprehensive report on *'Decentralisation in Kiribati'*.

This report has been described as reading:

> *'Something like an alternative national development plan, emphasising distribution of government activity and self-reliance, rather than the growth of government and foreign aid ... [but] its categories cut across the existing division of Government work by ministerial responsibility which increased the difficulty of making sure they were implemented'.*

Parts of the plan were implemented, nevertheless. The venerable system of District Administration, which had been instituted at the outset of colonial rule and had remained at its heart, was abolished and replaced by re-organised local government. However, other parts, such as the idea of 'Community High Schools on rural islands to promote non-academic secondary education, and aimed at enhancing island life', failed. Parents' aspirations had become wedded to academic education leading to a public sector job.

The plan did not however result in a major change in the basic system of governance from that of the colonial era:

- Ministries continued (with the exception of that for the Line and Phoenix Islands) to be functionally oriented, rather than territorial
- Although there were a number of agencies for co-ordination (including the Cabinet, the Planning Office, the new Ministry of Foreign Affairs and for legal matters the Office of the Attorney General) they were often of limited effectiveness
- Statutory bodies and local governments were both expected to balance their budgets. The number of statutory bodies had proliferated after the break-up of GIDA in 1976. In 1972 there had been four; by 1980 there were eighteen: and in terms of capital expenditure and employment they had become increasingly important instruments of government policy
- The role of the private sector in facilitating government policy continued to be negligible. Ideas of 'privatisation' that were beginning to become important in Europe and elsewhere at this time had not yet spread to Kiribati.

The limitations of 'micro-Statehood'

Kiribati is the 24th smallest of microstates as defined by land area (i.e. there are 23 recognised states with a lesser land area); and 15th by population, as of 2019. The limitations of micro-states are well documented, but are nevertheless very real:

- First, there is simply the problem of resources and coverage. Small states do not have the manpower comprehensively to cover all issues and international organisations. Lack of resources imposes severe limitations on the 'bandwidth' of intelligence and analysis available to officials and politicians

- It means spotty attendance at meetings, and, simply due to lack of staff on the ground, missing informal processes such as discussions in the corridors and participation in smaller working groups (often an important aspect of international engagement)
- It imposes an impossible demand for 'multi-tasking' by individuals, who have to cover individually an enormous range of topics to which, in larger countries, specialist teams would be assigned [192]
- There is also – and perhaps less widely recognised – a real problem of 'institutionalism', which has, for Kiribati, intensified in the past decades. International institutions and aid donors frequently demand that Kiribati establish formally separate 'counterpart' domestic institutions to work with and extend their programmes. Where this demand is acceded to, it results in a proliferation of small, ill-equipped offices; and where it is not, absence of a dedicated and separate institution is taken as a sign that the issue is not being taken seriously. Two examples of this problem are the rating of Kiribati by the Transparency International Corruption Index (pages 482 - 484); and that absence of 'counterpart' institutions caused the withdrawal early in the 21st century of Voluntary Service Overseas, which had been a very valuable form of 'hands-on' assistance in Kiribati since the 1960s.

Mitigation of the limitations of 'micro-statehood' are a strategy of working with other small states, which Kiribati has increasing done; and the cynical fact that a small state can exercise a 'nuisance' strategy, through the world press, for example, that is relatively cheaply bought off; or, as Kiribati soon showed, in 1985, there are opportunities to exploit geopolitical rivalries.

---

[192] I have frequently, in relation to my own work as Honorary Consul, referred to this as the 'Nancy Bell Syndrome'. *'The Yarn of the Nancy Bell'*, by W. S. Gilbert (of Gilbert and Sullivan, rather than Gilbert and Ellice, fame) has a chorus which runs:
> "Oh, I am a cook and a captain bold,
> And the mate of the Nancy brig,
> And a bo'sun tight, and a midshipmite,
> And the crew of the captain's gig."

Foreign affairs

A wholly new set of responsibilities created by Independence was I Kiribati control over foreign relationships, which exemplify these issues of micro-Statehood.

The Gilbert and Ellice Islands had, via Britain, been party to some 55 international treaties, some of them (such as the *International Convention for the Suppression of Counterfeiting Currency*) of dubious relevance; and some, such as ILO Regulations against compulsory labour (see p. 230) of doubtful utility.

The Gilbert and Ellice Islands had also been admitted to the Asian Development Bank as an associate member, in 1974.

It had been an early and enthusiastic supporter of the University of the South Pacific (USP), founded in 1968. USP is the only university in the Oceania region (other than Australia, New Zealand, Hawaii and Guam) to be internationally recognised. As well as sending students to the main campus in Fiji, a USP Centre was first opened in Kiribati in 1976 with the appointment of a resident Centre Director. In 1978 the Centre moved to its current location at Teaoraereke, South Tarawa; this Kiribati Centre formally became a USP Campus in 2006.

At Independence the new country joined the Commonwealth, and also became a full member of the principal regional organisations, such as the South Pacific Forum [193]. It was decided that Kiribati should not incur the costs of establishing Missions abroad; but the government did appoint a number of Honorary Consuls, in the UK, Australia, New Zealand and Japan. The UK, Australia and New Zealand established High Commissions on Tarawa, later joined by China and Cuba. Kiribati also soon rattled some regional feathers by entering into a dialogue with the Soviet Union over fish licensing (p. 323 below).

It was also initially decided not to become a full member of the IMF, World Bank or United Nations, primarily because the country had not funds, nor

---

[193] Now the Pacific Islands Forum. Kiribati hosted the Eleventh South Pacific Forum on Tarawa, on 14-15 July 1980, immediately after the celebration of the first anniversary of Independence

could it spare key staff, to participate. Kiribati eventually joined the first two of these in 1986 but did not become a full member of the UN until 1999.

Kiribati did not directly contribute either to the United Nations Convention on the Law of the Sea (UNCLOS), negotiations around which had begun in 1973 but did not conclude until 1982. A crucial part of the convention set the definition of Archipelagic States drawing up a baseline between the outermost points of the outermost islands, subject to these points being sufficiently close to one another, and including all waters inside this baseline as Archipelagic Waters. Kiribati thus acquired an Exclusive Economic Zone in four distinct parts (the Gilberts archipelago, the Phoenix Islands and two smaller zones in the Line Islands: at 3,441,810 square km. this is the twelfth largest in the world, and the largest in the Pacific Region. This EEZ has been vital to the long-term success of the Kiribati economy.

An early foreign affairs priority was to conclude the Treaty of Tarawa, whereby the US Government gave up its claims to various islands. This was ratified by the U S Senate in 1983.

In 1985, Kiribati was one of the nine initial endorsers of the Treaty of Rarotonga, creating the South Pacific Nuclear Free Zone.

The government also secured national ownership of all its territory by acquiring Washington and Fanning Islands (as they were then still known) from the Burns Philp family, for a reported sum of $400,000; this purchase was completed in March 1983. The islands were renamed Teraina and Tabueran respectively; and Christmas Island officially became known by its I Kiribati rendering, Kiritimati.

Defence and security

The issue of security had dominated thinking about independent states in the 1950s and early 60s, during the early days of decolonisation. This would have ruled out statehood for all the Pacific island countries. By the time most of them were along the path to independence, however, the big powers and the UN had accepted the concept of micro-states, and the issue of their defence needs had receded into the background.

Chapter 18: The Newly Independent Country

Despite its own decision to abjure military forces, Kiribati has participated since Independence [194] in the development of a regional security framework by the Pacific Islands Forum. This has been designed to ensure the cooperation of national law enforcement authorities with each other, and to ensure a standard regional approach to security activities. The 2000 Biketawa Declaration, one of four key instruments governing regional security arrangements, relates to regional crisis management and conflict resolution initiatives, is indeed named after the islet on Tarawa Atoll where it was signed; and Kiribati contributed a small number of police to the Regional Assistance Mission to Solomon Islands (RAMSI) (*Operation Helpem Fren*), between 2003 and 2016.

There is additionally an Australia-Kiribati Security Partnership, signed in 2010, which provides for security cooperation between the two countries.

The principal continuing security concern has been policing of the Kiribati EEZ and the closed areas of the *Nauru Agreement Concerning Cooperation in the Management of Fisheries of Common Interest* to which the United States Coastguard has also given assistance.

An object lesson – philately

Another, and less welcome, consequence of the assumption of sovereignty was the exposure of Kiribati and other small countries to fraudsters.

Philately had long been a useful source of revenue to the Gilbert and Ellice islands – in fact it was the fourth largest source of government revenue at Independence, at some AUD$ 500,000 per year. However at this time newly emerging countries were aggressively being recruited by a company called Philatelists Limited with a supposed offer of a much more lucrative philatelic service, complete with 'wise' policies (sic), recommendations on more frequent and populist stamp issues (many of which were wholly unconnected with Kiribati, such as one celebrating Princess Diana), and staff training. Gibraltar, Saint Kitts-Nevis, Saint Vincent and the Grenadines, Montserrat, the Virgin Islands, and St. Lucia as well as Kiribati and Tuvalu were all recruited by this company.

---

[194] As defence is an issue that seldom surfaces in Kiribati, this section has summed up how it has engaged the country in the 40 years since Independence; and the topic is not addressed again in subsequent Chapters of Part 3.

Unfortunately, the company's methods were, to say the least, unorthodox (such as deliberate printing of defective stamps, which were then sold for a premium). After a brief rise (in 1982 philatelic revenue was AUD$ 1, 047,000) the reputation of Kiribati (and that of other countries who had signed up) was shot and the market for such stamps collapsed; and by 1983 revenue from them had been reduced literally to zero. Philatelists Ltd. itself went bankrupt in 1987, at which time it was involved in litigation with the Tuvalu Government, for whom a similar collapse in philatelic revenue had been much more significant. Eventually UK criminal proceedings were taken against it.

The episode was heeded and it proved to be a warning to politicians in Kiribati to beware of 'get rich quick' approaches from abroad. Kiribati has been wary since [195].

Summary: a micro - 'MIRAB' state?

The MIRAB model of Pacific island micro-economies was developed in the mid-1980s by the New Zealand academics Bertram and Watters [196], and has for a long time dominated the literature on the economics of small island nations and economies.

MIRAB is an acronym for migration (MI), remittance (R), foreign aid (A) and the public bureaucracy (B). Proponents of the model have recognised that it exists in many variants. In relation to Kiribati at Independence and since, of the components of the model:

- Opportunities for permanent *migration* from Kiribati were, in 1979, very limited, unlike those from many of the Polynesian Islands formerly governed by New Zealand, who had already exported a significant part of their population to there [197]. Chapter 23 describes

---

[195] Although successive I Kiribati politicians, as in many other countries, have not been immune from spending very large sums on utterly unviable nationally-branded external air services.

[196] Ray Watters was one of the principal authors of the Rural Socio-Economic Survey described in the next Chapter, and had spent six months on Abemama in 1972.

[197] Indeed the then principal avenue of permanent migration – identified as a drain on stocks of the tertiary educated – was identified in the 1983-86 Development Plan as *'intermarriage with expatriates'*.

the growth of a permanent diaspora more recently, since about the year 2000; such a diaspora scarcely existed in 1979, except on Rabi and through the Phoenix Islands population's moving to the Solomon Islands. Small numbers of I Kiribati had moved permanently to Fiji and the then New Hebrides whilst they were still under British rule, but migration was not a significant factor
- Temporary migration, especially by seamen, but also students studying abroad, was by contrast growing; and as a result of such temporary migration, *remittances* were indeed a significant source of income: their value to rural villagers had already overtaken that of the copra crop
- Foreign *aid* was indeed a significant factor in the economy; and it has remained so since, although (and again unlike many of New Zealand's ex-colonies), since 1986 Kiribati has not received it to fund recurrent expenditures; nor, until much later, did the country receive food aid (p. 348)
- *Bureaucracy* was, and has remained, the principal source of employment.

Kiribati at and since independence has thus clearly exhibited most of the features of the model, but it should perhaps more accurately be represented as a 'MIRRAB' economy – with the second 'R' representing *'royalties'*; from the BPC operations before Independence, and from the Kiribati EEZ that effectively has replaced this. It is referred to by this new acronym, as MIRRAB, in subsequent Chapters.

Development of royalty regimes for fisheries has been very successful and, unusually for MIRAB states, this has led to recurrent budgetary surpluses becoming the norm for successive governments, thus avoiding the need to draw down funds from the RERF, the value of which (other than a wobble in 2008) has increased ever since.

Chapter 18: The Newly Independent Country

Further Reading

1. **Winding Up The British Empire In The Pacific Islands,** by W David McIntyre, published by the Oxford University Press, 2014
2. **Politics in Kiribati**, collection of essays by multiple authors, published by the Kiribati Extension Centre Tarawa, and the Institute of Pacific Studies of University of the South Pacific 1980
3. **Atoll Politics – The Republic of Kiribati**, collection of essays by multiple authors, edited by Howard Van Trease, published by the Macmillan Brown Centre for Pacific Studies, University of Canterbury and Institute of Pacific Studies, University of the South Pacific, 1993
4. **An Island In The Autumn**, by John Smith, Librario Publishing Ltd., 2011
5. **Kiribati: Aspects of History**, multiple authors and editors, published jointly by the Institute of Pacific Studies and the Ministry of Education, Training, and Culture, 1979
6. **Decentralisation in the Gilbert Islands**, Green et al, published by the Development Planning Unit, University of London, 1979
7. **Report on Urban Management in South Tarawa, Kiribati** by Peter Larmour, published by the United Nations Development Advisory Team (UNDAT), 1982
8. **The Last District Officer**, by John Pitchford, published by Librario, 2013
9. **Little Boat, Big Ocean**, by Alan Rush, published by Grosvenor House Publishing Ltd, 2010
10. **Tuvalu And The Leaders Of The World – A Philatelic Scandal**, compiled by Brian Cannon, at http://tuvaluislands.com/stamps/LOW_story.htm
11. **Fourth (1978-82), Fifth (1983-86) and Sixth (1987- 1991) Development Plans**, published by the Government Printer
12. **The MIRAB Model of Small Island Economies in the Pacific and their Security Issues: Revised Version**, by Clement A Tisdell, published as Working Paper No. 58 by the University Of Queensland, 2014

Chapter 19.

VILLAGE AND URBAN SOCIETIES AT INDEPENDENCE

'Te maiu *ni Kiribati*' and *'Te maiu ni imatang'* influences

This Chapter assesses the balance of traditional and modern influences - on daily living, on attitudes to further 'development', on the balance of authority (traditional, governmental and church) and on changing governance - at the time of Independence [198].

These clearly differed for those who had migrated to South Tarawa, from those who had remained on their own islands. In 1979 however the first group accounted only for 32% of the whole population [199], so the balance of daily living was still weighted towards villages, rather than the urban population.

A *Rural Socio Economic Survey*, originally commissioned as one of the first actions of the National Economic Planning Office in 1971, reported in 1979; the analysis of rural life in the first part of this Chapter is largely based on the evidence that it provided. [200]

---

[198] The *'te maiu ni'* concepts were introduced on p. 199; see also the discussion on the I Kiribati as *'satisficers'* rather than *'profit-seekers'* (pages 121 -122). The use of these terms in this Chapter is mine rather than that of the sources quoted.

[199] Including of course also those who were *'kain Tarawa'* to start with

[200] The Survey fieldwork was conducted between 1972 and 1974. It was undertaken by the Departments of Geography and Anthropology at Victoria University in New Zealand, and covered five islands: Butaritari, Abemama, Tabiteuea and Tamana; and Nanumea, which was part of the Gilbert and Ellice islands when the studies were commissioned, but by the time of publication had become part of Tuvalu. For various reasons, the final report was much delayed from its original targeted date of 1974, but the conclusions are still valid.

Chapter 19: Village And Urban Societies At Independence

A pattern of migrations

The most recent Census – that of 1973 - had reported 16,148 people as 'economically active'. Of these 11, 745 were primarily active in the 'village' economy, and 6,403 in the 'monetary' economy, mostly in the public sector, and with more than 60% of these living on South Tarawa. However, the Socio-Economic Survey emphasised that at that time:

> *'Any realistic assessment of island population must take account of the people who temporarily reside elsewhere but who nonetheless retain, as will their descendants, the right to share in island resources.... It appears that in 1973 in the Gilbert islands studied, from 28% to 40% of all potential residents were away from their home islands ... The reasons ... include temporary visits to kinsmen on other islands in the group as well as absences to obtain education and medical care...*

> *'On all the islands studied, circular migration has been thoroughly incorporated into the local lifestyle. Periodic employment off their home islands has become part of the expectations of most males. Most of these overseas absences are temporary and constitute but a segment of the individual's life cycle rather than a permanent alternative to life on his home island.'*

Before 1979, both Banaba and Nauru had been major components of this migration, as people migrated to work in the phosphate operations; but not for long after independence.

By the time of the 1983-86 Development Plan (the first such since independence), it was, however, already beginning to be questioned how far the circularity of migration was holding up in relation to Tarawa. The long term evolution of such migration patterns in the 40 years since independence, and the emergence of permanent 'diasporas', both internal and abroad, is the subject of Chapter 23.

Life in the village

In 1979, it could be said with confidence that *'the village economy, in spite of changes through Christianity, foreign trade and British administration, is still intact'*.

Chapter 19: Village And Urban Societies At Independence

The balance between subsistence and cash-funded consumption

The cash economy had nevertheless started to influence village life. The Rural Socio-Economic Survey found that, as always, there were differences between the islands studied, but there were also many underlying similarities. The following summary of time use analysed by the Survey (as median percentages of a 12-hour day) illustrates them.

Use of time	Abemama	Butaritari	N. Tabiteuea	Tamana
Earning cash	9.45	15.27	8.70	7.29
Subsistence	28.01	42.71	38.70	50.44
Social	36.79	14.84	11.20	21.12
Other [201]	31.75	29.18	41.40	21.15

This table appears to confirm the observation made 150 years earlier by the Wilkes expedition that *'the greater proportion of their time is spent in pastimes'*, although subsistence activities dominate towards the south.

As noted by Wilkes, as well, certain tasks were seen as appropriate for people of different ages and seldom performed by others; the 1972 survey noted that *'in households lacking adult males tasks normally associated with adult males are not done and the household is usually supplied with items such as fish or toddy from the surplus produced by related households ... young people become increasingly involved in economic activities from about the age of 12 years .... Full responsibility is assumed from about 19 years of age ... activity usually tapers off at 50 years'*.

With the partial exception of Butaritari, where opportunities for export of locally grown commodities to Tarawa had begun to be exploited, the survey concluded, however, that:

> 'Cash-earning is, for most households, irregular and intermittent. It bears little relation to family size or workforce and depends on such individual circumstances such as need for money, access to alternative sources of income, and the ease with which money can be earned at any time. There can be little doubt that at present considerable surplus labour exists ... the availability of time is not a limiting factor.'

---

[201] Includes such items as care of others, cooking and eating, school, sickness, time in gaol, etc.

Chapter 19: Village And Urban Societies At Independence

People thus still regarded the subsistence (*Te maiu ni Kiribati*) and cash (*Te maiu ni Imatang*) ways of life as largely separate - although *kabirongorongo* (see below) had become established as part of the former, to fund a few luxuries and occasional imported food 'treats'.

People who were *kaubai* (rich in land and other local resources) did tend to participate less in the cash economy; but the Surveys also found that, contrary to many perceptions at the time, that *'on none of the investigated islands was land in short supply, though it has been noted that should all absentee landowners return, land pressures would increase dramatically.'* Typically, by the late 1970s, a village household would only use about half the lands available to it, and even less of their *babai* pits: *'many pits have fallen into a state of disrepair... only on the island of Butaritari does* babai *appear to be a major subsistence food'*.

Within the monetary sector, fine distinctions about uses and roles for cash were articulated by villagers, especially in the report on Tamana:

'Money is treated as belonging to different 'funds' depending on method of earning, size of sums, and goals sought. Thus on Tamana kabirongorongo *('money that you spend') denotes small sums of money that can be earned at any time from the sale of copra or handicrafts and which is spent on everyday needs* [202]. Karinimane, *on the other hand, is 'money that you keep'. This involves larger sums of money which are banked or help to pay taxes, school fees or for major expenses. Significantly* karinimane *is associated with work off the island and is not to be had on Tamana. Thus it is capital or a form of nest egg and is not productive capital, being simply money in the bank kept for future needs.*

In 2002 it was found that 60% of households owned a radio, 55% a sewing machine, and 15% a handcart. Bicycles were the most important mode of local transport, although longer journeys would be made by canoe.

---

[202] This was an evolution of the word from its original meaning, when, especially in Southern Kiribati, it had once referred to storage of processed foods like *tuae* (pandanus cream cake), *kabubu* (pandanus powder), *kaaka* (pandanus slices), etc. and also other preserved foods like *ota* (dried grated coconut) and *manikinam* (dried grated coconut mixed with pandanus cream). These were all used to guard against bad times such as droughts, so by extension in the mid-1970s, the word was applied to 'cash' droughts.

Chapter 19: Village And Urban Societies At Independence

Food sources

Food represented the bulk of consumption.

My wife recalls that when she was a young child, *bwabai* had remained prominent in her staple diet, along with fish, coconut, and other subsistence foods. Rice (usually with bully beef) was a rare and occasional treat for very special events. By the end of the 1960s, however, urban families had become habituated to rice: *'when I visited my relations in North Tarawa or Abaiang, and went back to a wholly traditional diet, I distinctly missed rice as a daily food'.*

This experience is confirmed by the Rural Socio-Economic Survey, which found that:

> *'The islands with higher mean household income do not consume subsistence foods less frequently. The differences in frequency of consumption of coconuts are very small and coconuts are consumed more frequently on higher income islands. The pattern for babai and breadfruit bears little relation to income levels and is complicated by the effect of environmental differences and their effect on cultivation. Some decline in the importance of* babai *and the substitution of flour or rice has occurred on Abemama and possibly on Tamana and Tabiteuea North. On the latter,* babai *maintains its importance in ceremonial activities…*

> *'The frequency with which fish and shellfish are eaten reflects differences in quality and accessibility of marine resources … the importance of the subsistence element in all households' diets suggests that it is still vitally important; and as yet there is no evidence to suggest that as income rises, the importance of the subsistence sector declines'.*

Of imported foods:

> *'Flour was eaten far more regularly than rice … [it was] consumed mainly in household meals as prepared dishes with coconut, toddy, te bero, pandanus or other local products, and appears in feasts or communal meals only in the form of bread, pancakes, and some babai puddings.*

> *'In contrast, rice, although eaten occasionally at household meals, is still something of a special food prepared for communal meals or feasts'.*

The Survey presciently commented: *'if incomes were to rise to the point where consumers felt they could afford rice for everyday consumption, a situation could*

Chapter 19: Village And Urban Societies At Independence

occur ... which could have significant dietary consequences'. They have been proved right: I Kiribati genetic make-up is not well adapted for rice, flour, sugar, and other forms of imported carbohydrate.

Enterprise in the village

At that time, the co-operative movement and its informal equivalent, the *mronron* (see below) dominated the village cash economy as forms of enterprise. Any individual who set up a private enterprise on their own account (other than copra production or handicrafts) was likely to be at the receiving end of village disapproval, especially if they were seen to be 'out of line' in terms of renumeration from it.

Island co-operatives at a primary level, designed primarily for consumer marketing and also as a vehicle for copra sales, then had a virtual monopoly in rural areas (they might also run a few services such as transport for hire, cinemas, and were also a means for villagers to sell handicrafts). The co-operative movement was however reaching a peak in the 1970s and early 1980s. Membership of consumer and marketing co-operatives rose from 15,553 in 1980 to a peak of 17, 554 in 1983, when it began to decline – and fragment. From most islands then having just one Co-operative (a few, such as North Tabiteuea, had two) there are now some 276 registered societies, but with an average membership of only 30 individuals (closer to the pattern of *mronron* in 1979, see below).

At a secondary level the Kiribati Co-operative Wholesale Society was then still much the largest importer of consumer items into Kiribati; and except in the Line islands, the Kiribati Copra Co-operative Society handled the transfer of all copra to Tarawa for export, and all copra sales abroad; it also administered copra support schemes.

Less information is available about *mronrons*, although they were in many ways an equally important – to villagers - supplement to the government sponsored and controlled co-operatives [203]. This was an indigenous form of enterprise, but structured according to I Kiribati norms rather than any concept of 'western' private enterprise.

---

[203] Partly because these operated 'below the radar' of the government – I cannot find a single mention of them in any development plan, for example.

Chapter 19: Village And Urban Societies At Independence

The Rural Socio-Economic Survey commented:

> *'Most are at least in part engaged in selling store goods and perhaps a few prepared foods in exchange for nuts or cash. It is unknown when* mronron *as they exist today first originated. However early this* [i.e. the 20th] *century groups of Gilbertese were purchasing goods in bulk quantities from traders and reselling them, usually for coconuts; and especially since the 1930s various indigenous co-operatives sprang up ...* [there is] *a considerable range of types of* mronron*'.*

They had an important function as 'convenience' stores where the higher prices of very small quantities of goods (such as a matchbox of tea, or individual cigarettes) were not noticeable. Mronrons in some cases also granted credit and loans to their members, and it was reported (in marked contrast to the government SOEs) that *'persistent debtors are relentlessly pursued for payment'*.

Motivations for joining a *mronron* included investment: *'the hope to villagers of earning substantial amounts of money in an environment that strongly discourages individual profit-seeking ... some mronron never distribute their profit until the time of dissolution and over a period of years the protection of the investment, the long deferred reward to come, and the satisfaction and status of operating a successful enterprise provide sufficient return'.*

Economic strategies of the villagers

The Rural Socio-Economic Survey summed up villagers' typical economic strategies at this time as follows:

> *'Given the dominance of 'unearned' income from remittances and gifts over sources of locally generated and 'earned' income for many households, it is no surprise that this plays a significant role in household economic strategy and will continue to exert an influence on future economic response as long as substantial quantities of income flow in ... thus local responses to factors affecting local markets, income earning opportunities and returns is and will continue to be unpredictable ... many of the case studies cited illustrated a willingness on the part of individuals when confronted by the need for cash for taxes, school fees or fines (the major demand for cash in large sums experienced) to delay cash-raising activities in the hope that a windfall remittance will arrive ... on*

> *Abemama and Butaritari only was there evidence of some households seeking to maintain particular levels of cash use'.*

The Rural Socio-Economic Survey was explicit about *'two basic conceptions of development: innovations that come from government, and a greater opportunity to pursue Gilbertese ends'*. (These equate to *'Te maiu ni Imatang'* and *'Te maiu ni Kiribati*). Its summary continues:

> *'The idea of 'development' is ... wholly associated with 'Tarawa' (synonymous with government) - what government does and institutes from outside'.*

Where a new source of income was compatible with traditional ways of living, it might at least initially be adopted (for example, sea weed growing); but none has replaced or even supplemented copra to any marked extent. Ventures such as lobster exports or bêche-de-mer have been tried (mostly organised by Europeans married to locals) but all seem to fall foul of 'satisficing': once taxes and school fees have been paid, and perhaps a sack of rice purchased, initial enthusiasm has evaporated; villagers were and remain indifferent to the very *concept* of needs for a constant supply of a product, if export markets are to be sustained.

Changes to the Mwaneaba system, and acceptance of traditional authority

Change and adaptation had already begun to impact on traditional governance by the 1970s: but the *unimane* still controlled much of rural life.

There were 23 island councils, but most struggled to provide the basic infrastructure for which they had become responsible, in contrast to urban areas where the infrastructure was mostly provided by national government.

External ideas about 'pump-priming' – that aid or government funds to island councils would create a bit of infrastructure which they and villagers would then maintain – had gained no traction. A village view was that if such a development was originally funded by government, then it was wholly the responsibility of the government to keep it going.

Chapter 19: Village And Urban Societies At Independence

The District Officers were abolished as an institution soon after independence but writing of his experiences in the 1970s, John Pitchford described attitudes of local governments as being largely 'philosophical':

> 'Island governments often asked for bye-laws which I drafted before submission to the Attorney-General. All too often my efforts were refused on the grounds that a bye-law contravened human rights. When I returned to the islands with the sad news, I was surprised to find the unimane quite philosophical about it. This upset me more than the Island Council. I thought we were well on track to regularise essential survival practices and strategies along with environmental conservation under the laws of a newly independent nation but apparently, the United Nations had other ideas and so did the unimane.
>
> 'Obviously the old folks would prefer to operate in the old ways and apparently, the elected Island Council would happily go along with that. When a smart Alec or Alice returned from Tarawa or Taiwan with Imatang ideas and refused to comply with village discipline, labour, and organisation, they would soon be brought into line. There were many ways of doing this, many pretty brutal. A bad one I came across was a public beating in the Maneaba.'

Despite the requirement that the young and the female (as well, of course, as the old and male) remain respectful of the *mwaneaba*, ways were changing. Age (and to a lesser extent sex) were becoming less important for participation in community affairs; and there emerged a willingness by the *unimane* to listen in the *mwaneaba* and at Islands Councils to the educated, and to those who had experience off the island - provided that their opinions were tactfully expressed (the first Beretitenti, who had toured extensively to speak at *mwaneabas* before his election, was after all then still in his twenties).

In 1985 Nakibae Tabokai commented that '*Kiribati is still essentially a traditional society ... the village organisation still functions effectively. It focusses on the maneaba where important community matters are discussed ... recent attempts to strengthen these island systems, especially since independence, seem to be associated with a developing national and cultural pride*'. The 2002 *Monetization in an Atoll Society* (see Further Reading) found that two thirds of households were still members of a *mwaneaba* association in 2002 (compared to less than half of households on South Tarawa).

Chapter 19: Village And Urban Societies At Independence

Keith Dixon says more recently of Nikunau:

> 'I-Nikunau social and community groups … have adopted these arrangements and adapted them to some extent; for example, serving in governance groups has been extended to include persons of both gender who exhibit knowledge and ability, rather than be restricted to men on the basis of age (i.e., to unimane). Similar [change] has run right through to the top of formal institutions, with women and younger men occupying a significant proportion, if not the majority, of senior positions in the administration, control and governance of schools, hospitals, businesses.'

In 2002 *Monetization in an Atoll Society* noted the beginnings of change in wider attitudes especially towards participation of women, as the effect of equal access to education, especially, began to be apparent:

> 'In the outer islands, the role of women is generally still confined to domestic duties and food gathering … but women take on additional duties … when men leave home to work at sea. Peer and social pressure within the community appeared at one time to influence girls to accept a domestic role rather than to aspire for a career, but the pattern now seems to be changing. Girls outnumber boys through all secondary and tertiary levels and are making headway in participation in paid employment.'

Ten years on, the effects of this educational equality were becoming apparent at senior levels of the national public service which was still, at the time of independence, largely a male preserve. However formal elected participation by women in Island Councils is still minimal; as late as 2018, only 3.5% of councillors were female.

The *unimane* also continue to have a reserved seat on the councils, as a nominated member, and local government arrangements mostly continue to blend traditional with modern democratic governance. When their influence is threatened, they can still bring influence (and action) to bear on island affairs, most recently exemplified by the rejection of (and burning down of the house of) a Mayor [204] on Maiana, within the last decade.

---

[204] As the President of each Island and Urban Council has been redesignated in recent years.

Urban life

Most evidence about urban dwellers after independence comes from a decade later than the *Rural Socio-Economic Survey*; it is from the comprehensive study *Monetization in an Atoll Society* which was published rather later after independence, in 2002.

The 1983 - 86 Development Plan had already (and again, with an unusually brutal honesty for an official publication) diagnosed problems to come from sources other than the distribution of government expenditures, and the incidence of hidden subsidies (see previous Chapters).

Education had also emerged as an urban / rural issue also, following its expansion over the previous decade:

> *'Government policies are supposedly aimed at generating development and entrepreneurial activities at the commercial sector and at the village level. At the moment we have a most unhealthy situation in which the government absorbs virtually the whole output of ... secondary schools. There is very little hope for much advancement where all the educated people are employed within the comforting fence erected by the government or government controlled organisations; ... [and are] looking over the fence at the uneducated people outside, and wondering why those people are not making more progress in the enormously difficult and complex task of developing commercial enterprises ...*

> *'This point has been made before: the result being the short-lived community high schools. The CHSs aimed to provide a secondary education on the outer islands more aligned to the needs of the majority of pupils who will spend most of their lives combining subsistence and commercial agriculture (copra) and fishing. The rejection of the CHSs by parents is not surprising; but the aspirations of individual parents cannot always be met because the number of public sector jobs is limited. Parents doubtless recognise this but they estimate that a small chance of their children obtaining a public sector job is better than none.'*

The 'circular' nature that had characterised migration to urban areas (as well as overseas) was by then coming to an end:

> *'It is permanent employment for large numbers that has created many of the most serious problems of urbanisation. The interruption of the*

> *circular migration pattern manifested in the number of older people who are considering retirement on Tarawa is an alarming feature of urbanisation today.'*

By 2002, these trends were still apparent. By this time employment was the main source of income for two-thirds of household in South Tarawa, with income from 'own businesses' accounting for another 20%: these compared with figures on other Gilbert islands of 15% and 5%. Less than 1% of South Tarawa households earned income from copra, and only 5% from handicraft production.

Diets were becoming distinct. Three quarters of rural households grew breadfruit and bwabai, 83% cut toddy, and 25% grew bananas. The equivalent figures on South Tarawa were 39% for breadfruit and only 2% for bwabai, 47% for toddy, and 8% for bananas. Even for fishing, where 43% of rural households had fishing nets and 37% access to a canoe, on South Tarawa the figures were 10% and 30%.

Social conditions had begun to diverge. On Tarawa, the average size of a household was 8.1 people (and in 30% of households, there were more than 10), as opposed to an average of 5.9 in rural areas. Anti-social behaviours such as underage drinking, fights, and crime generally (including what was once the most heinous of all crimes, theft) were rising. A group of landless persons was beginning to emerge: some *kain* Tarawa had been persuaded to sell all their lands, and had exhausted the proceeds on daily living. Divorce rates had risen.

Despite poorer access to medical services (all but one of the doctors in the country were based on South Tarawa, and he was on Kiritimati), the less crowded and stressful conditions on rural islands, absence of 'junk' food, more exercise from a traditional lifestyle generally, together with the more 'primitive' - but in fact less polluted - water supply and sanitation meant that health outcomes were on average better than those in the city.

South Tarawa society was becoming less communal and more individualistic: by 2002, less than half of households on South Tarawa were members of a *maneaba* association and membership of womens' associations had fallen to 40% (60% in rural areas).

Chapter 19: Village And Urban Societies At Independence

Church influence at, and since, independence

In *A Changing Atoll Culture* (see Further Reading), in 1985, Baranite Kirata observed that:

> *'The modern ways of I Kiribati are very different from the customs followed by their ancestors who lived 50 or 100 years ago. It is also true that attitudes towards the Christian norms are changing today ... amongst those converted who profess to call themselves committed Christians, quite a number of I Kiribati came into the fold who still observe strong elements of the old religious beliefs ... it remains true even today that ... quite a good number of them find that they return to their traditional beliefs when faced with unusually difficult situations in their lives'.* [205]

By the time of independence the church in fact had relatively little influence on where people lived, how and when they danced, nor over the regulations that had controlled the population before the Japanese occupation. However, one visible influence of the rivalry between churches was that most villages of mixed religion have long since ceased to have a single *mwaneaba*.

Keith Dixon (see Further Reading) writes of Nonouti:

> *'While many of the Nikumanu district mwaneaba's formal uses have ceased, that is more than can be said for mwaneaba in the other kawa. A few standing stones on overgrown sites are all that remain of them, their place having been usurped by churches. Thus, each te kawa, including Nikumanu, has a church associated with the Kiribati Protestant (or Uniting) Church (KPC/KUC) and four—Tabomatang and Tabutoa are the two exceptions—have a Roman Catholic (RC) church.*

---

[205] When HM The British Queen visited Kiribati in October 1982, it was unusually wet. The government employed a traditional rainmaker to ensure her visit would not be impaired, and it is a recorded fact that the rainstorms abruptly ceased at the moment she landed on Bairiki wharf, and only recommenced precisely as she stepped off it again some hours later. The rain maker had succeeded brilliantly! The Queen herself was rather bemused on this visit that instead of the usual clapping and smiling to which she was accustomed, she was respectfully greeted by the I Kiribati crowds with silence and bowed heads, as was due respect in custom to someone of high rank.

Chapter 19: Village And Urban Societies At Independence

> *'Associated with each church is a dwelling for the pastor or cleric, including their companions, families, etc., which are more like Imatang house types than traditional ones, and a structure, almost as noticeable as the church itself, referred to, for obvious reasons of appearance, as the church mwaneaba, or simply te mwaneaba. Indeed, these church mwaneaba are seemingly in more frequent use than the churches themselves, for various administrative, social and recreational activities'.*

Although visitors frequently remark on the piety of I Kiribati (*'The islanders sang hymns, as they were inclined to do for the next five days afloat. After the twelfth time of listening to* Abide with me *in I Kiribati you get a little tired of the cadences of the language, but the choir was too pleasant, and their faith too great, for me to ask them to sing something else'*), the high tide of Mission and church influence has somewhat ebbed since independence. Certainly in the decade after 1979, church exhortations at elections, or against the fishing deal with Russia, or pre-selection of candidates for elected office, seemed to have little influence on voting patterns in either general elections, or in the Maneaba ni Maungatabu (Chapter 20); and decreasingly in local elections.

Soon after independence, also, many of the long-standing Roman Catholic European priesthood, and also nuns who had come to Kiribati in the 1930s or sometimes earlier (and who had lived through the Japanese and American occupations) retired to their home countries. Their I Kiribati successors had different attitudes towards I Kiribati culture, leading to the spectacle of clergy of both main denominations being filmed dancing!

Inter-church rivalry has declined. A first step toward tolerance had been taken in 1975, when the first combined church service was held in the Catholic Cathedral at Teoraereke on Tarawa. In 1989 the Roman Catholic Church and the Kiribati Protestant Church founded the Kiribati National Council of Churches to promote unity among the Christian denominations. In the 1980s there was nevertheless some tension between the growing Mormon presence and, particularly, the Kiribati Protestant Church which distributed anti-Mormon propaganda at that time.

As the government took over primary education, and with the expansion of government schools at secondary level, the Missions' grip on education – once total – also declined. Nonetheless the Catholic Church in Kiribati still runs six secondary schools which educate almost one third of the secondary school population; and the Mormon school on Tarawa, Moroni High School, also stands out. Its facilities are above the standards of other Kiribati schools, and this is a major attraction for people to convert.

The 2010 Census recorded that about 96% of the Kiribati population professes a religious affiliation, mostly either Roman Catholic (57%) or as members of the Kiribati Uniting Church, as the Kiribati Protestant Church has been renamed (31%). The Seventh Day Adventists also retained about 2% of the overall population. The only substantial non-Christian population remains the Ba'há'í Faith (which claims a following of 10,000, in 38 local spiritual assemblies). These affiliations have remained largely unchanged since independence, but other faiths have emerged as well.

There has been a proliferation of small, mainly Pentecostal, Christian Churches; and religions such as Jehovah's Witnesses (Te Kouau), Assembly of God, and Church of God, were recorded in the 2010 Census; there is also a small group of Muslims, of recent origin.

The Mormon Church is however now by far the largest 'new' religion. It was introduced to Kiribati when Waitea Abiuta, a school teacher and headmaster, asked if graduates from his school could attend Liahona High School in Tonga; 12 students were approved. They became Mormon converts at the high school, and began serving as missionaries in Kiribati in 1975. In August 1976 two Mormon educators set up a separate school on Tarawa. In 1982, a new church building was completed, and Buren Ratieta, Gilbertese branch president, held services. In 1996, a Tarawa Kiribati Stake (equivalent to a diocese) was created. The Mormon website claims a current following of more than 20,000 in Kiribati (15% of the population), spread over 32 Congregations throughout the islands. However in the 2015 Census only 5,857 people self-identified as Mormon.

In law, any religious group representing more than 2% of the population (about 2160 people as of the 2015 census) must register with the government, although there are no penalties for failure to do so; and the government generally has been perceived to be even-handed between denominations, even although at times since independence, the Churches have taken overtly political positions. Among 250 people who attended the Mormon dedicatory service in 1982 was the then Beretitenti, Ieremia Tabai. He is reported to have then said that government leaders at first feared a new church would divide the people, but they saw value in the social and educational contribution the church had made, and they were willing to accept it.

Chapter 19: Village And Urban Societies At Independence

Worldwide movements in churches has not in recent years been altogether a transfer of western ideas about religion to Kiribati: various elements of the Roman Catholic Mass have gradually also 'indigenised' in some places in Kiribati. Kiribati cultural elements are reported to have been involved in both the service and in daily home rituals. Such elements include liturgical dancing in traditional costume, particularly during the offertory procession. Many Roman Catholic communities have a charismatic song-and-dance group that leads meetings and other feasts. In an effort to draw youth to the church, the KPC has also encouraged the use of new music forms, such as rap music, in services. However, especially amongst the Protestant church, members are still expected not to consume alcohol; and the church has criticized the increasing consumption of kava.

It has also been claimed that the churches are still a major source of financial stress for families, echoing the criticisms advanced more than 100 years ago when the Protectorate was declared. Average offerings, for example, are said in a recent report to be up to 28% of household cash income on the rural islands (nearly a triple tithe), and significantly more for poor households. A 2005 government report stated that demands from churches to pay fees could be almost $300 a year.

N. Kuruppu (see Further Reading) has argued that: *'to maintain their power-base, the church has gradually exploited "collectivism" to serve its own interests rather than the needs of its followers'* and notes that church income is not used to help those in need, but instead to build and maintain elaborate buildings, and to cover staff and other costs.

A remaining area of controversy surrounds the issue of family planning—an issue with growing significance, given Kiribati's small land area and rapidly increasing population. The Roman Catholic Church in Kiribati, as in the rest of the world, frowns upon preventative methods; and although the Mormon church has now modified its previous opposition to any form of birth control (the current church stance is that 'decisions about birth control and the consequences of those decisions rest solely with each married couple') it 'strongly discourages' some control methods such as surgical sterilization.

Chapter 19: Village And Urban Societies At Independence

Further Reading

1. **Rural Socio-economic Change: Team Report**, published by Victoria University of Wellington, 1979
2. **Rural Socio-economic Change: Butaritari Report**, by Betsy Sewell, published by Victoria University of Wellington, 1979
3. **Rural Socio-economic Change: Abemama Report**, by Ray Watters, published by Victoria University of Wellington, 1979
4. **Rural Socio-economic Change: North Tabiteuea Report**, by Bill Geddes, published by Victoria University of Wellington, 1979
5. **Rural Socio-economic Change: Tamana Report**, by Roger Lawrence, published by Victoria University of Wellington, 1979
6. **Kiribati: A Changing Atoll Culture**, multiple authors, published by the Institute of Pacific Studies, 1985
7. **National Development Plan 1983-1986**
8. **Sixth National Development Plan 1987-1991**
9. **The Last District Officer**, by John Pitchford. Published by Librario, 2013
10. **Kiribati: Monetization in an Atoll Society**, published by the Asian Development Bank, 2002
11. **Worldmark Encyclopedia of Religious Practices**, 2nd Edition, Volume 3, 2014
12. **A Mad World, My Masters: Tales from a Traveller's Life**, by John Simpson, published by MacMillan, 2000
13. **Adapting water resources to climate change in Kiribati: the importance of cultural values and meanings** by N. Kuruppu, published in Environmental Science and Policy, 2009.

Chapter 20.

THE TABAI AND TEANNAKI YEARS 1979 – 1994

The first and second Beretitenti

Ieremia Tienang Tabai [206]

Ieremia was born in 1949, on Nonouti. He was one of those to be selected when the Resident Commissioner Val Andersen recommenced the policy of sending promising students overseas for their education. He went to St Andrew's College in Christchurch, New Zealand, from where he obtained entry to Victoria University, in Wellington: there, he qualified as an accountant. On his return to Kiribati in 1971 he worked initially in the Treasury Department.

He was elected to the House of Assembly to represent Nonouti in 1974, and soon became the *de facto* leader of the opposition, a post formalised after the election in 1976.

He then took office as Chief Minister in 1978, after winning the election in that year. At Independence he was made a Companion of the Order of St Michael and St George (CMG); he was also granted an honorary knighthood by the UK in 1982 and appointed as an honorary Officer of the Order of Australia in 1996. He was Beretitenti from 1979 until 1991, by which time he had served the maximum term allowed by the Constitution and had to step down. Ieremia briefly remained as an MP and Minister under Teatao but soon resigned to serve as Secretary-General of the Pacific Islands Forum, from 1992 until 1998.

He returned to I Kiribati politics and was re-elected to parliament in 1998, again representing Nonouti. He has retained this seat in elections since.

Teatao Teannaki

Teatoa was born in 1935 and worked in the Co-operative movement until he was elected in 1974 to represent Abaiang in the House of Assembly.

---

[206] In the modern orthography, now more correctly spelled as Tabwai

After Independence he served as Vice President, as well as successively holding the portfolios of Home Affairs and Finance. He was narrowly elected to succeed Ieremia as the President of Kiribati; he held office as Beretitenti from 8 July 1991 until 1 October 1994, continuing many of the policies of the previous administration. He lost the 1994 presidential election and was succeeded by Teburoro Tito, although he retained his parliamentary seat for another 20 years until the election of 2015.

He was then chosen to be Speaker of the *Mwaneaba ni Maungatabu*, in February 2016; but he died in office (at the age of 80) in October of that year.

Initial issues

Chapter 18 set out the self-reliance philosophy of the Tabai government. To achieve it, the government had to confront a number of issues.

The state of industrial relations

First casualties – at least as they saw it – of the desire to achieve a locally funded budget, and thus economic independence, were the members of the principal Trades Union, the BKATM.

The BKATM had been successful in organising public sector unskilled and semi-skilled workers, who comprised some 70% of those employed in the monetary sector, nearly all on South Tarawa. In the last few years of the colonial era, industrial action had been effective in pushing up urban wages. The Trades Union members were by the date of independence widely perceived by the general public to be better off than their peers who were not employed in the public sector (especially people outside Tarawa). By 1980 there were many willing 'strike breakers'.

The principal instrument for negotiations with the BKATM and other Trades Unions was the Industrial Relations Code, which had been published in 1974, and supplemented during 1978 - 1980 by a codified National Conditions of Service. However, the procedures of such control were seen as overly legalistic and, more importantly, as providing too much discretionary power to Ministers. Despite the fact that after independence several union leaders had themselves been appointed as Ministers (in particular, the Minister of Labour and Manpower, Abete Merang, was a former teacher who had been the original organiser of the BKATM), the Tabai government's initial sympathy for the Trades Unions soon turned to exasperation.

Chapter 20: The Tabai And Teannaki Years 1979 – 1994

After independence, disputes increased rather than diminished. There were continued, and as the government and much of the country saw it, unreasonable demands: in relation to pay, management discipline, and state enterprise organisation. Giving in to these demands would have seriously undermined the objective of self-reliance, for the benefit of a labour elite. A showdown came within a year: there was a one-day (then unlawful) strike, followed by a five-week (lawful) stoppage, but one that spiralled dangerously out of control. Awira (see Further Reading) described the events of the strike:

'The strike went on for five weeks and it proved a nightmare experience for the whole country. The powerhouse attendants withdrew their labour and the police mechanics took charge of powerhouse operation. The shipping and port services were disrupted, including the servicing of overseas ships.

'Arson and sabotage of public property were rampant, several buildings were set on fire, and a trade union member was shot by police during a night chase. The Kiribati government introduced emergency measures, including the recruitment of extra policeman, during the strike to combat militant action by the union.

'The union members spent most of their time fishing to support their families; however the loss of pay to the strikers began to take its toll from the third week'.

In the end, the government simply dismissed between 400 and 500 of the striking workers. It was a crushing defeat for the BKATM. The loss of Trades Union power was a vital factor in the ability of the government to squeeze urban living standards over the next decade.

The new state had survived its first major crisis, and was (just) able to host a meeting of the 11th South Pacific Forum a month later, on the first anniversary of independence.

Squeezing of urban living standards

The timing of Independence coincided with an upsurge in worldwide inflation, reflected in the price of imports; although the source of most consumer staples, Australia, did have lower rates of inflation than many other countries. Inflation would have been higher had there not been price controls on many of these staples, including rice, flour, sugar and fuel.

Chapter 20: The Tabai And Teannaki Years 1979 – 1994

Between 1979 and 1990, the consumer price index rose by between 4% and 7% each year – with a blip of more than 10% in the year 1980. In the decade of the 1980s the cumulative increase in prices was about 80%, while public sector salaries increased by a cumulative 50% for lower paid staff, and 35% for higher paid staff. The purchasing power of salaried employees thus fell on average by about 30%: more for those in the higher ranks of the public service. As wages and salaries accounted for some 40% of public spending, the squeeze in turn was a major factor in rebalancing of public finances over the decade.

Those still within the subsistence sector were not squeezed as hard, but their living standards fell also. The government continued to subsidise copra [207] : so that villagers were also to an extent protected from low world prices during this decade (and from bad weather in some years; for example, in 1987 copra production fell by half). New opportunities for cash from growing seaweed also contributed to living standards, as did continued remittances.

Tackling of the 'hidden subsidies'

As well as public sector salaries, the Tabai administration was at last successful in reducing hidden subsidies, although it was unable wholly to eliminate them.

Budgetary subsidies actually increased early in the administration because of the losses incurred in a new international air service (p. 332), and they briefly topped 10% of GDP. The airline was retrenched; cuts were made in payments to the shipyard and telecommunications enterprises; and more flexible pricing policies, coupled with decisive efforts to cut operating costs, reduced the drain through other public enterprises and services to less than 2% of GDP.

Ending UK budgetary aid

The cumulative effects of these measures, together with the jolt given by the Tabai government to efforts to increase revenue from foreign fisheries (see below) resulted in the government ceasing to request budgetary support from the UK earlier than had been agreed at independence.

---

[207] Copra was included in the European Community STABEX programme, to which Kiribati as an ACP country now had access; so until 2000 (when STABEX was abolished) the European Commission rather than the Government paid for much of the price stabilisation programme.

Ieremia comments:

> 'We had plans and we put them there. Because of our determination to be rid of the financial aid we got, we gave up the aid ahead of schedule – because of my belief that political independence must be accompanied by economic independence as well. Even though we weren't economically independent, that was to show we were on our way towards doing things for ourselves'.

The incentive created by the independence financial settlement with the UK resulted in a policy whereby drawdowns were limited, and priority was given to building the capital value of the fund. In fact the Tabai and Teannaki governments adopted a conservative stance even after UK Budgetary aid was halted: they took only about 2% of the value of the fund each year as a budgetary supplement, rather than the 4 -5% which could have been withdrawn annually if policy had been just to maintain its real value.

New Sources of national income

The decade-long search for new sources of income also began at last to bear some fruit, albeit changes in access to international regimes (e.g. the Law of the Sea, and the European Commission STABEX scheme) were as much the causes as developmental actions taken within Kiribati. The Kiribati government made the most of these - in a way in which the Gilbert and Ellice Islands, constrained as it had been by the need to work through the UK, could not.

Agriculture

Copra producers had mixed fortunes in the years following independence. The price paid to producers in the Gilberts group at independence was 38¢ per lb., but this fell as low as 11¢ in 1983, before gradually climbing back up to 40¢ by the final years of the period of this Chapter, in 1993. The value of copra production (as measured by GDP by sectoral origin) varied widely: from a low of only AUD$ 655,000 in 1980, to just under AUD$ 6 million in the best year of the decade, 1984.

The coconut replanting schemes were finally abandoned in the mid-1980s; they had resulted in the replanting of 9% of the total available area, far less than had been anticipated in the 1970-72 Development Plan – and much of this 9% consisted of land with poor soils. The schemes had been more useful as a means of channelling money to villagers than in improving agricultural productivity.

As well as copra production, the new government attempted to improve the quality of livestock (i.e. chickens and pigs), and to stimulate subsistence cultivation of a wider range of foodstuffs. This too had limited success, and it has taken another generation to stimulate an acceptance of 'green leaves' in people's diets.

Fisheries

The 1983-86 Development Plan was unequivocal: *'The wealth of the 1,015,000 square nautical miles encompassed by the 200 mile nautical fisheries zone declared around the Gilbert, Line and Phoenix Island groups provides the greatest single prospect for the development needed to re-establish economic independence for Kiribati.'*

At that time, catches were simply unknown; but research by the South Pacific Commission had suggested that *'there is a potential stock of 4 million tonnes of skipjack within the Central and Western Pacific area ... there are ample resources for the local industrial skipjack catch to exceed 800 tonnes per month throughout the Gilberts group'*. Similar stocks were believed to be available in both the Phoenix and the Line Islands.

Te Mautari

Initially, the main vehicle for the local development of an industrial fishery was through a new government-owned company, *Te Mautari*. In addition, foreign vessels were becoming increasingly active in the Pacific fisheries, exploiting the then relatively new (to the Pacific at least) technology of industrial purse-seining, rather than the pole and line techniques long used by Japan, Taiwan and Korea in the area. (In using this technique, a vertical net 'curtain' is used to surround the school of fish, the bottom of which is then drawn together to enclose the fish, rather like tightening the cords of a drawstring purse. It is thus more efficient and less labour intensive than pole and line fishing, which fishing method catches tuna one fish at a time. With this technique, when a school of target fish is located, water is sprayed from the back of the fishing vessel and small bait fish scattered onto the surface of the water, creating the illusion of an active school of prey fish. This process, known as chumming, in turn sends the target fish into a feeding frenzy during which they will bite anything they see. Fishers line up along the back of the boat each with a hand-held wooden or fibreglass pole with a short line and barbless hook attached. Once a fish is hooked it is flicked up and over the head of the fisher and onto the deck. Both techniques continue to be used up to the present time. A third technique, also employed in the Pacific, is longlining: a drifting longline is kept near the surface by means of regularly spaced floats with baited hooks evenly spaced on it.)

Te Mautari was set up in 1979 and commenced operations in 1981. It operated four pole and line ships (provided by UK and Japanese aid), together with a 'mothership' to freeze the tuna and carry it to market, principally a US cannery in American Samoa. Although it rapidly built up exports, it was never profitable. There was a major review in 1994, and despite further injections of aid, the company dwindled and became moribund by the early 2000s. By then attention had turned to training of I Kiribati fishing crews to work on foreign vessels, on the model of the Marine Training School.

Licensing of foreign fisheries

In addition to development of this indigenous industry, Kiribati had agreed, bilaterally, payments for access by distant water fishing nations - the first Pacific nation to do so. Agreements were concluded with Japan and Korea. While it resulted in a reliable and stable financial return, this was (at less than AUD$ 1 million per year) not one large enough to resolve the budgetary problem. Ieremia concluded that Kiribati must become *'forceful and uncompromising'* in its dealings with distant water fishing nations. He refused to renew the Japanese agreement in 1980; this paid off in 1981 when Japan agreed to more than double its fees, and increased its aid to Kiribati. Later, he made the controversial deal with the Soviet Union described below.

At this time, the US refused to recognise coastal state sovereignty in relation to 'highly mobile species' of pelagic fish, on the grounds that such fish were not 'territorial'. This policy had been formalised in the Magnuson Act of 1976, and was coupled with the Fisheries Protective Act of 1954 which sought to recover from the country concerned, either directly or by deducting them from aid disbursements, the costs of confiscation or fines for illegal fisheries. As late as 1985, when the US seiner *Carol Linda* ran aground in Kiribati territorial waters, having entered them illegally, the US Government refused even to acknowledge the Kiribati Government's protest and claimed that it accepted no responsibility for the actions of its fishermen.

Chapter 20: The Tabai And Teannaki Years 1979 – 1994

The US American Turnboat Association (ATA) was left to negotiate with Pacific governments without involvement of their own government.

The *Nauru Agreement Concerning Cooperation in the Management of Fisheries of Common Interest* (usually referred to with the less cumbersome title of the Nauru Agreement) thus came into being in 1982 as an Oceania sub-regional agreement between the Federated States of Micronesia, Kiribati, the Marshall Islands, Nauru, Palau, Papua New Guinea, Solomon Islands and Tuvalu. The eight signatories collectively controlled 25–30% of the world's tuna supply and approximately 60% of the western and central Pacific tuna supply. Under its auspices, Kiribati in 1983 joined a sub-group consisting of itself, the Federated States of Micronesia, and Palau to license the ATA to operate purse seiners over the next two years. However, this was at a lower level of fees than the Japanese and Koreans were paying, and the ATA were determined to pare fees down even further. Negotiations to extend the agreement beyond 1984 broke down. In this year also there were stand-offs between ATA vessels and the Solomon Islands and PNG. The US found itself described as *'intransigent and bullying'*.

The loss of revenue from the ATA agreement and its resulting impact on their budget prompted the Kiribati Government to seek new distant-water fishing partners. The Soviet Union had been seeking such a partner for some time, but had been rebuffed by several countries, including Fiji, PNG, the Solomon Islands and Samoa. Kiribati entered into negotiations and a one-year agreement was signed in Manila in August 1985. In contrast to the US, the agreement explicitly acknowledged the right of Kiribati to develop and manage resources in its EEZ and the responsibility of the Soviet Government for the actions of its vessels. The political repercussions of the government's actions both regionally and domestically are discussed later in this Chapter; and in fact the Soviets did not renew the agreement beyond a single year (they claimed it was not worth their while).

The perceived 'threat' of the Soviets did however radically change US and other regional metropolitan countries' approach to fish licensing. In 1987 the US accepted their obligations to pay royalties for pelagic fish caught in territorial waters, and concluded a Multilateral Fishing Agreement. Catches and associated fisheries royalties began to increase markedly, including those from newly monitored fisheries activity in the Phoenix Islands EEZ. Attention began in the 1990s to turn to conservation of stocks, and investigation of better ways to manage the licensing regime, with the intent to maximise the long-term value to participants in the Nauru Agreement.

Introduction of seaweed growing

In addition to pelagic fisheries, the new government also provided support to artisanal fishermen; and in 1986 introduced commercial aquaculture of seaweed, based on the species *Kappaphycus alvarezii*. *Kappaphycus* farming was chosen because this species requires a low level of technology and investment, can be operated at the family level, has relatively little environmental impact, and does not need refrigeration or postharvest processing within the country. It was thus promoted as an economic boost for the outer islands.

Commercial exports commenced in 1990 when the government-operated Atoll Seaweed Company was established to foster the industry; in that year some 100 metric tonnes were shipped to Denmark. Production increased significantly in 1995, following the establishment of a new programme of technical support by the government. Seaweed production was very active in the late 1990s to early 2000: but as with so many developmental initiatives, although in part also due to the unfavourable El Nino weather conditions, production in the Gilberts archipelago stalled; and after this period it fell dramatically. Production by 2000 was 1,435 metric tonnes; but by then 1,381 tonnes came from the Line Islands, principally Tabuaeran.

Commerce and development banking

The bulk of commerce in Kiribati remained in the hands of the Co-operatives and an increasing number of State owned enterprises. When GIDA was broken up, only the bus service was transferred to private enterprises; and later in the 1980s, private shipping began to emerge, although this too struggled to compete with subsidised government-owned shipping services. On the other hand, less and less retail of groceries and other commodities was channelled through the *boboti*, and the vast bulk of private ventures were in retail.

Although the government supported private enterprise in principle, in practice little was done to foster it or to alter cultural obstacles to successful private sector businesses. The Sixth Development Plan acknowledged that *'many public servants view government assistance to the private sector as a deliberate design to make a few people richer'*.

The National Loans Board was allowed to become moribund in the early years of independence; it was resuscitated with assistance from the Asian Development Bank and became the Development Bank of Kiribati (DBK) in 1986. However, by the 1990s, the DBK was again in serious financial difficulties, with high arrears, inadequate funding and staffing; it needed a further restructuring programme, this time funded by New Zealand.

Responsibility for housing loans transferred from the National Loans Board to a new Kiribati Housing Corporation at the time of independence, and provision of subsidised housing for employees (other than expatriates) diminished as a drain on government budgets, as it increasingly became the norm for better-off families to build their own houses. This had the side effect that land between villages on South Tarawa began to fill up, including, gradually, the reclaimed land enclosed by the Temaiku bund.

Foreign Investment

Attraction of foreign investment was (perhaps surprisingly, given the development philosophy of the government) the second of the three main stated goals of the 1979 – 82 Development Plan (after development of new industries based on marine and other resources).

Lack of opportunity as well as the low score of 'ease of doing business', and often subsidised competition from State Enterprises, means that such investment never took off, then or indeed since (in fact recorded foreign investments were precisely zero through the lifetime of that Plan). In 2016 the IMF reported that *'Over the past 37 years, the value for this indicator has fluctuated between $6,662,198 in 2010 and ($4,944,768) in 2009'*.

Rather, Kiribati has itself remained as a net foreign investor, through the Reserve Fund and the National Provident Fund.

Public Services

The third objective of the 1979 – 82 Development Plan was *'to control Government expenditure to a level that can be sustained in the long term'*. The principal means by which the government implemented this goal were:

- Holding down of public sector pay
- New mechanisms for industrial relations (see below)
- The policy to build up rather than to draw down the Reserve Fund

- Re-orientation of health services towards prevention rather than cure. Although it was relatively efficiently run compared to many parts of the public sector, health took up a significant part of recurrent expenditure. Per capita expenditure in 1979 was US$ 30, as opposed to a then average figure of $9 in comparable low income countries – and unlike in many of these – health care was available free of charge. The issue of pay was a particular problem in this sector since medical skills were more easily transferable to other, higher-paying countries than the skills of other professions; and retention of doctors became a significant problem
- Taking more seriously the long standing aim that household services in urban areas should, in principle, be paid for by their consumers.

New mechanisms for industrial relations

As part of public sector management, and in the aftermath of the 1980 strike, the Tabai government did address the weaknesses of the Industrial Relations Code: it took measures both to increase employee input into problem solving at the workplace, and to establish a mechanism for review of the National Conditions of Service.

In 1982 a number of unions – including the BKATM - formed the Kiribati Trade Union Congress (KTUC) and gradually began again to increase their influence, but with lesser militancy. A turning point took place in 1989, when a seminar on reform chaired by Kevin Hince (see Further Reading) was held in Tarawa at the University of the South Pacific Extension centre. Dr Hince commented that:

> ' The breakthrough came in an unexpected way, when the participants separated into groups to discuss the traditional i-Kiribati approach to resolution of family conflicts ... the seminar recognised that processes of negotiation, conciliation/mediation and arbitration were central to the traditions of dispute resolution for the i-Kiribati. Moreover, there was an identification of a specific process for a particular type of dispute and, if needed, a natural progression of stages towards final resolution...

> '... In traditional Kiribati society a failure of the discussions and decisions of the Maneaba to resolve the issue could lead to outright conflict (fighting) between the families. With some humour, but clear understanding of the coercive similarities, participants equated the modem notion of 'the strike' to this fighting, suggesting that the

availability, potential, and ultimate threat of a withdrawal of labour could play a key role in provoking an earlier settlement. It was at this point that the complexities of the Industrial Relations Code and the unilateralism of the JCC and SRC [the two principal avenues for dispute resolution] *were recognised, and the focus of the seminar shifted to establishing an agreed basis of change'.*

Although formal changes took some years to complete, the challenges that industrial strife had raised receded; and they have not been a major issue since. Not for the first or last time in the history of Kiribati, it was through turning to tradition, rather than by adopting Western ideas, that problem-solving became possible.

Infrastructure development in the early post-Independence years

Independence also saw the completion of a number of important infrastructure developments:

- The South Tarawa Water Supply project, designed to improve supplies of potable water up to 1990, and to identify and make into water reserves areas to meet demand after then, was completed in 1987. Water supply projects were also undertaken on a number of other islands

- The government took over air services, setting up Air Tungaru as a national flag carrier with the aim of unifying the country, as well as providing services. A regular service was provided to all 16 domestic airports in the Gilbert Islands; and, using a Boeing 727-100 aeroplane, the airline also operated an international service between Tarawa and Honolulu, via Kiritimati island. However, this service failed to pay for itself and was shut down in the mid-1980s as part of the programme for eliminating subsidies

- The long-mooted Betio-Bairiki causeway finally opened in 1989

- The Central Hospital was redeveloped, and opened at a new site in 1991.

Chapter 20: The Tabai And Teannaki Years 1979 – 1994

The political consequences of the Soviet Union / Kiribati fisheries agreement

The I Kiribati gambit of licensing the Soviet fishing fleet had consequences both domestically, and in its relations with the metropolitan powers of the region, despite Ieremia's insistence throughout that the arrangement was purely economic in nature and was preferable to external aid. He argued that it allowed Kiribati to achieve self-reliance: *'we want to earn our living. Earning a fishing living from the Russians is better than having to ask our traditional friends to support us… we feel insulted if* [the US] *fish our waters without an agreement'*.

The US, Australia and New Zealand had no desire to see the USSR gain any purchase in the region, and applied significant diplomatic pressure on Kiribati to try to prevent the deal being signed. Australia was concerned less with the fishing deal than a fear that it would lead to establishment of a Russian land base in Kiribati, and was worried enough to promise *'additional aid to the equivalent value of the deal if it did not go ahead'*. New Zealand was even more fearful of *'considerable diplomacy on the part of the Russians to establish a preserve unrelated to their economic interests'*. (When challenged by Kiribati as to why New Zealand itself had a similar fisheries arrangement with the USSR, the then Prime Minister made the arrogant statement that *'it is not my view that the smaller island states have the means that we have to preserve their interests'*). Clearly Australia and New Zealand had not yet adjusted to independence, and Ieremia had no hesitation in describing their attitudes as *'neo-colonial'*. The US called the deal *'disturbing'* and when the deal was completed declared somewhat menacingly that *'it was well known that Russia would do anything to expand its influence and that there would be unforeseen consequences'*.

But although the deal with Russia only lasted for a year, it did much to rebalance the relationship with metropolitan powers, and not just for Kiribati, but for other island countries. It forced President Reagan to acknowledge to Congress that the US fishing policy had resulted in *'a serious erosion of our good relations with the countries in the region'*; and in 1987 the US and 16 Pacific country negotiators completed a long-sought multilateral fisheries treaty, to run for five years.

The other major diplomatic gain - from the viewpoint of Kiribati - was that the proceeds of the Soviet agreement allowed for the early cessation of budgetary aid from the UK, avoiding the national humiliation of having to negotiate each year. As well, its signing provoked greater developmental aid flows from all the countries that had objected (those from the US being channelled through Save the Children to prevent any suggestion that Kiribati had *'played the Russian card'*).

Internationally the bold I Kiribati exploitation of geo-political rivalries had thus been very successful. Domestically, the deal was controversial as well.

Opposition was led by the Roman Catholic Church, whose bishop issued a manifesto against 'anti-Christ communists'. An expatriate local businessman resident in Kiribati, Brian Orme, claimed in *Pacific Islands Monthly* that it would result in *'loss of confidence and respect of our Pacific island neighbours, the total withdrawal of all aid from Western democratic countries, and sanctions which would affect travel, work, trade, diplomatic relationships and recognition'* [208].

Despite some protests against visitors from the government (notably on Marakei), the government easily won a vote of no confidence over the deal in the *Maneaba ni Maungtabu*, in August 1986. Also, despite the non-renewal of the agreement, it played out successfully. Babera Kirata, who as Minister for Natural Resources and Development had led the negotiations with the Russians, was able to report that:

> *'They complied with the terms of the agreement. Their reporting was in accordance with the agreement, and they payed up according to the agreement. There were no reports of landings by them.'*

Although the Roman Catholic Church had attempted to use the issue to introduce a religious divide into Kiribati politics, as the next section shows, their intervention appears to have had little long-term effect on voting patterns. Most I Kiribati people, regardless of their religion, seemed to agree with Ieremia that:

> *'While I admit that we are certainly poor, I cannot agree that we are for sale, to be manipulated or bribed against what we believe to be in our national interest ... that is definitely outside our concept of development'.*

---

[208] In fact, as noted above, it had resulted in exactly the opposite: Kiribati was taken much more seriously by other Pacific countries; it resulted in increased aid from metropolitan powers, including the US; and it was diplomatically a major victory, not least by persuading the US to change its policy on fishing rights in the Pacific.

Chapter 20: The Tabai And Teannaki Years 1979 – 1994

The maturing of politics 1979 - 1993

Over this period the National Progressive Party governed, although not without crises.

These crises were however on a much lower scale than other Pacific ex-colonies: this was a period in which there were two Fijian coups d'état; there was much instability in the governance both in Papua New Guinea, including an armed insurrection in Bougainville, and also in Vanuatu, which had a difficult transition to independence requiring foreign military intervention – and both of these also had recurring bouts of unstable government; meanwhile the five-year civil conflict in Solomon Islands, which eventually erupted from 1998 to 2003, was building up.

Competing influences on politics

The three sources of pre-Independence authority and influence on politics had evolved. After 1979 - or 1985 if the budgetary position is considered - that of British colonial authority had gone; and Kiribati robustly had seen off neo-colonial attempts by Australia and New Zealand to influence its policies (see above).

Over the period, an unusually sophisticated electorate reacted against influencing of results by all three; and this electorate also had no hesitation about deselecting sitting members of the *Maneaba ni Maungtabu*.

Trades Unions for a time replaced the colonial service as a competing source of authority, along with the continuing influence of the *unimane* and the churches. The BKATM strike in 1980 was indeed the first political test for the government: but the government easily then defeated a motion of no confidence in its handling of the dispute, and their influence waned.

Attempts by the Roman Catholic Church to influence political choices in favour of candidates of their faith only had very limited success; and as well the staunchly Protestant islands of Arorae and Tamana were by 1991 quite prepared to cast over 90% of their votes in support of two Roman Catholic presidential candidates, which would have been unthinkable two decades earlier. Fewer elections also came to be 'fixed' by the *unimane*: by the 1991 election, no constituency again returned a member unopposed, the *unimane* having made a choice in advance of nominations – and there could be as many as 20 candidates on an island.

Although the personal qualities of a prospective MP continued to be important (such as being local to the constituency, his or her level of education, family connections, and the candidate's observance of the customs of *mweaka* and *te nouete)* the organisation and impact of political party membership became increasingly decisive.

In all the elections in the first fifteen years of independence - 1982, 1983, 1987, 1991 and 1994 - both aspiring candidates for the *Maneaba ni Maungtabu* and the presidency, and their electors, showed an advanced attitude, especially given that I Kiribati participation through universal suffrage and national elections was less than two decades old.

An early action of the government after independence was to model its broadcasting and newsletter model along the lines of the British Broadcasting Corporation (BBC); so that news from official sources remained (generally) unbiased, as opposed to the slanted political reporting that had characterised the Ratieta government.

However, stung by attacks against the government in a newspaper called the 'Plain Truth' launched by Brian Orme, the government was less tolerant of the emergence of a partisan press. A Newspaper Act was enacted during in 1988, which provided that no newspaper could operate without registration.

Tolerance of independent (and hostile) sources of news has occasionally wavered under successive governments, but Kiribati is still recorded (2018) as having a 'free' press by the US-based non-governmental organization Freedom House.

Continuity and controversy over four general and Presidential elections

The first General Election – and thus chance for the country as a whole to judge the government – took place in 1982. The strike continued to be a major election issue, with the unions organising meetings against government supporters in both Tarawa and the outer islands (some of the latter, however, refused to receive visits from union members).

The results of the election to the *Maneaba ni Maungatabu* resulted in a large turnover of members, and on Tarawa Abete was defeated by a prominent union activist. Elsewhere, 17 out of 35 sitting members lost their seats – but those of these who were not government supporters were as many as those

Chapter 20: The Tabai And Teannaki Years 1979 – 1994

who had been supporters; and of the 11 government supporters who were re-elected, 7 had been Ministers.

Similarly Ieremia easily won the subsequent election for Beretitenti, after he and Teatoa had stood against Naboua Ratieta (attempting a come-back), and a union-backed candidate, Etera Tengana. In the event Naboua won only his home island of Marakei; Etera Tengana did not win any island (and only 12% of the votes); whilst Ieremia and Teatao collectively won all the other constituencies and a total of 77% of the electorate. It was a substantial victory and endorsement of their administration.

Surprisingly, therefore, they lost another vote of no confidence only seven months later. This arose, moreover, from what seemed an unimportant issue (concerning salaries of six statutory officers). It has been suggested that the opposition had not appreciated the clause in the Constitution that their action would result in another election, not by the opposition replacing the government as had happened in other Pacific countries where such a constitutional provision was not in place.

The 1983 Election that resulted had a significantly lower turnout, and again more opposition members lost their seats than government supporters, so they strengthened their position in the Mwaneaba. At the elections for Beretitenti, Ieremia and Teatao as candidates faced Harry Tong, a medical doctor and newly elected member for South Tarawa; and Tewareka Tentoa, member for Onotoa. Again, turnout fell; but Ieremia's share of it rose.

Ieremia's final election (as he hit the term limits of the Constitution) took place in 1987, after the controversy caused by the Soviet fishing licences (see below). For the first time, there was an organised opposition party, the Christian Democratic Party, which brought a High Court case claiming that he had already exceeded term limits (if his pre-independence term was counted). This case failed, although with allegations of skulduggery, in that a NZ lawyer brought to Tarawa by the Opposition to argue their case was refused entry. The Roman Catholic Church also tried to influence its members to vote against Ieremia. As a result of both of these, the election took place in a highly charged atmosphere.

Allowing for the addition of three seats, 21 members including 13 government supporters were re-elected; and 18 new members, only five of whom supported the government. Following a change of their policy, a Banaban representative sat in the Maneaba for the first time. With the Attorney-

Chapter 20: The Tabai And Teannaki Years 1979 – 1994

General, the government could therefore only rely on the votes of 20 of the 41 members. This time around, as well, there were three rather than four candidates for Beretitenti: in addition to Ieremia and Teatao, the newly elected member for South Tarawa, Teburoro Tito, represented the opposition. There followed another contest in which the Catholic Church again became – controversially – involved, urging support only for members of its faith. In fact Ieremia again won, with an increased share of the vote, including support in many 'Catholic' areas; but Teburoro greatly increased his share of the vote also, gaining more than 40%. Teatao was squeezed between them.

Ieremia managed to govern for the next four years despite his lack of an assured majority in the Maneaba, as he could normally count on the support of the group of independent members. The third I Kiribati government completed its term on 6 April 1991.

No fewer than 227 candidates stood for the next *Maneaba ni Maungatabu*. However the principal focus of voters was who was to become the next *Beretitenti*, rather than who would become members of the Maneaba; but there was no shortage of potential candidates here also. Although party allegiance was not always a decisive factor in the casting of votes, there were three principal groupings: the government party (*National Progressive Party*, the official opposition who were now labelled as '*Social Democratic*' rather than '*Christian Democratic*'; and a third grouping, albeit an organised one, of independents who called themselves *Reitan Kiribati* (Uniting Kiribati).

After two rounds of voting, no party seemed to have won a clear victory. As had become a pattern, many sitting members failed to be re-elected. After some manoeuvring, eight members emerged as potential presidential candidates of whom only four could stand. A tie-up between the NPP and a new grouping of freshly elected independents, *Waaki ae Boou*, resulted in elimination of both the leader of the opposition, Teburoro Tito, and of *Reitan Kiribati*, Tewareka Tentoa, from candidacy. Roniti Teiwaki and Teatao Teannaki thus became the two principal contenders (the other two, Beniamina Tinga and Boanareke Boanareke, being 'dummy' candidates for the NPP and *Waaki ae Boou* respectively); and the latter won by less than 1,000 votes (ironically, the two were brothers-in-law). Kiribati had narrowly opted for continuity.

The new administration under Teatao did not have a big majority (22 members against yet another newly coalesced post-election opposition party,

Chapter 20: The Tabai And Teannaki Years 1979 – 1994

the *Maneaba Party*, with 19), but it survived until 1994, when power passed to the opposition.

Further Reading

1. Interview transcript at https://www.radionz.co.nz/collections/u/new-flags-flying/nff-kiribati/ieremia-tabai
2. **The 1980 BKATM Strike and Its Implications on the Development of Industrial Relations in Kiribati,** by N. Awira, unpublished 1988 research report, Victoria University
3. **Industrial Relations in Kiribati**, by Kevin Hince, published in the New Zealand Journal of Industrial Relations, 1992
4. **Politics in Kiribati**, collection of essays by multiple authors, edited by Howard Van Trease, published by the Kiribati Extension Centre Tarawa, and the Institute of Pacific Studies of University of the South Pacific, 1980
5. **Atoll Politics – The Republic of Kiribati**, multiple authors, edited by Howard Van Trease, published by the Macmillan Brown Centre for Pacific Studies, University of Canterbury and the Institute of Pacific Studies, University of the South Pacific, 1993
6. **Economic Development in Seven Pacific Island Countries**, by Christopher Browne with Douglas A Scott, published by the International Monetary Fund, 1989
7. **FAO Fisheries Country Profiles**
8. **Capturing Wealth from Tuna: Case Studies from the Pacific**, by Kate Barclay with Ian Cartwright, published by the Australian National University, 2007
9. **Some Aspects and Issues Concerning the Kiribati/ Soviet Union Fishing Agreement,** by Dr David Doulman, published by the East-West Centre, 1986
10. **When the 'tuna wars' went hot: Kiribati, the Soviet Union, and the fishing pact provoked a superpower** by Jeff Willis, published in Pacific Dynamics, 2017
11. **Advances in seaweed aquaculture among Pacific Island countries**, by Timothy Pickering, published in the Journal of Applied Phycology, 2006
12. **Fourth (1978-82), Fifth (1983-86) and Sixth (1987- 1991) Development Plans**, published by the Government Printer.

Chapter 21.

THE TITO YEARS 1994 – 2003

The third Beretitenti

Teburoro Tito [209] was born on Tabiteuea in 1953, a son of Tito Teburoro, who had been prominent in politics in the later colonial period.

Teburoro attended the University of the South Pacific in Fiji from 1971 to 1977, graduating with a Bachelor of Science degree (he was one of the first I Kiribati people to study science to degree level), followed by a graduate certificate in education. He entered politics in the 1987 election; and he continued to represent the same South Tarawa constituency (rather than his home island) for more than 30 years, until he resigned in 2017 to become Kiribati ambassador to the United Nations – a position that he still held at the time of publication of this book.

Teburoro immediately became Leader of the Opposition upon his first election and first stood as a candidate for Beretitenti in 1987; he stood again in 1991, when he narrowly lost. He was elected Beretitenti with 51% of the vote (easily ahead of his three rivals) at his third attempt in 1994. He served as Beretitenti and foreign minister of Kiribati from October 1994 to March 2003 after being re-elected, firstly, in 1998 with 52% of the vote; and again in February 2003, with 50% of the vote.

Through his speeches at the UN, and his active participation at International Climate conferences, he began to address the issue of global warming on his and other South Pacific island nations, and through this and more generally to raise the profile of Kiribati within the international community.

Development strategy

The new government saw a change in the rule of Kiribati, from that of the *National Progressive Party* to the *Maneaban Te Mauri Party*. In 1993, shortly

---

[209] In the modern orthography, now more correctly spelled as Tiito, and of course pronounced as 'Seetoh'

before he assumed power, Teburoro (then Leader of the Opposition) wrote in *Atoll Politics* that:

> '... The opposition agrees with many of the policies of the government, because they look right and people would benefit if they were implemented correctly ... the workforce is quite capable of performing whatever task is required but there appears to be low morale, due to poor working conditions and inadequate income to meet basic living needs ...
>
> 'There are a number of policies that the opposition is unable to support. The first concerns the employment of our people on projects being carried out in Kiribati by overseas building contractors on conditions which are less than those prescribed by the National Employment Act ... the second policy of concern is the taking away of land from people who need it very badly for their living ... the third policy of concern is the privatisation of bodies which carry out or provide essential public services ... the fourth policy of concern relates to the curative and surgical services at the main hospital ... many local doctors have left.
>
> 'As people become more politically aware, it will become much more difficult for politicians simply to stand up and make promises. A better pattern of governing will develop which will reflect the fundamental values of Kiribati culture ... for some time this will be clouded as people get used to the foreign elements which have come into their lives, such as the Maneaba ni Maungatabu, the cabinet, the opposition and the island councils. They will eventually recognise that these institutions belong to them and that they have the right to expect them to function properly'.

On the face of it, therefore, the change of government was driven as much by perceived competence as it was a proposal to take Kiribati in a wholly new direction; but it was a signal to those in the public sector whose living standards had fallen significantly since independence that there would be less restraint of public sector pay. In fact early actions of the new government were to increase both copra prices, and public sector salaries.

Nevertheless after Teburoro's election there was a change – at least in terms of his government's declared objectives - of emphasis and tone. The last development plan of the previous administration, the Sixth Development Plan of 1987-1991, had still given highest priority to self-reliance.

Its successors, the National Development Strategy of 1996 and the Action Programme through to the Year 2000, which was published in November 1997, were much more oriented towards the conventional 'western' development thinking championed by the World Bank and IMF - both of which Kiribati had recently joined.

Without entirely discounting the need for self-reliance, Tebururo stated in an early 1994 interview that:

> 'Our main economic concern in Kiribati is our ability to improve and sustain the living standards of our people. It is not sufficient to aspire for improved standards of living when this cannot be sustained in the long run. We must have the necessary infrastructure and the productive sectors developed to support what we want to aspire for. At the same time, our human resources must be trained and our civil servants paid sufficient remuneration ...

> 'No country can isolate itself from the rest of the world. It goes without saying therefore that the influence of western-style development will continue to be felt, and it is important for Government to identify those western styles of development that will be useful to Kiribati and disregard those that have the potential to affect the cultural identity of the people of Kiribati.'

> 'The risk that I see in the western style of development is where such developments do not help us to secure a better quality of life and at the same time do not conform with our culture and identity as I-Kiribati people.

> 'But in saying this it is important to realise that it is not always a good idea to insist on maintaining a certain cultural aspect for the sake of maintaining our identity, if this would undermine all other efforts to achieve our desired goals, including our aspiration for improved living standards'.

The National Development Strategy and Action Programme

Public sector reform in Kiribati had begun in the late 1980s as part of a global trend towards reassessing the role of government in the economy, in part because of the perceived inefficiency and constant loss-making of the many state-owned enterprises (SOEs) in Kiribati. The National Development

Strategy of 1996 and its 2000 successor were aimed at speeding up such reform.

The overriding goal of the National Development Strategy, which covered the period from 1996 to 1999, was *'to generate a sustained, positive, real rate of economic growth per person'*. Priorities to achieve such an outcome were:

- Reducing the relative size of government
- Reform of public enterprises
- Facilitating the development of the private sector
- Having a foreign investment friendly environment
- Improving the availability and supply of land for productive purposes
- Alignment of sectoral policies with overall strategies.

It was intended that:

> *'The adoption of the strategy mark a significant shift in the approach to economic development, away from comprehensive five-year plans which emphasised the role of government and focussed on identifying projects, towards a strategic planning approach where emphasis is placed on implementing key policies which will drive private sector led growth.*
>
> *'This approach recognises that it is the private sector which is the engine of growth, and that government's role must consequently be to facilitate the private sector rather than to control, direct or duplicate its efforts'.*

Public sector reform and the economy 1994 - 2002

It must be said that neither the programme of reform, nor the hoped-for sustained increases in living standards set out in the National Development Strategy, materialised.

Seven years later, in 2001, the IMF commented that:

> *'Kiribati's economy is deeply rooted in community oriented values ... this strategy has managed to provide a stable macro-economic environment, the build-up of substantial official external assets, and a relatively equitable intra- and inter-generational distribution of income.*
>
> *'However this strategy has also yielded a stagnant economy with inefficient state-owned enterprises and a small private sector that has been unable to raise living standards ... Over the last decade, economic expansion has barely kept up with population growth'.*

Chapter 21: The Tito Years 1994 – 2003

Its recommendations were for an intensification of the 'western' economic policy model, a more determined approach to replacing SOEs, and 'removal of obstacles' to the private sector (such as traditional land tenures) - as well as reductions in subsidies and an end to price controls. The UN Regional Co-ordinator, however, recognised more realistically in his 2002 report that *'official government policy, strongly endorsed by (and in part developed by) the donor community may conflict ... with local cultural norms'.*

As a prime example, the National Development Strategy had identified a number of SOEs as candidates for privatisation, most of which, as the following list demonstrates, would have been private sector-led in most market economies: Abamakoro Trading Limited, Atoll Motor Marine Services, Atoll Seaweed Company, the Broadcasting and Publication Authority, Kiribati Oil Ltd, Kiribati Housing Corporation, Kiribati Supplies Company, Solar Energy Company, Tarawa Biscuit Limited, the Otiintai Hotel, Captain Cook Hotel in Kiritimati, Kiribati Insurance Corporation, and the Government Plant and Vehicle Unit Ltd.

Teburoro comments, with the benefit of hindsight:

> *'After independence the Tabai administration created a huge number of SOEs partly through corporatisation of a number of departments of the government that could operate on a self – financing basis with minimal state subsidy; and partly through creation of completely new companies and corporations. By the end of the Tabai and Teannaki administrations there were 26 SOEs ...*
>
> *'A number of Commissions of Inquiry were established to examine the extent of mismanagement and corruption in the SOEs and found that the SOEs examined were indeed suffering mainly from the failure of the Managers and Board members to act properly and honestly in their functions and duties for the public asset under their care... So when the new leadership [his!] came ... [it had a] preference for I Kiribati private sector over a foreign private sector which meant allowing more time for the local businesses to build their capacities and resources before an SOE within their line of business was advertised for sale. The change to the privatisation was not on the principle of privatisation but on the approach to be used, one that moves at the right pace and with minimum inconvenience to the people for whom all development models including privatisation are there to serve'.*

Chapter 21: The Tito Years 1994 – 2003

Meaua Tooki in her MA Thesis (see Further Reading) also casts some doubt as to whether the Cabinet had really bought into the new strategy (which had been drafted largely by consultants from the World Bank and ADB):

> *'The election of President Tito ... was based on anti-privatisation policy ... President Tito gained the support of the majority of the people because the policy of privatisation would involve the change of the existing community ties to individualism. Such change is a threat to many people, especially in alienating public assets to private entrepreneurs. However, with the influence of external aid donors (World Bank, IMF and ADB) this anti-privatisation vision came under attack.'*

Thus despite support in principle for the idea, no significant action was taken in these seven years to proceed with privatisation of any of them. Nor was action taken to break up other utility (rather than commercially) focused, organisations such as the Public Utilities Board, the Betio Shipyard, the Shipping Corporation, or the Public Works Department.

Towards the end of the second Tito administration, moreover, restraints on government expenditure and action to reduce the relative size of government were considerably relaxed: government revenues in 2000-2, although they had substantially increased (with fishing licence fees in particular reaching $47m in 2001), were fully spent on increases in personnel costs, in building a new parliament house and through substantially increased expenditures in support of SOEs. These included construction of a publicly owned copra mill, acquisition of an aircraft for Air Kiribati to venture into regional air services, and the rehabilitation of the collapsed fish exporting enterprise, again an SOE (p. 318). In fact total budget outlays at this time greatly exceeded income, and a draw-down of AUD$12.6m was made from the RERF.

The aircraft expenditure, in particular, led to the downfall of the newly elected government: on 24 March 2003, the government, which had been in office since February 2003, fell after losing a vote on a supplementary budget at the first sitting of *Maneaba ni Maungtabu*, by 21 to 19. Beretitenti Tito contested the procedure in court but the Kiribati Court of Appeal, sitting in New Zealand, ruled the vote had been correctly held and gave the go-ahead for the general elections. It also ruled that Teburoro's latest term in office constituted a 'full term' despite lasting just one day; as it was his third term, the constitutionally prescribed limit, he could no longer stand for the presidency.

Chapter 21: The Tito Years 1994 – 2003

The strategy in MIRRAB terms

Although the government's experiment with 'conventional western development' might therefore be judged not to have delivered the step change in GDP growth which was its object, in 'MIRRAB' terms the picture is quite different. It demonstrates considerable success.

Although reported GDP per capita hardly grew, and in 1998 hit the lowest real level since statistics had been collected in the early 1970s (US$ 702), fishing revenues meant that up to 2000 the budget had generally remained in surplus without recourse to the RERF:

- Overseas **migration** continued to be limited during this time, although migration flows to New Zealand intensified partly as a result of a work permit scheme in New Zealand in the 1990s and early 2000s. In 2002 New Zealand introduced the Pacific Access Category (PAC), which replaced the previous work permit and visa-waiver schemes. There was also internal migration to the three inhabited Line Islands, as well as continued migration into South Tarawa from other islands in the Gilberts. These migrations are the subject of Chapter 23 below
- **Remittances** from abroad (mainly from overseas seamen) reached a plateau of about AUD$ 12 – 13 million over the decade of the 1990s. Although the amounts had ceased to grow, they still remained important in terms of poverty reduction. Some 22% of households, mainly in rural areas, were estimated to have received remittance incomes from abroad in 2002. Figures for internal remittances from those employed on South Tarawa to other communities are not available, but probably increased in line with wages there (see below)
- Between 1995 and 1999 the RERF increased in value from AUD $ 375, 700 to AUD $ 616,500. By the end of 2000, returned investment income was about AUD$ 24m., equivalent to a third of GDP
- Fisheries **royaltie**s also expanded considerably, and had reached more than 50% of government expenditure by 2000. However, the level of revenue was variable year on year, depending on the El Niño conditions
- **Aid** flows during this period were also variable, but grew from AUD$ 17.2 million in 1995 to AUD$ 27.6 million in 1999
- **Bureaucracy** continued to be the primary source of employment. The public service (including SOEs) accounted for more than 80% of paid employment – most of which was on South Tarawa. Copra producers

were also subsidised through much of the period through government schemes. As the recurrent expenditure of the government expanded, so did the wage bill. However a survey in 1996 found that while on South Tarawa an average household had a weekly income of AUD$ 143 this dwarfed that of the average household on Onotoa, where there was a parallel study. Average household cash income there was only AUD$ 6.80 per week.

Political and social developments

While Kiribati continued to have a relatively good record in regard to human rights, in 2002 the government passed a controversial law enabling it to shut down newspapers, and it also blocked proposals for a privately run radio service. This legislation followed the launching (by Ieremia Tabai) of Kiribati's first successful non-governmental newspaper, which was becoming critical of the government.

The law passed in 2002 was an amendment to Newspaper Act of 1988. The 2002 amendment defined a set of ethical standards to be observed by newspapers, and provided administrative relief for anyone affected by wrongful reporting, including the right of reply to such misreporting; and a legal obligation for the newspaper concerned to publish such correcting statement at the same level and prominence as the article over which the complaint was made.

The amending Act also established a Newspaper Complaints Commission. The Commission had power to recommend to the Registrar of Newspapers for a newspaper that wilfully failed to observe and respect such standards to be struck off the register, subject to appeal to the High Court.

At this time allegations of corruption also surfaced, although the UN in 2002 concluded that there was *'little evidence that [politicians] have assets beyond levels accumulated by other members of the politico-bureaucratic elite ... within the public service cases of fraud are regularly detected, but few involve sums of more than a few hundred dollars ... politicians are often under financial pressure but seemed to resort to indebtedness rather than corruption'*.

In terms of social indicators:

- Kiribati continued to have one of the lowest life expectancies in the Pacific, 62.8 years at birth; high child mortality rates caused principally by respiratory diseases and diarrhoea contributed particularly to this
- By contrast, school attendance continued to exceed that of comparable countries, and any gender gaps below the age of 19 (imbalance in favour of males continued at tertiary level); and both the quality of education they had received, and a 'poverty of opportunity' for those who had completed secondary school, had emerged
- Environmental issues – especially pollution of Tarawa lagoon – were also emerging (see below).

International relations

Kiribati was admitted as the 186th member of the United Nations in September 1999. (It had already joined the IMF and the World Bank in 1986).

As one of the world's most vulnerable nations in terms of the effects of climate change (see below), Kiribati has been an active participant from their outset in international diplomatic efforts relating to climate change, most importantly the United Nations Framework Convention on Climate Change (UNFCCC) 'Conferences Of The Parties' (COP) since. The UNFCCC entered into force as an international agreement on March 1994 and entered into force for Kiribati in May 1995.

Kiribati also joined the Alliance of Small Island States (AOSIS), an intergovernmental organisation of low-lying coastal and small island countries established in 1990 to consolidate the voices of Small Island Developing States (SIDS), specifically to address global warming. AOSIS has been very active from its inception, putting forward the first draft text in the Kyoto Protocol negotiations (see below) as early as 1994.

Changing of the International Date Line

The choice of the 180° meridian as the basis for the change of day had been taken in 1884 in Washington, D.C. at an International Meridian Conference attended by 26 countries (but not, obviously, Tungaru). The 180° meridian was selected as the International Date Line precisely because it mostly runs through the sparsely populated central Pacific. However, various 'zigzags' were introduced from the outset: to avoid dissection of Russian possessions

Chapter 21: The Tito Years 1994 – 2003

in its far east; and, further south, to accommodate various inconveniently placed Polynesian islands where the line was diverted to the east of 180°, at its 'narrowest' passing between Samoa and American Samoa. In much of this area, the dateline follows the 165°W meridian, before reverting to the 180°meridian across empty ocean, and finally bisecting Antarctica.

There had been changes in which day countries operated before Kiribati extended the common day to its eastern borders: notably (and long before the 1884 Conference) the Philippines, together with the Mariana Islands, Guam and Caroline Islands (all then administered by the Spanish authorities in Mexico) had until 1844 been deemed to be on the 'east side'. Kwajalein in the Marshall Islands, although formally part of the Trust Territory of the Pacific Islands after World War II, was considered by the US (who had a military base there) to be in the same 'eastern' day and time as Hawaii.

Although the traditional homeland of Tungaru is entirely to the east of the International Date Line, inclusion of the Phoenix and Line Islands meant that the state of Kiribati, initially, straddled it. Government and commercial concerns on opposite sides of the line could only conduct business for four days of the week. To eliminate this anomaly, the Tito government introduced a change of date for its eastern half by removing Saturday, 31 December 1994 from the calendar: so that the dateline in effect moved eastwards, to go around the entire country.

Leasing of space for a Chinese satellite-tracking station

Kiribati had first established official diplomatic relations with the People's Republic of China in 1980, and maintained them for twenty-three years. For the PRC, relations with Kiribati became relatively important after Beijing had established a satellite-tracking station on Tarawa in 1997. The installation was on a back road at Temaiku, near the airport. Although Chinese officials claimed that the base was solely for space telemetry tracking and to be a command station for its space programme, there was local suspicion that it was actually intended to monitor the US missile range at Kwajalein. When the Tito administration was replaced by that of Beretitenti Tong in 2003, the Kiribati government switched to support of Taiwan rather than the PRC, and both the base and the PRC presence in Kiribati were abruptly terminated (p. 345 below).

Chapter 21: The Tito Years 1994 – 2003

Leasing of Kiritimati island facilities for space programmes

As early as the 1950s, Wernher von Braun had proposed using Kiritimati as a launch site for manned spacecraft; and it was also briefly considered as a stop-off point for a projected British Airways Concorde service across the US to Australia [210].

In November 1999 the Japanese space agency NASDA began to make payments for the use of Kiritimati island facilities to obtain meteorological information, and later proposed to use the abandoned Aeon Field as a landing site for their HOPE-X space shuttle project. This project, however, never came to fruition and was officially abandoned in 2004. There is still a Japanese JAXA satellite tracking station on Kiritimati.

International sport [211]

'European' sports were slow to replace traditional ones (page 69) in I Kiribati culture [212], although a large portion of the Kiribati population now plays football (the national football team is part of the Oceania Football Confederation); and volleyball is also popular.

The idea of winning in these sports (as opposed to traditional ones) also took time to emerge. John Pitchford records from the 1980s:

> 'Our housegirl, a keen volleyball player, returned late one day covered with sweat. 'Who won?' I asked. She just raised her eyes at such a stupid Imatang question. Nobody wins. Everything had to end in a sort of draw otherwise villages would be at loggerheads for generations.'

Competing with strangers was another matter:

> 'Later on this changed completely when national sport became organised and Tabnorth geared itself up to wipe the floor against all other islands'.

---

[210] The UK Government in fact briefly (and secretly) considered before independence whether they could detach Kiritimati from the GEIC, and keep it as a British territory, to avoid having to pay for its use for this purpose.

[211] I am grateful to David Little for providing me with the background for this section.

[212] Although Herbert McClure commended the prowess of the cricket team on Banaba in the 1920s

Chapter 21: The Tito Years 1994 – 2003

Kiribati first began systematically to compete in international sporting events in the late 1990s, although I Kiribati athletes had in fact competed in international events since at least 1963, when six sportsmen had gone to the first South Pacific Games held in Suva; and after independence the Kiribati Bank had also sponsored several athletes to compete overseas. In 1990, annual Secondary School Championships were instituted.

International sporting links, however, began in earnest when Kiribati first participated in the Commonwealth Games, held in 1998 in Kuala Lumpur (where it was represented by a single weight-lifter) [213]. The Kiribati Athletics Association joined the International Association of Athletics Federations (IAAF) in 1999. In 2002, the Kiribati National Sports Council became the Kiribati National Olympic Committee and Kiribati first participated in the Olympic Games in Athens in 2004 [214]. Six sports then had international affiliations (needed for Olympic acceptance): Athletics, Basketball, Tennis, Table-Tennis, Volleyball, and Weight-Lifting. More have been added since 2004: Archery, Badminton, Amateur Boxing, Football, Power-lifting, Taekwondo and Wrestling.

In 2014, the first medal at a major worldwide event, the gold medal won by David Katoatau at the Commonwealth Games in Glasgow provided another milestone for sport in Kiribati. [215]

The 'first dawn' of the third millenium

What caused the government's decision to change the dateline (see above) to be controversial was the impending millennium. Probably quite inadvertently, the change meant that the most easterly and southerly island

---

[213] Teburoro was himself a keen sportsman. In 1997 he was due to play a match with the British Prime Minister Tony Blair at the Commonwealth Heads of Government Meeting in Edinburgh, which was the subject of much speculation in the UK press. However, Flight Lieutenant Rawlings of Ghana spoke for so long at the Leaders' Retreat that this match had to be cancelled!

[214] With its name famously mispronounced to a worldwide TV audience (as 'Kireebarti') in at least three languages!

[215] Making Kiribati at one stroke the third in the Commonwealth Games for highest medal points when adjusted for population (Nauru being at the top of the list, and Dominica – whose population is about two-thirds that of Kiribati - second).

Chapter 21: The Tito Years 1994 – 2003

in Kiribati, Caroline Island, became a candidate for the 'first dawn' [216]. Because a number of countries claimed this prize, in most cases because they hoped to capitalise on a commercial opportunity, the decision by Kiribati came under attack [217]. Indeed, and giving some credence to the claim of opportunism, Caroline Island was officially renamed in 1999 as Millennium Island. The Beretitenti, ministers, and over 70 Kiribati singers and dancers travelled there, accompanied by approximately 25 journalists; and with the temporary infrastructure for them to occupy the otherwise uninhabited island for a few days. The celebration, as the sun rose at 0543 hrs on 1st January, was broadcast worldwide by satellite - and had an estimated audience of more than a billion viewers.

One of the broadcasters was John Simpson, the veteran BBC Foreign Correspondent. In his memoir he recalls:

> *'Our desert island had been inhabited for a week or so by a small group of television people from APTN, satellite engineers, cameramen, sound recordists, directors and others. As we staggered up the beach in the hot sunshine, lugging our equipment and our suitcases across the soft white coral sand ... we felt like interlopers on Robinson Crusoe's island.*

---

[216] At midnight on the 1st of January 2000 by general acclamation, although technically 2001 would have been more accurate!

[217] As I had by this time become the Kiribati Honorary Consul in the UK, I became sucked into the debate (including my only experience, so far, of some extremely hostile radio interviews); and eventually I became a bit of an expert on the 22 places of the world that the Royal Observatory considered might have a claim. These places ranged from the area within the Antarctic circle, where the sun had been up for several months; the uninhabited Balleny Islands just outside that circle, where the sun was to fall below the horizon on 31st December for less than an hour before rising again; to a most ingenious theory, that since the new millennium was to begin on January 1st at the stroke of midnight along the Greenwich meridian, the 'first dawn' would take place where the sun was rising at that midnight in Greenwich. This turned out to be Katchal Island, one of the Nicobar islands in the Indian Ocean. The more commercial contenders were all in the Pacific: the Chatham Islands, Fiji, Tonga and the NZ city of Gisbourne (this last on the - to me - curious grounds that only cities mattered!). Kiribati was widely accused (not least, of course, by this last group) of itself cynically making the move of its dateline in order to make money from it. Kiribati did not in actuality make a single tourist cent from its event at Caroline Island (although I had by then gathered a list of 72 people from the UK who would have paid large sums to be present, and worldwide there were many others).

Everything had been set up, including a kitchen range with huge amounts of food, shower stalls and a lavatory sheltered by woven coconut palms.

'The islanders had scarcely put down their red and blue plastic bags and their mats down in the shelter of the trees before they headed out to hunt the [coconut] crabs ...

'By the time the whole expedition, all eighty of us, television people and dancers and I Kiribati politicians, packed up and left, the islands had been occupied for eleven days. During that time our presence had had a lasting effect on its ecological balance ... [it was] estimated that the clam population had dropped by 40%, and that it would require ten or fifteen years of complete peace and isolation to recover. The outlook for the coconut crabs was worse: at least 70% of them had been killed or captured. Given that it took 50 or 60 years for each crab to reach its full size, it would take almost a century for their population to reach the level it had been at on the day our brief occupation had begun.

'Irony was wrapped in irony. We had violated Millennium Island's isolation in order to celebrate a new phase of human existence, and in doing so had stripped it of some of its chief characteristics'.

Wider issues for Kiribati in the new Millennium

By the late 1990s it was apparent that regardless of the strategy – 'western' or MIRRAB - some serious 'downsides' had been caused by the developments in the past two decades:

- Firstly, the changes in diet and nutrition due to substitution of imported for local foods were not improving the health of the population and both obesity and diabetes were becoming serious concerns
- Secondly, new diseases were entering Kiribati, including HIV/AIDS
- Thirdly, the effect of land reclamations at Temaiku and elsewhere, and the construction of the Betio-Bairiki Causeway, when combined with the continued growth in the urban population of Tarawa, were having a devastating effect on the health of Tarawa lagoon
- Finally, there was a recognition that the isolation of Kiribati had not insulated the country from the potential changes in the global climate, although the effects of these were only just starting to become apparent.

Impact from dietary changes

In 1994 the then Finance Minister commented that:

> 'Large quantities of imported rice, flour, sugar and canned food are modern additions, and are appreciated because they both vary the choice and are easy to prepare ... [but] the effects of this fattening fare on the physique are all too often apparent ... it has taken modern medicine and nutritional science to detect the hidden dangers to health. Obesity brings the risk of cardiovascular conditions, and an unbalanced diet undermines the organism in other ways: the vitamin A shortage produced by the absence of green vegetables in the local food, for example, has left 14% of all children in Kiribati suffering from night blindness'.

Kiribati ranks 10th in the world for the population percentage who are classified as obese, although below that of six other Pacific countries [218]. The percentage has been steadily increasing: from an estimated 37.9 % of women in 1997, to 50.4 % of them in 2016 (39% of men were similarly classified). This has implications for heart disease, and even more so for the incidence of diabetes. A high proportion of I Kiribati people have a high-risk profile in relation to diabetes: this consists of high blood pressure, obesity, lack of exercise, poor nutrition and heavy smoking.

Micronesians are also particularly susceptible to Type 2 diabetes. As early as 1984, attention was being drawn to the high prevalence of non-insulin-dependent diabetes in Kiribati. The then age-standardised prevalence was over twice as high in an urban as compared with a rural sample (9.1% versus 3.0% in men, 8.7% versus 3.3% in women). The findings were clear: the rural population was leaner, had higher habitual physical activity, and derived a lower percentage of daily energy intake from imported foods. Obesity alone did not explain the rural-urban difference. Since then diabetes rates have steadily increased and they are currently (2019) more than 22% of the population in urban areas (or more - in fact 30% by some estimates).

---

[218] In mitigation it is recognised that the BMI measures used to appraise obesity in Caucasian bodies probably needs to be adjusted for to allow for larger bone and muscle mass in those of Micronesians.

Imported diseases

Kiribati had imported a range of new diseases in the late 19th century. After independence others started to arrive. Major health concerns by the 1990s include tuberculosis, dengue fever, leprosy [219], malaria and typhoid. Recently, there has been a chikungunya outbreak, and an estimated 43% of the South Tarawa population carry this virus.

The first reported incidence of HIV also occurred in 1991, and a cumulative total of 60 cases were identified between then and 2015; of these 33 have died of AIDS-related illnesses. However, the government's response was transparent, rapid and effective. Under the EU AIDS programme, Kiribati was supplied with blood testing equipment in 1992, and there was a widespread information campaign. There were just 23 people in Kiribati in 2016 who are known to be living with HIV.

Pollution

A study conducted by the South Pacific Commission in 1979 had been able to report that then *'a variety of chemical indices all suggested that ecological damage due to the release of sewage and domestic rubbish into the lagoon was insignificant'* (although they commented that *'its localised visual and olfactory impact leave something to be desired'*). They warned that this situation could deteriorate without purposeful action, if the population continued to increase. It has.

Although there was a programme to relocate latrines to the Ocean side after the cholera outbreak of 1977, until the late 1990s there was little action: there were neither controls in place on pollution, nor much in the way of waste management systems. Solid waste was dumped on the beach, and there were no facilities for recycling glass, plastic and oil waste. Scrapped buses, lorries and cars were (and still are) simply left on wasteland to rust. As the government's environment unit then put it: *'everything that comes into this country by ship stays here.'*

Moreover, the Temaiku bund had been built in the late 1960s without regard to the environmental impact, and by 1970 other causeways across islets on South Tarawa had blocked off the passages to and from the open sea through which the lagoon waters used to be naturally regenerated. The Betio-Bairiki

---

[219] Kiribati is one of only four countries where leprosy remains common

causeway blocked the last major gap in the south of the atoll. In all, South Tarawa now has approximately 5.1 km of causeways that have closed such naturally occurring channels between islets.

As a result, since independence, Kiribati has developed one of the highest rates of diarrhoeal diseases in the Pacific, with 766 and 634 cases per 1000 population in 2008 and 2009 respectively. For example, in 2009 62,723 diarrhoeal diseases required inpatient care, with 11,594 of these occurring in children under 5 years, resulting in 9 deaths; Typhoid outbreaks also occurred in both 2009 and 2010. The vast majority of these cases were considered to be directly attributable to unsafe drinking water, inadequate sanitation and poor hygiene.

A report in 2011 concluded that:

> *'These incident rates have increased substantially over the last few years and have also seen an increase in other pathogenic-related symptoms such as cold and flu symptoms; skin, eye and ear problems; and, in particular, an increase in festering of cuts and sores after immersion in lagoon water'.*

Or, as a current travel guide to Tarawa puts it:

> *'Probably the most oft-repeated piece of advice to travellers here is: "Whatever you do, don't swim in the lagoon."'* [220]

Climate change

Scientific discovery of climate change began as early as the 19th century, when ice ages and other natural changes in paleoclimate were first suspected and the natural 'greenhouse effect' first identified; it was in fact argued that human emissions of greenhouse gases could change the climate even before 1900. Many other theories of climate change were advanced in the 20th century, involving forces from volcanism to solar variation. In the 1960s, the warming effect of carbon dioxide gas became increasingly convincing. During the 1970s, scientific opinion increasingly favoured the viewpoint that temperatures were increasing. By the 1990s a consensus had formed:

---

[220] Those who savour the scatological details may read the book *'The Sex Lives of Cannibals'* (see Further Reading). Of course this advice does not apply to lagoons on other islands, nor to North Tarawa.

greenhouse gases were deeply involved in most climate changes and human-caused emissions were bringing discernible global warming.

Kiribati recognised the threat early and (in contrast to its non-participation in the equally important Law of the Sea negotiations a decade before) was active in intergovernmental action from the outset. It took part in negotiation of the 1997 Kyoto Protocol, the first international treaty to extend the 1992 United Nations Framework Convention on Climate Change (UNFCCC). This committed state parties to reduce greenhouse gas emissions, based on the scientific consensus that firstly, global warming is occurring; and that, secondly, it is extremely likely that human-made CO_2 emissions have caused it. Since then, and especially after the change of government in 2003, climate change has become an existential issue. Actions including a Climate Change Adaptation Programme, which started in 2003, were developed over the next decade and are described further in Chapter 22.

Further Reading

1. **Atoll Politics – The Republic of Kiribati**, multiple authors, edited by Howard Van Trease, published by the Macmillan Brown Centre for Pacific Studies, University of Canterbury and the Institute of Pacific Studies, University of the South Pacific, 1993
2. **Sixth (1987- 1991) Development Plan**, published by the Government Printer 1987
3. **National Development Strategy** published by the Government Printer 1996
4. **Medium Term Strategy – An Action Programme For the National Development Strategy Through To The Year 2000**, published by the Government Printer 1997
5. **Kiribati: 2001 Article IV**, published by the International Monetary Fund, 2001
6. **Public Sector Reform In Kiribati And Its Impact On Public Enterprise: A Case Of The Public Utilities Board (PUB) In Kiribati, MA thesis** by Meaua Namane B. Tooki, 2005
7. **United Nations Committee for Development Policy: Report on the fifth session (7-11 April 2003)**, published by the UN 2003
8. **Kiribati – Country Report on Human Rights Practices 2001,** published by the US State Department 2002
9. **An Assessment of Where People Will Witness the First Sunrise of the New Millennium** by Peter D. Lechner, Philip A. Blain, Norris D. McWhirter and Ingrid S. Kristament published in The Geographical Journal 1997, published by the Royal Geographical Society
10. **Press Release** by the Royal Observatory, reported in the Independent 28 Dec 1997
11. **A Mad World, My Masters – Tales from a Traveller's Life** by John Simpson, published by Macmillan 2000.
12. **Non-insulin-dependent Diabetes (NIDDM) in a Newly Independent Pacific Nation: The Republic of Kiribati,** by Hilary King, Richard Taylor, Paul Zimmet, Karen Pargeter, L Robin Raper, T Beriki and J Tekanene, published in Diabetes Care, 1984
13. **Common Country Assessment Kiribati**, published by the Office of the UN Resident Coordinator, Suva, Fiji, 2002
14. **The Impacts Of Human Activities On Tarawa Lagoon,** by R. Johannes, W. Kimmerer, R. Kinzie, E. Shiroma, and T. Walsh, published by the South Pacific Commission 1979
15. **Increased flushing of Tarawa Lagoon: The potential for improving public and lagoon ecosystem health outcomes,** by Doug Ramsay, published by the Ministry of Foreign Affairs International Development Group, 2011
16. **The Sex Lives of Cannibals,** by J. Marten Troost, published by Broadway Books 2004.

Chapter 22.

THE TONG YEARS 2003 - 2015

The fourth Beretitenti

Anote Tong was born in June 1952 on Tabueran (then known as Fanning Island). He was, like the first Beretitenti, selected for overseas education in the 1960s: he went to St Bede's College and then took a BSc degree at Canterbury University, both in New Zealand. Anote joined the public service after his return from New Zealand, starting his career in the National Economic Planning Office in 1973 and rising rapidly, to become a Permanent Secretary at an early age. In mid-career he undertook an MA degree in Economics at the London School of Economics.

He entered politics in 1998, and was elected as MP for his home island of Maiana; he soon after became (albeit for a short time) a minister in the government of Teburoro Tito, but he resigned and joined the opposition - his new party being *Boutokan te koaua*. After Teburoro lost a vote of no confidence in 2003, Anote stood for election as Beretitenti and won in July of that year with a slim plurality of votes cast (47.4%) against his older brother, Dr Harry Tong (43.5%); and Banuera Berina (9.1%). The elections were contested by the new opposition, with allegations of electoral fraud; but these allegations were rejected in the High Court.

Anote was re-elected on 17 October 2007 for a second term (64%) and in 2012 for a third term, although with a significantly smaller percentage (42%, but 7% more than his closest rival) than in the previous two elections. He stood down as Beretitenti on reaching his term limits in 2015; and also (unlike previous Beretitenti) did not wish to continue as an MP. This was in order to continue his efforts internationally to raise global awareness of the threats posed by climate change - the issue that had, above all others, defined his presidency.

Chapter 22: The Tong Years 2003 – 2015

Initial actions after the 2003 election

The incoming government made a number of swift changes.

Cancellation of the Air Kiribati lease

Because of the mounting losses of the atoll nation's international carrier Air Kiribati over the lease of its French-manufactured aircraft, the turbo-prop ATR-72, Beretitenti Tong confirmed his government's intention to re-negotiate the lease arrangement. The ATR-72 French manufacturer had indicated its willingness to review the lease agreement on the aircraft, but Tong claimed that *'the cost of the lease of the aircraft is certainly much higher than other ATR-72 aircraft leased by airlines in the region, so we certainly hope it will be possible to reduce this.'* An ultimatum was issued to Air Kiribati: break even or close down. The lease was cancelled.

Switching alliances with China

In November 2003, Kiribati established diplomatic relations with the Taiwanese government in Taipei (the Republic of China, ROC). This brought the number of states in the Pacific Region recognising the ROC to six, as opposed to eight that had relations with the People's Republic of China (PRC).

For three weeks Beijing called upon Kiribati to break off relations with Taiwan and re-affirm support for the 'One China' policy. After those three weeks PRC severed relations, thereby losing the right to maintain its satellite-tracking base in Kiribati.

The PRC also pulled out of a half-completed sports stadium it was building on Bairiki, as well as recalling six medical doctors from the national hospital. The ROC quickly filled the gap, announcing it would provide AUD$8 million needed to complete the sports complex (four times as much as the PRC had given annually), as well as giving the government an additional AUD$400,000 for the hiring of expatriate doctors to replace their Chinese counterparts.

Revisiting the development strategy

The government also made a policy statement on taking office, to reset the overall aim of development: this was to be as an increase in *kabwaia* — well-being—*tibwatibwaan raoi* — equitably distributed — among the people of Kiribati *'according to principles of good governance'*. It was consciously a re-assertion of I Kiribati rather than 'western' concepts of development.

Chapter 22: The Tong Years 2003 – 2015

The statement recognised that efforts to achieve sustainable development can be undermined by lawlessness, and therefore also emphasised the need *'for a peaceful and law-abiding environment for growth'*.

Achievement of well-being was to come from:

- Partnership of public and private investment in infrastructure and production
- Equitable distribution of services and economic opportunity
- Improved efficiency in the public sector
- Equipping I Kiribati people to manage social and economic change: as individuals, as communities and as a nation
- Using natural resources and physical assets sustainably, and
- Preserving financial reserves while making use of them to finance development.

The programme was further developed and set out in a third National Development Strategy, covering the period 2004 - 2007; further Development Plans were produced for 2008 – 11 and 2012 - 15.

Acting on climate change

Kiribati had already been active in climate change discussions for a decade. By 2002, however, the impacts of rising sea levels and storm surges were becoming all too apparent, and the National Development Strategy for 2004-2007 recognised the potentially costly risks to economic growth. Kiribati was one of the first countries formally to articulate a Climate Change Adaptation Policy and Strategy; and to institute, with assistance from the World Bank, an Adaptation Programme. These are described below.

The National Development Strategies of the Tong years

It is instructive to compare the summary statement of the 2004 -2007 strategy with those of its predecessors from the pre-independence period (page 321), immediately after independence (pages 408 - 409); and from 1996 (pages 421 – 422). By 2004 the assessment was that:

> *'Kiribati is changing rapidly. Money incomes have risen through improved communications, monetised trade and financial transactions with a globalising world economy. The same factors have weakened traditional systems of redistribution and mutual support, while facilitating population growth and urbanisation, with serious*

consequences for the physical and social environment and for the well-being of poorer people. Appropriate skills, understanding, structures and codes of conduct are required in all areas of public and private life to enable the Kiribati economy to meet its people's needs for a sustainable livelihood'.

This plan was also much more explicit than any of its predecessors about the MIRRAB nature of the economy (although it did not itself use this term). It recognised also that:

'Changes in the national income of Kiribati are determined more by earnings from abroad than by domestic production of goods and services. Investment earnings of the government's reserve fund and other external reserves, EEZ access fees and other resource rents ... and remittances of Kiribati seamen and fishers on overseas ships, crucially underpin current levels of public and private disposable income, which in turn yield domestic tax revenues. GNP, which includes that foreign income, is therefore a more useful indicator of the current condition and capability of the Kiribati economy than GDP, which covers only incomes from domestic production. Moreover, estimates of GDP are strongly affected by movements in the public sector payroll, which is a weak indicator of changes in real economic activity... Alongside foreign earnings, development aid from foreign governments and international financial institutions plays a key role in the social and economic development of Kiribati. In the three years 2000 -2 official grants and loans from abroad amounted to $105m, providing about 30% of the annual budget expenditures of the Government, equivalent to more than one-third of GDP. The importance of foreign earnings and official aid in determining the development capacity of the economy highlights the need for purposeful management of Kiribati's external relations.'

The emergence of poverty

These national development strategies were also the first to recognise that an unwanted side effect of the MIRRAB economy, poverty, had emerged for the first time in Kiribati; and that the traditional redistribution mechanisms - through family networks - were struggling to contain it.

The 2010 Census found that 70% of adult I Kiribati were being supported by the income-generation efforts of the other 30%. Once children were added, this implied an extremely high dependency ratio, whereby the income generation efforts of approximately 20,000 people were supporting more than five times their number, some 103,000.

Health and poverty are also closely linked, even though basic health care (and also primary education) remained fee-free; and the government continued to subsidise the provision of water and electricity, intra-island shipping, and domestic air travel (after 2016, the Maamau government has also made secondary education fee-free).

A report in 2016 opened with the words:

> *'There is no translation for the word 'poverty' in Kiribati …. many do not consider themselves or those around them poor. In Kiribati, there is a prevalent belief that you are not poor unless you cannot maintain a subsistence living by going out and fishing or foraging for basic needs from the land. To most of those who call the island home, poverty means having nothing at all'*

The rise in poverty in Kiribati was mostly related to urbanisation and lack of employment. However traditional agro-forestry is now threatened by environmental degradation and depletion of natural resources, as well as by preferred diets (there are many unused babai pits in Kiribati); and since the 1980s the emergence of a generation who have grown up without 'subsistence' skills.

There are very few people who are 'destitute', in the sense that they have nothing at all (*te kain nano ni kannano*), but a Household Income and Expenditure Survey (HIES) in 2006 found that 22% of I Kiribati people were living in *'basic needs'* poverty; and that if the 'basic needs' poverty line was doubled, 66% of the population would be considered as poor. The highest rates then reported were in the Southern Gilbert islands (29% of households), although many stakeholders were then surprised that this was higher than in urban Tarawa which had the second highest poverty incidence (17% of households); but given that Tarawa was the largest population centre, by far the largest absolute number of poor people lived there.

The nature of hardship and poverty in South Tarawa were also very different to that experienced on the outer islands. Based on the 2010 Census and 2006 HIES, a typical household in South Tarawa:

- Was larger than a typical household than on the rural islands;

- Had one to two members earning a salary (71% of household income coming from wages)
- Received more remittances from seafaring (this is a sharp change from the situation at independence)
- Still supplemented cash with non-monetary activities (26% of household income);
- Were more likely to have health issues
- Had very limited access to land.

Traditional landowners have become some of the most vulnerable people in South Tarawa. Where their land is on long lease to the government they no longer benefit from it for subsistence, and the rent they have received (set many years ago without review clauses) is sometimes as little as $20 a year.

In both Tarawa and outside it, monetisation of the economy had as well led to high levels of household debt, even though credit was frequently expensive.

Malnutrition and diet-related diseases had – almost unnoticed – thus become a major social problem. The sudden rise in food prices, following the global financial crisis in 2008, brought the issue into focus. A 2010 United Nations Children's Fund (UNICEF) survey reported that more than half of households did not have enough to eat. In 6% of households, children missed meals because there was no food and in another 15% of households, adults sometimes cut back or skipped meals so children could eat.

In May 2011 the World Bank recorded that as global prices for commodities had soared, many households were spending more than half of their budgets on groceries. In response, the Bank provided US$2m (£1.2m) emergency food aid to more than 60,000 residents, 60% of the population: the first time that Kiribati had had to accept such assistance. Even so, the Health Information Unit of the Ministry of Health, in August 2017, revealed rates of malnutrition (including stunting) of 4.7% in 2015 and 5.9% in 2016 among children under age five.

The only governmental social protection scheme in Kiribati had been the Provident Fund; but this only provided for retirement of the 30% who had employment. The Provident Fund had existed since before independence, but like the SOEs had been experiencing persistent deficits, reflecting high crediting rates that were inconsistent with the sustainable rate of return on its investments.

The government thus formalised, and honestly described as a social security programme, the long-standing subsidy for copra. This was intended to keep rural populations employed, monetised and motivated to stay where they were, rather than add to overcrowding in the urban areas. It was viewed as a means of transferring cash to Kiribati residents, rather than as a development tool, unlike the intent of early development plans. It was initially set at $1 per kilo of copra (and the Maamau government has since doubled that amount, so that by 2018 the programme was a transfer equivalent to 12% of GDP).

In addition, the Tong government instituted the first conventional western-style social security payment, the Elderly Fund, a monthly pension now of AUD $40 to those over 67 years of age, and AUD $50 for those over 70.

Social issues

During this period, downsides from urbanisation and monetisation also appeared, giving rise to a wide range of dietary and social issues.

Health and poverty are closely interrelated in Kiribati. While healthcare is free, there are large economic costs on the family due to income losses. A 2014 Asian Development Bank study of the economic costs of inadequate water and sanitation in South Tarawa estimated the annual cost in South Tarawa to be between AUD$ 600 and AUD$1,300 per household.

The limited availability and affordability of nutritious foods has had a major bearing on both adult and childhood malnutrition. A survey of risk factors for diabetes and other non-communicable diseases showed that average consumption of fruit and vegetables among almost the entire population was well below internationally recommended levels. Research has also shown a strong association between diabetes and tuberculosis: both are linked to urban poverty, over-crowding, and poor sanitation and hygiene.

A large proportion of the adult population had other personal risk factors for non-communicable diseases. Almost one in 5 adults over 25 years of age had an elevated blood sugar level (or was already on treatment for diabetes); 80% were overweight (with 46% obese); around one-third had elevated blood pressure and/or serum cholesterol levels; 71% of adult males and 43% of adult females smoked; and 50% did not exercise sufficiently. Lower limb amputation due to the combined effects of diabetes and smoking had become the most rapidly growing reason for surgical admission at the Tungaru Central Hospital.

Child and maternal health was an equally important issue. Child mortality rates were higher than in any other Pacific Island country, due largely to deaths during the first 28 days of life (28% of all under-5 deaths), of which severe malnutrition (15%), and common, life-threatening infections associated with poor quality urban sanitation, water supply and hygiene (pneumonia, 15%; childhood diarrhoea, 15%) predominated. About one-quarter of urban residents and almost half of outer island residents accessed water from unimproved sources, while 40% of urban residents and three-quarters of those living on rural islands lacked access to improved sanitation. As a result, diarrhoea remained an issue. A study of 97 households in 2012 found that one in four children younger than five years had experienced diarrhoea in the previous month.

Domestic overcrowding and poor urban ventilation and sanitation were also reflected in high rates of tuberculosis and leprosy. The prevalence of tuberculosis was the highest or second-highest in the Pacific in most years, with most cases reported from South Tarawa.

By contrast the prevalence of HIV infection was stable and low, but high rates of sexually transmissible infections (up to 15% among antenatal mothers) and potential vulnerability (particularly among women who engaged in sex for payment on foreign fishing vessels) were cause for concern.

SOE Reform

The new government inherited some 32 SOEs. They operated in most sectors of the economy: transport, utilities, telecommunications, manufacturing, tourism, finance, media, wholesaling, and retailing. Most were not fundamentally unviable businesses, but there were many problems which the government had been slow to address. The biggest problem was build-up of debts; the government itself, and the Tarawa Urban Councils, were themselves often poor at paying. Cash flow, rather than profit and loss, was therefore often the most continuing concern.

Moreover the SOEs tended to regard any 'loan' from the central government as a grant; when they faced a cash shortfall, their first response was usually to approach the minister responsible for their affairs for a bail out. SOEs often also received financing for capital expansion from foreign aid donors as a

Chapter 22: The Tong Years 2003 – 2015

grant, and expected that these donors would also fund asset replacement. These made it not only difficult for the private sector to compete, but also positively rewarded poor SOE performance. Over the period 2008–2011, it was estimated that the cost of government bailouts and budget-financed transfers to SOEs totalled more than 9% of GDP, taking hidden subsidies back to levels not seen since the time of independence.

A series of technical assistance projects addressed problems under both the Tito and Tong administrations. A policy framework for SOE reform was developed that included a 'decision tree' to help government decide if public ownership was warranted or not. The 'tree' was ultimately adopted by the Cabinet as the basis for decision-making on divestiture, closure and other forms of SOE privatisation.

As an example, the Kiribati Supply Company Limited had faced growing private sector competition for several years, did not cut its costs as its market share declined, and eventually ran out of cash and was unable to pay its creditors. With private firms active in providing hardware, there was little justification for the government to operate a lossmaking business in that sector. Using the decision-tree approach, it was decided that KSCL should be liquidated. The government then played an active role in preparing the company for liquidation, including through the assumption of responsibility for the company's debts. This cleared the way for the sale of the company's assets, which included valuable long-term leases of prime land. Acknowledging the adverse social impact of staff redundancy, the government also agreed to a policy of providing minimum redundancy payments equivalent to six months' salary.

Betio Shipyards Limited provided another example of successful reform of a distressed SOE, this time without divestiture. Over the previous decade work volumes had declined but staffing levels had been maintained; eventually BSL ran out of cash leaving insufficient funds to pay creditors and to buy the materials needed to complete two vessels under construction. A restructuring programme was implemented, requiring around two-thirds of the staff being made redundant, and the government paying creditors and supplying working capital to enable materials to be purchased so that existing construction contracts could be completed. Those made redundant received a minimum of six months' pay. With a lower core staff level, BSL operated at lower output volumes but broke even.

After another stock-take in 2012, the government proposed further action plans for non-performing SOEs. Private-public partnership (PPP) agreements were designed to support the continued operation of some SOEs, while others were selected as candidates for either sale, liquidation or future joint ventures. Legislation to provide an improved governance framework for SOEs was passed at the April 2013 session of the Maneaba ni Maungtabu. Substantial progress was, as a result, made in improving SOE performance and reducing large ad hoc subsidies.

In 2014 the IMF commented that:

> *'The closures of underperforming SOE have significantly reduced fiscal risks, including through the reduction of outstanding government guarantees. Government plans for the near term include privatising certain enterprises and effectively implementing key provisions of the new SOE Act, particularly in the areas of SOEs' strategies formulation and financial reporting.*
>
> *Measures towards commercialization of SOEs and improving the operational efficiency of some others are all steps in the right direction. Nevertheless, realistic expectations need to be made about the commercial viability of those public enterprises that fulfill social mandates, including the shipping company that services the outer and dispersed smaller islands.'*

Reform has continued and the overall financial performance, with an increased percentage of SOEs reporting profits. Further reforms proposed at the end of the Tong administration included reduction in operational SOEs from twenty-five to sixteen, the merger of the two SOEs in the copra sector, and the privatisation of the telecommunications company, all of which were achieved.

The private sector

The private sector in Kiribati still remained small over this period, and continued to be concentrated in fisheries, retail trade, and copra; although there was some increase in tourism (if evidenced only by a growing number of private hotels and resorts).

The Chamber of Commerce estimated that there were some 2,000 businesses at the end of the Tong administration, but that only two of them employed over 200 people; and most remained family concerns, or were effectively (even if not described as such) *mronron*. Tarawa saw nevertheless its first shopping mall (complete with the first-ever escalator in Kiribati); and there were a number of new Chinese-run businesses.

In 2015, the final year of the Tong administration, the IMF repeated its annual litany:

> *'Kiribati's investment climate ranks 134th out of 189 economies globally and 8th out of 11 within the Pacific region in the World Bank's 2015 Doing Business Report. Its ranking has fallen each year since 2010, although primarily as a result of lack of improvements rather than worsening in the country's regulatory regime.*
>
> *'Starting a business, for example, takes 31 days, against the regional average of 26 days and the regional best practice of 9 days. Land sales are prohibited except between Kiribati citizens and are only allowed after the consent of the Land Court, which applies strict eligibility criteria. It takes on average 153 days to register a property and almost a year to settle a contract dispute.*
>
> *'Getting credit is costly and a large proportion of the population remains outside the formal banking system. Businesses are also subject to price controls that cover a wide range of goods and are subject to irregular revisions issued by the Minister of Commerce.'*

Enhancing fisheries revenue

Fishing license revenue increased significantly, especially between 2011 and 2013. A large share of this increase was due to the implementation of minimum fishing license fees under the Parties to the Nauru Agreement (PNA).

In 2007, PNA members introduced a new mechanism, the vessel day scheme (VDS), to increase the PICs' bargaining power and ensure sustainability of its marine resources. Instead of only setting a limit on the number of vessels in the region as was done previously, the new scheme also limited the total number of 'fishing days'. Under the VDS, Nauru Agreement members jointly consented to allocate a fixed number of transferable fishing days for their combined Exclusive Economic Zones (EEZs), apportioned to members according to the individual sizes of their EEZs and historical catch. The fishing companies were to pay a flat fee, per vessel per day, with adjustment for the size of the vessel.

Chapter 22: The Tong Years 2003 – 2015

The PNA members further strengthened the VDS in 2011 by introducing a minimum fee for fishing per vessel-day. The minimum fee was set at US$5,000 in 2012 and raised to US$6,000 in January 2014. In addition, this revision included annual revisions both of total fishing days for the combined EEZs of the parties, and of the VDS minimum prices.

Fallout and recovery from the 2008 financial crisis

Kiribati was badly affected by the global financial crisis that began in 2008. It was affected by a fall in remittances; large declines in the value of its wealth and pension funds—the Revenue Equalisation Reserve Fund (RERF) and the Kiribati Provident Fund; and by a spike in food and fuel prices, which (see above) led to the first-ever need for food aid. The RERF's losses from the Global Financial Crisis amounted to 25% of Kiribati's GDP, mostly because of investments in Icelandic banks (Kiribati had been the single largest non-Icelandic investor in Icelandic banks). Food and fuel imports rose from 30% of GDP and, as a share of total imports, from less than 40% to nearly 60%.

By 2011, however, despite the rise in world food and fuel prices, inflation had plunged from 2008 'crisis highs' into negative territory, reflecting the strong appreciation of the Australian dollar - and a decline in the world price of rice, which accounted for 20% of the CPI food basket. The RERF also recovered, buoyed up by record fisheries royalties in 2013 and 2014 and the large budgetary surpluses that these enabled.

This episode underlined the status of Kiribati as the most economically vulnerable country in the world (see Chapter 24).

Economic outcomes 2003 – 2015

Economic performance in this period is again best seen through the lens of MIRRAB, rather than that of a conventional, western-style, assessment of Gross Domestic Product. In fact GDP grew at a very slow pace in this period: it managed only an average of 1½% per annum between 2002 and 2014.

There were other causes for concern. After staying broadly stable at around 19% of GDP in the two decades leading to 2007, tax revenues started declining in 2008, and had dropped to about 14% of GDP in 2014. A Value Added Tax (VAT) was introduced in 2014, largely replacing the Import Duties that had been the mainstay of government revenue collection for nearly 100 years. Implementation of the VAT is reported to have been broadly successful in diversifying the revenue base.

Chapter 22: The Tong Years 2003 – 2015

VAT revenue outcomes in 2014–15 were in line with expectations - and the new tax also had positive spillover effects on other revenue collection through improved record keeping and tax compliance. However, the VAT implementation was hampered by SOE exemptions reintroduced in late 2015, which were estimated to have reduced VAT collection by around 15 % in 2016.

The non-monetary economy remained important, but in the 2010 Census, 71.7% of households reported their main income as being derived from wages; in the Gilbert islands other than urban Tarawa, the figure was 34.8%. The copra subsidy from the government enhanced rural incomes: households relied on sale of fish or crops (49.2%), but as well from support by family members living in South Tarawa. Some 30% of rural income came from remittances – 9% from seafarers, and just under 20% from other remittances).

Migration patterns in this period are the subject of Chapter 23. Albeit from a small base, opportunities to live, study and work overseas – either temporarily or permanently – were expanding in both New Zealand and Australia.

Kiribati's long-standing partnership with the South Pacific Marine Services nevertheless continued to provide the bulk of offshore employment opportunities for I-Kiribati. In 2012, 865 seafarers were employed on merchant shipping vessels. The average annual income for these workers was $15,000, of which an estimated $10,000 was saved or remitted home. (By way of comparison, the highest salary earned by a teacher was $12,818). Remittances from this source thus equated to an estimated $8 million in supplementary income, about the same as those from the copra subsidy. Remittances from seasonal workers added an unknown, but lesser, amount.

The second 'R', royalties, reached record levels after its hiccup in 2008 (see above). The balance of the sovereign wealth fund (Revenue Equalisation Reserve Fund, "RERF") was 86% of GDP at end-2017; cash reserves had reached 77%; and public debt stood at 23%. The government's net financial worth - calculated as the balances of the RERF and cash reserves minus public debt—rose to 440% of GDP. Royalty income from fisheries (see above) was even more spectacular, also at record levels.

Aid flows had also increased, with the rolling out of some important new infrastructure projects, especially reconstruction of the main road along South Tarawa and investment in both Bonriki airport and the port at Betio (all of which were aid funded). Kiribati also began to invest in renewable energy sources: 38% of the rural population in the outer islands were recorded to have access to electricity from a stand–alone solar PV home system.

Bureaucracy continued to sustain the economy as well: by 2014, government budgetary expenditures were close to 60% of GDP, and SOE revenues about 40% of GDP. Overall, the public sector still provided nearly 80% of the jobs in the formal sector.

The emergence of gender as a policy issue

It is only in recent times that gender issues have risen to prominence. Earlier chapters of this book discussed how the Churches and the colonial administration downgraded the traditional status of women in I Kiribati society. *Consuming Ocean Island* (see Further Reading) detailed personal testimony as to how girls attempting to join the school on Banaba in the pre-war period were physically turned away on the instructions of the Resident Commissioner; and it was the mid-1960s before girls were able to follow the same secondary education curriculum at KGV/ EBS as boys. Early development plans ignore the issue.

By the beginning of this century, however, full gender parity in primary education had been reached, and soon more girls than boys attended secondary education. Partly as a result, the proportion of women in non-agricultural employment reached 51% of the total in 2010; and, currently, probably a majority of senior public servants are female (by one account, a higher proportion than any other country in the world). More generally, women's decision-making roles, previously marginalised under both maneaba authority and Christianity, have also been transforming as more women become educated.

In 2004, Kiribati acceded to the Convention on the Elimination of all Forms of Discrimination Against Women.

Despite the patriarchal structure of the Missions, women's efforts have been significant within the churches, the KPC in particular. Nei Tenikotabare Bokai of Tabiteuea and Nei Ota Tioti of Onotoa were ordained in 1984, becoming the first women pastors.

However, some 68% of women aged 15-49 who have had, or have, a partner then reported experiences of physical or sexual violence. The passing in 2014 of a Family Peace Act for Domestic Violence has improved the prosecution of offenders, but the issue remains. In 2017, it was reported that 90% of women have experienced some form of controlling behaviour; 31% of women had experienced rape involving physical force; and 41% reported that they had been forced into sexual intercourse with a partner because of fear.

In 2012, a separate Ministry of Women, Youth and Social Affairs was established. This ministry is responsible for progressing women's empowerment and implementing the Strategic Action Plan (2011–2021) to support the elimination of sexual- and gender-based violence. Additional initiatives addressing gender issues in Kiribati included a 2013 National Gender Equality Policy, as well as the National Approach to Eliminating Sexual and gender-based Violence in Kiribati. This has been further supported by the aim of *'ensuring gender main-streaming'*[sic] as part of environmental policy.

Climate change adaptation

An Intergovernmental Panel on Climate Change was established by the UN in 1988, and its First Assessment Report was published in in 1990. Early reports were largely based on data based on analysis of the composition of air enclosed in bubbles in ice cores from Greenland and Antarctica, and the first evidence of global warming was very much focused on the polar regions: as Anote Tong remarked, *'discussion was all about polar bears, not remote communities on the equator'*.

As further work had been done, and models of the impact of various scenarios improved, it has become possible to make much more specific predictions for Kiribati, rather than general ones for the earth as a whole. Reproduced below are the latest ones, from the government's revised *Climate Change Policy* of 2017.

They project that:

- Air temperature will continue to increase. Annual and seasonal mean temperature will increase by 0.3 – 1.3° for the Gilbert islands and 0.4 – 1.2° for the Phoenix and Line islands, by 2030. This prediction has a high degree of confidence
- Sea-surface temperatures will increase by 0.6 – 0.8° by 2030 and by 1.2 – 2.7°, by 2100
- Rainfall patterns will change with increases in wet / dry season variations. This prediction also has a high degree of confidence

Chapter 22: The Tong Years 2003 – 2015

- There will be noticeable increases in extreme rainfall events and very hot days: the intensity and frequency of days of extreme heat, and warm nights, will increase and periods of cooler weather become less frequent
- The mean sea level will rise by 5-15 cm. by 2030 and 20-60 cm. by 2090. In addition there will be increased sea-surges and flooding
- Ocean acidification will continue to increase to the extent that coral reefs in Kiribati will degrade, by more than 25% by 2030 and more than 50% by 2050.

The long-term effects of these predictions on different islets and atolls in Kiribati will be influenced by a number of factors: variability in sediment dynamics and the composition of reefs (see Chapter 1), but also human modification of shorelines (both ancient and modern, such as settlement of previously uninhabited tidal flats, which has been caused by population pressure and its need for additional land space.

Islets composed of sand and rubble have been shaped over time by prevailing winds and waves, but can as well change very quickly; coastal erosion and wave run-up may also be particularly sensitive to the complexity and height of the reef crest, which will in turn be affected by the reef degradation predicted above.

Of human modifications, land reclamation and engineered physical barriers like sea walls can be effective in short-term protection of land and buildings during sea-surges; in Kiribati such sea walls, built from coral rock, sand bags and concrete blocks probably currently provide some 95% of engineered coastal structures. However, without measures to reduce wave energy, like vegetation or breakwaters, sea walls exacerbate or displace beach erosion over time and are unlikely to be a permanent solution.

Mangrove restoration or planting can reduce erosion by stabilising the sediment and by modulating wave energy; and they will also eventually reduce flooding as they build land up through sediment accretion. However mangrove plantations provide little immediate protection and will take at least five years to show a noticeable improvement in coping with rises or surges.

Another form of 'human modification' is simply for the population to leave. Under Beretitenti Tong, importance was given to the concept of *'migration with dignity'*. This emphasised that I Kiribati migrants should be sought after by the countries to which they wish to relocate, not dumped in squalid camps; for this to happen people must be in a position to provide the skills needed in receiving countries, so both Kiribati and the receiving country benefit. The issues around migration, and the experiences of migrants, are discussed in Chapter 23.

'Leaving' could also – at least in theory - mean abandonment of the land in favour of local artificial floating cities. One of the supposed advantages of floating architecture is its sustainability compared to land reclamation, which can harm the marine ecosystem, since it usually means dumping sand on the seabed, annihilating corals and plankton at the bottom of the food chain. There are however many reasons to be sceptical about the idea that floating architecture can help communities adapt to sea level rise: firstly, there are issues of cost and complication (although the growth in solar and floating home technologies point to prices reducing with time). Perhaps more fundamentally, however, they would represent a total disconnect with I Kiribati culture and the attachment of I Kiribati people to their ancestry.

The challenges arising directly from climate change can thus be summarised as:

- Dealing with the disruptions caused by king tides flowing over the atolls
- The need for physical protection of the shoreline
- Severe restrictions on the availability of fresh water (at an affordable price)
- Food security
- The very habitability of the atolls, and the continuing survival of Kiribati as a nation, if these other issues cannot be overcome in time.

The Climate Change Adaptation Programme

The KAP began in 2003 under the auspices of the World Bank using Global Environment Facility and donor funds. From the World Bank's viewpoint, it was explicitly a 'demonstration project'.

After an initial phase of consultations and project development, the US$8.7 million Phase II of the KAP focused on the development of pilot projects in several sectors and implementation of adaptation policies. Phase II underwent restructuring in 2009 after which the focus of the programme was narrowed to include only freshwater systems and coastal planning and protection. It concluded in 2011.

Substantial natural hazard risk assessment has been part of the KAP projects. Site-specific technical studies have evaluated the possible impact of several specific natural hazards: coastal erosion, coral reef and ecosystem degradation, types of coastal engineering with potentially adverse effects, uncontrolled beach mining and over-exploitation and degradation of groundwater resources have been some of the issues assessed. Many of these were classified as environmental stress symptoms by the National Adaptation Programme of Action (NAPA) process, completed in January 2007.

A US$10.8 million third phase of KAP began. The UN Development Programme's National Adaptation Plan of Action for Kiribati and other bilateral adaptation-related projects were integrated with KAP activities, and started to report directly to a centralised climate change planning office within the Office of Te Beretitenti. Phase III had the specific objectives of strengthening Kiribati's ability to provide its citizens with safe water and to maintain resilient coastal infrastructure.

By scaling up measures from the two previous phases, the programme was designed to build resilience to climate change at national, island and community levels, including:

- Improving water use and management by installing groundwater and roof rainwater harvesting systems to ensure cleaner, safer drinking water in selected areas, including during periods of drought; reducing water leakages and waste in existing systems; protecting water reserves, and improving long-term planning for local-level water management
- Protecting against coastal erosion by investing in protection such as seawalls and mangrove planting at priority sites
- Strengthening government and community capacity to manage the effects of climate change and natural hazards, by supporting the development and adoption of a national coastal management policy, as well as the development and implementation of locally managed adaptation plans
- Supporting and assisting the government in managing, monitoring and evaluating the programme.

By supporting education programmes and facilitating the preparation and implementation of locally managed adaptation plans, part of the programme focused also on building skills within communities to manage the effects of climate change and natural hazards.

Creation of the Phoenix Islands Protected Area

A further strand of climate change related actions by the Tong administration was the creation, in 2008, of the Phoenix Islands Protected Area (PIPA). PIPA encompasses one of the world's largest intact coral archipelago ecosystems, 14 known seamounts, and other deep-sea habitats. The area constitutes 11.34% of Kiribati's Exclusive Economic Zone (EEZ); with a size of 408,250 km2 (157,630 sq. mi.) it is one of the largest marine protected areas (MPA), and one of the largest protected areas of any type (land or sea) on Earth. Since January 2015, all commercial extractive activities (including tuna fishing) have been prohibited other than a small sustainable-use zone around Kanton, which allows for limited artisanal fishing to support the resident population. *Underwater Eden* (see Further Reading) makes clear how vulnerable the islands and reefs were before this: between a first reconnaissance voyage in 2000, and the second in 2002, the population of sharks was severely depleted by just a single vessel operating out of American Samoa.

At sea, PIPA contains roughly 200 coral species, some 514 identified species of reef fish (including several new species), 18 species of marine mammals, and 44 bird species. It serves as a migration route and reservoir of these and other marine life.

On land, five of the eight Phoenix islands have been designated as *Important Bird Areas*. There are 19 species of resident seabirds, and many other species migrate through there, including shearwaters and mottled petrels from Australia and New Zealand; and the endemic, but endangered, Phoenix petrel.

In mid-2008 rats and rabbits were eradicated on McKean and Rawaki; and in 2011, rats from Enderbury and Birnie. The responses from plant and bird life were spectacular, with seabirds nesting successfully on McKean for the first time in nearly 10 years; on Rawaki, the vegetation recovery has enabled birds such as blue noddies to find suitable nest sites throughout the island. Frigatebirds now nest on the recovering plants. These restoration efforts will enable populations of Phoenix petrel, white-throated storm petrel, and other important seabird populations to recover.

Chapter 22: The Tong Years 2003 – 2015

Underwater Eden comments:

> *'We reflected at how Rawaki's prolific bird life has survived for millennia, offering a window into what many Pacific islands may have looked like before the arrival of man.'*

In August 2010 the Phoenix islands were listed as a UNESCO World Heritage Site, the largest and deepest such marine area in the world.

Purchase of land abroad

Another strand of the programme involved the purchase, in 2014, of about 7 sq. miles of land in Fiji by the Kiribati government. The purchased land is the 2,210 hectare (5,500 acre) Natoavatu Estate on Vanua Levu that, unusually for Fiji, was freehold rather than native land.

It is currently the home of some 500 ethnic Solomon Islanders who are descendants of 'blackbirded' islanders made to work on Fiji's sugar plantations in the 19th century, and who will remain; but in the immediate future, the land purchased by Kiribati is intended to be used for agricultural and fish-farming projects, so as to provide greater food security, and protection against imported inflation via food commodity prices. The prospect has been questioned, although Kiribati will not be the first country to go down this route – for example, Brunei has for similar reasons invested in cattle ranches in Australia.

The property was visited in 2017 by Beretitenti Mamau partly to reassure the village of Naviavia, which is next to the purchased land, that development of the land would be mutually beneficial. He said that *yaqona (kava)* and vegetables were the major commercial crops envisioned; however, production for export to Kiribati has not yet started in earnest.

Further Reading

1. **Kiribati: 2001 Article IV Reports**, published annually by the International Monetary Fund, 2001- 2018
2. **Kiribati Social and Economic Report 2008**, published by the Asian Development Bank
3. **Public Sector Reform In Kiribati And Its Impact On Public Enterprise: A Case Of The Public Utilities Board (PUB) In Kiribati, MA thesis** by Meaua Namane B. Tooki, 2005
4. **Kiribati Program Poverty Assessment** published by the Department of Foreign Affairs and Trade, Australia, 2014
5. **Reducing the Risk of Disasters and Climate Variability in the Pacific Islands:** Republic of Kiribati Country Assessment, published by the World Bank, 2015
6. **Historical Overview of Climate Change Science,** multiple authors, published by the IPCC at https://www.ipcc.ch/site/assets/uploads/2018/03/ar4-wg1-chapter1.pdf
7. **Mental preparation for climate adaptation: The role of cognition and culture in enhancing adaptive capacity of water management in Kiribati** by N. Kuruppu, and D. Liverman, published in Global Environmental Change, 2010
8. **Obstacles to Climate Change Adaptation Decisions: A Case Study of Sea-Level Rise and Coastal Protection Measures in Kiribati,** by Simon Donner and Sophie Webber, published in Sustainability Science, July 2014
9. **National Adaptation Program Of Action (NAPA),** published by the Environment And Conservation Division, Ministry Of Environment, Land, And Agricultural Development, Government Of Kiribati, January 2007
10. **Report On The Kiribati 2010 Census of Population and Housing,** published by the National Statistics Office, Ministry of Finance and Economic Planning, 2012
11. **Kiribati Climate Change Policy,** published by the Government Printer, 2018
12. **Underwater Eden**, by Gregory Stone and David Obura, published by The University of Chicago Press, 2013

Chapter 23.

THE I KIRIBATI DIASPORA

Pacific diasporas

A 'diaspora' has been defined as *'a scattered population whose remembered origins lie in a geographic locale different to where that population now lives'*.

During the 20th century, and into the 21st century, New Zealand in particular saw a steady stream of immigration from Polynesian countries: Samoa, Tonga, the Cook Islands, Niue, Tuvalu, and French Polynesia. In the 2013 New Zealand census, 7.4% of the population identified with one or more Pacific ethnic groups, even though 62.3 % of these respondents had been born in New Zealand. Those with a Samoan background make up the largest proportion, followed by Cook Islanders, Tongans, and Niueans. Some smaller island populations, such as Niue and Tokelau, now have the majority of nationals living in New Zealand; the extreme case is the Cook Islands where a population of less than 20,000 domestically resident is supplemented by an estimated 70,000 ethnic Cook Islanders living abroad [221].

Part 1 of this book detailed some of the known early movements of the Tungaru people away from the Gilbert islands. In pre-contact times these were to Tuvalu and the Marshall islands (and a very few to other parts of Micronesia). After contact in the nineteenth century labour was recruited for Hawaii, Samoa, Guatemala, Reunion, New Caledonia and Peru. Some I Kiribati 'blackbirded' for the last of these were involuntarily dispersed to the Northern Cook islands. All these populations were however either eventually repatriated, or have been absorbed to the extent that individuals with I Kiribati ancestors do not retain even memory of their roots. The exception is those of mixed descent on the island of Nui, who now identify entirely with Tuvalu, despite having undergone a language shift which means they spoke a variant of I Kiribati.

---

[221] These proportions are nevertheless far less than other diasporas elsewhere in the world relative to their home populations; for example there are more than over 100 million people who have Irish ancestors, more than fifteen times the population of the actual island of Ireland, which is about 4.6 million.

By contrast those who were taken (voluntarily or not) to Fiji in the nineteenth and twentieth centuries have often retained both familial and cultural links, as have those who moved to the Solomon islands (via the Phoenix islands).

In the twentieth century there was also quite extensive intermarriage of I Kiribati with Nauruans and other Pacific islanders, as well as with Europeans and Hong Kong Chinese, which has resulted in settlement outside Kiribati.

Types of migration

Qualities which may distinguish between various types of diaspora include:

- The extent to which emigrants expect to return home, at least at some point
- Their continuing use of their own language and culture (and whether this is passed on to subsequent generations)
- Their relationships with other communities in their new environment, compared to their association with an I Kiribati community
- The degree to which they achieve success in, and become integrated into, host countries, including the incidence of intermarriage with host communities.

There are two very different 'diasporas' of I Kiribati, both of which are documented in this Chapter: 'internal' diasporas on urban Tarawa, and also the Line Islands; and the communities of those who go further, to other countries.

Thirdly, there are smaller pockets of diaspora (mainly in the UK, EU, USA and Hong Kong) where the main driver has been personal (inter-marriage with citizens of those countries, rather than 'economic' migration). Another, albeit minor, source of migration is Church-inspired (e.g. there is a small community of I Kiribati Roman Catholic nuns posted to Slovakia, and there are at least temporary migration opportunities for Mormon I Kiribati to undertake missionary work worldwide).

A comprehensive survey of both internal and external migrants was carried out in 2015 by the United Nations University (see Further Reading). Findings were based upon quantitative and qualitative fieldwork carried out in Kiribati by a team of researchers, and involved 377 household surveys: in South Tarawa, North Tarawa, Marakei, Kiritimati and Butaritari.

Chapter 23: The I Kiribati Diaspora

After weighting, the household survey estimated that some 10,480 movements had taken place from the sampled islands in the period 2005-2015, i.e. that approximately 10% of the population had migrated in this decade. 79% of the movements had been internal migration, within Kiribati; 13 % were external; and 8 % were connected to seafaring. A similar proportion of those interviewed reported that they would have wished to migrate but were unable to: usually because of a lack of money. Indeed, on the 'outer islands' lack of money represented almost 90% of the reasons quoted for *not* moving.

At the time of the survey, a big majority (some 70%) of migrants were aged between 15 and 50 years. It was reported that 63% of these migrants had also completed at least some secondary education, compared to just over half of the overall sample of people of this age group. Migration is thus clearly associated with education (although it might be that both are associated with access to funds): migrant households are also associated with higher median per capita incomes than those who stay put.

The survey also found that the vast majority (95%) of households had been affected by one or more natural hazards in the period 2005-2015. Sea level rise is the hazard which has impacted the most house-holds, affecting approximately 80%. Saltwater intrusion impacted just under half of all households.

The impact of migration: a case study of the Nikunau diaspora

There has also been a detailed analysis, by Keith Dixon (see Further Reading) of the worldwide community who have ancestral links with the island of Nikunau in the Southern Gilberts, and their experiences. While the experience of other island diasporas might differ in detail, there is no reason to think Nikunau is atypical.

Keith Dixon estimates that the island is the 'life world' of at least 85% of its permanent 2,000 inhabitants; but that it has continuing significance for at least another 4,000 who, if not born on Nikunau themselves, are descended from someone who was born there within the last three or so generations and would therefore be regarded traditionally as being *te utu ae kan*.

These 4,000 comprise a diaspora which, over the past few decades, has steadily extended to other parts of Kiribati (especially urban Tarawa but also the Line Islands, other Pacific countries, and further afield to metropolitan countries such as Australia, New Zealand, and the UK).

Chapter 23: The I Kiribati Diaspora

Internal diasporas

Chapter 19 discussed the manner in which periods of temporary and 'circular' migration had already characterised I Kiribati society at the time of independence. In the 40 years since, the relentless increase in the proportion of urban Tarawa has as well created more permanent 'mini-diasporas' of people there who identify with another Gilbert island - but have never actually visited it (nor, often, do they ever intend to do so).

Urban Tarawa

At the time of the 2015 Kiribati Census, it was reported that two-thirds of those living on urban Tarawa had been born there, while 34% had migrated in at some point, having been born elsewhere [222]. However, there was also significant evidence of 'out-migration' from urban areas as well, suggesting that a proportion of those had been born in urban areas when they and their parents were only temporary urban residents (e.g. to take advantage of the better medical facilities for birth).

Studies agree that people now migrate to South Tarawa for work, for education, and because of climate change, in approximately equal proportions.

The experience of the I Nikunau diaspora on Tarawa is summed up by Keith Dixon (see Further Reading):

> 'South Tarawa is ... where 95% of the 2,600 strong I-Nikunau diasporic community lives, many of the other 5% making up the increasing overspill of people and mwenga northwards, across the as yet uncausewayed [sic] lagoon-ocean channel at Buota, onto lower North Tarawa.
>
> 'In contrast to Nikunau, their mwenga are dispersed along Tarawa, and interspersed between them are mwenga of I-Kiribati from other islands and the aforementioned multiplicity of premises of various bodies. In these circumstances, I-Nikunau are less likely to have any historical kinship ties with neighbouring mwenga, and so their interactions are often less substantial and may be insubstantial, varying with other factors, such as

---

[222] Table 52 of the census does not however distinguish those who were temporarily on Tarawa at the time of the census, rather than having moved there permanently.

Chapter 23: The I Kiribati Diaspora

children playing together and young adults being freer to socialise and even inter-marry….

'Compared with Nikunau, their *mwenga (in the sense of households) are larger, typically comprising between 6 and 12 persons, usually of three generations, and sometimes even four. As more I-Nikunau have immigrated, or grown up and had children themselves, the area of land occupied and the number of* **mwenga** *have increased. However, these increases have not kept pace with the growth in persons, and so the numbers in each te mwenga have gradually increased, living conditions have become increasingly crowded and strains have been put on incomes, [and] the amounts of victuals available …*

'*These are among reasons for members of the oldest generation(s) moving from one te mwenga to another at infrequent intervals, and indeed for others to do so, in contrast to practices on Nikunau. However, other reasons for this fluidity are at least as important, including their adult offspring taking it in turns to look after the older generation according to* **te katei ni Nikunau,** *the traditional role of grandparents in teaching grandchildren, the modern need for unaine, in particular, minding grandchildren while parents attend places of paid employment, social tensions between the generations and the possibility of each te mwenga sharing in the pensions of these old people.*

'*In adapting their social organisation to their surroundings on Tarawa, various phenomena are noteworthy. I-Nikunau are engaged in te mwenga activities and other economic, social, cultural, religious and political pursuits, more in keeping with* **te katei ni Nikunau,** *albeit a much modernised version of tradition, including seeming almost as oblivious as I-Nikunau on Nikunau are to time as measured in hours and minutes.*

'*I-Nikunau journey along Tarawa frequently to visit each other and help each other in many other ways socially and economically—this includes being loyal member-customers of* **mronron,** *and working in these and on other tasks (e.g., child-minding, house construction) without receiving wages. Within and among* **mwenga,** *they spend much time on storytelling,* **maroro/winnanti** *(informal chatting/gossiping), [and] playing games'.*

Chapter 23: The I Kiribati Diaspora

The Line islands

The most recent development Plan for the Line and Phoenix islands starts with an assessment that:

> *'For more than one hundred years the Line and Phoenix Islands have been either managed as coconut plantations or occupied for government and military purposes, with no indigenous population. A range of infrastructure was developed during these specific periods of occupation (telecommunications staging, war, bomb testing, Trans-Pacific Aviation, resettlement) with much of it having been adapted to modern day uses.*
>
> *'Increasing population pressures on islands in the 'Gilbert Group' and small Government resettlement programmes on Kiritimati Island, from Kanton, and on Teraina (also known as Washington) and Tabuaeran (also known as Fanning Island) have resulted, with occasional exceptions, in the population of the Line and Phoenix islands growing steadily year on year between the 1950s and today.*
>
> *'Those who have settled on Kiritimati are either government workers, a small number of perpetual or short term leaseholders, church leaders, or an embryonic group of business people and their respective families, with the remaining population of the Line and Phoenix Islands having no land occupation rights'.*

The acquisition by the Gilbert and Ellice Islands government (and thence the state of Kiribati) of the inhabited islands in the Line Group, and a physical description of them, was set out in pages 140 – 141; and the story of Operation Grapple (nuclear tests on Kiritimati) in Chapter 13 (pp. 208 – 209). The remaining Line islands have no permanent residents.

Since 2005, the government of Kiribati has been promoting migration to the Line Islands, especially from South Tarawa, as they are considered less at risk from climate change and offer more space than other islands (Kiritimati alone has a larger land mass than all of the other islands of Kiribati combined). Migration occurs overwhelmingly for work, although in a few cases the motive for relocation was reported as environmental factors (only half of households surveyed there had been affected by sea level rise in Kiritimati, for example, compared to 85 % on South Tarawa, and 95 % on the 'outer' Gilbert islands).

Chapter 23: The I Kiribati Diaspora

The total population of the Line Islands was in 2015 about 10,500, of which the population of Kiritimati (6,356 residents enumerated in the 2015 Census) was the largest component, followed by Tabuaeran (2,317) and Teraina (1,712). Kiritimati is intended to become an economic hub for the development of Kiribati and this population is expected to grow. There are reported to be about 40 private businesses there; although as in the rest of Kiribati the bulk of employment is still provided by the public sector.

The established population of Kiritimati seems to have developed its own sense of unity. A focus group was held on Kiritimati by the 2105 Survey team where participants did not identify *any* beneficial impacts of further migration for them as the receiving community. They highlighted instead the negative impacts of migration, such as migrants related to them coming to the island without money and relying on family support, or as bringing and consuming *kava* and other drugs.

Fortunes on the two smaller inhabited Line Islands, Teraina and Tabuaeran, have been mixed.

Teraina has a combined land area of 9.55 square km. and a population (in 2010) of 1,690, giving a population density of 177 people per square km., making it one of the more densely populated islands in Kiribati. Because immigration is recent it has an unusual age structure; in 2015 nearly half the population (44%) was aged under 15 and one in five (19%) were under five years.

However Teraina also has vegetation that is lush by the standards of Kiribati. A 2012 study reported that:

> 'Coconut trees grow untamed and so high in the forest, they form a canopy, preventing sunlight from reaching the ground, so the soil is always moist. Concealed in this forest's vastness is a forest of breadfruit (Artocarpus altilis) trees that compete with the surrounding coconut trees for sunlight. The freshwater lake is surrounded by swampy areas where the 'babai' grow, some wildly and others cultivated, and bulrushes as far as the eye can see.'

Land use policies of the government have been designed to encourage migration to Teraina. In 2012, about a third of households (29%) live on land that they now have the right to call their own, while the remaining two thirds live on government leases or privately arranged subleases.

However, there are very few jobs on Teraina and only one in five families received income from wages at the time of the 2010 Census. Remittances, either from seamen or from other family members working abroad or on South Tarawa are a very important source of income. Sale of fish, crops (mainly copra) and handicrafts are the most common sources of income generated on the island.

Teraina probably better reflects the 'Maude migration design' (in which it is intended that a diaspora replicate the life its people once led in the Gilbert Islands) than any other of those covered in this Chapter. Perhaps it is no accident that it now has the healthiest population in Kiribati, including for infants, with few of the introduced diseases found elsewhere in the country.

The eight small villages of Tabuaeran are spaced along the lagoon coast on the western side of the island. The more exposed eastern side is set aside as a nature reserve. On the ocean side of the villages, there is ample government land which is available to households under a 'harvest permit' system to collect coconuts and to cultivate *bwabwai*.

Between 2005 and 2010, the population fell markedly due to people leaving the island following the temporary closure of the Mereang Tabai Secondary School (which has since re-opened); the closure of the Norwegian Cruise Liner Company that had called at the island; and the weakness of the Atoll Seaweed Company. Cruise liners have now also recommenced visits.

The ample land and marine resources of Tabuaeran, as well, provide for a life of *'affluent subsistence'* with plenty of food available to all households; and the island has land resources to support a much larger population than currently live there. Like those of Teraina residents of Tabuaeran have a low cash income and find it hard to pay for imported food, tobacco and fuel.

Because Tabuaeran was settled only recently, most of the residents identify themselves as being from another island of Kiribati. Of the people currently living on Tabuaeran in 2010, 725 had been born there, but only 374 identified themselves in the census as being *'kain Tabuaeran'*.

In addition to the three Line Islands, about 20 people live on Kanton, in the Phoenix islands; however, this is not a necessarily permanent population and thus not a 'diaspora'.

Chapter 23: The I Kiribati Diaspora

Migration experiences outside Kiribati

The motives for, incentives given, and way in which resettlement schemes outside of Kiribati have been designed have changed considerably since those of colonial times, which encompassed the eventually aborted resettlements in the Phoenix Islands, and the transfer of this population to the Solomon islands; and the resettlement of the Banabans on Rabi.

The intent of these schemes was that communities of I Kiribati be transplanted to new sites where, so far as their new environment permitted, their material and social culture would replicate that which they had left behind.

It is only in the past two or three decades that planned migrations to regional 'metropolitan' countries (New Zealand and Australia) have instead been based on the needs and lifestyles of the receiving communities. In this type of migration, individuals or nuclear families move piecemeal, and consciously to adopt 'western' lifestyles (e.g. work, housing, diet); it is expected that their I Kiribati identity, certainly that of succeeding generations, will be gradually replaced by that of their new homes.

Estimated numbers and whereabouts of the external I Kiribati diaspora in 2019

Over the past 70 years, therefore, the number of I Kiribati permanently residing outside its territory has grown from very few to nearly 15% of the number who live inside it. There are increasing numbers of second and third generations of migrants, and some studies have started to chart the extent to which they maintain links to their original islands.

The table on the next page estimates the current numbers and whereabouts of the diaspora outside Kiribati. This has been compiled from a number of disparate sources, both official and unofficial, and should be regarded as indicative only [223].

---

[223] The table omits the estimated 870 speakers of the I Kiribati language in Nui, in Tuvalu, who would consider themselves part of that country, rather than as ethnically I Kiribati.

Chapter 23: The I Kiribati Diaspora

Country of residence	Approximate number of people of recent I Kiribati descent	Source of estimate
Fiji	6,500	Estimate of I Kiribati language speakers in Fiji.
Solomon islands	6,000	Based on projection from 2009 Census
New Zealand	2,200	Estimate by NZ Ministry of Foreign Affairs
Australia	1,700	Estimate by Australian Bureau of Census and Statistics
United States	150	My estimate (probably underestimated)
UK	200	My estimate (60 born in Kiribati, 140 children/grandchildren born outside Kiribati)
EU (other than UK)	30	My estimate
Elsewhere	200	Includes I Kiribati resident in Hong Kong, other East Asian countries, the rest of Micronesia, and Vanuatu
TOTAL	17,480	

Fiji

The bulk of I Kiribati migrants to Fiji are Banabans or the descendants of the 300 others who relocated with them to the island of Rabi in the 1940s. They were joined by a second wave of migrants between 1975 and 1977, with a final migration between 1981 and 1983, following the ending of phosphate mining. Worldwide, it is estimated that there are now some 7 - 8,000 Banabans. A sizeable community can be found in Suva, and a few now also live in Australia, New Zealand and the US.

With a current population of around 5,000, Rabi itself is home only to the migrants and their descendants; the indigenous Fijian community that formerly lived on the island was moved to Taveuni after the island was purchased by the British using money from the Banaban Trust Fund.

Chapter 23: The I Kiribati Diaspora

The Banaban claim, in the run-up to Kiribati independence, that they were a separate nation from the I Kiribati (Chapter 17) has affected them in several ways. Their leader when they first arrived there, Rotan Tito, was adamant that they '*did not come to Fiji to be workers on the land, but to get our money*'. They were allowed to fish on the reef, and did so, but were subject to restrictions on gaining their living from any other form of marine enterprise. In any case, quite apart from the different nature of agro-forestry and fishing on Rabi compared to that of Banaba, most of the population had largely abandoned subsistence living during the pre-war and war period.

On Rabi they had soon acquired the soubriquet '*tin openers of the Pacific*'. They also – unlike most islanders - lived in permanent materials houses, and had both piped water and electricity. Until the 1980s, and with a boost at the time of Kiribati independence through the ex-gratia payment (p 282), royalties were sufficient to sustain this lifestyle. However, the $10 million ex-gratia payment and the Banaban Trust Fund were dissipated by a series of council chairmen: in *Consuming Ocean Island*, Katerina Teaiwa describes how:

> '*Corruption in the council became rampant, and a slew of con men presenting themselves as financial advisers targeted the Banabans, often making off with thousands of the community's dollars … the Fiji government had to step in and appoint three administrators*'.

For a period, the Council of Elders also largely excluded those not deemed to be of wholly Banaban descent from voting or holding positions in the Council.

Since the 1980s, when it became clear that they could no longer exist solely on past royalties because of the depletion of their Fund (and that they did need to become '*workers on the land*'), the Banabans have devised new strategies. In the last 30 years a modified form of traditional subsistence has emerged, with a range of 'Fijian' crops especially *taro* (*dalo* in Fijian) replacing those from Banaba. The New Zealand Geographic reported in 2011 that

> '*There is no cash economy here other than a limited number of jobs paid for by the Rabi Council of Leaders, but a subsistence economy keeps people industrious and fed, and tolerates no waste. After fish and dalo for breakfast, it will be fish and maybe rice for lunch, and fish and breadfruit for dinner.*'

A decision was made by the Fijian Cabinet in early 2005 to grant citizenship to all the residents of Rabi and Kioa Islands, concluding a decade-long quest by the people of both islands for naturalisation. This entitles the islanders to provincial and rural development assistance from the government of Fiji. On 15 December 2005, sixty years to the day since the arrival of the first Banabans, more than 500 Rabi Islanders were granted citizenship at a ceremony led by Minister for Home Affairs Josefa Vosanibola and fellow-Cabinet Minister Ratu Naiqama Lalabalavu, who was also the Tui Cakau, or Paramount Chief of Cakaudrove and Tovata, to which Rabi belongs. These islanders, who had not previously been naturalised, came from the second and third waves of migration, which were technically illegal but had been tolerated by the Fijian government on humanitarian grounds.

Banabans are represented in the Fijian House of Representatives, classified as General Electors (an omnibus category for Fijian citizens who are neither indigenous nor of Indian origin). Rabi Island forms part of the North Eastern General Communal Constituency, one of three reserved for General Electors, and of the Lau Taveuni Rotuma Open Constituency, one of 25 seats elected by universal suffrage.

Rabi remains, however, anomalous in political terms in Fiji: though part of the Province of Cakaudrove, it has a degree of autonomy, with its own council controlling local affairs (though this council is to be merged with its counterpart from Kioa, a nearby island purchased and settled by people from Tuvalu).

It is even more anomalous because of the dual citizenship of its residents: although citizens of Fiji, the Rabi Islanders may still hold Kiribati passports; they remain the legal landowners of Banaba; and they send one representative to the Kiribati parliament. Furthermore, the Rabi Council municipally administers the island of Banaba.

Of all the various diasporas covered in this Chapter, the Banabans thus retain the strongest links to their homeland – although many still claim that only the island of Banaba is their homeland, and that they are not part of Kiribati. Some 250 of them have returned to and now reside on Banaba, and a few have settled on Tarawa. Language and culture have been sustained, compared, for example, to the experience of second- and third generation I Kiribati in the Solomon islands (see below) and elsewhere.

Chapter 23: The I Kiribati Diaspora

Other I Kiribati in Fiji

There is little information about other people of I Kirbati descent in Fiji: anecdotal evidence suggests that most are probably from relatively well-off families (often part-European) who moved there because of superior educational facilities, and mostly to Suva.

No I Kiribati have yet moved to Naviavia village, now on land which is owned by Kiribati. The current inhabitants are reported to have mixed feelings towards the idea of future migrants from Kiribati. Adi Ulamila Wragg, a Fijian chief, is quoted as saying that *'Most are wondering what is going to happen? Are they going to be part of us or part of our community or are they going to have their own set up rules?'*. On the other hand *'We see that they bring new knowledge with them, traditional knowledge. That's something they can share with us'*.

In 2017, Fiji's Prime Minister Frank Bainimarama gave a pledge that all those forced to leave Tuvalu and Kiribati because of climate change will be allowed to settle permanently in Fiji.

The Solomon Islands

The first wave of I Kiribati migrants to the Solomon islands arrived in the Western Province in 1953. They were assigned land to the west of Gizo. Subsequent settlements were created at White River, Honiara, Wagina Island at the southeastern end of Choiseul, at Titiana on Gizo, and at Kamaliae in the Shortland Islands.

In 1971 the Governing Council of the Solomon Islands (then in its own trajectory to independence) stopped further migration. The 1976 census recorded 2,753 Gilbertese in the Protectorate.

The settlements in Titiana and Wagina adopted as far as they could the 'Maude' concept of translocation of I Kiribati - not fundamentally changing their way of life. They largely recreated their original lifestyles, building *maneabas* and maintaining distinct cultural ways, particularly singing and dancing (indeed I Kiribati dancing has become a tourist mainstay in Honiara and Gizo).

They were however unaccustomed to forested land and found it difficult to adapt their skills to Solomons-style agriculture, which was aggravated by the poor quality of land they had been allocated. They have however adopted (or readopted, see p 78 in Chapter 7) the habit of chewing betel nut; and they are reported to have adapted their daily fishing styles to local conditions. Seaweed farming has become important as a source of cash, especially on Titiana; and I Kiribati are said to be the main sellers of fish in Gizo.

The Melanesian host communities have generally got on fairly well with the settlers in the Western Province, yet the growing I Kiribati communities are only able to settle on the plots of land given to the original settlers during the 1950s and 1960s. They do not own, and cannot acquire, alternative land; there is concern that future population pressures may cause friction between host and settled groups, as resources become stretched. Gilbertese settlers have begun to intermarry with indigenous Solomon Islanders, and are becoming increasingly integrated into that nation.

In his study of the diaspora in the Solomons (see Further Reading) Tommy Tabe concludes of the new generation:

> *'Pidgin has become the dominant language in conversations among the youth … most I Kiribati descendants have never been to Kiribati and have little, if any, knowledge about the place … 90% of my informants strongly suggested they were Solomon islanders, while the remaining 10% claimed they were both I Kiribati and Solomon islanders'.*

New Zealand

In 1986 New Zealand began providing a small work permit scheme for I Kiribati. A significant number of those entering New Zealand legally on such work visas became permanent residents, but the Pacific Access Category (PAC) that was implemented in 2003 provided a new and more certain migration route. Under the PAC, up to 75 citizens of Kiribati per year are selected by ballot. They must then meet stated employment, income, health, basic English skills, and character requirements before being invited to apply for residence.

Largely as a result, the Kiribati ethnic population has increased by nearly 90% between 2006 and 2013, when the Census identified 2,115 people of I Kiribati birth and descent. Of the group, 93% lived in the North Island, with 76% in the main urban centres. The 2013 Census also confirmed that *'this ethnic population is largely a migrant group with 67.2 percent being born overseas and 32.8 percent born in New Zealand. Of those born overseas, 36.3 percent had arrived in New Zealand less than five years ago, compared with 52.8 percent in 2006'.* The Kiribati ethnic group is significantly younger than the New Zealand population, with 37.9% under the age of 15 years compared to 20.4% for the total New Zealand population.

Each year more than 100 I-Kiribati also go to New Zealand temporarily to work in horticulture and wine industries under the Recognised Seasonal Employer Scheme (RSE), which Kiribati joined in 2011; sometimes New Zealand horticulture companies who need to find regular workers have then offered continuing employment for I-Kiribati - for example, the Southern Paprika company, the largest exporter of capsicums in New Zealand. Once I Kiribati are established in New Zealand they have had a high retention rate of employment.

In 2011, Korauaba Taberannang published the results of a survey he had conducted of Kiribati people in New Zealand.

Amongst the most important findings were:

- The lack of recognition of I Kiribati qualifications in New Zealand. Very few Pacific or Kiribati qualifications are recognised; for example, a Masters degree from the University of the South Pacific counts only as an undergraduate degree in New Zealand. Many qualified workers like teachers, nurses and builders are unable to work in New Zealand without full retraining
- However in order to undertake training or retraining, I-Kiribati need to make do on a training allowance or no income at all. Further, many training schemes are not free. This catch-22 situation is preventing many I-Kiribati from retraining for a more rewarding occupation.

The 2013 Census confirmed that I Kiribati are still concentrated in low-paying industries, working as labourers (35%) and community and personal service workers such as carers (18%). Consistently with this employment profile, 56% aged 15 years and older received an annual income of less than $20,000, with only 3.6% receiving an annual income of more than $70,000.

In terms of their evolution as a diaspora, a study by the Presbyterian Church of Aotearoa (see Further Reading) suggests that the experience of Kiribati migrants is different to that of other migrants in several ways.

Firstly, in the degree of their reliance on those who had come earlier to New Zealand. Such host I Kiribati families are important in providing support to newcomers, by offering direct assistance financially and also helping with newcomers' adaptation to their new environment. A key priority for host families is reported to be actively helping the migrants gain paid employment.

Hosts often share their own houses with migrants: the accommodation arrangements often result in crowded conditions, with multiple families sharing one house. Many of the host families had hosted multiple migrants, some of whom were directly related to the host family and some of whom – against tradition - were not:

> *'The general consensus is that within a couple of generations the Islands of Kiribati will no longer be able to support much of a human population. The feeling is that the move is on, and that it is up to the first emigrants to set up networks in New Zealand for those who will follow'.*

Migrants often also tend to rely on church networks rather than government help. Pacific churches and community organisations contribute significantly to the positive settlement, providing such services as employment support, legal advice, language tutoring, immigration assistance, family support, and fellowship.

As with those in the Solomon Islands, a language shift is underway. It is already commonplace for New Zealand-born I Kiribati children to speak only English. Feelings on this are mixed, with some I Kiribati thinking it is a natural change while others struggle to maintain the language ability of their children.

Over 70% of Kiribati citizens who had taken up residence between January 1998 and December 2004 had never been out of New Zealand again, a much lower percentage than other island migrants.

Australia

In the 2016 Census, 505 residents were enumerated who were born in Kiribati, but larger numbers, 1,014 whose mother, and 694 whose father were born in Kiribati. (Some of these may be of European ethnicity, born on Banaba to Australian parents employed by the BPC).

Australia was late in acceptance of Pacific migration. Until well into the 20th century, the philosophy of Sir John Robert Seeley (p. 125) prevailed: *'This country shall remain forever the home of the descendants of those people who came*

Chapter 23: The I Kiribati Diaspora

here in peace [224] *in order to establish in the South Seas an outpost of the British race'*, as the WWII Prime Minister John Curtin put it. It was not until 1973 that the Whitlam government passed laws, for the first time, to ensure that race would be totally disregarded as a component for immigration to Australia; and in 1975 passed the Racial Discrimination Act, which made racially-based selection criteria unlawful.

The possibilities for migration of the Pacific island-born to Australia increased steeply about a decade later, mainly in response to labour shortages which island immigrants were prepared to fill; by 2016 the number of people in Australia claiming Pacific islands ancestry had grown strongly: from 112,133 in 2006, to 150,068 in 2011, and to 206,673 in 2016.

For temporary migration, the Seasonal Worker Programme (piloted from 2006, formalised in 2012) connects I Kiribati and other Pacific island workers with Australian employers experiencing labour shortages. A new Pacific Labour Scheme (from 2018) also enables citizens of Kiribati and other Pacific island countries to take up low and semi-skilled work opportunities in rural and regional Australia, for up to three years. Pacific Islanders stay up to six times longer at a farm than backpackers and are on average 20% more productive. In 2013-2014 34 I Kiribati workers used Australia's SWP but this number is increasing; and a new scheme, The Pacific Labour Scheme, commenced on 1 July 2018 following a successful pilot programme in northern Australia, building on the success of the Seasonal Worker Programme. The stated intent was that up to 2,000 workers from Kiribati, Nauru and Tuvalu would have first access to the scheme.

In 2019 it was reported that businesses on Hayman and Hamilton Islands currently employ 54 I Kiribati workers in hospitality roles and that *'these workers provide much-needed skills to keep Australian businesses running following the devastating effects of Cyclone Debbie'*. Workers on this scheme also benefit from the opportunity to enhance their skills while in Australia: I Kiribati workers have completed a Certificate III in Hospitality through an intensive on-the-job training programme, providing workers with an internationally recognised qualification.

---

[224] It is rather doubtful if the original inhabitants of Australia saw much of the 'peace' aspect; or indeed if those transported, as criminals, to Australia from Britain and Ireland saw the 'outpost' quite in that way.

Chapter 23: The I Kiribati Diaspora

Under the Kiribati Australia Nursing Initiative (KANI), Australia has also offered scholarships to study a Bachelor's degree in nursing in Australia. The aim of KANI was to provide a high quality education and employment opportunities overseas to I-Kiribati and also address the global skill shortage in nursing. A pilot programme was concluded in 2014 with an investment of AUD20.8 million, which achieved a completion rate of 81% over a total of 84 students.

Australia is also helping Kiribati to build a skilled workforce through technical and vocational training and scholarships (Australia Awards). These awards provide opportunities for I-Kiribati students to study at tertiary institutions in the Pacific or Australia. At present some 30 - 55 I Kiribati study each year at Australian or regional universities, supported by Australian scholarships.

The I Kiribati diaspora in Australia is thus of more recent origin than the others described in this Chapter, and there are few pointers as to the experience of second and third generation diaspora members.

The United Kingdom

The UK is wholly an example of the third type of migration outlined at the outset of this Chapter – driven by personal rather than economic reasons. It comprises I Kiribati wives (and a few husbands) of British and Irish people who worked in Kiribati in the past, mostly in the 1970s and early 1980s.

A Kiribati Tungaru Association is active there in promoting I Kiribati culture and dance. The Association was set up in 1994 by several families of mixed marriage to bring together similar families and other Imatang who had lived and worked in, or otherwise have links to Kiribati.

It has been highly successful in maintaining the interest of part-I Kiribati in their traditions, and its dance group has performed in a number of prestigious events, including the Millennium Dome, Commonwealth Day, and the RL Stephenson Centenary celebrations. Keith Dixon (see Further Reading) comments about the younger generation in the UK:

> *'... Not only do the young know something of its culture and language, and maintain links with each other through identifying with Kiribati, but also many have visited Kiribati, usually as still young adults. These visits are facilitated through the regular verbal contact senior I-Kiribati in the*

community in particular have maintained with utu, *etc., mostly on Tarawa but even on their home islands, including Nikunau, particularly since the coming about of low-cost or even free modern technology applications (e.g., Skype, Facebook Messenger, WhatsApp Messenger).*

'Otherwise, in many respects the lives of most members of the community, particularly those brought up in Britain are generally 'normal' for the many places they have settled in and for the socio-economic class (mostly middle, professional or skilled working) with which they have most to do'.

The majority, however, like second and third generation diaspora in the other countries surveyed above, have very limited fluency in the I Kiribati language.

Summary: the experiences of I Kiribati diasporas abroad

In so far as it is possible to generalise, the following conclusions apply to I Kiribati and their descendants abroad:

- Few emigrants expect to return home, and few do
- Use of networks of those I Kiribati already in the country are vital for helping new arrivals to settle
- The I Kiribati language is not generally passed on to subsequent generations of diaspora, and seems usually to be lost even amongst the first generation growing up overseas. The main exceptions to this are where there are large groups of I Kiribati living together, as on Rabi and to a lesser extent in the Solomon islands
- Transmission of I Kiribati culture (especially dances, but also good manners) is more common than language transmission, particularly where older members of the emigrant community are consciously teaching new generations. Dances have however started to evolve with new forms of dress and musical background
- I Kiribati mix well with other communities and readily intermarry. Church links are also important, especially in New Zealand
- Employment prospects and income vary considerably, depending on the original 'type' of migration. Education (but also recognition of existing educational qualifications) plays a vital role in the ability of I Kiribati to prosper abroad, just as it does at home.

Chapter 23: The I Kiribati Diaspora

Further Reading

1. **Gilbertese language – Wikipedia** at https://en.wikipedia.org/wiki/Gilbertese_language
2. **Census Report 2015 Volume I Final Report,** by Orebwa Morate, Census Commisioner, published by the National Statistics Office, Kiribati, 2016
3. **Kiribati Climate Change And Migration: Relationships Between Household Vulnerability, Human Mobility And Climate Change,** by Robert Oakes, Andrea Milan, and Jillian Campbell, published by ESCAP, 2016
4. **A pressure release valve? Migration and climate change in Kiribati, Nauru and Tuvalu** by Richard Curtain and Matthew Dornan, published by the Development Policy Centre Crawford School of Public Policy ANU College of Asia and the Pacific, 2019
5. **Circumstances of a Pacific atoll people in diaspora**: A retrospective analysis of I-Nikunau by Keith Dixon, University of Canterbury
6. **Line and Phoenix Islands Integrated Development Strategy 2016 – 2036,** prepared by the Ministry of Line and Phoenix Islands Development, 2016
7. **Fiji Census Data 2007 at** https://www.statsfiji.gov.fj/
8. **Consuming Ocean Island,** by Katerina Martina Teaiwa, published by the Indiana University Press, 2015
9. **The Banabans of Rabi**, by Jennifer Shennan, New Zealand Geographic, 2006
10. **Sapon Riki Ba Kain Toromon: A Study of the I Kiribati Community in the Solomon Islands,** by Tammy Tabe, 2011
11. **New Zealand Census 2013**
12. **Kiribati Migration to New Zealand: experience, needs and aspirations**, prepared for Presbyterian Church of Aotearoa New Zealand by Matt Gillard and Lisa Dyson, 2011
13. **Housing and Health of Kiribati Migrants Living in New Zealand,** by Mary Anne Teariki, published in International Journal of Environmental Research and Public Health, 2017
14. **Maximizing the Development Impacts from Temporary Migration: Recommendations for Australia's Seasonal Worker Programme,** published by the International Bank for Reconstruction and Development/The World Bank, 2017
15. **Overview of Australia's aid program to Kiribati** – published by the Department of Foreign Affairs and Trade at https://dfat.gov.au/geo/kiribati/development.../development-assistance-in-kiribati.aspx

Chapter 24.

THE NEXT FORTY YEARS

Kiribati as a nation and as a Sovereign State

The continuance of Tungaru, the Gilbert islands, and the Republic of Kiribati - as a nation, and retention of its culture - has been written off several times in the past - as recorded in earlier Chapters of this book:

- They achieved one of the densest populations in the Pacific, despite living in one of its most marginal habitats (Chapters 1 and 7)
- Through the 19th and early 20th century there was the notion that, like all Pacific islanders, they were a *'dying race'*, and that all the Europeans (who were to inherit the Pacific Ocean as a *'White Man's lake'*) could do was to *'smooth the pillow'* until they had disappeared
- There was then a confident assertion by 19th and 20th century missionaries that the I Kiribati would be transformed into pseudo-European Christians who would eschew *'depraved'* cultural activities such as dancing (*'a sign of heathen decadence to be swept away'*); and who would take only *'the same sort of interest in their ancestors as our French students might take in the ancient Gauls'*
- Colonial administrators did not believe that the I Kiribati could govern themselves without prescriptive rules and European supervision; and later, there was the metropolitan countries' view that even if the I Kiribati could be trusted to run themselves at island level, they were *'too small, too weak in resources, and too remote to be Sovereign'*
- Concerns after independence that without the *'guiding hand'* in foreign affairs and defence of Australia and New Zealand Kiribati would somehow fall into the orbit of predatory outsiders
- Having overcome all of these, there then arose in the 1990s for the Kiribati nation the issue and impact of climate change; this convinced the fourth Beretitenti and many others that *'to plan for the day when you no longer have a country is indeed painful, but I think we have to do that'*.

In 2016, the opposition replaced a sitting government (for the third time in the history of Kiribati; fourth if the pre-independence election of 1978 is counted), showing that representative democracy at least remains in good health. The new government, led by Beretitenti Taneti Maamau, soon published a new 'vision' for the nation: this was Kiribati Vision 2016 - 2036 (KV20). The core tenets of KV20 are summarised below; progress towards it has, though, only just commenced - so it will be for a successor to this book to evaluate it.

KV20 is very much predicated, not on *'no longer having a country'*, but that the impact of climate change will be manageable:

> *'In order to reduce vulnerability to climate change, Government will continue to implement and build on existing policy measures towards building adaptive and mitigation capacity, particularly of the most vulnerable people. The policy measures will also reduce exposure or sensitivity to climate impacts. In addition, Government will mainstream climate change adaptation and mitigation through development and effective implementation of strategies that fully integrate climate change concerns into various programmes, to ensure that the working environment is sensitive to climate change and sustainable development given the overreliance on tourism and fisheries sectors which are highly vulnerable to the impact of climate change. Sufficient technical capacity and human resources to successfully mainstream climate change adaptation and mitigation measures will also be heightened for effective implementation of climate change related adaptation measures.*

'Vision 20' for 2016 - 2036

The vision for Kiribati is that it will become:

> *'A wealthy, healthy and peaceful nation ....*
> *'The Vision is anchored on four pillars: Wealth; Peace and Security; Infrastructure; and Governance. 'The Wealth Pillar aims to develop the natural capital, human capital and cultural capital to improve economic growth and reduce poverty ... The human capital component seeks to create a highly educated and skilled population, increase access to decent employment; develop a highly skilled, qualified and efficient work force and accessible and affordable quality healthcare system; .... [and] to develop cultural capital by implementing measures to safeguard and revive traditional skills and knowledge...The Peace and Security Pillar aims to create a secure, safer and peaceful Kiribati .... The Infrastructure Pillar aims at improving connectivity and accessibility... The Governance Pillar aims to create a corruption-free society by*

strengthening national and local traditional governance policy and legislative frameworks.'

When compared to previous iterations of development plans and strategies in the past 50 years, the most radical innovations of KV20 are principally in two policy areas. Firstly, it gives a much higher priority to development of tourism than governments have done in the past; and secondly, the 'Governance Pillar' takes aim squarely at the issue of corruption.

Tourism

Development of tourism has never before had a very high priority in the developmental aims of Kiribati, compared to countries in the region such as Fiji - and in marked contrast to similar sized island economies in the Caribbean. Kiribati is the sixth least visited country in the world (although numbers of visitors are ahead of those to the Marshall Islands, Tuvalu and Nauru).

Successive governments took the view that the returns would be low (since most of the things consumed by tourists would be imported, with little added value); and that even a modest expansion of tourism would make unaffordable demands on scarce natural resources, especially of fresh water [225]. The inevitable social consequences that many politicians had observed overseas were also not desired. The exception to this policy has been the small-scale but productive tourist industry on Kiritimati, based on the very niche market of sports fishermen.

The tourism sector has thus long been very limited; and, like all monetary activity in Kiribati, focused on South Tarawa and Kiritimati. Growth in holiday arrivals has been largely static, with total such arrivals recorded as just 1412 people in 2015. 'Business related' travel is the dominant motive of all visitors, while more conventional tourists (the 1412) are largely the fishermen (although there is a small but steady stream of 'country completists'

---

[225] When I wrote the first government official policy about tourism in 1973, I worked on the established basis that the average tourist then (in pre-ecotourism days) used more than 200 gallons of water per day; at that time, we on Tarawa were rationed per household to 12 such gallons. It did not take a lot of calculation to show that even a medium sized hotel, would, on this basis, pre-empt the entire fresh water supply of a typical atoll. Since then the experience of the Maldives in combining tourism and desalinisation (now to be solar-powered) have altered these perceptions.

Chapter 24: The Next Forty Years

who wish to record a visit to every country in the world). The Phoenix Islands Protected Area remains wholly unexploited as a potential eco-tourism destination.

KV20, by contrast, aims at increasing the contribution of tourism to GDP from 3.6% in 2016 to 50% by 2036, based on investment in experiences and facilities for cultural and also eco-tourism:

> *'Development of cultural industry on the outer islands could bring to life an important cultural heritage site and create additional economic opportunity for the local people. The cultural industry can revive and connect intangible cultural heritage and knowledge, while at the same time creating employment opportunities for traditional craftspeople, composers, dance groups and their dancers, musicians and singers'.*

Corruption

The first comprehensive assessment [226] of 'national integrity systems' was produced by Uentabo MacKenzie, on behalf of Transparency International, in 2004. Its introduction begins with the statement that *'there is no specific translation for the term 'corruption' in the language of Kiribati though the indigenous terms* babakanikawai, kamangao *and* anonikai *clearly indicate deviant and dishonest behaviour. The public is therefore generally aware of what kinds of acts qualify as corruption (though traditional custom blurs the line between activities and legitimate gift-giving'.*

The customs which cause most difficulty are *te mweaka* (a gift which is obligatory, whether it is election time or not; it was defined by Hiram Bingham as *'a gift presented to persons visited after long absence, to a new host, [and] formerly to the spirit of a place visited*). Typically, it would be publicly presented to designated recipients in the form of sticks of tobacco, and would be given on the day of arrival – and only once. Secondly, *te nouete* represents a gift given at a specifically fund-raising gathering to which the donor has been invited, and is given publicly at that gathering. It might take the form of cash.

Court cases after allegations of corrupt practices had entered the electoral processes as early as 1982, attempting to distinguish between such *'respect for*

---

[226] Also the only full assessment by TI I have been able to find, so that it is still reflected on their website.

Chapter 24: The Next Forty Years

customs and tradition' and *'intention to influence voters'*. For example, the custom of *bubuti* makes it *'acceptable for someone lacking in* [certain] *resources to make a specific request to another who is better endowed'* (Chief Justice Williams, 15 October 2003). Such requests had been made in the form of a 'fine' demanded of a candidate visiting a Maneaba, and had involved gifts including a chainsaw and a video set. In the case then before the High Court, it was decided that the issue depended on the intention of the giver and that the gifts in this case *'were made because of custom. The candidates had no choice'*. [227]

The bulk of the 2004 report was based on a Transparency International questionnaire which focused almost entirely on the presence or absence of anti-corruption institutional structures (rather than case studies or statistics as to the actual occurrence of corrupt behaviour, admittedly harder to gather).

It thus provided a classic example of 'institutionalism' in relation to micro-states (page 375) [228].

The general absence of formal rules, legislation, codes of conduct and dedicated monitoring authorities - no fewer than 107 questions about the presence or absence of these were addressed in the questionnaire - were adduced as evidence that problems must be being ignored, rather than accepted as a statement about the capabilities of micro-states to produce and monitor the same level of formal regulation as that appropriate for large developed countries.

It resulted in Kiribati being given a low score in Transparency International's widely used Corruption Perceptions Index, which has in turn been picked up by many other bodies as 'proving' the existence of widespread dishonesty.

---

[227] I must however declare an interest in this case, as one of the candidates referred to in this judgement is my brother-in-law.

[228] Another interest declaration - I do feel strongly about the issue of 'institutionalism' in relation to micro-states such as Kiribati – i.e. the idea that unless you have dedicated laws, codes of conduct, regulations and (especially) government monitoring units – the issue is not being taken seriously. Kiribati cannot have unlimited separate units of government to deal with all issues. (One personal memory of this is being excoriated by one international body in 1974, because the then Gilbert islands had no regulations for 'trucks crossing international borders by road'!).

Chapter 24: The Next Forty Years

For example statements such as this, from the US Freedom House, are common on external websites:

> *'Official corruption and abuse are serious problems, and the government has not shown a commitment to addressing them'.*

This is not to say that there have been no areas for concern, as KV20 recognises. Allegations of electoral malpractice, doubtful involvement of ministers and senior civil servants in granting business licenses, and nepotism (particularly affecting the award of overseas scholarships but also more generally), have periodically arisen both before and since 2004; they have been subject to investigation, and a number of instances of small-scale official petty corruption (albeit rather fewer of abuse of office in decision-taking) have been prosecuted. Misuse of publicly funded foreign travel is probably the most common form of dishonesty. Audit reports also regularly highlight 'missing' government funds, although late and inadequate submission of accounts are frequently the causes, as well as fraud.

What Kiribati does not have is a culture in which bribes routinely need to be paid for businesses or individuals to access government services.

At a macro-level, there are equally valid concerns about competition between the two Chinas (PRC and ROC) supporting different political parties [229]. Another curious incident early in the life of the new administration was the approach of the shadowy 'Romanov Empire' (a would-be micro-state hoping to recreate Tsarist Russia elsewhere in the world); its representative held a series of talks with the government of Kiribati in 2016 about a proposal to invest US$350 in return for a grant of sovereignty to them over Malden, Caroline and Starbuck islands in the Line Group. In February 2017, the Kiribati government rejected the proposal.

The Leadership Commission

Kiribati acceded to the United Nations Convention against Corruption in 2013 and set up a Public Service Integrity and Corruption control unit in the Public Service Office. Accused persons have been suspended from public office pending criminal proceedings.

---

[229] As this book was going to the publisher, it was announced that Kiribati was again to revert to the People's Republic of China and would be breaking off its relations with Taiwan.

Chapter 24: The Next Forty Years

One of the first actions of the new Maamau administration, in 2016, was to pass a Leaders Code of Conduct Act, and to appoint a Leadership Commission, in March 2018. In its first twelve months, the Commission has received a total of 20 complaints involving 28 cases. The most common forms of violation reported related to unfair decisions (25%), and abuse of power (21%), rather than bribery or other 'economic' corruption. In June 2019, the new arrangements achieved their first major public impact, when the Vice-President left office following allegations of misuse of public funds overseas.

Graduation from Least Developed Country Status

Kiribati was included in the United Nations list of Least Developed Countries (LDCs) when this was created as a category in 1986. Kiribati's graduation from Least Developed Country status was under review when this book was being written; and given the 'write-offs' itemised at the start of this Chapter, it would be a major achievement.

A country becomes eligible for graduation from the LDC category when it meets any two of three criteria in two consecutive triennial reviews.

In the 2018 review, the criteria were as follows:

- Gross National Income per capita of US$ 1,230 or above (the income threshold)
- Human Assets Index (HAI) of 66 or above
- Economic Vulnerability Index (EVI) of 32 or below

Kiribati has been found eligible for graduation in 2006, 2012 2015 and 2018, based on its GNI per capita (well over double the threshold) and its score on the human assets index. With the exception of child mortality all components of the HAI score rank high amongst other LDCs, and Kiribati has an unequalled secondary school enrolment ratio of 86%.

However, as the UNCTAD assessment commented:

'This level of human capital development is more the consequence of good governance and proper targeting of social investment with external support, than a dividend of structural economic progress'.

The economic implications

If Kiribati were to graduate, the country would lose access to various international support measures covering market access and trade, development assistance and general support. Offsetting this are potential soft benefits, such as a heightened sense of national progress and pride as Kiribati moves off the 'lowest official rung of the development ladder'. It would increase the country's political standing in regional and international institutions.

The most significant export effect would be on fish exports of tuna loins and related processed fish products, which constitute major elements of the current fisheries development strategy. While products currently sent to Australia and the US would be unaffected, products sent to Japan and the EU would face higher tariffs. Copra exports are not currently subject to tariffs and so would not face any changes.

Graduation would not impact Kiribati residents working abroad, as the preferential access to Australia and New Zealand through seasonal workers schemes is independent of LDC status, and Kiribati seafarer and fishing crews do not receive any preferential treatment already.

Other impacts of LDC graduation would be minor: the loss of aid-for-trade coordination, needing to pay for attendance at the UN General Assembly and related conferences, loss of some minor UNDP programmes, and small increases in payments to some international organisations, and a liability for contributions to UN peacekeeping operations.

Graduation is also not expected to impact aid flows, as all the significant bilateral development partners (Australia, New Zealand, Japan, and China) have confirmed that their support to Kiribati does not depend on its LDC status. Similarly, all significant multilateral partners either do not use the LDC category for operational activities (World Bank and Asian Development Bank) or confirmed their continuing support at current or increased levels (the EU and its institutions). Almost all United Nations entities confirmed that they will continue to support Kiribati after a possible graduation. In fact the only significant impact on ODA appears to be the UN Framework Convention on Climate Change LDC Funding window, which is currently implementing one project in Kiribati under the UNDP. Under transition arrangements, funding already approved under the LDCF would not be removed.

Economic Vulnerability

The principal reason that Kiribati has not yet made the move out of LDC status is that it is rated economically as the *'most vulnerable country in the world'*: it scored only 45% of the 'graduation threshold' under the economic vulnerability criterion in 2015, and a provisionally estimated 43% in 2018.

The Economic Vulnerability Index is based on criteria that include smallness in population terms, geographical remoteness, physical exposure to sea-related risks for people living in low-lying areas, and the ratio [to population] of victims of natural disasters (including those caused by climate change). These four are the components of the index which weigh most heavily against Kiribati.

The 2015 Economic Vulnerability Index also however indicates that exports of goods and services have been more unstable in Kiribati than other LDCs, by a margin of 18%, and three times more unstable in Kiribati than the average for other small island developing states. Such export instability has been caused by both supply-related and price-related factors. Another component of the index is tourism (see above).

The 2018 UNCTAD assessment concludes:

> *'Kiribati is more a permanently fragile economy as a consequence of its geography than an unstable economy, and there is little scope for improvement of its EVI score under the graduation line...*
>
> *'At 200% of the graduation threshold relevant to the per capita income criterion in 2015 and 248% in 2018, Kiribati statistically demonstrates a level of continued relative prosperity. The 2012 review of the list of LDCs by the United Nations was the point of history when an impression of irreversible prosperity in Kiribati began to percolate internationally, with a surge in the country's score above the same graduation threshold in that year (before further peak effects in 2015 and 2018).*
>
> *'Yet in the absence of significant productive capacities and of commensurate progress in the standards of living of Kiribati nationals, the impression of prosperity is fallacious. Rental income sources (notably fishing license fees), aid and private remittances are the main monetary wealth of Kiribati, and that wealth is barely sufficient for meeting the high costs associated with the challenges of smallness, remoteness, and climate change'.*

The remainder of this Chapter thus examines the vulnerability issues (other than remoteness) which KV20 sets out to overcome – or which might become critical to survival of the nation as a Sovereign State.

Vulnerability issues

Issues which might impact Kiribati over the next decades fall into four main categories:

- Physical: the fabric of the islands and surrounding oceans
- Demographic: what population density can be sustained, and the likely incidence of poverty as a result of population pressure
- Cultural: whether cultural networks can sustain a situation where the wages of a few sustain an ever-increasing dependency ratio; how far I Kiribati norms will (or need to) evolve to embrace an individualistic, private sector-driven, and less culturally egalitarian society; and/or whether government-funded social security schemes could provide a substitute for the lack of employment opportunities for the majority
- Pressures to 'homogenise' with the culture and lifestyles of the rest of the world, and to lose the distinctive culture of Kiribati.

These are assessed below.

The final section of this Chapter assesses whether there are, as yet, observable limits to the sustainability of the current 'MIRRAB' model because of any, or the combined effect of, the issues listed above.

The physical fabric of the islands and oceans

Climate change deniers frequently argue that *'global warming is a hoax'* because atolls in the Pacific are accreting (getting larger) rather than being swept away and disappearing, as is often claimed.

Statements such as this, in the popular press, and by many websites, are typical: *'rising sea levels due to climate change are causing the islands to become smaller each year'*. Such statements are also wrong.

Accretion and erosion

In fact, the climate change deniers are correct about one thing: accretion in most atolls is based on solid fact.

Chapter 24: The Next Forty Years

A study (see Further Reading) in 2015 concluded that:

> 'Over two thirds (106) of the 146 islands [studied in this report] [230] can be regarded as being in a steady state or stable condition. In most instances, the change in island size was less than 0.5 hectare, with 50 islands changing by less than 0.1 hectare.

> 'Of the remaining 40 islands 28 indicate island expansion while the other 12 islands decreased in size... All of the latter are concentrated in the group of the smallest islands, [of] less than 1 hectare in area ....

> 'Accretion occurred across all island sizes, and none of the islands larger than 1 hectare recorded a reduction in area. These results show the preponderance of accretion over erosion in the sample islands'.

This is due to the common sense idea that the sedimentary products of island erosion— skeletal sand and coral rubble— do not 'disappear' with local erosion. Instead, they must go somewhere, and in atolls this may be that they are:

- Transported off-reef into deep water
- Moved along the island shore
- Returned to the seaward reef flat
- Deposited in the nearshore lagoon
- Transferred to the island surface.

Only the first of these possibilities – very rare - results in permanent loss to the island sediment system.

The 2015 study concluded that:

> 'By the end of the 21st century, we expect the majority of the present atoll islands in the central and western Pacific to be still there, providing the scale of future climate–ocean processes does not accelerate much beyond those projected in the IPCC Fifth Assessment. While some islands may reduce in size, it is likely there will be an equal or greater number that remain the same size, or increase in area'.

---

[230] By which they mean *islets divided by reef passages*, rather than a whole atoll regarded as a single island, as more normally expressed in I Kiribati usage. Three Gilbert island atolls were included in this study.

Man-made structures also affect both accretion and erosion. Earlier (2010) studies of Majuro and Tarawa clearly demonstrated the distinction between the urban and rural zones on those two 'urban capitals', and other islands in their groups (the main islet on Majuro has the same sort of density as Betio).

On both Majuro and South Tarawa, changes in island area and shoreline position have been unequivocally attributed to human activities. Reclamation, construction of seawalls, groins, and causeways between islands have resulted in large increases in local island area and have also altered patterns of sediment movement creating both accumulation and erosion. Erosion is amplified by sand and aggregate mining of beaches and reefs.

On Tarawa, there is an observable urban–rural distinction. The total land area on Tarawa atoll had increased by nearly 20% from 1968 to 1998, as shown by changes in the shoreline position over the past 30 years. All of this increase has taken place in urban South Tarawa, where reclamation of sandy intertidal areas of the lagoon and causeway construction between islands, as well as seawall construction and backfill, have resulted in expanded land area. By contrast, in North Tarawa, 25 of the 40 islets were classified as 'stable'; 13 islands showed net accretion; and two (both small) displayed net erosion over the 30-year period.

Another 2005 study (see Further Reading) on Maiana and Aranuka also showed that village shores on those islands had been modified by groins, seawalls, and other structures; and that in some cases these had had the unintended consequence of stopping or slowing sediment transfers: so actually resulted in enhanced local erosion.

Storm surges and salt water intrusion into the water lenses

Since there are no rivers or streams on atoll islands, the only natural source of fresh water, besides collecting of rainwater or desalinisation, exists in the form of the thin aquifers of fresh groundwater described in Chapter 1. Over the past 80 years, 13 major droughts have been recorded in Kiribati, with an average duration of 20 months; the consequences range from ground water contamination to fatal illnesses.

Five major tropical cyclones and four extreme tide events have been recorded as well in this period, mostly in recent years.

Mean significant wave height (defined as the average of the highest one-third of wave heights) is projected to be 5 – 10% higher than the present-day mean

Chapter 24: The Next Forty Years

in the tropical South Pacific and Southern Ocean by the end of this century. Projecting how atoll islands will physically respond to future rises in mean and extreme sea level, changes in wave conditions, and human-induced pressures - as well as to increases in cyclone intensity, sea surface temperature, and ocean acidity - is a critical but complex issue. Modelling of it is in its infancy, but yields worrying results (see, in Further Reading, the article by Ting Fong May Chui and James P. Terry).

As Kiribati has increasingly discovered surges and flooding ('king' tides) already cause saltwater intrusion directly into the freshwater aquifers. Smaller islands are at a far greater risk of extensive saltwater intrusion - there is a non-linear relationship between island width and thickness of the freshwater lens.

At the opposite climatic extreme, extended dry periods diminish the receipt of moisture needed to recharge the aquifer. In Kiribati, rain failure is caused by shifts in the regular weather patterns associated with the El Niño-Southern Oscillation, which seems to be becoming more frequent as a result of global warming. A depleted lens may need over eighteen months to be replenished after the re-establishment of normal rainfall.

While actual casualties from violent events such as tropical cyclones or sea swells have been few, growing numbers of people have been suffering from loss and poverty as a result.

In the longer term, if more and more of the potable groundwater becomes saline, there will be a substantial reduction in available water resources from the lenses, affecting agro-forestry systems as well as potable water for humans. A 40 cm. rise in sea level is likely to have a drastic effect on the shape and thickness of the typical freshwater lens, reducing its size by up to 50%, and encouraging the formation of brackish zones. Saline plumes can form at the bottom of the freshwater aquifer when the lens thickness is compromised by drought and saltwater intrusion. Even after a full year of groundwater recharge, the saline plume may not completely dissipate. Sea level rise will likely lead to sustained, possibly irreparable, damage to freshwater lenses due to an increase in cyclone-generated wave wash-over, rendering many islands uninhabitable because of the loss of potable water for both humans and for a range of crops.

Thus claims that the islands are 'drowning' are indeed wrong. They are not drowning; but, humans and plants alike, they may well die of thirst.

Chapter 24: The Next Forty Years

Demographic pressures and poverty

The population of Kiribati in 2019 is estimated at 117,600. The nation as a whole has a population density of 135 people per square km. (350/sq mi.), which is actually only the 73rd highest in the world. However it is not the overall density that is at issue, but that in South Tarawa, home to half this population.

The rate of natural increase is currently estimated at 2.2%, with net annual permanent emigration of 0.1% (a little over 120 people a year) barely making a dent on increases in population growth of some 20,000 people per decade.

Population growth and the 'demographic transition'

Fertility in Kiribati appears to have peaked around 1968, when it reached 7.4. Over the following decade, the total fertility rate (TFR) - the number of children born or likely to be born to a typical woman in her life - declined rapidly, to 4.5; it then fluctuated around this rate for the following 20 years, to the late 1990s. By 2000-2005 the TFR had declined to 3.5, although it seems since to have increased again, to 3.9, as recorded by the most recent census in 2015.

Fertility in Kiribati has thus dropped below 4 children per woman: but at the present time this seems to be a plateau. There is no sign that Kiribati is near a 'demographic transition' of the kind that has transformed the population profiles of Europe and more recently of Asia.

The concept of 'demographic transition' has arisen from a well-established historical correlation between falling total fertility rates and social and economic development. The TFR model posits four stages, or in some iterations, five. The ones relevant to Kiribati are:

- Stage one, pre-industrial society, when death rates and birth rates are high and roughly in balance
- Stage two, when death rates drop quickly and produce an imbalance; the countries in this stage experience a large increase in population
- Stage three, when birth rates fall due to various fertility factors such as access to contraception; increases in wages; urbanisation; a reduction in subsistence living; an increase in the status and education of women; a reduction in the value of children's work; an increase in

Chapter 24: The Next Forty Years

parental investment in the education of children; and other social changes.

Kiribati left stage one about 100 years ago; but although some of the factors listed as features of stage three are in place, there is little sign that they are having any great impact on the TRF. This means that the population of Kiribati, if present trends continue, will be between 160,000 and 170,000 by 2040. Again, if current patterns persist unchanged, the population of urban Tarawa could rise from some 50,000 today to more than 100,000.

Much of the land in urban Tarawa is not available for use, including the water reserves and airport runway, the causeways, and some of the reclaimed land at Temaiku, the eastern corner of the atoll, which is too swampy and low-lying. If these areas are excluded, the land area of South Tarawa is only just over 1,000 hectares (10 square km or 2,500 acres) and the current population density is 49 people per hectare or 4,905 per square mile, which is almost equal to the density of London. Unlike London, however, there are no high-rise buildings to house this population; and very little scope for in-filling by building more low-rise ones.

The much-used phrase 'South Tarawa is full' is unfortunately correct [231].

Dependency ratios and transfer networks

The continuation of present trends would result in a stark picture. If current population growth and employment trends continue, the dependency ratio will increase from the current situation, where the income of one employed person must support five, to at least twice this, with one person's income supporting ten or more other adults and children. That is far from the traditional concept of households being *toamau*—balanced in age and gender so there is a good division of labour, and everyday needs can be met by household members dividing their labour. It is no longer sufficient for each household to ensure that it has enough members to carry out essential tasks such as fishing, agro-forestry, cutting copra and toddy, cooking, and making crafts; where, moreover, if a household was missing someone, the extended family could be asked for help.

---

[231] Although visiting consultants were already saying this in the early 1970s, so it is all relative to perceptions!

Chapter 24: The Next Forty Years

Family care systems are already under stress: and there is a wide perception that the informal structures are weakening because of the increasing dependency ratios, as well as other factors. It seems doubtful whether systems would hold up if the number of dependents per person with a cash income were to double, which on present trends it will do within a generation.

The alternative is to turn to publicly-funded social security. Existing provisions for social transfers were summarised above in this Chapter. It has been estimated that the Elderly Fund costs a little less than 1% of GDP per annum, and the Copra Fund Subsidy, 2.8% of GDP. The benefits of the latter are unevenly distributed and it is not accessible to households with restricted labour capacity or without access to land, who are most likely to be amongst the poorest. Likewise the National Provident Fund only benefits those in formal employment.

The Maamau administration took early actions in this field, firstly, to double the copra subsidy, and secondly, to abolish secondary school fees; but it is likely that more radical solutions will have to be found within a decade.

Other forms of potential state-provided social security

The case study published in March 2012 as part of the AusAID Pacific social protection series (see Further Reading) costed some possible additions to the social security now provided by the Kiribati state.

These included:

- Child grants: It has been estimated that a grant of $15 a month to all Kiribati children aged 0 to 4 years would reach 56% of the population and would reduce the national poverty rate by 6%
- Work programmes addressing youth unemployment (along the lines of India's Employment Guarantee Scheme). Such a program in Kiribati could provide a daily wage to people—including young people—working on public infrastructure programmes and guarantee a maximum number of days of employment a year (in India, it is 100 days)
- Disability grants: a Kiribati National Disability Survey, carried out in 2004–05, found 3,840 people living with disability—including 723 children aged 0 to 14 years— comprising around 4% of the population. Traditional care structures for such people with disability appear to be breaking down. A grant of $40 a month aimed at the 1000 people with

the most severe disability in Kiribati, who are under 70 years of age, would only cost around $0.5 million a year, or 0.3% of GDP
- Greater support to the elderly: households with residents over 65 years of age had a poverty rate of 23%, compared to a poverty rate of 15% for households without older people. Reducing the age of eligibility to 60 years would significantly increase the fund's impact on poverty: the fund would reach a quarter of households nationally and would reduce the national poverty rate by 11%.

Basic income schemes

In addition to these, the debate currently taking place in many countries on the desirability and affordability of basic income schemes for all citizens may have some applicability.

The idea of a state-run basic income dates back at least to the early 16th century: Sir Thomas More's *Utopia* depicted a society in which every person receives a guaranteed income. In the late 18th century, English radical Thomas Spence and American revolutionary Thomas Paine both declared their support for a welfare system that guaranteed all citizens a certain income.

Basic income schemes are a live topic in a number of developed countries at the present time, albeit caused more by worries about the employment prospects for all as automation and artificial intelligence displace jobs, than by population pressures.

Perhaps the closest actual example of a state-run basic income scheme in the world today, is in the United States: the Permanent Fund of Alaska provides a kind of basic income to nearly all state residents based on the oil and gas revenues of the state, which are analogous to the fishing royalties of Kiribati. Such a scheme might be one way of recycling the income from the 'royalties' component of MIRRAB - without engendering the current and prospective dependency ratios predicted by current trends and the ensuing cultural stresses on redistribution networks.

I Kiribati culture

Earlier Chapters have recorded many cultural shifts in Kiribati, generally from *'Te maiu ni Kiribati'* towards *'Te maiu ni Imatang'*, over the past two hundred and fifty years.

Chapter 24: The Next Forty Years

It is a long list, with changes from:

- Endemic warfare to a peaceful society
- A society in which even the idea of 'money' played no part, to one where cash income has become essential
- Identification with *kaainga* and *utu*, to the exclusion of other I Kiribati, to a strong I Kiribati consciousness and sense of nationhood
- Moving from family-based living to multi-family villages, and now to crowded suburbia, at least on Tarawa
- Acceptance of governance and justice based on laws rather than rule by *unimane*, and replacing of concepts of compensation by the family for violation of custom with fines or imprisonment for the individual.

More recent cultural changes, which are still working their way into society and societial norms, include:

- A shift from a wholly Austronesian vocabulary to modern I Kiribati: the language now spoken by younger people, laced as it is with English language words, would probably be incomprehensible to their great-grandparents
- Moving from a society in which everyone had subsistence skills, and if necessary could live off their own land and resources (and did in the days of Tungaru, and up to and during WWII), to one where living depends on access to imported goods, and where a new generation has not been taught how to practice agro-forestry and fishing
- Looser social control of young people, with a sharp drop in 'arranged' marriages
- Limited consumption of sour toddy by the old, to a culture of drinking by the young; and, latterly, similar abuse of the *kava* that it was hoped would be more beneficial than alcohol (but which now, it appears, has equally deleterious effects on the liver if over-used)
- More recently still, an increased exposure to 'world' culture (at least in urban areas): in 2016, a survey in South Tarawa showed that 41% of households in South Tarawa had a desktop or laptop computer, 25% had a tablet computer, and 29% had a television (used for watching video films as there is no indigenous TV service).

Another current feature of I Kiribati culture is a comparatively passive response to litter and pollution: piles of tins, plastic, and rusting vehicles, and

Chapter 24: The Next Forty Years

even discarded nappies, all left in piles on the beach, are not generally seen as visually offensive by I Kiribati. This may also change.

The rise of 'economic man (or woman)'

In this book, it has been argued that the branch of economic theory most applicable to I Kiribati culture and behaviours is that of *'satisficing'* (pp. 121 - 122). Since at least the Tito administration, outsiders have urged its replacement [232], often with stark statements such as this:

> *'It is necessary to rapidly introduce a culture of enterprise and business principles'.* [233]

The traditional social protection system in Kiribati (see above) is seen by such outsiders as a challenge, and as a tax on working people, reducing their willingness to invest in business. They observe that I Kiribati entering into business are often subjected to the demands of *bubuti* (or for credit which is never repaid) from extended family members, and that this has led to many businesses failing. So, in this view, is people's attachment to their land inimical to business growth; proponents of change would like to see land fully commoditised like any other factor of production.

Despite the intentions that the private sector become the engine of individual prosperity, espoused by successive governments since at least the 1990s, this has not happened.

While the private sector in Kiribati is small in relation to the public sector, its contribution to GDP has increased, from 47.3% in 2005 to 54.5% in 2015. Also, private sector formal employment is currently increasing at a rate of over 12% per year: the number of private sector contributors to the Kiribati Provident Fund (KPF) has grown from 2,130 in June 2010 to 3,982 in June 2016, a rise of 87%; although the number of contributors from the public sector is still much larger and rose from 6,789 in 2010 to 6,917 in 2016. Additionally, other than a few businesses on North Tarawa and some tourist facilities which are

---

[232] Often with all the enthusiasm and disdain for tradition ('to be swept away') of the 19th century Missionaries

[233] Presumably by waving a magic wand; see page 192.

Chapter 24: The Next Forty Years

developing on Abaiaing, and about 40 businesses on Kiritimati, the private sector is almost entirely confined to urban Tarawa.

Income distribution

Despite their historically strong egalitarian cultural values, any perception that income levels in Kiribati are nowadays equal is no longer correct: the richest 10% of households were calculated in 2006 to be 10 times better off in income terms than the poorest households [234].

The latest calculation of the Gini coefficient [235] in Kiribati was made in 2006, and gave a score of 0.37; this is not below, but is about the average of all countries – and perhaps surprisingly suggests that income in Kiribati is actually less equal than that in Australia or the UK. The coefficient is well below the level of inequality in many Asian countries, and in the USA; in the Pacific region, income disparities are reported to be slightly wider in PNG, Tuvalu and Tonga. Fiji, however, despite its much larger private sector contribution to GDP, was calculated have a more equal distribution of income than did Kiribati.

Perhaps a *'nation of entrepreneurs'* might have identified them; but other than (and then temporarily) seaweed, no crop, besides now cultivation of a few vegetables, has prospered since the original Austronesian package of pre-historic times; and no animal husbandry other than the pigs introduced in the 19th century.

Artisanal fisheries have grown, but do not have the attractions of public service jobs. Import substitution projects have mostly come and gone, at least without continuing subsidy. It is difficult to see what new ventures might

---

[234] This is as measured by the Lorenz curve, a graphical representation of the distribution of income or wealth developed by Max O. Lorenz in 1905 for representing inequality of the wealth distribution.

[235] The 'Gini coefficient' is a statistical measure of distribution developed by the Italian statistician Corrado Gini in 1912. It is often used as a gauge of economic inequality, measuring income distribution among a population; or, less commonly, wealth distribution. The Gini coefficient is expressed as a number between 0 and 1, where 0 corresponds with perfect equality (where everyone has the same income) and 1 corresponds with perfect inequality (where one person has all the income—and everyone else has zero income).

Chapter 24: The Next Forty Years

prosper given the well-known disadvantages of scale, remoteness, and so on [236].

Without a 'great wall of protection' (historically in the form of subsidies to SOEs) import substitution, with an exception for renewable energy, struggles to compete with the imports; and however entrepreneurial the I Kiribati might become, the assessment of UNCTAD that the most important issues are geographical and size-related, rather than cultural, seems apt.

As with many 'cultural' predictions it is difficult to say what will evolve, but societal acceptance of inequality in Kiribati seems to be growing, but much faster than any idea of admiration for 'entrepreneurship' and 'getting rich'.

For how long will the MIRRAB model be sustainable?

The Kiribati economy is essentially sustained by external money – via royalties (the second 'R' that I have suggested be added to the Bertram and Watters model). The largest current component of this is fishing licenses.

Revenue collected from such licenses increased from AU$ 29.5 million in 2009 to AU$ 167.5 million in 2017, and has continued upwards since. This increase has been mainly the result of successful implementation of the vessel day scheme.

Although recent figures reflect an unusually long favourable ENSO cycle, modelling by the IMF in its 2108 annual assessment suggests that even if revenue (as seems likely) falls back somewhat when this cycle ends, fisheries revenues and the RERF can sustain other elements of the MIRRAB model up until 2030 (the end date of their model) - at least at current levels of the 'bureaucracy' component.

Subject to fish spawning and migration patterns, the amount of rent that the Kiribati government can extract from the fisheries resource (currently about 12% of its value) must however eventually be capped by the:

- Sustainability of the stock: although the latest (2017) assessment of the current stock concludes that the central and western Pacific Ocean

---

[236] Possibly, telecommunications advances might make labour-intensive service industries (e.g. call centres, professional services) a source of employment, but not at current standards of wages and education. There are no current proposals for development of such enterprises.

skipjack and yellowfin tuna stock is not yet overfished, although in some years catches have been near the maximum sustainable yield
- Willingness of distant water fishing fleets to pay ever-higher prices on tuna fishing days
- Limited capacity of Kiribati to derive onshore (processing) benefits from its fish stock.

Growth in fisheries revenue must reach a plateau at some point, but that point is not yet in sight. There are other possible sources of 'Blue Economy' revenue, but (as, however, was fishing licensing forty years ago, at the time of independence) these are not yet proven.

For example, mineral extraction from sediments and structures across the deep sea has been proposed at several habitat types—the abyssal plains, hydrothermal vents and seamounts along the mid-ocean ridges. Three main resources are of commercial interest: manganese nodules on the abyssal plains; seafloor massive sulfide deposits at hydrothermal vents; and cobalt-rich crusts, which are found at seamounts worldwide, with the largest deposits in the Pacific Ocean. Kiribati has possibilities for all of these. They are not proven to be commercially exploitable, and there may be severe environmental downsides: the extent of mining on seamounts will dictate the level of impact, but it is likely that intensive mining could disrupt the pelagic species from which existing fisheries royalties derive. Impacts will include removal of benthic fauna because of the presence of machinery; and disruption to fish as a result of noise and the presence of light and suspended sediments in the water column [237].

It nevertheless seems that the essential underlying 'feed' of the MIRRAB model, **royalties**, is sustainable for at least one or more decades to come. As regards other elements of the model:

- If current **migration** trends are extended into the future, only a few thousand people will have migrated by 2050
- The trend in temporary migration with its associated **remittances** is upwards, but in the absence of major policy change in New Zealand and Australia, not transformative in terms of employment or reduction in dependency ratios for those in receipt of remittances.

---

[237] Indeed deep sea mining seems to bear a strong relation to nuclear fusion, as an industry that somehow always remains 30 years into the future as a practical possibility. (I remember getting excited about manganese nodules in the early 1970s).

Unfortunately the trend for the best-paid overseas jobs, as seafarers, seems downwards as technology and automation in that industry evolves

- **Aid** flows seem similarly to be stable and reliable, even when Kiribati does graduate from LDC status (see above)
- **Bureaucracy.** The expansion of public service jobs continues, and (as the 2018 IMF assessment discusses) there have in recent years been particularly sharp increases in the public wage bill (in 2018, such increases alone amounting to 6% of GDP). The issue for the future, as discussed above, is how far such increases (even if affordable in MIRRAB terms) will 'trickle down' to the poorest through an ever-increasing dependency ratio; or whether, also as discussed above, traditional welfare will need to be supplemented by state social security measures.

Chapter 24: The Next Forty Years

Further Reading

1. **Population and Development Profiles: Pacific Island Countries,** published by the United Nations Population Fund Pacific Sub-Regional Office, 2014
2. **Kiribati Social and Economic Report 2008**, published by the Asian Development Bank
3. **National Integrity Systems: Transparency International Country Study Report Kiribati 2004,** by Ueantabo MacKenzie, published by Transparency International 2004
4. **Corruption : expanding the focus,** various authors, edited by Manuhuia Barcham, Barry Hindess and Peter Larmour, published by the Australian National University 2012
5. **Leadership Commission Annual Report for 2018,** published by the Kiribati government 2019
6. **Ex-ante Impact Assessment of likely Consequences of Graduation of Kiribati from the Least Developed Country Category**, paper for the UN Committee for Development Policy, 2018
7. **Kiribati: what will it lose when it graduates?** by James Webb at http://www.devpolicy.org/kiribati-what-will-it-lose-when-it-graduates-20190620/, 2019
8. **Destruction or persistence of coral atoll islands in the face of 20th and 21st century sea-level rise?** by Roger McLean and Paul Kench published in WIREs Climate Change, 2015
9. **Influence of sea-level rise on freshwater lenses of different atoll island sizes and lens resilience to storm-induced salinization** by Ting Fong May Chui and James P. Terry, published in the Journal of Hydology, 2013
10. **Vulnerability Of Freshwater Lens On Tarawa – The Role Of Hydrological Monitoring In Determining Sustainable Yield,** by Eita Metai, published in Proceedings of the Pacific, Regional Consultation on Water in Small Island Countries Theme 2 Case Studies, 2003
11. **Morphological Development of Reef Islands on Tarawa Atoll,** by Naomi Biribo, PhD thesis published by the University of Wollongong, 2012 at https://pdfs.semanticscholar.org/49d6/df0358e576a7429df5d35dd41dd123206af4.pdf
12. **Kiribati country case study AusAID Pacific social protection series: poverty, vulnerability and social protection in the Pacific**, by Stephen Kidd and Ueantabo Mackenzie, 2012
13. **How healthy are Hawai'i's oceans?** The 2018 Hawai'i OHI at www.oceanhealthindex.org/news/how-healthy-are-hawaiis-oceans
14. An Overview of Seabed Mining article in Frontiers at https://www.frontiersin.org/articles/10.3389/fmars.2017.00418/full

Chapter 24: The Next Forty Years

15. **Underwater Eden**, by Gregory Stone and David Obura, published by The University of Chicago Press 2013
16. **Kiribati Staff Report For The 2018 Article iv Consultation,** published by the IMF, 2018
17. **A Sustainable Future for Small States: Pacific 2050,** various authors, edited by Resina Katafono, published by the Commonwealth Secretariat, 2017

Epilogue

It is easy to be nostalgic about the 'rural idylls' of one's youth [238]. Nor is it a new phenomenon: see the comments of the second Western Pacific High Commissioner Sir John Thurston (page 171), or many of Maude's later writings.

I find it too tempting, however, not to quote Oliver Goldsmith's poem *'The Deserted Village'*, written about the time when the first European exploring vessels were coming across the Gilbert archipelago 250 years ago, and with many resonances to the themes of this book:

> *Ill fares the land, to hastening ill a prey,*
> *Where wealth accumulates and men decay:*
> *Princes and lords may flourish or may fade;*
> *A breath can make them, as a breath has made;*
> *But a bold peasantry, their country's pride,*
> *When once destroyed, can never be supplied.*
>
> *A time there was, ere* [Kiribati] *griefs began,*
> *When every rood of ground maintained its man;*
> *For him light labour spread her wholesome store,*
> *Just gave what life required, but gave no more:*
> *His best companions, innocence and health;*
> *And his best riches, ignorance of wealth.*
>
> *But times are altered; trade's unfeeling train*
> *Usurp the land and dispossess the swain;*
> *Along the lawn, where scattered hamlets rose,*
> *Unwieldy wealth and cumbrous pomp repose;*
> *And every want to opulence allied,*
> *And every pang that folly pays to pride.*

---

[238] I was but 22 years' old when I arrived first on Tarawa, to shock the colonialists by refusing to wear white shirts/shorts/stockings, in favour of colourful shirts and jeans (and also to play subversive songs on the 5-string banjo). But that is a story for my memoirs....

Epilogue

> *These gentle hours that plenty bade to bloom,*
> *Those calm desires that asked but little room,*
> *Those healthful sports that graced the peaceful scene,*
> *Lived in each look and brightened all the green;*
> *These, far departing, seek a kinder shore,*
> *And rural mirth and manners are no more.*

However, tempting though such nostalgia is, it would be wrong to conclude with it.

Te maiu ni Kiribati is still alive and well, and living in the three groups of Kiribati. It is not just about the survival of I Kiribati dances.

There are roughly 7,000 spoken languages in the world today – but only half of them are expected to survive this 21st century. Use of the I Kiribati language is growing rapidly, and it will surely be one of the language survivors, wherever its people are then living (and my bet is that most will somehow still be on the islands where they are today).

John Simpson starts the book from which his description of the Millennium celebrations is taken with the words:

> 'Once we had a planet. Now at the start of the third Christian millennium, we're left with a suburb. ... the differences between us are disappearing as fast as the animal, bird and insect species we share our planet with...'

In the 1930s, Eric Bevington recounted how the *unimane* on Beru reacted to his question:

> 'What is the I Matang's most wonderful invention? ...
>
> 'The discussion ... must have gone on for a full two hours, and I probably dozed off. At last it dawned on me that a consensus of opinion had arisen: "in our opinion, the most wonderful thing that the I Matang has made is the penny ... because every single one is exactly the same. We can never make two things exactly the same"'.

May this very last *Te maiu ni Kiribati* statement persist!

Epilogue

Further Reading

1. **'The Deserted Village',** by Oliver Goldsmith, published in 1770 (at https://www.bl.uk/collection-items/the-deserted-village-by-oliver-goldsmith)
2. **A Mad World, My Masters – Tales from a Traveller's Life** by John Simpson, published by Macmillan 2000.
3. **The Things We Do For England – If Only England Knew**, by Eric Bevington, published by the Laverham Press, 1990

Index

Note: in accordance with their custom, names of I Kiribati individuals are indexed by *First Name* followed by *Father's name* (or *Surname* if one has been adopted): i.e. Ieremia Tabai rather than Tabai, Ieremia; European names are expressed as the reverse i.e. Smith, John; and Chinese names by the ordering by which they were usually known within Kiribati (not always correctly), e.g. Jong Kum Kee

NB: Page numbers in **bold** and *italic* indicate a footnote reference

Abaiang, 4, 7, 33, 37, 54, 56, 95, 99, 121, 127, 131, 136, 138, 146–51, 151, 169, 211, 215, 238, 248, 288, 314, 384, 399
Abemama, 4, 29, 37, 47, 50, 52, 54, 85, 90, 112, 134, 136, 168, 174, 215, 250, 251, 255, 262, 276–78, 288, 304, 309, 313, 314, 386, 389
Accelerated decolonisation, policy of, 274, 356
'African Influence', the, 276, 282, 326, 339, 342, 357
Ah Sam, 169, 287
Aid
  As component of MIRAB/MIRRAB model (q.v.), 379, 426, 440, 486
  Budgetary aid from UK, 359–60, 402
  Colonial Development and Welfare Acts, 276
  Post WWII concept of, 272
  Problems caused by diversification of donors, 325, 370–71, 373, 375, 423
Air Kiribati, 424, 439
Air Transport Services
  Establishment in Kiribati, 309, 333, 428
  Trans - Pacific via Kanton, 242
Air Tungaru, 410
Andersen, Val, 293, 296, 298, 305, 312, 313

Anderson, John, 44, 133
Anote Tong
  And climate change, 440, 452–56, 480
  Biographical details, 312, 438, 453
  Development strategies of, 302–14
  Initial actions of Tong government, 439–40
Arorae, 4, 7, 24, 35, 50, 67, 103, 113, 130, 140, 145, *213*, 313, 413
Asian Development Bank (ADB), 370, 376, 408, 423, 444, 486
Aspects of History, iii, v, **14**, 203, 249, 293, 307, 328
Australia, iv, 1, 18, 142, 146, 162, 164, 167, 171, 188, 190, 197, 236, 242, 255, 257, 267, 288, 297, 301, 303, 310, 334, 371, 376, 378, 411, 451, 480, 487, 501
  I Kiribati diaspora in, 468, 475–76
Ba'há'í faith, 288, 396
Babai / bwabwai, 46, 97, 105, 110, 152, 385–86, 442, 465
Babera Kirata, ix, 359, 412
Baggallay, Anna, ix
Bailey, Eric, vii, 267, 349
Banaba
  As GEIC Headquarters, 193, 235
  Droughts on, 113–14
  Impact of phosphate workings on, 184, 191, 194
  Physical characteristics of, 1, 4
Banabans

507

And the British Phosphate
   Commission, 67, 200, 259
And the Pacific Phosphate
   Company, 166, 175, 179, 181,
   186–95
And WW11, 246, 248–49, 256–57
Claims to independence from
   Kiribati, 296, 302, 352–55, 359–61,
   414
Granting of leases by, 121, 181, 186,
   189, 191, 193–94, 196, 232–35,
   278, 303
On Rabi, 260, 469
Pre-contact history and culture, iv,
   24, 31, 35, 36, 38, 47, 53, 54, 94,
   100, 104, 354
Banking services, 334, 385, 408
Baranite Kirata, 394
Barley, Jack, 210, 219, 238, 247
Beia Mwa Tekaai, iii, 68
Beniamina Tinga, 416
Bernacchi, Michael, 265, 279, 283,
   285, 292, 298, 303–5, 304, 307, 312
Beru, 4, 7, 15, 23, 24, 35, 36, 37–38, 44,
   49, 50, 51, 53, 64, 140, 205, 211, 214,
   220, 223, 238, 289, 314, 505
Bevington, Eric, 205, 220, 223, 238,
   246, 247, 506
Bingham, Rev Hiram, 27–28, 98, 131,
   138, 143–44, 219
Binoka, Tem, 38, 47, 136, 138
Boanareke Boanareke, 416
Boti, iii, 35, 48, 50–52, 53, 55, 56, 61,
   64, 66, 79, 88, 133
Boundaries of Kiribati, evolution,
   171, 181–82, 344–55
British Phosphate Commission
   Establishment of, 197, 201
   GEIC revenues from, 236, 302–3
   Influence over Colonial
      Administration, iv, 209, 231, 238,
      237, 239, 259
   Pricing policies, 232, 296, 310, 335
Bruce, Thomas, 209

Bubuti, **custom of**, 46, 56–57, 57, 121,
   123, 153, 483, 497
Bureaucracy, 380, 425, 452, 501, 503,
   See also under **Regulations**
   As component of MIRRAB model,
      379, 425, 432, 443, 449–51, 489,
      497, 499–501
Butaritari, 4, 6, 15, 25, 29, 33, 34, 37,
   39, 46, 49, 50, 53, 54, 90, 98, 111, 113,
   123, 124, 134, 135, 139, 163, 167, 168,
   169, 175, 213, 215, 227, 230, 246,
   248–49, 252–53, 261, 262, 287, 289,
   309, 384, 389, 460
Butler, Ian, 266, 283, 287, 288
Bwebwentekai Tutu Tekanene, ix
Byron, Commodore John, 127, 129
Campbell, William Telfer, 176–78,
   185, 192, 193, 202, 203, 204, 206, 210,
   215, 220
Canoe design and sailing. See under
   Proa
Carlson Raid, 249
Caroline Island (in Kiribati), 1, 185,
   432
**Caroline Islands (in Northern
   Micronesia)**, 14, 20, 29, 33, 36, 97,
   100, 105, 111, 161, 164, 428
Cartland, B C, 276–78, 296
Cary, Captain James, 127, 129
Chatfield, Norman, 229, 279
Christmas Island. *See* under
   Kiritimati
Churches, 25, 56, 86, 143–45, 161, 173,
   210–15, 288–90, 297, 393–96, 412,
   413, 451, See also **Missionaries**
Cinderellas of the Empire, iii, vi, 178,
   179, 216, 285, 326, 340, 348
Climate change, 369, 427, 435, 440,
   452–56, 462, 464, 480, 488–92
Coconut (*Cocos nucifera*)
   As part of Austronesian package,
      11, 20, 32, 114, 466

Improvement and Replanting Schemes, 265, 305, 316, 323, 329, 403
Names for in I Kiribati, 104, 106–8
Oil and copra as traded commodities, 131, 136–39, 228
Uses in I Kiribati material culture, 68, 71, 75, 78, 85, 91, 98, 106–8, 115–18
Cogswell, R H, 177, 192, 208
Colonial Office, 164, 165–67, 170, 176, 179, 180, 185, 188–89, 193–97, 204, 209, 219, 231, 235, 236, 254, 260, 274, 277, 290, 301, 302
Colonial service in the GEIC, characteristics of, 56, 175, 179, 201, 205, 219, 276, 279, 284, 316, 339
Colony, status of, 180, 201, 236, 254, 273–74, 276–78, 279, 292, 338–39, 367
Committee of Twenty-Four, 273, 349
Commonwealth, 271, 358, 376
Constitutional development, 273–74, 290, 293–95, 320, 338
Cook, Captain, 36, 115, 265
Co-operative movement, 230, 285, 287, 294–307, 306, 325, 387, 407
Copra
As a vehicle for development, 228–30, 285–86, 307, 316, 321, 323, 329, 332, 387, 392, 403, 424, 447
Replacement for coconut oil, 135, 139, 228
Subsidies, 298, 402, 421, 425, 444, 450, 494
Taxes, 174, 228, 237, 286
Coral lens, 3, 8, 489 92
Corrie, Robert, 138, 148, 169–70
Corruption, prevalence of, 375, 426, 482–84
Corvée, imposition of, 202, 213, 292, 295
Cowell, Reid, 27, 61
Dance
And I Kiribati culture, 75, 84–86, 169, 477, 506
European attitudes towards, 84–86, 169, 212, 262, 394
Ornaments and costumes, 77–79
Types of, 81, 84–85
Darwin, Charles, 184
Davis, Captain, 37, 56, 146, 168–70, 212, 227
de Grijalva, Hernado, 127
de Quiros, Pedro, 127
de Roburt, Hammer, *294*, 303
Development Authority (GEIDA/GIDA), 317, 325, 327, 330, 339
Development of I Kiribati national consciousness, 56–57, 200, 201, 273–74, 293–95, 338–39, 354, 357, 361, 368, 376, 390, 497
Development planning, 304, 317, 321–22, 368, 373, 392, 403, 420, 465, 481
Development, attitudes towards
International and expatriate attitudes, 172, 184, 272, 276, 304, 329
Villagers' attitudes, 321–22, 389–91, 439, 442
Diseases in Kiribati, 11, 124, 426, 433–35, 442, 444, 465
District Administration, 205, 215, 216, 220, 222, 266, 283, 285, 291, 297, 373
Dixon, Keith, 391, 394, 462, 476
Droughts, 7, 8, 12, 105, 111, 113–14, 124, 141, 175, 225, 243, 265, 455, 490
Duperrey, Captain Louis, 127
Durant, George, 135
Earhart, Amelia, 241
Eastman, George, 211, 214
Economic vulnerability, 480, 486, 489
Education
And government, 204, 239, 289, 304, 453

And missions, 200, 212, 289, 395
And the BPC, 236, 239
Primary, 289, 313
Purposes of education, debate about, 239, 275, 286, 312, 372–73, 391, 427, 478
Secondary, 314, 444
Tertiary, 296, 314, 375

Eliot, Edward, vii, 43, 53, 113, 180, 195, 196, 204, 208, 226, 232, 239

Ellice Islands (see also **Tuvalu**), v, vii, 2, 140, 143, 151, 163, 168, 171–74, 201, 210, 216, 225, 230, 238, 239, 251, 264, 280, 286, 294–95, 296, 310, 313, 338, 344–50

Ellis, Sir Arthur, 186–87, 190–93, *193*, 302, 310

Empire, British, 164, 196, 205, 220–21, 222, 233, 242, 246, 271, *274*, 302, 346

Employment
Cash economy, in, 200, 284, 310, 372, 380, 392
On Banaba, 201, 228, 236, 309
Overseas, 141, 310, 332, 372, 451, 474–77
Public sector, in, 466, 498
Village economy, in, 53, 383, 387

Equality, culture of, 43, 53, 340, 391, 499–500

Exclusive economic zones, 329, 376, 405, 449, 457, 479

Fairclough, Hugh, 135

Family in I Kiribati society
Family knowledge as asset, 14, 38, 46, 48, 55, 61, 66, 76, 101, 106
Obligations, 44–46, 49, 91, 122, 200, 441–43, 473, 494, 498
Structure of, 42, 43, 45, 55–57

Family planning, 319, 321, 323, 331, 369, 397

Fanning Island, 181, 246, 255, 264, 276, 377, See also **Tabueran**

Field, Sir John, 295, 319, 337, 345

Fiji, 141, 163, 314, 457

I Kiribati diaspora in, 469–72

Fish and mollusc resources and their exploitation
Importance as food source, 86, 97, 99, 112, 225
Occurrence as a household activity, 122, 386, 393
Resources available, 9, 261, 458
Techniques for catching, 100–103

Fisheries development programmes
Government programmes to develop internal fisheries, 317, 323, 330, 404
Licensing regimes for foreign fishing vessels, 328, 376, 380, 405–6, 425, 501

Fletcher, Sir Murchison, 221, 234, 237

Foreign Office (FCO), British, 165–66, 167, 253, 290, 346, 349, 352, 356, 360

Foreign relations of independent Kiribati, 371, 373, 376–78, 405, 412, 428, 440, 442, 474–77, 485

Fox-Strangways, Lt Col Vivian, 254, 260, 261, 262

Gallagher, Gerald, 243

'Gaming' of colonial regulations, examples of, 217, 221, 227, *230*, 286, 289, 297

Garvey, Ronald, 210, 247

Gaze, Alfred, 192, 236, 237, 301, 302, 310

GEIDA (later GIDA).. *See* under **Development Authority**

Gender issues. *See* also **Status of Women**

Gilbert islands archipelago, v, 4, 14, 31, 127, 377

Gilbert, Captain Thomas, 127, 129

Goronwy-Roberts, Baron, 360, 362

Goward, William, 211, 212

Grantham, Alexander, 254, 263, 278

Grimble, Sir Arthur

As anthropologist, iv, 16–17, 28, 30, 32, 34, 52, 56, 61, 68, 69–70, 72, 79–80, 87, 91, 98, 116–19, 228
As Colonial Official, 69–70, 201, 204, 213, 217–18, 226, 232–36, 239, 274, 276
Personal experiences in the Gilberts, 52, 79–80, *102*, 209, 228
Guano Islands Act, 163, 241, 243, 264, 265
Gulick, Dr, 137, 220
Guns (firearms), 38, 47, 54, 151, 170, 190
H.M.S. Royalist, 168–70
Hamann, Nicolas, iv, vi, 37, 73, 78
Hambruch, Paul, 94–95, 146
Hamilton-Gordon, Sir Arthur, 166, 185, See also **Stanmore, Lord**
Harry Tong, 415, 438
Highland, Frank, 253
Holland, F G L, 239, 254, 260
Housing
Policies for, 195, 286, 298, 301, 304, 315, 326, 333, 334, 408
Standardisation of, 200, 202
Hudson, Lt. William, 132
Ieremia Tabai
Actions of Tabai government, 359–61, 401, 403, 409, 426
Biographical details, 312, 338, 342, 359, 396, 399
Development strategies of, 368, 404, 423
Foreign relations of, 405, 411–12
Later career, 415, 426
Incest, prohibitions against, 32, 38, 44, 48
Indirect rule, 174, 263
Industrial relations, 401, 409
International Date Line, vi, 1, 428
International Monetary Fund (IMF), 368, 376, 408, 421, 422, 424, 427, 445–47, 499, 503

Jaluit Gesellschaft, 175, 188, 191, 227, 229
Justice system
Colonial, 146, 171, 199, 200, 206–8, 214, 226, 295
Post-independence, 414, 424, 439, 483
Traditional concepts of justice, 42, 49, 199, 200, 496
Kaainga, 42, 44–46, 50, 52, 53, 54, 66, 77, 90, 91, 94, 122, 153, 200, 221, 496
Kabunare Koura, 258
Kakiaman, Te, 95
Kanton Island, 241–43, 456, 464, 466
Kanzaki (Japanese trader and spy), 248
Kapui (Hawaiian missionary), 145, 170
Karangoa *boti*, iii, 55, 62, 79
Kennedy, D G, 230, 239, 260
Kershaw, Sir Anthony, 346
King George V/Elaine Bernacchi school (KGV/EBS), 239, 246, 250, 304, 311, 314, 452
King tides, 7, 454
Kingsmill Group, 127, 147
Kirby, John, 123, 133
Kiribati Vision 20 (KV20), i, 480–84, 487
Kiritimati Island, 241, 263, 265–68, 331, 377, 428, 464, 481, 498
Kleis, Sione Tui, 338, 344
Koch, Gerd, 55, 75, 77, 81, 88, 102
KorauabaTaberannang, 473
Kosrae, 20, 25, 29, 31, 32, 120, 211
Kuria, 4, 37, 38, 47, 54, 90, 133, 136, 169, 215
Lambert, Dr B, 123
Lambert, S M, 202
Land ownership in I Kiribati society
As economic resource, 45, 55, 121, 228, 264, 276–78, 329, 403, 408, 421, 423, 449, 454, 458, 467–68, 498

511

Cultural significance of, 14, 42, 47, 53, 57, 276–78, 448
Forms of ownership, 47, 53, 188–89, 466
Leases of, 180, 190, 191, 195, 232–34, 277, 444
Shortages of land, 240, 384, 423, 454, 494
Lands Commissions, 47, 200, 209, 226, 240, 275, 276
Latouche, Jean-Paul, iv
Law of the Sea, UN Convention on, 328, 377, 403, 436
Layng, Tom, 350
Lestor, Joan, 352
Lever, William, 185, 191, 194
Licensing of foreign fisheries. *See* **Fisheries Development Programmes**
Line Islands. See also entries on **Kiritimati Tabueran, Teraina** and **Caroline Islands**
Development of, 185, 264, 309, 331, 377, 407
Incorporation into GEIC, 181–82
Physical characteristics, 1, 454
Resettlement onto, 356, 465–68
US claims to, 164, 181–82, 264–67, 356
Use for nuclear testing, 268
London Missionary Society, 67, 143, 162, 289
Lowther, James, 138
Luke, Sir Harry, 220, 235, 238, 243, 246
Luomala, Katherine, iv
Macdonald, Dr Barrie, iii, 130, *201*, 209
Magic wands, transforming I Kiribati culture by waving of, 191, *497*
Magic, uses in I Kiribati society, 15, 37, 38, 46, 49, 61, 68–70, 199, 213, 221

Mahaffy, Arthur William, 177–78, 193
Maiana, 4, 37, 68, 73, 78, 82, 136, 138, 139, 140, 148, 168, 170, 391, 438, 490
Makin, 4, 7, 29, 32, 33, 39, 46, 50, 53, 54, 85, 90, 98, 111, 113, 127, *131*, *137*, 139, 145, 169, 213, 215, 230, 248, 314
Mara, Ratu, 355, 361
Marakei, 4, 8, 33, 37, 69, 99, 110, 127, 139, 175, 248, 255, 292, 314, 359, 412, 415
Mariana Islands, 20, 26, 33, 34, 110, 161, 164, 428
Marine Training School, 142, 309, 311, 321, 323, 332, 344, 370, 372, 405
Marshall Islands, 2, 10, 14, 20, 25, 29, 32, 33, 36, 110, 139, 140, 170, 175, 228, 229, 246, 249, 251, 255, 261, 369, 428, 481
Marshall, Captain John, 127
Massing, Professor J M, vi
Matang, uea of Tarawa, 37, 78
Maude, Harry
As anthropologist and historian, iv, 25, 34, 35, 36, 38, 50–52, 58, 66, 87–88, 128, 134, 136–38, 225, 228, 354–55
As Colonial administrator, 206, 209, 214–16, 219, 240, 242–43, 273, 275–77, 279, 282, 290, 304, 307, 466, 468, 470
Maude, Honor, 87–88, 215, 275, 282
McClure, Herbert, vii, 36, 151, 209, 222, 239, ***429***
McIntyre, Professor W David, vii, *274*
Medical services
Attitudes towards, 238
Establishment of, 205
Expenditure on, 304, 314, 315, 345
Impact of, 240, 261, 333, 393, 409, 434, 439
Meyer, Anton, 206, 228, 229
Micro-states, 271, 374–75, 377, 484

Migration. See also **Phoenix Isalnds Resettlement Scheme**
   As component of MIRRAB model, 379, 425, 432, 443, 451–52, 489, 497, 501–2
   In colonial period, 140, 142–43, 275, 297
   Pre-contact, 14, 17, 19, 25, 29, 30, 33, 34, 35
   Since independence, 370, 379, 383–84, 392, 424, 450, 453–54, 456, 461–78, 492, 501–2

MIRAB / MIRRAB States
   Definition of, 380
   Performance of Kiribati as MIRRAB state, 425, 432, 441–43, 449–51, 488, 495, 499–501

Missionaries, foreign
   And I Kiribati orthography, 26
   Attitudes and behaviours of, and towards, 25, 43, 73, 168, 176, 289, *312*
   Authority of, 201, 210–15
   Bahá'í, 288
   Mission financing, 146, 174, 228
   Mormon, 395, 461
   Protestant, 143–44, 162, 170, 212, 288
   Roman Catholic, 145, 213–15, 288
   Seventh Day Adventists, 288

Missions. See under **Churches**
Mitchell, Sir Philip, 273–74, 277, 293, 301, 312
Monetary policy, 334
Money, role of in I Kiribati scoiety, 56–57, 120–21, 174, 178, 199, 221, 235, 320, 327, 384, 388, 402, 442, 460, 485
Monson, Sir Leslie, 347
Mooring Report, 316, 319, 324, 331, 337, 339, 370
Mooring, Sir George, 316
Motufoua school, 314, 351

Murdock (or Murdoch) George, 92, 138, 177
Murray, David, 101, 357, 360
Mwaneaba (maneaba) organisation and customs
   First establishment of, 36, 54
   Functions in society, 23, 50–52, 53, 66, 154, 200, 215, 220, 389–90, 395, 409, 452, 484
   Types, 44, 51

Na Rakobu, 85
Nabetari, 256
Naboua Ratieta, 311, 317, 338, 342, 350, 351, 354, 357, 358, 415
Nareau, 11, 14, 15, 61, 64, 87
National Economic Planning Office, ii, 317, 319, 323, 345, 374, 382, 438
National Provident Fund, 334, 443, 449, 494, 497
Native administration, 174, 201, 203–4, 206, 209, 213–15, 217–19, 255, 263, 273–74, 277, 286, 292, 295, 313
'Natives', attitudes of Europeans towards, 42, *53*, 55, 132, 146–51, 194, 226, 236, 279, 282, 286
Nauru, 25, 30, 33, 176, 186, 189, 190, 196, 237, 247, 250, 256, 257, 259, 294, 297, 313, 351, 460
Nauru Agreement, 406, 448
Neli Lefuka, 251
New Zealand, 162, 163, 181, 190, 197, 247, 254, 271, 297, 312, 370, 371, 376, 411, 424, 450, 459, 467, 479, 486
   I Kiribati diaspora in, 473–74, 477
Nikunau, iii, 4, 23, 24, 30, 103, 127, 129, 130, 141, 145, 287, 391, 463–64, 476
Nonouti, 4, 34, 37, 38, 49, 71, 75, 91, 127, 129, 138, 139, 140, 143, 152, 212, 297, 338, 399
Ocean Island. *See* Banaba
Onotoa, 4, 23, 24, 37, 49, 68, 75, *112*, 129, 138, 141, 213, 415, 426, 451
Operation Dominic, 268

513

Orme, Brian, 412, 414
Overseas Development, Ministry of, 290, 306, 359
Pacific Islands Company, 184, 241
Pacific Islands Forum, 378
Palau, 14, 20, 25, 33, 75, 120, 161, 164
Pandanus *(Pandanus tectorius)*, 9, 11, 30, 32, 47, 75, 76, 77, 81, 88, 98, 104–5, 116, 192, 193, 194, 386
Peel, Sir John, vii, 205, 229, 279, 281
Phelan, Nancy, 284, 289
Philately, 379
Phoenix Islands, 1, 2, 24, 163, 240, 241–42, 251, 263, 355, 374, 377, 404, 407, 428, 453, 464, 467
Phoenix Islands Protected Area, 242, 456–57, 482
Phoenix Islands Resettlement Scheme, 227, 242–43, 296, 380
Pitchford, John, vii, 54, 297, 332, 340, 373, 390, 429
Pohnpei, 20, 29, 33, 110
Political parties, 297, 413, 414, 417, 419, 439
Pollution of Tarawa Lagoon, 427, 434–35
Population of Kiribati. See also Censuses
   Perceptions of, 143, 225, 226, 228, 240–42, 276, 304, 306, 369, 372, 383, 423, 432, 442, 488, 494
   Pre-contact, 124, 140, 142–43, 151
Posnett, R N, 353
Poverty in Kiribati, 332, 368, 425, 441–43
Press, freedom of, 414, 426
Prison, attitudes to, 201, 208, 217
Private sector, 288, 304, 307, 309, 321, 324, 328, 334, 370, 372, 373, 387, 407, 422–23, 439, 446, 448, 464, 488, 497
Proa (sailing craft, canoe), 17, 22–23, 31, 34, 55, 114–15, 172
Protectorate
   Administration of GEIP, 154, 171, 175, 176–78, 191, 200, 220
   Establishment of, 141, 151, 167, 169–70, 188–89
   Legal status of, 170, 180
   Replacement of by colonial status, 180, 194
Public sector. See also Bureaucracy
   Dominance of, 298, 325, 371, 373, 392, 422–24, 451, 497, 501
   Role assigned in development strategies and plans, 401, 408, 420, 422, 440, 447–48
Public Works Department, 205, 206, 305, 317, 325, 326, **327**
Quayle-Dickson, John, 179, 193–94, 209
Rabi island
   Life on, 303, 351, 354, 359, 469–70
   Resettlement of Banabans on, 236, 259
Randell, Richard, 124, 136–39
Regulations, for I Kiribati villagers, 201, 204, 210, 213, 216–19, 236, 238, See also under 'Gaming'
Reitaki movement, 297
Religion, I Kiribati
   And magic, 15, 46, 68–70, 75
   Deities (anti), 60, 61–64
   Observance of, 60, 66–67, 289
Remittances, 311, 319, 321, 332–33, 323, 380, 388, 425, 443, 450, 451, 466, 488, 501–2
   As component of MIRRAB model, 425, 432, 443, 451–52, 490, 498, 501–2
Replanting schemes, coconut, 316, 329, 403
Reuben Uatioa, ix, 263, 294, 297, 319, 337, 338, 349, 351
Revenue Equalisation Reserve Fund (RERF), 301, 320, 335, 359, 371, 380, 425, 450, 452, 501

514

Rice, as part of diet, 20, 97, 250, 386, 433
Richards, Sir Arthur, 236, 238, 241
Rongorongo, school at, 211, 239
Roniti Teiwaki, 339, 341, 359, 416
Rotan family, 235, 359, 469
Rowlands, Ted, 351
Royal Navy, 146, 166, 170, *See* also **HMS Royalist**
Royalties, as component of MIRRAB model, 425, 432, 443, 451–52, 489, 498, 501–2
Rural Socio-Economic Survey, 323, 333, 384–91
Sabatier, Fr Ernest, vi, 34, 36, 61, 64, 65, 67, 71, 91, 102, 152, 239, 240
Sadd, Alfred, 250
Samoa, 14, 16, 20, 21, 27, 29, 33, 35, 50, 52, 64, 65, 97, 98, 101, 117, 140, 141, 143–44, 162, 164, 167, 171, 172, 196, 211, 239
Satisficing
  Definition of, as branch of economics, 119, 122
  Examples of satisficing behaviours, 228, 329, 407, 499
Schutz, Paul, 307
Schutz, Willie, 247
Seaweed farming, 402, 407, 466, 469
Seeley, Sir John, 161, 476
Seligman, Rosemary (nee Grimble), ix, 17
Smith, Charles, 135
Smith, John, vii, ix, 43, 330, 339, 343, 348, 349, 350, 352, 355, 356
Social control
  In colonial society, 221, 297
  In traditional society, 56, 122, 221, 498
Social security and welfare
  In modern times, 444, 489, 494–96, 503
  In traditional I Kiribati society, 112, 121, 123, See also **Bubuti**

Solomon Islands, 14, 20, 34, 120, 161, 165, 167, 190, 243, 282, 378, 412
  I Kiribati dispora in, 296, 380, 460, 468, 473, 474
South Pacific Forum, 376, 401
Soviet Union, 267, 376, 405, 406, 411–12
Sport, 88, 429, 441
Stanley, Henry, 353
Stanley, Sir Robert, 312
Stanmore, Lord, 184, 185, 188, 194, 196, See also **Hamilton-Gordon, Sir Arthur**
State Owned Enterprises, 326, 387, 407, 422–24, 445, 447–48, 452, 499, See also **Development Authority**
Status of women in society, 55–56, 122, 200, 354, 451
Stevenson, Fanny, 83
Stevenson, R L, 38
Subsidies, 298, 307, 320, 326, 410, 423, 447, 499
Swayne, Charles, 171, 175, 178, 221, 295
Swinbourne, Charles, 210
Tabakea, 14, 62
Tabanea, 214
Tabiteuea, 4, 6, 15, 24, 34, 35, 37, 44, 54, 90, 98, 128, 136, 139, 140, 144, 168, 170, 212, 284, 288, 289, 297
Tabueran, 264, 406, 466–68
Tabunawati Tokoa, 206
Taiwan
  As ancestral home of Austronesian culture, 18, 19, 22, 25, 26, 31–32, 97, 109, 119
  Relations with modern Taiwan, 428, 440, 487
Tamana, 4, 6, 25, 29, 31, 32, 36, 50, 103, 113, 127, 129, 130, 139, 140, 145, *213*, 225, 229–30, 313, 354, 383, 385, 386, 413
Taneti Maamau, 480
Tangitang, 307

515

Tantarabe of Abaiang, 169
Tapiria, Nei, 37
Tarawa
   As colonial HQ, 101, 175, 193, 207–8, 275, 276, 281, 304, 356
   Concentration of people and resources onto, and impact on *kain* Tarawa, 226, 238, 239, 279, 284, 287, 289, 298, 304, 307, 313, 314, 317, 319, 320, 326, 333, 369, 371, 383, 392, 400, 444, 449, 451, 482, 493, 498
   Diaspora communities on, 461, 463–64, 472, 477
   In WWII, 247, 251–55, 260, 262–63, 278
   Other references to, 175, 206, 213, 228, 229, 247, 390, 414
   Physical characteristics of, 4, 6, 408, 427, 432, 434–35, 490, 494
   Pre-colonial history, iii, 15, 29, 35, 37–38, 50, 61, 64, 67, 79, 90, 118, 128, 136, 139, 147, 151, 170
Teaeki, 44
   Te maiu ni Imatang, concept of
      And colonial authority, 215, 217, 220–22, 297, 307, 383–90, 495
      And sport, **75**, 429
      And WWII, 285–86, 295
      Definition, 199
   Te maiu ni Kiribati, concept of. See also under **Satisficing**
      19th century changes, 152–53
      20th century changes, 201, 217, **249**, 295, 307, 383–90
      21st century changes, 497–98
      Definition, 199
Teatao Teannaki, 399, 415, 416
Teburoro Tito
   Actions in government, 426–54, 421
   And the Millennium, 430–31
   Biographical details, viii, 419, **430**
   Development strategies, 420–25
   Early career in ploitics, 400, 416
   Foreign relations, 428–30
Tekarei Russell, 338, *339*
Temati of Banaba, 187, 189
Teraina, 1, 377, 464, 465
Teurikan, Nei, ix
Thomas, Dr Frank, ix
Thurston, Sir John Bates, 166, 168, 170, 171, 174, 203, 504
Tione Baraka, iii
Tito Teburoro, 311, 338, 419
Toalipi Lauti, 311, 339
Toamati Iuta, ix, 359
Tokelau Islands, 181–82
Tommy Tabe, 472
Tonga, 21, 27, 29, 33, 34, 36, 98, 172
Tourism, 448, 482
Trades Unions, 341, 400, 409
Trading companies, 121, 131, 134–39, 153, 229–30, 246, 275, 285, 306
Trainer, Captain, 134
Treaty of Tarawa, 163, 267, 377
Turpin, Dick, ix, 284
Turpin, Nei Beta, ix
Turpin, Peggy, ix, 284
Turpin, Richard, ix, 284
Tutu Tekanene, 253, 281, 289
Tuvalu, ii, 10, 21, 29, 34, 172–74, 350, 377, 460
Uakeia, 36, 90
Unimane, authority of
   In colonial times, 200, 216, 291, 297
   In modern times, 389–91, 413
   In traditional society, 42, 189
Union Islands, 181–82
United Nations and its institutions, v, 271, 272, 377, 427, 436–37, 444, 486, 488
United States of America
   And pelagic fish, 405
   Claims to islands in Kiribati, 163, *167*, 240, 263, 264, 267, 355

For **US Exploring Expedition** see **Wilkes Report**.
US presence in GEIC in WWII and cold war, 241–43, 251–55, 268
Urbanisation, 285, 333, 369, 373, 392, 400, 401, 410, 433, 443, 445–46, 463–64, 490, 494, 498
Urswald, Brother, 95
Utu **(extended family)**, 45–46, 52–53, 57, 123, 462
Vanuatu (as a place of origin of the I Kiribati people), 14, 19, 20, 25, 32, 33
von Krusenstern, Admiral Adam, 127
Walker, William, 132
Walsh, Nei Rotee, vii, *4*, *60*, *73*, *76*, 85, 110, *112*, *131*, *213*, *217*, 282, 284, 290, 314, *337*, 386
Ward, Vic, 24, 267

Washington Island. *See* Teraina
Wernham, David, 253, 278
Western Pacific High Commission, 142, 165–67, 188, 197, 207–8, 219, 232, 236, 237, 238, 241, 273, 275, 278, 283, 294–95, 312
Visits to GEIC by High Commissioners, 171, 220, 221, 254
Whales and whaling, 99, 130, 226
Wholesale Society, 283, 285–86, 307, 325, 387
Wilkes Report, 33, 44, 49, 54, 56, 64, 72, 75–76, 90, 98, 120, 122, 132–33, 383
Wood, Robert, 134
World Bank, 376, 421, 424, 427, 442, 444, 449, 455, 487
Yap, 20, 33, 120

Printed in Great Britain
by Amazon